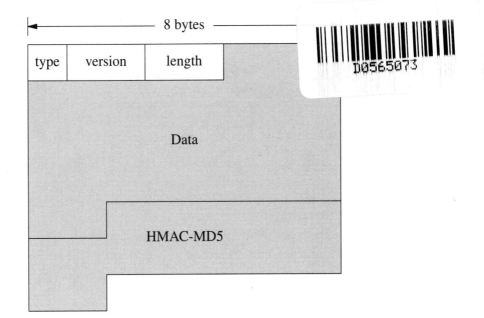

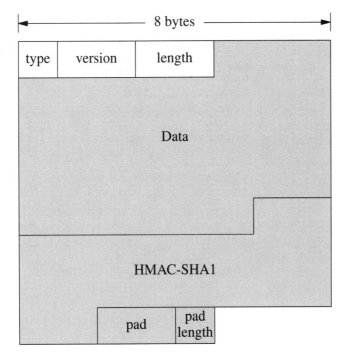

Record with stream cipher and HMAC-MD5

Record with block cipher and HMAC-SHA1

SSL and TLS

SSL and TLS

Designing and Building Secure Systems

Eric Rescorla

Addison-Wesley

Boston • San Francisco • New York • Toronto • Montreal
London • Munich • Paris • Madrid
Capetown • Sydney • Tokyo • Singapore • Mexico City

The publisher offers discounts on this book when ordered in quantity for special sales. For more information please contact:

Pearson Education Corporate Sales Division
One Lake Street
Upper Saddle River, NJ 07458
(800) 382-3419
corpsales@pearsontechgroup.com

Visit us on the Web at www.awl.com/cseng

Library of Congress Cataloging-in-Publication Data

Rescorla, Eric, 1972-
    SSL and TLS: designing and building secure systems / Eric Rescorla
        p. cm.
    Includes bibliographical references and index.
    ISBN 0-201-61598-3 (alk. paper)
    1. Computer networks—Security measures. 2. World Wide Web—Security measures
3. Computer network protocols. I. Title.
TK5105.59.R47 2000
05.8—dc21   00-057593

ISBN 0-201-61598-3

Text printed on recycled paper.
1 2 3 4 5 6 7 8 9 10-CRS-04 03 02 01 00
First printing, October 2000

For Lisa

Contents

Preface

The *Secure Sockets Layer* (SSL) is by far the most widely deployed security protocol in the world. Essentially every commercial Web browser and server supports secure Web transactions using SSL. When you buy online using "secure" Web pages (an estimated 20 billion dollars' worth of such transactions will occur in 2000), you're almost certainly using SSL.

Although its most common use is for securing Web traffic, SSL is actually quite a general protocol suitable for securing a wide variety of kinds of traffic. File transfer (FTP), remote object access (RMI, CORBA, IIOP), e-mail transmission (SMTP), remote terminal service (Telnet) and directory access (LDAP) are just some of the applications that have already been secured with SSL or its successor, *Transport Layer Security* (TLS).

The effort to secure all these protocols has taught us a number of significant lessons. First, doing a good job of using SSL/TLS to secure a protocol requires having a fairly deep knowledge of how it works. It is not possible to simply treat SSL/TLS as a black box that somehow magically provides security when used.

Second, although each application is slightly different, there seems to be a set of security problems that are common to every application you wish to secure. For instance, we usually need to figure out some way for the insecure and secure versions of an application protocol to coexist. Although there aren't cookie-cutter solutions to these problems, the security community is starting to develop a common set of techniques for solving these problems using SSL/TLS.

These techniques can often be applied to a new application protocol with minimal modification. In essence, we've developed a set of *design patterns* for securing protocols. Much of the work of securing a system is in recognizing which pattern most closely matches the system you're working with and then using the appropriate techniques.

The purpose of this book, then, is to address both of these needs. After reading this book, you should know most if not all of what you need to know in order to design secure systems using SSL/TLS. You'll know enough about SSL/TLS to understand what security features it can deliver and what it can't deliver. Further, you'll be familiar with the common design patterns for using SSL/TLS and be ready to apply them to new situations.

What This Book Provides

This book is intended for anyone who wants to understand and use SSL/TLS.

- For designers, it provides information on designing systems that use SSL/TLS as well as a library of the techniques that have already been used.

- For programmers who program with SSL/TLS, it provides information on what your libraries are doing under the covers and what those functions you're calling are really doing. Understanding these details is critical for obtaining acceptable and predictable application performance.

- For SSL/TLS implementors it acts as an adjunct to the standard, explaining obscure sections and describing both common practice and why things are the way they are.

Intended Audience

This book assumes a basic familiarity with how the TCP/IP protocols work. Readers who are unfamiliar with TCP/IP would be best served to consult one of the many fine books describing TCP/IP. *TCP/IP Illustrated, Volume 1* [Stevens1994] is a good choice. RFC 791 [Postel1991a], RFC 792 [Postel1991b], and RFC 793 [Postel1991c] provide the definitive reference for TCP/IP. Although some of this book will be understandable without a deep understanding of TCP/IP, much of the discussion of performance will be difficult to follow without an understanding of TCP behavior.

Because SSL/TLS is a cryptographic protocol, properly understanding it requires at least basic familiarity with cryptographic algorithms, including public key cryptography, symmetric cryptography, and digest algorithms. Chapter 1 provides an introduction to cryptography and communications, but space is too limited to do a complete job. We attempt to cover the requisite cryptographic details for understanding SSL/TLS; however, readers interested in a broader understanding of the cryptographic issues should consult a cryptography text such as [Schneier1996a] or [Kaufman1995].

Organization of the Book

This book is written in two halves, matching the two primary goals described previously: understanding the protocol and understanding how to use it. The first half, Chapters 1–6, is devoted to describing SSL and TLS. We concern ourselves with the technical details of how they work and their security and performance properties in isolation.

The second half of the book, Chapters 7–11, covers the design of application protocols and systems that use SSL/TLS for security. First we describe general guidelines for using SSL/TLS and then we discuss several protocols that have already been secured using SSL/TLS.

Chapter 1 — Security Concepts provides an introduction to cryptography and communications security, with an eye toward its use in SSL/TLS. If you're already familiar with communications security, you may want to skip this chapter. If, on the other hand, you're not familiar with security, you'll want to read this chapter carefully so you don't get lost later.

Chapter 2 — Introduction to SSL is a broad overview of the history of SSL/TLS and what sorts of security features it provides. We also provide a snapshot of the status of SSL/TLS-secured protocols as of the time of this writing.

Chapter 3 — Basic SSL covers the most common SSL/TLS operational mode. We describe an entire SSL/TLS connnection from start to finish. This chapter should give you a very good idea of how SSL/TLS works in practice. All the other operational modes can be easily understood once you understand this chapter.

Chapter 4 — Advanced SSL covers the rest of the major operational modes. We cover session resumption, client authentication, and a number of algorithms that are only now seeing deployment with SSL/TLS, such as DH/DSS and Kerberos.

Chapter 5 — SSL Security describes the security benefits that SSL offers as well as (even more important) those it doesn't offer. Whereas previous chapters mostly focused on describing how things work, this chapter focuses on what you need to do to make a system that uses SSL/TLS secure.

Chapter 6 — SSL Performance describes the performance profile of TLS-based systems. It's been widely observed that security imposes significant performance demands on systems, but it's not widely understood that this impact is limited to certain parts of the protocol. We'll discuss these issues with an eye to getting better performance while preserving good security.

Chapter 7 — Designing with SSL is a guide to using SSL/TLS to secure application layer protocols. We focus on identifying the required security properties and on well-understood design techniques for satisfying these properties.

Chapter 8 — Coding with SSL discusses the common programming idioms required to write software that uses SSL/TLS. We provide complete sample programs in C and Java using the OpenSSL and PureTLS toolkits.

Chapter 9 — HTTP over SSL describes the application that started it all. SSL was originally designed by Netscape to work with HTTP, and we cover both the traditional way of doing things and the replacement that's currently being proposed.

Chapter 10 — SMTP over TLS describes the use of TLS to secure the *Simple Mail Transport Protocol* (SMTP), which is used for transporting e-mail. SMTP is a bad match for TLS, and this chapter illustrates some of the limitations of SSL and TLS.

Chapter 11 — Contrasting Approaches is devoted to describing other alternatives to securing your applications. SSL/TLS isn't always the best solution and part of knowing how to use a protocol is knowing when not to. This chapter tries to give you a perspective on your other choices. We discuss IPSEC, S-HTTP, and S/MIME as alternatives to SSL/TLS.

How to Read This Book

This book is suitable for a number of audiences of different technical abilities and requirements. You should read any section that interests you, but depending on your needs you may want to focus on specific sections.

Protocol Designers

If you're designing a new application-level protocol or securing an existing protocol with SSL/TLS, you should read the first parts of Chapters 1–6 so that you have a good general understanding of how SSL/TLS works. Then carefully read Chapter 7 for a guide to SSL/TLS design principles. You can skip Chapter 8 unless you intend to implement your design, but be sure to read Chapters 9 and 10 so you can see real-world examples of how SSL/TLS should and should not be used in practice. Finally, before you start to design, read Chapter 11 to make sure that SSL/TLS is appropriate for your design and that you wouldn't be better served by using another security protocol.

Application Programmers

If you're writing an application that uses a preexisting SSL/TLS toolkit you can safely read only the first parts of Chapters 1–6. You should also read the summaries at the end of each chapter. These sections discuss SSL/TLS and SSL/TLS implementation techniques in overview form. This will provide enough information to understand what your SSL/TLS toolkit is doing. You should carefully read Chapters 7 and 8, paying special attention to the programming techniques discussed in Chapter 8. If you are implementing HTTP or SMTP over SSL, you should also read the chapters that deal with those protocols.

SSL/TLS Implementors

If you're implementing SSL/TLS from scratch, you should read the entire book. If you're already familiar with cryptography you can skip Chapter 1; however, if you don't have a detailed knowledge of cryptography you should read the entire chapter. You should pay particular attention to Chapters 2–6, which provide a detailed description of SSL/TLS and of the various implementation techniques required to produce a fast and secure implementation.

Just Curious

If you just want to learn about SSL/TLS you can skip around in the book. If you don't already know about cryptography, read all of Chapter 1. Then read Chapters 2–6 so you know how SSL/TLS works. Then you can read as much or as little of the rest of the book as interests you. It's probably worth reading Chapter 11 to get some perspective on how SSL/TLS compares to other security protocols.

SSL/TLS Versions

By now you've no doubt gotten tired of seeing the name SSL/TLS. We've been using it to avoid being specific about exactly which version we mean. There are currently two versions of SSL in wide deployment: SSL version 2 (SSLv2) and SSL version 3 (SSLv3). TLS, a modification of SSLv3, was standardized by the *Internet Engineering Task Force* (IETF) in 1999. Despite what you might think from the names, SSLv2 and SSLv3 are completely different protocols, and TLS is extremely similar to SSLv3. SSLv2 is essentially obsolete, and TLS isn't really in wide deployment as of this writing. In general, we'll use the term SSL to refer to SSLv3/TLS interchangeably. When we mean one or the other, we'll specify it explicitly. In the few instances when we're talking about SSL version 2, we'll use SSLv2.

Typographical Conventions

This book contains a number of network traces of real SSL or TLS sessions. In the presentation of such traces, we use a constant-width font to show the output of the program (CONSTRUCTED), and an italic font for comments inserted afterwards (*Comment*). Where the network trace displays a hexadecimal representation of the protocol data, we render that in a bold constant-width font (**01 02 03**). When we display encrypted data in plaintext form, we'll use an italic constant-width font (*data*).

Excerpts from standards (e.g., Internet RFCs) and protocol structure definitions in the main text are rendered in a sans serif font: (helvetica). In figures, we use Times for readability. Code snippets are rendered in a constant-width font (int). In a few special cases we'll need to wrap long lines, in which case we'll use the symbol ↵ at the end of the wrapped line to indicate that the text continues.

> Historical notes and asides will be indented and rendered in this smaller font.

Network Traces

The network traces in this book are all traces of real sessions, mostly captured on the author's home ethernet. A variety of client and server programs were used, including OpenSSL, Netscape Navigator, Internet Explorer, and qmail. The traces were captured using the tcpdump program and stored to disk. The author's ssldump SSL decoding package was used to generate the traces shown in the text. tcpdump can be obtained from http://www.tcpdump.org/. ssldump can be obtained from http://www.rtfm.com/ssldump/.

Source Code

This book contains a number of snippets of source code. The source code in Chapters 8 and 9 were written by the author and are Copyright © 1999–2000 Eric Rescorla. They may be used and reproduced for any purpose and without fee but no warranty of any kind is provided. Machine-readable versions are available from the author's Web site at http://www.rtfm.com/sslbook/examples.

The Java source code in Chapter 5 is part of the PureTLS Java SSL/TLS implementation. It may be obtained at http://www.rtfm.com/puretls. This source code is covered by the following copyright.

The SSL session caching example in Appendix A is from Ralf S. Engelschall's (rse's) Mod_ssl package, available at `http://www.modssl.org/`, The version used is 2.6.1-1.3.12. It is subject to the following copyright.

```
LOSS OF USE, DATA, OR PROFITS; OR BUSINESS INTERRUPTION)
HOWEVER CAUSED AND ON ANY THEORY OF LIABILITY, WHETHER IN CONTRACT,
STRICT LIABILITY, OR TORT (INCLUDING NEGLIGENCE OR OTHERWISE)
ARISING IN ANY WAY OUT OF THE USE OF THIS SOFTWARE, EVEN IF ADVISED
OF THE POSSIBILITY OF SUCH DAMAGE.

=====================================================================
```

Acknowledgments

It's impossible to write any book, much less a technical book, without the assistance of many people. As is customary, I'd like to use this space to acknowledge some of them.

My technical reviewers not only kept me honest but also ensured that my writing was as clear as I could make it. Joshua Ball, Joe Balsama, Douglas Barnes, Debasish Biswas, Andrew Brown, Robert Bruen, Megan Conklin, Russ Housley, Paul Kocher, Brian Korver, Chris Kostick, Marcus Leech, Robert Lynch, Joerg Meyer, D. Jay Newman, Tim Newsham, Stacey O'Rourke, Radia Perlman, Mark Schertler, Win Treese, Tom Weinstein, and Tom Woo all reviewed sections of the manuscript.

A number of people generously provided answers to technical questions that I had while writing, often without even knowing that they were doing so. In particular, I'd like to thank John Banes, Steve Bellovin, Burt Kaliski, Paul Kocher, Bodo Moeller, Dan Simon, and Robert Zuccherato for helping to fill in gaps in my knowledge. Special thanks goes to Terence Spies who provided valuable comments on the entire manuscript and answered numerous technical questions about Microsoft's SSL implementation.

This book makes extensive use of OpenSSL to generate demonstration SSL traffic. OpenSSL wouldn't exist without the hard work of Eric Young and Tim Hudson in creating SSLeay as well as the OpenSSL team in maintaining and improving OpenSSL after Eric Young's departure for greener pastures.

Brian Korver and Stacey O'Rourke from Network Alchemy/Nokia provided significant assistance in collecting some of the performance data in Chapter 6. Not only did they allow me to use their machines and network, they graciously reconfigured them in obscure ways so that I could produce particular cases.

Although I never met him, the late W. Richard Stevens nevertheless contributed greatly to this book. The idea of showing network traces to illustrate the protocol is taken from Stevens's fine *TCP/IP Illustrated* series. I've striven throughout this book (with only limited success) to emulate his clear and accessible style.

It wouldn't be possible to publish anything without the publisher and I've been quite pleased to be working with Addison-Wesley. I'd particularly like to thank Mary Hart for first suggesting this project to me and then putting up with the endless delays as the book exploded from a trim 200 pages to break through the 400 barrier. I'd also like to thank my production manager, Kathy Glidden, who patiently answered my endless typesetting questions.

Although they didn't contribute directly to the writing of this book, I'd like to thank Allan Schiffman, Marty Tenenbaum, and Jay Weber. Jay and Marty gave me a chance when I had talent and no experience. Over the eight years I've known him, Allan has taught me an immeasurable amount about computer science. In a similar vein, had my parents not taught me how to think, I wouldn't be able to do anything useful at all.

Jennifer Gates played a major part in keeping me sane during the writing—an unenviable task. In the past few years, she and her husband Lee have many times provided hospitality and friendship above and beyond the call of duty.

The other major factor in my continued sanity was triathlon. Kevin Joyce and Kyle Welch provided valuable advice and motivation in the upkeep of my habit.

Finally, I'd like to thank Lisa Dusseault and Kevin Dick. Lisa and Kevin both read the entire manuscript and helped take my rough drafts and turn them into readable chapters. Without them, I would most likely never have finished at all and the text would certainly be far worse than it is now.

Camera-ready copy was produced by the author using James Clark's Groff package. I welcome electronic mail from readers with comments, suggestions, etc.

Mountain View, CA   Eric Rescorla
September 2000   `ekr@rtfm.com`

1

Security Concepts

1.1 Introduction

This chapter is intended to provide a basic introduction to communications security and cryptography. Communications security is a complicated topic and many fine books have been written about it. Our intent here is not to provide an exhaustive discussion of the topic but rather to teach you enough to understand the concepts and terminology that will be used throughout the rest of the book. Readers who are already familiar with cryptography and communications security should feel free to skip this chapter entirely.

We start by explaining the sorts of threats we're concerned about and the various sorts of security services we can provide. Next we provide a broad overview of cryptographic algorithms and how to put them together to provide these security services. Finally, we discuss some details of the various algorithms which will be relevant when we discuss their use in SSL/TLS.

1.2 The Internet Threat Model

The first thing that we need to do is define our *threat model*. A threat model describes what resources we expect the attacker to have available and what attacks the attacker can be expected to mount. Nearly every security system is vulnerable to some threat or another. To see this, imagine that you keep your papers in a completely unbreakable safe. That's all well and good, but if someone has planted a video camera in your office they can see your confidential information whenever you take it out to use it, so the safe hasn't bought you that much.

Therefore, when we define a threat model, we're concerned not only with defining what attacks we are going to worry about but also those we're not going to worry about. Failure to take this important step typically leads to complete deadlock as designers try to figure out how to counter every possible threat. What's important is to figure out which threats are realistic and which ones we can hope to counter with the tools available to us.

Designers of Internet security protocols typically share a more or less common threat model. First, it's assumed that the actual end systems that the protocol is being executed on are secure. Protecting against attacks where one of the end systems is under the control of the attacker is extraordinarily difficult, if not impossible. This assumption comes with two caveats. First, compromise of any single end system shouldn't break security for everyone. There should be no *single point of failure*. For instance, if an attacker breaks system A, then all communications between B and A may be compromised, but communications between B and C should be safe. If we must have a single point of failure it must be possible to harden it against attack. Second, attackers may control systems that attempt to pose as legitimate end systems. All we're assuming is that users can expect that their own machines haven't been compromised.

Other than that, we assume that the attacker has more or less complete control of the communications channel between any two machines. He can certainly inject packets into the network with arbitrary address information, both for the sender and the receiver, and can read any packet that is on the network and remove any packet packet he chooses. Any packet you receive must be assumed to potentially come from the attacker and any packet you send might be modified in transit. An attack that depends on the attacker writing data to the network is known as an *active attack*. An attack that merely involves reading data off the network is known as a *passive attack*.

An obvious corollary of the assumption that the attacker can modify traffic is that the attacker can shut down all communication between any pair of machines simply by removing all relevant packets. This is one form of *denial-of-service* attack. Another form would be to force you to use up enormous CPU resources responding to connections. Conventionally, protocol designers don't worry about denial-of-service attacks, not because these attacks aren't important but because they're extraordinarily difficult to prevent.

One of the most important functions of a threat model is to arrange that security doesn't become more expensive than it is worth. Security measures should be employed only up to the point where the cost to implement them doesn't exceed the expected risk. Failure to make this judgment correctly can easily lead to a situation where no risk is judged acceptable and thus no acceptable system can be designed.

Part of the risk calculation is the effort required by the attacker to mount a given attack, and cost generally increases with each attack prevented. No security system is resistant to every attack. The function of a security model is to allow designers to determine which attacks are worthwhile to prevent.

However, accurately estimating how much security you need requires accurately estimating the attacker's capabilities. If an attack that was originally considered impractical is discovered to be simple, then there will be a window of vulnerability while people adjust their security models and implementations to compensate.

1.3   The Players

To make it easier to understand the various examples we'll be discussing in this chapter, we'll use the same names repeatedly for the various parties. By convention, the two communicating parties are referred to as Alice and Bob, after the names used in the original RSA paper [Rivest1979]. The attacker is known merely as "the attacker."

1.4   The Goals of Security

Most people speak of security as if it were a single monolithic property of a protocol, but as the previous discussion shows, that's clearly not true. Depending on precisely what capabilities the attacker has, he poses different risks to the security of our data. Communications security consists of a number of distinct but somewhat related properties. Exactly how these are partitioned depends on whom you're talking to. The partitioning we've found most useful is to divide them into three major categories: *confidentiality*, *message integrity*, and *endpoint authentication*.

Confidentiality

When most people think of security, they think of *confidentiality*. Confidentiality means that your data is kept secret from unintended listeners. Usually, these listeners are eavesdroppers. When the government taps your phone, that poses a risk to your confidentiality. (Incidentally, it's also a passive attack, unless the Fed on the line starts trying to imitate your voice.)

Obviously, if you have secrets, you're concerned that no one else knows them and so at minimum you want confidentiality. When you see spies in the movies go into the bathroom and turn on all the water to foil bugging, the property they're looking for is confidentiality.

Message Integrity

The second primary goal is *message integrity*. The basic idea here is that we want to be sure that the message we receive is the one that the sender sent. In paper-based systems, some message integrity comes automatically. When you receive a letter written in pen you can be fairly certain that no words have been removed by an attacker because pen marks are difficult to remove from paper. However, an attacker could have easily added some marks to the paper and completely changed the meaning of the message.

On the other hand, in the electronic world, since all bits look alike, it's trivial to tamper with messages in transit. You simply remove the message from the wire, copy out the parts you like, add whatever data you want, and generate a new message of your choosing, and the recipient is no wiser. This is the equivalent of the attacker taking a letter you wrote, buying some new paper, and recopying the message with changes. It's just a lot easier to do electronically because all bits look alike.

Endpoint Authentication

The third property we're concerned with is *endpoint authentication*. What we mean by this is that we know that one of the endpoints in the communication (typically the sender) is the one we intended. Without endpoint authentication, it's very difficult to provide either confidentiality or message integrity. For instance, if we receive a message from Alice, the property of message integrity doesn't do us much good unless we know that it was in fact sent by Alice and not the attacker. Similarly, if we want to send a confidential message to Bob, it's not of much value to us if we're actually sending a confidential message to the attacker.

Note that endpoint authentication can be provided asymmetrically. When you call someone on the phone, you can be fairly certain that you have the right person—or at least that you got a person who's actually at the phone number you called. On the other hand, if they don't have caller ID, then the receivers of a phone call have no idea who's calling them. Calling someone on the phone is an example of recipient authentication, in which you know who the recipient of the call is (it's difficult but not impossible to compromise the phone network), but they don't know anything about the sender.

On the other hand, cash is an example of sender authentication. A dollar bill is like a message signed by the government. The government has no idea who's got any given dollar bill, but you can be fairly certain that any bill was actually printed by the U.S. Mint because currency is difficult to forge.

A Physical Example

To make this all a little clearer, let's examine a physical system that provides all three properties together and see how the various physical security features interact to provide each property. We'll start with a system with no security features and keep making changes until we have all the security features we want.

You receive a postcard in the mail, addressed to you, ostensibly from Alice. What can you know about it and its contents? Not much. Any random eavesdropper could have read it, and they could have changed it as well.

One potential improvement might be for Alice to write a letter instead of a postcard and put the letter in an envelope. Does this improve the situation? Not much, actually. By examining the envelope, you can be fairly confident that it wasn't tampered with (it could have been steamed open, but you can get envelopes that are resistant to this), so you might think that you've got confidentiality and message integrity for the contents. This isn't necessarily true. The attacker could have opened the original envelope, read the message or modified the contents, and then resealed it in a new envelope. So, in fact, you can't have any confidence in the message at all. Both message integrity and confidentiality have collapsed because you don't have sender authentication.

Note that from Alice's perspective, the situation is even worse. As far as she knows, the message was opened as soon as the mail carrier picked it up from her door. We'll show how to fix this problem a little later.

The traditional way to ensure that a letter is not opened in transit is to affix a wax seal across the envelope flap. It's possible to open and reattach such seals, but let's assume for the moment that it wasn't possible. Another more modern approach is for the sender to sign across the flap. Assuming that you recognize either the seal or the sender's signature, you can have some confidence that the envelope arrived unopened, because signatures are difficult to forge.

However, we can have this confidence only if we have some way of knowing who ought to have sent us the message. What if the attacker opened the envelope and then resealed it with his own envelope, and signed his own name across the flap? If we didn't know that the signature should in fact be Alice's, we wouldn't be able to detect this attack.

To see why this would be useful, imagine that the envelope contains an order form for something, along with Alice's credit card number. The attacker changes the message to have his shipping address but Alice's credit card number and reseals the envelope. You incorrectly ship to the attacker and bill Alice. This attack is very difficult to stop with the sorts of technology we've discussed so far.

The mechanisms we've been talking about so far—envelopes, seals, etc, are *tamper-evident*. The receiver can tell that the contents were tampered with, but can't stop it from happening. The easiest way to stop this new attack is to use packaging that's *tamper-resistant*. (The phrase *tamper-proof* is often used, but that seems overly optimistic.) Imagine that instead of sending a letter, Alice sends us a safe containing the letter. The only two keys to the safe are in Alice's and our possession.

This pretty much fixes the problem entirely. Because you have the only other key and you know that you didn't send the letter yourself, you can be quite confident that Alice sent it, so you have sender authentication. Because no one besides you or Alice can open the safe, you know that it hasn't been opened and read or modified in transit, so you've got confidentiality and message integrity as well. Similarly, Alice knows that no one else but you can open the safe, so she can be assured that she has recipient authentication, confidentiality, and message integrity.

This approach has (at least) one serious problem. You have to exchange one of a pair of keys with everyone with whom you might ever want to communicate. If you think about how many messages the typical business sends in a day, you'll see that this method is inconvenient.

This example is useful for two purposes. First, it illustrates the various security services we might wish to provide. Just as important, it illustrates the concept of the threat model. Because it's fairly expensive to go around mailing safes, this isn't a very practical approach, and people typically settle for lower levels of security and just assume that the postal service is trustworthy. For particularly confidential information, they might use a courier, but that's about the typical limit of their concern. Attackers who are able to open the mail and arbitrarily change it just aren't part of the standard business threat model. The cost of providing high security for every message mailed is simply so high that no company can afford to do so.

1.5   Tools of the Trade

Note that we haven't even mentioned cryptography yet. We're going to get to it now. *Cryptology* is the theory of designing the various algorithms we use to provide security. *Cryptography* is the study of using these algorithms to secure systems and protocols. This section is going to provide a broad overview of the types of cryptographic algorithms available to us. The next section will discuss how to use them to provide security services.

Encryption

Conceptually, the easiest sort of algorithm to understand is encryption. The idea is simple: an encryption algorithm takes some data (called *plaintext*) and converts it to *ciphertext* under control of a *key*. The ciphertext looks like random data and no useful information about the plaintext (except possibly the length) can be gathered without knowing the key. The key is usually just a short random string, usually on the order of 8–24 bytes. The relationship between these elements is shown in Figure 1.1.

$$\text{Plaintext} \xrightarrow{\text{Encrypt}} \text{Ciphertext} \xrightarrow{\text{Decrypt}} \text{Plaintext}$$

Figure 1.1 Encryption and decryption

An encryption algorithm should be viewed as providing pure confidentiality. The exact effects on the plaintext of tampering with the ciphertext vary depending on the exact encryption algorithm used, but such tampering is often quite difficult to detect. Thus, when we receive a message that has only been encrypted, we don't know that it hasn't been tampered with.

A good encryption algorithm should have its security totally determined by the number of possible keys. The fastest attack should be *exhaustive search*: given a ciphertext, the attacker tries each key one at a time until he finds a key that produces a plausible decryption. The security of the algorithm should depend solely on the secrecy of the key. The algorithm should not need to be secret to be secure.

An attack in which the attacker knows the plaintext corresponding to the ciphertext is called a *known plaintext* attack. An attack in which the attacker doesn't know the plaintext is called a *ciphertext only* attack. Even if the attacker doesn't know the details of the plaintext, he may know something about it, which would allow him to mount a ciphertext only attack. For instance, the attacker may know that the plaintext is ASCII, in which case any decryption that includes non-ASCII characters must be using the wrong key.

Because the sender and the recipient share the same key (which key must be kept secret), what we've just described is sometimes referred to as *secret key cryptography*, as opposed to *public key cryptography*, which we'll talk about in a little bit.

Encryption algorithm design has been a very active field, and there are tens if not hundreds of available algorithms. The most popular algorithms include the *Data Encryption Standard* (DES) [NIST1993a], *Triple-DES* (DES repeated three times) [ANSI1985] , *RC2* [Rivest1998], and *RC4* (no official RC4 specification has ever been published but see [Schneier1996a] for a description).

Message Digest

A message digest is simply a function that takes as an input an arbitrary length message and outputs a fixed-length string that is characteristic of the message. The most important property of a message digest is *irreversibility*. It should be extremely difficult to compute a message given its digest. It's easy to show via a counting argument that the digest value doesn't give enough data to generate the original message; the number of possible messages (of arbitrary length) is far longer then the number of fixed-length digests; many messages must map to a single digest, making it impossible to reverse the function. However, for a digest to be secure, it must be difficult to generate *any* of the messages that digests to this value. By difficult, we mean that you need to search a message space of proportional size to the size of the digest in order to find a matching message text.

The second important property of a message digest is that it should be difficult to produce two messages M and M' such that they have the same digest. This property is known as *collision-resistance*. It turns out that the strength of any message digest against finding collisions is only half the size of the digest, so a 128-bit digest is only 64 bits strong against collisions; it requires roughly 2^{64} operations to generate a collision. As a consequence, the limiting factor in choosing a digest length is usually strength against collisions rather than strength against reversibility.

The primary uses for message digests are for the computation of digital signatures and *message authentication codes* (MACs), both of which we'll talk about later in this chapter. However, there's at least one use of simple digests that's obvious now: they can be used to prove possession of a secret without revealing the secret. Imagine that you've invented something new and you want to show that you invented it first without actually telling anyone what it is. You write the secret down, compute the digest, and publish the digest in the newspaper classified ads. Then, if anyone challenges your primacy, you can show them the original text and they can independently verify the digest.

The most widely used message digest algorithms are Message Digest 5 (MD5) [Rivest1992] and Secure Hash Algorithm 1 (SHA-1) [NIST1994a]. The term *hash algorithm* is often used synonymously with the term *message digest*, because digest algorithms are superficially similar to normal hash algorithms. I'll be using the terms *hash* and *digest* interchangeably throughout the text.

Message Authentication Codes

Imagine that Alice and Bob share a key and Alice wants to send Bob a message that he will know is from her. If she wanted to encrypt it, that would be straightforward—she'd just use the key they share as an encryption key. But as we said, this doesn't provide any real assurance that the message hasn't been tampered with, and only some assurance that it's from Alice. What we need is a new tool, the *message authentication code* (MAC). A MAC is sort of like a digest algorithm, but it also incorporates a key into the computation, so the MAC is dependent on both the key being used and the message being MACed. Actually, MACs are usually constructed from digest algorithms.

Although there have been a number of attempts to construct MACs based on various digest algorithms, the Internet security community seems to be settling on a construct called HMAC [Krawczyk1997], which describes how to create a MAC with provable security properties based on any digest for which a certain somewhat reasonable set of assumptions holds. A variant of HMAC is used in SSLv3, and HMAC itself is used in TLS.

The Key Management Problem

With the addition of a MAC to our toolbox, we now have an electronic system equivalent to mailing safes around, as we discussed at the beginning of the chapter. Naively, Alice can take our message, encrypt it with our shared key, add a MAC also based on the shared key, and send it to Bob. She knows that only Bob can read it because only Bob has the shared key needed to decrypt it. Similarly, Bob knows that only Alice could have sent the message because only Alice has the shared key needed to create the MAC on the message. Thus, he knows that Alice sent the message and that it hasn't been tampered with.

So, we have everything we need, right? Wrong. Although these messages are lighter than safes and thus cheap to mail around, we still have the problem of sharing a key with everyone we communicate with. This is inconvenient because it means having all those keys floating around. But more important, it means that you must actually meet everyone with whom you want to communicate in order to exchange keys. This puts a damper on your being able to buy anything over the Internet unless you've personally met the vendor. This inconvenience is referred to as the key management problem.

Key Distribution Centers

The most popular solution to the key management problem is *public key cryptography* (PKC), which we'll talk about in the next section, but there is also a fix for the key management problem using only the tools we've talked about so far. The basic idea is that we use a *trusted third party*, which we trust to authenticate other parties to us. The third party is usually implemented as a secure machine somewhere on the network. This machine is called a *key distribution center* (KDC). Each person who wants to communicate securely shares a key with the KDC. When Alice wants to communicate with Bob, she sends a message to the KDC, protected with the key she shares with the KDC, requesting to communicate with Bob. The KDC generates a new encryption key for the Alice-Bob communication and returns it in a message called a *ticket*.

A ticket consists of two messages in one. The first is a message to Alice with the new key. The second is a message to Bob encrypted under Bob's key containing the new key. Alice forwards Bob's half of the ticket to Bob and now Alice and Bob share a key. The basic version of this protocol was invented by Needham and Schroeder [Needham1978], but the most widely deployed variant is Kerberos, which is used extensively for authentication and encryption at MIT, among other places (see [Miller1987]).

This scheme has two primary drawbacks. First, the KDC must be online all the time because no communication can be initiated when it's offline. Second, the KDC can read all the traffic sent by any two parties. It can also forge traffic between two parties. Worse yet, if the KDC is ever compromised, all traffic sent between any two KDC users is compromised. This is not good. Nevertheless, there has been a fair amount of interest in this type of protocol for closed systems.

Public Key Cryptography

In 1976, some very smart people at Stanford figured out a better way to solve the key management problem. In the article "New Directions in Cryptography" [Diffie1976], Whitfield Diffie and Martin Hellman suggested what we now know as public key cryptography. The basic idea is that you have a function in which encryption and decryption use different keys. You publish your encryption key (the *public key*) but keep your decryption key (the *private key*) secret. (Because the public and private keys are different, public key cryptography is sometimes called asymmetric cryptography and secret key cryptography is sometimes called symmetric cryptography). This means that anyone can send you a secret message without ever meeting you. This solves the confidentiality part of the equation while eliminating the inconvenience of preshared keys.

> As it turns out, public key cryptography was also invented by one of the British intelligence agencies, the *Communications-Electronics Security Group* (CESG) during 1970 to 1974. They referred to the practice as *non-secret encryption* (NSE). Interestingly, the techniques invented include both Diffie-Hellman and a variant of RSA, which implies that these methods are somehow fundamental. However, the results were classified and the academic community reinvented both techniques independently. The prior existence of these techniques in the intelligence community was only revealed in 1998. [Ellis1987] details the history of NSE. [Ellis1970] describes a demonstration that NSE was possible. [Cocks1973, Williamson1974, Williamson1976] describe the specific techniques.

It turns out that PKC has a solution to the authentication part of the problem, too. Your private key can be used to create something called a *digital signature*, which bears the same relationship to a MAC that public key encryption bears to secret-key encryption; you use your private key to *sign* a message and the receiver uses your public key to *verify* your signature. Note that a digital signature has one important property that a MAC does not: *nonrepudiation*. Either sender or receiver can generate a MAC, but only the signer can generate a signature. Thus, the recipient can prove that the sender signed the message and the sender cannot deny it.

Certification

Unfortunately, what we have so far doesn't completely solve the key management problem, though it gives us the tools we need to solve it. The easiest way to see what is still wrong is to ask how the parties get each other's public keys. If the keys are published electronically or if they're exhanged by the communicating parties, then an attacker can tamper with them while they are in transit to the receiver. When two parties want to communicate, the attacker intercepts their keys and instead sends his own key to each party. Thus, each party encrypts to him and then he reencrypts to the real recipient, as shown in Figure 1.2. This is called a *man-in-the-middle* attack.

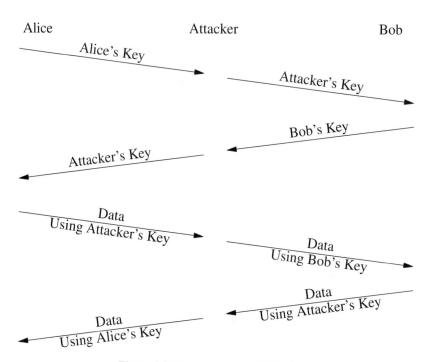

Figure 1.2 The man-in-the-middle attack

However, if keys are published physically, it's a major inconvenience. The solution is (again) to have a trusted third party, called a *Certificate Authority* (CA). The CA publishes a directory signed with the CA's private key. In actual practice, rather than signing a directory, what the CA does is sign individual messages which contain both the name of the key owner and his public key. These messages are generally known as *certificates*, hence the name certificate authority. The primary standard for certificates is X.509 [ITU1988a] profiled for the Internet in RFC 2459 [Housley1999a].

The CA's public key is published in some physical form, but there aren't many CAs and they don't change their keys often, so it's not such a big problem. In actual practice, CA keys are usually compiled into the software that needs them so that they are distributed with that software. This makes a lot of sense when the software is shipped on CD-ROM or floppy, but sometimes that software is just downloaded, in which case we're right back where we started—which just goes to show that people often don't act rationally.

Figure 1.3 shows an expanded view of a public key certificate. The details aren't that important, but notice the basic structure: The certificate contains an *issuer name* (the name of the signer of the certificate, in this case "Secure Server..."), *subject name* (the name of the holder of the key that the certificate vouched for, in this case "www.amazon.com..."), the *subject public key* (the key itself), a bunch of control information such as expiry date and serial number, and a *signature* over the whole data object.

```
version:                          v1
serial number:                    2A 17 EF 73 97 07 74 7B E2 4B FB
    61 95 DB 4D 77
signature
    algorithm:                    md5WithRSAEncryption
issuer:
    C=US
    O=RSA Data Security, Inc.
    OU=Secure Server Certification Authority
validity
    not before:                   Sat Jan 28 02:21:56 1995
    not after:                    Thu Feb 15 02:21:55 1996
subject:
    C=US
    ST=Washington
    L=Seattle
    O=Amazon.com, Inc.
    OU=Software
    CN=www.amazon.com
subject public key
    algorithm:                    rsaEncryption
    modulus
        bit length:               1024
        value:
            00 C8 1B 8B FA 40 C3 5B E3 46 3F 17 10 56 19 64 C4 F4 F9
            CC AE CA F7 0B 02 1C C3 2D 27 60 91 16 C0 A1 23 8B CA 90
            77 31 25 CA D9 DE B0 87 F5 25 C9 12 7A 95 DF DC 6C E4 1C
            C3 31 9F 77 BE 69 3E 9F BB 35 BF F3 3D BA 7A 72 DA 5D 0C
            60 91 29 F8 89 67 50 5C 32 46 63 F2 FF 42 9D 24 F2 DC 6F
            E5 CA D3 CD 3A AB 9D 5F A9 4D B0 82 91 E3 D3 EA AA EF 78
            8A C1 06 B6 6D EA 56 B8 7E 68 5D AF 4D 85 AF
    public exponent:
        bit length:               2
        value:                    03
signature
    value:
            03 43 60 4B 5B 4B F1 78 56 BF B4 9B 81 E6 EE 0D 19 1B 4E 43 BD
            D9 C7 62 62 55 32 C7 15 A4 33 3A CA 0E 60 E5 FE D7 53 94 C6 AC
            17 D0 CE 7B 11 27 0C 3B 26 19 6D 35 55 4C D8 26 F4 5F F0 90 0D
            90 7F FC 39 47 FE EE B4 72 92 93 BF 93 7F 5C 56 38 10 F5 E5 58
            B5 6C 3E E0 B4 55 8D 74 BE 84 F1 53 67 49 5B 14 12 E6 A7 59 A9
            97 9E 6C E4 59 A6 8F 4E 7E B5 D9 2D 80 3F 38 3C 4C 11 A7 37
```

Figure 1.3 A public key certificate

Public key solutions involving certification still involve a trusted third party (the CA), but they do fix the primary problems we described with KDC-based systems. Because the same certificate can be used to prove one's public key to anyone, the CA doesn't have to be online in order for Alice and Bob to communicate. And because the CA doesn't have access to anyone's private keys, it can't read any of the messages.

Distinguished Names

The subject name and the issuer name in the certificate are X.500 *distinguished names* (DNs) [ITU1988b]. The idea behind a distinguished name is to provide a unique name for every network entity. In order to do this, a DN has a hierarchical structure. A DN consists of a series of *relative distinguished names* (RDNs). RDNs are like components of DNS names. Each RDN specifies the name of the entity in the namespace of some other entity. Thus, the highest-level RDN must be globally unique, but each RDN under that must be unique only within the scope of the previous RDNs. RDNs have structure as well. Each RDN consists of a series of *attribute-value assertions*. An AVA is basically a key/value pair. Figure 1.4 shows a possible sample DN.

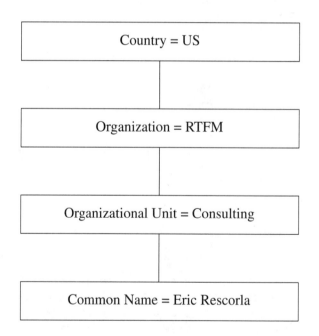

Figure 1.4 A sample DN

Each box in Figure 1.4 represents an RDN. Thus, the top-level RDN contains one AVA, with the *attribute* being *Country* and the *value* being *US*, and so on. Note that although in theory each RDN may have multiple AVAs, in practice, they almost always have just one. Similarly, although in theory any AVA may appear at any level, in practice they go from least specific (country) to most specific (common name—roughly corresponding to your name—or e-mail address). It's quite common to render distinguished names in text form, in which case the attribute names are abbreviated. The name in Figure 1.4 would be rendered

```
C=US, O=RTFM, OU=Consulting, CN=Eric Rescorla
```

Extensions

Certificates contain a standard set of values, but it's quite common to want to put other information in them. X.509 version 3 provides for an arbitrary series of *extensions*. Extensions are simply type-value pairs. Although X.509 allows for private extensions, a number of standard extensions have been provided. The three important ones for our purposes are

subjectAltName contains other names for this user. These may be other DNs, but may also be other name forms, including dNSName (a DNS hostname) and emailAddress (an e-mail address).

keyUsage contains a bitmask of acceptable uses for this key, including signing, encryption, etc.

extendedKeyUsage allows a list of arbitrary *object identifiers* (OIDs), (see the *ASN.1, BER, and DER* section) listing detailed possible uses for this key.

Certificate Revocation

Consider the case where user's key is compromised by being lost or exposed. We'd like to have some way to communicate to other users that a public key and the certificate verifying it were no longer to be trusted. The most common way to approach this problem is to use something called a *Certificate Revocation List* (CRL, pronounced "krill").

A CRL is a signed, dated list of all the certificates that have been *revoked*, that is, they are no longer considered to be valid. Assuming that the CA in question issues CRLs, verifying a certificate requires obtaining the appropriate (latest) CRL and checking that the certificate doesn't appear on that list.

Unfortunately, CRLs don't work very well, for two reasons. First, they need to be issued periodically, which means that there is a window of vulnerability between the time period when a CRL issues and the next CRL is due. The key might have been compromised but users can't tell because the CRL on which it would have appeared has not been issued. Second, CRL distribution is problematic. CRLs can get rather large and either protocols need to carry them around or users need to get them from the CAs, which requires the CA to be online.

If the CA is going to be online, it can also provide *online certificate status*. This can provide completely up-to-date revocation status. The user can make a request of the CA for the status of a given certificate and the CA provides a signed response. The *Online*

Certificate Status Protocol (OCSP) [Myers1999] can be used to do this job. However, the need to sign these responses creates a high load on the server CPU. Obviously, this is undesirable. Some optimizations that reduce this load [Kocher1996a] have been described but are not in wide deployment.

ASN.1, BER, and DER

ASN.1 falls into the category of "highly unpleasant things that it is sometimes necessary to know." A lot of our basic security tools, in particular X.509 certificates, end up being defined using ASN.1. ASN.1 was designed as part of the International Telecommunications Union's *Open Standards Interconnect* (OSI) effort as a description language for the OSI protocols. The basic idea was to create a system for describing data structures that would allow machine generation of data encoders and decoders (generically, *codecs*).

This seemed like a good idea at the time: you have a language which can be used to describe data formats as structured types, much like that for C structs and Java classes. This language is called *Abstract Syntax Notation 1* (ASN.1). You also describe how to map structures in this language into data encodings on the wire. This allows you to write a compiler that does two things:

1.   Generate mappings from ASN.1 structures to whatever language you're using

2.   Automatically generate codecs for the structures

Unfortunately, ASN.1 is complicated and counterintuitive, making it hard to write the ASN.1 specifications themselves as well as making compilers fairly complicated. Worse yet, apparently on the theory that more is better, the people who designed ASN.1 defined not one but upwards of four different sets of encoding rules for laying out the data on the wire. Each encoding serves a slightly different set of goals, but the result is a confusing mess.

The two ASN.1 encoding rules we'll be concerned with are *Basic Encoding Rules* (BER) and *Distinguished Encoding Rules* (DER). Whereas BER allows several ways to encode any given piece of data, DER is a subset of BER that picks one and sticks with it so that you can be sure that any given structure will be encoded the same way by any codec. The advantage of BER is that it is often more efficient to BER encode data than to DER encode it. However, if you are digitally signing data, you want semantically equivalent messages to always have the same encoding, and so you need DER.

We're not even going to try to describe how to read ASN.1 in any detail. In order to get the general idea, all you really need to know is that it's like C structures except that the type definitions are backwards: the name comes first and the data type comes second. Figure 1.5 shows a sample ASN.1 structure. What it says is that Foo is a sequence of two elements, bar and mumble. bar is of type INTEGER and mumble is of type BIT STRING.

```
Foo ::= SEQUENCE {
    bar INTEGER,
    mumble BIT STRING
}
```

Figure 1.5 A sample ASN.1 structure

This example should give you enough information to get the general idea of what ASN.1 structures mean. If you're interested in the details, your best bet is to refer to [RSA1993a]. The actual standard is in [ITU1988c] and [ITU1988d].

For the purposes of this book, you only really need to know about one other thing: *object identifiers* (OIDs). OIDs are globally unique byte strings assigned to any kind of object, such as algorithms, keyusages, etc. The OID space is *federated*—ISO has assigned sections of the OID space to various entities who can further divide the space among other entities. Thus, a large number of organizations can assign OIDs and it's possible to get your own OID section (called an *arc*) if you want to assign private but unique OIDs.

1.6   Putting It All Together

We now have enough pieces to build some simple security systems. The system we're about to describe sounds complicated, but it's important to realize that nearly every piece of communcations security technology we'll be discussing is built from one of four simple pieces: *encryption*, *digest*, *public key encryption*, and *digital signature*. These pieces are often called *security primitives*, and primitives can be combined to build more complicated structures.

For instance, public key methods are much slower than secret key methods, so it's convenient to combine the two techniques, using public keys to exchange secret keys. To encrypt a message, Alice generates a random secret key (variously called a *session key*, *message encryption key*, *content encryption key*, or *data encryption key*) and encrypts it under Bob's public key, which she gets from Bob's certificate. She then encrypts the message with a symmetric algorithm using the session key. This combination of public key encryption and symmetric encryption provides fast message encryption with the benefits of certificate-based key management.

Similarly, digital signature algorithms are very slow and can only be used with small messages. But combined with message digests, they can be used to efficiently sign large messages. To sign a message, Alice computes the message digest of the message and signs that digest with her private key. The combination of message digests and digital signatures provides message integrity and sender authentication without shared keys.

1.7   A Simple Secure Messaging System

Let's start by designing a simple secure messaging system that would be suitable for sending secure e-mail messages. A large number of such protocols have been designed, including S/MIME [Dusse1998], PGP [Atkins1996], and PEM [Linn1993, Kent1993, Balenson1993, Kaliski1993]. All of them follow the same basic model, which we will now describe.

The sending process, shown in Figure 1.6, closely follows the description of the previous section.

1. Alice computes the message digest.

2. She signs the message digest and attaches the resulting digital signature plus her certificate to the message.

3. She produces a random session key and uses it to encrypt the signed message, certificate, and signature.

4. Finally, she encrypts the session key under Bob's public key and attaches the wrapped session key to the message. She now has a message she can send to Bob.

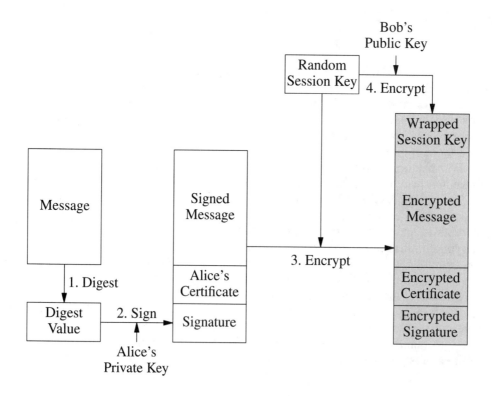

Figure 1.6 The message sending process

The receiving process, shown in Figure 1.7, reverses these steps.

1. Bob uses his private key to decrypt the session key.

2. He uses the session key to decrypt the message, certificate, and digital signature.

3. He computes the message digest of the message himself.

4. He verifies Alice's certificate and extracts Alice's public key.

5. He uses Alice's public key to verify Alice's digital signature.

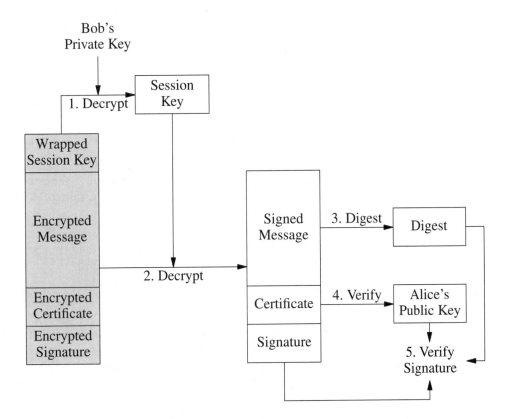

Figure 1.7 The message receiving process

1.8   A Simple Secure Channel

The system we've just described works pretty well if all we're doing is sending single messages around, as with e-mail, but it rapidly becomes inadequate if what we want is to have a communications channel over which we can pass arbitrary messages. We'd like to be able to establish a set of secret keys that we could use for the entire connection. This would let us avoid doing expensive public key operations for every packet, which is especially important for interactive applications where each keystroke might generate a packet.

A second improvement we'd like to add in an interactive protocol is the ability to do *certificate discovery*. In the messaging protocol we described in the previous secion, Alice needs to be able to get Bob's certificate before she can send him a message. This is done either by consulting a directory or by having Bob send a nonencrypted message containing his certificate. In an interactive protocol, though, Bob can send Alice his certificate as the first thing he does.

A typical design for such an interactive system is to have a handshake phase where Alice and Bob authenticate each other and establish a set of keys. They then move on to a data transfer phase where they use those keys to actually transmit the data they're interested in. The rest of this section builds a simple protocol that does this job. We'll call it *Toy Security Protocol* (TSP).

The basic stages in our protocol will be

Handshake. Alice and Bob use their certificates and private keys to authenticate each other and exchange a shared secret.

Key derivation. Alice and Bob use the agreed upon shared secret to derive a set of cryptographic keys which can be used to protect the traffic.

Data transfer. The data to be transmitted is broken up into a series of *records*, each of which is individually protected. This allows data to be transmitted as soon as it is ready and processed as soon as it is received.

Connection closure. Special protected closure messages are used to securely close the connection. This prevents an attacker from forging closes and truncating the data being transferred.

A Simple Handshake

The first thing that Alice does is to send Bob a message saying that she's ready to communicate. There's no cryptographic content here. It's just a "Hello." Bob responds with his certificate. We've now accomplished certificate discovery, so we could go back to sending around individual messages like we did before, but there's a better way; what we actually want to do is arrange that Alice and Bob share a single secret, which we'll call the *master secret* (MS). Afterwards, Alice should know that only Bob knows the MS and vice versa. Then we'll use the MS to create a set of keys that we can use to encrypt the data.

The first step is for Alice to generate a random number to be the MS. Actually doing this requires having a *cryptographically secure* random number generator, which is trickier than it sounds. There are a number of techniques, but they border on magic and we won't discuss them here. Once Alice has the master secret, she simply encrypts it under Bob's public key to produce the *encrypted master secret* (EMS). We've now done the first half of the job. Alice knows that only she and Bob have the MS. If Bob doesn't care about her identity, she could just send the EMS to Bob and they could start communicating. This is called *one-way authentication* (see Figure 1.8.) This sort of authentication would be useful (for example) if Bob were running an Internet store and only needs Alice's credit card number.

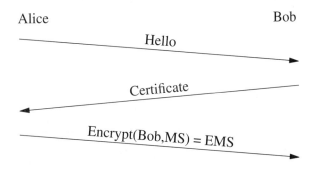

Figure 1.8 A handshake with one-way authentication

On the other hand, if Bob does care about Alice's identity, we need to add one more feature to the protocol to let him have that assurance. If Alice signs the EMS with her private key, then Bob can verify the signature and be sure that Alice vouches for the EMS she just sent.

This new protocol also contains one new subtlety: Bob sends Alice a random number called a *nonce* along with his certificate (see Figure 1.9.) The idea here is to stop an attacker from retransmitting all of Alice's messages to Bob and convincing him that he's engaging in a new conversation. This attack is known as a *replay attack*. We'll use the nonce when we make keys to ensure that the keys produced by this handshake are different from the keys produced by any other handshake.

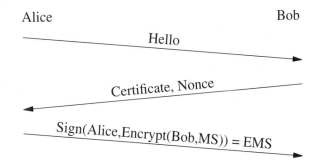

Figure 1.9 A handshake with mutual authentication

A Simple Data Transfer Protocol

At the end of the handshake, Alice and Bob share a master secret, but what good is that? The purpose of the exercise is for Alice and Bob to transfer data, not random numbers. In order to achieve that goal, we need an entirely different protocol whose job it is to arrange that. The rest of this section describes how to build a simplified one.

Making Some Keys

The first thing we need to do is to make some keys. In general, it's considered a bad idea to use the same key for more than one type of cryptographic operation. We'll see one reason for this in the discussion of stream ciphers later on, but you can consider it a form of insurance. Imagine that the attacker figured out how to break one algorithm (say the encryption algorithm). If you use the same key for MAC and encryption and the encryption is broken, then the communication is totally insecure. If you use different keys, then the MAC will still be secure even if the encryption is broken.

In this case we need four keys, one for encryption in each direction and one for MACs in each direction. In order to do this we need a tool we haven't seen yet, which is typically called a *key derivation function* (KDF). A KDF takes the master secret and (usually) some other random data and creates the appropriate keys out of it. In this case, the KDF takes the master secret and the nonce that is transmitted by Bob. KDFs are usually constructed using message digests and we'll skip the details here.

For convenience, we'll label these keys as follows:

E_{cs}—encryption key for data sent from client to server
M_{cs}—MAC key for data sent from client to server
E_{sc}—encryption key for data sent from server to client
M_{sc}—MAC key for data sent from server to client

Data Records

The next task is to describe how we're going to package the data. If we're working over a reliable protocol like TCP, we might imagine that we could just encrypt the data in a constant stream as we write it to the network. But then where would we put the MAC? If we simply transmit it at the end, then we don't have any message integrity until we've processed all the data. This isn't really any good because we can't safely act on received data if we don't know it hasn't been tampered with.

The solution to this problem is to break up the data into a series of records, each of which carries its own MAC. When we've read a record and checked its MAC, then we know that it's ok and we can act on it. What we're about to describe is the minimal record format that does this job.

When we read data off the wire, we need to be able to tell which data bytes are the encrypted data and which are the MAC. If we were willing to commit to a constant amount of data in each record, we could simply know which was which, but this doesn't work very well: in some circumstances, we want to be able to transmit one byte at a time, and having one-byte-long records would mean that we expanded the data something like twenty times when we transmitted it. This really isn't acceptable if we want to transmit a lot of data in bulk.

Since fixed-length records are so inefficient, we need some way to have variable length records. This means that we have to have a length field to tell us where the record data ends. This field has to come before the record so we know how much data to read. The MAC can come before or after, but it typically comes after to allow it to be appended to the message after it's computed. (This is a matter of programming convenience). This leaves us with the record format shown in Figure 1.10.

Length	Data	MAC

Figure 1.10 A simple record format

So, when the client wants to encrypt a data block D of length L, it goes through the following process:

1. Compute a MAC over the data using M_{cs}. We'll call this MAC M.

2. Encrypt D using E_{cs}. We'll call this C. We're assuming here that encrypting the data doesn't expand it. As we'll see in Section 1.13, this sometimes isn't true.

3. Transmit $L\|C\|M$ (the $\|$ stands for concatenation).

To read the data, the server goes through the reverse process.

1. Read L from the wire. We now know that D is L bytes long.

2. Now read C and M from the wire.

3. Decrypt C using E_{cs} to recover D.

4. Compute M' over D using M_{cs}.

5. If $M' = M$ then everything is ok. Process the record. Otherwise report an error.

In other words, the MAC computation is as shown in Figure 1.11 where x is either cs or sc depending on which direction we're sending the data.

Sending:
$$M = MAC(M_x, D)$$

Receiving:
$$M' = MAC(M_x, D)$$
compare M to M'

Figure 1.11 MAC computation

Sequence Numbers

Unfortunately, this simple protocol has a security hole. Because the records aren't labelled by the order they're transmitted in, an attacker can take a record off the wire and send it again to the receiver. (Remember, this is called a *replay attack*.) To see why a replay attack might be used, consider the case in which the messages are financial transactions and the attacker might want to arrange to be paid twice. Without protection against replay attack, the attacker could simply replay the message requesting payment.

The current protocol also allows the attacker to remove records or reorder them. It's easy to think up situations in which reordering or replay attacks might be useful and we'll leave it as an exercise for the reader. In order to fix this problem, we need to use a *sequence number*. The first record that each side transmits is numbered 1, the second 2, etc. When you receive a record, you check that its sequence number is the one you expect. If it's not, you report an error.

Of course, the sequence number has to be part of the input to the MAC in order to prevent the attacker from changing the sequence number. The easiest way to do this is simply to prepend the sequence number to D before it's encrypted and MACed. However, if we're communicating over a reliable protocol (like TCP), then the sequence number is implicit and we don't even have to transmit it. Messages will always be delivered in order, so we can just maintain a counter on either side and use it as part of the MAC computation:

$$M = MAC(M_x, Sequence\|D)$$

Note that the sequence number doesn't prevent the attacker replaying *all* of Alice's messages. However, because Bob generates a new nonce for each handshake with Alice, if the attacker tries this attack, Bob will generate a different set of keys (because his nonce will be different) and so when he goes to decrypt the data records, he'll get garbage rather than the plaintext, and the MAC check will fail.

Control Information

We have one more security problem to deal with. Remember that it's easy for the attacker to forge packets. Well, TCP connection closes are just another packet, so it's easy for the attacker to forge connection closes. That means that the attacker can mount a *truncation attack*, in which the attacker convinces one side (or both) that there is less data than there actually was. In order to fix this problem, we need to have some way for Alice to tell Bob (or vice versa) that she's done sending data. Then, if the attacker forges a TCP close, the victim can tell that something is wrong because the end of data message never arrives.

There are a number of tricks we could use to prevent this attack. For instance, we could say that a zero-length record means that you're done. However, in general it would be nice if we had some place to transmit *control messages* that aren't part of the data stream. For instance, we might want to have some way to report errors. An easy way to accomplish this is to have each record be *typed* by what kind of data it carried, regular or control. We can do this by adding a *type field* to each record, and the type field has to be MACed in order to protect it, as shown in Figure 1.12.

Length	Sequence Number	Type	Data	MAC

Figure 1.12 Improved record format

The MAC would then be computed using:

$$M = MAC(M_x, Sequence\|Type\|D)$$

Of course, the type field isn't much good if we don't define some types. We'll go with something simple. If the type field is 0, that means just treat the record as if it were ordinary data. If it's 1, that means that this record is control information. The data portion of the record needs to be scanned by the protocol to figure out what to do next. We'll adopt a simple convention that all control data consists of a simple number. We'll reserve 0 to indicate that the connection is closing, and use nonzero numbers to indicate errors, as shown in Figure 1.13.

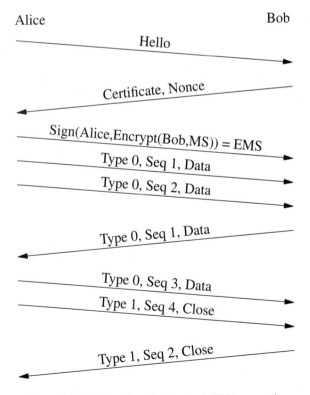

Figure 1.13 Full Toy Security Protocol (TSP) connection

Summary

As the astute reader will probably have guessed, we've now reproduced most of the essential features of SSL. We've got handshaking, key exchange, mutual authentication, and secure data transfer. What's left?

First, TSP isn't complete. We haven't specified enough detail for someone to actually implement it. Some of these details aren't that important. For instance, how long is the length field? Two bytes? Three? Variable? This governs the maximum record length, so it's not unimportant, but mainly it has to be big enough—and we all have to agree. Some of the other details are a little more tricky. Exactly what algorithms are we going to use for key exchange, authentication, etc.? In any case, we'd have to fill in a lot of detail before this protocol would even work.

TSP is skimpy on details, but more important, it is missing some desirable features. The most important thing it's missing is *negotiation*. We'd like to be able to support a number of different algorithm choices for each essential task. That way, if one algorithm is broken, we can switch over easily. We'd also like to be able to choose whether clients are authenticated or anonymous. Nevertheless, it's an interesting and instructive toy and captures most of the idea.

1.9   The Export Situation

Because so much computer software is written in the United States, the U.S. export situation has had a dramatic impact on the design of communications security systems. Export policy in the U.S. has been historically driven by the National Security Agency (NSA). NSA has responsibility for securing the government's communications and snooping on the communications of others. The actual enforcement of export policy is always left to someone else, originally the State Department and now the Bureau of Export Administration (BXA) of the Commerce Department, but all the important decisions are made by NSA.

The Stone Age

Up until September of 1998, the general idea behind export policy was simple. It was legal to export encryption technology for use in authentication, but confidentiality was severely restricted. If your product included any confidentiality at all, it had to be reviewed before export. The rules for what would pass review were never published but it was generally understood that the limits were 40-bit-strong encryption and 512-bit-strong key exchange.

Provided you met these criteria, you could get what was called *commodities jurisdiction*, which basically meant that you could apply to the Department of Commerce for a general license to export your software without having to seek approval. If you wanted to sell your software widely as a mass market product or have it downloaded over the net, this was the approval you needed. Even with this classification, you still couldn't export your software to a few embargoed countries: Cuba, Iran, Iraq, Libya, North

Korea, Sudan, and Syria. Also, some countries such as France heavily restricted cryptography.

The NSA also had a special approval process for a few ciphers (RC2 and RC4). If you used one of them (in 40-bit mode, of course) with key exchange of no stronger than 512 bits, then your review went faster and you were almost certain to get approval. It was possible to get approval for other algorithms and IBM got approval for a reduced-key DES called CDMF [Johnson1993] but in general things went more smoothly if you used RC2 or RC4. It was widely assumed that NSA had done extensive analysis of RC2 and RC4 and perhaps knew how to break them quickly, either via cryptanalytic attack or custom hardware. In any case, NSA made it easy to export RC2 or RC4 and difficult to export other ciphers. This is why you see RC2 and RC4 in so many systems.

There was one notable exception to the general weak cryptography rule. If the system you were exporting was solely for financial transactions (this basically meant it would be used only by banks), it could use stronger cryptography.

Medieval Times

In September of 1998 the encryption rules were amended to allow the export of 56-bit encryption and 1024-bit key exchange. Products were still required to undergo review, but they could at least use semi-strong algorithms. However, at the time DES was known to be weak, so it still wasn't permitted to export really strong algorithms.

The Modern Age

Many times after the 1998 relaxation, rumors were floated that the export controls would be repealed completely. Finally, in January 2000, they were substantially relaxed. Publicly available source code ("open source" software) could be simply posted on the net. "Retail" software still had to undergo a one-time technical review (it's not clear what this was really for), but in practice the BXA has allowed the export of a number of commercial products with strong cryptography. Thus, in practice it is now legal to export strong cryptography from the U.S., except to the embargoed seven countries mentioned earlier.

Despite these liberalizations, the impact of export controls lives on. Many protocols contain features designed to let them work in an exportable environment. SSL is no exception. First, it contains some weak algorithms as well as strong ones so that SSL implementations could be exported. Second, it contains a number of hacks such as ephemeral RSA and Server Gated Cryptography (both discussed in Chapter 4), which are designed to preserve as much security as possible while remaining exportable.

1.10 Real Cryptographic Algorithms

So far, we've been acting as if all cryptographic algorithms of a given type were more or less the same. Unfortunately, that's not true. For instance, each digital signature algorithm is slightly different, as is each key exchange algorithm and each symmetric encryption algorithm. These details turn out to be security-relevant, as we'll see in Chapter 5. In the rest of this chapter we'll give a brief overview of the most popular algorithms so that when they're discussed later in the text you'll be familiar with them.

If you're not interested in the details, you can completely skip this section and read the summary at the end of the chapter. When we talk about security issues in other sections of the text, you should be able to understand the implications of the discussion without understanding the algorithm details.

1.11   Symmetric Encryption: Stream Ciphers

Symmetric ciphers come in two major variants, *stream ciphers* and *block ciphers*. Stream ciphers are the easiest type to understand, so we'll cover them first. The way that a stream cipher works is very simple. You have a function that generates a stream of data one byte at a time. That data is called the *keystream*. The input to the function is the encryption key, which controls exactly what keystream is generated. Without the key, you can't predict the keystream. You take each byte of keystream and combine it with a byte of plaintext to get a byte of ciphertext. Exactly how you combine them turns out not to matter much, but the most popular way is to use exclusive-or (XOR).

$$C[i] = KS[i] \oplus M[i]$$

$$M[i] = KS[i] \oplus C[i]$$

We'll be using this notation throughout the rest of the chapter, so we'll take this opportunity to explain it. $C[i]$ refers to the ith unit of ciphertext. (In this case unit means byte.) $KS[i]$ refers to the ith unit of the keystream and $M[i]$ refers to the ith unit of message. $\oplus$ is the symbol for exclusive-or. So, what this means is take the ith byte of keystream and XOR it with the ith byte of message to get the ith byte of ciphertext. $A \oplus B \oplus A = B$, so we can decrypt the plaintext simply by XORing the ciphertext with the key.

Unfortunately, the symmetry of encryption and decryption causes stream ciphers to have some dangerous security properties. The worst of these is that you can never *ever* reuse the same section of keystream to encrypt two different messages. Imagine that we've encrypted two messages M and M' with the same key. If the attacker learns M, he can easily compute KS simply by computing $M \oplus C$. Once the attacker knows KS, he can compute M' given C':

$$M' = (M \oplus C) \oplus C'$$

This situation occurs surprisingly often because many communications formats contain large amounts of predictable and repetitive data which allows the attacker to guess a large amount of a given message. If another message is encrypted with the same key, the attacker can then leverage this knowledge to recover that message as well.

Worse yet, the attacker can mount an attack even if he doesn't know plaintext of either message. XORing the two ciphertexts together eliminates the effects of the key entirely:

$$C \oplus C' = M \oplus M'$$

Because there are well-known methods for decrypting two plaintexts given their XOR, having two such ciphertexts is disastrous. If you want to encrypt multiple texts with a stream cipher, you must either use separate keys or different sections of keystream.

Even if you use a keystream only once, it's still trivially easy to tamper with data encrypted with a stream cipher. Imagine that you, the attacker, know the text of a message M and the ciphertext C, and you want to change the message so that it decrypts to a new message M', it's trivial to compute the ciphertext C' that achieves this.

$$C' = C \oplus (M \oplus M')$$

Even if you don't know the plaintext, you can make predictable changes in it because each ciphertext bit maps one-to-one with a plaintext bit. Consequently, any plaintext bit can be flipped by changing the corresponding bit in the ciphertext. As a consequence, if you use a stream cipher, you absolutely must use a strong MAC along with it.

RC4

The only stream cipher to have received widespread attention and use is RC4. RC4 was designed by Ron Rivest and was used for quite some time as a proprietary cipher in RSA Data Security's (RSADSI) products. In 1994 someone anonymously posted a cipher that he claimed to be RC4 to the Cypherpunks mailing list. Subsequent testing has demonstrated compatibility between the cipher and RSA's RC4 implementation, and it is widely assumed that the cipher was either reverse engineered from a disassembled version of RC4 code or that someone leaked RSA's source. Because RSADSI has a trademark on the term RC4, the cipher is generally referred to as Alleged RC4 or Arcfour.

RC4 is a variable-key-length cipher, with a key that can be anywhere between 8 and 2048 bits long. Whatever the key length, the key is expanded into an internal state table of constant size, and so the algorithm runs equally quickly with any key. SSL and TLS always use RC4 with a 128-bit (16 byte) key length. RC4 is extremely fast; a Pentium II/400 can achieve speeds on the order of 45 MB/s.

1.12 Symmetric Encryption: Block Ciphers

The other major type of symmetric cipher is a *block cipher*. A block cipher can be thought of as a huge lookup table. The data to be encrypted is processed in blocks of bytes (typically 8 or 16) and each possible plaintext block corresponds to a row in the table. The key is used to select a column in the table. So, to encrypt a block, you find the column corresponding to the key, run down the table to find the row corresponding to the block you want to encrypt, and the entry at that point is the ciphertext. Of course, such a table would be unmanageably huge, so in practice you've got a function that does the computation for you, but the idea is to have a function that simulates a randomly permuted table.

Another way to look at this is that a block cipher is a function of two variables, the key and the input block. You have two functions E (for encryption) and D (for decryption). M is the plaintext and C is the ciphertext.

$$C = E(K, M)$$

$$M = D(K, C)$$

What we've got so far gives us the ability to encrypt only eight bytes or so. Usually the message we want to encrypt is far longer than that, so we've got to find a way to do that. The obvious way is what's called *Electronic Codebook* (ECB) mode. Simply speaking, we break the message up into block-sized chunks and individually encrypt it using our encryption algorithm:

$$C[i] = E(K, M[i])$$

$$M[i] = D(K, C[i])$$

This is straightforward, but it has an obvious disadvantage. Imagine that we have two blocks $M[j]$ and $M[k]$ that are the same. In that case, $C[j]$ and $C[k]$ will also be the same. If we've got a pattern that appears frequently, the attacker can detect this and learn something about our plaintext. We'd rather not have this property.

Cipher Block Chaining (CBC) mode fixes this problem. In CBC mode, the encryption of each plaintext block depends on the ciphertext for the previous block of ciphertext. This is accomplished by XORing the previous ciphertext block with the plaintext before encryption:

$$C[i] = E(K, M[i] \oplus C[i-1])$$

$$M[i] = D(K, C[i]) \oplus C[i-1]$$

In CBC mode, even if we have two plaintext blocks that are the same, they most likely won't encrypt to the same result because the previous ciphertext blocks will be different. Consider the case where $M[j]$ and $M[k]$ are equal, but $M[j-1]$ and $M[k-1]$ are not. In that case, $C[j-1] \neq C[k-1]$ and so $C[j] \neq C[k]$.

The only remaining question is what to do with the first ciphertext block. Since there is no preceding block of ciphertext to XOR in, we can't follow our usual procedure. We could just use a block of all zeros, but then attackers would be able to tell if the first cipher blocks of two messages were identical. To solve this problem, we generate a random block, called an *initialization vector* (IV). The IV is XORed with the first cipher block of the message before encryption. Typically the IV is just sent with the message, but it can also be generated from some value shared by both sides. IVs do not have to be secret, but they should be *fresh*, which is to say different for each message.

There are a large number of other modes for operating block ciphers in, including *Output Feedback* (OFB) and *Cipher Feedback* (CFB), but CBC is by far the most popular one and is the only one relevant for SSL.

Block ciphers in CBC mode always expand the data a little bit, whereas stream ciphers don't. The reason for this is that the data input must be a multiple of the block size. Since most data isn't a multiple of the block size, you need to *pad* the final block out until it ends on a block boundary. This is slightly tricky, because when you decrypt you want to be able to remove all the padding, but nothing else. The way this is typically done is to pad the message with a byte value equal to the number of pad bytes added. If the message actually ends on a block boundary, you have to pad with a full block. The data expansion isn't a problem when encrypting large messages, but if you encrypt one byte at a time then you'll see a lot of data expansion as each byte in produces an encryption block out. This can waste network bandwidth.

Block ciphers in CBC mode are easier to use safely than stream ciphers. It's perfectly safe to use the same key for different data as long as you change the IV. Even if you don't change the IV, pretty much all the attacker learns is that two messages are the same, whereas reusing a key would totally compromise a stream cipher.

Block ciphers perform better under integrity attacks too. The attacker can't make predictable changes to the plaintext by changing the ciphertext. Any change damages both the block that was changed and the next block. An important exception to this rule is the first block. If the IV is in the message and isn't integrity protected, then the attacker can make predictable changes to the first block by changing the IV. Because the IV is XORed in, the attacker can flip any bit of his choosing by flipping the same bit in the IV. In general, it's still important to use a MAC when encrypting with block ciphers. However, the attacker can't mount as precise an attack on block cipher-encrypted data as on stream cipher-encrypted data.

When using CBC mode, you need to worry about *CBC rollover*. Imagine that two data blocks $M[i]$ and $M[j]$ encrypt to the same value C. If $M[i+1] = M[j+1]$, then $C[i+1] = C[j+1]$. Thus, the attacker will be able to know that $M[i+1] = M[j+1]$. On average, a cipher with an X-bit blocksize will have two ciphertext values collide every $2^{X/2}$ (2^{32} for DES) blocks. Thus, it's important not to encrypt more than this amount of data with a given key.

DES

By far the most widely used symmetric cipher is the *Data Encryption Standard* (DES). DES was designed by IBM in the 1970s in response to a request for proposals by the National Bureau of Standards (NBS), now the National Institute of Standards and Technology (NIST). Although IBM had patented DES, they agreed to make it freely available and it was standardized in [NIST1993a].

DES is a 64-bit block cipher with a 56-bit key. This means that data is encrypted in blocks of 8 bytes and the key space is 56 bits. DES keys are actually 64 bits long, however, with the low order bit of each byte used as a parity check to attempt to detect transmission and key wrapping/unwrapping errors. In practice, because DES keys are usually wrapped with public key techniques, the parity check is redundant and the parity bits are usually ignored.

DES is certainly the most widely analyzed public cipher. When it was proposed, it was known that NSA had provided design assistance and some of the design decisions were both unobvious and unexplained. The IBM cryptographers who developed DES were silent on what attacks they knew about, and it was clear that they knew about potential weaknesses that the rest of the world didn't. Naturally, there was concern that DES had been intentionally weakened.

Early attention focused on a particular part of the algorithm called the S-boxes, and for a long time there was concern that the S-box structure had been designed to provide the NSA a *back door* for cryptanalysis. Finally, in 1990–1993, Eli Biham and Adi Shamir used their *differential cryptanalyis* technique on DES [Biham1991a, Biham1991b, Biham1993a, Biham1993b] and it became clear that the DES S-boxes had been optimized to resist differential attack. Only extremely paranoid people still worry about the design of the S-boxes.

No really good analytic attack has ever been found against DES. However, DES is now quite weak, basically as a consequence of having too short a key (56 bits) and of computers getting faster. In 1997 a distributed effort (dividing up the search space between a large number of machines on the Internet) recovered a single DES key using exhaustive search and in 1998 Deep Crack, a custom-built DES search machine, recovered a DES key in 56 hours. As of this writing, the record is below 24 hours. DES is now useful only for low-value or short-lived information.

3DES

Because DES has withstood such aggressive analysis, when the key length became too short a very attractive prospect was just to run the data through more than once, a process called *superencryption*. Unfortunately, just using DES twice (2DES) turns out not to be that much more secure than DES. There's an attack called the *meet-in-the-middle* attack that allows you to break 2DES in the same time as DES if you have 2^{56} blocks of memory to work with. As a consequence, people were forced to encrypt the data three times (3DES). 3DES has an effective strength of 112 bits, the strength that you would naively expect 2DES to have.

> Actually, there's a time-memory tradeoff for the meet-in-the-middle attack. If you're willing to use more CPU time, you can reduce the memory requirement. The time-memory product remains at 2^{112}, however (see [Menezes1996]).

What we've just said doesn't completely specify how 3DES works: not all three operations have to be encryption. The most popular version of 3DES uses what's called *Encrypt-Decrypt-Encrypt* (EDE) mode. What this means is that you encrypt with Key 1, Decrypt with Key 2, and Encrypt with Key 3. This turns out to be just as safe as *Encrypt-Encrypt-Encrypt* (EEE) and has one major advantage: If you set all three keys equal, this is the same as single DES, which means that 3DES hardware can be made to interoperate with DES hardware. This variant is usually referred to as 3DES-EDE.

3DES is (not surprisingly) about three times slower than DES. DES wasn't very fast to start with, and so people are often wary of using 3DES in performance-critical applications. Also, using 192 bits of keying material (168 bits of key and 24 bits of parity) to get 112 bits of security seems unaesthetic to many people.

It's possible to use 3DES with two keys (the two encrypts are done with one key and the decrypt with the second) but there is a known weakness on two-key 3DES that requires $O(t)$ space and $2^{120-lg(t)}$ operations. This attack isn't really practical, but it can't be mounted at all against three-key 3DES. Thus, conservative practice is to use three-key 3DES.

RC2

RC2 is a block cipher invented by Ron Rivest, who also invented RC4. Like RC4, RC2 was a trade secret of RSADSI, and like RC4 it was eventually published by persons unknown. Subsequently, Ron Rivest published an RFC describing RC2. However, because RSADSI holds a trademark on the name RC2, the RFC refers to it as RC2(r).

RC2 is a variable-length cipher with a twist. It also has a variable *effective key length*. So, you can use it with a 64-bit key but it can be broken with 2^{40} operations. This makes it convenient for export reasons. Like DES, it has a 64 bit block size. In SSL, RC2 is always used with a 128-bit key and a 128-bit effective key length.

AES

As mentioned previously, although DES has no known severe cryptographic weaknesses, the key length is too short, and it's long past time to replace it. In 1997 NIST put out a call for submissions for an *Advanced Encryption Standard* (AES). The AES is to have a minimum block size of 128 bits and three key lengths of 128, 192, and 256 bits, making it strong enough for the foreseeable future. Moreover, AES algorithms are supposed to be fast in software and nearly all the submissions are faster than DES.

As of this writing, NIST has narrowed the field to five finalists, MARS [Burwick1999], Serpent [Anderson1999], Twofish [Schneier1998], Rijndael [Daemen1999], and RC6 [Rivest1995]. NIST is expected to determine a final standard in 2000. One of the requirements for submission is that the algorithm must be offered for use on a royalty-free basis if chosen, so use of the AES will be free.

Cipher	Key Length	Speed(MB/s))
DES-CBC	56	9
3DES-CBC	168	3
RC2-CBC	variable	.9
RC2-CBC	variable	3*
RC4	variable	45

* The faster RC2 benchmark is on Celeron 450 running Windows 2000[Dai2000]. The rest of the benchmarks were generated with OpenSSL.

Figure 1.14 Some common cryptographic algorithms (OpenSSL, FreeBSD, Pentium II 400)

Summary

Figure 1.14 summarizes the symmetric algorithms we've discussed. As you can see, RC4 is by far the fastest algorithm and 3DES and RC2 are really quite slow. Although RC2 and RC4 have variable key sizes, they run at the same speed no matter what key size you use. By contrast, 3DES is much slower than DES, but correspondingly more secure. Now that 128-bit ciphers have been cleared for export, there really isn't any reason to use RC2, except for compatibility with 40-bit systems, because it has neither security nor performance advantages over 3DES.

1.13 Digest Algorithms

As far as protocol design is concerned, all digest algorithms are very similar. The only difference is the size of the output. The two most popular algorithms are MD5, which was designed by (guess who) Ron Rivest, and SHA-1, designed by NIST (presumably with help from NSA).

MD5 and SHA-1 both derive from a common ancestor, MD4, also designed by Rivest. MD5 is basically a stronger version of MD4. It has a 128-bit output, as does MD4. SHA-1 is based on MD4, but has a 160-bit output. This makes it somewhat stronger. Because of what's called the *Birthday Paradox*, the difficulty of finding two messages that digest to the same value (a collision) is approximately the square root of the key space. Consequently, it requires about 2^{64} operations to find a collision with MD5 and 2^{80} operations with SHA-1. Recently, there have been some indications that there may be an easier way than brute force to find collisions in MD5 [Dobbertin1996]. Conservative designs all use SHA-1.

> The name *Birthday Paradox* comes from a mathematical party trick. If you have more than 23 randomly chosen people in a room, the probability that some two will have the same birthday is over 50%. This result surprises most people, who expect the required number of people to be around 128. The key insight is that we're computing the probability that *some* two people will have the same birthday, not that someone will have a given birthday, and that the space of birthdays that have already been assigned to someone gets depleted each time you add a person. A similar effect on a larger scale applies with hash collisions, where we're interested in the probabiliity that *some* two messages will have the same digest.

An older MD4-like algorithm called MD2 is sometimes used to sign very old certificates. No modern systems use it. There also used to be an older version of SHA, but it was revised to correct a weakness, creating SHA-1. Figure 1.15 compares MD5 and SHA-1.

Digest	Output size (bits)	Speed (MB/sec)
MD5	128	65
SHA-1	160	31

Figure 1.15 Digest algorithm comparison (OpenSSL, FreeBSD, Pentium II 400)

1.14 Key Establishment

The two primary uses of public key cryptography are key establishment and digital signatures. This section talks about key establishment and the next section talks about digital signatures.

There are really two flavors of key establishment. In *key exchange* or *key transport*, one side generates a symmetric key and encrypts it using the public key of the other side. In *key agreement*, both sides cooperate to generate a shared key. We'll be talking about two algorithms, RSA and Diffie-Hellman (DH). RSA can be used as a key transport algorithm. DH is a key agreement algorithm.

RSA

RSA is the public key algorithm most people think of when they think of public key cryptography. It was invented in 1977 by Ron Rivest, Adi Shamir, and Len Adelman (hence RSA) [Rivest1979]. From a high level, RSA is very simple. Each user has a public key and a private key. The public key can be distributed freely and the private key must be kept secret.

RSA public keys actually consist of two numbers, the *modulus* (usually represented by the letter n) and the *public exponent* (usually represented by the letter e). The modulus is the product of two very large prime numbers, conventionally represented by the letters p and q. p and q also need to be kept secret. The security of RSA is based on the difficulty of factoring n to get p and q.

The private key is another number, usually called d, which can be computed only if you know p, q, and e. When we talk about the key length of an RSA key, we're talking about the length of the modulus. The RSA public exponent (e) must be relatively prime to e and $(p-1)(q-1)$. For convenience, e is usually chosen to be one of a few small prime numbers (usually 3, 17, or 65537). Having a small e makes operations performed with the public key faster. With e chosen, d is computed as

$$d = e^{-1} mod((p-1)(q-1))$$

To encrypt a message M using RSA and the public key (e,n), you compute $C = M^e mod\ n$. What the *mod n* means is that the computation is done *modulo n*, which means that you take M to the eth power and then divide by n and take the remainder. Decrypting the message requires the corresponding private key. For example, $2^5 mod\ 10 = 2$ and $2^5 mod\ 7 = 4$. To decrypt the message, you compute $M = C^e mod\ n$. Just take our word for it that this works.

One thing that this explanation glosses over is that it assumes that the message is a number, when actually it's just a string of bytes. You need some rules to convert the message into a number. This number should be more or less the same size as (but not greater than) n. The reason for this requirement is that we want to ensure that $M^e > n$. If this isn't the case, then $C = M^e mod\ n = M^e$ (i.e., the *mod n* doesn't do anything). It's easy for the attacker to recover M by taking the integer e^{th} root of C. On the other hand, if $M^e > n$, then this attack isn't possible. Making M approximately the same size as n ensures that $M^e > n$.

The standard procedure for how to do this conversion is specified in PKCS #1 [RSA1993b]. We'll summarize it here, because it turns out that there are security problems with this procedure when applied to SSL. PKCS #1 version 2 [Kaliski1998a] fixes these security problems but isn't currently in wide use.

The first thing to do is to compute how large the formatted encryption block needs to be. If n is an L-bit number, then the encryption block is $L/8$ bytes long (rounded up). The first (high order) byte is always 0. The second byte is set to the *block type*. For encryption, this is 2 and for signature it's 1. This ensures that the number formed is just slightly smaller than n.

The message goes in the low-order bytes of the encryption block and is prepended with a zero byte. (Figure 1.16 shows this padding in pictorial form.) The bytes in between are filled with *pad bytes*. For block type 1, the pad bytes have the value 255. For block type 2, the pad data consists of random nonzero bytes. The idea here is that when a message is signed repeatedly, the signature should be the same, but if you encrypt the same message repeatedly, the encryption block should be different. When you recover the encryption block, you can find where the data begins by starting at the third byte and moving to the right until you find a zero byte. This is the last byte of padding.

There must always be at least 8 bytes of padding for encryption to prevent plaintext guessing attacks. Without the padding, the attacker would try encrypting a plaintext guess with the public key to see if it produced the given ciphertext. With the padding, the attacker must try 2^{64} different padding combinations for each plaintext, which makes this attack much harder.

Once you have the encryption block formatted, you convert it into an integer by taking the first byte as the most significant and the last byte as the least significant. This is the same as *big-endian* byte order.

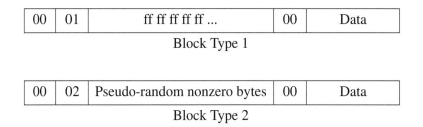

Block Type 1

Block Type 2

Figure 1.16 PKCS-1 padding

RSA was patented in the United States; however, the patent expired on September 20, 2000 [Rivest1983]. The patent was held by RSADSI. Despite this patent, RSA became the de facto standard for public key cryptography and has been licensed by nearly every company that does public key.

To use RSA for key transport, generate a random session key and encrypt that (appropriately padded) under the recipient's public key. The recipient then decrypts the message and removes the padding with the result that you now share a session key.

Diffie-Hellman

Diffie-Hellman (DH) is the first public key algorithm ever published [Diffie1976]. DH is a key agreement algorithm rather than a key exchange algorithm. Instead of the sender generating a key and encrypting it for the receiver, the sender and receiver collectively generate a key that is private to them. The sender and the receiver each have key pairs. To compute the agreed key, the sender combines his private key with the receiver's public key. The recipient combines his private key with the sender's public key. A DH public key is often called a *share*, because it's one side's share of the key agreement.

DH also uses modular exponentiation, but the modulus is a large prime (usually called p). The modulus is publicly known and has to be shared between the sender and the receiver. There is also another number called the generator (g) which must be shared between sender and receiver. g is chosen such that for any value $Z < p$ there exists a value W so that $g^W \bmod p = Z$. Thus, it "generates" all the numbers from 1 to $p - 1$. To generate a key, you generate a random number (X) smaller than p and compute $Y = g^X \bmod p$. X is the private key and Y is the public key. We'll use Xs and Ys to refer to the sender's keys and Xr and Yr to refer to the receiver's keys.

To compute the shared key (ZZ), the sender computes

$$ZZ = Yr^{Xs} \bmod p = (g^{Xr})^{Xs} \bmod p = g^{Xr \cdot Xs} \bmod p$$

The recipient computes

$$ZZ = Ys^{Xr} \bmod p = (g^{Xs})^{Xr} \bmod p = g^{Xs \cdot Xr} \bmod p$$

It should be easy to convince yourself that these numbers are the same and that the sender and the recipient thus share the same number. It's more difficult to show that an attacker can't compute ZZ. In fact, it's not known that this is the case. However, it is widely believed that to do so would require having either Xs or Xr, which would require computing X given Y, a problem known as *discrete logarithm*. Currently, there are no known efficient ways of computing discrete logarithms.

The most important operational difference between RSA and DH is that in DH all the communicating parties must share g and p (collectively known as the *group parameters* or just *group*.) Often this means that a community of people will all use the same group. However, it is possible for the recipient to simply randomly generate his own group, in which case he must arrange to transmit g and p to the sender, often in his certificate. The sender generates a temporary key in the recipient's group, which he uses to encrypt to the recipient only. This is called *ephemeral-static* DH. If the recipient also makes up a key just for this transaction, it's called *ephemeral-ephemeral* DH.

Ephemeral-ephemeral mode has the advantage that if the parties delete their keys when they are done communicating, then even if their machines are subsequently broken into, the attacker cannot read any old traffic, since there won't be any private keys on the machine. If one of the keys is static, the attacker might be able to break into the machine with that key and recover it. This property is called *Perfect Forward Secrecy* (PFS). Note that with DH, unlike in RSA, the recipient must know the sender's public key to decrypt the message.

The strength of DH keys depends on two values, the size of p and the size of X. X is often chosen to be the same general size as p, and so only the size of p is relevant. However, X can be chosen to be much smaller than p for performance reasons. In that case, the length of X must be chosen to be about twice the length of the symmetric key you want to generate from ZZ. For instance, if you're agreeing on DES keys, X must be at least 112 bits long. Note that this doesn't mean that X must be greater than 2^{112}, but merely that it must be randomly chosen over an interval at least as large as 2^{112}. It's also desirable that X be chosen so that its size makes it as strong against attack as p (see [Menezes1996]). Because attacking X is harder than attacking p, X can still be much smaller than p, however. For a 1024 bit p, an X of 160 bits would be quite appropriate. Note that this statement implies that a 1024-bit DH key is really too short to provide full security for a 3DES key. The DH key will be the weakest link in the chain. Similar comments apply to using 1024-bit RSA keys to secure 3DES keys.

1.15 Digital Signature

RSA

Using RSA for digital signature is almost exactly the same as using it for key transport, except with the roles of the public and private keys reversed. To sign, one computes a message digest and "encrypts" it using one's private key. To verify, the receiver "decrypts" the digest and compares it to the message digest he has independently computed on the message. If they match, the signature is valid.

The only part of RSA signature that's a bit obscure is the block formatting. Rather than just encrypting the message digest, you encrypt a DER encoded DigestInfo structure [RSA1993b]. The DigestInfo structure is a combination of the algorithm (e.g., MD5 or SHA-1) rendered as an *algorithm identifier*, which is just a specific series of bytes and the digest value itself (see Figure 1.17).

```
DigestInfo ::= SEQUENCE {
  digestAlgorithm DigestAlgorithmIdentifier,
  digest Digest }

DigestAlgorithmIdentifier ::= AlgorithmIdentifier

Digest ::= OCTET STRING
```

Figure 1.17 DigestInfo structure

To see why things are done this way, consider what would happen if we signed the digest directly. Imagine that there exists digest algorithm $H1$ that was widely used for signing. Now, suppose that $H1$ is catastrophically broken—that is, it became possible to generate random messages that digested to a chosen value. Now, suppose further that we had signed a message M with a different digest algorithm $H2$, which was still strong. The attacker could generate a new message M' with the property that $H1(M') = H2(M)$. If he attached our signature to his new message M' (labelled as being signed with the broken hash $H1$) the signature would still verify! Thus, the attacker would have succeeded in generating a message of his choice that apparently was signed by us. Including the identifier of the digest in the signature itself stops this attack.

DSS

The *Digital Signature Algorithm* (DSA) was invented by NSA and proposed by NIST in 1991. The idea seems to have been to have an algorithm which could be used for digital signature but not for key establishment. This algorithm was intended to replace RSA, which could be used for both. This would have satisfied the NSA's goal of having widely available authentication technology but restricted encryption technology. The DSA was standardized as a *Federal Information Processing Standard* (FIPS-186) called the *Digital Signature Standard* (DSS), and DSA is now widely known as DSS.

DSS is based on the same cryptomath as DH: modular exponentiation in a prime field. We won't bother to describe it, because it's fairly complicated and the details aren't that relevant. The important thing to know is that the keys are more or less the same as those for DH with one notable difference: p (the large prime) is constructed such that $p-1$ is divisible by another (smaller) prime called q. This allows the algorithm to be made faster.

DSS signatures consist of two large (160 bit) numbers called r and s. Unlike RSA, which can be used with any digest, DSS can be used only with SHA-1. (Actually, it could be used with any 160-bit digest, but the standard requires SHA-1). DSA signatures do not include a digest identifier, so allowing multiple digests would open DSA up to the substitution attack described previously.)

It is important to know that DSS differs from RSA in the general way that the signature is verified. With RSA, you recover the message digest from the signature and compare it to the computed message digest. DSS requires you to perform a computation based on the message digest and the signature and returns a yes or no answer. There is no way to recover the sender's calculated message digest using DSS. This has led to confusion in converting RSA-based protocols and implementations to DSS.

The patent status of DSS is unclear. NIST claims that it's free, but RSADSI has claimed that it's covered by Claus Schnorr's patent [Schnorr1991], to which RSADSI happens to have exclusive license rights.

Summary

Figure 1.18 summarizes the performance of RSA, DH, and DSS using Wei Dai's Crypto++ [Dai2000] on a Celeron 450 running Windows 2000 Beta 3. The first thing to notice is that RSA public key operations (encryption and signature verification) are much faster than private key operations (decryption and signature). This isn't an inherent property of RSA, but it might as well be. It's actually a property of the way people choose RSA keys, but because it makes public key operations much faster, pretty much everyone chooses keys the same way.

DSS performance is much more symmetric, with the performance for private and public operations being worse than RSA private operations for small key sizes but better

Algorithm	Key length	ms/operation
RSA encryption	512	.2
RSA decryption	512	4
RSA encryption	1024	1
RSA decryption	1024	27
DH agreement	512	5
DH agreement	1024	19
RSA signature	512	4
RSA verification	512	.3
RSA signature	1024	27
RSA verification	1024	.7
DSS signature	512	4
DSS signature (w/ precomputation)	512	2
DSS verification	512	5
DSS signature	1024	15
DSS signature (w/precomputation)	1024	5
DSS verification	1024	18

Figure 1.18 Public key algorithm comparison (Celeron 450)

for large key sizes. Because DH is the same on both sides, performance is usually symmetric (though see a special case in Chapter 6 where it is not). In general, if you're worried about performance, RSA is a better choice. However, if you're worried about performance, you may well want to purchase cryptographic hardware, in which case the speed difference isn't relevant.

1.16 MACs

The only MAC algorithm we'll be using is HMAC [Krawczyk1997], which uses digest algorithms to construct a MAC with provable security properties. Before HMAC was introduced in 1996, protocol designers used a variety of ad hoc MAC constructions, but were never very confident of their security. The sole exception to this was an algorithm based on DES called DES-MAC [ANSI1986], which was widely analyzed but quite slow. HMAC is quickly replacing all those other algorithms in most applicatons.

HMAC uses a nested keyed digest. What this means is that we compute a digest whose input is both the key and the data and then we use that digest value as the input to another keyed digest. The actual algorithm is

$HMAC(K, M) = H(K \oplus opad \| H(K \oplus ipad \| M))$
H = the digest algorithm we're using
$ipad$ = a string consisting of the byte 0x36
$opad$ = a string consisting of the byte 0x5c

K is 64 bytes long for all common message digests. If your K is shorter than 64 bytes, you pad it to the right with zero bytes.

1.17 Key Length

The most common way to talk about the strength of an algorithm is by talking about its key length. This turns out to be fairly deceptive because not all key lengths mean the same thing. Nevertheless, it's a useful metric and it's the one that's most commonly used. What we're trying to achieve here is to have an idea of the computational resources needed to attack a cipher. The key length provides an upper bound on how hard that is. It measures the difficulty of breaking it by *brute force*, which simply means throwing computational power at breaking the system.

It is important to remember that computers are getting faster, so algorithms gradually get weaker as the computers used to attack them get better. It is commonly estimated that computer speed doubles every 18 months. This observation is referred to as *Moore's Law* in honor of Gordon Moore, who first noticed the phenomenon. It's widely expected that eventually the rule of performance growth will start to slow down, but a number of predictions as to when have been wrong and it's certainly not safe to predict that speeds will stop increasing any time soon.

> Actually, what Moore observed was that the number of components on a chip doubled every 18 months, but Moore's Law has grown to refer to a set of rules of thumb about performance trends in computers.

Symmetric Algorithms

The only way to attack a well-designed symmetric cipher is to try each key until we find one that works. In this case, the length of the key directly controls how strong the cipher is. A key length of 40 bits allows 2^{40} different keys and therefore requires 2^{40} cryptographic operations to search through all possible keys. A 56-bit key requires 2^{56} operations, and so on.

The most important thing to realize here is that the strength of a cipher increases exponentially with key length, not linearly. A 56-bit cipher is roughly 65000 (2^{16}) times stronger than a 40-bit cipher: it takes 2^{16} times more resources to attack. So, if a 40-bit cipher can be cracked with X machines in time Y, and a 56 bit cipher can be cracked with aX machines in bY time, then the *ab* product must equal 2^{16}.

In 1996, an expert panel of cryptographers known as the "Group of Seven" (Matt Blaze, Whitfield Diffie, Ron Rivest, Bruce Schneier, Tsutomu Shimomura, Eric Thompson, and Michael Weiner) concluded that 90 bits should provide adequate security for 20 years [Blaze1996]. For information with a shorter lifetime, 75 or 80 bits should be enough. Anything shorter than 70 bits is questionable and anything shorter than 56 bits is known to be vulnerable to commercial attackers. Several widely used ciphers have 128-bit keys, which are certainly plenty long, and the new Advanced Encryption Standard will have a 128-bit key.

It's very important to remember that key length is not the only determinant of cipher strength. Many ciphers with long keys have been broken by new analytic techniques. For instance, LUCIFER, the predecessor to DES, had a 128-bit key but was vulnerable to differential cryptanalysis. Nevertheless, if you're using a cipher with too short a key, then you're definitely in trouble.

Asymmetric Algorithms

Key lengths for asymmetric ciphers are not directly comparable to key lengths for symmetric ciphers. Because of the math required to make asymmetric ciphers work at all, the keys tend to be quite long. For ciphers such as RSA and Diffie-Hellman, key lengths will typically be between 512 and 2048 bits. This definitely does not mean that 512-bit RSA is stronger than 128-bit RC4. On the contrary, it is likely far weaker.

Unfortunately, we're not sure how much weaker. With symmetric ciphers, it's fairly clear what a brute force attack looks like: You search every key until you find the right one. With asymmetric ciphers, this isn't how it's done. With RSA, for instance, the best known attack is to factor the RSA modulus. The development of a new factoring algorithm or just an improvement on the current algorithms automatically makes all existing keys weaker.

That said, we've got some rough idea of RSA's strength. RSADSI has a factoring challenge where they publish a large number of "challenge numbers" and award cash prizes for the factorization. To date, the largest RSA modulus number that is publicly known to have been factored was RSA-155, a 155-digit (512 bit) number. At Eurocrypt 1999, Adi Shamir described a design for an RSA key breaker called "Twinkle" capable of factoring 512-bit numbers [Shamir1999]. These results show that 512 bit RSA keys are at the outer edge of breakability using current technology. In general, 768 or 1024 bits are the minimal acceptable key lengths. DH and DSA keys are about as strong as RSA keys of equivalent length. Current information suggests that 1024-bit asymmetric keys are about as strong as 80-bit symmetric keys.

1.18   Summary

This chapter has provided a basic introduction to communications security. At least some comprehension of this material is required to understand the rest of this book.

Communications security has three primary objectives: confidentiality, message integrity, and endpoint authentication. Confidentiality means that the data you're sending is kept secret. Message integrity means that you can detect when a message was tampered with in transit. Endpoint authentication means that you can be confident you are speaking to the right person.

The network cannot be trusted. A basic assumption of Internet security is that the attacker may have control of the network. In order to retain security in such an environment, we use cryptographic techniques.

We deal in four fundamental types of algorithms: symmetric ciphers, message digests, public key ciphers, and digital signatures. All of our more complicated constructs are built from these four primitives. There are many different algorithms of each type.

Public key systems are usually used in tandem with symmetric systems. Public key cryptography provides capabilities that cannot be attained with symmetric cryptography but it is too inefficient to be used alone.

For noninteractive (messaging) applications, we generate self-contained messages. We use public key cryptography to wrap the symmetric keys we use to encrypt the message. We use message digests in concert with digital signature functions to provide message integrity.

For interactive applications, we establish keys with a handshake and then use symmetric algorithms. We use public key cryptography in a handshake to authenticate both sides and exchange keys. We then use those keys to protect individual data records using symmetric techniques.

2

Introduction to SSL

2.1 Introduction

This chapter provides an introduction to SSL and TLS as well as background for the rest of the book. We first provide a general overview of how SSL works and then we describe the history of SSL and its variants, culminating in TLS. We also cover the implementation and deployment status of the various versions.

We then provide a brief overview of the use of SSL with the *HyperText Transfer Protocol* (HTTP), the native protocol of the World Wide Web and the protocol to which SSL is best matched. Finally, we describe the movement to deploy other non-Web protocols over SSL.

2.2 Standards and Standards Bodies

Most of the standards we'll be discussing in this book were produced by the *Internet Engineering Task Force* (IETF). IETF documents are easily recognizable because they have names of the form RFC #### (RFC 2246 is the TLS document). Note that not all IETF RFCs are standards. Some are merely informational documents which are published in archival form. This allows vendors to document their protocols in a stable and public way.

IETF Standards Track documents actually go through three stages, *Proposed Standard*, *Draft Standard*, and *Standard*, and a document can go through changes at any point in the cycle. However, the process of progressing a document has started to take so long that anything at Proposed level or above is generally treated as a standard by implementors, and we'll mostly do the same here.

IETF documents have two useful features that documents produced by other standards bodies don't have. First, they're typically written either by implementors or by their close colleagues, so they usually address immediately relevant problems. Second, IETF documents are free and can be downloaded from Web and FTP sites all over the world. The main site is at http://www.ietf.org/.

The two other sorts of standards that we'll be dealing with are those produced by the *American National Standards Institute* (ANSI) and those produced by the *International Telecommunications Union* (ITU). ANSI standards typically have names like X9.42 (the standard for Diffie-Hellman key exchange). ITU standards have names that look like X.509 (the standard for certificates). Being able to identify which is which isn't that important unless you want to buy one of the documents; neither organization produces free documents.

Soapbox: It's difficult to overstate the importance of having free documents. It's quite common for implementors of IETF protocols to be unwilling or unable to pay for the non-free protocol documents that the IETF protocols depend on. As a consequence, bootleg copies and summaries of the non-free standards are passed around from hand to hand, with the result that implementations of these (often very complex) standards tend to be non-standard.

For this and other cultural reasons, IETFers tend to look down on ANSI and the ITU (especially the ITU), but a number of their documents cover important space and have been incorporated by reference into IETF documents, so it's important to be aware of them.

2.3   SSL Overview

Secure Sockets Layer (SSL) is a protocol that provides a secure channel between two machines. It has facilities for protecting data in transit and identifying the machine with which you are communicating. The secure channel is *transparent*, which means that it passes the data through unchanged. The data is encrypted between client and server, but the data that one end writes is exactly what the other end reads. Transparency allows nearly any protocol that can be run over TCP to be run over SSL with only minimal modification. This is very convenient.

SSL has gone through a number of revisions, beginning with version 1 and culminating in its adoption by the IETF as the *Transport Layer Security* (TLS) standard. All the pre-IETF versions of SSL were designed by engineers at Netscape Communications. Version 1 was never widely deployed, and so we'll begin our discussion with version 2 (SSLv2). Appendix B contains a brief discussion of version 1.

2.4   SSL/TLS Design Goals

SSLv2 Design Goals

SSL was originally designed for the World Wide Web environment. Netscape's intent was to provide a single solution for all their communications security problems, including Web, mail, and news traffic. However, their immediate problem was Web traffic, and SSL was designed to fit those needs. This meant that SSL had to work well with the main protocol used by the Web, *Hypertext Transfer Protocol* (HTTP) [Fielding1999].

When SSLv2 was first designed in 1994, the Web security problem that people were most worried about was how to pass information from the client to the server without disclosing it to attacking third parties. The paradigmatic usage scenario is providing a credit card number for online shopping. Consequently, the first major design goal was to provide *confidentiality* for traffic between client and server.

The credit card case also motivates the second and third design goals. Because credit card numbers are inherently valuable, it's important that they be revealed only to someone with whom you intend to do business—and it had better be the right person. This requires that the customer (the Web browser) be sure that he's sending his credit card to the correct merchant (the Web server). On the other hand, there was no need for the server to know who the user is because the credit card number is all the identity information required to bill him. Thus, the second major design goal: *server authentication*. Optionally, SSL also provided *client authentication*.

Because customers will often want to do business with merchants with whom they have never done business before, it was very important that the protocol be able to handle this situation automatically, with a minimum of hassle to the user. This design goal is best referred to as *spontaneity*.

Because Netscape wanted to use SSL as a unified security solution, it also had to work correctly for other protocols besides HTTP. The designers observed that most popular Internet protocols ran over TCP connections, so a protocol that provided a secure, transparent channel could be used to provide security for all such protocols. This property, *transparency*, is probably the single largest reason for SSL's success, because it made it relatively simple to provide some security for almost any protocol merely by running it over SSL. Indeed, immediately after introducing SSL, Netscape started using it to protect not only HTTP traffic but also Usenet news traffic over *Network News Transfer Protocol* (NNTP).

Unfortunately, not all protocols require the same security properties, and so the results of "just" running a protocol over SSL are often undesirable, either from a security or a performance perspective. Much of the purpose of this book is to give you enough information to design faster and more secure systems than a naive use of SSL would allow.

SSLv3 Design Goals

The wide popularity of SSLv2 more or less assured that all of the original SSLv2 design goals would be retained in SSLv3 [Freier1996]. The primary job of the SSLv3 designers was to fix a number of security problems in SSLv2 (see Appendix B for more on this). This meant designing a system that was both stronger and easier to analyze. In particular, the SSLv3 designers explicitly wanted to design a mechanism for securely negotiating multiple cryptographic algorithms. The result is that SSLv3 supported a far greater number of algorithms than SSLv2. In the end, these desires led to SSLv3 being completely different from SSLv2, retaining only the basic protocol flavor.

2.5   SSL and the TCP/IP Suite

All versions of SSL and TLS share the same basic approach: they provide a secure channel between two communicating programs over which arbitrary application data can be sent. In theory, an SSL connection acts very like a "secured" TCP connection. As the name *Secure Sockets Layer* makes clear, SSL connections are intended to act just like sockets connected by TCP connections.

The primary purpose of having SSL semantics mimic TCP semantics is to make the application programmer's life easier. In recognition of this goal, most SSL implementations provide an *application programming interface* (API) consciously modeled after the most popular networking API, *Berkeley sockets*. Figure 2.1 provides an example of some calls from a typical SSL API (OpenSSL) and the corresponding Unix API calls.

Sockets API   OpenSSL

```
int socket(int, int, int)                 SSL *SSL_new(SSL_CTX *)
int connect(int, const struct sockaddr *, int)   int SSL_connect(SSL *)
ssize_t write(int, const void *, size_t)  int SSL_write(SSL *, char *, int)
ssize_t read(int, void *, size_t)         int SSL_read(SSL *, char *, int)
```

Figure 2.1 Sockets API compared to SSL API

From the application programmer's perspective, in a perfect world, he would be able to replace all sockets calls with SSL calls and get security more or less automatically. It would even be possible to secure an application merely by relinking with a library that provided secure (but otherwise indistinguishable) versions of the ordinary sockets call. Unfortunately, although this is possible to some extent, SSL semantics do not *precisely* match TCP semantics, which can lead to problems and confusion, as we'll see in Chapter 8. Figure 2.2 shows SSL's place in the protocol stack, just below the application and just above TCP.

Application
TCP
IP

Normal Application

Application
SSL
TCP
IP

With SSL

Figure 2.2 SSL's place in the protocol stack

SSL assumes that the underlying packet delivery mechanism is *reliable*: data written to the network will be delivered to the program on the other end in order, with no data being dropped or delivered twice. In theory, there are any number of transport protocols that could provide this service, but in practice SSL nearly always runs on top of TCP. SSL cannot run over UDP or directly over IP.

SSL's dependence on a reliable transport protocol to deliver its data has been a point of contention in the past and at least two attempts have been made to remove the dependency. In general, what this involves is arranging for acknowledgments and retry time-outs so that lost messages can be resent. Microsoft's STLP and the Wireless Applications Forum's WTLS [WAP1999a] are both SSL variants that are intended to work correctly over a datagram transport such as UDP.

2.6   SSL History

Figure 2.3 shows the family tree of various SSL variants, with the earliest (SSLv2) at the top and the latest (WTLS) at the bottom The original SSLv2 specification was first publicly released in November 1994, and deployed in Netscape Navigator 1.1 shortly thereafter in March 1995. The primary design was done by Kipp Hickman, a Netscape employee, with a minimum of public comment.

> The original Netscape Navigator SSLv2 implementation was badly broken. It seeded its pseudo-random number generator from the time of day and a few other sources. Wagner and Goldberg [Goldberg1996] showed how to break an SSL connection from Navigator 1.1 in under an hour.

Because SSL had been developed with a minimum of vendor input, as other vendors started implementing SSL, a number of somewhat incompatible independent variants were developed to fix problems with the protocol. The most important of these was Microsoft's *Private Communications Technology* (PCT) [Benaloh1995], published in October of 1995.

PCT

PCT's authors (Josh Benaloh, Butler Lampson, Daniel Simon, Terence Spies, and Bennet Yee) had significant cryptographic experience and they applied it to the protocol. In general, PCT had better-thought-out security properties than SSL, though it was backward compatible with SSL.

Although SSLv2 had version numbers, Netscape had control of the version number space, and behavior of a server upon seeing a newer version number than it supported was never well specified. As a consequence, an implementation indicated that it spoke PCT by sending a special PCT_SSL_COMPAT cipher in its cipher list. SSLv3's semantics for version upgrading are better defined; however, there is still no way to indicate that one supported specific new features, meaning that there was no good way to

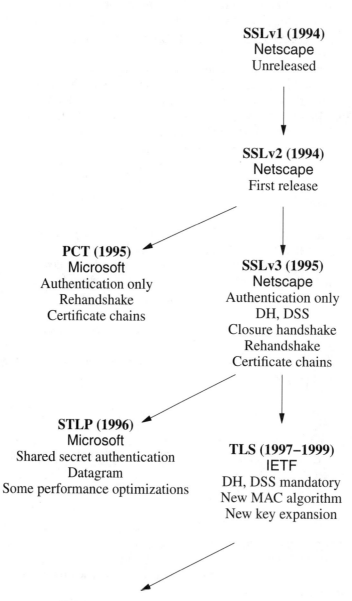

Figure 2.3 Family tree of SSL variants

add experimental features. As a result, this hack is occasionally used by TLS and SSLv3 implementations as well.

Three significant changes were made. First, PCT included a non-encrypted operational mode, providing only data authentication. Second, it tightened up the key expansion transform. Due to United States export restrictions, SSLv2 had an *export* mode in which the encryption security was limited to 40 bits. Unfortunately, SSLv2 used the same key for encryption and authentication, and thus authentication security was also limited to 40 bits. PCT allowed weak encryption to coexist with strong authentication. Third, PCT improved performance by decreasing the number of required round trips. For more on SSLv2 and PCT, see Appendix B.

SSLv3

Although an abortive first draft of "SSLv2.1" as a modification of SSLv2 circulated around Netscape, Netscape eventually decided to burn everything and start over again. They hired Paul Kocher, a noted security consultant, to work with Allan Freier and Phil Karlton to develop a new version of SSL, to be called SSL version 3 (SSLv3). SSLv3 was released in late 1995.

PCT had preserved the general style of SSLv2 to the extent that it used the same specification language and some of the same messages, but SSLv3 invented a completely new specification language and an all-new record type and data encoding. It also addressed some of the same issues as PCT, including adding an authentication-only mode and completely redoing the key expansion transform.

SSLv3 also added a number of new features not in PCT, including a number of new ciphers (*Digital Signature Standard* (DSS), *Diffie-Hellman* (DH), and the National Security Agency's *FORTEZZA* cryptographic token), and support for a *closure* handshake to prevent *truncation attacks* on the data stream. With SSLv2, it was possible for an attacker to forge a TCP connection closure and make it appear that less data was transmitted than in fact was. SSLv3's closure handshake allows this attack to be detected. As with PCT, SSLv3 was backward compatible with SSLv2.

> Backward compatibility in SSL has traditionally been fairly limited. The sense in which it's usually meant is that an SSL client/server pair can safely interact even if they are different versions, provided that they share a common version. It does not mean that valid messages in a previous version are always valid in a newer version, and in fact that has traditionally not been the case.

TLS

In May of 1996 the *Internet Engineering Task Force* (IETF) chartered the *Transport Layer Security* (TLS) working group to try to standardize an SSL-like protocol. Although the official working group charter said otherwise, it was widely understood that this would be an attempt to harmonize the Microsoft and Netscape approaches, and although a number of other approaches were proposed, they received essentially no support. The intention was to be finished by the end of 1996.

Microsoft produced a submission called *Secure Transport Layer Protocol* which was a modification of SSLv3, adding a number of features that Microsoft considered critical. Primary among them were support for datagrams (e.g., UDP) and support for client authentication using shared secrets. Although it was always possible to send the shared secret over an encrypted SSL connection, this meant that in the exportable case, the secret was encrypted with only a 40-bit key. STLP incorporated a mode that allowed a much stronger shared-secret-based authentication for clients. STLP also incorporated some modest performance improvements and improved cipher extensibility as well as allowing the TCP "client" to be the STLP "server."

In late 1996 the major players (and a number of minor ones) met in Palo Alto at a rump group meeting chaired by cryptographer Bruce Schneier. Typically, IETF working groups meet face to face only three times a year at the IETF meetings, but sometimes they'll meet informally when the job is particularly urgent. This was such a meeting.

It rapidly became clear that there was very little support for changing any of SSLv3, except for a few obvious (and minor) bugs. In particular, there was a lot of resistance—largely in the name of backward compatibility—to the sort of changes Microsoft had proposed. The primary open issue seemed to be what the name of the new protocol could be, since using either SSL or PCT seemed too much like saying that Microsoft or Netscape had won. Whatever the name, however, the new protocol would just be a minor cleanup of SSLv3.

Eventually, after several more working group meetings, the TLS working group decided to name the protocol TLS, which all parties were equally unhappy with. A number of minor changes were made to the document, in the name of security, with the effect that the key expansion and the message authentication computations are totally incompatible with SSLv3, destroying most backward compatibility.

By far the most contentious change made in TLS was the decision to require implementations to support DH, DSS, and *Triple-DES* (3DES). This was problematic for two reasons. First, Netscape had only implemented RSA for authentication and key exchange. Because Netscape constituted the vast majority of browsers in the field, interoperability with Netscape's SSL implementation was the de facto minimal standard. Because interoperation with older clients and servers was required by the market, this meant that implementors would have to implement both RSA and DH/DSS.

Far more inconvenient at the time, however, was the requirement to add 3DES. At the time, United States export regulations forbade general export of cryptography stronger than 40 bits. Thus, it was illegal to export a TLS implementation containing 3DES. The result was that an implementation could either be TLS compliant or U.S. exportable, but not both.

To understand why these controversial changes were made, you have to understand how the IETF works. The IETF is organized into a number of working groups working on specific tasks (e.g., to develop TLS). Each working group is part of one or more general *areas*. Currently, there are eight areas: Applications, General, Internet, Operations and Management, Routing, Security, Transport, and General Services. Each area has one or more *area directors*, who oversee work in that area. The area directors collectively form the *Internet Engineering Steering Group* (IESG), which must approve any document before it becomes an Internet archival document, a *Request For Comment* (RFC).

At the April 1995 IETF meeting in Danvers, Massachusetts, the IESG adopted what came to be known as the *Danvers Doctrine*, which stated that the IETF would design protocols that embodied good engineering principles, regardless of exportability. At the time, this doctrine implied support for DES at a minimum and over time it came to mean 3DES. Moreover, the IETF had a longstanding preference for unencumbered (i.e., free) algorithms when possible. When the Merkle-Hellman patent (covering all of public key cryptography) expired in 1998, but RSA was still patented, the IESG began pressuring working groups to adopt free public key algorithms. Finally, many IETF members felt it was good practice for protocols to have a mandatory set of options to ensure that any two implementations could talk to each other.

When the TLS working group had finished its work, in late 1997, it sent the document off to the IESG, and the IESG sent it back with instructions to add a mandatory cipher—DSS for authentication, DH for key agreement, and 3DES for encryption, thus solving the above three issues. Much discussion on the mailing list ensued, with Netscape in particular resisting mandatory algorithms in general and 3DES in particular. After a prolonged standoff between the IESG and the working group, grudging consensus was reached and the document was sent back with the appropriate changes.

Unfortunately, in the meantime, another obstacle appeared. The IETF *Public Key Infrastructure* (PKIX) working group, which was standardizing a profile for X.509 certificates, was winding up its work. TLS depended on certificates and hence on PKIX, and IETF rules forbid protocols advancing ahead of other protocols on which they depend. PKIX finalization took rather longer than expected and added an additional delay. Finally, in January of 1999, over two years late, TLS was published as RFC 2246 [Dierks1999]. As of this writing, deployment has been less than spectacular. Internet Explorer supports TLS but Netscape Navigator does not. Most toolkits do support TLS.

2.7 SSL for the Web

The primary use of SSL is to protect Web traffic using HTTP. We discuss this topic extensively in Chapter 9. Here we do so to provide a brief overview of a typical application in order to explain some of the choices that were made in SSL design.

The process is simple. In HTTP, a TCP connection is created and the client sends a request. The server responds with a document. When SSL is used, the client creates a TCP connection, establishes an SSL channel on top, and then sends the same HTTP request over the SSL channel. The server responds in a similar fashion over the SSL connection.

Because the SSL handshake looks like garbage to an ordinary HTTP server, in order for the process to work correctly the client needs some way to know that the server is prepared to accept SSL connections, as not all servers do so. A Web address (technically known as a *Uniform Resource Locator* (URL)) beginning with `https` rather than `http` is used to indicate that SSL should be used, for example

`https://secure.example.com`

As a consequence, the combination of HTTP running over SSL is often referred to as *HTTPS*.

If all goes well and the server and client can communicate, the user is typically rewarded with some sort of user interface indication that security is in use. In older versions of Netscape, a blue bar was displayed below the toolbar and a key appeared in the lower left-hand corner of the browser. In newer versions of Netscape, the open lock in the lower left-hand corner closes. In Internet Explorer, a lock appears in the lower right-hand corner of the screen. These are all indications that the current page was fetched using SSL.

Although nearly all modern commercial Web servers implement SSL, initially Netscape charged a significantly different price for their SSL-enabled server (*Netscape Commerce Server*) than for their ordinary server. Moreover, due to patent reasons, none of the free servers in the United States support SSL with RSA. (And since RSA is the de facto standard, this might as well mean not at all.) Even if you have a server that implements SSL, you might choose not to enable security. HTTPS puts a much higher load on the server machine than does pure HTTP, and obtaining the required certificate is fairly inconvenient. Moreover, certificates aren't cheap. Verisign, the biggest CA as of this writing, charges over $300 U.S. for a single certificate.

In January 2000, Netcraft's survey [Netcraft2000] found about 1.5 million servers running SSL, but only about 60,000 of them were certified by a well-known third party. The rest were self-signed or issued by a private CA. A client would require special configuration to connect to these servers.

2.8   Everything over SSL

Because so many protocols run over TCP, and SSL connections act so much like TCP connections, securing a preexisting protocol by layering it over SSL is a very attractive design decision. In addition to HTTP over SSL and NNTP over SSL (often referred to as *SNEWS*), proposals soon appeared for using SSL to secure all the major Internet protocols, including SMTP [Hoffman1999a], Telnet [Boe1999], and FTP [Ford-Hutchinson2000]. Many vendors also use SSL to secure their proprietary protocols.

In order to accommodate connections from clients who do not use SSL, servers must typically be prepared to accept both secured and non-secured versions of the application protocol. All of the protocols mentioned in the previous paragraph use one of two basic strategies: *separate ports* and *upward negotiation*. Both of these strategies have advantages and disadvantages, which we'll discuss in Chapter 7.

In a separate-ports strategy, the protocol designer simply assigns a different *well-known port* to the protocol and the server implementor has the server listen both on the original port and on the new secure port. Any connections that arrive on the secure port are automatically SSL negotiated before application protocol traffic begins. HTTPS uses this strategy, as we'll discuss in Chapter 9. Figure 2.4 shows the port assignments for some commonly used protocols.

Name	Port	Use
ftps-data	989/tcp	ftp protocol, data, over TLS/SSL
ftps-data	989/udp	ftp protocol, data, over TLS/SSL
ftps	990/tcp	ftp protocol, control, over TLS/SSL
ftps	990/udp	ftp protocol, control, over TLS/SSL
nntps	563/tcp	nntp protocol over TLS/SSL
nntps	563/udp	nntp protocol over TLS/SSL

Figure 2.4 Port number assignments for SSL-ized protocols

When using an upward negotiation strategy, the protocol designer modifies the application protocol to support a message indicating that one side would like to upgrade to SSL. If the other side agrees, an SSL handshake starts. Once the handshake is completed, application messages resume over the new SSL channel. SMTP over TLS uses this strategy, as we'll discuss in Chapter 10.

2.9   Getting SSL

By far the easiest way to get an SSL implementation is to download it. The OpenSSL Project at `http://www.openssl.org/` provides a high-quality, free, source implementation of SSLv2, SSLv3, and TLS available for worldwide downloading. OpenSSL is based on Eric Young's SSLeay library, which was first released in 1995. The code is written in more or less ANSI C and has been widely ported. OpenSSL is licensed under a BSD-style license and is therefore free for commercial and noncommercial use. Until very recently, due to patent reasons, OpenSSL could not be used inside the United States in RSA mode. However, since RSA's patent expired in September 2000, it is now legal in the U.S. as well.

The following vendors sell C/C++ SSL/TLS toolkits.

- Certicom (`http://www.certicom.com/`)
- Netscape Communications (`http://home.netscape.com/`)
- RSA Security (`http://www.rsasecurity.com/`)
- SPYRUS/Terisa Systems (`http://www.spyrus.com/`)

Netscape had the first SSL implementation. RSA has hired Eric Young and their toolkit is based on SSLeay. Consensus and SPYRUS/Terisa's implementations were both independently developed.

Full disclosure: The author worked at Terisa for three years and was the primary author of Terisa's SSL product.

Similarly, the easiest way to get a Java implementation is to download it. The author's free Java SSLv3/TLS implementation, PureTLS, is available at `http://www.rtfm.com/puretls`. The following vendors also have Java implementations.

- Baltimore (`http://www.baltimore.com/`)
- Certicom (`http://www.certicom.com/`)
- Phaos Technology Corporation (`http://www.phaos.com/`)
- Sun (`http://www.javasoft.com/`)

As of this writing, Sun's is royalty-free for "non-commercial" use but is available in binary form only.

Both Netscape and Internet Explorer implement SSL as do Netscape's Web servers and Microsoft's IIS. Microsoft also allows programmers to call their SSL implementation (SChannel), but that's only an option for Windows programmers. Several free source implementations of SSL (based on OpenSSL) for the free HTTP server Apache are available.

- ApacheSSL (`http://www.apachessl.com/`)
- mod_ssl (`http://www.modssl.org/`)

A number of commercial Apache-based SSL implementations are available.
- Raven (`http://www.covalent.net/`)
- Stronghold (`http://www.c2.net/`)

What's Implemented

Nearly every currently available SSL implementation supports SSLv3 with RSA. A notable exception is some installed Web servers (typically old versions of Netscape Commerce Server) that support only SSLv2. Most implementations support SSLv2 for backward compatibility, though some newer implementations omit SSLv2 support. Most SSL toolkits support the TLS protocol changes, but support for DSS and DH isn't always available. Microsoft's implementations also support PCT and TLS, and the versions of IIS and IE shipping with Windows 2000 also support DSS and DH. As of this writing, Netscape's products still support only SSLv3 and do not support DSS and DH.

For maximal compatibility, it's important to support SSLv2 and SSLv3. There are essentially no implementations that support only TLS, so support for TLS is not necessary, although it is desirable because it's an IETF standard.

2.10 Summary

This chapter has provided an overview of SSL and its place in the networking universe, providing the context into which the material we'll be discussing for the rest of the book fits.

SSL and TLS provide a generic channel security mechanism on top of TCP. Any protocol that can be carried over TCP can be secured using SSL or TLS.

SSL was originally designed by Netscape. SSLv2 and SSLv3 were basically Netscape-only productions, but TLS is the product of an IETF working group starting with SSLv3.

SSL provides server authentication, encryption, and message integrity. Optionally, there is support for cryptographic client authentication.

SSL APIs are typically designed to mimic normal networking APIs. In C, SSL APIs typically emulate Berkeley sockets, and in Java they emulate the Java socket abstraction. This makes it very easy to convert an insecure application to SSL.

SSL is very widely used for HTTP traffic. However, more and more protocols are now being secured with SSL/TLS. TLS is slowly replacing SSL.

A large number of SSL and TLS implementations are available. There are free implementations in both C and Java and a number of commercial implementations are available.

3

Basic SSL

3.1 Introduction

This chapter provides a detailed account of SSL operation for the most common case, server-only authentication using RSA. By titling this chapter Basic SSL, we mean that this is the basic mode of SSL, not that we're not going to go into depth about the protocol (we are). This chapter covers only the simplest mode of SSL. The next chapter will discuss several more-complicated modes.

This chapter is organized into two primary sections. The first is an overview of how SSL works and how the various pieces fit together. We'll broadly describe each protocol message and its general purpose. The second section dissects a sample SSL connection in detail. We use an automated tool to generate a session trace and then examine each protocol message in detail, seeing how the individual fields fit together to accomplish the job of the protocol. If you're reading this as an implementation guide or want a really detailed understanding of what's happening, you should read both sections. If your primary interest is simply in using SSL, you can probably safely skip the second half.

3.2 SSL Overview

The basic design of SSL should look fairly familiar from the Toy Security Protocol we designed in Chapter 1. A connection is divided into two phases, the *handshake* and *data transfer* phases. The handshake phase authenticates the server and establishes the cryptographic keys which are used to protect the data to be transmitted. The handshake must be completed before any application data can be transmitted. Once this has been done, the data is broken up and transmitted as a series of protected records.

3.3   Handshake

The purpose of the SSL handshake is threefold. First, the client and the server need to agree on a set of algorithms which will be used to protect the data. Second, they need to establish a set of cryptographic keys which will be used by those algorithms. Third, the handshake may optionally authenticate the client, as we'll see in Chapter 4. First, we'll discuss the handshake process in general terms without discussing specific protocol messages and then we'll show how it breaks down into messages.

The overall process works something like this (see Figure 3.1 for a pictorial representation).

1.   The client sends the server a list of the algorithms it's willing to support, along with a random number used as input to the key generation process.

2.   The server chooses a cipher out of that list and sends it back along with a certificate containing the server's public key. The certificate also provides the server's identity for authentication purposes and the server supplies a random number which is used as part of the key generation process.

3.   The client verifies the server's certificate and extracts the server's public key. The client then generates a random secret string called the pre_master_secret and encrypts it using the server's public key. It sends the encrypted public key to the server.

4.   The client and server independently compute the encryption and MAC keys from the pre_master_secret and the client and server's random values.

5.   The client sends a MAC of all the handshake messages to the server.

6.   The server sends a MAC of all the handshake messages to the client.

So, what has this process accomplished? Remember that our two goals were, first, to agree on a set of algorithms and, second, to establish a set of cryptographic keys. Steps 1 and 2 accomplish the first goal. The client gets an opportunity to tell the server which algorithms it supports and the server chooses an algorithm. When the client receives the message the server sent in step 2, it also knows the algorithm, so both sides now know what algorithm to use.

The second goal, establishing a set of cryptographic keys, is accomplished by steps 2 and 3. In step 2 the server provides the client with its certificate, which allows the client to transmit a secret to the server. After step 3, the client and the server both share the pre_master_secret. The client has the pre_master_secret because it generated it, and the server has the pre_master_secret because it decrypted it.

Note that step 3 is the key step in the whole handshake. All the data that is going to be protected depends on the security of the pre_master_secret. What's going on is very simple: the client uses the server's public key (extracted from the certificate) to encrypt a shared key, and the server uses its private key to decrypt the shared key. The rest of the handshake is mainly devoted to ensuring that this exchange can happen safely. In step 4 the client and the server then separately use the same *key derivation function* (KDF) (see Section 3.11) to generate the master_secret. The master_secret is used to generate the cryptographic keys, again using the KDF.

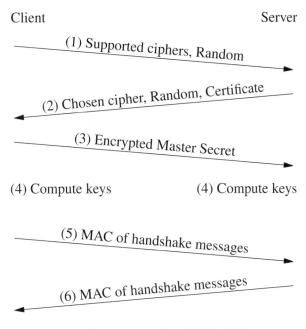

Figure 3.1 Overview of the SSL handshake

Steps 5 and 6 serve to protect the handshake itself from tampering. Imagine an attacker who wished to control the algorithms used by the client and the server. It's quite common for the client to offer a range of algorithms, some weak and some strong, so that it can communicate with servers that only support weak algorithms. The attacker could delete all the strong algorithms from the client's offer in step 1 and thus force the server to choose a weak algorithm. The MAC exchange in steps 5 and 6 stops this, because the client's MAC will be computed over the original messages and the server's MAC will be computed over the messages the attacker modified, and they won't match when checked. Because the client- and server-provided random numbers are inputs to the key generation process, the handshake is secure from replay attack. These messages are the first messages encrypted under the newly encrypted algorithms and keys.

So, at the end of this process, the client and the server have agreed on the cryptographic algorithms to use and have a set of keys to use with those algorithms. More important, they can be sure that an attacker hasn't interfered with the handshake and that therefore the negotiation reflects their true preferences.

Handshake Messages

Each step of the description we've just given is accomplished by one or more handshake messages. We'll briefly describe here which messages map to which steps and then cover each individual message in detail later in this chapter. Figure 3.2 shows the individual messages.

- Step 1 corresponds to a single SSL handshake message, ClientHello.

- Step 2 corresponds to a series of SSL handshake messages. The first message the server sends is the ServerHello, which contains its algorithm preferences. Next it sends its certificate in the Certificate message. Finally, it sends the ServerHelloDone message, which indicates that this phase of the handshake is done. The reason that the ServerHelloDone is needed is that some of the more complicated handshake variants involve other messages being sent after the Certificate message. When the client receives the ServerHelloDone message, it knows that no such other messages will be arriving and so it can proceed with its part of the handshake.

- Step 3 corresponds to the ClientKeyExchange message.

- Steps 5 and 6 correspond to the Finished message. The Finished message is the first message that's protected using the just-negotiated algorithms. To protect the handshake from tampering, the content of the message is a MAC of *all* the previous handshake messages. However, since the Finished message is protected using the negotiated algorithms, the message itself is also MACed with the newly negotiated MAC keys.

   Note: This diagram omits two messages, the ChangeCipherSpecs. We'll cover them later, but they're not important at this stage in the discussion.

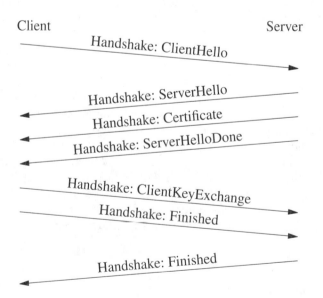

Figure 3.2 SSL handshake messages

3.4   SSL Record Protocol

All we've managed to do so far is to authenticate the server and share some keying material. Remember that the point of having SSL in the first place is to be able to exchange encrypted and authenticated *data*. The purpose of the handshake is to set up the shared state required to make sending and receiving protected data possible. In SSL the actual data transfer is accomplished using the *SSL Record Protocol*.

The SSL Record Protocol works by breaking up the data stream to be transmitted into a series of *fragments*, each of which is independently protected and transmitted. On the receiving end, each record may be independently decrypted and verified. This approach allows data to be transferred from one side of the connection to the other as soon as it is ready and processed as soon as it is received.

Before a fragment can be transmitted, it must be protected against attack. To provide integrity protection, a MAC is computed over the data. The MAC will be transmitted along with the fragment and must be verified by the receiving implementation. The MAC is then appended to the fragment and the concatenated data and MAC are encrypted to form the *encrypted payload*. Finally, a header is attached to the payload. The concatenated header and encrypted payload are referred to as a *record*. Records are what is actually transmitted. Figure 3.3 shows the transmission process.

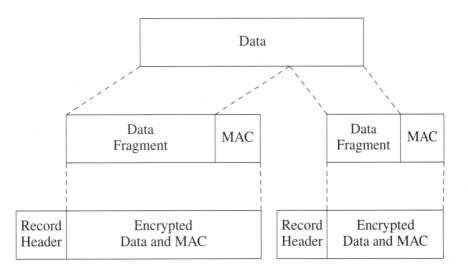

Figure 3.3 SSL data fragmentation and protection

Record Header

The job of the record header is to provide information that is necessary for the receiving implementation to interpret the record. In practice, this means three pieces of information: the *content type*, the length, and the SSL version. The length field allows the receiver to know how many more bytes to read off the wire before it can process the message. The version number is simply a redundant check to ensure that each side agrees on the version.

The content type field identifies the type of the message. As we discussed in Chapter 1, it's convenient to be able to send other kinds of traffic over the same protected channel. In particular, we'd like to be able to send protected messages to indicate errors and connection closure termination. The content type field allows implementations to distinguish this sort of management traffic from data that is intended for the higher-level application.

Content Types

SSL supports four content types: application_data, alert, handshake, and change_cipher_spec. All data sent and received by software that uses SSL is sent as application_data. The other three content types are used for management traffic, such as performing the handshake and signaling errors.

The alert content type is primarily used for signalling various types of error. Most alerts signal things that went wrong in the handshake, but some indicate errors that occurred when trying to decrypt or authenticate records. The other use of alert messages is to signal that the connection is about to close. This is necessary to prevent the truncation attack discussed in Section 1.8.

The handshake content type is used (unsurprisingly) to carry handshake messages. Even the initial handshake messages that form the connection are carried by the record layer as records of type handshake. Because no cryptographic keys have been established, these initial messages aren't encrypted or authenticated, but otherwise the processing is the same. It is possible to initiate a new handshake over a preexisting connection (see Section 4.5) in which case the new handshake records are encrypted and authenticated just as any other data would be.

The change_cipher_spec message has a special purpose. It indicates a change in the encryption and authentication of records. Once a handshake has negotiated a new set of keys, the change_cipher_spec record is sent to indicate that those new keys will now be used. This is covered in more detail in Section 3.10.

3.5   Putting the Pieces Together

As we've seen, SSL is a *layered* protocol consisting of a record layer and a number of different message types which are carried on top of the record layer. In turn, the record layer is carried on top of some reliable transport protocol such as TCP. Figure 3.4 shows the structure of the protocol.

The rest of this chapter is a detailed look at a particular SSL connection. It covers similar territory to the first part of the chapter, but at a much deeper level of detail. The material covered here is primarily the contents of the specific handshake messages. Thus, if you're interested in implementing SSL, analyzing the protocol, or designing an SSL variant, you should read on. Otherwise, you can safely skip to Chapter 4 where we cover the rest of the handshake modes. First, we discuss the general features of the

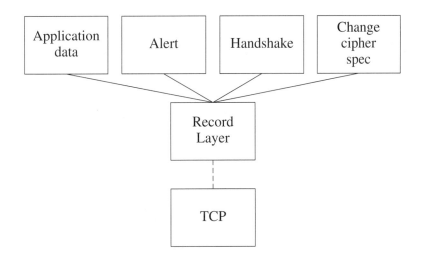

Figure 3.4 SSL protocol structure

connection and then move on to discussing the individual messages in detail.

As before, we'll cover the handshake first, describing how algorithms are negotiated by means of cipher suites and how the server's key is used to establish a shared pre_master_secret which can be used to create the cryptographic keys for the connection. Then we'll cover the cryptographic transformations that the SSL Record Protocol uses to protect the data being communicated.

3.6   A Real Connection

Figure 3.5 shows a ladder diagram for the connection we'll be studying. As with previous such diagrams, messages from the client (speedy) to the server (romeo) are shown as going from left to right and messages from server to client are shown as going from right to left.

The first message sent is the ClientHello, which contains the client's proposed cryptographic parameters, including the ciphers it's prepared to use. It also contains a random value to be used in key generation. The server responds with three messages: first, it sends the ServerHello which selects a cipher and a compression algorithm. This message contains a random value from the server.

The reason why SSL includes compression is that encrypted data is random for all practical purposes and thus incompressible. Thus, link-level compression such as is found in most modems doesn't work on SSL data. If you want to compress the data before transmission you must do so before encryption. Unfortunately, due to intellectual property considerations, neither SSLv3 nor TLS defined any compression algorithms.

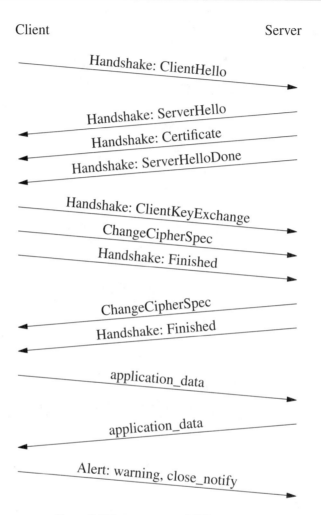

Figure 3.5 Time sequence of SSL messages

Thus, compression is almost never used with SSL. As an exception, OpenSSL does support compression, so if both sides are based on OpenSSL and suitably configured, compression can be used.

Next, the server sends the Certificate message, which contains the server's public key, in this case an RSA key. Finally, it sends the ServerHelloDone, which indicates that no more messages will be sent in this phase of the handshake.

The client now sends a ClientKeyExchange message, which contains a randomly generated key encrypted under the server's RSA key. This is followed by a Change-CipherSpec message, which indicates that all messages that the client sends afterwards will be encrypted using the just-negotiated cipher. The Finished message contains a check value for the entire connection so that the server can tell that the ciphers were securely negotiated.

Once the server has received the client's Finished message, it sends its own Change-CipherSpec and Finished messages and the connection is ready to begin sending application data.

> The SSLv3 specification allows a party to start sending application data as soon as that party's Finished message is *sent*. However, this creates a security risk for client data if the connection has been attacked. If the attacker has changed the handshake to negotiate a weaker cipher suite, the client can't detect this until it receives the server's Finished message. To fix this, in TLS the client must wait until it has received the server's Finished message before it can send its first byte of data. Note that this isn't a security problem if the server chose the most secure of the client's ciphers, but rather than trying to detect this case, it's safest to simply wait for the other server's Finished message.

The next two messages are application data sent by the client and server, respectively. In this case, these were the result of typing data at the client and server programs, but in an actual transaction, this would be when the application protocol data was sent.

Finally, the client shuts down the connection, but first it sends a close_notify alert to indicate that the connection is about to close. The close_notify is followed by a TCP FIN (not shown here). The server responds with its own TCP FIN. The FINs indicate that the host's TCP implementation has closed its side of the connection and will not send any more data.

> Note that the server did not send a close_notify. The SSL specification is a little unclear on exactly whether close_notifys are required, but under perfect circumstances, both the server and client would send close_notifys.

3.7   Some More Connection Details

In order to understand the protocol messages we'll be examining, it's convenient to have a piece of software that can break apart the various messages and display their contents. We've used the ssldump program for this purpose.

Figure 3.6 shows an ssldump trace of all the messages in a simple SSL connection. We'll be talking about each message in detail in a little bit, but here we present a trace of the whole connection so you can get a feel for the flavor.

Since this is the first ssldump trace presented in the book, we'll take a moment to describe the output. The first line simply indicates the setup of the underlying TCP connection that the SSL session will use. In this case it's a connection between romeo and speedy, two machines on the test network. The name of the host (romeo) that initiated the TCP connection (i.e., the host which called connect()) is printed first, and the host (speedy) that accepted the TCP connection (i.e., the host which called accept()) is printed second. In normal SSL operation, the initiating host takes the client role and the accepting host takes the server role.

Each numbered line represents an SSL record. Thus, this connection consists of 12 different records. The first number is the number of the record in the sequence that was processed. This is followed by two timestamps, the first being the time since the creation of the TCP connection and the second being the time since the last record. Both times are represented in seconds and to four decimal places. Next is an indication of which direction the record was sent: C>S indicates client to server (in this case romeo to speedy) and S>C indicates server to client (speedy to romeo). Next is the record type, which corresponds to one of the layers described in the previous section.

```
New TCP connection: speedy(3266) <-> romeo(4433)
1 0.0456 (0.0456) C>S   Handshake
      ClientHello
        Version 3.1
        cipher suites
                  TLS_DHE_RSA_WITH_3DES_EDE_CBC_SHA
                  TLS_DHE_DSS_WITH_3DES_EDE_CBC_SHA
                  TLS_RSA_WITH_3DES_EDE_CBC_SHA
                  TLS_RSA_WITH_IDEA_CBC_SHA
                  TLS_RSA_WITH_RC4_128_SHA
                  TLS_RSA_WITH_RC4_128_MD5
                  TLS_DHE_RSA_WITH_DES_CBC_SHA
                  TLS_DHE_DSS_WITH_DES_CBC_SHA
                  TLS_RSA_WITH_DES_CBC_SHA
                  TLS_DHE_RSA_EXPORT_WITH_DES40_CBC_SHA
                  TLS_DHE_DSS_EXPORT_WITH_DES40_CBC_SHA
                  TLS_RSA_EXPORT_WITH_DES40_CBC_SHA
                  TLS_RSA_EXPORT_WITH_RC2_CBC_40_MD5
                  TLS_RSA_EXPORT_WITH_RC4_40_MD5
        compression methods
                  NULL
2 0.0461 (0.0004) S>C   Handshake
      ServerHello
        session_id[32]=
          74 6d 09 76 1d 2a c9 02 4a a1 a3 4e
          27 5c 18 63 8a d9 4a 59 f9 c3 14 a5
          c4 b3 a4 f6 61 ef f5 cd
        cipherSuite           TLS_RSA_WITH_DES_CBC_SHA
        compressionMethod          NULL
3 0.0461 (0.0000) S>C   Handshake
      Certificate
4 0.0461 (0.0000) S>C   Handshake
      ServerHelloDone
```

```
 5 0.2766 (0.2304) C>S    Handshake
      ClientKeyExchange
        EncryptedPreMasterSecret[64]=
            17 4d 00 32 bc b2 af 95 09 0a 45 24
            97 d8 34 dc 73 20 4d 00 91 a5 0d ed
            c3 f0 b4 f5 32 6f 13 cc ea 41 00 5e
            bb 05 f1 b7 e2 c4 fa 1b 40 c1 2a f3
            00 20 83 43 2d 8c 2a 53 3b 33 cc 5f
            0b bc db a2
 6 0.2766 (0.0000) C>S    ChangeCipherSpec
 7 0.2766 (0.0000) C>S    Handshake
      Finished
 8 0.2810 (0.0044) S>C    ChangeCipherSpec
 9 0.2810 (0.0000) S>C    Handshake
      Finished
10 1.0560 (0.7749) C>S    application_data
11 6.3681 (5.3121) S>C    application_data
12 7.3495 (0.9813) C>S    Alert
        level           warning
        value           close_notify
Client FIN
Server FIN
```

Figure 3.6 A simple SSL connection

For some record types, `ssldump` performs further decoding, and this is shown on subsequent indented lines. In particular, if the record type is handshake, `ssldump` does a fair amount of decoding. The next line is the handshake type, and subsequent lines contain decodings of some relevant fields. Exactly how much information is conveyed is controlled by command line flags. This particular trace was generated with settings that show only a moderate amount of detail. The intent in this session is to show message flow, so some fields are elided from the trace. Later in the chapter we discuss each message in detail and show all fields in each message.

For example, the first record is a handshake message. The next line shows that it's a ClientHello, sent from `romeo` to `speedy`. It offers a number of cipher suites, ranging from ephemeral Diffie-Hellman with 3DES to RSA with RC4-40, but only one compression method, NULL.

Because `ssldump` was written partially in order to generate traces for this book, the traces are more or less direct program output, with the occasional addition of comments in *italics*. The message trace displayed here was generated by using OpenSSL's `s_client` and `s_server` programs, which are simple command-line client and server programs. Encrypted data is rendered in `fixed-width italic`.

3.8   SSL Specification Language

It's fairly common practice for protocols to be described in terms of a specification language which describes the various fields of the protocol messages and how they appear on the wire. This is intended to provide an unambiguous and concise description of the protocol. One example of such a language is ASN.1.

Both TLS and SSLv3 use the same specification language to describe their messages. Although the syntax is vaguely reminiscent of C type definitions, the language was invented for SSLv3 and the only definition is in the specifications.

> The TLS specification describes the syntax as "somewhat casually defined," and although most of the specification is obvious, new constructs are introduced several times without much introduction. At one point, the author attempted to write a grammar-driven parser (using YACC) for the language, with the aim of mechanically generating a decoder, but abandoned the project in frustration.

Basic types

The specification uses five basic types, opaque, uint8, uint16, uint24, and uint32. opaque is simply a single uninterpreted byte. uint8, uint16, uint24, and uint32 are unsigned 8-, 16-, 24-, and 32-bit integers respectively and are represented on the wire by sequences of 1, 2, 3, or 4 bytes. All numbers are represented in "network byte order"—high byte first—so the number 1 is represented as a uint32 by the hex bytes 00 00 00 01. The constructs /* and */ bracket comments just as in C.

Vectors

A vector is simply a sequence of elements of a given type. Vectors come in two flavors, fixed-length or variable-length. Fixed-length vectors are represented using [] and variable-length vectors are represented using <>. It is important to note that all lengths are in bytes, not in number of elements. As a consequence, the declaration uint16 foo[4] refers to two 16-bit integers, not four. This allows the decoder to be layered; it can treat structures as opaque strings (since it knows their length) and pass them on to another layer for parsing.

Variable-length vectors can be represented either by specifying both an upper and lower length bound or just an upper length bound. For example:

```
opaque stuff<1..20>  /* A string of between 1 and 20 bytes */
uint32 numbers<16>   /* Up to 4 32 bit integers */
```

Fixed-length vectors are encoded on the wire simply by concatenating their elements end-to-end with the first element coming first. Variable-length vectors are encoded in the same way, except that a length field is prepended. A length field is an integer type just large enough to encode the upper bound length of the vector. For instance, opaque vec<300> would require a uint16 length field.

Enumerateds

An enumerated type is simply a field that can assume only a specific series of values. Each value is named. For example:

enum { red(1), blue(2), green(3) } colors;

specifies a type called colors which can take on the values red, blue, and green, which are represented on the wire by the integers 1, 2, and 3. When an enum is encoded on the wire, it is represented by an integral type just large enough to hold its largest value. So, colors would be represented by a uint8, one byte.

It is possible to specify an explicit maximum size for an enum, by including an unnamed value:

enum { warning(1), fatal(2), (255) } AlertLevel;

As a special case, it is possible to define an enum with no values at all. This is used occasionally in the specification to refer to state values that are internal to an implementation. Obviously, such an enum can never be encoded on the wire, because there are no definitions for how to encode the values.

enum { high, low } security;

Structures

Constructed types may be made by using the struct definition, which is very similar to C `struct` syntax:

```
struct {
  type1 field1,
  type2 field2,
  type3 field3,
  ...
} name;
```

structs are encoded on the wire simply by concatenating the encodings of the various fields, in the order that they appear in the struct definition. struct definitions can also be nested. The name field of a struct may be omitted if it is directly included in another struct.

Variants

Structures may be defined with variant contents which change depending upon some external information. This is done with a construct that looks superficially like C's `switch` statement, but is really more like a C `union` or an ASN.1 `CHOICE`.

```
select (type) {
    case value1: Type1
    case value2: Type2
    ...
} name;
```

The type that controls the contents of a select is always an enum. Here's an example:

```
struct {
    select (KeyExchangeAlgorithm) {
        case rsa: EncryptedPreMasterSecret;
        case diffie_hellman: DiffieHellmanClientPublicValue;
    } exchange_keys;
} ClientKeyExchange;

enum { rsa, diffie_hellman } KeyExchangeAlgorithm;
```

This switches the definition of the ClientKeyExchange struct based on the value of KeyExchangeAlgorithm. If KeyExchangeAlgorithm is rsa, then the value is of type EncryptedPreMasterSecret. If it is of diffie_hellman then the value is of type Diffie-HellmanClientPublicValue. Note that the value of KeyExchangeAlgorithm is not represented anywhere in the message, but is merely part of the system context. Some variants, however, refer to other fields in the message.

3.9   Handshake Message Structure

Each SSL handshake message consists of a simple header followed by a body which is dependent on the message type. Figure 3.7 shows the definition for the message:

The header is 4 bytes long and consists of a 1-byte type field followed by 3 length bytes. The length field refers to the length of the rest of the handshake message (not including the type and length fields). The contents of the rest of the message are completely dependent on the msg_type field. The length field is not strictly necessary because the end of the handshake message can be determined from the components. However, having an explicit length field makes it much easier to implement the protocol. The implementation can break apart sequential handshake messages in one layer and then process them in another. Note that the mapping of handshake messages to SSL records is not fixed. Multiple handshake messages may appear in a single record. Theoretically, a single handshake message might span multiple records, but in practice this does not occur.

```
struct {
    HandshakeType msg_type;
    uint24 length;
    select (HandshakeType) {
        case hello_request:      HelloRequest;
        case client_hello:       ClientHello;
        case server_hello:       ServerHello;
        case certificate:        Certificate;
        case server_key_exchange: ServerKeyExchange;
        case certificate_request: CertificateRequest;
        case server_hello_done:  ServerHelloDone;
        case certificate_verify: CertificateVerify;
        case client_key_exchange: ClientKeyExchange;
        case finished:           Finished;
    } body;
} Handshake;

enum {
    hello_request(0), client_hello(1), server_hello(2),
    certificate(11), server_key_exchange (12),
    certificate_request(13), server_hello_done(14),
    certificate_verify(15), client_key_exchange(16),
    finished(20), (255)
} HandshakeType;
```

Figure 3.7 SSL Handshake Message

3.10 Handshake Messages

The first step in creating an SSL connection is the handshake, which establishes the algorithms and keying material for the rest of the connection. This section covers the SSL handshake we showed earlier in detail. For each handshake message, we show the relevant piece of specification language and the expanded trace of that handshake message. Then, we explain the meaning and values of each field.

There are two ways to read this section. If you want to really understand what's going on, then read each piece of specification and match it up with the ssldump trace, using the accompanying text as a guide. If all you want to do is get the general idea, then just read the text, referring to the structure definitions and the protocol traces as a guide.

ClientHello

```
struct {
   ProtocolVersion client_version;
   Random random;
   SessionID session_id;
   CipherSuite cipher_suites<2..2^16-1>;
   CompressionMethod compression_methods<1..2^8-1>;
} ClientHello;

struct {
   uint8 major;
   uint8 minor;
} ProtocolVersion;

struct {
   uint32 gmt_unix_time;
   opaque random_bytes[28];
} Random;

opaque SessionID<0..32>;
uint8 CipherSuite[2];
enum { null(0), (255) } CompressionMethod;
```

```
ClientHello
  Version 3.1
  random[32]=
    38 f3 cb de 80 4c b4 79 0a 07 9f b3
    51 ba b8 62 69 e3 8f bf ce c7 ff 25
    3c 3b 84 16 38 b2 5e f7
  cipher suites
            TLS_DHE_RSA_WITH_3DES_EDE_CBC_SHA
            TLS_DHE_DSS_WITH_3DES_EDE_CBC_SHA
            TLS_RSA_WITH_3DES_EDE_CBC_SHA
            TLS_RSA_WITH_IDEA_CBC_SHA
            TLS_RSA_WITH_RC4_128_SHA
            TLS_RSA_WITH_RC4_128_MD5
            TLS_DHE_RSA_WITH_DES_CBC_SHA
            TLS_DHE_DSS_WITH_DES_CBC_SHA
            TLS_RSA_WITH_DES_CBC_SHA
            TLS_DHE_RSA_EXPORT_WITH_DES40_CBC_SHA
            TLS_DHE_DSS_EXPORT_WITH_DES40_CBC_SHA
            TLS_RSA_EXPORT_WITH_DES40_CBC_SHA
            TLS_RSA_EXPORT_WITH_RC2_CBC_40_MD5
            TLS_RSA_EXPORT_WITH_RC4_40_MD5
  compression methods
            NULL
```

The first handshake message sent is always the ClientHello message. The main purpose of this message is for the client to communicate its preferences for connection parameters. After sending the ClientHello, the client waits for the server to send its hello message. In SSLv3 and TLS, the client presents its acceptable parameters and the server chooses the final set. The three negotiable parameters are the version, represented by the client_version field, the cryptographic algorithms, represented by cipher_suites, and the compression algorithm, represented by compression_methods. Figure 3.8 lists the main TLS cipher suites.

The client_version field should contain the highest SSL version number that the client is prepared to speak. For SSLv3, this means major=3 and minor=0. For TLS, major=3 and minor=1. In this trace, the client has indicated that it speaks TLS. In general, it is expected that an implementation speaks all lesser versions. SSL provides no facility for indicating that you do not speak previous versions. This means that if a client knows that (say) version 2.0 is insecure, there's no way to tell the server: use version 3.0 or above. You simply have to try out the server and terminate the connection if the server chooses version 2.

All cryptographic selections for a connection are bundled together into Cipher-Suites, which are represented by arbitrarily chosen 2-byte constants. The CipherSuite specifies the server authentication algorithm, the key exchange algorithm, the bulk encryption algorithm, and the digest (message integrity) algorithm. The suites are listed in the order of descending client preference. Figure 3.8 shows a list of the TLS cipher suites.

The cipher suites marked with a † are not part of the TLS standard. They were introduced in [Banes1999] in response to the liberalization of U.S. export policy that allowed 1024-bit key agreement and 56-bit symmetric encryption. These cipher suites allow 1024-bit RSA and DH combined with either DES or 56-bit RC4. [Banes1999] also adds support for DSS/DH with RC4-128, which had been omitted in the TLS standard. Although these algorithms are widely implemented, the full liberalization of U.S. export policy has rendered them unnecessary, so it's unclear if they will ever be standardized. Note that because these algorithms are labelled export, they go through the export key derivation procedure described in Section 3.11.

The final negotiable parameter is the compression algorithm. Compression algorithms are represented by 1-byte constants. In actual practice, due mainly to patent considerations, no compression algorithms have ever been defined for SSL, and so the only supported algorithm is the mandatory NULL algorithm, which does not change the data. Some proprietary implementations implement private compression algorithms, as does OpenSSL.

The second parameter in the ClientHello is a 32-byte value, (called random) which is used as one of the inputs to the key generation procedure. The first 4 bytes of the value are the time of day when the message was generated (in seconds since the Unix epoch, 12:00 midnight, January 1, 1970 GMT) and the other 28 bytes are supposed to be randomly generated. Note that the protocol will operate correctly even if the first 4 bytes are not time. Client and server clocks do not have to be synchronized. The purpose of the random data is to ensure that even if the same pre_master_secret is used the generated encryption and MAC keys will be different. This prevents replay attack.

Cipher Suite	Auth	Key Exchange	Encryption	Digest	Number
TLS_RSA_WITH_NULL_MD5	RSA	RSA	NULL	MD5	0x0001
TLS_RSA_WITH_NULL_SHA	RSA	RSA	NULL	SHA	0x0002
TLS_RSA_EXPORT_WITH_RC4_40_MD5	RSA	RSA_EXPORT	RC4_40	MD5	0x0003
TLS_RSA_WITH_RC4_128_MD5	RSA	RSA	RC4_128	MD5	0x0004
TLS_RSA_WITH_RC4_128_SHA	RSA	RSA	RC4_128	SHA	0x0005
TLS_RSA_EXPORT_WITH_RC2_CBC_40_MD5	RSA	RSA_EXPORT	RC2_40_CBC	MD5	0x0006
TLS_RSA_WITH_IDEA_CBC_SHA	RSA	RSA	IDEA_CBC	SHA	0x0007
TLS_RSA_EXPORT_WITH_DES40_CBC_SHA	RSA	RSA_EXPORT	DES40_CBC	SHA	0x0008
TLS_RSA_WITH_DES_CBC_SHA	RSA	RSA	DES_CBC	SHA	0x0009
TLS_RSA_WITH_3DES_EDE_CBC_SHA	RSA	RSA	3DES_EDE_CBC	SHA	0x000A
TLS_DH_DSS_EXPORT_WITH_DES40_CBC_SHA	RSA	DH_DSS_EXPORT	DES_40_CBC	SHA	0x000B
TLS_DH_DSS_WITH_DES_CBC_SHA	DSS	DH	DES_CBC	SHA	0x000C
TLS_DH_DSS_WITH_3DES_EDE_CBC_SHA	DSS	DH	3DES_EDE_CBC	SHA	0x000D
TLS_DH_RSA_EXPORT_WITH_DES40_CBC_SHA	RSA	DH_EXPORT	DES_40_CBC	SHA	0x000E
TLS_DH_RSA_WITH_DES_CBC_SHA	RSA	DH	DES_CBC	SHA	0x000F
TLS_DH_RSA_WITH_3DES_EDE_CBC_SHA	RSA	DH	3DES_EDE_CBC	SHA	0x0010
TLS_DHE_DSS_EXPORT_WITH_DES40_CBC_SHA	DSS	DHE_EXPORT	DES_40_CBC	SHA	0x0011
TLS_DHE_DSS_WITH_DES_CBC_SHA	DSS	DHE	DES_CBC	SHA	0x0012
TLS_DHE_DSS_WITH_3DES_EDE_CBC_SHA	DSS	DHE	3DES_EDE_CBC	SHA	0x0013
TLS_DHE_RSA_EXPORT_WITH_DES40_CBC_SHA	RSA	DHE_EXPORT	DES_40_CBC	SHA	0x0014
TLS_DHE_RSA_WITH_DES_CBC_SHA	RSA	DHE	DES_CBC	SHA	0x0015
TLS_DHE_RSA_WITH_3DES_EDE_CBC_SHA	RSA	DHE	3DES_EDE_CBC	SHA	0x0016
TLS_DH_anon_EXPORT_WITH_RC4_40_MD5	-	DH_EXPORT	RC4_40	MD5	0x0017
TLS_DH_anon_WITH_RC4_128_MD5	-	DH	RC4_128	MD5	0x0018
TLS_DH_anon_EXPORT_WITH_DES40_CBC_SHA	-	DH	DES_40_CBC	SHA	0x0019
TLS_DH_anon_WITH_DES_CBC_SHA	-	DH	DES_CBC	SHA	0x001A
TLS_DH_anon_WITH_3DES_EDE_CBC_SHA	-	DH	3DES_EDE_CBC	SHA	0x001B
TLS_RSA_EXPORT1024_WITH_DES_CBC_SHA †	RSA	RSA	DES_CBC	SHA	0x0062
TLS_DHE_DSS_EXPORT1024_WITH_DES_CBC_SHA †	RSA	RSA	DES_CBC	SHA	0x0063
TLS_RSA_EXPORT1024_WITH_RC4_56_SHA †	RSA	RSA	RC4_56	SHA	0x0064
TLS_DHE_DSS_EXPORT1024_WITH_RC4_56_SHA †	RSA	RSA	RC4_56	SHA	0x0065
TLS_DHE_DSS_WITH_RC4_128_SHA †	RSA	RSA	RC4_56	SHA	0x0066

Figure 3.8 Available TLS cipher suites

The ClientHello also contains a session_id parameter. The session ID is a byte string of up to 32 bytes which can be used by the client to indicate that it wishes to reuse the cryptographic keying material from a previous connection rather than generate new material. This is typically much faster because public key operations are computationally expensive. In this trace, the client and server had no previous session to resume and so the session_id field was zero length. We'll see an example of a resumed session in Chapter 4.

ServerHello

```
struct {
    ProtocolVersion server_version;
    Random random;
    SessionID session_id;
    CipherSuite cipher_suite;
    CompressionMethod compression_method;
} ServerHello;
```

```
ServerHello
  SSL version 3.1
  random[32]=
      38 f3 cb d1 33 63 1c c7 2e 8c 56 43
      9e fb 20 70 cc 4b 16 06 4d 5a 8b 15
      e3 9f 0d 47 39 16 5f 5c
  session_id[32]=
      74 6d 09 76 1d 2a c9 02 4a a1 a3 4e
      27 5c 18 63 8a d9 4a 59 f9 c3 14 a5
      c4 b3 a4 f6 61 ef f5 cd
  cipherSuite              TLS_RSA_WITH_DES_CBC_SHA
  compressionMethod            NULL
```

The ServerHello message is used by the server to choose from the various options offered to it by the client. The server_version, cipher_suite, and compression_method fields in this message are the version, ciphers, and compression algorithms that will be used for this SSL connection.

In this trace, the client and the server both speak TLS, so the chosen version is 3.1. The server has chosen the cipher suite TLS_RSA_WITH_DES_CBC_SHA: RSA key exchange with DES-CBC for message encryption and SHA for message digest. Note that the server is under no obligation to choose the client's preferred cipher suite, even if it is supported. The SSL specification is silent on how the choice is made among the client's supported ciphers. The server is free to defer to the client's preferences or impose its own preferences. Common practice, however, is for the server to choose the client-supported cipher that it prefers most. This is somewhat inconvenient for client implementors because they cannot predict which cipher the server will choose. Among other things, this means that they can't give the user feedback about the likely consequences of making a given connection until the connection process has started.

Finally, the server has chosen the only available compression algorithm, NULL. The server also provides a random value. Together with the client's random value and the pre_master_secret (to be discussed later), it is used to generate the keying material to be used for this connection. This ensures that even if the client is broken and uses the same random value for two handshakes, the final cryptographic keys will be different. This also serves to protect against attempts to replay the handshake, as discussed in Section 1.8.

Typically, the server provides a session_id which the client could later use to resume the session. If a server doesn't want to resume sessions, a zero-length session ID can be provided. In this case, the server has provided one, indicating that it's prepared to resume this session. Exactly how session IDs are generated is left up to the implementation. Although they're often generated purely randomly, it is possible for them to have some structure that makes it easier for the server to look up the session in its cache.

Certificate

```
struct {
    ASN.1Cert certificate_list<1..2^24-1>;
} Certificate;

opaque ASN.1Cert<2^24-1>;

Certificate
  Subject
    C=AU
    ST=Queensland
    O=CryptSoft Pty Ltd
    CN=Server test cert (512 bit)
  Issuer
    C=AU
    ST=Queensland
    O=CryptSoft Pty Ltd
    CN=Test CA (1024 bit)
  Serial            04
  certificate[493]=
      30 82 01 e9 30 82 01 52 02 01 04 30
      0d 06 09 2a 86 48 86 f7 0d 01 01 04
      05 00 30 5b 31 0b 30 09 06 03 55 04
      06 13 02 41 55 31 13 30 11 06 03 55
      04 08 13 0a 51 75 65 65 6e 73 6c 61
      6e 64 31 1a 30 18 06 03 55 04 0a 13
      11 43 72 79 70 74 53 6f 66 74 20 50
      74 79 20 4c 74 64 31 1b 30 19 06 03
      55 04 03 13 12 54 65 73 74 20 43 41
      20 28 31 30 32 34 20 62 69 74 29 30
```

```
1e 17 0d 39 38 30 36 32 39 32 33 35
32 34 30 5a 17 0d 30 30 30 36 32 38
32 33 35 32 34 30 5a 30 63 31 0b 30
09 06 03 55 04 06 13 02 41 55 31 13
30 11 06 03 55 04 08 13 0a 51 75 65
65 6e 73 6c 61 6e 64 31 1a 30 18 06
03 55 04 0a 13 11 43 72 79 70 74 53
6f 66 74 20 50 74 79 20 4c 74 64 31
23 30 21 06 03 55 04 03 13 1a 53 65
72 76 65 72 20 74 65 73 74 20 63 65
72 74 20 28 35 31 32 20 62 69 74 29
30 5c 30 0d 06 09 2a 86 48 86 f7 0d
01 01 01 05 00 03 4b 00 30 48 02 41
00 9f b3 c3 84 27 95 ff 12 31 52 0f
15 ef 46 11 c4 ad 80 e6 36 5b 0f dd
80 d7 61 8d e0 fc 72 45 09 34 fe 55
66 45 43 4c 68 97 6a fe a8 a0 a5 df
5f 78 ff ee d7 64 b8 3f 04 cb 6f ff
2a fe fe b9 ed 02 03 01 00 01 30 0d
06 09 2a 86 48 86 f7 0d 01 01 04 05
00 03 81 81 00 95 be f7 e4 19 27 b6
18 78 03 15 f9 8e b9 ae 08 b2 36 fd
25 58 48 99 63 00 4a 23 82 96 46 65
30 44 83 26 3b 2c ce 0f fa f9 df d6
fb c4 eb 6c e6 e1 6b 3a 65 f7 91 62
bd 70 55 b9 c6 e3 f5 db 9d 87 b0 0e
21 9b b5 87 53 00 3e 5c a4 9d cf 54
77 cd 7a bf 3d c5 7a 30 78 aa a5 28
69 78 e7 96 4a c8 80 46 eb fe e9 fb
8d 24 bc e9 63 9e d2 14 61 c0 79 09
15 41 9c 3d 97 fd 34 3d b6 12 d7 3e
01
```

The Certificate message is simply a sequence of X.509 certificates. The certificates are presented in order, with the first certificate being the certificate belonging to the server and the next certificate (if there is one) containing the key that certifies the server's certificate, and so on. In all common SSL and TLS cipher suites, the server must send its certificate (there are several rarely used cipher suites where the server remains anonymous). The key in the certificate is then either used to encrypt the pre_master_secret or to verify the ServerKeyExchange, depending on which cipher suite was chosen.

In this case, the server has sent only one certificate, for *Server Test Cert (512 bit)*. It's assumed that the client already has the CA certificate for *Test CA (1024 Bit)*. What's presented here is a summary of the most important certificate information. More detail about the structure of X.509 certificates can be found in Chapter 1.

ServerHelloDone

```
struct { } ServerHelloDone;
```

The ServerHelloDone is an empty message that indicates that the server has sent all the handshake messages it will send in this phase. This is required because there are some optional messages that can appear after the Certificate message. We'll see some examples of that in Chapter 4.

ClientKeyExchange

```
struct {
   select (KeyExchangeAlgorithm) {
     case rsa: EncryptedPreMasterSecret;
     case diffie_hellman: DiffieHellmanClientPublicValue;
   } exchange_keys;
} ClientKeyExchange;

struct {
   ProtocolVersion client_version;
   opaque random[46];
} PreMasterSecret;

struct {
   public-key-encrypted PreMasterSecret pre_master_secret;
} EncryptedPreMasterSecret;

enum { implicit, explicit } PublicValueEncoding;

struct {
   select (PublicValueEncoding) {
      case implicit: struct {};
      case explicit: opaque DH_Yc<1..2^16-1>;
   } dh_public;
} DiffieHellmanClientPublicValue;
```

```
ClientKeyExchange
  EncryptedPreMasterSecret[64]=
     17 4d 00 32 bc b2 af 95 09 0a 45 24
     97 d8 34 dc 73 20 4d 00 91 a5 0d ed
     c3 f0 b4 f5 32 6f 13 cc ea 41 00 5e
     bb 05 f1 b7 e2 c4 fa 1b 40 c1 2a f3
     00 20 83 43 2d 8c 2a 53 3b 33 cc 5f
     0b bc db a2
```

The ClientKeyExchange message provides the client's contribution to the creation of the pre_master_secret. When RSA key exchange is being used, this simply means that the client generates a PreMasterSecret structure and encrypts it under the server's RSA key. The pre_master_secret is a 48-byte quantity consisting of two version number bytes followed by 46 randomly generated bytes. It is critical that these bytes be chosen using a cryptographically secure RNG (see Chapter 5 for information on RNGs.) RFC 1750 [Eastlake1994] provides guidance on random number generation. Wagner and Goldberg's successful attack on Netscape's SSLv2 implementation [Goldberg1996] was based on flaws in Netscape's RNG. We provide some guidance on generating strong random numbers in Chapter 5.

> Wagner and Goldberg disassembled the Netscape RNG and observed that the RNG was seeded with the time of day and the process ID. Since both of these numbers are fairly limited in range, it was fairly easy to search the entire space and recover the SSL session key. This process took about an hour at the time and would be faster now.

The public-key-encrypted operator in the EncryptedPreMasterSecret struct means that the pre_master_secret field is to be encrypted using the recipient's public key. The encrypted key is then represented as a variable length vector:

```
opaque encrypted_data<0..2^16-1>
```

The ClientKeyExchange message is one of only two messages that are different between SSLv3 and TLS. This difference is due to a bug in Netscape's SSLv3 implementation that was mimicked by other SSLv3 implementors. When RSA is being used for encryption, the length of the encrypted data is redundant because the length of the Encrypted-PreMasterSecret is unambiguously determined both by the length of the Client-KeyExchange message and by the length of the server's RSA key. As a consequence, Netscape's SSLv3 implementation omitted the length bytes when encoding the EncryptedPreMasterSecret, and most other SSLv3 implementations followed their (incorrect) lead. That is to say that most SSLv3 implementations violate the SSLv3 specification. An implementation note in the TLS specifcation points out that most SSLv3 implementations are broken and requires that TLS implementations correctly include the length bytes. The trace we are looking at is from an implementation in TLS mode, and therefore the length bytes are included.

ChangeCipherSpec

```
struct {
    ChangeCipherSpecType type;
} ChangeCipherSpec;
```

```
enum { change_cipher_spec(1), (255) } ChangeCipherSpecType;
```

The ChangeCipherSpec message indicates that the sending implementation has switched to the newly negotiated algorithms and keying material and that future messages will be protected using those algorithms. The ChangeCipherSpec message is unique in that it is not properly part of the handshake but rather has its own content type. This is described as a performance improvement in the specification, which says:

Note: To help avoid pipeline stalls, ChangeCipherSpec is an independent TLS Protocol content type, and is not actually a TLS handshake message.

However, only one implementation known to the author (Netscape's) makes use of this feature in any interesting way. Netscape uses this feature to make sure that the ChangeCipherSpec message is transmitted separately from the Finished message. Because the ChangeCipherSpec message must not be encrypted and the Finished message must be encrypted, they cannot be transmitted in the same record. Having them in different layers ensures this.

   This trick is useful only if your implementation attempts to send multiple handshake messages in the same record. As we'll see in Chapter 6, it's sometimes a performance win to send multiple handshake messages in the same TCP segment, and sending them in the same record is one way of doing this. However, many implementations instead opt to transmit multiple records in the same TCP segment, which has much the same effect. For such implementations, this protocol feature is an inconvenience which complicates the handshake state machine.

   A typical implementation is to have the handshake state machine read only handshake type traffic. However, it also needs to be aware that the ChangeCipherSpec has been received, and this information must be carried out of band from the record layer processing. If the ChangeCipherSpec message were a handshake message, the handshake layer could simply read it off the network. Instead, the record layer code needs to have special support for recognizing the ChangeCipherSpec message and either telling the handshake layer or throwing an error depending on whether the handshake is in the right state.

   The ChangeCipherSpec message consists only of a single type byte, which is mainly a placeholder since it can currently have only a single value of 1. No expansion of the use of this message has been publicly proposed.

Finished

```
SSLv3:
struct {
  opaque md5_hash[16];
  opaque sha_hash[20];
} Finished;
```

```
TLS:
struct {
   opaque verify_data[12];
} Finished;
```

Finished
  verify_data[12]=
    03 3b 69 b7 26 e3 0e 23 fc 03 79 27

The Finished message is the first message encrypted with the new cryptographic parameters. It allows an implementation to verify that none of the handshake messages have been tampered with by an attacker.

Although the details of the SSLv3 and TLS Finished messages are different, the general concept is similar. Each side sends a digest of the negotiated master secret and the concatenated handshake messages to the other, which compares it to the same result computed locally. If they differ, the handshake has been tampered with.

```
enum { client(0x434C4E54), server(0x53525652) } Sender;

md5_hash = MD5(master_secret + pad2 +
          MD5(handshake_messages +
             Sender + master_secret + pad1));
sha_hash = SHA-1(master_secret +  pad2 +
          SHA-1(handshake_messages +
             Sender + master_secret + pad1));
```

Figure 3.9 SSLv3 Finished computations

The SSLv3 Finished message is modeled after the popular cryptographic message authentication function HMAC [Krawczyk1997], which uses nested hashes to create a construction which provably has certain security properties. Figure 3.9 shows the SSLv3 computation. The plus sign indicates concatenation, so the input to the first invocation of MD5 (the inner one) is the string created by concatenating all the handshake messages, the Sender constant, the master secret, and some pad bytes (pad1 is a string of the byte 0x36 repeated 48 times). The input to the second invocation of MD5 is the string created by concatenating the master secret, some pad bytes (pad2 is the a string of the byte 0x5c repeated 48 times), and the output of the first MD5 computation. The SHA-1 computation is identical except that the pad bytes are repeated 40 times instead of 48. The purpose of the Sender constant is to ensure that the client and server produce different Finished messages. This prevents an attacker from reflecting a Finished message back to its sender.

Although the SSLv3 Finished message is based on HMAC, it was modified to be usable for SSL. In particular, because the master secret is available only midway through the handshake, the handshake messages are the first input to the inner digest, whereas in HMAC, the key is always the first input. Consequently, some of the security properties of HMAC may not apply. Comments from the HMAC designers were the primary reason why the computation was changed in TLS.

```
verify_data =
  PRF(master_secret, finished_label, MD5(handshake_messages) +
      SHA-1(handshake_messages)) [0..11];
```

Figure 3.10 TLS Finished computation

TLS makes wide use of an HMAC-based *pseudo-random function* (PRF) for a number of cryptographic computations, including the Finished message (see Figure 3.10). (We'll see more of the PRF in the section on key derivation.) This PRF is used to create the verify_data value. The inputs are the master secret, an ASCII string for the finished label ("client" or "server") and an MD5 and SHA-1 digest of the handshake messages. The [0..11] indicates that the first 12 bytes of PRF output are used to create the verify_data.

Note that both MD5 and SHA-1 are used in the creation of the Finished message. The rationale for this is to provide additional security against weaknesses in the digest algorithm. This way, an attacker must break both MD5 and SHA-1 in order to forge a Finished message.

Programming Note: Processing Finished

Note that although the Finished message must include the digest of all the handshake messages so far, it does not include its own digest. However, the second Finished message must include a digest of the first. This creates an interesting programming problem for implementors. A naive implementation might write its handshake handler something like the code in Figure 3.11.

Unfortunately, when the recipient goes to compute the Finished value, the digest will include the just-received Finished message, and so the values won't match. However, the server can't just stop digesting because it needs to include the digest of the first Finished in its response to the client's Finished. Thus, it must either maintain two sets of digests or make a copy of the digest objects before processing the Finished message, as shown in Figure 3.12.

3.11 Key Derivation

Once the pre_master_secret has been exchanged, each implementation needs to expand it into the individual cryptographic keys that will be used for encryption, authentication, etc. This expansion is accomplished using a key derivation function. The SSLv3 and TLS key derivation functions are similar, but differ in the precise cryptographic transformations they use. We'll describe the TLS key derivation function with an aside at the

```
receive_handshake_message(context,message) {
  digest_handshake_message(context,message);
  switch(message.type){
    case ClientHello:
      handle_client_hello(context,message);
      break;
      ...
    case Finished:
      handle_finished(context,message);
      break;
  }
```

Figure 3.11 Naive Finished handling

```
receive_handshake_message(context,message) {
  if(message.type==Finished){
    digests=copy_digests(context);
  }
  digest_handshake_message(context,message);

  switch(message.type){
    case ClientHello:
      handle_client_hello(context,message);
      break;
      ...
    case Finished:
      handle_finished(context,message,digests);
      break;
  }
```

Figure 3.12 Correct Finished handling

end describing the differences from the SSLv3 process. You can refer to Figure 3.13 for a graphical representation of the process.

The PRF

The entire TLS key derivation process uses PRF as the key derivation function. The point of this is to expand the pre_master_secret into another secret called master_secret, and then expand the master_secret into the cryptographic keys that we

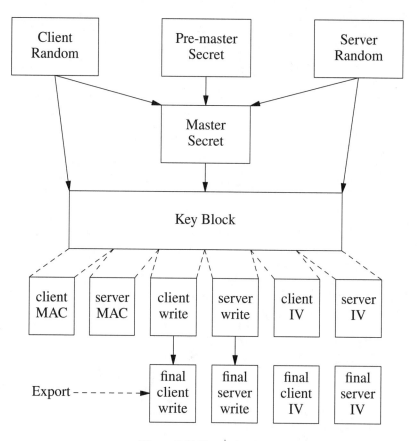

Figure 3.13 Key derivation

need for the various encryption and MAC algorithms. As with the key derivation function in Section 1.8, the client and the server each independently use the same key derivation function to generate the keys from the shared master_secret. The PRF takes three arguments, a secret (presumably random), a fixed ASCII string (the label), and a seed (presumably random, but public), as in PRF(secret, label, seed). The purpose of the label is to allow you to use the PRF to generate different keys from the same secret material simply by using different labels for each key. The label is simply digested as the corresponding ASCII string.

The PRF generates an arbitrary length string of pseudo-random bytes, which are referred to by using the TLS vector notation. So, PRF()[0..9] refers to the first 10 bytes of the PRF output. The PRF computation is fairly complicated and not that interesting except to implementors. We cover it here only for completeness, so feel free to skip over this stuff. It won't be on the exam.

First, the secret part is split into two halves, S1 and S2. S1 is the first half of the secret and S2 is the second half. If the original secret is odd-sized, then the last byte of

S1 and the first byte of S2 are the same.

Each half is used as the secret component in an expansion function P_hash, which is based on HMAC. P_hash generates an arbitrary length byte string by the process shown in Figure 3.14.

```
P_hash(secret, seed) = HMAC_hash(secret, A(1) + seed) +
                HMAC_hash(secret, A(2) + seed) +
                HMAC_hash(secret, A(3) + seed) + ...
```

A() is defined as:
```
    A(0) = seed
    A(i) = HMAC_hash(secret, A(i-1))
```

HMAC_hash means HMAC using a given hash algorithm, e.g., HMAC_MD5 means HMAC using MD5.

Figure 3.14 P_hash function

Now that we've got these functions defined, we construct PRF by XORing a P_MD5 and a P_SHA-1:

```
PRF(secret, label, seed) = P_MD5(S1, label + seed) ⊕
                P_SHA-1(S2, label + seed);
```

Because MD5 digests are 16 bytes long and SHA-1 digests are 20 bytes long, P_MD5 and P_SHA-1 don't line up. So, if you want to produce an 80-byte output, you have to run P_MD5 five times and P_SHA-1 four times.

The three non-fixed inputs to the key derivation function are the pre_master_secret, the client_random, and the server_random. The pre_master_secret is simply a secret byte string. When RSA key exchange is being used, it's a 48-byte string generated by the client. It's encrypted under the server's public key. The pre_master_secret is the only source of secret information in this process. The other two inputs, the client_random and server_random, are the random values from the ClientHello and ServerHello messages.

The first step in the key derivation is to transform the pre_master_secret into the master_secret. This is done by applying the pseudo-random function PRF to the pre_master_secret, client_random, and server_random:

```
master_secret = PRF(pre_master_secret, "master secret",
                client_random + server_random) [0..47];
```

We now use the PRF with the master_secret to give us enough keying material for all the algorithms we'll need. Depending on the cipher suite being used, we might need up to six values, an encryption key, a MAC key, and an initializaton vector (IV) for both client and server. First, we add up the lengths of all the values we need and produce that many bytes using the PRF. For instance, if we're using DES and MD5, we need 8 bytes for each encryption key, 16 bytes for each HMAC-MD5 key, and 8 bytes for each IV, for a total of 48 bytes:

```
key_block = PRF(master_secret, "key expansion",
        server_random + client_random)
```

Note that the order of the client_random and server_random is different here from the master_secret computation.

Once we have the key block, we simply slice and dice it one key at a time, in the following order: client_write_MAC_secret, server_write_MAC_secret, client_write_key, server_write_key, client_write_IV, server_write_IV.

Exportable Algorithms

Due to U.S. export restrictions at the time of the SSLv3 and TLS design, exportable ciphers needed to have their encryption keys shortened so that they could be broken with no more than 2^{40} operations. In order to do this, we first generate a short intermediate and then reexpand it using the PRF. This approach prevents a precomputation attack in which the attacker simply builds a big table for all 2^{40} keys. The server and client random values act as a *salt* preventing this attack. The attacker can still attack the key by trying all of the intermediate keys but the time/memory tradeoff won't work.

> The export situation has changed since the design of SSL/TLS. 40-bit keys are essentially worthless for data security. Attacking a 40-bit key is easily within the range of the most modest commercial attacker. In 1998 a dedicated DES keysearch machine was built [Gilmore1998], showing that 56-bit keys could be compromised by a dedicated attacker. In response to this, the U.S. government decided that cryptographic systems with 56-bit keys would now be exportable. Changes have been proposed to the TLS spec to include 56-bit exportable ciphers. These ciphers also allow 1024-bit RSA keys instead of 512-bit RSA keys. In January 2000 the U.S. government essentially removed all export restrictions. However, there is still a lot of old software that has only exportable modes so it's important to know about them. The Bureau of Export Administration Web site describes them and can be reached at
>
> http://www.bxa.doc.gov/Encryption/Default.htm/.

Also, we're required (again for export reasons) to use a non-secret IV (normally the SSL IV is generated partially from secret data and is therefore secret) so we derive it purely from the public client_randomand server_random values. The first half of the iv_block is used to generate the IV that the client uses to encrypt data, and the second half for the IV that the server uses to encrypt data (see Figure 3.15).

```
final_client_write_key =
    PRF(client_write_key, "client write key", client_random + server_random)
final_server_write_key =
    PRF(server_write_key, "server write key", client_random + server_random)

iv_block = PRF(0, "IV block", client_random + server_random)
```

Figure 3.15 Export keying material derivation

SSLv3 Key Derivation

SLv3 key derivation is similar to TLS key derivation, except that the PRF is replaced with a series of expansion functions based on a combination of MD5 and SHA-1. The use of the constants "A","BB", etc. ensures that the output of each digest is different, even though the secret data is the same. This process is shown in Figure 3.16.

```
master_secret =
    MD5(pre_master_secret + SHA-1("A" + pre_master_secret +
        client_random + server_random)) +
    MD5(pre_master_secret + SHA-1("BB" + pre_master_secret +
        client_random + server_random)) +
    MD5(pre_master_secret + SHA-1("CCC" + pre_master_secret +
        client_random + server_random))

key_block =
    MD5(master_secret + SHA-1("A" + master_secret +
        server_random + client_random)) +
    MD5(master_secret + SHA-1("BB" + master_secret +
        server_random + client_random)) +
    MD5(master_secret + SHA-1("CCC" + master_secret +
        server_random + client_random)) +
    ...
```

Figure 3.16 SSLv3 key derivation

Note that the order of the client_random and server_random is opposite for these two computations.

As with TLS, when being used with exportable ciphers, SSLv3 postprocesses the keying material to weaken it, as shown in Figure 3.17.

```
final_client_write_key =
    MD5(client_write_key + client_random + server_random);
final_server_write_key =
    MD5(server_write_key + server_random + client_random);
```

```
client_write_IV =
   MD5(client_random + server_random);
server_write_IV =
   MD5(server_random + client_random);
```

Figure 3.17 SSLv3 export key derivation

Note that even though the SSLv3 key derivation was changed for TLS, no known weaknesses exist in the SSLv3 key derivation.

3.12 Record Protocol

The SSL record protocol is a fairly simple encapsulation protocol. It consists of a series of encrypted, integrity-protected records. Each record consists of a small header block and an encrypted data block which itself contains the content and a MAC. Figure 3.18 shows an example record. The header is shown in white and the encrypted payload is shaded. We've drawn the various pieces of the encrypted payload as they would appear if the encryption were removed.

The record shown has been encrypted with a block cipher such as DES using MD5 as a MAC. Therefore, the record needs to be padded out to fit the DES block length. Note that although the encrypted data must be a multiple of the block length, the record itself is not aligned on block boundaries.

In this trace, we have the client and the server writing one record each. The cipher suite, as we know from the ServerHello message, is TLS_RSA_WITH_DES_CBC_SHA.

SSL data is broken up into a series of *fragments*. The protocol definition provides a maximum fragment size but otherwise doesn't specify how to determine what fragment boundaries are, but usually they're one-to-one with application data write calls. However, boundaries of calls to SSL_write() (or equivalent) need not be preserved. Consequently, the record layer may break up any given write into multiple records or conversely aggregate the input from multiple calls into a single record. The maximum fragment data size is 2^{14} bytes, so larger writes must be fragmented into pieces of this size or smaller. Note that the length field is long enough to indicate records up to $2^{16} - 1$ bytes. Indeed, older versions of Internet Explorer incorrectly generated records of greater than 2^{14} bytes.

Once the data has been fragmented, it's compressed—or it would be if any compression algorithms were defined. Because none are, no compression is done. A MAC is computed over the compressed data fragment and concatenated with the data. The MAC covers the data and the headers, as well as including a sequence number to prevent replay and reordering attacks. Figure 3.19 shows the MAC algorithms.

```
TLS MAC = HMAC_hash (MAC_write_secret, seq_num + type + version +
           length + content)
```

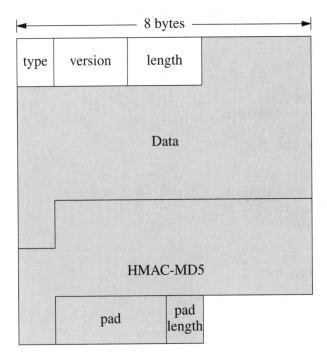

Figure 3.18 Diagram of an SSL record

SSLv3 MAC=hash(MAC_write_secret + pad_2 +
        hash(MAC_write_secret + pad_1 + seq_num + content_type +
            length + content));

Figure 3.19 MAC computations

seq_num is a 64-bit sequence number, which is independent for the client and server (i.e. the first message that both the client and server send has sequence number zero). The content type here is one of the content types listed in Figure 3.20. The version is simply the SSL/TLS version number. The length is the length of the content (i.e., the data in the record); it is *not* the same as the length in the record header, because that length includes the MAC and possibly padding.

The TLS MAC is standard HMAC. The SSLv3 MAC is based on an early draft of HMAC. pad_1 is the byte 0x36 repeated 48 times for MD5 and 40 times for SHA-1. pad_2 is the byte 0x5c repeated the same number of times. The intention of the padding is to ensure that the MAC key plus pad fills the entire first block of the message digest. Because MD5 and SHA-1 blocks are 64 bytes long, a 16-byte key means a 48-byte pad. Note that this implies that the padding for SHA-1 (a 20-byte key) should be 44 bytes, but it's 40 in the specification. This is an error in the SSLv3 specification, but it became part of Netscape's implementation and thus the specification was never changed. Once again, we can see that Netscape's implementation constituted the real baseline for SSLv3.

```
struct {
   ContentType type;
   ProtocolVersion version;
   uint16 length;
} RecordHeader;

enum {
   change_cipher_spec(20), alert(21), handshake(22),
   application_data(23), (255)
} ContentType;

struct {
   uint8 major;
   uint8 minor;
} ProtocolVersion;
```

Figure 3.20 The record header

The sequence number serves to prevent various attacks on the message stream, including *replay* attacks, where the attacker repeats a record, and *reordering* attacks, where the attacker exchanges the order of one or more records. Note, however, that although the sequence number allows these attacks to be detected, because the sequence number isn't in the record, it does not allow them to be corrected. Thus, SSL must be run over a transport protocol that provides *reliable* transport (i.e., it must deliver data to the receiving application in the order it was transmitted without duplicates or omissions). TCP meets these requirements (the data may arrive in any order, but the kernel ensures that the application sees it in transmission order). However, UDP does not, and so SSL cannot be successfully run over UDP, because records might be arbitrarily lost or reordered, which would look like an active attack to the SSL implementation.

Note that the TLS specification describes records somewhat differently, without breaking them up into header and body. This presentation is intended to be easier to follow, and is more typical of how network protocols are usually presented.

The different type values correspond to the different types of data that can be carried over the TLS record layer, as shown in Figure 3.4. The length and version fields we've seen before. The length in the header is the total length of all the data following in the record, including the MAC and padding.

Stream Ciphers

Stream ciphers don't need any padding, so the MAC is simply appended to the data and the entire data block is encrypted. Because the stream cipher keystream can never be reused, the cipher encryption state must be retained from record to record. Logically, it is as if all the data to be encrypted were encrypted in a single pass by the cipher.

Block Ciphers

The length of the input to a block cipher must be a multiple of the block size (typically 8 bytes). Since the input data can be of arbitrary size, the data usually does not line up on a block boundary, and it is necessary to add a number of padding bytes. The most padding bytes that will ever be needed is 7, but up to 255 bytes can be added to hide the plaintext length from sniffers. The number of pad bytes used is recorded in the pad length byte. The value of the pad bytes must be equal to the value in the pad length byte.

For example, if the block length is 8 bytes, the length of the data is 16 bytes, and the MAC length is 16 bytes, then the length before padding is 33 bytes, because the length byte must always be included at the end. At least 7 bytes of padding will be needed, but 15, 23, etc., may also be used. Assuming that the minimum pad length of 7 bytes is used, the last 8 bytes would be 07 07 07 07 07 07 07 07 (7 pad bytes plus the pad length byte) for a total data length of 40 bytes. Note that this padding construct is incompatible with standard block cipher padding (see [RSA1993c]) which does not use a pad length byte, but merely records the total number of pad bytes in the padding. In the example here, the standard algorithm would give the pad 08 08 08 08 08 08 08 08.

All the current block ciphers use *cipher-block chaining* (CBC) mode. The chaining must be continued from record to record: The last cipher-block of record X is used as the IV for record X+1.

Null Cipher

As a special case, the Null cipher simply passes the data untransformed from input to output, with no padding. The starting cipher suite TLS_NULL_WITH_NULL_NULL doesn't even add a MAC, but simply puts the plaintext directly in the record. Note that TLS_NULL_WITH_NULL_NULL is available only during the handshake at the start of a connection. It is illegal to negotiate to it.

3.13 Alerts and Closure

The alert protocol is designed to allow one side to alert the other to exceptional conditions. Alert messages are very simple, conveying a severity level and a description. On receiving an alert message of level fatal, an implementation must terminate the connection and the session cannot be resumed. A warning message may be ignored; however, an implementation may choose to treat warnings as fatal. Figure 3.21 shows the TLS alert message structure. The SSL alert message structure is identical, but fewer alerts are defined. See Chapter 4 for detailed coverage of all the alerts.

```
enum { warning(1), fatal(2), (255) } AlertLevel;

enum {
    close_notify(0),
    unexpected_message(10),
    bad_record_mac(20),
    decryption_failed(21),
    record_overflow(22),
    decompression_failure(30),
    handshake_failure(40),
    no_certificate(41),  SSLv3 only
    bad_certificate(42),
    unsupported_certificate(43),
    certificate_revoked(44),
    certificate_expired(45),
    certificate_unknown(46),
    illegal_parameter(47),
    unknown_ca(48),
    access_denied(49),
    decode_error(50),
    decrypt_error(51),
    export_restriction(60),
    protocol_version(70),
    insufficient_security(71),
    internal_error(80),
    user_cancelled(90),
    no_renegotiation(100),
    (255)
} AlertDescription;

struct {
    AlertLevel level;
    AlertDescription description;
} Alert;
```

Figure 3.21 TLS alert message

Closure

The close_notify alert is used to signal that the sender has sent all the data that it is going to send on this connection. The purpose of this alert is to prevent a truncation attack in which the attacker inserts a TCP FIN before the sender is finished sending data, forcing the receiver to think that all data has been received. As a consequence, unless the receiver receives a close_notify it can never be sure that more data wasn't forthcoming. If an implementation receives a TCP FIN without first receiving a close_notify it must mark the session as not resumable.

In practice, many protocols contain their own end-of-data markers, and it's fairly common practice for an implementation receiving one to simply send a close_notify and close the connection immediately without waiting for a close_notify. This behavior is implicitly allowed by the SSL and TLS specifications. This is what has happened in the trace we provided at the beginning of the chapter, where the client provided a close_notify but the server did not. Normally, the closure alert is sent with a level of warning.

Other Alerts

All the other alerts signal errors of various kinds. Although in theory implementations can continue past a non-fatal alert, in practice even such alerts indicate that one side requested something that the other side couldn't fulfill and so they result in connection closure. The TLS specification provides a complete list of all the available alerts and we'll discuss each alert in detail in Chapter 4.

Figure 3.22 shows an example trace terminating in an alert. The client has been configured to require DSS/DH, and the server only supports RSA. Thus, the server rejects the connection with a handshake_failure alert. Note that the server closes the connection immediately after sending the alert.

```
New TCP connection: speedy(1085) <-> romeo(4433)
1 0.0168 (0.0168) C>S   Handshake
      ClientHello
        Version 3.0
        cipher suites
                TLS_DHE_DSS_WITH_DES_CBC_SHA
        compression methods
                NULL
2 0.0171 (0.0002) S>C   Alert
        level        fatal
        value        handshake_failure
Server FIN
Client FIN
```

Figure 3.22 A connection ending in an alert

3.14 Summary

This chapter has provided a detailed discussion of the most basic mode of SSL, RSA server-only authentication. This provides the background for our discussion of future modes, all of which share many features with the basic mode.

The SSL handshake negotiates cryptographic algorithms and establishes keying material between client and server. The client offers a choice of cryptographic algorithms and the server selects the algorithms to be used. The server provides its public key using a Certificate message.

The pre_master_secret *is encrypted under the server's public key.* A *key derivation function* is used to convert the pre_master_secret into the cryptographic keys used for the connection.

A Finished *message is used to provide integrity for the entire handshake.* The Finished message contains a message digest of all the handshake messages, preventing an attacker from tampering with the handshake.

The data stream is segmented into records. Each record is individually encrypted and MACed, providing both confidentiality and message integrity. The MAC is computed over a sequence number to prevent replay and reordering attacks.

Errors are signalled via alerts. Alerts are a special type of record distinct from the main data stream, and they are used to signal handshake errors or problems with MACing or decryption.

A close_notify *alert is used to signal the end of the connection.* This prevents truncation attacks where the attacker forges a close on the underlying transport layer.

4

Advanced SSL

4.1   Introduction

The previous chapter covered the simplest type of SSL connection, server-only authentication using RSA. This chapter presents the rest of the major operational modes. As with the previous chapter, this chapter is divided into two sections. The first section covers the modes in overview form and the second describes each message in gory detail. Most readers will want to read the entire first section and skim the second section. Those who wish to challenge themselves should read the entire second section.

Both sections follow the same order of presentation. First, we discuss session resumption, which allows a new SSL connection to be formed without performing a full handshake. Next, we cover client authentication, which allows the client to authenticate itself using its public key and digital certificate.

Because United States export regulations restricted the size of keys that could be used by applications exported from the U.S., SSL has two modes designed to provide maximum security while still remaining exportable, Ephemeral RSA and Server Gated Cryptography. Although these modes are no longer necessary, they're still in widespread use. We show how these work and describe their benefits. We also show the TLS standard DH/DSS key exchange and less-used cipher suites that use Elliptic Curves, Kerberos, and FORTEZZA. We finish with a detailed discussion of all the SSL alerts and of SSLv2 backward compatibility.

A note on presentation: although the timelines we show will include all the messages in the handshake, the detailed presentation will only show the messages which are new or different from the basic handshake.

4.2   Session Resumption

As we'll see in Chapter 6, the full SSL handshake can be very expensive, both in terms of CPU time and in terms of the number of round trips required to execute. In order to reduce this performance cost, SSL incorporates a session resumption mechanism. If the client and server have already communicated once, they can short-circuit the full handshake and proceed directly to data transfer.

The most expensive part of the handshake is the establishment of the pre_master_secret, which usually (except in the case of Kerberos) requires public key cryptography. A resumed handshake allows a new connection to use a master_secret established in a previous handshake. This avoids the computationally expensive operations required by public key cryptography.

Sessions versus Connections

SSL makes a distinction between a *connection* and a *session*. A *connection* represents one specific communications channel (typically mapped to a TCP connection), along with its keys, cipher choices, sequence number state, etc. A *session* is a virtual construct representing the negotiated algorithms and the master_secret. A new session is created every time a given client and server go through a full key exchange and establish a new master_secret.

Multiple connections can be associated with a given session. Although all connections in a given session share the same master_secret, each has its own encryption keys, MAC keys, and IVs. This is absolutely necessary for security reasons, because reuse of symmetric keying material can be extremely dangerous. Resumption allows the generation of a new set of symmetric keys and IVs from a common master_secret because the keys depend on the random values which are fresh for each connection. The new random values are combined with the old master_secret to produce new keys.

How It Works

The first time a client and server interact, they create both a new connection and a new session. If the server is prepared to resume the session, it gives the client a session_id in its ServerHello message and caches the master_secret for later reference. When the client initiates a new connection with the server, it uses that session_id in its ClientHello message. The server agrees to resume the session by using the same session_id in its ServerHello. At this point, the rest of the handshake is skipped and the stored master_secret is used to generate all the cryptographic keys. Figure 4.1 shows the timeline for this process.

4.3   Client Authentication

So far, all the handshakes we've discussed authenticate only the server. SSL also provides a mechanism for cryptographically authenticating the client. This would be useful

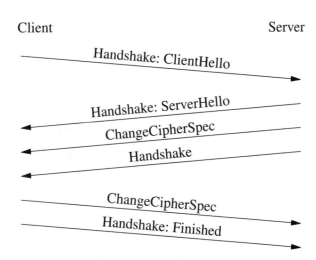

Figure 4.1 Resumed SSL session timeline

if a server wanted to restrict access to some services to only certain authorized clients and could use client authentication to do so. The idea here is that the client uses its private key to sign something, thus proving that it has possession of the private key corresponding to the certificate. Client authentication is initiated by the server sending a CertificateRequest message to the client. The client responds by sending a Certificate message (the same message that the server uses to transmit its certificate) and a CertificateVerify message. The CertificateVerify message is a string signed with the private key associated with the certificate that it transmitted. Client authentication is *always* initiated by the server. There is no mechanism for the client to unilaterally offer client authentication. Figure 4.2 shows the timeline for this process.

4.4 Ephemeral RSA

When SSL was designed, United States export regulations limited RSA encryption key lengths to 512 bits for exportable applications. Unfortunately, a 512-bit permanent RSA key presents an attractive target for attack. Thus, a server that wished to communicate with both domestic and exportable clients would have liked to have two key exchange keys, one 1024-bit and one 512-bit, assuming that it wanted to have strong cryptography when possible.

Although SSLv2 simply forced such a server to have two certified keys if it wanted to communicate at the highest possible security with both export and domestic clients, SSLv3 and TLS incorporate a feature called *ephemeral RSA* which allows

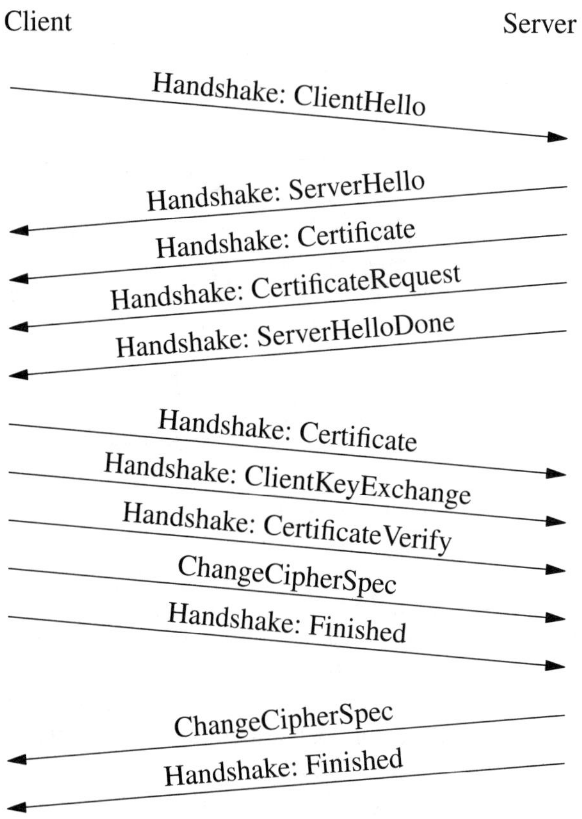

Client   Server

Figure 4.2 Client authentication timeline

communication between an exportable client and a domestic server with a permanent strong key. The way this works is that the server generates a temporary 512 bit key which it signs with its strong key. When communicating with domestic clients, it simply uses its strong key as discussed in Chapter 3.

The only difference in the handshake between ephemeral RSA mode and normal RSA mode is the presence of a single new message: ServerKeyExchange. The server uses the ServerKeyExchange message to transmit the signed RSA key. When the client receives the ServerKeyExchange message, it verifies the server's signature over the ephemeral key and then uses it to wrap the pre_master_secret exactly as described in Chapter 3. Figure 4.3 shows the timeline for this process.

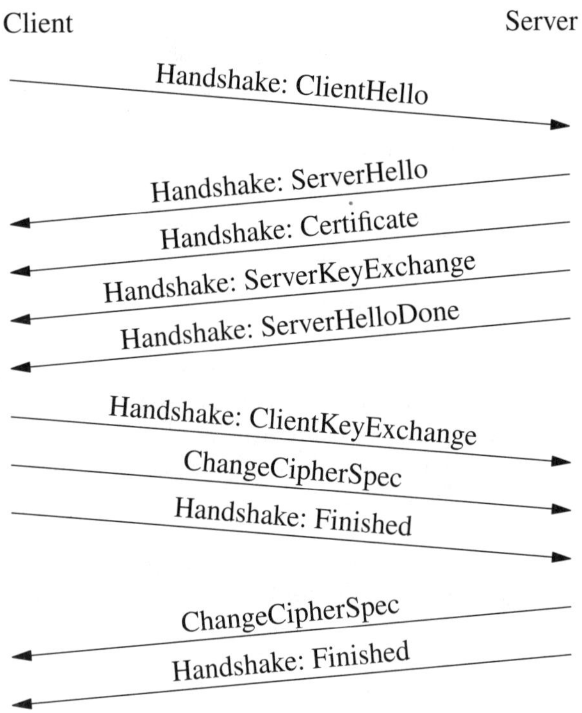

Client   Server

Handshake: ClientHello

Handshake: ServerHello

Handshake: Certificate

Handshake: ServerKeyExchange

Handshake: ServerHelloDone

Handshake: ClientKeyExchange

ChangeCipherSpec

Handshake: Finished

ChangeCipherSpec

Handshake: Finished

Figure 4.3 Ephemeral RSA timeline

4.5 Rehandshake

Once an SSL connection has been established, it's possible to perform a *rehandshake*. A rehandshake is simply a new SSL handshake performed over the current protected connection. Thus, the handshake messages are encrypted in transit. Once the new handshake has finished, data will be protected using the new session state.

```
struct { } HelloRequest;
```

The client can initiate a new handshake simply by sending a new ClientHello message. If the server wishes to initiate a rehandshake, it must send the empty HelloRequest handshake message. The client responds to a HelloRequest with a ClientHello, after which the handshake proceeds normally. There's no requirement that either client or server agree to rehandshake. An implementation which does not wish to rehandshake can simply ignore the message or send a no_renegotiation alert. The next section shows an example of a client-initiated rehandshake. Chapter 8 shows an example of a server-initated rehandshake.

4.6   Server Gated Cryptography

Even before they were liberalized, the United States export regulations provided an exception allowing for the use of strong cryptography for certain financial transactions. In order to accommodate this, many SSL implementations include a feature that allows otherwise weak clients to detect that they're talking to a special server and upgrade to strong cryptography. This feature is variously referred to as *Server Gated Cryptography* (SGC) by Microsoft and *Step-Up* by Netscape. Actually, SGC and Step-Up are different variations of SSL. However, the difference isn't relevant at the moment and we'll simply refer to them collectively as SGC for the rest of this section.

SGC relies on the server having a special certificate that indicates that it is allowed to engage in strong cryptography with exportable clients. This certificate is tagged in two ways. First, it must be issued by one of a very short list of trustworthy CAs. Currently, Verisign and Thawte are the only permitted issuers. In the non-SGC situation, CAs merely need to be trusted by the user. However, in this case the CAs need to be trusted by the U.S. government not to issue SGC-capable certificates to non-financial servers. Second, the certificate contains an extension indicating that the certificate-holder is SGC-capable.

Note that this means that SGC-capable clients must actually contain all the code to do strong cryptography. Whether it is used or not actually depends on a simple test in the code. Actually, because the key reduction stage happens in the handshake, even export-only clients must contain strong versions of the symmetric encryption algorithms. In practice, then, browsers contain all the strong crypto. In Netscape, a compiled-in table controls which algorithms are available. In 1998 a program called *Fortify* was released, which takes advantage of this fact to turn on the strong cryptography in an exportable Netscape by patching this table in the binary.

SGC works by using the rehandshake feature of SSL. In the first handshake, the client offers only weak ciphers. Once the client has seen the server's certificate and can verify that SGC is appropriate, it initiates a second handshake, offering strong ciphers in its ClientHello. The messages for the second handshake are transmitted over the current protected session. Figure 4.4 shows a timeline of a Netscape client doing Step-Up.

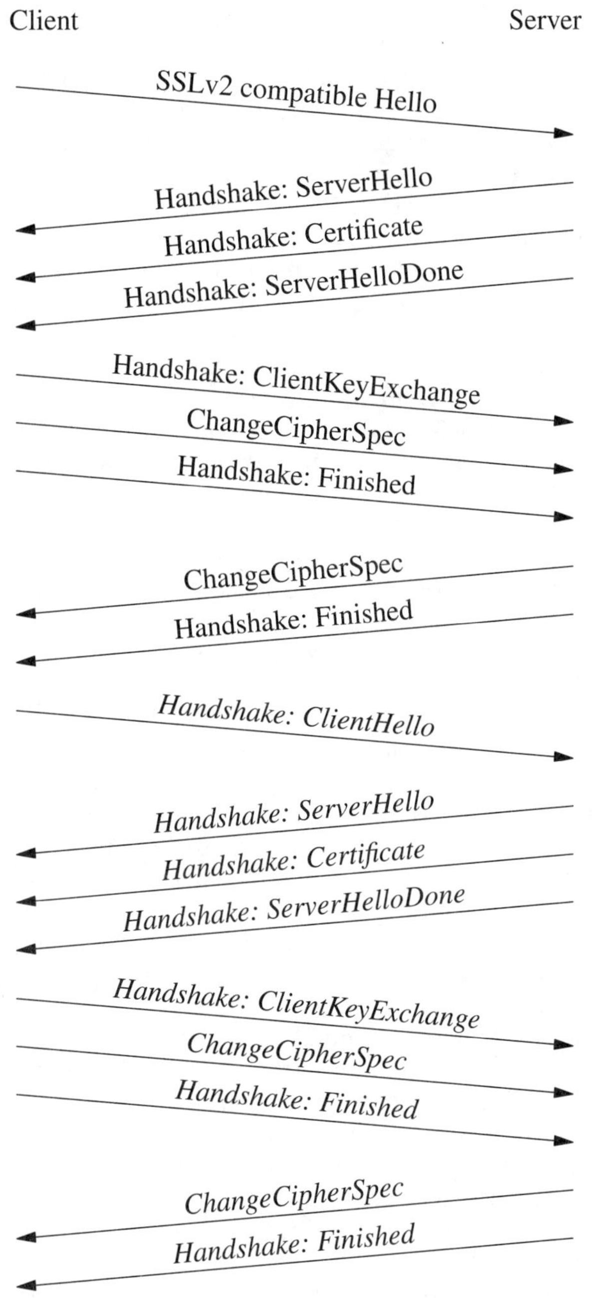

Client   Server

SSLv2 compatible Hello

Handshake: ServerHello

Handshake: Certificate

Handshake: ServerHelloDone

Handshake: ClientKeyExchange

ChangeCipherSpec

Handshake: Finished

ChangeCipherSpec

Handshake: Finished

Handshake: ClientHello

Handshake: ServerHello

Handshake: Certificate

Handshake: ServerHelloDone

Handshake: ClientKeyExchange

ChangeCipherSpec

Handshake: Finished

ChangeCipherSpec

Handshake: Finished

Figure 4.4 Step-Up timeline

4.7   DSS and DH

Although RSA is by far the dominant public key algorithm supported by SSLv2 and SSLv3 implementations, SSLv3 supports a number of cipher suites based on other algorithms, notably Digital Signature Standard (DSS) and Diffie-Hellman (DH). As discussed in Chapter 2, support for these ciphers was made mandatory in TLS. The main idea here was to avoid patented algorithms—in particular RSA. The patent on Diffie-Hellman expired in 1997. The patent situation of DSS is unclear in that RSA Data Security has claimed that the Schnorr patent (U.S. Patent 4995082) [Schnorr1991] covers DSS, but the U.S. National Institute of Standards and Technology claims otherwise. With all that in mind, the IETF decided to go with the devil it *didn't* know and mandate DH/DSS. Since the RSA patent has since expired, this motivation is no longer compelling, but support for DH/DSS lingers on.

Unlike RSA, which can be used for either key exchange or signature, DH can only be used for key agreement and DSS can only be used for digital signature. As a consequence, in order to get a complete solution, DH and DSS are typically used together. In such a system, the certificates are also usually signed with DSS.

There are two primary ways to use DH and DSS in SSL. The most common is to use *ephemeral DH* keys, which are analogous to ephemeral RSA keys. In this case, however, the server generates a temporary DH key and signs it with its DSS key, transmitting the signed key in the ServerKeyExchange message. The client then uses that DH key for key agreement. It is also possible to have a long-term DH key. In this case, the server will have a certificate (signed with DSS) containing its DH key. The client then uses the key in the certificate for key agreement.

The process of key agreement is the same no matter how the client gets the server's DH key. The client needs a DH key in the same group. Normally it won't have one, in which case it will have to generate one. It then transmits the DH key in the ClientKeyExchange message. At this point, the client and the server each have their own private key and the other side's public key, so they can independently compute the DH shared secret. This shared secret is used as the pre_master_secret. From there, the rest of the connection proceeds exactly as with RSA. Figure 4.5 shows the timeline for a handshake using ephemeral DH/DSS.

Note that the cipher suite numbers for DH/DSS are different from those for RSA, even if the symmetric algorithms are identical. Furthermore, the numbers for static DH/DSS are different from those for ephemeral DH/DSS. This highlights an unfortunate consequence of specifying all the algorithms together as a single cipher suite: there is no guarantee that symmetric algorithm support is orthogonal to public key algorithm support. For instance, RFC 2246 specifies five symmetric ciphers that can be used with RSA key exchange (DES, 3DES, RC2, RC4 and IDEA) but only two (DES and 3DES) for use with DH/DSS.

This situation is partially a result of resistance on the part of the working group to using proprietary algorithms such as RC4 and IDEA and partly a result of simple omission. Because positive action had to be taken to provide a full set of symmetric ciphers for DH/DSS, the WG only bothered to standardize the ciphers for which there was significant support and minimal resistance.

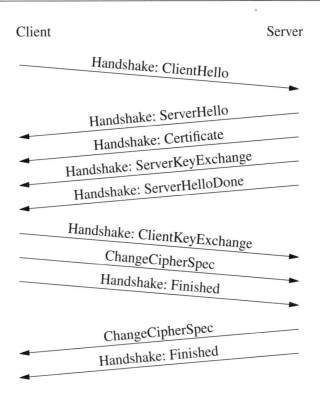

Figure 4.5 DSS/ephemeral DH timeline

4.8 Elliptic Curve Cipher Suites

Recently there has been a fair amount of interest in Elliptic Curve (EC) ciphers. To grossly oversimplify, EC ciphers replace the prime integer field of DH and DSS with a field composed of points on an elliptic curve. The discrete logarithm problem may be harder in such a group, so keys can be shorter and the public key operations comparatively faster. This is especially useful for smartcards where both memory and processing power are extremely limited, but even on fast servers the cost of the modular exponentiations in conventional public key crypto systems is quite high. The idea is that an EC system can be dropped in as a replacement for DH and DSS.

As of this writing, an Internet-Draft has been published for adding several EC-based cipher suites, but no such cipher suites have been standardized. One of the primary obstacles to standardizing such ciphers is that the intellectual property situation is rather vague. At the very least, Certicom and Apple both hold important patents on efficient implementation of EC ciphers, and there is some concern that the ciphers themselves may be patent encumbered.

4.9   Kerberos

Kerberos [Miller1987] is a popular symmetric-key-based authentication system developed at MIT. The general idea is that there is a central server (called a *Ticket Granting Server* (TGS)) that is trusted by every entity in the system. Each entity shares a symmetric key with the TGS. When a client wishes to communicate with a server, it requests a *ticket* from the TGS. The ticket is encrypted using the target's shared key and contains authenticating information for the requestor and a session key to be used for further communication between the two entities. The requestor then sends the ticket to the target.

RFC 2712 [Medvinsky1999] describes how to use Kerberos with TLS. The Client-KeyExchange contains both the ticket and an encrypted pre_master_secret. The shared key found in the ticket is used to encrypt the pre_master_secret. The server extracts the shared key from the ticket and decrypts the pre_master_secret. From that point on the handshake proceeds as usual. The Kerberos cipher suites have not seen wide deployment. Figure 4.6 shows the Kerberos cipher suites defined in RFC 2712.

Cipher Suite	Authentication	Key Exchange	Encryption	Digest	Number
TLS_KRB5_WITH_DES_CBC_SHA	Kerberos	Kerberos	DES_CBC	SHA	0x001e
TLS_KRB5_WITH_3DES_EDE_CBC_SHA	Kerberos	Kerberos	3DES_EDE_CBC	SHA	0x001f
TLS_KRB5_WITH_RC4_128_SHA	Kerberos	Kerberos	RC4_128	SHA	0x0020
TLS_KRB5_WITH_IDEA_CBC_SHA	Kerberos	Kerberos	IDEA_CBC	SHA	0x0021
TLS_KRB5_WITH_3DES_EDE_CBC_MD5	Kerberos	Kerberos	3DES_EDE_CBC	MD5	0x0022
TLS_KRB5_WITH_DES_CBC_SHA	Kerberos	Kerberos	DES_CBC	SHA	0x0023
TLS_KRB5_WITH_RC4_128_MD5	Kerberos	Kerberos	RC4_128	MD5	0x0024
TLS_KRB5_WITH_IDEA_CBC_MD5	Kerberos	Kerberos	IDEA_CBC	MD5	0x0025
TLS_KRB5_EXPORT_WITH_DES_CBC_40_SHA	Kerberos	Kerberos	DES_40_CBC	SHA	0x0026
TLS_KRB5_EXPORT_WITH_RC2_CBC_40_SHA	Kerberos	Kerberos	RC2_40_CBC	SHA	0x0027
TLS_KRB5_EXPORT_WITH_RC4_40_SHA	Kerberos	Kerberos	RC4_40	SHA	0x0028
TLS_KRB5_EXPORT_WITH_DES_CBC_40_MD5	Kerberos	Kerberos	DES_40_CBC	MD5	0x0029
TLS_KRB5_EXPORT_WITH_RC2_CBC_40_MD5	Kerberos	Kerberos	RC2_40_CBC	MD5	0x002A
TLS_KRB5_EXPORT_WITH_RC4_40_MD5	Kerberos	Kerberos	RC4_40	MD5	0x002B

Figure 4.6 The Kerberos cipher suites

4.10   FORTEZZA

The FORTEZZA card is a U.S. government–designed cryptographic token in a PCMCIA form factor. It uses DSA and SHA for signature and message digests but NSA-designed key agreement and encryption algorithms. The key agreement algorithm is a variant of Diffie-Hellman called *Key Exchange Algorithm* (KEA) and the encryption algorithm is a block cipher called SKIPJACK.

FORTEZZA was originally designed by the NSA to provide strong cryptogaphy while allowing the NSA to intercept communications. The conflict between these goals was resolved by incorporating a *key escrow* feature into the device. Each card had its own key, which was escrowed with the NSA. Thus, when the NSA wished to decrypt a communication, it could recover the key for the card used to encrypt it, but the encryption would be secure against all other attackers.

The FORTEZZA cipher suites require that the client be authenticated. This can happen in one of two ways. The client can either have a KEA certificate or it can have a DSA certificate and use its DSA key to sign a KEA share. In either case, the client will have a certificate to the server. Figure 4.7 shows a FORTEZZA handshake.

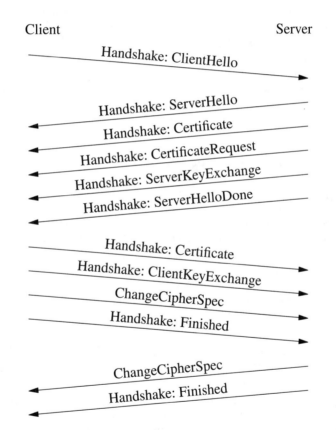

Figure 4.7 FORTEZZA handshake

Even though the server's KEA key is in its certificate, the server still sends a ServerKeyExchange message. This is used to transmit a random value which is used as part of the KEA key agreement process. Also, because the client must be authenticated, the server sends a CertificateRequest message. However, since client authentication happens via key agreement, no CertificateVerify is sent.

When FORTEZZA cards were originally released, SKIPJACK and KEA were classified. FORTEZZA support was specified in SSLv3 but removed for TLS because IETF won't standardize algorithms that aren't fully specified. Netscape did deliver FORTEZZA-capable versions of Navigator and Netscape Server, but they never saw wide use outside the U.S. government. Nevertheless, using FORTEZZA with SSL presents some interesting technical challenges so we'll discuss the details in Section 4.17.

4.11   The Story So Far

As we've seen, in addition to the basic RSA server-only authentication mode, SSL supports a number of other modes with special properties. All of these modes require a different handshake than that required for server-only RSA. The next half of the chapter covers these modes in detail, showing the contents of each new message and how they work together to provide new handshake functionality. The important thing to remember through all this is that, with the exception of FORTEZZA, these variations are simply changes to the handshake. Key derivation from the master_secret and data protection at the record layer are identical no matter which handshake variant you use.

4.12   Session Resumption Details

Session resumption is accomplished using the session_id field of the ClientHello and ServerHello messages. On the initial handshake between any client and server pair, the client's session_id field is absent because the client has no session cached. If the server is willing to allow resumption—it almost always is—it generates a session_id and returns it in the session_id field of the ServerHello. When the handshake is finished, both the client and the server store the session information (the keying material and negotiated ciphers) somewhere that they can get to them later if the session is resumed.

When a client wishes to resume a session, it uses the appropriate session_id in the ClientHello. If the server is willing to resume the session, it responds with the same session_id in the ServerHello. The server then skips the rest of the handshake and immediately sends a ChangeCipherSpec message. The key_block is recomputed using the stored master_secret and the new client and server random values, so all the keys are different.

Figure 4.8 shows the detailed handshake messages for a resumed TLS session. Note that the session_id field in the ClientHello matches the session_id in the ServerHello. If the server did not want to resume the session, it would simply generate a new session_id and continue with the handshake as if the client had not attempted to resume. Typically this happens because the server no longer remembers the session that the client wants to resume, either because it maintains a limited size cache or because the session has timed out.

When resuming a session, the client is required to offer at least the cipher suite that was originally negotiated. If the server agrees to resume, it must choose that cipher suite. In this case, the client has offered a full set of cipher suites. If the server were to choose not to resume the session, it could choose any of the offered cipher suites.

```
New TCP connection: romeo(1300) <-> speedy(4433)
1 0.0022 (0.0022) C>S   Handshake
      ClientHello
        resume [32]=
            6d f3 02 8a 44 a7 42 94 14 7b 59 ad
            8f 00 32 71 e9 a5 d1 bc 3f c0 23 0c
            50 fa 4f 9f 27 cf 45 c4
        cipher suites
                  TLS_DHE_RSA_WITH_3DES_EDE_CBC_SHA
                  TLS_DHE_DSS_WITH_3DES_EDE_CBC_SHA
                  TLS_RSA_WITH_3DES_EDE_CBC_SHA
                  TLS_RSA_WITH_IDEA_CBC_SHA
                  TLS_RSA_WITH_RC4_128_SHA
                  TLS_RSA_WITH_RC4_128_MD5
                  TLS_DHE_RSA_WITH_DES_CBC_SHA
                  TLS_DHE_DSS_WITH_DES_CBC_SHA
                  TLS_RSA_WITH_DES_CBC_SHA
                  TLS_DHE_RSA_EXPORT_WITH_DES40_CBC_SHA
                  TLS_DHE_DSS_EXPORT_WITH_DES40_CBC_SHA
                  TLS_RSA_EXPORT_WITH_DES40_CBC_SHA
                  TLS_RSA_EXPORT_WITH_RC2_CBC_40_MD5
                  TLS_RSA_EXPORT_WITH_RC4_40_MD5
        compression methods
                  NULL
2 0.0288 (0.0266) S>C   Handshake
      ServerHello
        session_id[32]=
            6d f3 02 8a 44 a7 42 94 14 7b 59 ad
            8f 00 32 71 e9 a5 d1 bc 3f c0 23 0c
            50 fa 4f 9f 27 cf 45 c4
        cipherSuite            TLS_RSA_WITH_RC4_128_SHA
        compressionMethod            NULL
3 0.0288 (0.0000) S>C   ChangeCipherSpec
4 0.0288 (0.0000) S>C   Handshake: Finished
5 0.0293 (0.0005) C>S   ChangeCipherSpec
6 0.0293 (0.0000) C>S   Handshake: Finished
```

Figure 4.8 Resumed TLS session handshake messages

Session ID Lookup

Servers and clients use different information to retrieve sessions. When a client initiates an SSL connection, the only available information is the server's hostname (or IP address if no hostname was used) and port, so these must be used to look up the session ID. However, when a server receives a request for a resumed session for the client, the session_id is available and can be used to look up the session. Since the lookup is based on the session_id, session resumption will work even when the client is connecting from a different IP address and port than the one used for the initial handshake.

Because initiating TCP ports are sequentially chosen, the client's port will almost always be different from the port used for the original connection. Usually the client's IP address will be the same for every connection. However, because many clients have their IP addresses dynamically assigned via DHCP or similar mechanisms it is quite possible for a client to attempt to resume a session using a different IP address than the one it used to create it. Servers should support this.

Although permitting resumption from a client with a different IP address may seem dangerous, it is actually secure: first, it's trivial for an attacker to forge messages from a given IP address, so checking the IP address offers little value. More important, the server checks the client's Finished message at the end of the handshake. In order to correctly generate the Finished message, the client must have access not only to the new encryption and MAC keys (in order to encrypt and MAC the message) but to the master_secret in order to compute the Finished hashes. Since an attacker with access to the master_secret could easily take over an existing connection, this is equally secure. Note that to reduce the effect of compromise of any given master_secret, servers typically expire sessions after some period of time (a day is common.)

4.13 Client Authentication Details

As we've seen, SSL client authentication uses two new messages that we haven't seen before, as well as a new usage for an old message. The first new message is the CertificateRequest message which is used by the server to request client authentication. The client responds by sending the Certificate message (which we previously saw being used by the server) to send its certificate and the CertificateVerify message to authenticate itself.

CertificateRequest

```
struct {
    ClientCertificateType certificate_types<1..2^8-1>;
    DistinguishedName certificate_authorities<3..2^16-1>;
} CertificateRequest;
```

```
enum {
  rsa_sign(1), dss_sign(2), rsa_fixed_dh(3), dss_fixed_dh(4),
  (255)
} ClientCertificateType;

opaque DistinguishedName<1..2^16-1>;
```

```
CertificateRequest
    certificate_types            rsa_sign
    certificate_types            dss_sign
  certificate_authority
    C=AU
    ST=Queensland
    O=CryptSoft Pty Ltd
    CN=Server test cert (512 bit)
  certificate_authority
    C=US
    O=AT&T Bell Laboratories
    OU=Prototype Research CA
  certificate_authority
    C=US
    O=RSA Data Security, Inc.
    OU=Commercial Certification Authority
  certificate_authority
    C=US
    O=RSA Data Security, Inc.
    OU=Secure Server Certification Authority
  certificate_authority
    C=ZA
    ST=Western Cape
    L=Cape Town
    O=Thawte Consulting cc
    OU=Certification Services Division
    CN=Thawte Server CA
    Email=server-certs@thawte.com
  certificate_authority
    C=ZA
    ST=Western Cape
    L=Cape Town
    O=Thawte Consulting cc
    OU=Certification Services Division
    CN=Thawte Premium Server CA
    Email=premium-server@thawte.com
```

The CertificateRequest message indicates to the client that the client should perform client authentication and provides guidance as to what sorts of certificates the server is willing to accept. The server is allowed to specify both the cryptographic algorithm that should be used and a list of the certificate authorities which it trusts to sign client certificates.

The certificate_types field is an array of single byte values, each of which describes a permitted signature algorithm. In this case, the server has specified rsa_sign and dss_sign, indicating that it is prepared to accept a response signed with either RSA or DSS. Note that this value also specifies the algorithm which was used to sign the certificate.

The other two possible values, rsa_fixed_dh and dss_fixed_dh actually do not involve a signature at all. Rather, they indicate that the client and server will use fixed Diffie-Hellman key pairs to agree on the pre_master_secret. If these methods are chosen, the client does not send a CertificateVerify because the connection is implicitly authenticated by the ability to generate the appropriate keys from the pre_master_secret. However, see Section 4.16 for an explanation of fixed DH.

The certificate_authorities field specifies a list of certificate authorities (CAs) from which the server is willing to accept certificates. These CAs are specified by using a BER encoded version of the CA's distinguished name. See Chapter 1 for more information on distinguished names and certificates. It is important to note that if certificate chains are being used, then the CA name specified in the CertificateRequest message need not refer to the CA that signed the client's certificate, but may instead refer to one of the parent CAs.

Certificate

```
struct {
    ASN.1Cert certificate_list<1..2^24-1>;
} Certificate;

opaque ASN.1Cert<2^24-1>;
```

We saw the Certificate message before when the server used it to provide its certificate to the client. Here it is used by the client to send its certificate for client authentication. This message has exactly the same structure as the server's Certificate message, although the certificates themselves are different.

CertificateVerify

```
select (SignatureAlgorithm) {
    case anonymous: struct { };
```

```
      case rsa:
        digitally-signed struct {
          opaque md5_hash[16];
          opaque sha_hash[20];
        };
      case dsa:
        digitally-signed struct {
          opaque sha_hash[20];
        };
} Signature;

struct {
  Signature signature;
} CertificateVerify;
```

```
CertificateVerify
  Signature[64]=
      5a a7 6a 48 54 17 c9 a3 09 87 90 37
      42 17 45 c7 bf de 24 0f 4d 73 9b a8
      69 a6 c7 f3 a0 41 c5 26 fc 6a 48 0d
      e1 02 4f 9d 1b d2 17 55 dc 4e 55 11
      6f 89 7c ed 68 59 70 db b4 e7 fe 11
      d7 2f f6 83
```

The CertificateVerify does all the actual work of client authentication. It contains a digest of the handshake messages signed by the client's private key (the one that corresponds to the certificate in the client's Certificatemessage). This is what the digitally-signed operator means. Because only the holder of the private key corresponding to the certificate could sign this message, the server can conclude that the entity named in the certificate is connecting.

In SSLv3, we compute the hashes of the handshake messages as shown:

```
CertificateVerify.signature.md5_hash =
  MD5(master_secret + pad2 +
    MD5(handshake_messages + master_secret +
      pad1));

CertificateVerify.signature.sha_hash =
  SHA-1(master_secret + pad2 +
    SHA-1(handshake_messages + master_secret +
      pad1));
```

Including the master_secret in the messages actually doesn't add much security value because it's implied by the other handshake messages. TLS uses a simple digest of the handshake messages.

CertificateVerify.signature.md5_hash = MD5(handshake_messages);
CertificateVerify.signature.sha_hash = SHA-1(handshake_messages);

The details of the signature computation depend on which signature algorithm is being used. In this handshake, the client is signing using RSA, so the signed object is the concatenation of MD5 and SHA-1 digests of the handshake messages up to this point in the handshake. Because DSS requires a 160-bit input, when DSS is being used, only the SHA-1 digest of the messages is used. Because the digest covers the server's random value, the server can be sure that this signature is *fresh* (that is, not replayed) as long as it used a fresh random value in its ServerHello.

It is important to note that this form of RSA signature is different from the usual RSA signature described in [RSA1993b], which only includes one digest. In PKCS #1, the signature is typically computed over a DER encoded DigestInfo structure which also contains the algorithm identifier for the digest. Because the MD5 and SHA-1 digests are mandated as part of the SSL protocol, the digest algorithm identifier is unnecessary (and because there is no identifier for the MD5 and SHA-1 combination, it is also problematic). As a result, the concatenated hash value is signed directly without being first encoded in a DigestInfo. This can cause problems with hardware implementations or all-in-one PKI toolkits, which often want to perform the DigestInfo encoding as part of the signature.

Failure Conditions

If the client has no suitable certificate, a Certificate message containing no certificates should be sent. At this point, the server can either proceed with the connection, using some other means of authentication (for instance, prompting for a password in the application layer) or no authentication at all. If the server is unwilling to continue, it sends a fatal handshake_failure alert.

4.14   Ephemeral RSA Details

```
struct {
    select (KeyExchangeAlgorithm) {
        case diffie_hellman:
            ServerDHParams params;
            Signature signed_params;
        case rsa:
            ServerRSAParams params;
            Signature signed_params;
    };
} ServerKeyExchange;
```

```
struct {
   opaque RSA_modulus<1..2^16-1>;
   opaque RSA_exponent<1..2^16-1>;
} ServerRSAParams;

select (SignatureAlgorithm) {
   case anonymous: struct { };
   case rsa:
      digitally-signed struct {
         opaque md5_hash[16];
         opaque sha_hash[20];
      };
   case dsa:
      digitally-signed struct {
         opaque sha_hash[20];
      };
} Signature;

enum { rsa, diffie_hellman } KeyExchangeAlgorithm;
enum { anonymous, rsa, dsa } SignatureAlgorithm;
```

```
ServerKeyExchange
  params
    RSA_modulus[64]=
        c9 61 5e 58 08 6a 5c f0 76 a4 5d 6e
        ae 99 51 f9 ae c6 2c 8a e5 34 1e 9d
        a6 cb 68 b4 d6 47 b2 01 d4 5d 9b 32
        3c 49 2a 90 ac c2 41 cd b4 20 4f 54
        c2 a0 26 e4 b8 ee 69 61 04 23 64 72
        f2 40 e3 9f
    RSA_exponent[3]=
        01 00 01
  signature[128]=
        09 6d 34 ee 8c 2f 14 e5 52 05 26 25
        4c 34 72 35 ef 79 1f 07 c1 71 82 cd
        3d f6 7c 67 05 ff eb 02 bc da bf 8e
        3a e7 c8 37 14 5c ca 05 4a 69 5f 09
        f3 b0 fa 53 33 50 ab 41 e8 63 6b f5
        5a 5d c1 5d f0 09 6d aa bd d8 0b e2
        bb 13 0d e6 09 f8 91 11 b1 ec 25 58
        1f 7e b3 56 81 4e c0 03 71 a4 95 e4
        be 1f 2e 10 75 80 75 1a 65 ed c4 70
        09 0b 19 64 3f dd f0 42 4a 32 73 36
        82 b1 2b 24 2c a4 6b 3a
```

The ServerKeyExchange message contains a signed version of the server's ephemeral public key. Because this message is also used for ephemeral DH, the specification permits both RSA and DH keys. We'll see an example of ephemeral DH in Section 4.16. The message is signed using the server's long-term key, in this case an RSA key. The permitted algorithms are RSA signature, DSS, or anonymous, which simply means that the message is unsigned. Note that the anonymous mode offers no security at all against active attack. The attacker can trivially pose as the server to the client using a man-in-the-middle attack.

Although the specification permits cipher suites that mix-and-match key exchange and signature algorithms, the common combinations are RSA signature with RSA key exchange (shown at the beginning of this section) and DSS signature with DH key exchange (TLS implementations must implement DH/DSS). Cipher suites are defined for RSA signature with DH key exchange, but they are not commonly used. No cipher suites are even defined for DSS signature with RSA key exchange.

The RSA key is presented in the message as a pair of byte strings representing the RSA modulus and exponent. Following Internet convention, the large integers are mapped to byte strings in "network" byte order, with the first byte representing the most significant byte of the integer. The size of the RSA modulus is the important number, and it's 64 bytes long, consistent with a 512-bit key. As we saw in Chapter 1, standard practice is to use a very small public exponent for performance reasons, and here 65537 has been chosen. See Chapter 1 for more information on RSA keys.

The RSA signature shown in the message is computed using a pair of hashes as in the CertificateVerify message, but the input data to the hashes are different. The ServerKeyExchange hash incorporates only the parameters to be signed and the client and server random values. The random values serve to prevent replay of a previous ServerKeyExchange message in a new handshake:

```
md5_hash =
   MD5(client_random + server_random + ServerParams);

sha_hash =
   SHA(client_random + server_random + ServerParams);
```

Because generating RSA keys is computationally expensive, SSL server implementations typically use the same ephemeral key to service a large number of clients. This isn't as secure as generating a fresh key for each client, because a large number of transactions (often as much as a day's worth) are protected under the same 512-bit key. However, the cost of generating a fresh key for each transaction would almost always be prohibitive.

There are two conditions under which ephemeral RSA can be used: first, the cipher suite used must be one of the export cipher suites (i.e., the key exchange algorithm is RSA_EXPORT). Second, the signing key must be longer than 512 bits. Otherwise, normal RSA must be used.

Before we get too excited about ephemeral RSA, it's worthwhile to do a back-of-the-envelope computation as to how much security it adds. Typical key lifetimes are on the order of a year or two and servers usually generate a new ephemeral RSA key at most once a day (though on a modern CPU it's possible to do it far more frequently, say every few minutes). Often, they'll generate it at server startup only, and servers can stay up for weeks. So, if you wanted to read all the traffic to a given server, ephemeral RSA would increase your workload by less than a thousand times given typical use patterns. On the other hand, if you want to read a specific message, and you know when that message was sent, ephemeral RSA doesn't make your job any more difficult at all.

4.15 SGC Details

The difficulty faced by SGC/Step-Up is that the client must send its ClientHello before it knows whether the server is a normal SSL server or an SGC/Step-Up capable server. Thus, it must offer only export cipher suites. Otherwise, a normal server might select a strong cipher suite that the client couldn't use. Only when the client receives the server's Certificate message can it detect that the server is SGC/Step-Up capable. At this point, SGC and Step-Up differ. We'll discuss Step-Up first.

Step-Up

The server signals to the client that it's willing to do Step-Up by providing a special value in the extendedKeyUsage extension. When the client sees this value, it knows that it can Step-Up. The browser completes the SSL handshake that it's currently doing (which negotiates an export cipher suite) and then immediately rehandshakes to negotiate a strong cipher suite. Figure 4.9 shows a Step-Up connection in action.

```
New TCP connection: romeo(4290) <-> romeo(443)
1 0.0004 (0.0004) C>S SSLv2 compatible client hello
  Version 3.0
  cipher suites
      SSL2_CK_RC4_EXPORT40
      SSL2_CK_RC2_EXPORT40
      TLS_RSA_EXPORT1024_WITH_RC4_56_SHA
      TLS_RSA_EXPORT1024_WITH_DES_CBC_SHA
      TLS_RSA_EXPORT_WITH_RC4_40_MD5
      TLS_RSA_EXPORT_WITH_RC2_CBC_40_MD5
2 0.0058 (0.0053) S>C    Handshake
      ServerHello
        session_id[32]=
          5e ae 37 80 c5 30 ff 35 59 65 2a 8c
          9b a1 8a 73 ad 2d 88 30 59 9a f9 58
          45 ac 8d a3 85 5f ca e9
        cipherSuite           TLS_RSA_EXPORT1024_WITH_RC4_56_SHA
        compressionMethod          NULL
```

```
3 0.0058 (0.0000) S>C    Handshake
      Certificate
        Subject
          C=US
          O=RTFM, Inc.
          CN=romeo.rtfm.com
        Issuer
          C=US
          ST=California
          O=RTFM, Inc.
          CN=Step-Up CA
        Serial          03
        Extensions
          Extension: X509v3 Subject Alternative Name
            <EMPTY>
          Extension: X509v3 Basic Constraints
            CA:FALSE, pathlen:0
          Extension: Netscape Comment
            mod_ssl generated custom server certificate
          Extension: Netscape Cert Type
            SSL Server
          Extension: X509v3 Extended Key Usage
            Netscape Server Gated Crypto
4 0.0058 (0.0000) S>C    Handshake
      ServerHelloDone
5 0.0248 (0.0189) C>S    Handshake
      ClientKeyExchange
        EncryptedPreMasterSecret[128]=
            a1 40 7c 99 2f 40 4d 01 dd b0 0a 7b
            f8 8e ee e3 1d f1 ed 35 04 ea 56 5f
            1a 3f 62 75 cf 6e bc b9 58 cf ad 33
            ba be 30 3c 63 d0 85 ea a7 a4 24 e2
            b5 dd d1 21 03 e1 87 bd cb cf 56 54
            8d ed 02 f9 67 d7 bc 9a 73 cb 51 a6
            c2 d6 c2 12 b6 96 06 45 db a3 ed d8
            40 0c ea 11 22 09 61 7c 98 85 8f ed
            ca 4a 51 52 bd e9 14 0a b3 5d 04 be
            58 79 1e 51 cd fd dc ae 66 23 b8 4f
            1b ea 68 10 eb 8a e7 87
6 0.2199 (0.1951) C>S    ChangeCipherSpec
7 0.2199 (0.0000) C>S    Handshake
      Finished
8 0.2223 (0.0023) S>C    ChangeCipherSpec
9 0.2223 (0.0000) S>C    Handshake
      Finished
```

First handshake completed.

Client initiates a new handshake offering strong cipher suites.

```
10 0.2231 (0.0008) C>S    Handshake
      ClientHello
        Version 3.0
        cipher suites
                  TLS_RSA_WITH_RC4_128_MD5
                  value unknown: 0xffe0 Netscape proprietary cipher suite
                  TLS_RSA_WITH_3DES_EDE_CBC_SHA
                  TLS_RSA_EXPORT1024_WITH_RC4_56_SHA
                  TLS_RSA_EXPORT1024_WITH_DES_CBC_SHA
                  TLS_RSA_EXPORT_WITH_RC4_40_MD5
                  TLS_RSA_EXPORT_WITH_RC2_CBC_40_MD5
        compression methods
                  NULL
11 0.2271 (0.0039) S>C    Handshake
      ServerHello
        session_id[32]=
          de 59 fc ef 7f b5 59 e0 92 f9 31 20
          da a3 f1 82 bf 78 ba 53 8b b6 8a a9
          d6 69 82 af 55 8b 99 27
        cipherSuite             TLS_RSA_WITH_RC4_128_MD5
        compressionMethod            NULL
12 0.2271 (0.0000) S>C    Handshake
      Certificate
        Subject
          C=US
          O=RTFM, Inc.
          CN=romeo.rtfm.com
        Issuer
          C=US
          ST=California
          O=RTFM, Inc.
          CN=Step-Up CA
        Serial          03
        Extensions
          Extension: X509v3 Subject Alternative Name
            <EMPTY>
          Extension: X509v3 Basic Constraints
            CA:FALSE, pathlen:0
          Extension: Netscape Comment
            mod_ssl generated custom server certificate
          Extension: Netscape Cert Type
            SSL Server
          Extension: X509v3 Extended Key Usage
            Netscape Server Gated Crypto
```

(continued)

Figure 4.9 *(continued)*

```
13 0.2271 (0.0000) S>C    Handshake
       ServerHelloDone
14 0.2381 (0.0110) C>S    Handshake
       ClientKeyExchange
         EncryptedPreMasterSecret[128]=
             98 29 0c 5f 72 b0 46 03 fd 3d ed 62
             c6 fc ec d3 e3 73 d3 f5 c8 a0 60 0a
             f7 94 de 18 0a 9c 3c db db 7c f4 9c
             34 65 90 dd 11 fd a2 d3 ae 50 f1 d6
             e8 22 79 72 fe 99 b8 e1 03 a4 4a 64
             22 4d e8 a5 58 d5 80 22 d5 da d4 dc
             fc 42 a0 f3 f3 50 a6 56 4f f4 ae 69
             37 7b 9c 8c 53 c8 d7 7a ac 91 2d 7b
             48 8b 10 e5 b0 55 65 45 99 3e ca 69
             f7 c5 9e ae 0b fe f1 36 7b 4c 1c 6d
             7e 4d 42 96 6b 21 55 d4
15 0.4199 (0.1818) C>S    ChangeCipherSpec
16 0.4199 (0.0000) C>S    Handshake
       Finished
17 0.4215 (0.0015) S>C    ChangeCipherSpec
18 0.4215 (0.0000) S>C    Handshake
       Finished
```

Figure 4.9 A connection using Step-Up

Figure 4.9 shows a Step-Up connection between a Netscape client and an Apache server with mod_ssl. Note that in the initial message, the client sends an SSLv2-compatible hello offering only export cipher suites. It must do this on the initial connection because it doesn't yet know that the server is Step-Up capable. On future connections, of course, it could offer strong ciphers immediately if it remembered that the server had a Step-Up certificate.

The server's certificate, shown in record 3, contains the Step-Up extension (shown here as `Netscape Server Gated Crypto`), so the client knows it can do Step-Up. However, the client and the server have already agreed to a set of cipher suites, so this information isn't immediately useful because there's no way in SSL for the client to change its mind at this point. The client could drop the connection and reconnect, but that's not the way that Step-Up works. Instead, the client completes the handshake.

Once the handshake is completed, the client initiates a rehandshake over the newly established encrypted channel. The rest of Figure 4.9 shows that rehandshake. In record 10 the client sends a new ClientHello. This time it offers strong cipher suites as well as weak ones and naturally the server accepts one. From there, the handshake completes as usual.

Note that the client does not attempt to resume the session. Most of the export cipher suites use ephemeral RSA, in which case resuming is impossible, because we need to establish a new master_secret using the server's 1024-bit RSA key. However, the new (and still unstandardized) EXPORT1024 cipher suites use the long RSA key for key exchange, so this session could technically be resumed. However, the client doesn't offer this. As a consequence, an entirely new RSA key exchange must be performed. Thus, Step-Up handshakes are (at least) twice as expensive computationally as ordinary handshakes.

This trace also shows the SSL feature of *rehandshake*. At any time during a connection, SSL implementations can initiate a new handshake. The new handshake is carried over the currently protected channel. Thus, the second handshake is entirely encrypted. The reason we're able to read it is that ssldump has been given the server's private key and is automatically decrypting the data for us. All the encrypted records are rendered in a *fixed-width italic* font to show that we've decrypted them. At the end of the handshake, all traffic switches over to the newly negotiated connection.

Careful inspection of Figure 4.9 reveals that the server's certificate was signed by the author's local CA. However, we said earlier that Step-Up certificates must be signed by specific trusted CAs. Surely the author's CA is not one of them! We've taken advantage of a weakness in Netscape's implementation. The CAs are stored in a database and being able to issue Step-Up certificates is simply a database attribute. We've changed that attribute in our local database, thus allowing ourselves to issue Step-Up certificates. We could have just as well connected to a legitimate Step-Up server, but then we wouldn't have the server's private key and be able to decrypt the traffic.

SGC

In the previous section, we saw that Step-Up requires two key exchange stages. This is expensive and the first stage isn't really adding much security value. Microsoft noticed this and SGC used only one key exchange stage. Figure 4.10 shows an SGC connection between IE and Internet Information Server (IIS).

```
New TCP connection: swagger(1897) <-> 151(443)
1 0.3679 (0.3679) C>S SSLv2 compatible client hello
   Version 3.0
   cipher suites
       TLS_RSA_EXPORT_WITH_RC4_40_MD5
       TLS_RSA_EXPORT_WITH_DES40_CBC_SHA
       TLS_RSA_EXPORT_WITH_RC2_CBC_40_MD5
       SSL2_CK_RC4_EXPORT40
       SSL2_CK_RC2_EXPORT40
```

(continued)

Figure 4.10 *(continued)*

```
2 0.7508 (0.3829) S>C    Handshake
      ServerHello
        session_id[32]=
          22 00 00 00 4b 66 29 fe 02 a7 f3 cc
          56 38 a6 4e 41 ad d8 fd 55 08 75 5d
          fe e3 41 02 fe 4e 27 62
        cipherSuite            TLS_RSA_EXPORT_WITH_RC4_40_MD5
        compressionMethod            NULL
      Certificate
        Subject
          C=IT
          ST=Milano
          L=Assago
          O=BANCO AMBROSIANO VENETO
          OU=INNOVAZIONE TECNOLOGICA
          OU=Terms of use at www.verisign.com
          RPA (c)99
          CN=HB.AMBRO.IT
        Issuer
          O=VeriSign Trust Network
          OU=VeriSign, Inc.
          OU=VeriSign International Server CA - Class 3
          OU=www.verisign.com
          CPS Incorp.by Ref. LIABILITY LTD.(c)97 VeriSign
        Serial       69 5a a3 c0 d8 8e bf ac 6b 64 ca cc
        ce ec 1b 59
        Extensions
          Extension: X509v3 Basic Constraints
            CA:FALSE
          Extension: 2.5.29.3
            value omitted
          Extension: Netscape Cert Type
            SSL Server
          Extension: X509v3 Extended Key Usage
            Netscape Server Gated Crypto, Microsoft Server Gated Crypto
          Extension: 2.16.840.1.113733.1.6.7
            value omitted
        Subject
          O=VeriSign Trust Network
          OU=VeriSign, Inc.
          OU=VeriSign International Server CA - Class 3
          OU=www.verisign.com
```

```
                  CPS Incorp.by Ref. LIABILITY LTD.(c)97 VeriSign
              Issuer
                C=US
                O=VeriSign, Inc.
                OU=Class 3 Public Primary Certification Authority
              Serial          23 6c 97 1e 2b c6 0d 0b f9 74 60 de
              f1 08 c3 c3
              Extensions
                Extension: X509v3 Basic Constraints
                  CA:TRUE, pathlen:0
                Extension: X509v3 Key Usage
                  Certificate Sign, CRL Sign
                Extension: Netscape Cert Type
                  SSL CA, S/MIME CA
                Extension: X509v3 Extended Key Usage
                  2.16.840.1.113733.1.8.1, Netscape Server Gated Crypto
                Extension: X509v3 Certificate Policies
                  Policy: 2.16.840.1.113733.1.7.1.1
                  CPS: https://www.verisign.com/CPS
                  User Notice:
                  Organization: VeriSign, Inc.
                  Number: 1
                  Explicit Text: VeriSign's Certification Practice Statement, ↵
                  www.verisign.com/CPS, governs this certificate & is ↵
                  incorporated by reference herein. SOME WARRANTIES DISCLAIMED ↵
                  & LIABILITY LTD. (c)1997 VeriSign
          ServerKeyExchange
          ServerHelloDone
```

Client aborts first handshake and initiates a new one on the same connection, offering strong cipher suites.

```
3 0.7599 (0.0090) C>S    Handshake
      ClientHello
        Version 3.0
        cipher suites
                  TLS_RSA_WITH_RC4_128_MD5
                  TLS_RSA_WITH_RC4_128_SHA
                  value unknown: 0x80    Microsoft proprietary cipher suite
                  value unknown: 0x81    Microsoft proprietary cipher suite
                  value unknown: 0x80    Microsoft proprietary cipher suite
                  TLS_RSA_WITH_DES_CBC_SHA
                  TLS_RSA_EXPORT_WITH_RC4_40_MD5
                  TLS_RSA_EXPORT_WITH_DES40_CBC_SHA
                  TLS_RSA_EXPORT_WITH_RC2_CBC_40_MD5
        compression methods
                  NULL
```

(continued)

Figure 4.10 *(continued)*

```
4 1.1402 (0.3802) S>C    Handshake
      ServerHello
        session_id[32]=
            22 00 00 00 4b 66 29 fe 02 a7 f3 cc
            56 38 a6 4e 41 ad d8 fd 55 08 75 5d
            fe e3 41 02 fe 4e 27 62
        cipherSuite              TLS_RSA_WITH_RC4_128_MD5
        compressionMethod           NULL
      Certificate
        Subject
          C=IT
          ST=Milano
          L=Assago
          O=BANCO AMBROSIANO VENETO
          OU=INNOVAZIONE TECNOLOGICA
          OU=Terms of use at www.verisign.com
          RPA (c)99
          CN=HB.AMBRO.IT
        Issuer
          O=VeriSign Trust Network
          OU=VeriSign, Inc.
          OU=VeriSign International Server CA - Class 3
          OU=www.verisign.com
          CPS Incorp.by Ref. LIABILITY LTD.(c)97 VeriSign
        Serial        69 5a a3 c0 d8 8e bf ac 6b 64 ca cc
      ce ec 1b 59
        Extensions
          Extension: X509v3 Basic Constraints
            CA:FALSE
          Extension: 2.5.29.3
            value omitted
          Extension: Netscape Cert Type
            SSL Server
          Extension: X509v3 Extended Key Usage
            Netscape Server Gated Crypto, Microsoft Server Gated Crypto
          Extension: 2.16.840.1.113733.1.6.7
            value omitted
        Subject
          O=VeriSign Trust Network
          OU=VeriSign, Inc.
          OU=VeriSign International Server CA - Class 3
          OU=www.verisign.com
          CPS Incorp.by Ref. LIABILITY LTD.(c)97 VeriSign
```

```
        Issuer
          C=US
          O=VeriSign, Inc.
          OU=Class 3 Public Primary Certification Authority
        Serial        23 6c 97 1e 2b c6 0d 0b f9 74 60 de
        f1 08 c3 c3
        Extensions
          Extension: X509v3 Basic Constraints
            CA:TRUE, pathlen:0
          Extension: X509v3 Key Usage
            Certificate Sign, CRL Sign
          Extension: Netscape Cert Type
            SSL CA, S/MIME CA
          Extension: X509v3 Extended Key Usage
            2.16.840.1.113733.1.8.1, Netscape Server Gated Crypto
          Extension: X509v3 Certificate Policies
            Policy: 2.16.840.1.113733.1.7.1.1
            CPS: https://www.verisign.com/CPS
            User Notice:
            Organization: VeriSign, Inc.
            Number: 1
            Explicit Text: VeriSign's Certification Practice Statement, ⏎
            www.verisign.com/CPS, governs this certificate & is ⏎
            incorporated by reference herein. SOME WARRANTIES DISCLAIMED ⏎
            & LIABILITY LTD. (c)1997 VeriSign
        ServerHelloDone
5 1.1459 (0.0057) C>S    Handshake
        ClientKeyExchange
          EncryptedPreMasterSecret[128]=
            7d 4f fb ae fb 3e 5c 5b 9f 72 82 86
            04 c7 7e 5e 72 e0 81 d3 8a 1a a0 10
            97 36 d3 ab 0a 8b d8 e3 ba 83 1b 1c
            8e 82 73 34 0a 4e 74 ec 0c 57 08 f7
            ce 61 13 cf 8b c2 7b 5e 8a 14 29 28
            94 5f 8a ff 93 42 59 93 12 ee 6d d4
            d6 15 c2 90 c1 b1 df 2a 73 1e fb 11
            bc e1 83 81 cd c7 4e ec 2c 1c e2 ba
            14 ab fa 7c 80 b1 e5 8e 52 9b 55 bf
            b7 84 b3 60 98 67 58 29 cd 50 ab 4d
            2e 3f 21 09 4a 16 a0 57
6 1.1459 (0.0000) C>S    ChangeCipherSpec
7 1.1459 (0.0000) C>S    Handshake Finished
8 1.4361 (0.2901) S>C    ChangeCipherSpec
9 1.4361 (0.0000) S>C    Handshake Finished
```

Figure 4.10 A connection using SGC

The first two records in the handshake are more or less the same as those in Figure 4.10. The client offers export cipher suites and the server provides its certificate showing that it's SGC-capable. (Although note that IIS transmits all of the handshake messages in a single record rather than in separate records as OpenSSL does. This is a matter of taste. There's no real technical reason to do one or the other.) However, instead of completing the connection, IE immediately responds in record *3* with a new ClientHello offering strong cipher suites. At this point, the old handshake is aborted and an entirely new one takes place. Note that IE is also offering the proprietary cipher suites 0x0080 and 0x0081. These are from a precursor to SGC used for Microsoft Money [Banes2000].

This seems like a clever trick, and it is. Unfortunately, it also violates the SSL specification, which has no provision for sending ClientHellos in the middle of a handshake. Thus, to preserve interoperability, Microsoft had to use a different extension from Netscape to signal that not only was a server allowed to use Step-Up, but that it could also do SGC. Note that the certificate in Figure 4.10 contains both the Netscape and Microsoft SGC extensions. Thus, when talking to this server, Step-Up only clients will do Step-Up but SGC-capable clients will do SGC. OpenSSL only added support for SGC in OpenSSL 0.9.5.

4.16 DH/DSS Details

```
struct {
    opaque DH_p<1..2^16-1>;
    opaque DH_g<1..2^16-1>;
    opaque DH_Ys<1..2^16-1>;
} ServerDHParams;

ServerKeyExchange
  params
    DH_p[64]=
        da 58 3c 16 d9 85 22 89 d0 e4 af 75
        6f 4c ca 92 dd 4b e5 33 b8 04 fb 0f
        ed 94 ef 9c 8a 44 03 ed 57 46 50 d3
        69 99 db 29 d7 76 27 6b a2 d3 d4 12
        e2 18 f4 dd 1e 08 4c f6 d8 00 3e 7c
        47 74 e8 33
    DH_g[1]=
        02
    DH_Ys[64]=
        98 5a ee fc ce ac cf f1 05 cf 08 07
        63 18 dd 50 53 66 a5 b8 0b 88 4d 7e
        7d ea 11 3e 2a 99 63 e8 92 7a 56 cb
        f1 36 74 97 36 4a f0 3e 4e 29 3e a2
        e2 53 36 d8 9c a0 40 aa 8c fc eb c0
        93 b6 c3 e8
```

```
signature[47]=
   30 2d 02 14 78 bb 87 40 13 e4 8d e9
   73 16 4e 0c dd 1c 9e a8 bd 58 99 a1
   02 15 00 95 10 42 e1 cb b9 1d 26 34
   d4 5f b1 0d b8 66 ba 8c 61 20 c3
```

Ephemeral DH with DSS is conceptually very similar to ephemeral RSA. Only the details of the messages are different.

A DH/DSS ServerKeyExchange message contains Diffie-Hellman parameters signed with a DSS key. The provided parameters are the prime modulus (p), the generator for the group (g) and the server's public key (Ys). Because DSS requires a 160-bit input, the DSS signature is computed over the sha_hash value only. Recall that DSS signatures consist of two large integers, called r and s. The SSL representation of these in the message is the DER encoding of an ASN.1 structure defined in ANSI X9.57 [ANSI1995].

```
Dss-Sig-Value ::= SEQUENCE {
   r    INTEGER,
   s    INTEGER
}
```

Note: The description of how to encode DSS signatures in the SSLv3 specification is insufficiently specific and Netscape interprets it differently from most other vendors. Instead of DER encoding r and s, Netscape merely concatenates them into a single 40-byte field. Thus, although Netscape implements DSS for client authentication, it is not interoperable with other implementations. Despite widespread agreement on the "right thing," Netscape has refused to change their implementation, claiming that it complies with the SSLv3 specification and citing installed base. The TLS specification clears up this issue; all TLS implementations must DER encode DSS signatures.

ClientKeyExchange

```
struct {
   select (KeyExchangeAlgorithm) {
      case rsa: EncryptedPreMasterSecret;
      case diffie_hellman: DiffieHellmanClientPublicValue;
   } exchange_keys;
} ClientKeyExchange;

struct {
   select (PublicValueEncoding) {
      case implicit: struct {};
      case explicit: opaque DH_Yc<1..2^16-1>;
   } dh_public;
} DiffieHellmanClientPublicValue;
```

```
ClientKeyExchange
  DiffieHellmanClientPublicValue[64] =
     14 ea e2 18 c1 69 b3 60 fc ea c7 54
     f7 18 db b9 47 c7 cf 95 80 2a 32 b7
     0c 07 11 ab 7a 9d dc 0a 1c 82 a1 35
     23 1f 90 71 2a 94 6d d8 86 b4 e2 84
     e9 a6 a2 00 5e bb 82 09 a3 8a ba f2
     e8 29 87 61
```

Because Diffie-Hellman requires that the client and the server share a common set of parameters (g and p, found in the ServerKeyExchange), the client needs to send only its public key (Yc) in the ClientKeyExchange message. Yc is represented in the usual SSL style for big integers, high byte first.

Fixed DH Keys

Because the client has a DH key, it is possible for the client to have a certificate binding the key to the client's identity. This certificate can be used to perform client authentication, using the rsa_fixed_dh and dss_fixed_dh certificate types. These certificates are certificates containing DH keys signed with RSA and DSS respectively. The client sends its certificate in response to the CertificateRequest but does not send a CertificateVerify. Rather, it proves that it possesses the corresponding private key by being able to produce the pre_master_secret using its private key. Because the client's public key is present in the Certificate message, no public key is present in the ClientKeyExchange message (the implicit choice in the DiffieHellmanClientPublicValue structure).

Similarly, it is also possible for the server to have a static DH key that is contained in its certificate. The server's identity is proven by being able to reproduce the pre_master_secret. Neither of these operational modes is as common as the ephemeral DH modes using DSS.

4.17 FORTEZZA Details

The FORTEZZA support described in [Freier1996] does not work. It was apparently written without ever being tested. The various changes required for successful operation are described in [Relyea1996].

The FORTEZZA command interface has a number of properties that make FORTEZZA difficult to use with SSL. The most important one is that the card will not use arbitrary keys. Thus, keys must either be generated on the card by the card random number generator or received encrypted from another card. As a result, it's not possible to use the standard SSL key generation procedure to generate the FORTEZZA encryption keys.

The second important limitation is that the card must generate the IV. This requirement was imposed by the escrow feature. The escrowed session is carried in something called the *Law Enforcement Access Field* (LEAF). The LEAF contained the session key used to encrypt the actual traffic. The session key was wrapped in the card key. In order to ensure that the LEAF is carried along with the ciphertext, it was embedded in the IV, resulting in a 24-byte IV. The card automatically extracts the actual 8-byte IV from the IV given to it.

> In 1997, the NSA bowed to pressure over the escrow issue and removed the LEAF. However, for compatibility, the 24-byte IV remained with a dummy LEAF. Finally, on June 23, 1998, SKIPJACK and KEA were declassified.

```
struct {
  opaque r_s [128];
} ServerFortezzaParams;

struct {
  opaque y_c<0..128>;
  opaque r_c[128];
  opaque y_signature[40];
  opaque wrapped_client_write_key[12];
  opaque wrapped_server_write_key[12];
  opaque client_write_iv[24];
  opaque server_write_iv[24];
  opaque master_secret_iv[24];
  block-ciphered opaque encrypted_pre_master_secret[48];
} FortezzaKeys;
```

The ServerFortezzaParams structure is used to carry the server's random value r_s to the client. The FortezzaKeys structure is carried in the ClientKeyExchange message. It contains all the information that the server will need to derive the same keys as the client.

The y_c value contains the client's KEA public key if it's not in the client's certificate. If it is, this field is empty. The r_c value contains the client's random value. y_signature contains the client's signature over y_c. The specification is unclear on what the value of y_signature should be if the client's KEA public key is in its certificate. In KEA, the client and server public keys are combined with the random values to generate a *Token Encryption Key* (TEK) which can then be used to encrypt other keys.

wrapped_client_write_key and wrapped_server_write_key contain the encryption keys wrapped under the KEA-generated shared key. client_write_iv and server_write_iv contain the IVs for these keys (with the LEAF embedded in them). Finally, the FortezzaKeys structure contains the pre_master_secret encrypted under the shared key with an IV given in master_secret_iv. The pre_master_secret is used only to generate the MAC keys.

The FORTEZZA command interface imposes one other limitation: IVs are intended to be generated by the sender and read by the recipient. Thus, it's possible to load an IV onto the card when decrypting but not encrypting. However, both keys and IVs are generated by the client. The result is that the first block of data encrypted by the server uses an essentially random IV—which the client has no way of knowing. In order to synchronize the CBC state, the server first transmits a dummy encrypted block that is discarded by the client. From then on, the cipher states will be synchronized.

Note that the encryption of this dummy block means that the server never needs to use the server_write_iv. [Relyea1996] says that the server implementation should load the IV in decryption mode to verify the IV and then change over to encryption mode. This step is not required for interoperability. Its purpose is to verify that IV correctly matches the key, thereby preventing a rogue client from using a fake IV (with a bogus LEAF) and thereby thwarting the escrow provisions.

The inability to use random keys also means that ordinary session resumption will not work, since there is no way to use the newly generated keys. [Relyea1996] describes two options:

- Don't resume sessions at all.

- Resume but continue encrypting and decrypting as if the data were a continuation of the previous session. Note that if this approach is taken it is not possible to have two simultaneous connections with a given session, as it ordinarily would be. This is problematic for systems such as HTTPS which use a number of simultaneous connections.

Only two FORTEZZA cipher suites were defined, one with SKIPJACK and one with NULL encryption. Figure 4.11 shows them.

Cipher Suite	Authentication	Key Exchange	Encryption	Digest	Number
SSL_FORTEZZA_DMS_WITH_NULL_SHA	DSA	KEA	NULL	SHA	0x001c
SSL_FORTEZZA_DMS_WITH_FORTEZZA_CBC_SHA	DSA	KEA	SKIPJACK	SHA	0x001d

Figure 4.11 FORTEZZA cipher suites

4.18 Error Alerts

In Chapter 3, we discussed alerts in general without discussing the specific alert cases other than close_notify. All the other alerts indicate errors of some kind. This section presents a detailed discussion of those alerts.

Recall that alerts may have a level of warning or fatal. A fatal alert always terminates the connection, whereas implementations may continue past a warning alert. While in theory implementations can continue past a non-fatal alert, in practice even warning alerts indicate that one side requested something that the other side couldn't fulfill and so they usually result in connection closure.

The specification requires some alerts to be fatal whereas others may be either fatal or warning. An implementation which receives an alert which should be fatal but which is incorrectly tagged as warning should nevertheless treat it as fatal. In practice, since many implementations treat all alerts as fatal, implementations should refrain from sending warning alerts unless they're willing to have the other side terminate the connection.

This section describes each SSL error alert in detail. Although some of the alerts could signal an attack in progress, if you're debugging your SSL implementation, they most likely represent bugs. Where appropriate we'll attempt to identify the common implementation errors that these alerts might indicate. Reading this section may allow you to determine what's happened when your implementation receives or generates one of these alerts. See Figure 4.12 for a list of all the alerts.

Alert Name	Level	SSL Version	Number
close_notify	either	either	0
unexpected_message	fatal	either	10
bad_record_mac	fatal	either	20
decryption_failed	fatal	TLS	21
record_overflow	fatal	TLS	22
decompression_failure	fatal	either	30
handshake_failure	fatal	either	40
no_certificate	either	SSLv3	41
bad_certificate	either	either	42
unsupported_certificate	either	either	43
certificate_revoked	either	either	44
certificate_expired	either	either	45
certificate_unknown	either	either	46
illegal_parameter	fatal	either	47
unknown_ca	fatal	TLS	48
access_denied	fatal	TLS	49
decode_error	fatal	TLS	50
decrypt_error	either	TLS	51
export_restriction	fatal	TLS	60
protocol_version	fatal	TLS	70
insufficient_security	fatal	TLS	71
internal_error	fatal	TLS	80
user_cancelled	fatal	TLS	90
no_renegotiation	warning	TLS	100

Figure 4.12 All SSL/TLS alerts

unexpected_message

The unexpected_message alert signals that an inappropriate message was received. This alert almost always signals that one of the implementations is broken and generating inappropriate messages or sending messages in the incorrect order. You might see this message often when debugging an SSL implementation but should never see it in working systems. As a special case, a non SGC-capable server might send an unexpected_message to a client attempting SGC. This alert must always be sent as fatal.

bad_record_mac

The bad_record_mac alert is transmitted if an implementation receives a record with a bad MAC. This might represent an attack. Thus, this alert must be treated as fatal.

If you're testing your implementation and you receive a bad_record_mac alert, it most likely indicates an error in your MAC code. However, if the alert is sent in response to a Finished message, it could also represent an error in key derivation. Even if the encryption keys are also wrong, the decryption may appear to succeed. However, the MAC will fail. In fact, even if the MAC key is correct but the encryption key is wrong, the error will still most likely appear in the MAC check (see the decryption_error alert for a discussion of decryption errors).

Finally, some SSLv3 implementations use the bad_record_mac message to signal an error in verifying the Finished message itself. In TLS, failure to verify the Finished is signalled with the decrypt_error alert. Thus, when debugging a bad_record_mac error, it's important to consider other culprits besides the MAC computation itself.

decryption_failed

The decryption_failed signals that the ciphertext couldn't be decrypted. This error must be fatal. This error is really only relevant with block ciphers. RC4 decryption always appears to succeed whatever the decryption key. The output is simply wrong.

Block cipher decryption can fail in a number of ways. First, the block cipher input length can be something other than a mutiple of the block length. This is an obvious message formatting error. Also, after the data is decrypted, the padding check may reveal errors resulting from incorrect padding or the use of the wrong encryption key.

If the wrong encryption key is used, the padding bytes will be essentially random. However, it's possible that they will still appear correct, particularly if the implementation chooses to examine only the length byte and then remove the padding without examining it. (This procedure is safe because the data is covered by the MAC anyway.) Note that the padding does not have to actually be the same as the original padding. It merely has to be consistent.

In this case, the receiver will have the wrong plaintext but this will only be discovered when the MAC check and a bad_record_mac alert will be received. Obviously, since RC4 decryption always appears to succeed, errors in RC4 keying always show up in the MAC check.

record_overflow

This alert indicates that the record was larger than allowed by the SSL specification. This message must be fatal. In practice, this message almost always represents a bug in the SSL implementation since an attack would likely be caught in the MAC check. Note that early versions of Internet Explorer generated incorrectly long records and so it's not uncommon to see an unsuspecting implementation generate this alert when talking to IE. This alert is new with TLSv1.

decompression_failure

This alert indicates that a record could not be decompressed. It is always fatal. However, since compression is almost never used, this error will rarely be seen in practice.

handshake_failure

The handshake_failure alert is the all-purpose alert used in SSLv3 to indicate problems handshaking. TLS introduced a number of finer-grained alerts to indicate what actually went wrong. In TLS, the handshake_failure alert is only used when no common cipher can be negotiated.

When debugging a handshake_failure alert, you need to examine which stage of the handshake went wrong and from there determine what happened. If you received a handshake_failure alert after sending a series of messages at once, it's often useful to send each message individually, checking for the alert after each one using a network sniffer. This alert must always be fatal.

no_certificate

The no_certificate alert is an SSLv3-only alert sent to indicate that "no appropriate certificate is available." It has been replaced in TLS with certificate_unknown which serves essentially the same purpose.

bad_certificate

The bad_certificate alert indicates that a certificate was corrupt or the signatures were wrong or some similar error. In theory this alert may be a warning. An implementation might choose to ignore the bad certificate but issue the alert as a warning. However, in practice implementations either silently accept the certificate or send an alert. Thus, this alert is really always fatal. This comment applies to the next four alerts as well. Interestingly, Internet Explorer doesn't use this alert at all. Instead, it simply closes the connection. We'll see an example of this in Chapter 8.

unsupported_certificate

This alert means that the implementation received a certificate which was of an unsupported type. Since SSL only supports X.509 certificates, this alert means that an unsupported algorithm was used. Because the algorithm used to sign certificates is not specified in the cipher suite, it's possible to have (for instance) a certificate for an RSA key signed with a DSA key. An implementation which did not support DSA would send an unsupported_certificate error. However, in practice such mixed certificate regimes nearly never occur and an unsupported_certificate error represents a bug in one of the implementations.

revoked_certificate

This alert indicates that the sender received a certificate that was revoked. Most real life SSL implementations do not currently support revocation so this alert almost never appears.

certificate_expired

This alert indicates that one of the certificates has expired. Implementations shouldn't send expired certificates, but sometimes they are misconfigured. This alert is the result.

certificate_unknown

This alert is a catch-all certificate error introduced in TLSv1. Certificate errors that don't fall into any of the previous classes or the unknown_ca class described below generate a certificate_unknown error. SSLv3 implementations would generate a bad_certificate alert for those conditions.

illegal_parameter

The illegal_parameter alert indicates that one of the handshake fields was out of range or inconsistent with some other fields. The handshake obviously can't complete so this error is fatal.

unknown_ca

The unknown_ca alert is sent when an implementation receives a certificate signed by a CA it doesn't recognize or can't find the certificate for. This alert must be fatal. Note that this treatment is inconsistent with the other certificate errors which can be sent as warnings. I know of no reason for the inconsistency. In my opinion, best practice is to either silently accept certificates or to reject them with an alert. Note that in this context *silent* refers only to SSL messages. An implementation might accept a bad certificate only after prompting the user or sending error messages to a logging facility. The unknown_ca message is new with TLS. SSLv3 implementations send the no_certificate alert instead.

access_denied

This alert means that although a valid certificate was received the identity in the certificate fails access control checks so the connection is being rejected. This alert is always fatal. I know of no implementation which generates this alert.

decode_error

This alert indicates that a message couldn't be decoded because one of the fields was out of range or the length was incorrect. In most cases this represents some sort of implementation error. This alert is always fatal. decode_error was introduced in TLS and it's not clear what to use with SSLv3. OpenSSL and PureTLS both use handshake_failure, presumably on the theory that most of these errors occur in the handshake.

decrypt_error

The decrypt_error alert indicates that one of the handshake cryptographic operations failed. The likely cases are failure to decrypt a ClientKeyExchange, verify a signature, or check a Finished message. This alert is always fatal. decrypt_error was introduced with TLSv1. SSLv3 implementations usually use handshake_failure instead. Note that if you receive a decrypt_error in response to a Finished, this means that your encryption and MAC keys and code are correct but that your Finished computation is broken.

export_restriction

This alert indicates that one of the implementations tried to violate export restrictions. The example provided in RFC 2246 is trying to use a 1024 bit ephemeral key with RSA_EXPORT key exchange. This is a new alert type for TLSv1 and isn't seen much. Note that this is not the alert that you will see when an implementation that supports only strong ciphers tries to talk to one that supports only weak ones. That will be either insufficient_security or handshake_failure. This alert is always fatal.

protocol_version

The protocol_version alert is sent by the server to indicate that the client used an unrecognized protocol version. Because the client can only supply the maximum version that it supports, the server will only send this alert when the client asked for a version older than it will support. For instance, if the client offered only SSLv3 and the server supported only TLS, the server would generate a protocol_version alert. Since essentially all TLS implementations are also SSLv3 implementations, this alert is only seen if one of the sides has been explicitly configured to support only TLS or if there is a bug. There is no value in configuring for TLS-only support.

Note that if the server only supports a version older than the client offers, it will *not* send a protocol_version alert. Instead, it will simply respond with its version in the ServerHello. If the client does not want to support the server's version choice, it will have to send an alert (presumably protocol_version but the SSLv3 and TLS specs don't specify). The protocol_version alert is always fatal. The protocol_version alert was added in TLS. SSLv3 implementations usually use handshake_failure for this purpose.

insufficient_security

The insufficient_security alert is used to indicate that the cipher suites offered by the client were weaker than required by the server. This alert is new with TLS. SSLv3 implementations use handshake_failure. Since the insufficient_security alert indicates failure to negotiate a cipher suite, it is always fatal.

internal_error

The internal_error alert is used to indicate that the transmitting implementation encountered some sort of internal error such as a memory allocation or hardware failure. This alert is new with TLS so SSLv3 implementations need to use some other error. The internal_error alert is always fatal.

user_cancelled

The user_cancelled alert is used when the user cancels the handshake for some reason. This alert is new for TLS. RFC 2246 says that it should be used as a warning, which is confusing—if the user cancels the handshake then the connection will be unsuccessful so the alert should be fatal.

no_renegotiation

As we'll see in Chapter 4, SSL allows either client or server to initiate a new handshake at any time other than during a handshake. The client initiates renegotiation by sending a new ClientHello. The server initiates renegotiation by sending a HelloRequest message. RFC 2246 says that the client can silently refuse to renegotiate or send a no_renegotiation alert. RFC 2246 is unclear on how the server should respond to an unwanted ClientHello but presumably it should send a no_renegotiation alert as well.

The no_renegotiation alert is new for TLS. SSLv3 implementations simply ignore unwanted renegotiation requests. Since most existing TLS implementations are actually upgraded SSLv3 implementations, they typically silently ignore renegotiation rather than sending the no_renegotiation alert. In any case, the no_renegotiation alert is always a warning.

4.19 SSLv2 Backward Compatibility

SSLv2 had already been widely deployed when SSLv3 was invented. Thus, one of the requirements for SSLv3 was for SSLv3 clients and servers to automatically talk to SSLv2 clients and servers. However, the message formats were totally different. (See Appendix B for a discussion of SSLv2.) It's fairly straightforward for servers to auto-detect whether they are talking to an SSLv3 or SSLv2 client. The SSLv2 and SSLv3 length bytes are in different locations and SSLv3 records appear to be unreasonably long when interpreted as SSLv2 handshake messages. Thus, the server can wait for the client's first message and respond appropriately.

Clients, however, must speak first and so cannot auto-detect. Thus, the SSLv3 specification contains support for sending the ClientHello in a format that was backward-compatible with SSLv2. In essence, the backward-compatible ClientHello maps all the SSLv3 fields onto SSLv2 fields in the SSLv2 CLIENT-HELLO. Thus, when a server receives a backward-compatible CLIENT-HELLO, it can either interpret it as an SSLv2 message and continue with the SSLv2 handshake or translate the fields to SSLv3 values and perform the SSLv3 handshake. Figure 4.13 shows the SSLv2 CLIENT-HELLO.

```
char MSG-CLIENT-HELLO
char CLIENT-VERSION-MSB
char CLIENT-VERSION-LSB
char CIPHER-SPECS-LENGTH-MSB
char CIPHER-SPECS-LENGTH-LSB
char SESSION-ID-LENGTH-MSB
char SESSION-ID-LENGTH-LSB
char CHALLENGE-LENGTH-MSB
char CHALLENGE-LENGTH-LSB
char CIPHER-SPECS-DATA[(MSB<<8)|LSB]
char SESSION-ID-DATA[(MSB<<8)|LSB]
char CHALLENGE-DATA[(MSB<<8)|LSB]
```

Figure 4.13 SSLv2 CLIENT-HELLO

The CLIENT-HELLO shown is in the SSLv2 specification language of [Hickman1995]. Unlike SSLv3, SSLv2 places all the object lengths in one part of the message and all the objects in another. Also, the high and low bytes of lengths are represented individually. Thus, the length of the CIPHER-SPECS-DATA field is given by computing

(CIPHER-SPECS-LENGTH-MSB << 8) | CIPHER-SPECS-LENGTH-LSB

All of the SSLv3 handshake parameters can be mapped to SSLv2 values.

Version

The SSLv2 version number is 2 (MSB=0, LSB=2). To represent SSLv3 or TLS compatibility, we use the appropriate version numbers from the SSLv3 or TLS Version field: 0x300 and 0x301 for SSLv3 and TLS, respectively.

Random

The SSLv2 CHALLENGE value is used as part of the SSLv2 key generation procedure in much the same way as the ClientRandom is used by SSLv3. It's randomly generated, so it can be used as a ClientRandom value. However, it's allowed to be between 16 and 32 bytes, whereas the SSLv3/TLS ClientRandom must be 32 bytes. To convert a CHALLENGE to a ClientRandom value, it is padded with zeros on the left.

Session ID

Whenever resuming an SSLv3 session, the SSLv3 ClientHello must be used. Thus, the SESSION-ID field should always be empty and the length zero.

Cipher Suites

SSLv2 CIPHER-SPECSs are analogous to SSLv3 CipherSuites. They specify the encryption and digest algorithms. (SSLv2 only supports RSA, so they don't specify key exchange or signature.) Thus, in backward-compatibility mode, the CLIENT-HELLO should contain both the SSLv2 and SSLv3/TLS ciphers that the client supports. SSLv2 CIPHER-SPEC values are 3 bytes, so 2-byte SSLv3 values are represented with a zero first byte.

It's also possible to use SSLv2 ciphers when using the backward compatibility handshake. Some of these ciphers correspond to SSLv3/TLS ciphers, but some do not. For instance, SSLv2 has an RC2-128 mode. SSLv3 does not define such a cipher suite. However, it's possible for two SSLv3 clients to negotiate it if they are using the SSLv2 backward compatible handshake. All these cipher suites use RSA for signature and key exchange. Figure 4.14 lists these ciphers.

Cipher Spec	Encryption	Digest	Number
SSL_CK_RC4_128_WITH_MD5	RC4_128	MD5	0x010080
SSL_CK_RC4_128_EXPORT40_WITH_MD5	RC4_40	MD5	0x020080
SSL_CK_RC2_128_CBC_WITH_MD5	RC2_128_CBC	MD5	0x030080
SSL_CK_RC2_128_CBC_EXPORT40_WITH_MD5	RC2_40_CBC	MD5	0x040080
SSL_CK_IDEA_128_CBC_WITH_MD5	IDEA_CBC	MD5	0x050080
SSL_CK_DES_64_WITH_MD5	DES_CBC	MD5	0x060080
SSL_CK_DES_192_EDE3_CBC_WITH_MD5	DES_EDE3_CBC	MD5	0x070080

Figure 4.14 SSLv2 compatibility cipher suites

Rollback Protection

SSL uses PKCS #1 padding to encrypt data using RSA. However, in order to protect against an active attack in which the attacker forces negotiation back to SSLv2, SSLv3- and TLS-capable client implementations must use the value 03 for the last 8 bytes of the padding when doing SSLv2. The server can check this to make sure that it really is talking to an SSLv2-only client (which would fill these 8 bytes with random data). Note that this unusual padding will not appear and does not need to be checked if doing an SSLv3 handshake. The purpose of all this is to prevent an attacker from forcing a client/server pair back to the (weaker) SSLv2 from SSLv3/TLS.

Compatibility

In order for the backward-compatibility handshake to work correctly, an SSLv2-only server must simply negotiate to SSLv2 if it receives a higher version in the CLIENT-HELLO. Unfortunately, the SSLv2 specification wasn't very clear on how servers should handle CLIENT-HELLO messages with version numbers higher than they support. This problem was made worse by the fact that Netscape's SSLREF reference implementation simply rejected connections with higher version numbers. Thus, it's not guaranteed that all SSLv2 servers will respond correctly to the backward-compatible handshake, although the vast majority will.

4.20 Summary

This chapter concludes our detailed coverage of SSL. Each of these modes offers some benefit over the traditional RSA server-only mode discussed in Chapter 3.

Session resumption allows a client/server pair to reuse keying material between connections. This makes subsequent handshakes between a client/server pair faster.

Client authentication uses the client's public key to prove the client's identity to the server. Traditionally, SSL connections have anonymous clients, but with client authentication, clients as well as servers can authenticate using certificates.

Ephemeral RSA allows a server to have a single long (>512 bits) RSA key but still to communicate with exportable clients which require 512-bit RSA keys, by generating a temporary 512-bit key and signing it with the long-term key.

Server Gated Cryptography allows exportable clients to use strong cryptography with specifically designated servers. These servers must have special certificates that indicate that they are SGC eligible.

DSS and DH cipher suites make it possible to implement SSL in the United States without infringing on the RSA patent. Support for DSS and DH has been mandated for TLS.

Elliptic Curve ciphers may be faster than either DH/DSS or RSA, but they have not yet been standardized by IETF as part of TLS.

Kerberos keys can be used to exchange keying material between client and server, while keeping the rest of SSL the same. This makes it possible to bootstrap a Kerberos infrastructure to authenticate SSL connections.

SSLv3 is backward-compatible with SSLv2. The SSLv3 ClientHello can be cast as an SSLv2 CLIENT-HELLO, thus permitting SSLv3 agents which also speak SSLv2 to communicate with SSLv2-only agents.

5

SSL Security

5.1 Introduction

This chapter discusses the security properties of SSL. This chapter is divided into three sections. The first section of the chapter provides general rules for using SSL securely. Understanding this material requires some understanding of cryptography and an understanding of SSL approximately equal to that provided by the first halves of the previous two chapters. The idea here is to explain the security properties of SSL and how to use it securely.

The second section discusses the security threats discussed in the first part in more detail. It's fairly easy to get an interoperable implementation that nevertheless has hidden vulnerabilities if you're not careful while writing it. Where the first part provides general guidelines, this section covers the attacks that are possible if those guidelines aren't followed and discussion of the various implementation techniques that are in common use.

The final part of the chapter covers some more exotic security threats in detail. Although there have been no good attacks on the SSL protocol itself, a number of SSL implementations have been successfully attacked and some care is required to ensure that one's implementation is not vulnerable to these threats. This section is fairly technical, but you can get a good understanding of the security properties of SSL merely by reading the first two-thirds of the chapter.

5.2 What SSL Provides

SSL provides channel-level security. What this means is that the two ends of the connection know that the data being transmitted is being kept secret and that it has not been tampered with. The server is nearly always authenticated so the client knows who's on the other end of the connection. The client can be required to authenticate using his certificate as well. SSL also provides for secure notification of exceptional conditions, including error alerts and connection closure.

All of these protections depend on certain assumptions about the system: we assume that the keying material has been correctly generated and is being kept secure. Failure to follow careful procedures can result in a significant loss of security.

5.3   Protect the master_secret

Nearly all the security of the protocol depends on keeping the master_secret private. If the master_secret for a session is compromised, then the session is completely vulnerable to attack. Remember that the master_secret is used to produce all the cryptographic keys used to protect the data. An attacker who knows it can therefore mount a large number of attacks.

Section 5.9 discusses the detailed consequences of master_secret compromise, but the short description is that if an attacker has the master_secret the data might as well be transmitted in the clear. Such an attacker can read all the message traffic and under most circumstances can undetectably forge traffic from either side. This is not good.

5.4   Protect the Server's Private Key

One obvious way for an attacker to get the master_secret is to acquire the server's private key. In order to prevent this, you have to keep the server's private key (surprise!) private. This sounds obvious, but it's one of the most widely violated rules and it's also surprisingly difficult to accomplish.

In general, an attacker who has the server's private key constitutes a serious threat to the security of the system. If the server is using the common static RSA mode discussed in Chapter 3, an attacker with the server's private key can recover the master_secret and undetectably read any traffic he can capture, as well as pose as the server at will. If the server is using ephemeral modes, the attacker can't passively read traffic but can mount an active attack posing as the server. In either case, compromise of the server private key is very dangerous.

Protecting the private key requires storing it securely. Most implementations encrypt the private key on disk and require a password/passphrase to decrypt it. This requires the user/administrator to generate and remember a strong passphrase, which turns out to be remarkably difficult to do. Other implementations store the key in secured hardware. Both approaches require intervention from the administrator to start the server, making unattended reboots in case of system crash or power failure problematic.

5.5   Use Good Randomness

Nearly all cryptographic protocols require *strong random numbers* to operate securely and SSL is no exception. Random number generators (RNGs) are used primarily to generate keys but also for key steps in other cryptographic operations. If the attacker can predict what numbers your RNG is going to output, then he can guess what your keys are, completely compromising the protocol.

SSL uses random numbers in a number of places. First, the private keys for the server (and optionally the client) need to be randomly generated. Second, the client needs to generate random data to perform the key exchange. If RSA is being used, then the client must generate the pre_master_secret and if using DH, it must generate an ephemeral private key. Third, if DSA is being used for signature, then a random number must be generated for each signature. Finally, the client and server both need to generate their handshake random values, but those do not in fact need to be securely generated because they are public.

Thus, both client and server need to be able to generate strong random numbers. If the server generates weak random numbers, then the attacker can guess the server's private key, leading to compromise of the pre_master_secret. If the client generates weak random numbers, then the attacker can guess either the pre_master_secret directly (if in RSA mode) or the client's ephemeral DH private key and transitively the pre_master_secret (if in DH mode). In either case, the protocol is completely compromised.

Most systems use software based *pseudo-random number generators* (PRNGs). A PRNG is an algorithm that provides a stream of unpredictable (though not random) numbers. These PRNGs must be *seeded* with some random data in order to produce a high-quality random stream. The seed data is usually collected from network traffic sampling, system internal variables, or user input timing. Hardware random number generators based on physical randomness are also available. See Section 5.12 for guidance on generating strong randomness.

5.6   Check the Certificate Chain

Let's assume that your SSL implementation is operating correctly, and you receive a certificate from the server. That certificate is signed by a *Certification Authority* (CA) that you don't recognize. This provides no assurances about the server's identity. Although the server has asserted its identity via its certificate, it's nothing more than a certificate because you can't verify that the assertion is correct. You can still establish a secure connection to the server, but you're vulnerable to an active (man-in-the-middle) attack where the attacker poses as the server to you and you to the server. Knowing the server's identity is absolutely necessary to avoid this attack.

A server without a certificate server is obviously unauthenticated, but there are more subtle ways in which a seemingly good certificate chain can provide less security than you might expect. The SSL implementation can help to protect you against these attacks, but often having complete security requires that the application get involved.

The most important countermeasure is to check that the identity being presented in the certificate matches the identity that the application expects. Imagine that you're trying to connect to a server operated by Bob and the server provides you with a certificate bearing the name Alice. The certificate is valid, but it's the wrong one. Consequently, you need to check that identity in the certificate corresponds to the expected identity of the other end of the connection.

Correctly checking the identity requires interaction with the application-layer protocol and potentially with the user. Only they have all the information as to the expected user's identity. Another case in which the user may need to be notified is expired certificates. In some cases, organizations may have policies forbidding the use of expired certificates, but in others the decision may be up to the user. We'll discuss the detailed interaction of the certificate chain with the application-layer protocol in Chapters 7, 9, and 10.

5.7   Algorithm Selection

SSL supports a variety of cipher suites, specifying the set of algorithms to be used for the connection. These algorithms vary in strength from very weak exportable ciphers such as RC4 in 40-bit mode to (hopefully) very strong ciphers such as 3DES. Moreover, asymmetric key pairs can use keys of a range of lengths. The security of an SSL connection is naturally totally dependent on the security of the ciphers it uses. It's therefore necessary to choose a cipher suite commensurate with the value of your data.

To do this, limit the set of cipher suites that your application is willing to support. Because both client and server have to agree on a common cipher suite in order to communicate, this ensures that you will obtain the appropriate level of security. However, a possible side effect is that the server and client may not have a common algorithm set and not be able to communicate. As a consequence, the best policy is typically to allow all cipher suites that provide security above an acceptable minimum level rather than merely choosing to support the strongest algorithms exclusively.

Our recommendation is to use either RSA or DH/DSS with minimum 768-bit keys. Use 3DES or RC4-128 for encryption, 3DES if you want maximum security, and RC4-128 if you want maximum performance. Use SHA-1 for message authentication. See Chapter 1 for performance numbers for these algorithms.

5.8   The Story So Far

We've covered a number of generally important rules for using SSL securely. This ought to provide some idea of the sorts of measures you need to take in order to achieve decent security. This isn't to say that the list is exhaustive—there are an infinite number of ways to screw up, mostly by not paying attention to what you're doing—but it covers a number of important issues that are easy to get wrong. The author has personally seen at least one implementation break each of the previously described rules.

5.9   Compromise of the master_secret

Compromise of the master_secret is disastrous. Let's reexamine key derivation for a moment to see how master_secret (or pre_master_secret) compromise can lead to compromise of the entire system. Figure 5.1 shows the key derivation process. Secret information is shaded, all other information is public.

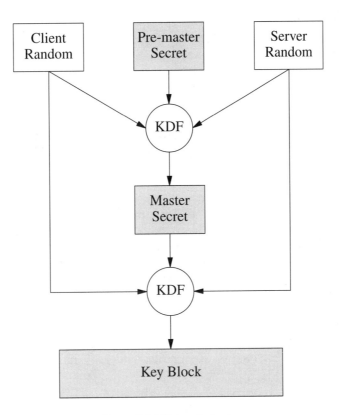

Figure 5.1 SSL key derivation

Recall that key derivation proceeds in two stages. First, the pre_master_secret is converted into the master_secret. The *key derivation function* (KDF) takes three parameters that are different for every handshake: the client_random and server_random values and the pre_master_secret. However, recall that the client_random and server_random values are exchanged before the master_secret is agreed upon, so they must be transmitted in the clear in the handshake. Thus, an attacker who can snoop on traffic already knows them. The only piece of secret information used to generate the master_secret is the pre_master_secret.

The second stage is to convert the master_secret into the individual cryptographic keys. As before, the KDF takes three inputs: the client_random and server_random values and the master_secret. Again, only the master_secret is a secret. An attacker who knows the master_secret can therefore compute all the cryptographic keys that are used to protect the connection. Similarly, an attacker who knows the pre_master_secret can compute the master_secret and transitively the keys.

So, if an attacker does recover the master_secret, the results are very bad. From the perspective of such an attacker, you might as well be transmitting your messages in the clear.

Confidentiality Attacks

As we said earlier, an attacker who knows the master_secret can compute all the cryptographic keys used for the connection. Naturally, this includes the encryption keys used to encrypt the data. Recall that our threat model assumes that attackers can read any data that is transmitted over the network. Of course, when we're using SSL, this data is encrypted, but this poses no problem to an attacker with the master_secret. Such an attacker has the encryption keys and can easily decrypt each record captured.

There is one trivial technical problem: If the attacker fails to capture every record, some work is needed to decrypt subsequent records. Recall that each record is encrypted as if it were part of a continuous stream. For a stream cipher, each record uses a different section of keystream. In order to decrypt a record, the attacker needs to know how many bytes have already been encrypted. However, even if the attacker misses a record, he can usually get a good guess at how many bytes he's missed from the TCP sequence number and do a little searching to find the exact right section of keystream.

With block ciphers, the situation is a little trickier. The IV of each record is the last cipher block of the previous record. If the attacker has missed that record, then he has no way of decrypting the first cipher block of the record, but he can decrypt the rest of the record and any records that come after that.

Note that this attack is completely passive. If the attacker is willing to interfere with network traffic, he can work around the missed records problem more easily by arranging for retransmits. On the other hand, if the attacker is willing to mount an active attack, he can also mount some significant integrity attacks. We'll discuss that next.

Integrity Attacks

Of course, an attacker who has the master_secret can compute the MAC keys. In combination with the encryption keys, such an attacker can mount a wide variety of integrity attacks. We'll describe a few here, but this list is not exhaustive.

The easiest form of attack is simply to take over the connection. The attacker forges a close on the underlying connection to one side (typically using TCP RST) and proceeds to impersonate that side to the other. The attacker can create convincing forgeries of whatever traffic it chooses. This attack isn't very subtle, but it can be very effective. Note that this sort of attack doesn't require very fine control of the underlying network: Techniques for TCP connection hijacking are well known (see [Joncheray1995]).

A variety of more subtle attacks are possible if the attacker has good control of the network. For instance, the attacker might be able to add and delete packets at will while preserving the connection. Then it's possible to change any record or even insert or remove records. Exactly what capabilities are required depends on what sort of modification the attacker wants to make to the traffic and what ciphers are being used.

If the traffic the attacker is modifying is encrypted using a stream cipher, the attacker can make point modifications to individual records simply by decrypting the record, changing the message text, generating a new MAC, reencrypting, and sending. Note that the attacker can't change the length of the record or all future records will be out of synch with the keystream.

On the other hand, the attacker can make arbitrary changes to any record he likes if he's willing to intercept and modify all subsequent records. There are a number of intermediate forms of attack that require modifying fewer records, but it should be clear by now that an attacker who knows the master_secret can make the traffic look however he wants it to look.

Pretty Scary, Eh?

We hope that at this point you're convinced that allowing an attacker to get hold of the master_secret is disastrous and that it must therefore be vigorously protected. The good news is that a *correctly* written SSL implementation makes recovering the master_secret very difficult if not impossible. The next few sections describe a few easy-to-make mistakes that allow master_secret recovery.

5.10 Protecting Secrets in Memory

Unless the SSL implementation resides largely in hardware, the master_secret will live in the host's main memory. This means that any attacker who can read the memory of the SSL process can read the master_secret. Thus, it's not possible to protect your SSL connection from an attacker who has administrator privileges on your machine. However, it's possible to make mistakes that potentially allow non-administrators to access the master_secret.

Disk Storage

In general, implementations should refrain from writing secret data to disk at all. However, in some circumstances (see Chapter 9), it's necessary. In such cases, the implementation should take care to set the permissions on the files so that no other users can read the data. Moreover, the implementation should ensure that the disk files are deleted before it exits. On operating systems which have an undelete function, the program should ensure that the files are erased beyond recovery. Good practice is to scrub the data by doing three overwrite passes: the first of zeros, the second of random data, and the third of zeros. This is of particular concern on single-user operating systems such as Windows 95 and 98, where permissions offer no protection and subsequent users can read the entire disk.

Locking Memory

On operating systems with virtual memory, it may be desirable to ensure that the memory containing the master_secret (and other secrets) is never swapped to disk. If it is, a subsequent user or the administrator might be able to read that data and thus recover the secrets. Many operating systems offer subroutine calls to *lock* sensitive data so it cannot be swapped to disk. However, in some cases these calls are actually inactive stubs. Consult your operating system documentation carefully for more information on this topic.

Note that locking memory doesn't offer any protection from an administrator who reads sensitive data from the process while it's resident in memory. It merely protects against an administrator subsequently deciding to recover the data.

Core Dumps

On many operating systems (UNIX in particular) when an application generates a memory error, a *core* image is written to disk. This image contains the entire memory state of the process, including any secret information. Anyone who can read those files can of course recover that information. Programmers may wish to install exception handlers that detect when the application is about to core dump and zero sensitive information.

5.11   Securing the Server's Private Key

The server's private key is the key to the security of the handshake. In static keying modes, it is used to protect the pre_master_secret directly. In ephemeral keying modes it is used to authenticate the ephemeral key which is in turn used to protect the pre_master_secret. Consequently, although compromise of the server's private key is always bad, it's worse when static keying is used because this compromises all the traffic encrypted under that key.

Static Keying

The most vulnerable situation is when the server has a *static* key pair that is used to establish the master_secret. The most common case is the one we covered in Chapter 3. The server has a single RSA key pair with the public key in its certificate. The client uses that public key to encrypt the master_secret so that only the server can read it. However, an attacker who has the private key can easily decrypt the master_secret and perform all the attacks described previously.

In this situation, compromise of the server's static private key compromises every SSL session that was ever established with that key, because the attacker can recover the master_secret offline at a time of his choosing. In other words, the attacker can mount a purely passive attack. It's trivial to write a program that takes the server's private key and a recorded message trace and outputs the plaintext. In fact, the ssldump traces in Chapter 4 were generated using exactly this technique.

Although static keying is mostly used with RSA, SSL also has a number of static Diffie-Hellman modes in which the static DH key is in the server's certificate. These modes are equally vulnerable to this sort of attack. However, most uses of DH in SSL use ephemeral DH. The next section discusses the results of private key compromise when ephemeral keying (as described in Chapter 4) is used.

Ephemeral Keying

Consider the case in which the server's private key is not used for key establishment but only for signature. The server generates an *ephemeral* key pair which is used for key establishment and uses its static key pair to authenticate the ephemeral public key to the client.

When ephemeral keying is used, there are actually two flavors of private key compromise, each with different consequences. Either the static key (used for authentication) can be compromised or the ephemeral key (used for key establishment) can be compromised. First consider the case where the static key is compromised. Knowing the static key is of no value for decrypting traffic because no data is ever encrypted under this key. It's only encrypted using the ephemeral key. However, the static key is also of no use in recovering the ephemeral key.

Recovering a static authentication key isn't useless, however. An attacker who has the server's static authentication key can take over any connection (posing as the server) during the handshake phase. He can then either simply act as the server or mount a man-in-the-middle attack where he poses as the server to the client and the client to the server, shuttling data back and forth between them. Figure 5.2 shows this process.

Figure 5.2 shows this man-in-the-middle attack in action with some of the irrelevant messages trimmed. The attacker copies most of the handshake messages directly from client to server and vice versa, but changes the ServerKeyExchange message to be a signed version of his own ephemeral key rather than the server's. He signs this with the compromised private key. He then decrypts all traffic from the client and forwards it reencrypted to the server, making whatever changes he wants. There is one subtlety here in that the attacker must generate a new Finished message because the handshake hashes that the client sees will be different from those the server sees due to the changed ephemeral key.

So, compromise of a static authentication key allows the attacker to actively attack any given session during the handshake phase but not afterwards. It's interesting to note that the attacker cannot mount this form of attack if client authentication is used. Because the client's signature is over all of the handshake messages, the messages that the attacker sends to the client are different than the messages that the server thinks it's sending to the client. Therefore, the server's signature check will fail.

Even if the server machine is completely compromised and the server's private authentication key is recovered, this knowledge cannot be used to attack any session that's already been established and shut down. This property is called *perfect forward secrecy* (PFS). Note that static key establishment keys do not have this property. However, PFS is obtained only if the traffic keys themselves haven't been stored somewhere. For instance, if the keys are in the session cache, then the attacker could still decrypt the connection. Deleting unused or expired keying material regularly is critical for PFS.

By contrast, if the attacker compromises one of the server's ephemeral keys, he can use it only to attack connections that were protected using that key. For all such connections, the attacker can recover the master_secret and mount the attacks described in Section 5.9.

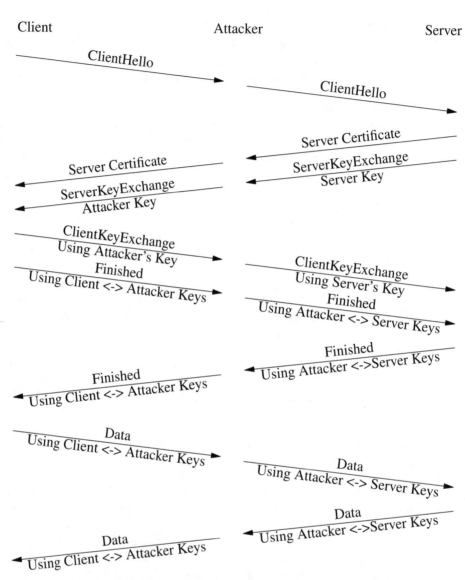

Figure 5.2 Attack using a compromised signing key

How many connections are affected depends entirely on the server's behavior. When ephemeral RSA is being used, the number of compromised connections can be very large. As we discussed in Chapter 4, generating RSA keys is expensive and servers will often generate one ephemeral RSA key when they start up and use that key until they're shut down, days or weeks later. Consequently, an enormous amount of traffic might well be compromised when one ephemeral key is compromised. Because ephemeral RSA is currently used only with exportable RSA encryption keys (<512 bits), and we know keys of this size to be at the outer edge of breakability, this is an area of some concern.

When ephemeral DH is used, it's fairly common to regenerate the ephemeral key frequently. Some implementations (OpenSSL for instance) have a mode in which they generate a new ephemeral key for every new session. When used this way, compromise of one session has no effect on any other session.

Private Key Storage

Most SSL servers run on general purpose computers. Like most server programs, they use the computer's filesystem to store their permanent data between invocations. This usually includes the server's private key. If the server machine is secure against attack and only trusted users are allowed on the system, this is a reasonably safe practice.

However, having a completely trusted server is difficult. Many organizations can't devote a machine solely to being an SSL server, and even if they could the machine might be compromised or stolen. To partially defend against these eventualities, common practice is to encrypt the private key on disk.

At this point, the astute reader will be wondering how this makes the situation any better. We've encrypted the private key, but now we need to protect the key to encrypt it under. Of course, we could encrypt that key, but then we'd need to protect the new encryption key, and so on. So, encryption alone isn't the solution to the problem.

Of course, we could force the user to memorize the key, but memorizing 128 random bytes is really a lot of work and most users won't accept that job. The usual approach is to use a password or passphrase to generate the encryption key that we use to encrypt the private key. Passwords are easily memorizable and we have a special key derivation function that we use to generate the key from the password.

Password-Based Encryption

There are a large number of ways to transform passphrases into encryption keys. However, the strong ones share a number of common features. The reason that these functions must be different from ordinary key derivation functions is that text usually has a very low *entropy*. That is to say that given part of a word or a phrase, the rest isn't completely unpredictable. (By contrast, cryptographic keys usually are constructed so that knowing part of a key provides no information about the rest of the key.) Several techniques have been designed to counter this problem.

Users are encouraged to choose longer passphrases than the keys to be derived from them. For instance, a 128-bit key can be represented in 16 characters, but passphrases are often 50 or more characters. This allows them to be both memorable and somewhat secure. Nevertheless, passphrases are probably more guessable than keys, particularly since users often choose short passwords. In order to provide some protection even if poor passwords are chosen, password-based key derivation functions typically use two techniques called *salting* and *iteration*.

Salting includes a public random value as part of the input to the key derivation function. This value is called a *salt*. The salt is simply stored with the key file. Even if two users use the same password, they won't have the same encryption key because they will be using different salt values. This prevents two attacks. First, the attacker might make a table of all common passwords and then could break a password merely by searching that table. Second, the attacker could collect a series of password files and search them all in parallel, thus doing the key derivation stage only once. Neither of these attacks works when salting is used.

Iteration slows down the key derivation function. Password-based key derivation functions are designed to be very slow, in order to make search of the password space expensive. Users won't notice if it takes a half a second to decrypt their private key, but this is a substantial burden if each of a hundred million passwords takes a half a second to check. Typical functions are designed with a basic primitive which can be applied (iterated) an arbitrary number of times, with the output of one stage being used as the input to the next stage. Each iteration takes some time, slowing down the entire process. Again, the iteration count is stored with the encrypted file.

The best-known algorithm for password-based encryption is RSA's PKCS #5 [RSA1993d], which included both the salt and iteration features. Unfortunately, PKCS #5 could generate keys of 160 bits at most, making it useless for 3DES. When Microsoft designed the PFX key storage standard (now PKCS #12 [RSA1999a]), they designed a new function that could generate arbitrary length keys. RSA has since updated PKCS #5 to support arbitrary length keys [RSA1999b].

Figure 5.3 shows a diagram of the salting and iteration process as used in PKCS #5 version 1. The process proceeds in two stages. First, the concatenated password and salt are hashed to produce T_1. This value is hashed repeatedly (*count* − 1 times) to produce T_n, which is the output of the function. T_n is simply equal to $Hash(T_{n-1})$. Obviously this transform cannot produce an output longer than the hash function, which is why it is not used to generate keys longer than the 160-bit output of SHA-1. The PKCS #12 and PKCS #5 version 2 transforms are similar in spirit but not identical and can produce keys of arbitrary length.

Storageless Key Recovery

Imagine that you want to run SSL on a device without any user-specific permanent storage whatsoever. There's no place to store a private key on disk, encrypted or otherwise. It's nevertheless possible for such a device to have a private key if we can derive the private key from the passphrase.

The simplest case is when using discrete log systems such as DH or DSA. Because the private key X is an arbitrary number, it's possible to simply generate it from the passphrase using the password-based KDFs we've just discussed. The group parameters

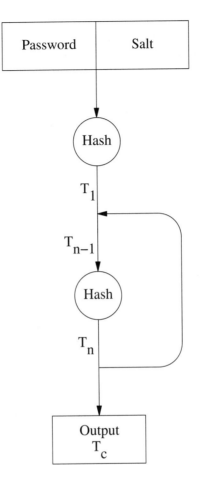

Figure 5.3 PKCS #5 transform

g, p, and q can be common to all device users and thus burned into permanent storage on the device when it's created.

This technique is less convenient for systems such as RSA where the key generation process is expensive, but it's nevertheless possible to use a passphrase to seed the PRNG that is used to generate the RSA key. As long as the passphrase is the same, the same RSA key will be generated each time.

This approach is primarily useful in situations in which a given user might use any number of different machines at any given time, such as kiosk machines or shared terminals. Because certificates can be stored in the clear on the network, the user can simply walk up to the machine and enter his passphrase.

Hardware Cryptography

Another approach to storing private keys is to use a hardware device. The device contains both permanent storage for the private key and some sort of processor capable of doing cryptographic computations. The private key is generated on the device, all private key operations are done on the device, and the private key never comes off the device.

Hardware crypto devices come in two basic flavors, permanent and removable. Permanent devices are intended to stay connected to the machine at all times, either as a card on the system bus or plugged into the back via a SCSI, parallel, or other interface. Removable devices typically are packaged as PCMCIA cards or smartcards (devices about the size of a credit card). A removable device has the obvious advantage that it can be taken away from the machine and locked up for extra security.

Either sort of device can be stolen, so the private keys are usually protected by a password or a *personal identification number* (PIN). The device won't operate correctly unless the user *logs in* with the correct PIN. Sometimes the private key is encrypted as it would be on disk and sometimes the device is simply programmed to forbid using the key unless the PIN is entered. Furthermore, the devices are typically designed to *zeroize* after some (small) number of incorrect attempts. Zeroizing means that they erase all of their sensitive internal state.

For additional security, hardware devices often incorporate a tamper resistance feature. The device is designed to detect attempts to open the case and directly access the hardware. If such an attempt is detected, the device zeroizes its memory. The idea is that even physical possession of the device is useless without the appropriate PIN. FIPS-140-1 [NIST1994b] provides standards for this sort of tamper resistance.

So, hardware devices have two primary advantages over software key files: Because the card zeroizes after some number of failed login attempts, the attacker cannot simply try all possible PINs as he can with the key file, so it's not necessary to choose a really good PIN. (This is good, because choosing good PINs is difficult.)

Second, even if the attacker does get the PIN, he needs physical access to the device. Say the attacker breaks into your server machine and guesses the PIN, but your key is in hardware. He can use the server to decrypt traffic, but once you discover the compromise, you can remove the device or change the PIN and the attack is over. With software, the attacker would have the private key and you would have to generate a completely new key pair.

Fixed devices usually are packaged (and marketed) as *cryptographic accelerators*. They're intended to be able to perform cryptographic operations faster than the host computer. As a consequence, they typically provide both increased security and a performance boost. By contrast, removable devices tend to be very slow (on the order of a few RSA operations per second) and therefore not really usable in a server environment, though they can provide convenient security and packaging for client-side keying material.

Some cryptographic accelerators have both a fixed and removable component. This provides added security because the device cannot be used without the removable key but is as fast as an ordinary fixed device.

Passphrase Entry

You may have noticed by now that both encrypted disk files and hardware devices usually require the operator to enter a passphrase in order to start the server. This is the weak link in the security of the entire system. It's extremely desirable for server systems to be able to restart cleanly without user intervention, but the requirement to enter passphrases to start the secure server makes this impossible.

There are only two known workable approaches: compromise security or compromise unattended reboot. Compromising unattended reboot is easy: require the operator to enter a passphrase to start the server. This means that the machine may restart correctly but an operator is needed on site to start the secure server portions.

Compromising security is similarly easy. You simply place the passphrase somewhere in the system startup scripts and arrange for it to be passed to the server when the server is started. The obvious disadvantage here is that anyone (for instance the administrator or attackers) who can read that file can read the password. Typically, such files are set to have very restrictive permissions, but most operating systems let the administrator read any file.

There's no known way to work around these two choices. Your organization simply has to choose one and accept the consequences.

Biometrics

Biometric authentication measures such as fingerprint identification and retinal scans are often used as secure access control measures. Although there is some doubt as to whether they can be securely implemented, they are nevertheless fairly widely used for access to secure environments and computers.

However, biometrics are singularly inappropriate for protecting private keying material. The measures we've talked about so far all depend on encrypting the private key based on some piece of data the user inputs. This piece of data must be identical each time because it is used to create an encryption key and encryption algorithms are specifically designed so that tiny errors in the key cause large errors in decryption.

However, biometrics cannot be easily used for this purpose because the characteristic being measured is not identical every time. Therefore, it's difficult if not impossible to recreate the same encryption key from the biometric each time. Biometric systems therefore have to keep the key in the clear and simply use the biometric to control access. This is inferior if the device containing the key is ever compromised, because the attacker doesn't need to decrypt the key. If the key is stored on disk somewhere, this is catastrophic.

There are two exceptions to this general rule. First, if the key is stored in trusted tamper-resistant hardware, then a biometric is safe because the hardware will zeroize the key before allowing it to be recovered. This requires having a lot of faith in your tamper resistance! Second, if a passphrase is used in conjunction with a biometric, then the key can still be encrypted using the passphrase and biometrics can be used as a secondary piece of access control. In this case, biometrics add valuable security.

Bottom Line

Understanding your threat model is critical to understanding which technique to use. For instance, if you have strong physical security for your system, you may not need to use as strong security to protect the keys. By contrast, if you're worried that your machine will be stolen or accessed by an unauthorized user, it's critical to protect the keys in hardware in order to limit the cost of compromise. This section gives you the information to evaluate various techniques, but you must choose the one that fits your security model.

5.12   Random Number Generation

The security of an SSL implementation depends completely on the quality of the random numbers it generates. Moreover, both the client and the server need to have strong random number generation. Exactly what is meant by "strong" random numbers isn't that obvious, but it's fairly obvious what it doesn't mean: The "random" number generators that most programming languages provide don't do the job. Special tools are required.

There are two general approaches to generating random data: you can have true randomness provided by some random or nearly random physical process, or you can have pseudo-randomness, which uses some algorithm to produce a stream of random-seeming numbers. In general, good hardware random number generators aren't available on most machines, so programmers settle for algorithmic *pseudo-random number generators* (PRNGs).

Whatever strategy we choose, we want to have at least the following properties.

The stream should be unbiased. The number of zero and one bit should be on average equal.

Output should be decorrelated. Knowing the value of the output of some section of the byte stream should not help you know the value of any other section.

Pseudo-Random Number Generators

The general idea with a PRNG is that you have some function that produces a stream of unpredictable bytes. In theory, this stream should be indistinguishable from a stream of bytes generated by a hardware device, such as flipping a coin.

Of course, this isn't the case because all PRNGs will eventually repeat the stream of bytes. The output of a PRNG is a function of the PRNG's internal state. Because their internal state can be no larger than the memory of the computer they are running on, they must repeat after outputting at most that many outputs. In practice, the internal state of the PRNG merely needs to be sufficiently large that an essentially infinite number of bytes can be generated without the state repeating. 256 bits of internal state is easily plenty to achieve this goal.

Typically, PRNGs are based on digest or encryption algorithms. A good example is described in [Kelsey1999]. There are a number of well-known PRNGs available, and we won't discuss the details here. However, they all have one thing in common—they need to be *seeded* with some amount of secret data. That data is used to set up their internal state. Knowing the seed data amounts to the same thing as knowing the internal state of the PRNG and allows the attacker to predict the bytestream completely. The major problem with using a PRNG is to seed it correctly.

In general, PRNGs are constructed so that they can be seeded with a large amount of low-quality random data and they will *distill* the randomness out of it. For instance, consider some data like the price of a stock from day to day. If the stock is at 85 on Monday, it's very likely that it will be somewhere between 80 and 90 on Tuesday, so the 10s digit isn't that random, but the 1s place is somewhat random and the fractions place is very random. A good PRNG can be seeded with this sort of data and collect all the good randomness out. This makes the job of collecting seed data somewhat easier.

A typical strategy for collecting seed data is to look at some fairly volatile piece of system state, such as network activity, the process table, or the screen, and distill that input into strong randomness. On an active system, this is probably good enough for generating keys to protect single sessions. Several operating systems (Windows 2000, *BSD, and Linux, at least) provide a kernel device that collects system events to continuously seed a PRNG in the background.

For high-security applications, such as private key generation, the implementations often require user input and measure the time between keystrokes or mouse movements. RFC 1750 [Eastlake1994] provides some guidance on collecting seed data.

Although most SSL implementations provide some way of seeding their PRNG from system data, they usually expect the application to provide most of the seed data and provide their own seeds only as a last-ditch effort. Even if you're using a toolkit, you may very well have to seed the PRNG yourself.

It's critical to note that a strong PRNG produces random-looking output even if it's poorly seeded. There are a number of statistical tests that are of some use in determining whether the PRNG you are using is strong. They are of little use in determining whether it has been well seeded.

Hardware Random Number Generators

The other popular strategy is to use a hardware source of randomness. Certain physical devices seem to act randomly at the quantum mechanical level, and this can be used to produce random data. The most obvious example is radioactive decay, which produces a steady stream of signals at random (but predictable on average) intervals. The time between signals (or their intensity over a given time window) can be used to produce random numbers.

Although radioactive decay is random, it's not unbiased, because the output clusters around a mean value. Some processing is usually needed to make sure that the output is unbiased.

Imagine that you have a random number generator that is random but biased in a simple way, such as an unbalanced coin that returns 60% heads and 40% tails. John von Neumann [Neumann1951] proposed a simple way to unbias it. Collect the output in pairs. Any pair that is the same (e.g., {heads, heads} or {tails, tails}) throw away. Any pair that is different, output the first one (e.g., {heads, tails} becomes heads.) The choice of first or second is arbitrary. It's easy to convince yourself that even if the generator is biased, this trick produces a balanced stream of output, because the probability of the sequence {heads, tails} is the same as the probability of the sequence {tails, heads}.

The easiest way to do this is simply to use the output of a hardware random number generator to seed a PRNG. This overcomes the bias problem as well as ensuring that you don't have to wait for the hardware device to do its thing whenever you want random data.

Recently, Intel Corporation added a hardware-based random number generation feature to their Pentium III processors. The RNG works largely as described above. A hardware random number device based on thermal noise is built into the chip. The data is post-processed through a mixing function based on SHA-1. Initial evaluations [Kocher1999] indicate that the system is secure, provided, of course, that the machine running it has not been compromised by an attacker who is forging RNG output.

5.13   Certificate Chain Verification

We've already established that an unverifiable certificate is little better than no certificate at all. However, merely being able to construct a certificate chain to some root isn't enough to verify a certificate. A number of other checks are required in order to be sure that you're communicating with the entity you think you're communicating with.

Server Identity

As we discussed earlier, the certificate presented by the server must contain an identity which is somehow connected to the expected identity of the server. The expected identity can't be carried over the wire, but must already be known to the client at the time the connection is initiated.

In most cases, when a client wants to connect to an SSL server, the destination is specified by a DNS domain name (see [Mockapetris1987a, Mockapetris1987b]) such as foo.example.com or by a *Uniform Resource Locator* (URL) [Berners–Lee1994] that contains a domain name. Thus, the expected identity of the server is the domain name and that must match the identity in the certificate.

Unfortunately, the *distinguished names* (DNs) in certificates aren't really that compatible with domain names. Recall from Chapter 1 that distinguished names are structured as a series of attribute-value pairs whereas domain names are essentially a single string. Moreover, there's no DN attribute for domain names. As a consequence, most CAs use the Common Name attribute to represent the domain name. This approach requires both client and server to be aware of the convention to work correctly.

If you're using X509v3 certificates, which allow extensions, there is another approach. Version 3 certificates can contain a subjectAltName extension which contains alternate name forms for the subject of the certificate. One such form is the dNSName, which is used to represent a domain name. It's permissible to leave the subject DN field blank and use only the subjectAltName to convey identity.

It's important to note that we're not using the server's IP address to denote its identity. The reason for this is that usually the client doesn't get the IP address from a trusted source. Rather, the domain name is trusted but the IP address is looked up using the DNS (a process called *name resolution*), which is easily compromised, as described in [Bellovin1995]. Thus, you can't safely compare the IP address to the IP address in the certificate.

Unfortunately, the original BSD sockets API required that clients specify which host to connect to using the IP address (forcing them to do name resolution themselves). Many SSL APIs mimic this behavior. Thus, because the SSL implementation doesn't know the domain name, it can't check it against the certificate and this check must therefore be done at the application layer. Figure 5.4 provides an example of this procedure using PureTLS. We'll talk more about server identity checking in Chapter 7 when we discuss the design of secure protocols.

```
public static SSLSocket connect(SSLContext ctx,String host,int port)
  throws IOException {
  // Connect to the remote host
  InetAddress hostAddr=InetAddress.getByName(host);
  SSLSocket s=new SSLSocket(ctx,hostAddr,port);

  // Check the certificate chain
  Vector certChain=s.getCertificateChain();

  // Length check
  if(certChain.size()>2)
   throw new IOException("Certificate chain too long");

  // Hostname check (using Common Name)
  Certificate cert=(Certificate)certChain.lastElement();
  String commonName=dnToCommonName(cert.getSubjectName());
  if(!commonName.equals(host))
   throw new IOException("Host name does not match commonName");

  return s;
 }
```

Figure 5.4 Java SSL identity checking example

Client Identity

Client identity obviously needs to be verified only when client authentication is used. Otherwise the client is completely anonymous. SSL doesn't really have anything to say about client identities. The application layer is expected to know how to interpret them. That said, the rest of the discussion of certificate chain verification holds as much for client certificate chains as for servers.

Choose Your Roots

All verified certificate chains must eventually terminate in a *root* certificate. This root certificate is configured into the application either by the application developer or by the user (or his system administrator.) For instance, most popular browsers come with upwards of 25 root certificates configured into the application.

These roots must be trusted to accurately certify the identity of the customers whose certificates they sign. If they don't, then the system becomes untrustworthy. For instance if a root provides an attacker with a certificate bearing Alice's name, then the attacker can impersonate Alice when you attempt to make a connection to his server.

In order to evaluate whether a root is acceptable, you need to evaluate the care with which they authenticate users (do they require positive physical ID, etc.) and the care with which they protect their keys. Neither Netscape nor Microsoft has published the rules that they use to determine which roots are compiled into their browsers. However, both Netscape and Microsoft allow the user to install their own roots. This is typically done by having the user dereference a Web page with a specific content type labelling it as a root certificate. Unless carefully handled, this practice represents a security vulnerability. The roots must be obtained from a trusted location over a trusted link or an attacker can convince the user to install a fake root. One common approach is to distribute a root *fingerprint*—a digest of the root key—offline and then allow the user to check that against the root when installing it.

Certificate Chain Depth

For management reasons, it's often convenient to use certificate chains that contain more than one certificate. This allows for distributed certification. For instance, imagine that Widgets, Inc. wants to issue certificates to all of its 20,000 employees at ten different locations. It might be convenient to have each location issue its own certificates.

One way to do this is to have a single root certificate for all Widgets certificates. That root would then sign the certificates for each location's CA. The location CA would then sign certificates for employees. Figure 5.5 shows a certificate hierarchy that uses this model.

In this example the Widgets Root CA certifies two location CAs, one for the Palo Alto office and one for the Seattle office. Each office has two employees, who are certified by their local CAs. Alice and Bob both work in Palo Alto and are certified by the Palo Alto CA. Charlie and Dave both work in Seattle and are certified by the Seattle CA.

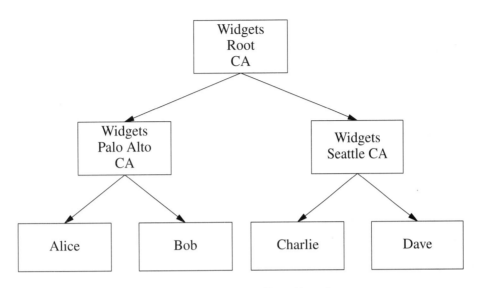

Figure 5.5 A sample certificate hierarchy

Realize that we now need to distinguish between two different classes of entities: those whom we trust to vouch for others and those whom we do not. For instance, in the above example, the certificate for the Widgets Palo Alto CA means "The Root CA asserts that this key belongs to the Widgets Palo Alto CA and this CA may in turn issue certificates." However, the certificate for Alice means "The Root CA asserts that this key belongs to Alice." The Widgets Palo Alto CA is trusted to sign certificates, but Alice is not. If Alice were allowed to sign certificates, she could create herself the certificate chain shown in Figure 5.6 and impersonate Bob.

The distinction between the two types of certificates can be made either implicitly or explicitly. Before X.509v3 certificates, the only real choice was to make it implicitly by controlling the *depth* of the certificate chain. That is to say, they would declare that certificate chains from their roots would be no more than *n* certificates long. In the current example, *n* would be 2: the location CA (signed by the root), and the user.

The primary problem with this approach is that it doesn't allow implementations to follow a single global policy. One CA might allow a depth of 2 and one might allow a depth of 1. Setting one's implementation's maximum depth to 2 allows impersonation attacks by individuals certified by the second CA, and setting it to 1 makes it impossible to verify certificate chains issued by the first CA. In practice, nearly all CAs use only one level deep certificate chains, and it's easy to add the next-level CAs as roots for those CAs who use longer certificate chains.

The newer approach is to use X.509v3 certificate extensions to indicate whether a certificate corresponds to a CA or not. In particular, PKIX (the IETF X.509 certificate profile described in [Housley1999a]) requires that the Basic Constraints extension must be present in all CA certificates. The Basic Constraints extension specifies whether or not a certificate belongs to a CA and how deep the certificate chain may extend from that path.

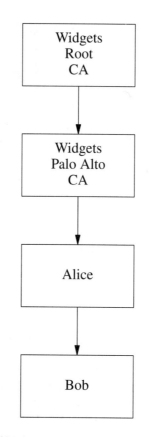

Figure 5.6 Impersonation by extending the hierarchy

Unfortunately, many currently available certificates and CAs do not follow PKIX and there are a large number of legacy certificates that don't. Consequently, if you have a closed system, you should try to use Basic Constraints, but otherwise you're pretty much stuck using hard-coded length constraints. Software that follows PKIX will reject otherwise legitimate CAs because they don't have Basic Constraints.

Key Usage Extensions

The X.509 key usage extensions restrict the purposes for which a key may be used. X.509 defines 8 key usage values that are combined into a bitmask of allowed operations. The values are: digitalSignature, nonRepudiation, keyEncipherment, dataEncipherment, keyAgreement, keyCertSign, cRLSign, encipherOnly, decipherOnly. No browser requires the keyUsage extension to be present but Netscape and Microsoft both check them if they are. Figure 5.7 shows the required bits for the various types of certificate for each type of operation.

Usage	Netscape	Microsoft
SSL Server	keyEncipherment	keyEncipherment
SSL Client	digitalSignature	keyEncipherment
Certificate Signing	keyCertSign	keyCertSign

Figure 5.7 Use of X.509 extensions

Note that Microsoft and Netscape expect different bits to be set to indicate that client authentication is permitted. The confusion as to what bit to use for client authentication derives from the fact that SSL client authentication involves signing a string that the client never sees. Arguably, the client's key is being used to authenticate the key exchange, so keyEncipherment is more appropriate. Netscape took the natural approach and used digitalSignature.

To add to the confusion, Netscape also defined their own certificate usage extension: netscape-cert-type. Documentation of Netscape's certificate practices can be found at [Netscape1995a]. The netscape-cert-type extension is a bit string. The relevant values are SSL Client (bit 0), SSL Server (bit 1), and SSL CA (bit 5). There are several other values that are used for S/MIME certificates and for something Netscape calls *object signing*. It's not clear how to behave if both extensions are present and disagree. In practice, however, this is unlikely to happen.

Certificates for root CAs are compiled into the browser. Certificates for intermediate CAs should contain basicConstraints. Netscape will also accept certificates with one of the CA bits in netscape-cert-type set as an intermediate CA. Many other implementations, including older versions of OpenSSL, are far less picky and will take any certificate as a CA provided they can construct a chain. As a rule, modern implementations should either manually limit certificate chain length or insist on some indication in the certificate that the certified entity is a CA.

Not all certificates contain the keyUsage extension. Most browsers will accept such certificates for either client or server but not for an intermediate CA.

Other Certificate Extensions

Netscape also defined a number of other certificate extensions, as shown in Figure 5.8. These extensions are described in [Netscape1999a]. Most of these extensions are URLs that the verifier can dereference to get information about the certificate, such as the policy under which it was issued and its revocation status. These aren't that widely used because revocation is actually quite uncommon. There is also a netscape-ssl-server-name extension. This field can be used instead of the Common Name to identify the server to which the certificate belongs. Thus, there are at least three ways to put the server's name into a certificate, the Common Name, the subjectAltName extension, and the netscape-ssl-server-name extension. In general, you should avoid using the netscape-ssl-server-name since it's completely nonstandard. Instead, use the Common Name for maximum compatibility or the subjectAltName for newly designed systems.

Extension	Purpose
netscape-base-url	The base for all URLs in the certificate—allows the other URLs to be shorter.
netscape-revocation-url	Contains a pointer to a URL that will return revocation information.
netscape-ca-revocation-url	Used to check revocation status of CA certificates.
netscape-cert-renewal-url	The URL that the certificate owner can use to renew the certificate.
netscape-ca-policy-url	The policy under which the certificate was issued, in text form.
netscape-ssl-server-name	The name of the SSL server.
netscape-comment	A comment to be displayed to the user.

Figure 5.8 Other Netscape certificate extensions

5.14 Partial Compromise

The security of SSL is completely dependent on the cipher suites used. Each cipher suite specifies four algorithms: a digital signature algorithm, a key establishment algorithm, a data encryption algorithm, and a message digest algorithm. Although these algorithms are not orthogonally specified, in general there are multiple choices for each type of algorithm and these choices vary in strength. Moreover, for both digital signature and key establishment algorithms, multiple key sizes are possible, and each key size represents a different security level. It's quite likely that one algorithm will be broken while the others remain secure. This section considers the effect on the security of the overall system of such a compromise.

When we talk about algorithm strength, we need to consider two factors. First, we can place an upper bound on the strength of an algorithm based on the best known attack against that algorithm. By that metric, RC2-40, RC4-40, DES, and RSA, DH, and DSS with 512-bit keys are already dangerously weak. That is to say that with a plausible amount of effort, an attacker might be able to recover a single key for such an algorithm.

The second factor is the possibility that an algorithm might be completely broken sometime in the future. That is to say, it might become possible to recover an arbitrary number of keys, regardless of key length, with a trivial amount of effort. This has happened to other algorithms. Most of the ciphers used in SSL have undergone fairly extensive analysis, so it's widely believed that we have some idea of their security properties. Nevertheless, the possibility that an algorithm might be catastrophically broken remains as a worst-case scenario.

Digital Signature Algorithms

SSL uses digital signatures for three purposes:

1. To authenticate certificates.
2. To sign ephemeral keys.
3. To sign CertificateVerify messages for client authentication.

Total compromise of a digital signature algorithm compromises all of these uses and renders the protocol completely vulnerable to active attack. The situation here is worse than compromise of a single-server private key, because compromise of a signature algorithm means that all certificates signed with that algorithm are also vulnerable. This means that any SSL connection where one accepts the compromised algorithm is subject to active attack.

Partial compromise of an algorithm is also possible. In some sense this has already happened with RSA and DSS keys of 512 bits or less, since recovering such keys is within the current capabilities of a wealthy and dedicated attacker. The effect of such a compromise depends on which key is compromised.

> Note that DSA keys can also be compromised due to incorrect usage. DSA computations require the generation of a random quantity k for each signature. This number must be kept secret. If it is revealed, or simply not randomly generated, then the DSA key can be totally compromised.

Compromise of a CA key leads to total compromise of all agents who trust that CA. Although the individual private keys corresponding to the certificates that the CA has issued are still safe, this is irrelevant because the attacker can mount an active attack and impersonate any client or server merely by signing himself a certificate with the appropriate CA key.

Compromise of a server's key allows that server to be actively attacked. We've already covered this situation previously in this chapter.

Compromise of a client's key allows the attacker to pose as the client. Note that this does *not* permit the attacker to take over connections that the client creates, but it does permit him to initiate his own connections and client authenticate as the client.

Key Establishment Algorithms

Total compromise of a key establishment algorithm means that the attacker can recover the master_secret for any connection encrypted with that algorithm and can thus mount any of the attacks described in Section 5.9. Similarly, if a key establishment key is compromised (even if the algorithm is strong), then the attacker can recover the master_secret for any session that uses a key established using that algorithm and can similarly mount any attack that involves knowing the master_secret. This is particularly bad when the key is a static key because that means that all traffic to a given server can be broken. Figure 5.9 shows a summary of the consequences of the exposure of various kinds of keys.

Key Type	Effect of Compromise
CA	Attacker can impersonate to all agents that trust that CA.
Key Establishment (Static Keying)	Total compromise of all traffic to the server.
Server Authentication (Ephemeral Keying)	Attacker can mount an active attack on any session at handshake time.
Key Establishment (Ephemeral RSA)	Total compromise of all traffic exchanged with this key (typically hundreds of connections).
Key Establishment (Ephemeral DH)	Total compromise of all traffic exchanged with this key (typically one connection).
Client Signature Key	Attacker can impersonate this client.

Figure 5.9 Summary of effects of private key compromise

Revocation

As we saw in Chapter 1, when a private key is compromised, some CAs issue *Certificate Revocation Lists* (CRLs) which can be checked to see if a certificate has been revoked. The issue then becomes how to get the CRLs to the end users. Some protocols such as S/MIME allow CRLs to be carried along with certificates in messages. SSL does not allow this. Agents must get CRLs in some undefined way, which often means not at all. This makes compromise of keys particularly problematic for SSL.

After Goldber and Wagner [Goldberg1996] showed that Netscape's PRNG was weakly seeded, servers that had used that PRNG to generate their private keys all had to generate key pairs. Since CRLs were not widely deployed, this led to a large number of certificates for weak keys floating around with no good way to take them out of service other than waiting for them to expire.

Encryption Algorithms

The broadest range of algorithm strengths in SSL is found for the encryption algorithms. At the strong end of the spectrum, SSL supports 3DES which has an effective key length of 112 bits under the best-known attacks. Moreover, DES has undergone far more analysis than any other public cipher, so it seems unlikely that a new good attack against 3DES will be discovered. At the weak end, SSL supports 40-bit RC4, which is breakable by attackers with minimal resources—a few high-end PCs.

Imagine that the attacker manages to recover the encryption key for one side of the channel (say the client_write_key). Obviously he can now read all traffic encrypted with that key (traffic sent from the client to the server), but the scope of the attack is limited to the confidentiality of that data.

The client_write_key and server_write_key are independently derived from the master_secret, so having the client_write_key is insufficient to recover the server_write_key. Similarly, you can't backtrack from any given encryption key to the master_secret because the master_secret is much larger than the encryption keys it generates, so there is a many-to-one relationship between master_secret and encryption keys.

Similarly, confidentiality and message integrity are independently provided. Even if the attacker breaks the encryption, he can only mount a passive snooping attack. That is, he can recover the encrypted data. He can't use this information to forge traffic. For that, he has to break the MAC algorithm.

The effect of encryption algorithm compromise can be limited by occasionally rehandshaking. Even if no new key exchange is performed, just refreshing the random values will result in new encryption keys and force the attacker to re-attack the keys in order to read the new traffic. Note that because of CBC rollover, if you're using a block cipher it's important to rehandshake every 2^{32} blocks or so. Note that doing a new key exchange while rehandshaking adds little value, because most attacks on key exchange algorithms break the entire private key and not just one exchange.

Digest Algorithms

Compromise of a digest algorithm can mean a number of things. In general, because message digests destroy information (the message space is larger than the digest space), it is impossible to recover a message given the digest. However, it is not known to be impossible to produce a message that digests to a given value, although it is not known how to do so for any currently used digest. It would totally compromise such a digest if such a method were known.

The effect of being able to produce messages with a given digest would be very bad, because it would be possible to forge certificates. The attacker would start with a certificate that had a valid signature and attempt to generate a new certificate with a name and public key of his choice that digested to the same value.

Imagine that you have certificates signed with a safe digest but that both sides accept a broken digest for message protection. This does not necessarily lead to system compromise. First, SSL uses a combination of digests (both SHA-1 and MD5) to protect the handshake, so the attacker would need to have broken both in order to actively attack the handshake. Thus, you would probably still have confidentiality, even if no message integrity.

Moreover, HMAC is believed to be immune to some forms of compromise of the underlying digest [Krawczyk1996], so a partial compromise of a digest might not even lead to message integrity problems. For instance, collisions in a digest do not lead to a weakness in HMAC based on that digest.

One other case is worth mentioning. Because DSS signatures are computed over a SHA-1 digest only, if SHA-1 were broken, then any ephemeral key exchanges signed with DSS would be subject to active attack, because the attacker could forge the ServerKeyExchange. Figure 5.10 summarizes the effects of symmetric algorithm compromises.

Algorithm	Effect of Compromise
Any digest algorithm	Attacker can forge certificates for CAs using that algorithm.
SHA-1	Attacker can mount an active attack on anything protected with DSA.
Any encryption algorithm	Confidentiality lost. Integrity intact

Figure 5.10 Summary of effects of symmetric algorithm compromise

The Weakest Link Principle

Although SSL provides a check on the handshake to prevent man-in-the-middle downgrade attacks, this does not provide total protection. Because all security is based on the master_secret, no SSL implementation can ever be more secure than the weakest key establishment mechanism that it supports. Imagine that a client supports RSA but is willing to accept certificates signed with 512-bit RSA keys. It's also willing to accept certificates with longer keys, but it doesn't distinguish between them.

An attacker who can compromise a 512-bit RSA key can thus attack connections such a client makes even though the client would be willing to support a longer key, because the client will accept a handshake made with a weaker key. If the attacker can break a key establishment (or signature) algorithm that one of the parties accepts, he can mount a man-in-the-middle attack. Note that if client authentication is required, then the attacker *also* needs to be able to forge a signature that the server will accept.

This concern does not apply to encryption algorithms. The check in the handshake protects attackers from downgrading the handshake to support a weaker encryption algorithm as long as the key establishment mechanism is strong.

5.15 Known Attacks

Although no good attacks are known on SSL itself, a number of attacks are known that are effective against specific implementations. The next several sections describe these attacks and the required countermeasures.

Of particular note are *timing cryptanalysis* and the *million message attack*. Timing cryptanalysis was developed in 1996, after SSLv2 was widely deployed and after SSLv3 had been published. The million message attack was developed after SSLv3 had seen wide deployment and TLS had been published. Neither of these attacks is known to have been used against production servers, and it's not even known that they are practical, but conscientious implementors should at least be aware of them and the appropriate countermeasures.

5.16 Timing Cryptanalysis

In 1996, Paul Kocher publicized a technique which he called *timing cryptanalysis*. The technique relies on the observation that cryptographic operations take varying amounts of time to complete depending on the keys and data that are being used. The attack is actually a general technique which must be tailored for the target cryptosystem. Kocher provided examples for RSA, DH, and DSS in his original paper [Kocher1996b].

Attack Overview

Kocher emphasized timing attacks on public key cryptosystems in his paper. To mount the timing attack, the attacker needs to time the victim using his private key. With enough samples (roughly 2500 for a 1024-bit RSA key) you can recover the entire key. The details of the attack are out of the scope of this book. Suffice it to say that Kocher describes how to mount timing attacks on RSA, DH, and DSS.

Naturally, there is some noise in these measurements due to other system activity that interferes with timing. Kocher describes how to filter out noise in the measurements, but this technique requires more samples. To be maximally effective, the attacker should be able to get accurate times for the operations in question, with as little noise added as possible.

For maximal convenience, the attacker would be on the same machine as the victim and be able to time the victim directly. Such favorable circumstances are rarely available, but network protocols such as SSL often allow the attacker to determine the same information by observing network traffic.

Applicability

Recall that the server's private key is the most valuable key to attack. Is it potentially subject to timing analysis? Yes. Consider first the static RSA case. The time between the receipt of the ClientKeyExchange and the sending of the server's ChangeCipherSpec message is primarily divided between three primary tasks: decrypting the pre_master_secret, using the key derivation function to create the keys, and processing the client's Finished message.

Because the time taken by key derivation and Finished verification is mostly constant—and, more importantly, random with respect to the server's private key operation—it can be treated as noise and filtered out with enough samples. After these are factored out, the attacker has some idea of the time taken for the private key operation and can use this to attack the server's private key.

Ephemeral keying is similarly vulnerable. Although the attacker can't get enough samples to attack the ephemeral key, he can attack the static signing key. The time between the server's receipt of the ClientHello and sending of the ServerKeyExchange is dominated by computing the signature in the ServerKeyExchange message. If DH is being used and a new DH key is generated for every session, this provides a source of random noise, but this can be filtered out. Ephemeral RSA typically reuses the same ephemeral key for every session, making this mode particularly vulnerable.

Note that this attack does not require the attacker to be active. He can collect all this information merely by monitoring the victim's network connection. The attack can be mounted with fewer samples if the attacker mounts an active attack and can therefore choose the ciphertexts that the victim decrypts. The timing attack does require the attacker to know a fair number of details of the victim's SSL implementation, but these are fairly easy to come by, either by downloading the source (e.g., OpenSSL) or reverse engineering a binary.

No reports of hostile timing attacks being mounted against operational servers have ever been published. In any case, a number of SSL implementations contain countermeasures to make this attack difficult.

Countermeasures

The most obvious countermeasure is simply to slow down all operations by a random time. This is distasteful for performance reasons and it also doesn't work that well. Precisely because the noise is random, if the attacker collects enough samples the noise can be filtered out using basic signal processing techniques.

A second approach is to make all operations take constant time. This is a feasible approach in hardware but not really in software. And again, it has undesirable performance consequences.

The most popular approach is to use *blinding* techniques. The victim transforms the data to be signed (or decrypted) in such a way that the private key operation now operates on data unknown to the attacker. The victim then *unblinds* the result to obtain the original result that would have been obtained if no blinding had been used.

5.17   Million Message Attack

In 1998, Daniel Bleichenbacher published an attack which came to be known as the *million message attack* [Bleichenbacher1998]. The attack is actually an attack on RSA using PKCS #1, but all versions of SSL that use RSA are susceptible to it. The effect of this attack is to allow the attacker to recover the pre_master_secret, for a given session. We assume that the attacker has captured the ClientKeyExchange message containing the relevant encrypted pre_master_secret. He does this by sending a series of *chosen ciphertexts* to the server. That is, he generates a series of messages and observes the server's responses. From this, he can recover the pre_master_secret.

Attack Overview

The attack proceeds as follows. The attacker generates a series of messages based on the encrypted pre_master_secret and then chooses a series of integers s and computes

$$c' = cs^e \bmod n$$

where c is the encrypted pre_master_secret and e is the RSA public exponent.

The attacker then uses the victim's server as an *oracle*: he probes it with these messages and examines the responses. The attacker initiates a handshake with the server and sends c' in his ServerKeyExchange message. When the server decrypts c' he recovers a new message m'. m' can be shown mathematically to be ms where m is the original message. However, since the server doesn't send us m', this information isn't directly useful. However, it can still be used to attack m.

The key to the attack is that the attacker needs to be able to use the victim server as an oracle to get information about m'. He can use this information to get an accurate picture of m. The information that this attack uses is whether m is correctly PKCS #1 formatted.

Recall that PKCS #1 (described in Chapter 1) contains as the first 3 bytes a zero and a block type indicator. For properly formatted public key encrypted data, these bytes will be 00 02. About one in 2^{16} s values will yield an m' that is properly formatted. Figure 5.11 shows the entire padded pre_master_secret for a TLS connection, including the version number.

00	02	Random nonzero bytes	00	03	01	rest of pre_master_secret (46 bytes)

Figure 5.11 TLS Formatted pre_master_secret

The attack proceeds by finding a series of s values that produce PKCS #1 conforming plaintexts. These values can be used to narrow down the range of the original message m until it is completely determined. The exact details of how this is done are out of scope for this book, but suffice to say that around 2^{20} messages are required. (This number is around a million, hence the name *million message attack*.)

Applicability

The attack depends on the attacker being able to determine the difference between correctly and incorrectly formatted messages. Conveniently for the attacker, implementations written before this attack was discovered sent an alert (and then closed the connection) when they encountered incorrectly formatted messages. This makes it very easy to mount such an attack against such servers.

Note that SSL formatted pre_master_secret contains three pieces of verifiable information, not one. Aside from the PKCS #1 formatting, the pre_master_secret must be 48 bytes long and the first 2 bytes of the pre_master_secret must be the version number. The probability of a randomly chosen message getting all three of these right is less than 2^{-40}, so an implementation which rejected all of these errors *identically* would be impractical to attack in this fashion.

The key word in the above sentence is *identically*. Some implementations have been experimentally determined to reject all of these cases but to behave differently. Such implementations are still vulnerable to this attack.

There are no known instances of this attack being used against live servers, but Bleichenbacher says that he has tried it experimentally against one of his own servers and successfully recovered the pre_master_secret [Bleichenbacher1999].

Countermeasures

The most widely adopted countermeasure (and the one recommended in RFC-2246) is to make all three checks but not to send any alerts. If an error is detected, the implementation fills the pre_master_secret with random data and proceeds with the handshake as usual. The server will throw an alert when the client's Finished message is received and decrypts to garbage, but this is the behavior it would exhibit if m' were correctly formatted but the pre_master_secret were wrong.

Note that setting the pre_master_secret to a constant value will not work. The attacker could then use that value as the pre_master_secret and check to see if the Finished message is accepted or not.

A stronger fix is to replace PKCS #1 with a different padding algorithm that is sensitive to any damage to the plaintext. If the plaintext is padded in this way, then all of the probe messages used by this attack will automatically be rejected because they fail integrity checks. The most widely accepted example, *Optimal Asymmetric Encryption Padding* [Bellare1995] has been included in PKCS #1 version 2 [Kaliski1998a]. Unfortunately, OAEP padding is incompatible with PKCS #1 version 1 padding, so there's little incentive for SSL to move to PKCS #1 version 2.

5.18 Small-Subgroup Attack

Under certain specialized conditions, it is possible for an attacker to compromise a static Diffie-Hellman key that is used for a large number of key exchanges. This attack is generally called a *small-subgroup attack* [Lim1997].

Attack Overview

The attack arises out of an optimization that can be made to improve DH performance. Recall that the DH shared secret is computed by: $ZZ = Y^X mod\ p$. The smaller X, the faster this computation is. Choosing too small an X can compromise security (X should be about twice as long as the largest key you want to generate) but Xs a lot smaller than 1024-bits (a typical size for p) are still quite secure.

The choice recommended in the ANSI X9.42 standard [ANSI1998] is to create p such that $p = jq + 1$ where q is a large prime. X is then chosen to be smaller than q. g must be chosen so that it generates a group of order q.

Under these circumstances, the attacker can obtain information about X if he chooses his public key appropriately. He chooses his Y such that $Y \ll q$. If he can convince the victim to send him ZZ, he can obtain information about X. With enough samples, he can recover all of X. This may take as little as a hundred trials. It turns out that it is not necessary for the victim to return ZZ. Simply returning information about decryption success or failure is sufficient.

Applicability

Small subgroups are only an issue for a very small number of systems that use Diffie-Hellman keys for multiple transactions and also use small exponents (X). Because static DH is almost unused, this in practice means only those implementations that use ephemeral DH keys for multiple transactions. Of those, only some use small Xs.

Countermeasures

There are a number of countermeasures available. The simplest is to always use a new key for every transaction. This also has the advantage of providing perfect forward secrecy.

If you must use a static DH key, then there are still several countermeasures available. The simplest is to choose a long exponent, thus avoiding the vulnerability. Choosing p such that $p - 1 = 2qj$ reduces the risk so that only a single bit of the private key is leaked. This is sufficient for most purposes. As a special case, if $j = 1$ then p is referred to as a *strong prime*. A more complicated technique called *compatible cofactor exponentiation* is described in [Kaliski1998b].

5.19 Downgrade to Export

An attacker who can factor 512-bit RSA keys can downgrade a client/server pair into 512-bit ephemeral RSA mode even if both sides support 1024-bit RSA keys. The following attack was described in [Moeller1998]. The attack requires both sides to also support export mode and the attacker to be able to factor the server's ephemeral RSA key.

Attack Overview

The attack, shown in Figure 5.12, requires the attacker to act as a man-in-the-middle. He intercepts the client's ClientHello and removes all but the export ciphers. He transmits the modified ClientHello to the server which chooses an export cipher and sends a ServerKeyExchange containing his ephemeral RSA key. The handshake sniffs the ClientKeyExchange. Because he has factored the server's ephemeral RSA key, he can recover the master_secret. He then forges new Finished messages, one to the server reflecting the modified ClientHello and one to the client reflecting the original ClientHello. Once the handshake has completed, the server can simply sniff traffic. Because he has recovered the master_secret the connection is completely compromised.

Applicability

This attack requires the client and server to support strong cipher suites but be willing to negotiate export cipher suites. If both sides support only strong cipher suites, then the attack cannot succeed. If either side supports only export cipher suites, then they would

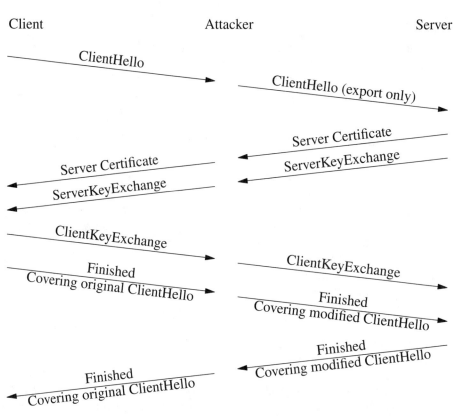

Figure 5.12 Downgrading to 512-bit ephemeral RSA

negotiate an export algorithm anyway. Moreover, the attacker must be able to factor the server's ephemeral RSA key during its lifetime. Thus, servers which frequently regenerate their ephemeral RSA keys will be safe. However, as factoring technology gets better, the safe lifetime becomes shorter.

Countermeasures

The safest countermeasure would be to fix the protocol so that the signature over the ServerKeyExchange covered more of the handshake, including the ClientHello. This would allow the client to detect that the attacker had modified the ClientHello. This change would also serve to strengthen SSL against similar attacks based on downgrading key exchange algorithms.

However, it's possible to protect against this attack without a protocol change. The ephemeral RSA cipher suites are doubly outdated. They have been replaced with the EXPORT_1024 cipher suites and strong ciphersuites can now be exported. Thus, there is no longer any real reason to support them, except for interoperability with old implementations.

In most cases, users can safely configure their browsers to support only strong cipher suites. Nearly all servers support 1024-bit RSA so this should not cause an inter-operability problem. Server administrators can protect themselves by frequently regenerating the ephemeral RSA so that it cannot be factored during its lifetime.

A Similar Attack

A similar attack is described in [Schneier1996b]. If the client supports both DH and RSA and the server supports DH, the attacker can tamper with the ServerHello to make the client believe that the server's ephemeral DH key is actually an RSA key. If the client is incautious, it will interpret the DH prime p as the RSA modulus and the DH base g as the RSA exponent. It's easy to recover the pre_master_secret from the resulting ClientKeyExchange.

For this attack to succeed the client would have to be quite careless. First, the server would likely use a DH modulus of longer than 512 bits, in which case the client should abort the handshake when it sees that the "modulus" is likely longer than 512 bits. This check is required by SSL to enforce export constraints. Second, the client would have to ignore the fact that the ServerKeyExchange contained more data than it should since it contains the server's public key Y. The moral of the story is that clients and servers should carefully check all protocol values.

5.20 Summary

This chapter has provided a description of the security properties of SSL. We start with some general guidelines for using SSL securely and then provide some detailed description of various potential attacks and how they are countered.

The master_secret *is everything.* Compromise of the master_secret compromises the entire protocol. An attacker who knows the master_secret can read traffic and forge messages at will.

Protect the server's private key. In the normal RSA mode and static DH mode, compromise of the server's private key leads to compromise of the master_secret. Even if ephemeral modes are used, an attacker who has the server's private key can pose as the server and attack traffic in real time.

Good randomness is essential. If either party doesn't use secure random number generation, the protocol is at risk. Good random numbers are especially important when generating long-term secrets such as private keys.

Just having a certificate isn't good enough. If you care about the identity of the other side, you must not only check that it has a valid certificate but that the certificate matches the expected identity of the other side.

Use good enough algorithms to protect your data. SSL supports a variety of algorithms with a variety of keylengths. Choose an algorithm such that the cost of breaking it is substantially higher than the value of your data.

There are no good known attacks on SSL. However, there have been a number of proposed attacks on certain implementations. Careful implementation can protect you from these.

6

SSL Performance

6.1   Introduction

This chapter discusses the performance properties of SSL. As with previous chapters, we divide the discussion into two primary parts. The first part discusses the performance properties of SSL in general terms and makes fairly broad observations about performance of various modes under various circumstances. The second part of the chapter covers the same territory in detail, using instrumented network traces and profiled implementations to show exactly where the time is going.

6.2   SSL Is Slow

The most common complaint that server administrators make about SSL is that it's slow. This criticism is not without some justice: Depending on the protocols being used, the server hardware, and the network environment, SSL connections can be anywhere between 2 and 100 times slower than ordinary TCP connections.

This performance cost translates directly into increased operational costs. Internet servers are usually heavily loaded even when insecure protocols are used. Computationally intensive security protocols necessarily mean that more server machines must be purchased and operated to maintain the same quality of service. This transition is particularly difficult when the original service ran on a single server machine. If security necessitates operation of multiple machines, this may mean arranging to share data between servers where this was previously unnecessary.

Unfortunately, some performance degradation is largely unavoidable. Cryptography is computationally expensive and the difference between simply writing data to the network and encrypting it before sending is usually nontrivial. However, it is often possible to minimize SSL's performance impact with careful systems design and configuration.

6.3   Performance Principles

Before discussing SSL performance, we'll first discuss some general principles of system performance, with a special emphasis on network protocols. This provides a background for understanding the contribution the various pieces of SSL make to the performance of the protocol as a whole.

Amdahl's Law

The most basic rule of performance tuning is Amdahl's Law, described in [Hennessey1996]. Roughly speaking, the speedup resulting from an optimization is equal to the improvement of the speedup multiplied by the fraction of the CPU time spent in the code sped up, as shown in Figure 6.1.

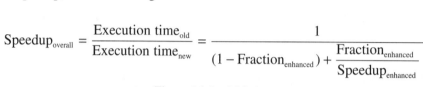

$$\text{Speedup}_{\text{overall}} = \frac{\text{Execution time}_{\text{old}}}{\text{Execution time}_{\text{new}}} = \frac{1}{(1 - \text{Fraction}_{\text{enhanced}}) + \dfrac{\text{Fraction}_{\text{enhanced}}}{\text{Speedup}_{\text{enhanced}}}}$$

Figure 6.1 Amdahl's law

Therefore, it is of crucial importance to determine which sections of the system consume the most time, because they represent prime targets for optimization. Once we have a picture of where the time is going, our strategy becomes clear: try to improve the performance of these sections of the system, either by making them run faster or using them less often.

As a corrolary, it should be clear that even very expensive operations aren't worth speeding up unless they also happen frequently. In the case of a network protocol, this means that we're primarily concerned with operations that happen with every transaction or protocol message. We'll ignore time consumed by system startup and shutdown, even though it may represent the equivalent of hundreds of transactions, because it's insignificant over the life of a server.

The 90/10 Rule

Amdahl's law wouldn't be very useful if all parts of a system consumed equal amounts of time. In such a system, we'd have to optimize a significant fraction of the system in order to see any improvement. This is very infrequently the case. Rather, most of a system's time is spent performing a few tasks.

A useful rule of thumb, the *90/10 rule* states that 90% of the execution time of a program is spent in 10% of the code. Combining the 90/10 rule with Amdahl's law, we can see that optimizing that section of the system would contribute greatly to the performance of the system. Focusing on on the other 90% is almost useless.

A particular case of this rule is what is termed a *bottleneck*. A bottleneck occurs when a system is performing a lot of different operations, but they all have to go through some central point or operation. Any time you see congestion before a certain point and free flow afterwards, suspect a bottleneck.

The Cost of I/O

Program performance tuning is normally accomplished with the aid of profilers (software that determines the amount of CPU time consumed by pieces of a program) and instrumented software. This allows the person tuning the code to identify sections of code that consume large amounts of CPU. Systems that perform extensive input/output (I/O) in general, and network protocols in particular, add another dimension to tuning: the cost of I/O. This must be balanced against the cost of CPU.

Consider the problem of transferring a file over a network between two computers. Under most circumstances, the factor that limits the performance of this transaction isn't the load placed on the CPU by the transmitting and receiving programs but rather the performance of the network between the two machines.

A 10 megabyte (10 MB) file takes roughly 3000 seconds to transmit over a 28.8 kilobit per second (Kb/s) transmission channel. Provided that the machines at either end meet some minimal standard of processing power (essentially any commercially available machine can do the job) the speed of transmission is constant because it's limited by the speed of the communications channel. In this case, then, it might be worth expending some CPU power to compress the data before (or during) transmission in order to reduce transmission time. Nearly any machine is fast enough to compress data at much faster than 28.8 Kb/s.

The laptop on which this was written can compress roughly 1 megabyte/second. Typical text files can be compressed by a factor of between two and four, so, compressing while encrypting will reduce the transmission time to between 750 and 1500 seconds, raising the effective data transmission rate to about 100 Kb/s—quite an improvement. Notice that the bottleneck is still the network: The machine can easily compress data faster than it can be transmitted over the network. In fact, compression is so much faster that nearly all commercial modems automatically compress the data as they transmit it.

Now, consider the same two machines connected by Fast Ethernet. Such a network can transmit roughly 100 megabits/s (Mb/s). In this case, then, the same file can be transmitted in about 1 second. By contrast, compressing the file before transmitting it will take roughly 10 seconds. In this case, then, we've made the situation far worse: the bottleneck is the CPU rather than the network.

As we can see, it is possible to trade off I/O bandwidth for CPU and vice versa. The optimal design and configuration for such a system depends on the relative amounts of CPU and I/O bandwidth available. If your system is deployed in a wide variety of environments, it may be advantageous to have it probe to see how much I/O and CPU are available before deciding which tradeoffs to make.

Latency versus Throughput

> *"Never underestimate the bandwidth of a station wagon full of tapes."*
> —*Dr. Warren Jackson*

Recall the problem of data transmission from the previous section. This time, let's consider a somewhat larger file of 100 MB. With compression, that file will take somewhere around three hours to transmit over a 28.8 Kb/s channel. With a file this large, it might be more efficient to simply write it onto a tape (this can be done in about ten minutes) and carry (or mail) it from machine to machine.

If we mail it, it will take somewhere between two and five days to move the file from machine to machine. This doesn't seem that good when compared to 3 hours, but imagine we have many such files to transmit. Over a modem, we can only move about eight files a day. If we mail them, we can move them as fast as we can copy them onto tape: around 100 files a day. True, the first file won't arrive for a few days, but they'll arrive at a steady (and fast) rate afterwards.

This example illustrates the difference between *latency* and *throughput*. Latency is the amount of time it takes to process a given transaction from beginning to end. Throughput is the number of total transactions you can maintain over a period of time. As you can see, they're not always related.

To make this difference more clear, suppose we Federal Express the tapes instead of mailing them. We've thus reduced latency to overnight. However, we haven't had any effect on throughput at all. By contrast, if we buy another machine to write tapes with, we can increase throughput without impacting latency.

With a little thought, it's easy to come up with examples of nearly any combination of throughput and latency. Figure 6.2 shows some examples:

	Low Latency	High Latency
Low Throughput	Modems	Pager
High Throughput	LANs	Satellite

Figure 6.2 Latency/throughput variations

Servers versus Clients

As a general rule, network systems have many clients and a few servers. In such systems, slowdown at the client side generally manifests as increased latency, whereas slowdown at the server side manifests as both increased latency and decreased throughput.

Recall our now familiar example of network file transmission, with one twist. Now we have a single server serving a large number of clients. The server has a T1 Internet connection (capable of carrying roughly 1.5 Mb/s) and each client is served by a

28.8 Kb/s modem. In such an environment, the server can service approximately 50 clients at a time and keep their network connections completely full. As before, each 1 MB file takes somewhere around 300 seconds to deliver. Thus, our throughput is roughly 1.5 Mb/s, and our latency is 300 seconds.

Now imagine that we double the number of clients. The server tries to service them all equally, so they now get only half as much data as before. This doubles the latency to 600 seconds. Notice, however, that although it takes twice as long to serve each client, we're serving twice as many clients at the same time, so throughput is unaffected.

Next, imagine that we halve the speed of each client's network connection to 14.4 Kb/s. Again, latency doubles to 600 seconds, but we can serve twice as many clients at this speed, so again throughput is unaffected.

Finally, consider the impact of halving the speed of the server's Internet connection. If we keep the number of clients the same, then we can serve them at only half the previous rate, doubling latency and halving throughput. This sort of effect applies equally when the bottleneck is CPU instead of I/O. Slow clients leave server resources available for other clients. Slow servers simply slow down the system as a whole.

Note that CPU and bandwidth aren't the only scarce resources for a server. Each client consumes some server resources, especially memory, so when the number of clients gets really large, the server can be overloaded just from trying to serve them all, even if there is plenty of CPU and bandwidth to go around.

6.4   Cryptography Is Expensive

In the first section of this chapter, we established that SSL was slow. In the second section, we introduced the concepts necessary to understand the factors that affect performance. In this section, we start to apply that general knowledge to SSL. As we hinted in the first section, the primary reason why SSL is slow is that cryptography, particularly the big number operations required for public key cryptography, is extremely CPU-intensive.

Profiling OpenSSL using gprof(1) shows this quite clearly. Consider a simple SSL connection using TLS_RSA_WITH_3DES_EDE_CBC_SHA. The vast majority of the time on both client and server is spent on cryptographic processing. In fact, the vast majority of time is spent on a single operation: RSA decryption.

The two phases of an SSL connection, handshake and data transfer, are worth considering separately. Handshake happens only once per connection, but is comparatively expensive. Each individual data record is comparatively cheap, but for connections involving large amounts of data the cost of the data transfer phase eventually dominates the cost of the handshake. Nevertheless, the cost of data transfer is mostly due to cryptography.

The costs of the handshake differ substantially between client and server, but the data transfer phase is symmetrical. Therefore, in the rest of this section, we'll first discuss the handshake for client and server and then the data transfer phase.

Server Handshake

The performance profile for the server side of the handshake is comparatively simple. Over half of the CPU time goes to a single operation: the RSA private decryption of the pre_master_secret. A distant second is the computation of the master_secret and the key schedules from the pre_master_secret.

Client Handshake

The situation on the client is far less straightforward. The client side operations are much faster than the server side operations. Thus, in many cases the client spends most of its time simply waiting for server messages.

Once this waiting time is factored out, we find that the two most expensive operations are verifying the server's certificates and encrypting the pre_master_secret. Although both of these involve RSA operations, these are public key operations and therefore are roughly an order of magnitude faster than the private key operations the server executes. As a consequence, the client's major computational burdens are two-fold: RSA computations and the ASN.1 decoding of the server's certificate.

The Bottleneck

Clearly, in this case, the server's performance limitations control the performance of the system as a whole. This situation would change somewhat if client authentication were used. In that case, the client would perform an RSA private key operation more or less equivalent to that performed by the server and this would become the dominant performance cost on the client. The server would incur almost no additional performance cost.

It's also worth noting that this particular division of labor really only applies to RSA. DSA operations are much more symmetrical between client and server, and we find that when DSS/DHE cipher suites are used, the computational load is similarly symmetrical between client and server.

However, in most production systems, the server is still the bottleneck. First, client authentication and DSS/DH are rarely used. More important, as we discussed previously, the server is accessed by many clients, whereas any client will have only a small number of connections open. Thus, even a very fast server will quickly achieve a load that slows it down below the speed of clients.

Data Transfer

In the data transfer phase, there are two relevant cryptographic operations, record encryption and the record MAC. Together, these account for the majority of the cost of data transfer. The relative importance of these depends on which precise algorithms are chosen and the implementation details. If a fast encryption algorithm (such as RC4) is chosen, then the HMAC will be the dominant cost. If a slow encryption algorithm such as 3DES is shown, then encryption and MACing will share the cost somewhat evenly. Record assembly and disassembly account for an insignificant amount of time.

6.5   Session Resumption

As we discussed in the previous section, the performance bottleneck in SSL handshakes is the public key crypto operations associated with the handshake itself. Most of these operations are associated with the exchange of the session key. The encryption and decryption of the master_secret are obviously directly related; however remember that the only need to verify the server's certificate is in order to use it for key exchange.

We can conclude from this that if we could do away with these operations, the handshake would be dramatically faster. As we discussed in Chapter 4, session resumption provides us with an opportunity to do exactly that. Because resumed sessions use the master_secret from a previous connection, we can omit the expensive public key computations.

As expected, this provides a dramatic performance improvement. In our test harness, using 512-bit RSA keys, we see a performance improvement of roughly a factor of 20 in the handshake. An even larger improvement would be observed with larger keys. More important, this improvement comes almost completely as a result of reduced load on the server. Consequently, in an environment where most sessions are resumed, we would expect to see a corresponding improvement in throughput.

Clearly, session resumption can provide a significant performance improvement. However, it's not appropriate in all cases. Rather, it's only appropriate when a reasonable number of clients will reconnect within some reasonable period of time.

The Cost of Session Resumption

The cost of session resumption is borne almost entirely by the server. As we indicated before, a client will only talk to some very small number of servers, so the cost of maintaining a cache is minimal. The server, however, needs to retain cache entries for a large number of clients, so the load is correspondingly greater.

Session resumption consumes two primary resources: memory to store the resumable sessions and CPU time to check the cache. Obviously, in an environment where resumption happens frequently, these resources have been well spent, but in an environment where sessions are never resumed, they're just waste.

The state for a resumable session requires somewhere on the order of 50–100 bytes in the session cache. This isn't a lot for any individual session, but in a server handling hundreds of transactions a minute, this could mean megabytes of data in an hour. Clearly, even if resumption pays off, it's worth limiting the size of the cache and timing out entries fairly frequently.

Accessing the cache takes time as well. The relevant issue is that the cache must be shared between multiple working threads or processes. This means that the cache must be locked, read, and then unlocked. Locking and unlocking are comparatively expensive operations. If the cache needs to be shared between processes, as with many UNIX servers, every read or write of the cache requires a context switch into the kernel. This is even more expensive. Again, if a cache entry is resumed, this time was negligible, but if sessions are never resumed, then the CPU time consumed was merely unnecessary overhead.

The moral of the story is that session resumption is nearly always worth doing on the client. On the server, however, it's only worth doing if there is a lot of repeat business within a fairly short period of time. Even in such situations, it's worth asking whether the protocol can be converted to simply leave those connections up rather than incurring even the minimal cost of a resumed handshake.

6.6   Handshake Algorithm and Key Choice

As we discussed in Section 6.4, the performance characteristics of an SSL connection depend substantially on the algorithms being used. In the handshake phase, this can dramatically affect the cost of the handshake, as well as changing the relative loads on the client and server.

RSA versus DSA

When deploying SSL systems, the choice of signature algorithm often depends on intellectual property or compatibility concerns. However, in cases where performance is the dominant concern, RSA is the algorithm of choice over DSS/DH. In general, RSA is *much* faster than DSA for verification and comparable for signature, as shown in Figure 6.3. However, this cost is paid primarily by the client, so it affects latency, not throughput.

Algorithm	Keysize	Signs/s	Verifys/s
RSA	512	342	3287
DSA	512	331	273
RSA	1024	62	1078
DSA	1024	112	94
RSA	2048	10	320
DSA	2048	34	27

Figure 6.3 Digital signature performance (Pentium II 400/OpenSSL)

However, the DSA cipher suites are nearly always run in ephemeral mode. This requires substantial extra work on both sides to generate, sign, and verify the ephemeral DH keys. This dramatically reduces throughput. In practice, DSA cipher suites tend to be between two and ten times slower than RSA cipher suites of comparable strength.

Fast or Strong, Choose One

The performance of public key algorithms declines dramatically with key size. RSA with 1024 bits is roughly four times slower than RSA with 512 bits. DSA performance is similarly reduced by longer keys. As a consequence, choosing your private key length is a compromise between security and handshake performance. As discussed in Chapter 1, 512 bits is almost certainly too short for valuable data. However, 768-bit keys are probably strong enough for most commercial transactions and are dramatically faster than 1024-bit keys.

Ephemeral RSA

Recall that when using RSA with a strong (>512) bit key and an export cipher, the standard requires you to use a 512-bit ephemeral RSA key. In essence, this adds a single 512-bit RSA operation to each side (a public one on the client side and a private one on the server side). This has some negative effect on throughput and latency.

Note that both sides must still perform all the operations they would have performed if ephemeral RSA were not being used. The slower these operations, the smaller the proportional effect will be of using ephemeral RSA. For 1024-bit keys, we expect to see between a 10% and 25% slowdown. Note that this is not a security/performance trade-off, as 512-bit ephemeral RSA is both weaker and slower than 1024-bit static RSA: 512-bit keys are much weaker than 1024-bit keys, and because the same 512-bit key is used for a large number of transactions, there is no compensating benefit of perfect forward secrecy.

6.7   Bulk Data Transfer

Algorithm Choice

Recall that cryptography consumes the bulk of the time in record processing. Unsurprisingly, the choice of MAC and encryption algorithms affects the performance of the system. In short, use RC4 for maximum speed and 3DES for maximum security. RC4 is about ten times faster than 3DES. Digest choice is less flexible as MD5 is being phased out. SHA-1 is fast enough in most real world scenarios, so it's a generally good choice. On modern systems, RC4 with SHA-1 is fast enough to saturate most networks.

Optimal Record Size

A surprising amount of the record computation is insensitive to the size of the data being transmitted. There is substantial fixed overhead, both from the cryptographic algorithms and from writing to the network. As a consequence, transmitting the data in small records results in bad performance. Up to a certain point, increasing the size of the record increases performance. On our test system, this point appears to be roughly 1024 bytes. Beyond this point, the advantage of using even larger blocks is small. If you're transferring bulk data, it pays to buffer it until you can encrypt fairly large records.

6.8   Basic SSL Performance Rules

Asymmetric algorithm choice. Use RSA.

Private key size. Use the shortest private keys with which you feel safe. 768 is good enough for most applications.

Symmetric algorithm choice. Use RC4 for best performance, 3DES for best security. Export versions compromise security without improving performance.

Digest algorithm choice. MD5 only improves performance about 40% over SHA-1. In most cases SHA-1 will be fast enough. Stick with SHA-1 for security.

Session resumption. Clients should always use session resumption. Servers should use it only if clients tend to reconnect within five to ten minutes.

Record size. Send data in the largest chunks possible.

6.9   The Story So Far

The general idea behind getting good performance is to perform as few operations as possible. This means minimizing the number of time-consuming operations and, whenever possible, making them faster. As we've seen, the time-consuming operations in SSL are mostly cryptographic. Session resumption allows us to remove a number of those operations and proper algorithm selection allows us to minimize the ones we still have to perform.

The first part of this chapter was intended to provide enough information to obtain good performance out of SSL as a server or client administrator. The rest of this chapter is geared toward the programmer and is intended to provide a more complete picture of the performance characteristics of SSL. We reexamine some of the material from the first part in more detail as well as discussing some of the fine points of the interaction of SSL with TCP.

6.10   Handshake Time Allocation

The next several sections provide detailed coverage of a number of different SSL handshakes. The data described in these sections was collected using a specially instrumented version of OpenSSL 0.9.4. The instrumentation records the time taken to generate and/or process each handshake message.

Test Environment

The test system is a 300 MHz Pentium running FreeBSD. The client and server programs are modified versions of the OpenSSL `s_client` and `s_server` programs. Both client and server are running on the same system, so network latency is insignificant. The instrumentation does not record the time taken to actually send and receive the network messages or to context switch between processes.

Serialization

As discussed in Chapters 3 and 4, the order of SSL messages is completely described by the standard. Moreover, at certain times the server must wait for a client message and vice versa. OpenSSL buffers network output for increased performance. On modern operating systems, network I/O requires a context switch to enter the kernel. This is expensive. Thus, it's often computationally cheaper to generate a number of messages and transmit them all at once. The traditional approach to buffering is to have a fixed size buffer and transmit the data when the buffer gets full. With SSL, it's also necessary to flush the buffer when transmitting the last message before waiting for a reply. Otherwise the implementations will deadlock.

Figure 6.4 shows this behavior in a simple RSA handshake (the same one we showed in Chapter 3). The ServerHello, Certificate and ServerHelloDone all have the same timestamp, meaning that they were transmitted to the network at the same time. Similarly, the client's ClientKeyExchange and ChangeCipherSpec were transmitted at the same time.

```
New TCP connection: speedy(3266) <-> romeo(4433)
 1  0.0456 (0.0456) C>S    Handshake       ClientHello
 2  0.0461 (0.0004) S>C    Handshake       ServerHello
 3  0.0461 (0.0000) S>C    Handshake       Certificate
 4  0.0461 (0.0000) S>C    Handshake       ServerHelloDone
 5  0.2766 (0.2304) C>S    Handshake       ClientKeyExchange
 6  0.2766 (0.0000) C>S    ChangeCipherSpec
 7  0.2766 (0.0000) C>S    Handshake       Finished
 8  0.2810 (0.0044) S>C    ChangeCipherSpec
 9  0.2810 (0.0000) S>C    Handshake       Finished
10  1.0560 (0.7749) C>S    application_data
11  6.3681 (5.3121) S>C    application_data
12  7.3495 (0.9813) C>S    Alert
Client FIN
Server FIN
```

Figure 6.4 Buffering of SSL handshake messages

However, when messages are buffered in this way, it's possible that one side is waiting for a message that has already been written by the other side, but is still in the output buffer. Thus, processing on the client and the server sometimes take place sequentially and sometimes in parallel, depending on whether the handshake messages completely fill the buffers or not. If the buffers fill, the messages will be sent immediately, in which case the host on the other side can process the message in parallel with the next message being generated. If the buffers don't fill, the messages will only be sent when the sending side stops to wait for a response, in which case the messages will be processed sequentially.

The version of OpenSSL used to generate these traces has had the buffer size increased from 1024 to 4096 bytes so that all handshake messages are processed sequentially. This makes the handshake traces much easier to read and allows us to show the CPU time used without the impact of context switching. The choice of 1024 bytes in OpenSSL is arbitrary and other implementations may use no buffering at all.

In some cases, this sort of buffering improves latency and in some circumstances it makes it worse. We'll discuss this issue in Section 6.23 when we discuss Nagle's algorithm.

6.11   Normal RSA Mode

The first mode that we'll be examining is the server-only RSA mode. Figure 6.5 shows the time allocation to process the various messages. Time allocated to client processing is in the left column and time allocated to server processing is in the right column. Indentation is used to indicate instrumentation of pieces of an operation. All times are in milliseconds. Thus, reading the server certificate consumed 8.11 ms. This included three verifies, each of which took about 2 ms.

In general, RSA operations come in two flavors: *private key operations* (digital signature and private key decryption) and *public key operations* (signature verification and public key encryption). This distinction is important in this context because private key operations are much slower than public key operations. However, all private key operations with a given key size take pretty much the same time, as do all public key operations with a given key size. We'll be using these terms throughout the discussion of RSA to avoid distinguishing between the various instances of each type of operation.

As we'd expect from the 90/10 rule and the discussion in Section 6.4, the vast majority of the CPU time is allocated to processing three messages: on the client side, the processing of the server's Certificate message and the generation of the ClientKeyExchange; on the server side, the processing of the client's ClientKeyExchange message. All the rest of the messages put together account for less than a millisecond of CPU time. We'll discuss each of the three important messages in turn.

> When we initially collected these traces, the majority of the time went to the creation of the ClientHello message. This was due to the one-time (on-demand) seeding of the OpenSSL PRNG. In reality, this is a startup cost and so we moved the seeding to a section of the code called before the handshake.

Certificate (Client)

Recall that the Certificate message contains the server's certificate chain. In order to process it, the client needs to parse and verify each certificate. Primarily this means performing RSA verifies. In this case the certificate chain is three certificates long, so three verifies are required. Each verify takes roughly 2 ms. The rest of the time goes mostly to ASN.1 parsing.

```
Client                 Server
0.07 Write client_hello
                       0.15 Read client_hello
                       0.07 Write server_hello
                       0.20 Write certificate
                       0.00 Write server_hello_done
0.05 Read server_hello
8.11 Read certificate
2.47   verify
1.95   verify
2.25   verify
0.00 Read server_hello_done
2.54 Write client_key_exchange
2.26   encrypt_premaster
0.15 Write finished
                       31.01 Read client_key_exchange
                       30.79   decrypt_premaster
                        0.00 Read finished
                        0.12 Write finished
0.00 Read finished

Client: 10.95       Server: 31.59
```

Figure 6.5 RSA server-only mode time allocation (ms)

This is an unusually long certificate chain. Normal certificate chains are one certificate long (a certificate signed directly by the root), requiring only a single verify. Under such circumstances the time taken to process this message is approximately the same as the ClientKeyExchange. Also, note that the limiting factor here is the length of the *CA* keys, not the server's key. The server's key isn't really processed in this stage.

As a performance optimization, it is possible to cache the results of certificate validation, thus saving the public key verification stage. This doesn't make sense when certificate chains are short because the number of server certificates one is likely to encounter is too large to be cached. However, when long chains are used, as in this handshake, it's often worth caching CA certificates.

> By default, s_client provides a callback to OpenSSL's certificate processing code. This callback outputs a lot of certificate debugging information to stderr. We had to disconnect this callback because the I/O was consuming significant amounts of CPU time and thus skewing the instrumentation results.

ClientKeyExchange (Client)

Recall from Chapter 4 that the ClientKeyExchange contains the pre_master_secret encrypted under the server's public key. The dominant operation here is this RSA encryption. Thus, the limiting factor is the length of the server's public key.

ClientKeyExchange (Server)

Unsurprisingly, the dominant operation here is the server's RSA decryption of the pre_master_secret, which takes up essentially all of the time allocated to this message. Note that the time this operation takes is directly related to the size of the server's RSA key. The longer the key, the longer the decryption takes. Note that this is a much slower operation than the encrypts and verifies performed by the client.

Note that because the decrypt is a server operation, it is the bottleneck in SSL throughput. The cost of the decrypt is dependent on the server's choice of key length, making the server's RSA key length the most important factor limiting performance in this mode.

6.12   RSA with Client Authentication

RSA with client authentication mode is basically normal RSA mode with some extra steps. From a performance perspective, one takes all the operations that were previously performed on the server and also performs them on the client and vice versa. As a consequence, client authentication mode substantially increases the load on the client but only slightly increases the load on the server. Figure 6.6 shows an instrumented client authentication trace. In this trace, and from now on, the operations that have changed from the previous trace will be rendered in bold.

All the operations we performed in normal mode still consume roughly the same amount of CPU time. The new time-consuming operations we've added are the client-side generation of the CertificateVerify message and the server-side verification of the client's Certificate and CertificateVerify message.

The CertificateVerify message consists of an RSA-signed message. The expensive stage here is, of course, the RSA signature. The comments in the previous section about the processing of the ClientKeyExchange apply here.

On the server side, the Certificate message is processed exactly as the client processes the server's Certificate message. That is to say that the dominant cost is the verification of the digital signatures. Finally, the server needs to process the CertificateVerify. This mainly consists of checking the client's digital signature, one public key operation.

Although the total computational cost of client authentication mode is roughly double that of server-only authentication, this cost is borne disproportionately by the client. In this case, the cost to the server is roughly 20% of that of the client. As a result, using client authentication substantially increases latency but has a much smaller effect on throughput. Overall, client authentication adds:

+1 Client-side RSA private key operation
+1 Server-side RSA public key operation
+1 Server-side RSA public key operation per client certificate

```
Client              Server
  0.07 Write client_hello
                    0.15 Read client_hello
                    0.17 Write server_hello
                    0.49 Write certificate
                    0.06 Write certificate_request
                    0.00 Write server_hello_done
  0.05 Read server_hello
  9.01 Read certificate
  2.44    verify
  1.94    verify
  2.24    verify
  0.18 Read certificate_request
  0.00 Read server_hello_done
  0.42 Write certificate
  2.61 Write client_key_exchange
  2.33    encrypt_premaster
 30.56 Write certificate_verify
  0.12 Write finished
                    8.65 Read certificate
                    2.38    verify
                    1.97    verify
                    2.24    verify
                   30.72 Read client_key_exchange
                   30.51    decrypt_premaster
                    2.23 Read certificate_verify
                    0.00 Read finished
                    0.14 Write finished
  0.00 Read finished

Client: 43.075     Server: 42.66
```

Figure 6.6 RSA client authentication mode time allocation (ms)

6.13 Ephemeral RSA

As we discussed in Chapter 4, ephemeral RSA uses a temporary short RSA key to encrypt the pre_master_secret. Effectively, this adds one short RSA operation to both client and server. However, this is accomplished by adding some operations and subtracting others, as we'll see in this section. In order to do that, we need to look at each message whose contents change in ephemeral mode. Figure 6.7 shows the trace of a handshake using ephemeral RSA.

```
Client               Server
 0.07 Write client_hello
                     0.15 Read client_hello
                     0.12 Write server_hello
                     0.49 Write certificate
                    30.45 Write server_key_exchange
                    30.43    sign
                     0.00 Write server_hello_done
 0.05 Read server_hello
 8.57 Read certificate
 2.34   verify
 1.94   verify
 2.23   verify
 2.23 Read server_key_exchange
 2.20   verify
 0.00 Read server_hello_done
 1.12 Write client_key_exchange
 0.86   encrypt_premaster
 0.11 Write finished
                     5.81 Read client_key_exchange
                     5.59   decrypt_premaster
                     0.00 Read finished
                     0.11 Write finished
 0.00 Read finished

 Client: 12.2                Server: 37.17
```

Figure 6.7 Ephemeral RSA mode time allocation (ms)

ServerKeyExchange (Server)

This message doesn't even appear in the normal RSA handshake, so whatever cryptographic processing it entails is new, and as we can see, it's quite an expensive operation. The reason for this is that we're signing the ServerKeyExchange using the server's private key, which is typically long (1024 bits or more).

Note that this does not include the time to generate the ephemeral RSA private key. On this platform it takes 200–400 ms, which is too expensive to do for each transaction. Instead, one conventionally generates the ephemeral key once a day or so. Thus, we don't count it in the per-transaction cost.

The score so far:
+1 server-side long RSA private key operation

ServerKeyExchange (Client)

On the client side we need to process the server's ServerKeyExchange message. The only interesting processing here is verifying the server's signature over the message. This adds a client side long public key operation.

The score so far:
+1 server-side long RSA private key operation
+1 client-side long RSA public key operation

ClientKeyExchange (Client)

This message existed in the normal RSA case, but in that case the client was doing a long RSA encryption. Now the client simply does a 512-bit RSA encryption, which is substantially faster. So, we've added a 512-bit RSA operation and subtracted a long RSA operation.

The score so far:
+1 server-side long RSA private key operation
+1 client-side 512-bit RSA public key operation

ClientKeyExchange (Server)

As we said above, we've substituted a short RSA operation for a short one with this message. This obviously applies on the server side as well. Thus, the final change is:

+1 client-side 512-bit RSA public key operation
+1 server-side 512-bit RSA private key operation

Because 512-bit operations are roughly 4 times as fast as 1024-bit operations, this isn't that big a difference. On this platform it works out to roughly 2 ms on the client side and 6 ms on the server side.

6.14   DSS/DHE

The following series of traces are handshakes using DSS/DHE mode. The DSA signing key and the ephemeral DH key are both 1024 bits long. As before, the client and the server are the same machine, and we've arranged the buffers so that the handshake happens sequentially.

Figure 6.8 shows the time allocation for a normal DSS/DHE handshake. The messages are the same as those for ephemeral RSA but the processing times are wildly different. This is accounted for by two factors: first, the performance characteristics of DSS and DH are dramatically different from those for RSA. Second, both sides are generating new ephemeral DH keys during the connection.

We can immediately make two observations: first, the DSS/DHE handshake is dramatically more expensive than an RSA handshake; we're spending roughly eight times as much CPU time. Second, the majority of the additional cost of the handshake is

```
Client                Server
  0.07 Write client_hello
                      0.18 Read client_hello
                      0.11 Write server_hello
                      0.26 Write certificate
                    113.90 Write server_key_exchange
                     96.67    generate_keys
                     17.15    sign
                      0.00 Write server_hello_done
  0.06 Read server_hello
  0.48 Read certificate
 21.24 Read server_key_exchange
 21.19   verify
  0.00 Read server_hello_done
196.95 Write client_key_exchange
 96.82   generate_keys
 99.86   key_agree
  0.18 Write finished
                    100.86 Read client_key_exchange
                    100.66    key_agree
                      0.00 Read finished
                      0.15 Write finished
  0.01 Read finished

Client: 219.02     Server: 215.51
```

Figure 6.8 DSS/DHE mode time allocation (ms)

borne by the client. Nevertheless, Figure 6.8 shows that the server consumes significantly more CPU (by a factor of five to seven) when using DSS/DHE than when using RSA.

ServerKeyExchange (Server)

Recall that in the ephemeral RSA ServerKeyExchange nearly all of the time was spent signing the message using the server's permanent key. In this handshake, we've added something new: the server generates the DH key on the fly, one for each connection. The primary cost of generating the ServerKeyExchange message is generating this key. In fact, a 1024 bit DSA signature is about twice as fast as the equivalent RSA signature.

It's worth examining the DH key generation process in more detail. Recall from Chapter 1 that DH (unlike RSA) relies on a publicly known group (p and g). The private key is simply a random number X. The public key (Y) is $g^X mod\ p$. The key generation we're talking about here is simply the generation of the pair (X, Y), not the generation of the group.

The generation of the group is extremely slow, because it requires making a 1024-bit prime (p). Moreover, it is often recommended that that prime have special properties which makes it take even longer to generate. On the test machine, OpenSSL took ten minutes to generate a 1024-bit DH group. Thus, group generation is done either at server startup or (preferably) when the server is originally installed.

Certificate (Client)

The client side certificate processing is the same with DSA as with RSA; the only difference is the algorithm. As we discussed previously, DSA is substantially slower than RSA for verification (roughly ten times slower at the 1024-bit ey length). Thus, the client processing of the Certificate message is much slower when using DSA.

ServerKeyExchange (Client)

As with the Certificate message, client processing of the ServerKeyExchange for DSS/DHE differs from RSA only by substituting DSA for RSA. Thus, the processing of this message is slower purely because DSA verification is so much slower.

ClientKeyExchange (Client)

In this trace, the processing of the ClientKeyExchange message actually consists of two operations, each consuming roughly half of the CPU time: generating the client's ephemeral DH key and computing the DH shared secret (ZZ). Generating the client's ephemeral DH key is exactly the same as generating the server's ephemeral DH key, and we see that the time allocated to this operation on the client is roughly the same as that on the server.

We've seen the computation of ZZ before. Recall that we compute

$$ZZ = Ys^X mod\ p = (g^{Xs})^{Xc} mod\ p = g^{Xs \cdot Xc} mod\ p$$

As you can see from the trace, this operation takes roughly the same amount of time as the generation of the client's DH key.

Note that we've missed an opportunity for parallelism. The generation of the ClientKeyExchange does not depend on knowing ZZ. ZZ is never transmitted over the wire and is used purely to compute the symmetric message keys. Computing ZZ before we send the ClientKeyExchange simply delays transmission of the message, increasing latency.

A better approach would be to send the ClientKeyExchange and then compute ZZ. That way the client can be computing ZZ while the ClientKeyExchange is in transit and/or the server is itself computing ZZ. Note that this change would primarily affect latency; unless the server is unloaded, it would not have much of an effect on throughput.

ClientKeyExchange (Server)

ClientKeyExchange processing on the server is simply the dual of processing on the client. We compute ZZ using the server's private key and the client's public key. Unsurprisingly it takes roughly the same amount of time to compute.

6.15 DSS/DHE with Client Authentication

The final handshake we'll cover is DSS/DHE with client authentication. Figure 6.9 shows that as with RSA client authentication, the only significant difference from the non-client authentication mode is the addition of several new messages: the client Certificate and the CertificateVerify.

```
Client              Server
  0.07 Write client_hello
                    0.17 Read client_hello
                    0.12 Write server_hello
                    0.26 Write certificate
                  113.96 Write server_key_exchange
                   96.63    generate_keys
                   17.26    sign
                    0.02 Write certificate_request
                    0.00 Write server_hello_done
  0.06 Read server_hello
  0.46 Read certificate
 21.36 Read server_key_exchange
 21.30    verify
  0.01 Read certificate_request
  0.00 Read server_hello_done
  0.23 Write certificate
193.21 Write client_key_exchange
 96.87    generate_keys
 96.07    key_agree
 17.06 Write certificate_verify
  0.18 Write finished
                    0.42 Read certificate
                   95.98 Read client_key_exchange
                   95.79    key_agree
                   21.00 Read certificate_verify
                    0.00 Read finished
                    0.15 Write finished
  0.01 Read finished

Client: 232.69     Server: 232.13
```

Figure 6.9 DSS/DHE client authentication mode time allocation (ms)

On the client side, the only substantial operation is the DSA signature on the CertificateVerify. The server's processing of the client's Certificate message is dominated by certificate verification. Because this is a DSS certificate, the verification is fairly slow. Similarly, the server's processing of the CertificateVerify is dominated by DSA verification. Note that with DSA (unlike RSA) the primary cost of client authentication is borne by the server because DSA verification is so slow.

6.16 Performance Improvements with DH

As we've seen, DHE performance is much worse than performance with RSA. It would be reasonable to ask why anyone would ever use this mode. Until very recently, there were two reasons: first, it's free. RSA was still subject to patent in the United States; DSA is not. Second, it provides one new feature, Perfect Forward Secrecy. PFS isn't practical with RSA due to the high cost of RSA key generation, but it is practical (though expensive) with DHE. Now that RSA's patent has expired the only reason is to get PFS. PFS is sometimes valuable, so it's worth considering whether we can improve DHE performance at all. The answer is yes.

Use Smaller Private Keys

Recall that all DH operations require exponentiating some number to $X \bmod p$. The larger the value of X the slower this operation. A common approach is simply to use an X of approximately the same size as p. To be more specific, X is chosen in the interval $(2, p)$. It is possible that X will be much less than p, but because X is randomly chosen over this interval, it will be about as long as p. However, if a smaller X is deliberately chosen, the operations are much faster.

This optimization is allowed only under certain specific circumstances, however. Otherwise, it is possible to greatly weaken the security of the key exchange. Recall from Chapter 1 that g and p must have special properties in order to use a short X.

However, the client cannot conveniently tell if the server has generated g and p appropriately because the server only sends it g and p in the ServerKeyExchange. Thus, the client cannot safely use a short X and therefore doesn't experience any speedup at all. Under most circumstances, only server performance would matter but if the client is a very limited device such as a palmtop or a cell phone, the load on the client from the DH operation may be substantial.

As a demonstration of this optimization, we modified OpenSSL, which chooses X over $(2, p)$, to choose a 256-bit X while still using a 1024-bit p. This simple change increased the speed of the server-side DH operations by roughly a factor of four, as shown in Figure 6.10.

Recall that we said in Chapter 1 that the length of X should be chosen so that it is twice the length of the desired keying material. However, in practice the strength of a DH key is also limited by the size of p. The strength of a DH key is governed by the minimum of the strength of p and the strength of X. An X of 160 bits is roughly equivalent to a 1024-bit p. Thus, with a 1024-bit prime, a 256-bit X is more than long enough. (See [Menezes1996].)

```
Client              Server
  0.07 Write client_hello
                       0.17 Read client_hello
                       0.12 Write server_hello
                       0.26 Write certificate
                      43.14 Write server_key_exchange
                      25.93    generate_keys
                      17.14    sign
                       0.00 Write server_hello_done
  0.06 Read server_hello
  0.47 Read certificate
 21.26 Read server_key_exchange
 21.21    verify
  0.00 Read server_hello_done
192.66 Write client_key_exchange
 96.60    generate_keys
 95.79    key_agree
  0.18 Write finished
                      25.57 Read client_key_exchange
                      25.38    key_agree
                       0.01 Read finished
                       0.15 Write finished
  0.01 Read finished

Client: 214.75      Server: 69.46
```

Figure 6.10 Performance effect of short DH keys

Reuse Ephemeral Keys

We improved performance without a significant effect on security by using shorter private keys (*X*). However, it's possible to improve performance even further by discarding Perfect Forward Secrecy. Recall that roughly a third of the server's computational load is consumed by generating the ephemeral DH key. Reusing that key reduces the load accordingly. Unfortunately, the server must still perform the signature on the ServerKeyExchange because the signature is also computed over portions of the handshake.

Reusing ephemeral keys only reduces server load, not client load. Because the group is determined by the server, in most cases each server will have a different group, so the client must still generate a new key for each server. Nevertheless, this optimization improves both throughput and latency because it makes the server faster.

Some might object that in order to get this performance improvement, we had to give up some security. However, note that RSA mode does not provide PFS at all, so although this sort of reuse is weaker than using a new key for each connection, it is comparable in strength to RSA. As a compromise, it's possible to regenerate the server's DH key periodically. Regenerating as frequently as every 20 or 30 connections will provide partial PFS with only a negligible impact on performance. Note that if you use a short X and reuse it for a number of connections, you must take care to prevent small subgroup attacks, as described in Chapter 5.

Precomputation for DH Key Generation

Even if we're not willing to reuse ephemeral keys, it's possible to improve key generation dramatically. In order to do so, you precompute a table of powers of the generator g. Because each public key computation requires exponentiating g, this optimization will reduce the time it takes to compute Y from X. Wei Dai [Dai2000] reports a speedup of a factor of about three for precomputed DH key generation versus ordinary DH key generation. As a special case, if the base is 2 it's possible to compute exponentials very quickly simply by left-shifting.

Static DH

A final option is to use a static DH key. Recall from Chapter 4 that it is possible to have the server's DH key in a certificate, exactly as is usually done with RSA keys. This dispenses with the ServerKeyExchange method completely, leaving the only computational load on the server as the computation of ZZ. Together with short Xs, this optimization reduces the load on the server to roughly comparable to that presented by RSA. The load on the client is still significantly greater because DSA verification is so slow. Note that if static DH is used, great care must be used to ensure that small subgroup attacks are not possible.

The primary deployment problem with static DH is that it requires static DH certificates, which are even less widely used than DSA certificates.

6.17 Record Processing

Algorithm Choice

Figure 6.11 shows the performance of OpenSSL on a Pentium 300 using various combinations of encryption and MAC algorithm. These numbers were generated by computing SSL records but not sending them to the network. Thus, they measure only record generation cost, not network overhead. They are intended as representative of the sorts of behavior you can expect. Obviously, each system and implementation will perform differently.

In short, RC4 with MD5 provides the best performance and it's roughly eight times faster than 3DES with SHA. The moral of the story is that you should use RC4 if you want reasonable security and high performance. Using MD5 instead of SHA-1 gets you about a 40% improvement.

Cipher/HASH	KB/s
RC4-MD5	15034
RC4-SHA	10831
DES-CBC-SHA	4758
DES-CBC3-SHA	2068

Figure 6.11 SSL record processing speed (Pentium 300)

Note that the processing time for the slowest cipher (3DES/SHA) is over 2MB/s. This is easily fast enough to saturate a 10 Mb Ethernet. The performance of RC4-MD5 on a reasonable machine is easily fast enough to saturate a 100 Mb Ethernet. On our test machine, even RC4 with SHA-1 will generate over 80 Mb/second of traffic. In practice, this is enough to saturate a 100 Mb network. A fast machine can easily handle the SSL record processing for even the fastest networks if RC4 is used, even with SHA-1.

It's important to note that there is no performance benefit from using the export variants of each cipher. SSL always uses the same version of each cipher and simply expands a shortened key out to the full key length. As a consequence, the export versions have exactly the same data transfer rate as the strong versions. This is different from the behavior with public key ciphers, where the export versions are notably faster.

Optimal Record Size

Both SSLv3 and TLS use HMAC (SSLv3 uses a variant, but the performance characteristics are roughly the same). As we discussed in Chapter 1, HMAC consists of a pair of nested digests. The first digest covers the key and the data. The second digest covers the key and the output of the first digest. The key is always processed as a separate digest block.

Therefore, the inner digest is dependent on the length of the message, but the outer digest isn't. Data is fed to the digests 64 bytes at a time. Up to a digest input of 64 bytes, 4 digest blocks need to be processed. For each 64 bytes after that, one more digest block is required. The point is that there is a lot of fixed overhead for the MAC.

When we encrypt the record, we need to encrypt both the MAC and the data. If we're using SHA, then this means we need to encrypt a minimum of 20 bytes. Again, there is significant fixed message overhead. Therefore, it pays to encrypt large payloads whenever possible in order to reduce the effect of the overhead. Figure 6.12 shows this quite clearly.

Transmission Rate (bytes/s)

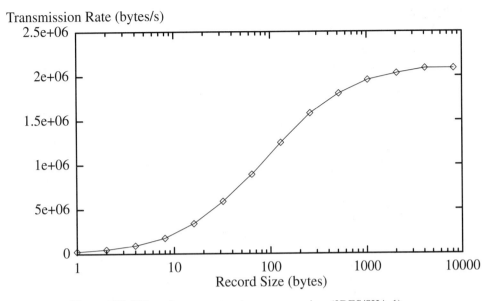

Figure 6.12 SSL performance at various message sizes (3DES/SHA-1)

The data for Figure 6.12 was collected using 3DES-CBC and SHA, but we could draw a similar picture using any set of ciphers. In order to show the effect at small record sizes, we're using a log scale for the X axis.

As Figure 6.12 shows, the performance with really small record sizes is terrible, and it gets progressively better until a point of diminishing returns around 600 bytes or so. The exact location of this point will of course depend on the implementation, operating system, compiler, etc., but the basic message should be clear. Using record sizes smaller than 32 bytes produces really terrible performance. For optimal performance, use record sizes of 1024 bytes or greater when possible.

6.18 Java

The Java performance situation is far worse than the C performance situation. Java code in general is slow, and crypto code is especially CPU intensive and therefore especially slow. Recall that on our test platform OpenSSL executes SHA-1 at roughly 22 MB/s. The fastest code for Java that the authors know of executes at roughly 2.3 MB/s on a Pentium II/450.

Operating System

Unfortunately, it's fairly difficult to get a clear picture of the situation since the performance of Java crypto code is VM and operating system dependent. DES is probably the most common algorithm implemented, and its speed varies from 37 KB/s running under Netscape Navigator on FreeBSD to 2.3 MB/s running under Internet Explorer on Windows NT. Figure 6.13 shows the performance of DES on various platforms.

Processor	OS	VM	Speed (KB/s)
Pentium II (400)	FreeBSD 3.4	Netscape 4.7	36
Pentium II (400)	FreeBSD 3.4	JDK 1.1.8	105
Pentium II (450)	Windows NT	JDK 1.2.2	2368
Pentium II (450)	Windows NT	Netscape 4.61	1856
Pentium II (450)	Windows NT	Internet Explorer 5	2334

Figure 6.13 Java DES performance on various platforms

Note that the performance of the Windows implementations is dramatically better than that of the FreeBSD implementations. Windows is one of the platforms on which Sun has delivered official JDKs, whereas the FreeBSD port is unofficial. Clearly, much more effort has gone into tuning the Windows implementations. However, even on Windows the difference between IE and Navigator is substantial.

Native Code Acceleration

Because the bottleneck in this process is the Java cryptographic primitives, an efficient and straightforward way to dramatically improve performance is to replace the Java primitives with fast native code. JNI (the Java Native Interface) provides a portable way to interface Java with native routines (typically with C code).

The GoNative Provider (see `http://www.rtfm.com/puretls/gona tive.html`) implements one approach to doing this: The Java Development Kit (JDK) provides a generic cryptographic provider interface called the Java Cryptography Architecture (JCA). Programs that use the JCA call the JCA to get a specific instance (a class object) which implements a given algorithm. Providers inform the JCA of which algorithms they implement and the JCA automatically arranges to use the right provider.

The combination of the JCA and JNI is what makes this form of acceleration easy. GoNative Provider is a JCA provider which acts as a bridge to OpenSSL (using JNI). It can be installed as a provider on a given machine and made accessible to all applications transparently without the application making any special effort. Cryptographic algorithms implemented in this fashion are far faster than the standard Java algorithms and are only about 10% slower than the equivalent code written directly in C. Note that the faster the algorithm, the more significant the overhead from JNI itself. Figure 6.14 shows the performance properties of some representative algorithms (platform: Pentium 300, FreeBSD).

Algorithm	OpenSSL	Java	GoNative Provider
DES (KB/s)	6792	31	5165
3DES (KB/s)	2392	10	2142
RC4 (KB/s)	32363	132	13872
SHA-1 (KB/s)	22838	93	10014
DSA (sign/s)	60	7	48
DSA (verify/s)	49	4	40

Figure 6.14 Relative performance of Java and C

One observation to make from this table is that there is significant overhead from calling into JNI itself. This is why 3DES performance is so close between GoNative Provider and C. As a corollary to this observation, it's especially important to use large record sizes if you want to get maximum benefit from JNI acceleration.

It's also important to buffer as much data as possible in Java before passing it into the C code. For instance, imagine you're given a large chunk of data to DES. It's important to pass it to the DES code all as one block rather than calling DES on the individual 8 byte blocks. Figure 6.15 shows the effect of input block size on DES encryption with GoNative Provider. Note that Figure 6.15 only shows performance for DES, not for SSL record encryption, which would include the MAC computation. However, similar block size effects hold true for message digests and MACs.

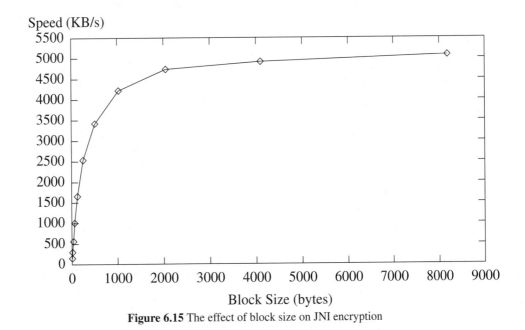

Figure 6.15 The effect of block size on JNI encryption

The end result of all this tuning is unfortunately still not as fast as pure C code, but it's not that far off, either. PureTLS with the GoNative Provider module is roughly half as fast as OpenSSL, depending on your algorithm choices.

6.19   SSL Servers under Load

Unsurprisingly, under heavy load, the cryptographic computations necessary for SSL become the bottleneck for server performance. Thus, a server that is capable of handling a given load can quickly become overloaded if those transactions are transitioned over to SSL. In order to simulate the impact of a large number of clients, we can use a *load generator*. We have a client machine (or machines) which connects to the server and makes requests. Each machine can generate a large number of requests at a given time, thus simulating a large number of users connecting to a given site. In this case, our client is a Pentium II/400 running FreeBSD 3.4.

We could perform this experiment using any SSL-enabled protocol, but for convenience we'll use HTTP over SSL. The traffic mix we've chosen simulates the behavior of a Web site when a large number of people decide to request a page at more or less the same time. In their paper on SSL performance, Abbott and Keung [Abbott1988] report that this is the scenario of most concern to their customers.

To produce this traffic mix, we arrange that each client connects to the server at a different *arrival time*. The arrival times are generated using a Poisson process with a mean of 3 seconds. Thus, all of the clients connect somewhere between 0 and 10 seconds after the start of the simulation.

Figure 6.16 shows the results of such a simulation on an ordinary HTTP server. The server is Apache 1.3.12 with mod_ssl 2.6.5 running under Linux 2.2.14-5.0 (Red Hat) on a Pentium III/650. The bar graph labelled "arrivals" represents the number of simulated client connections within each 1-second window. Thus, 23 connections were initiated in the first second of the simulation. The line graph labelled "queue" is the number of clients that were active during this time window. Thus, a client that connects at 1.5 s and disconnects at 2.5 s contributes to the queue during the 1–2 and 2–3 time windows.

When we examine Figure 6.16, we can see that the queue size closely tracks client arrivals. This is happening because the server is serving each request more or less as it comes in. This is a good indication that the server is handling the load successfully.

Compare this result to Figure 6.17, which shows the server behavior with 550 simulated HTTP/SSL clients. The cipher suite is TLS_RSA_WITH_3DES_EDE_CBC_SHA and the client has been set never to resume sessions, so every handshake requires an RSA operation. Initially, the queue size closely tracks the client arrival times, but as the number of clients increases during the simulation the queue size starts to increase dramatically. Note that although our client is significantly slower than our server, it nevertheless is capable of completely saturating the server machine. This is a nice demonstration of the asymmetry of SSL.

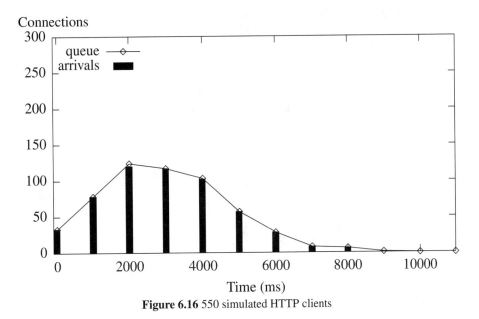

Figure 6.16 550 simulated HTTP clients

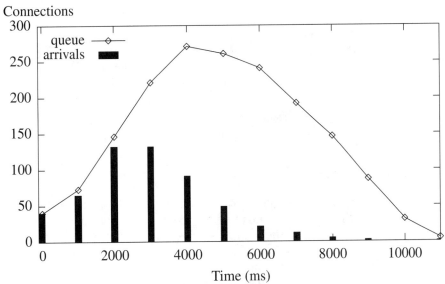

Figure 6.17 550 simulated HTTP/SSL clients

What's happening here is that the server CPU is saturated by the SSL handshakes it is already performing. Thus, more clients are arriving than are being successfully served, creating a backlog of unserved clients. As the number of new arrivals decreases, the server is able to work through the backlog of queued but unserviced connections and so the queue size slowly decreases. However, the server is only able to clear the queue because the number of arrivals trails off.

The server would not be able to handle the peak load shown in Figure 6.17 on a continuous basis. This is demonstrated by Figure 6.18, which shows the server under a continuous load of approximately 75 connections a second. Note that the size of the queue grows linearly with time, indicating that the server is not keeping up with load.

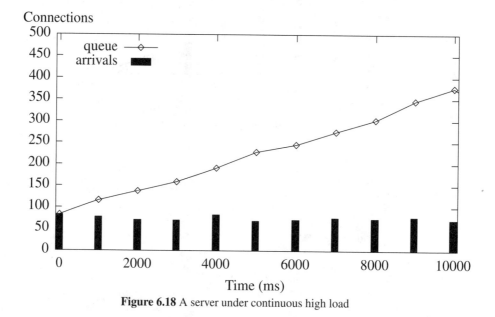

Figure 6.18 A server under continuous high load

6.20 Hardware Acceleration

Because the bottleneck in SSL performance is server CPU, it's natural to consider accelerating the SSL server by offloading the expensive crypto operations to a separate processor. Hardware acceleration not only increases the number of connections that a server can handle but also frees the server CPU to perform other tasks, such as interpreting the CGI scripts that are used to run many Web sites.

Typically, hardware accelerators are packaged as boards that may be plugged into the server machine, usually via the PCI bus on Intel architecture machines. Accelerators can also be attached to the server machine via an Ethernet connection or the SCSI bus. Accelerators are available from several manufacturers but the best known are Rainbow (http://www.rainbow.com/) and nCipher (http://www.ncipher.com/).

Figure 6.19 shows the same server as in the previous connection accelerated with a Rainbow SSL accelerator, capable of doing 200 RSA operations per second. Again, we use 550 simulated clients. However, with acceleration the queue size once again closely tracks arrival time. The server is handling the load, and thus no backlog is building up.

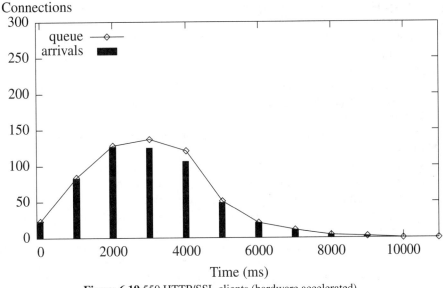

Figure 6.19 550 HTTP/SSL clients (hardware accelerated)

Because the most expensive computation in the SSL handshake is the RSA computation, accelerating RSA adds the most value. Rainbow and nCipher advertise that their high-end boxes can process up to 1000 SSL handshakes per second by accelerating the RSA computation. This acceleration is largely independent of the server CPU as long as it is reasonably powerful. By contrast, our Pentium III/650 system can perform 95 RSA operations per second. In practice, the number of connections per second it can handle will be substantially lower, because in real life the CPU would have to be running the server as well as performing crypto. Thus, 75 simulated clients per second is enough to overload the server.

Accelerators can also be used to offload symmetric operations. In most circumstances, merely offloading the asymmetric operations will be enough but if the network connection is very fast, it pays to accelerate the encryption and message digesting as well. Keung [Keung] reports that throughput nearly doubles when an accelerator is added to a 200 MHz Pentium on a 10 Mb Ethernet. Note that this effect will be less pronounced with modern faster processors. Nevertheless, if your server is handling a lot of secure traffic, it may be worth considering an accelerator to increase throughput. It's certainly worth accelerating some symmetric cryptography if you already have acceleration for asymmetric cryptography. RC4 is already so fast that it's probably not worth accelerating it at all.

Typically, the manufacturers of accelerators also provide drivers that allow popular servers to use their accelerators. A popular approach is to distribute patches or modified versions of OpenSSL that use the hardware device. This allows any OpenSSL-based system to be accelerated.

6.21   Inline Hardware Accelerators

Another approach to hardware accelerating SSL is to use a separate *inline accelerator*. The accelerator is a hardware device which sits between the clients and the servers. It listens for SSL connections from clients and accepts the SSL handshake. It then initiates an ordinary TCP connection to the server. This relieves the server of the requirement to do SSL. In order for this approach to work, the accelerator needs to have the server's keying material.

The primary virtue of an inline accelerator is that it does not require tampering with the server at all. By contrast, hardware acceleration boards must be inserted into the server, with the possibility of destabilizing it. The primary disadvantage of inline acceleration is that the coupling between the client and the server is broken. This makes it difficult for the server to make access control decisions based on the security properties of the SSL connection because there is no good way to communicate them from the accelerator to the server.

Inline accelerators are made by a number of manufacturers, including iPivot/Intel (`http://www.ipivot.com/`), F5 (`http://www.f5.com/`), and Network Alchemy/Nokia (`http://www.network-alchemy.com/`).

Configuration

Consider the problem of inserting an inline accelerator into an environment with an operational server. We must now arrange for connections from clients to terminate at the accelerator rather than the server. One approach would be to give the accelerator its own IP address. Then the DNS records could be adjusted to point to the accelerator rather than the server. Alternatively, we could give the server a new IP address and leave the DNS alone. Note that although the server and the accelerator may be on the same network segment, because traffic between them is unencrypted, that segment must be secure.

A more popular approach is to use a *transparent* configuration. In such a configuration, the accelerator must sit on a separate network physically between the client and server. The accelerator is configured to intercept a certain class of connections as if it were the server. However, it allows all other connections to simply pass through, as if it were a bridge. The transparent approach has the significant advantage that it does not require any changes to address assignments or DNS at all. You simply plug the accelerator into the network and plug the server into the accelerator, as shown in Figure 6.20.

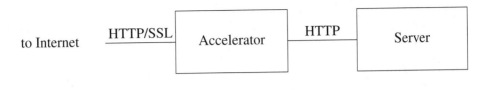

Figure 6.20 An inline SSL accelerator

Multiple Accelerators

A really busy server may have more traffic than a single accelerator can handle, even with hardware cryptography. In order to serve high loads, administrators may wish to use multiple accelerators. An additional benefit of this approach is that if one accelerator box fails, the server will still be able to handle requests, although the total number of requests it can serve will, of course, be smaller. There are two primary ways to use multiple accelerators, "chained" and "clustered."

Chained Accelerators

The first vendor to provide inline accelerators was iPivot, which has since been acquired by Intel, with their Commerce Accelerator. iPivot's box is a transparent proxy only. In order to use multiple boxes, one simply connects them in series, as shown in Figure 6.21.

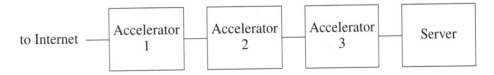

Figure 6.21 Chained SSL accelerators

If the load on a box gets too high, the box simply starts to pass traffic untouched to the next box in the chain. This process continues until all clients have been serviced. The last box in the chain can be configured to either refuse connections when the load gets too high or to pass them on to the server. The server should be configured to support SSL in order to allow it to process such requests.

iPivot's hardware is equipped with a "bypass" feature. If a box fails, the bypass feature goes into effect and all traffic is passed directly through the box as if it were not there. Thus, even if the box fails fairly catastrophically, the server will still be connected to the network and able to serve clients. However, because the server must be configured to accept raw HTTP, use of the bypass feature can lead to the server accepting HTTP connections while thinking that it's accepting decrypted HTTPS connnections. This is an obvious security problem.

Clustered Accelerators

Consider the situation where you have multiple chained accelerators and one box fails. Although the remaining accelerators will be able to handle new connections, all the SSL connections terminated at that box when it failed will be lost. Of course, neither the client nor server will know that this has happened, so when they attempt to send traffic they will get TCP RSTs. The idea behind clustered accelerators is to allow individual connections to fail over between boxes, so that no traffic is ever lost.

Full Disclosure: The author did significant development on Network Alchemy's clustered SSL accelerator under contract. This has the advantage that I am familiar with how it works and that I am able to describe it before it is released. It has the disadvantage that I have a conflict of interest. I have attempted to describe the advantages and disadvantages of the solution objectively, but the reader would do well to bear this fact in mind.

Network Alchemy/Nokia's clustered SSL accelerator, due out in Q1 2001 attempts to solve the problem of failover of active connections. Instead of connecting boxes in a chain, you connect multiple boxes in parallel, as shown in Figure 6.22. This configuration is called a cluster.

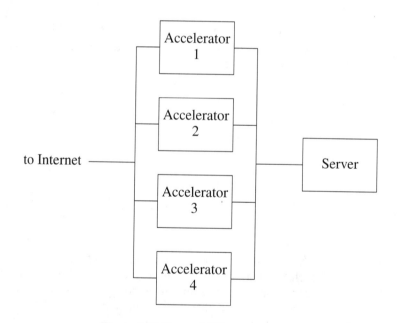

Figure 6.22 Clustered SSL accelerators

The entire cluster has a virtual ethernet MAC address and thus behaves as if it were a single piece of hardware. Each machine in the cluster listens to all traffic destined for that address. The cluster automatically distributes responsibility for handling each section of traffic between the machines in the cluster. If a box fails, its traffic is automatically picked up by the other boxes.

In order to enable failover, the clustered machines automatically propagate connection state from the machine handling the connection to the rest of the machines in the cluster. Thus, if one of the machines fails, the new machine assigned to handle the connection already has all of the connection state and can pick up where the other machine left off. Note that if the machine is handling traffic for a given connection when it fails, that IP packet will be dropped. However, when the packet is retransmitted the machine that is now handling the connection will automatically process it correctly. All the client and server will see is some delay while waiting for the retransmit.

Note that although a clustered solution handles single box failures more cleanly, it handles catastrophic failures less cleanly. As we saw in the previous section, if all the iPivot boxes fail, the network simply behaves as if they were not present. Because we want another box to pick up the load if a box fails, when individual clustered boxes fail, they fail in a disconnected state. Thus, if all the boxes in a cluster fail, the server will be denied service.

However, the probability that all the boxes in a cluster will fail is generally fairly low. The most likely situation would be some sort of power glitch that brought them all down together. In order to avoid this, the various cluster members must be on separate circuits so there is no single point of failure. By contrast, with the iPivot solution, each box is a single point of failure. Although the iPivot boxes are designed to fail safe, some conceivable problems (a broken internal wire, for instance) would bring down the entire system in such a way that bypass would not work.

The clustered solution has a number of other advantages. Because the cluster automatically shares workload, the load can be more easily and evenly distributed between cluster members. This is more difficult to accomplish with a chained solution. Also, the cluster can be configured as a single unit. Each individual box does not need to be configured with all the SSL information. You configure it as part of the cluster and the SSL configuration propagates automatically.

6.22 Network Latency

So far, we've concentrated on how SSL uses the processor, ignoring its interaction with the network. However, the characteristics of the network over which the SSL connection is running have a substantial effect on its performance characteristics. The rest of this chapter focuses on that interaction.

Although theoretically SSL can be run over any connection-oriented protocol, in practice it's nearly always run over TCP/IP. Therefore, we're going to focus almost exclusively on the performance characteristics of SSL running over TCP networks, although some of this material is also applicable to other types of networks.

The data we've been collecting so far comes from programs running on a single machine and communicating directly through the kernel without any network in the way at all. This differs from a real network in that it's much faster. Throughput is very high and latency is very low. By contrast, in a real network, throughput will be lower and latency will be higher.

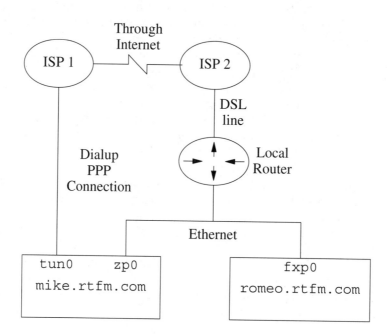

Figure 6.23 A slow test network

To demonstrate the effects of a slower network, we collected a number of traces on the network configuration shown in Figure 6.23. This network has two test machines, `romeo.rtfm.com` and `mike.rtfm.com`. `romeo` is connected to the network as usual, but `mike` has been specially configured to be *dual homed*. It has two IP interfaces. The primary network connection is the PPP dialup on interface `tun0`. All traffic between `mike` and the local network must go over the PPP interface.

However, `mike` is also connected directly to the local network via the Ethernet interface `zp0`. Under normal circumstances, traffic between `mike` and `romeo` would go through this interface. However, we've deliberately configured `zp0` with a private network to force traffic to go via PPP.

The point of this configuration is that `mike` can be configured to capture packets on both `tun0` and `zp0`. Thus, it can see each packet twice—when it appears on the PPP interface and again when it appears on the Ethernet. This allows us to directly observe the time it takes for a given packet to transit the network between `mike` and `romeo`. For instance, when a packet is sent from `romeo` to `mike` it is first transmitted from `romeo` to the local router on the Ethernet. The packet sniffer attached to `mike`'s interface `zp0` captures the packet. The packet is then sent through the DSL line to one ISP, through the Internet to another ISP, and finally down the PPP connection to `mike`. At this point the packet sniffer attached to `tun0` captures the packet.

Figure 6.24 shows a simple SSL handshake performed between `mike` (the client) and `romeo` (the server). Again, the cipher suite uses RSA for key exchange. Unlike previous timelines, this one is drawn to scale. The vertical displacement of each arrow represents the time that it takes to transit the network. The bars on the left and right of each arrow show the actual time from transmission to delivery. Thus, the ClientHello took 112 ms to get from `mike` to `romeo`.

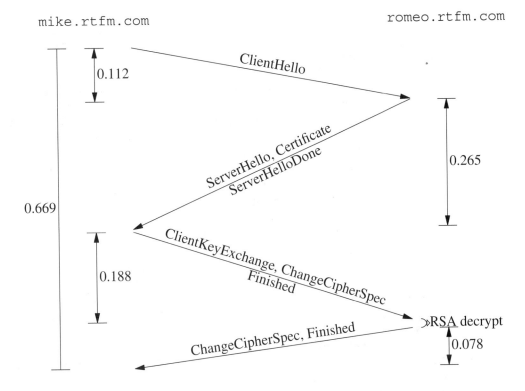

Figure 6.24 SSL handshake over a high-latency connection

Note that the total time of the handshake is vastly increased. In this case, the time from start to finish is 669 ms. A comparable handshake performed on a fast network might take 100 ms. However, the vast majority of the time is simple network latency. Packets are processed nearly as quickly as they are received. The only piece of computation that has any noticeable effect at all is the RSA decrypt, which takes perhaps 20 ms—an insignificant fraction of the total time for the handshake.

It's interesting to note that the transit time for the various handshake messages is wildly different. The combined ServerHello, Certificate, and ServerHelloDone takes 265 ms, whereas the server's ChangeCipherSpec and Finished take only 78 ms. This result is surprising at first but is easily explained: most of the latency in the system is introduced not by the Internet between the ISPs but by the PPP connection between `mike` and the first ISP. On a slow modem link, latency is dominated by transmission time. The larger the packet the longer it takes to transmit and thus the higher the latency. The Certificate is large and therefore introduces the most latency.

Note that although increased network latency slows down individual handshakes, it generally doesn't decrease server throughput. Provided that the server's network link isn't saturated, while the server is waiting for a response from one client it can be serving others. However, this isn't to say that high handshake latency is unimportant. Because it's perceived by the user as poor performance, if we can reduce latency we can improve the user experience.

6.23   The Nagle Algorithm

Under certain circumstances, SSL interacts poorly with various TCP congestion control measures. This interaction can cause the SSL handshake to stall even though both the client and server are idle. The culprit is Nagle's algorithm described in [Nagle1984].

The Nagle algorithm is intended to reduce *tinygrams*: small packets on the wire. The problem is the TCP packet header. TCP segments have a minimum header size of 40 bytes. Thus, when one character is sent per segment, 41 bytes must be sent to the network. This can rapidly lead to congestion. Under normal circumstances, whenever programs call `write()` (or equivalent), the TCP stack simply sends out the data immediately. However, if programs call `write()` with small data segments (such as when a user is typing) and kernel sends out one packet for each such write, the network can get clogged with such packets.

The Nagle algorithm prevents this in a very simple way. When there is outstanding data that has been sent but not acknowledged, the TCP implementation does not send small packets. Instead, it buffers the data and sends the entire buffer when it receives the ACK. Under normal circumstances, this works very well, but it can cause a problem with SSL, as we'll see shortly.

The second cause of the problem is a technique called *delayed ACKs*. Rather than generating an ACK as soon as a packet is received, the TCP implementation tries to *piggyback* it on a data segment it is already sending out. To facilitate this, the TCP implementation will wait for up to 200 ms for data to be written. If none shows up within that window, then the ACK will be written to the network anyway.

A good example of this interaction is what happens when SSL sessions are resumed. Figure 6.25 shows a network trace of such a connection. Note that although the client and server are on the same machine, the data still goes through the TCP stack and so we can observe the behavior of the Nagle algorithm. The important thing to notice here is the 148 ms delay between the client sending its Finished message (line 6) and the first application data record (line 7). This is far longer than it takes to prepare the record.

What's happened here is that the client TCP stack is waiting for the Finished message to be ACKed before it sends out the first application data record (due to the Nagle algorithm). The server TCP stack isn't sending out the ACK because it's implementing delayed ACK. But the server program isn't writing because it's waiting for the client to send its first application data record: We've got a deadlock.

The deadlock is finally broken at 0.1516 seconds, when the server's delayed ACK timer goes off. The server sends the ACK out anyway (between line 6 and 7) even

```
New TCP connection: localhost(2830) <-> localhost(4433)
1  0.0003 (0.0003)  C>S   Handshake      ClientHello
2  0.0028 (0.0024)  S>C   Handshake      ServerHello
3  0.0028 (0.0000)  S>C   ChangeCipherSpec
4  0.0028 (0.0000)  S>C   Finished
5  0.0039 (0.0011)  C>S   ChangeCipherSpec
6  0.0039 (0.0000)  C>S   Finished
   TCP ACK arrives at 0.1516
7  0.1517 (0.14777) C>S    application_data
8  0.1530 (0.0014)  S>C    application_data
```

Figure 6.25 The Nagle algorithm and session resumption

though it can't piggyback it. The client gets the ACK and at 0.1517 seconds it flushes its own buffers and sends the first record of application data. (Note that for clarity we've opted not to show the piggybacked ACKs on the data packets.)

Disabling the Nagle Algorithm

It's possible to disable the Nagle algorithm. (The sockets API uses the TCP_NODELAY option). If we disable it, then data will be written to the network as soon as it's presented to the TCP stack (provided there's room in the TCP window, of course). The effect is to avoid the sort of deadlock we saw in Figure 6.25. Figure 6.26 shows the same SSL handshake with the Nagle algorithm disabled on the client. As you can see, the client sends the application data immediately after sending the Finished message, drastically reducing the time it takes to complete the handshake.

```
New TCP connection: localhost(2850) <-> localhost(4433)
1  0.0006 (0.0060)  C>S   Handshake      ClientHello
2  0.0016 (0.0010)  S>C   Handshake      ServerHello
3  0.0016 (0.0000)  S>C   ChangeCipherSpec
4  0.0016 (0.0000)  S>C   Finished
5  0.0028 (0.0012)  C>S   ChangeCipherSpec
6  0.0028 (0.0000)  C>S   Finished
7  0.0046 (0.0018)  C>S   application_data
8  0.0059 (0.0013)  S>C   application_data
```

Figure 6.26 Session resumption with the Nagle algorithm disabled

The Right Layer

The obvious question to ask at this point is whether it's ever worth using the Nagle algorithm for SSL. In general, the answer is probably no. The purpose of the Nagle algorithm is to reduce the TCP overhead associated with the transmission of small datagrams.

However, SSL records are almost never small. Due to the addition of the header and the MAC, the absolute minimum size for an SSL data record is 22 bytes. Thus, if the SSL implementation packages one byte per record, we've already suffered an expansion of twenty-fold before we ever get to the TCP stack. Moreover, as we saw earlier, processing records one byte at a time is very cryptographically expensive.

Therefore, if we want to solve the tinygram problem for SSL we have to arrange to buffer data before the SSL implementation packages it into records. Exactly what is required depends on which protocol is being run over SSL, and we'll see more about that in Chapter 7.

6.24 Handshake Buffering

As we discussed in Section 6.10, some implementations buffer parts of the SSL handshake. OpenSSL uses a 1024-byte buffer. Most of the time this works fairly well, but there are a number of pathological cases where another strategy would produce significantly lower latency. Consider the DSS/DHE handshake shown in Figure 6.27. This handshake was carried out over a 10 Mb Ethernet, so transmission latency is minimal. However, we can still be hurt by the Nagle algorithm. The ServerHello, Certificate, and ServerKeyExchange cannot all fit in a single 1024-byte buffer. Thus, the ServerKeyExchange gets split into two pieces. The first piece is transmitted along with the Certificate. The second piece is buffered and sent to the operating system when the buffer is flushed after the ServerHelloDone.

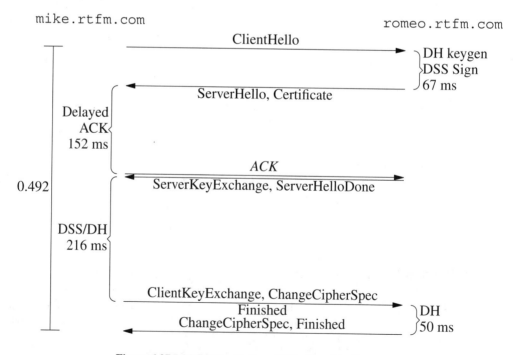

Figure 6.27 DSS/DHE with OpenSSL's normal buffers

However, because the buffer size is 1024 bytes, the first segment containing the ServerHello, Certificate, and part of the ServerHelloDone is also 1024 bytes. This is smaller than the Ethernet *maximum segment size* (MSS) and therefore this is considered to be a small packet for the purposes of the Nagle algorithm. Thus, the next segment containing the rest of the ServerKeyExchange can't be transmitted until the previous segment is ACKed. As described in the previous section, the client delays the ACK for 152 ms. During this period, both client and server are idle. As soon as the server receives the ACK it transmits the rest of the ServerKeyExchange and the ServerHelloDone.

Several features of OpenSSL conspire to produce increased latency in this handshake. First, the interaction of OpenSSL's small buffer size and the Nagle algorithm create a totally idle period where the server is waiting for an ACK and the client is performing delayed ACKs. The simple fix for this is simply to increase the buffer size. Figure 6.28 shows the same handshake except that the buffer size has been increased to 4096 bytes.

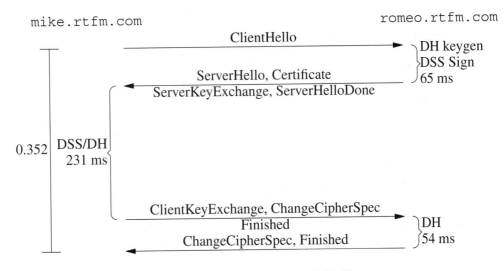

Figure 6.28 DSS/DHE with an expanded buffer

Now that we've increased the buffer size all four server messages fit in the same buffer. Thus, they are all sent at the same time. This eliminates the condition where the server waits for the client's delayed ACK, thus avoiding the temporary deadlock we saw previously. As a consequence, this handshake takes only 352 ms to complete instead of the 492 ms that we saw with the smaller buffer size.

Note that any fixed buffer size is a clumsy solution to this problem. No matter what buffer size choice we make, it's possible that the certificate will be large enough to fill it. A more tasteful solution would be to use a variable length buffer that automatically resizes and then flush the buffer manually after transmitting the ServerHelloDone. Note that it's possible that the data may be so large that it is transmitted in more than one TCP segment. However, this will not trigger the Nagle algorithm because all but the final segment will be full-sized.

An alternative to increasing the buffer would be to simply turn off the Nagle algorithm entirely. This has much the same effect as increasing the buffer size. It does increase server load very slightly because two calls to `write()` must be made instead of one. However, the high CPU cost of the rest of the SSL handshake renders the cost of a single additional context switch insignificant by comparison.

Increasing Parallelism

The second factor contributing to the latency of this handshake is a lack of parallelism between client and server. Essentially all the time that the server spends in the first phase of the handshake is consumed generating the ServerKeyExchange message. Only after the ServerKeyExchange is generated are any messages sent from the server. Even when we use a 1024-byte buffer, it's the ServerKeyExchange that fills up the buffer and forces the ServerHello and Certificate to be transmitted.

During the generation of the ServerKeyExchange, the client is completely idle. However, there is a task that it could be performing during this time: verifying the server's certificate. Recall from Section 6.14 that DSA verification costs a significant amount of CPU time. We could reduce latency if the client performed this verification while the server was generating the ServerKeyExchange. In order to do this, we must arrange that the server sends the ServerHello and Certificate before generating the ServerKeyExchange. A simple approach would be to modify the server to send each message separately. A more sophisticated approach would be to flush the write buffer after writing the Certificate message. In either case, the Nagle algorithm would need to be turned off.

With the server suitably modified, we should expect the client to verify the server's certificate entirely before it receives the ServerKeyExchange. Thus, latency should be reduced by the time it takes to verify the server's certificate. Experimentation with a modified client reveals the expected 20 ms improvement.

The DSS/DHE case is extreme in that significant processing is required on both client and server and thus parallelism offers significant performance gains. However, it demonstrates a general principle: SSL implementors need to be carefully aware of the interaction between their implementation and the network in order to get maximal performance. In particular, whenever one side is transmitting data that requires significant processing by the other side, that data should be written to the network as soon as possible to maximimize parallelism and thereby reduce latency. A good rule of thumb is to flush network buffers before entering any time-consuming operation.

6.25   Advanced SSL Performance Rules

Avoid ephemeral keying. Ephemeral DH slows down the server. Don't use it unless you need Perfect Forward Secrecy. Even DHE mode with a fixed DH key is an improvement.

Use short DH exponents. A 256-bit DH exponent improves performance dramatically with a trivial reduction in security.

Nagle algorithm. Always turn off the Nagle algorithm.

Handshake buffering. Transmit data before entering any significant computation. Beware of the interaction of buffer flushes with Nagle.

6.26 Summary

This chapter has provided a description of the performance properties of SSL. We started with some general observations about the factors controlling SSL performance and then covered these points in more detail using instrumented software and network traces to illustrate the important points.

Most of the time goes to cryptography. Cryptographic operations are the dominating factor in SSL performance. The protocol state machine and I/O contribute negligibly to the performance of the system.

Handshakes are very expensive. For sessions that don't transmit a lot of data, the SSL handshake consumes most of the CPU time.

Session resumption can reduce the cost of handshakes. The handshake for a resumed session is much faster than the handshake for an ordinary session. If a client/server pair are going to communicate repeatedly, resuming sessions pays off.

Server performance is more important than client performance. Slow servers increase latency and reduce throughput. Slow clients mainly increase latency.

Use large records. There is a certain minimal amount of cryptographic and network overhead consumed to process any record. The larger the record size, the fewer times this overhead is incurred.

Algorithm choice matters. For fast handshake performance, use RSA. For fast data transfer use RC4. Digest algorithm performance doesn't make a big difference.

If you want acceptable performance, use C. Java crypto performance is abysmal. The performance of Java implementations can be dramatically improved by calling to C using JNI.

If you want high performance, use cryptographic hardware. For high-load servers, hardware cryptographic engines can substantially improve performance.

7

Designing with SSL

*"First, figure out what you are trying to do (this is good advice
under most circumstances, and it is especially apropos here)."*
—NNTP Installation Guide

7.1 Introduction

So far we've focused on the mechanics of SSL itself. However, SSL isn't very useful in and of itself. Rather, it's used to carry application-layer protocols. It's these protocols that perform services for users. SSL's job is to allow those protocols to do their jobs securely while abstracting away as much security functionality as possible. SSL takes care of the mechanics of security in a generic fashion and the application-layer protocols run on top and take advantage of the security services it provides.

In practice, however, simply carrying the application data over an SSL connection often gives undesirable security and performance properties. Application-layer protocols (and protocol designers) need to know enough about SSL to be able to run on top of it securely. This chapter covers what you need to know in order to accomplish this task. As usual, we've broken the material up into two parts, with the first covering the basic concepts in overview form and the second covering some of the more technical material in more detail as well as introducing some fine points that were glossed over in the initial presentation.

All the material in this chapter addresses the problem of securing an application protocol from a protocol-level perspective. This presentation is aimed at the application protocol designer and system architect. Chapter 8 serves as a companion to this chapter and covers these techniques from a programmer's perspective, providing sample code which uses commonly available SSL implementations.

7.2 Know What You Want to Secure

The first thing you need to figure out is what security services you want to provide. In order to do that, you need to evaluate the threat model for your application. If you don't remember what a threat model is, go back and reread Chapter 1. With the threat model in hand, figure out what are the vulnerabilities of the system you're trying to secure. Your aim should be to secure all the vulnerabilities that can be secured economically.

As a template for this exercise, recall the three security services discussed in Chapter 1: *confidentiality*, *message integrity*, and *endpoint authentication*. Not every application will need all of these services (though an application that doesn't need any isn't worth securing), and to some extent they can be provided independently. Thus, it's important to identify which services you need. Part of this process is identifying the cost of providing those services. The cheaper the service, the smaller a need justifies providing it.

It's not necessary that all security services be provided by SSL. For instance, it's quite common for systems to provide client authentication using a username and password. Although the password encryption is provided via SSL, the application protocol is responsible for transmitting, receiving, and checking it. At this point you want to identify which security services are best provided by SSL and which are best provided by the application protocol.

Confidentiality

Confidentiality is useful in most applications. However, as we saw in Chapter 6, it comes with a nonzero performance cost, particularly if RC4 is unavailable. Moreover, there are some applications that do not need confidentiality. A good example is free software download. When you're downloading software, you want to know that it arrives unmodified from the vendor, but because anyone else can download it, there's no value in keeping the contents secret.

Message Integrity

Message integrity is a required part of SSL. Moreover, it's difficult to offer any security services without message integrity. Thus, there's really not any question about whether to use the message integrity feature of SSL.

Server Authentication

The only SSL modes that don't require server authentication are the anonymous DH modes. However, it is of course possible to use self-signed (and hence unverified) certificates and get the effect of an anonymous connection with any SSL mode. This is undesirable because it leaves the connection open to a man-in-the-middle attack. Therefore, in general, server certificates are required for nearly all SSL applications.

There are certain special cases where a man-in-the-middle attack can be prevented by the application-layer protocol. We'll discuss a technique for doing this in Section 7.16. These techniques typically require an especially tight integration between the application protocol and SSL.

Client Authentication

As we've said, using SSL pretty much locks you into certificate-based server authentication. However, certificates are not the only option for client authentication. Although SSL itself provides support only for certificate-based client authentication, many application protocols incorporate their own client authentication mechanisms, which can be run over SSL. Although these mechanisms may have been insecure when run over the net in the clear, they are often far more secure over SSL. The next section discusses some of the simpler client authentication options.

Rule of Thumb

As we've said, message integrity isn't optional, so there's no choice to be made there. In general, it's best to provide confidentiality. Many SSL implementations do not support the authentication-only modes, so you'll need to support confidentiality in service of interoperability. Moreover, it matches user expectations. Client authentication is in general a hassle for users, so avoid it unless you have some data that really needs to be restricted to specific users.

7.3   Client Authentication Options

Username/Password

The most traditional way to do client authentication is to use *username/password*. The user supplies a username and password to the network client, which in turn supplies it to the server the user wants to access. The server checks the user's password against its password database. If the password checks, then the network client is authenticated as the user.

This method is often combined with an *Access Control List* (ACL) mechanism. An ACL is simply a list of users and the permissions each user has. Each resource on the server has an ACL associated with it and when a client requests access to a resource the server checks whether the user associated with that client has permission in the appropriate ACL.

Username/password methods are vulnerable to a simple passive attack: the attacker sniffs the password off of the wire and then initiates a new session, presenting the username/password pair as his own. SSL prevents this attack because the password is sent over an encrypted channel. However, it's still possible for the attacker to mount an active attack by repeatedly guessing passwords, hoping to get a correct one.

Username/Password Variants

Because so many systems have been designed with username/password security systems, a number of complicated schemes have been designed to retain the general username/password model while improving security. The simplest example is one-time password schemes such as S/Key or SecureID cards. In general, these schemes are designed to make passwords safe in the face of arbitrary passive or active attacks on the connection carrying the password. Because SSL prevents such attacks, these schemes are generally without advantage in environments where SSL is being used. However, in a system with both insecure and secure connections, such schemes may be useful. Two examples of such schemes are described in [Jablon1996] and [Wu1998].

SSL Client Authentication

As with server authentication, client authentication in SSL depends on possession of a digital certificate. However, because of the large client-to-server ratio, this presents a larger operational challenge for client authentication than does server authentication. Certifying large numbers of clients often requires a special arrangement with a CA. To avoid making such an arrangement, many organizations choose to run their own certificate authorities, but this too presents an operational burden.

An additional problem with certificate-based client authentication is mapping certificates to user identities. ACLs can be used with certificates provided that you arrange to look up ACL entries based on the identities in certificates. This requires particular care in cases where certificate-based authentication will be used together with username/password-type authentication schemes, because the system must arrange to map both types of identity information into a common user format.

Rule of Thumb

In most circumstances it's easier to offer clients username/password-style authentication. Passwords are easier to integrate with most infrastructures and they're easier for users to understand. As an exception to this rule, automated clients are often just as easy to manage with certificates, particularly if no access control is required. A good example of such a client is a mail server, which runs unattended and should be able to authenticate itself when forwarding messages.

7.4   Reference Integrity

Server Identity

As we discussed in Chapter 5, ensuring a secure connection with SSL absolutely requires verifying the server's identity. Without this check, an active attacker can mount a man-in-the-middle attack on the connection. Moreover, it's imperative not only that you verify the server's certificate but that you verify that the server is the server you're expecting to talk to. Otherwise, it's possible for one server with a valid certificate to intercept connections verified for another.

Naturally, comparing the server's expected identity to the server's actual identity requires having some expectation about the server's identity. Thus, whatever application protocol you're using must allow you to have some expectation as to the server's identity.

Typically, this information comes in the form of the server's domain name, which must be matched against the certificate as described in Chapter 5. The domain name is usually supplied either directly by the user (e.g., the host name in a Telnet request) or indirectly via a URL. In cases where neither of these is possible, the situation becomes much more difficult. We'll consider a workable approach for such a case in Section 7.16.

Security Properties

For security reasons, the client needs to verify that the connection properties meet its security expectations. The exact details of these expectations will depend on the type of reference that the client has for the server. For instance, with a protocol such as Telnet the client may simply have the domain name of the server. However, with a protocol such as HTTP, the client often has an indication in the URL that the protocol should be HTTP over SSL (the URL begins with `https://`).

If the reference indicates that SSL is to be used, the client needs to check that it in fact was used. If a domain name is available, the client needs to check whether the domain name in the server's certificate matches the domain name in the reference—if the server cannot be authenticated somehow, then a man-in-the middle attack is possible.

It's important to note that enforcement of secure connections must generally be done on the client side. If the client doesn't enforce it, an attacker can man-in-the-middle the client's insecure connection and initiate a secure connection to the server. Thus, the server thinks it has a secure connection and can't tell that it's to the attacker and not to the client. This sort of attack makes server enforcement of security properties extremely problematic. The one case in which this can't happen is if the server demands SSL client authentication. If SSL client authentication is used, the attacker can make a connection to the server but cannot pose as the client.

Rule of Thumb

In general, you need to provide a reference that (1) concretely identifies the server the client can expect to connect to and (2) indicates that SSL is required. The server's identity needs to be able to be automatically compared to the server's certificate. Servers should be identified via domain name, and that's what should appear in certificates.

7.5   Inappropriate Tasks

Although SSL is useful for a wide variety of security tasks, there are also a fair number of jobs for which it's inappropriate. Recall that SSL provides a secure channel between two machines and that this channel is oblivious to the data passing over it. This creates some limitations on what can be done with it. This section describes those limitations. Chapter 11 provides a brief overview of some other technologies that can fill in these pieces of the puzzle.

Nonrepudiation

One common task that SSL cannot be used for is to provide *nonrepudiation* of data. Consider making an online purchase. The transaction is performed over an SSL connection so you can be certain that you are talking to the correct merchant. Typically, the merchant gives you a receipt and because that's carried over an SSL connection you can be sure that it hasn't been tampered with. However, you can't show the receipt to anyone else and have them externally verify its contents. Thus, if the merchant claims that you forged the receipt you can't prove otherwise.

End-to-End Security

Because the SSL handshake is interactive, it's not possible to send encrypted or authenticated data to a machine to which you cannot establish a network connection. Thus, if your machine is behind a firewall, you have to punch a hole in the firewall if you want to establish an SSL connection to the other end. The other option is to establish an SSL connection to the firewall and let it establish its own connection to the end machine. This approach has the major drawback that the firewall can now read all your traffic.

In general, SSL is bad at any task that involves protecting objects in such a way that they can be stored with their cryptographic properties intact and then recovered, verified, etc., at some later time. If you have such an application, you should strongly consider the possibility that using SSL is an inappropriate approach. A better approach is to use a message security protocol such as S/MIME. We'll discuss this sort of approach in Chapter 11.

7.6   Protocol Selection

Quite commonly, it's desirable to be able to run both an insecure and a secure version of the same application protocol at the same time. If this capability is desired for a given protocol, there must be some way to differentiate between connections that are going to use the native (unsecured) and the secured version of the protocol.

We have two requirements for parallel secure and insecure operation: first, we must be able to unambiguously distinguish secure and insecure connections. Second, security-oblivious clients and servers must be able to interoperate correctly with security-aware clients and servers.

The second requirement deserves a little explanation. Naturally, agents that know nothing about security cannot interoperate securely with agents that expect security. However, an attempt by one agent to use security with a security-oblivious agent must not break the oblivious agent. It's obviously permissible for an error to be thrown, but it should be an understandable error.

One approach would simply be to have the server auto-detect based on the first bytes sent by the client. This approach depends on the SSL ClientHello and the application protocol being sufficiently different that the server can distinguish them. This is not the case for all protocols.

Moreover, even for situations where they are distinct, this approach requires the server to be able to auto-detect the difference. This requirement makes retrofitting SSL to an application protocol difficult because preexisting servers will not know about the SSL handshake and will therefore return errors, or stall, which can be worse. Although auto-detection might be acceptable (though tasteless) when designing a new protocol, it's completely unacceptable when securing an existing protocol.

There are two common approaches to protocol selection: the *separate ports* approach and the *upward negotiation* approach.

Separate Ports

Most Internet protocols have what's called a *well-known port*. For instance, Telnet connections are on port 23 and SMTP (mail) connections are on port 25. See [IANA] for a list of all the currently assigned port numbers. This means that traffic for that protocol is expected to arrive at the server on that port. The *Internet Assigned Numbers Authority* (IANA) controls registration of these port numbers, thereby ensuring that no two registered protocols can share the same port. Obviously, if two different protocols were to collide on the same port, we could encounter the sort of errors that we discussed in the previous section.

A separate ports strategy, then, means that we assign a different TCP port to the secure version of the protocol from the insecure one. A server can figure out whether the connection is to be secure or insecure simply by seeing which TCP port the client is connecting on. It then knows whether to expect the SSL ClientHello or to start processing the application protocol immediately.

The separate ports strategy's main problem is that it doesn't scale well. The number of available ports is large (around 65000) but not infinite. If we define two ports for each protocol the number space will be depleted twice as quickly. Moreover, this sets a dangerous precedent. Imagine that we wish to add some other new feature. Will we define a new port for it as well? Do we need to define a nonsecure and secure version of this new feature? The potential for combinatoric explosion is substantial.

Upward Negotiation

Normally, when we want to add new protocol features to an existing protocol, we find some way to introduce them into the existing protocol in a backward-compatible fashion. Only when major protocol changes are afoot do we use a new TCP port. For instance, in SSL we can add new ciphers quite easily simply by defining new cipher suite numbers and their associated semantics. The protocol automatically determines whether these ciphers are usable or not.

Many other protocols allow for extensions of this sort. Therefore, it's natural to use these mechanisms to introduce security. In a typical such mechanism, one side will indicate that it supports SSL and the other side will indicate that it wants it. The SSL handshake will then occur and the rest of the application protocol will run over the secured connection.

Figure 7.1 shows a typical such negotiation in abstract form. In the first message, the client indicates that it's prepared to speak TLS. In the second message, the server agrees to speak TLS and tells the client to go ahead. In the next message, the client sends its ClientHello. The client and server complete the handshake and then the client sends the first application protocol message over the new TLS connection. This message is shown in italics to indicate that it's encrypted.

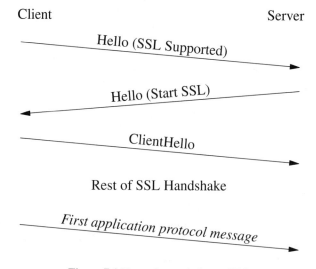

Figure 7.1 Upward negotiation to TLS

Upward negotiation requires that the protocol already have some mechanism for negotiating extensions. This is a common but by no means universal feature. If the protocol does not have such a mechanism, one will have to be inserted. Because the changeover to SSL happens during a normal protocol exchange, more care must be taken to ensure adequate security. No sensitive data should be passed until the SSL session has been negotiated and clients and servers may need to be configured to operate correctly (and safely) if the other side rejects the switch to SSL.

Rule of Thumb

In general, it's much easier to design and implement a separate ports strategy. If you're designing a protocol for largely internal usage or you're working with a protocol you can't change (not an uncommon case) use separate ports. The only time when it's really worth paying the design and implementation cost for an upward negotiation strategy is when you're designing for broad standardization.

7.7   Reducing Handshake Overhead

Recall from Chapter 6 that the primary performance cost in most SSL connections is the handshake. As an application protocol designer, the primary thing that you can do to reduce this overhead is to minimize the number of new SSL handshakes required by your protocol.

If you're designing a new protocol, reducing new connections is a first-order consideration. However, even if you're simply securing a preexisting protocol, it's important to bear it in mind. Some protocols (e.g., HTTP and SMTP) can process multiple transactions over the same protocol connection. This is a good idea in general, but is especially important with SSL.

7.8   Design Strategy

So far, we've discussed the major design considerations in securing a protocol using SSL. This section provides a broad overview of the design steps you should be going through and the order you should be going through them.

Identify your threat model. The first step in any security design is to figure out what sorts of security threats you're trying to protect against. You need to figure out the ways in which your data is sensitive. This procedure leads directly into the next step.

Figure out what you want to secure. First, figure out which security services you wish to provide in the abstract. Next, figure out which ones you can provide using SSL and which ones will have to be provided externally. Now is the time to consider the possiblity that SSL is inappropriate for your application.

Choose a protocol selection strategy. The first design decision you need to make is how to select secure versus insecure mode. As we've discussed, a separate ports strategy is easier to implement, but has some scalability problems.

Decide how (whether) to offer client authentication. If your threat model involves authenticating users, you'll need to use some sort of client authentication. If your application already uses username/password authentication, you may want to reuse this authentication model. Even if you choose to use certificates, you may want to leverage the username/password infrastructure for access control.

Identify servers and provide reference integrity. The next step is to figure out how servers will be authenticated. Almost certainly this will be done with certificates, but the important task is to figure out how to compare references with the identity in the certificates. This requires identifying what sort of references you have and arranging for the certificates to mirror them.

Optimize connection semantics. Finally, you want to take a look at performance considerations. At this protocol layer most of what you can do is arrange that the number of connections is kept to a minimum and that sessions are resumable where possible. Moreover, you want to make sure that closure happens correctly, both because this reduces rehandshake and to provide security against truncation attacks.

7.9   The Story So Far

The first part of this chapter dicussed general strategy for securing protocols using SSL. In general, it's possible to do a very basic job of securing a protocol with little effort, but there are a number of important details that should be considered. As we've seen, failure to consider some of them leaves substantial security holes while others merely result in bad performance.

The purpose of the first part was to provide an overview of the required tasks. The second part of this chapter discusses in detail various strategies for executing them. Most of the strategies that we'll discuss have been deployed effectively in one or more protocols and are part of the standard SSL design toolbox.

7.10   Separate Ports

The most popular method of operating parallel secured and unsecured servers is to use separate ports for each protocol variant. Implementing a separate ports strategy is trivial. You simply assign a new port to the secure variant of your protocol and arrange for your server to listen on both the non-secure port and the secure port. This can be implemented by having one server process listen to both ports or one process for each port. There's no need to be able to distinguish SSL traffic from ordinary traffic, because anything that comes in on the secure port must be SSL. Any insecure traffic that comes in on the secure port results in an error, as does any secure traffic on the non-secure port.

The only tricky issue is arranging for the client to behave correctly. First, the client has to know to use SSL. Second, it has to know to go to the secure port. If the secure port is well-known then the choice of port may be obvious, but otherwise the client will have to be specially notified. Finally, the client needs to know how to behave if it can't negotiate a secure conection. Does it fall back to an insecure connection or report failure? We'll cover this issue a little later in the chapter when we discuss reference integrity.

The primary advantage of this strategy is that it doesn't require any real modification to the application-layer protocol. You need to describe its behavior over SSL but all the protocol commands stay the same. Moreover, extant unsecured implementations simply work as is. There's no risk of bizarre interactions between secure and insecure implementations because they never interact at all.

The primary weakness of a separate ports strategy is that it consumes TCP ports twice as fast as an upward negotiation strategy. This is of special concern because many protocol designers prefer well-known ports with numbers less than 1024. On UNIX machines, only processes with effective user ID of 0 (the root user) can open ports with port numbers smaller than 1024. Thus, receiving a packet from a port less than 1024 was thought to imply that the sender had the permission of the root user. Similarly, connecting to a server on a low-numbered port is taken to mean that the server is officially sanctioned by the machine's owner because only a process owned by the root user could listen on that port.

Obviously, in the face of the Internet threat model, this is a laughable distinction. It's trivially easy to forge packets with low port numbers. Moreover, many other operating systems do not enforce the low-port-number convention and there's no way to tell whether you're talking to a machine with such an OS or not. Nevertheless, many designers have a sentimental attachment to low-numbered ports and worry about depleting them.

Another problem with this strategy is that it requires modifications to some firewalls. Many packet filtering firewalls are set not to allow TCP connections except on specific ports. Such firewalls will have to be modified to support this strategy. Finally, if you're designing a protocol for IETF standardization, you should be wary of a separate ports strategy. As of this writing, the IESG was strongly encouraging protocol designers to use upward negotiation.

7.11 Upward Negotiation

An upward negotiation strategy uses the same port for secure connections as for non-secure connections. This obviously has the advantage that it doesn't require allocating an extra port, eliminating the problems associated with that.

Furthermore, upward negotiation adds an important new feature: automatic discovery. Either the client or server can offer security, and if the other side accepts, then it can be automatically negotiated. By contrast, a separate ports strategy more or less requires the client to know that security is available. This feature adds substantial resistance to passive sniffing attacks. However, if not carefully implemented, it can make the protocol vulnerable to active downgrade attacks, as we'll see later.

An upward negotiation strategy requires substantial modifications to the code on both client and server. If the protocol doesn't have a mechanism for adding extensions, one must be added. If it does, support must be added for negotiating security. This doesn't always work correctly the first time it's designed; the mechanism in HTTP, called Upgrade, had not really been used prior to its use for TLS, and some problems were encountered as a result, as we'll discuss in Chapter 8.

Second, it's important to define the semantics of a failed handshake. Simply because both client and server support SSL does not mean that they support compatible cipher suites or keying material. If the SSL handshake fails, then the applications can disconnect and reconnect insecurely, try to continue with an insecure connection without reconnecting, or simply signal an error. The second approach requires being sure that the network buffers on either side are in a well-defined state so that SSL data is not inadvertantly processed as application protocol data.

Upward negotiation can come at a performance cost as well. When secure and insecure protocols run over separate ports, then the first packet of data is the ClientHello. However, if upward negotiation is employed, then the client and server must first establish that SSL is permitted. This can take up to one round-trip time to establish (it might be less than one round-trip if you piggyback the SSL ClientHello on the first protocol message).

Finally, although packet filtering firewalls do not need to be modified to support an upward negotiation strategy, the effect on application-layer firewall proxies is substantial. Because the application-layer proxy must be able to recognize the upward negotiation commands and get out of the way, this often requires not simply reconfiguration of the proxy but a change to the code as well. This can be a substantial deployment barrier.

7.12 Downgrade Attacks

Both methods of protocol selection are susceptible to an active downgrade attack. In this attack, the attacker convinces the client or the server that an SSL connection is not possible, thus forcing the parties to fall back and communicate via an insecure channel if they are to communicate at all. It's important to note that none of these attacks work by downgrading the SSL handshake itself. That's prevented by the digests in the Finished message. Rather, they work by making it appear as if it's impossible to negotiate an SSL connection. Thus, no SSL protocol measures can protect against them.

Separate Ports

The simplest attack to mount on a separate ports negotiation is simply to make it appear that the server isn't listening on the appropriate port at all. This is trivial to do for any attacker who can inject packets into the network. The attacker simply waits for the client to send the TCP SYN to open the connection and then forges an RST packet in response. There's no way for the client to detect that the RST came from the attacker rather than the legitimate server, so the TCP stack returns an error to the client code.

Under normal circumstances this would be a simple denial-of-service attack and of minimal concern. However, the client's (or user's) behavior can make it something far worse. The problem is illustrated by many Web pages for secure servers. Such servers want to be able to support SSL but also don't want to deny non-SSL transactions. For instance, amazon.com's Web server contains the following text:

If you received an error message when you tried to use our secure server, sign in using our standard server. If you select the secure server, the information you enter will be encrypted.

If the user follows these directions literally and clicks on the standard server link, an attacker can trivially force any connection to an insecure mode by simulating an error when the user tries the secure link. The situation can be made even worse if clients automatically fall back to insecure modes. In either case, the attacker has achieved much more than a denial-of-service attack. It's an active confidentiality and integrity attack.

Naturally, this isn't the only way that an attacker can make it appear that an SSL connection cannot be created. Other options would be to forge a ClientHello with no cipher suites or a server alert claiming that the negotiation was impossible.

Upward Negotiation

Downgrade attack on a protocol that uses an upward negotiation strategy is a little different from one using a separate ports strategy, but the theory is the same. The attacker forges a message from the server (or the client) indicating that it is unwilling to use SSL. This means that the attacker must be able to take over the TCP connection, but this isn't that difficult. Figure 7.2 shows the flow of protocol messages here.

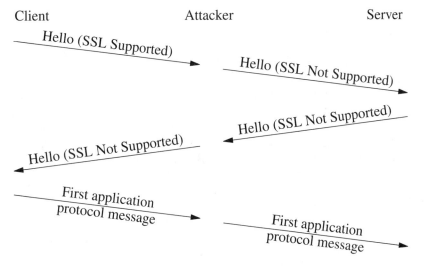

Figure 7.2 A downgrade attack on upward negotiation

As with the working upward negotiation example shown in Figure 7.1, the client attempts to form a TCP connection to the server. However, this time it forms a connection to the attacker. In Figure 7.2 we show the attacker connecting to the server posing as the client, but in many cases the attacker can just pose as the server. The client requests SSL but the attacker refuses. What happens next depends on how the client is configured.

In many cases, the client will be configured to proceed without SSL if it can't negotiate it. If all goes well, we'll *opportunistically* negotiate cryptography, but we won't worry if we can't negotiate it. In an environment where some but not all servers speak

SSL and the client has no prior knowledge about any server, this is the only sensible and interoperable way to configure it.

However, when it's configured this way, the client is completely open to this downgrade attack. As we show in Figure 7.2, it simply proceeds with an ordinary transaction. Thus, opportunistic cryptography provides excellent protection against passive attack but little protection against active attack. One partial solution to this problem (recommended in RFC 2487 [Hoffman1999a]) is to remember servers with which you have previously negotiated secure connections and insist on secure connections to them. This doesn't help when you're first encountering a new server, but it will protect against this downgrade attack against servers you've already contacted.

Even if the server requires SSL, the attacker can often mount a downgrade attack by posing as the server to the client and proxying the client's requests. This will work as long as the client doesn't demand SSL. The only case in which the server can enforce SSL successfully is if it requires SSL and client authentication. In that case the attacker will not be able to pose as the client. However, this requires all clients to have certificates as well as to support SSL. The result will be that the vast majority of clients will not be able to connect, which is often unacceptable.

Countermeasures

As we've seen, both protocol selection strategies can be vulnerable to downgrade attacks. With a separate ports strategy, all it takes is a little user inattention for security to be completely lost. The fact that legitimate servers encourage manual downgrading as a response to error makes this attack even easier.

When an upward negotiation strategy is being used, the situation is even worse. Under attack, the primary virtue of upward negotiation—automatic upgrade—becomes a weakness—automatic downgrade. Because references do not need to contain an indication that security is required in order to interoperate, it's quite common not to introduce such references at all. As a consequence, there's no way to automatically enforce security, leaving the protocol completely open to a downgrade attack.

There are two countermeasures required for this sort of attack, one technical and one social. The technical measure is straightforward; references to servers must include the fact that it is a secure site and some minimal expectations about what sorts of connection you can negotiate. The fact that SSL protects its negotiation provides some assistance here. If you can connect to the site and verify its certificate, then you can be sure that you have not been subject to a downgrade attack.

The social problem is harder. Users and programmers must be taught not to make insecure connections when secure connections fail. If you see a reference that indicates security, it's almost certainly not safe to reference it insecurely. This sort of behavior is difficult to teach users, but without it systems are ridiculously vulnerable.

7.13   Reference Integrity

The goal of reference integrity is to ensure that the server that you're connecting to is the same one that the user (or the program acting for some user) intended to connect to. This is a difficult task for several reasons.

First, the identities that servers present (distinguished names in certificates) aren't very user-friendly. More important, users aren't very motivated to pay attention to the identity of the servers they're connecting to, so the process has to be automated. Finally, many attempts to make software more user-friendly have resulted in representations of identity that are inherently difficult for software to parse. For instance, it's very easy for software to match domain names. However, software is increasingly hiding the domain names in favor of "Internet keywords," the name of the Web page, or a user's personal name. These name forms are much more difficult to map to domain names.

The overriding requirement for reference integrity is that there be a chain of trust between the identity that the application layer expects and the application layer that the certificate presented by the server. Optimally, this would consist of a single link: the identity in the certificate would match the application-layer identity. Unfortunately, this is only possible in some cases.

Failing that, the application-layer identity must be securely linkable to some other identity form. This identity form must in turn be linkable to a third identity form. This process continues until the identity can be compared to the server's certificate. Naturally, if this chain is at all long, it must be mechanically verifiable; users simply will not take the time to verify it. The major alternate forms we need to be concerned with are *IP addresses* (i.e., raw network addresses), *alternate DNS names*, and *human readable names*.

IP Addresses

As we discussed in Chapter 5, the requirement for a chain of verifiable identities is why certificates generally should not contain IP addresses. In general, DNS does not provide a secure way of mapping names to IP addresses. Secure DNS [Eastlake1999] provides some promise of fixing this problem but deployment has so far been underwhelming.

As a special case, if application-layer identities are expressed in terms of IP addresses, it's acceptable for certificates to contain IP addresses, because they can be securely compared. However, in general this is bad practice for several reasons. First, IP addresses are often obtained by dereferencing DNS names using `nslookup` or some similar tool. As we've just said, that's insecure. Second, they're subject to renumbering both when service providers change and when configurations change, so they may not be as persistent as domain names. It's difficult for users to know when such renumberings are legitimate and when they are not, so they are easily tricked into accepting spoofed connections.

Alternate DNS Names

Mapping domain names to IP addresses is not the only situation in which DNS insecurity comes into play. For a number of reasons, it's common for a single DNS name to map to a number of other DNS names. The two most common cases are CNAME and MX records. CNAMEs are usually used to provide a layer of indirection between a published name and a machine's actual name. MX records are used for e-mail routing, and we'll discuss their special problems in Chapter 10 where we discuss SMTP.

Two of the most common uses for CNAME records are simple aliasing and load balancing. Imagine that you run a very small company which is big enough to want its own Web site but not big enough to run it yourself. Instead, you farm that job out to your ISP. Nevertheless, you'd like your customers to be able to refer to your company's Web site by your company name, like so: `www.example.com`. In actuality, though, this machine is run by your ISP and it already has a name: `web1.isp.com`. A CNAME provides an alias between these two names.

> CNAME stands for *canonical name*. The idea here is that `web1.isp.com` is the canonical name of the machine and the CNAME record contains the canonical name.

Now when customers enter `www.example.com` into their browser, it automatically detects that it really needs to talk to `web1.isp.com` and so looks up its address and connects to it. If the ISP decides to move the Web site, it simply changes the target of the CNAME. Better yet, if you decide to host the Web site yourself, you just change the CNAME to point to the machine you're hosting it on, for instance `server.example.com`.

Now, imagine that your load gets so high that your single machine can't handle it any more. CNAMEs help here too because you can arrange for the name server to return a different CNAME every time, thus sharing the load between multiple servers.

Whenever we have this form of indirection, we need to carefully consider which name should appear in the certificate. From a security perspective the answer is clear but from an operational perspective it's difficult. Because DNS lookups cannot be trusted, it's not possible to create a chain of trust from the name `www.example.com` to any of these names pointed to by CNAMEs. Thus, the address that appears in the certificate *must* be `www.example.com`.

Unfortunately, using the original name (the CNAME) in the certificate is operationally problematic. In the case where the ISP is running your Web server, this would require them to obtain multiple certificates (one for each customer) or a single certificate with multiple aliases (multiple Common Names or subjectAltNames). In the case where you're running multiple servers, you'll need to share your certificate (and private key!) between all of those servers, thus increasing your security risk.

In the Web context, a common fix for this problem is to have an opening page that is accessible via HTTP only and have that point to a secure server using a URL that matches the secure server's one certificate. So, in this example the link that actually takes you to the secure server might be a link to `https://secure1.isp.com`. Of course, this sort of mismatch between URLs and the user's expectations has its own security issues which we'll take up partially in the next section and more in Chapter 9 when we discuss HTTP over SSL.

Human Readable Names

The final form of identity to consider is human readable names. Many application protocols and clients provide references to users that are in themselves representative but are
nearly meaningless to the software. For instance, it's very common for e-mail clients to
display user's names instead of their e-mail addresses. Similarly, users who view data in
Web browsers often look at the title of the document or the content of a link rather than
at the underlying URL.

Since this data is not securely bound to the server's certificate, it forms an inadequate basis for trust. Occasionally, an implementation will have access to a trustable
database that maps these names onto network names. (Even Secure DNS would not do
this, however.) Then and only then can these names be trusted. Otherwise, users need to
be presented with the opportunity to view the identity that was verified in untranslated
form. Only then can full security be provided.

7.14 Username/Password Authentication

As we stated previously, authenticating users (and clients) presents a difficult problem.
From a security perspective, it would be ideal to simply deploy certificates for every
client we wished to authenticate. However, this presents deployment problems in many
situations, so it's important to have other options available.

Username/Password

The most obvious (and commonly used) approach is simple passwords. As we stated
earlier, transmitting passwords over SSL removes the major problem with passwords—
passive sniffing attacks—but it still leaves open some other more difficult (but still possible) forms of attack.

There are three major types of attack worth considering. First, note that the security
of the channel depends on the client forming a secure connection to the right server.
This means that the client must carefully check the server's certificate. If this check is
not performed the channel is subject to a man-in-the-middle attack and the attacker can
recover the user's password.

A second variety of attack is a *password guessing* attack. As we said in Chapter 5,
users often choose very poor passwords (see [Klein1990]) such as their username, first
name, date of birth, etc. Such passwords are easily guessed. Therefore, an attacker can
simply initiate a connection to the server and try each of these easily guessed passwords
in sequence. Such an attack might not succeed with any given user, but if there is a large
user base, the probability that at least one user will choose a bad password is high.
There are a number of somewhat effective countermeasures against password guessing,
including proactive password checking, limited tries, and slowing down each password
check (to make guessing more time consuming), which we will not discuss here.

A final weakness with passwords is that they're transferable. When you authenticate
to a server you give it your password. If you've used the same password on multiple
machines (many users do) then any one of these servers can impersonate you to another

server. As you can see, although passwords are better over SSL than in the clear, they still have substantial weaknesses.

7.15 SSL Client Authentication

The other obvious approach is to use certificate-based SSL client authentication (SSL doesn't have any other kind of client authentication). This approach doesn't have any of the weaknesses we've just described for password-based authentication. In particular, there is no way that an attacker can use the attacker's client authentication information to impersonate the client—although it is of course possible for an attacker to trick the client into making an authenticated request for the attacker.

As we've said, the primary problem with certificate-based client authentication is operational. Each client who can authenticate needs to be issued a certificate. Moreover, in most cases you still need to maintain a user list on the server side, both to support access control and to support user deletion.

Certificate Issuance

The primary problem with issuing certificates is arranging to authenticate users before you issue them certificates. For obvious reasons, if you really want to map a person's physical identity to a certificate, you can't issue certificates online but rather have to see them physically. However, in most circumstances a weaker form of authentication will suffice. For instance, users might be required to provide a credit card number.

Once you've authenticated users, you need to arrange that only that user can get a certificate with that user's name. One straightforward approach to certificate issuance is to issue temporary passwords through some out-of-band mechanism. For instance, in a corporate setting, you might simply call them on the phone to deliver the password, thus providing authentication of a sort and password security in one. The password is then provided along with the certificate request (encrypted under an SSL connection, naturally). Note that if you already have a username/password-type infrastructure in place you can simply use those passwords to transition to certificates.

Access Control

In some circumstances merely knowing that a user has a certificate is enough, but in most cases administrators want to be able to provide different levels of access to different classes of users. A number of approaches have been described for embedding this information in certificates. [Blaze1999] and [Ellison1999] describe two such systems. However, in most cases it's simpler to maintain *Access Control Lists* (ACLs) that describe the actions permitted for each certificate holder. The primary advantage of this approach is that permissions can be changed simply by changing ACLs without issuing any new certificates to the clients.

This approach has the virtue that it permits you to have a mixed certificate and password infrastructure. In order to do this, all you need is a function that maps users authenticated via certificates to users in the username/password infrastructure.

Figure 7.3 shows a simple system that uses this approach. There are actually two types of lists: a user list (which also stores passwords) and ACLs. Normally, there would be one ACL for each object in the system, but we've shown only one for simplicity. In this infrastructure, Alice can authenticate by either password or certificate, Bob can authenticate by certificate only, and Charlie can authenticate by password only. ACL entries then refer to entries in the user list.

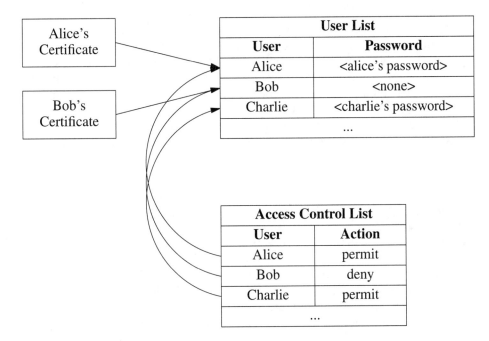

Figure 7.3 A mixed password and certificate infrastructure

Note that you can allow such users to authenticate by either method or flag users with certificates in such a way that password authentication is not allowed. The primary problem with this approach is that it requires user data to be maintained in two locations: the access control list and the CA. Thus, to create a user you have to both issue a certificate and modify the user list. Naturally, these databases can get out of synch, causing maintenance problems.

Revocation

In a dual architecture as described above, removing users is simple. You remove the entry in the access control list and do nothing else. Users can authenticate, but because their certificate doesn't map to any user, they have no permissions. The ACL entries become dangling references that can be garbage collected at some convenient later time. If you're not using ACLs (or some analagous technology), then the alternative is *Certificate Revocation Lists* (CRLs). However, as discusssed in Chapter 1, CRLs also present a significant operational problem which is exacerbated by the lack of direct support for CRLs in SSL.

Host to Host Communication

There is one special case in which certificate based authentication can be used with only minimal overhead: host to host channels. Imagine that you want to establish a secure tunnel (for a virtual private network) between two machines. In this case all you care about is the identity on the other end. In this case, the same identity checking procedures that you use for server authentication can be used for client authentication.

Moreover, if all you're interested in is authenticating the machine that is the source of a connection, you don't need to worry about access control (and therefore don't need any ACLs). Revocation is still a modest issue, but since most implementations ignore it for servers, it doesn't make much of a difference if you ignore it for clients as well.

7.16   Mutual Username/Password Authentication

So far, we've assumed that servers always authenticate via certificates. As we said in Section 7.1, this is absolutely required for secure password transmission using normal methods. However, SSL does allow operational modes in which the server remains anonymous: the SSL_DH_anon cipher suites. Under most circumstances, these cipher suites are completely vulnerable to an active attack. However, it's possible to combine passwords and anonymous cipher suites to provide a somewhat secure protocol.

Man-in-the-Middle

As discussed in Chapter 1, the primary weakness of DH is to active man-in-the-middle attack. In normal SSL operational modes, this attack is prevented by having the server sign its DH key with its static signing key. This prevents an attacker from mounting such an attack. However, if we're using anonymous mode, the server's DH key is no longer signed and so the attack again becomes possible. The only means of authentication we have left is the password shared by client and server. Somehow we have to leverage that to build a trusted connection.

One approach would be to simply use the password directly to sign the ServerKeyExchange message. Obviously, this would be a MAC rather than a digital signature, but it would have the same effect. The primary drawback to this approach is that it would require a change to SSL, because a MAC is not one of the defined methods for signing the ServerKeyExchange. Historically, there has been resistance to adding such password mechanisms directly to SSL. Thus, proposals have been made to solve this problem at the application layer.

An Approach That Won't Work

Consider the classic DH man-in-the-middle attack, shown in Figure 7.4. The attacker intercepts the DH public keys from client and server and substitutes its own public key. It is thus able to agree on a shared key (ZZ) with both client and server. Note that although the attacker is able to compute pairwise keys with both client and server, the ZZs aren't the same because the client and server private keys are not the same. Because SSL uses ZZ as the pre_master_secret, the client and server will compute different pre_master_secrets. It seems that one might be able to use this fact to protect against the man-in-the-middle attack.

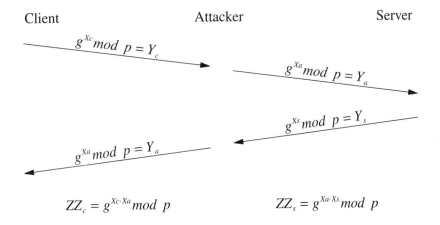

Figure 7.4 Classic DH man-in-the-middle attack

One approach that has been suggested is to use the password to compute a MAC over the master_secret (this is equivalent to computing one over the PreMasterSecret). The two sides would then exchange MACs and if they didn't match they would know they were under attack. The attacker does not know the password and therefore can't compute new MACs using it, even though he knows both ZZs.

Although this approach prevents the classic man-in-the-middle attack, there are variants for which it does not work. It turns out to be possible (by appropriate choice of forged keys) to force ZZ (as computed by both client and server) to be the same *and* to be one of a very small set of values. The signatures over ZZ will thus be the same and the attacker can just forward them from client to server and vice versa.

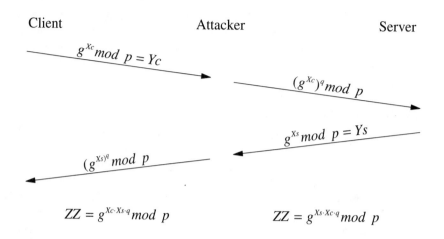

Figure 7.5 A more sophisticated man-in-the-middle attack

Figure 7.5 shows one sort of this attack. Consider the case where $p = 2q + 1$ where q is also prime and R is a relatively small number. It turns out that under these circumstances $g^q = -1$. Now, if the attacker replaces each of the public keys in transit (X) with X^q we force the resulting shared key (ZZ) to be $g^{2Xs \cdot Xy \cdot q}$. Note that ZZ is the same on either side. This is useful because

$$g^{Xs \cdot Xy \cdot q} = (g^q)^{Xs \cdot Xy} = (-1)^{Xs \cdot Xy} = 1 \; or \; -1$$

Thus the attacker has managed to force ZZ to be either 1 or -1 and can simply try them both. This attack can be extended to DH groups where $p \neq 2q + 1$.

An Approach That Will Work

We've seen that MACing the PreMasterSecret won't work. Although MACing the ServerKeyExchange would work, it requires modifying SSL, which is problematic. However, we can indirectly MAC the DH public keys by MACing the Finished message. Because the Finished message includes digests of the public keys this transitively MACs the public keys themselves. Because the public keys seen by the client and the server are not the same, this will detect this attack. This is a variant of the procedure used in the protocol STS, described in [Diffie1992]. The specific variant described here was first suggested by Bodo Moeller on the OpenSSL mailing list.

Figure 7.6 shows this process. After the SSL connection has been formed, the applications send MACs of the Finished message as their first application data. Note that it's important that each side MAC its own finished message. This method allows the construction of a secure channel without certificates, which is bootstrapped via a shared password. Moreover, both client and server know that the other side knows the password, providing for mutual authentication. This is in a sense superior to user-name/passwords with certificates because the server is forced to prove that it knows the password. Note that SSL does not have a mechanism for negotiating this technique. Client and server have to agree on it via some mechanism external to SSL.

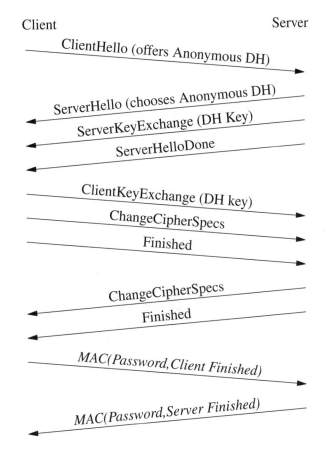

Figure 7.6 Password-based mutual authentication

An Active Dictionary Attack

Although this method is good, it does not provide total security for the password. It is possible for the attacker to mount an active attack against the connection and potentially recover the password. The attacker mounts an ordinary man-in-the-middle attack and thus shares a secret with both client and server. He then collects the MACed Finished message from either the client or server and uses this to mount his attack.

The attack is a simple variant of the dictionary search attack discussed in Chapter 5. The attacker knows the contents of the finished message but doesn't know the password used to compute the MAC. He thus tries out various potential passwords until he finds one that produces the right MAC.

Note that this attack is far superior to the password guessing attack available for regular username/password authentication because it can be carried out mostly offline. The only portion of the attack that's active is the collection of the Finished message. By contrast, the normal password guessing attack requires the server seeing every attempt.

7.17   Rehandshake

As discussed in Chapter 4, it is possible to initiate a new SSL handshake once the SSL handshake has already been completed. This is primarily useful if your server is configured such that different types of protocol requests require different types of security. Because the SSL connection is negotiated before the first byte of application data is written, there is no way of knowing which security properties to apply to the connection during the first handshake. Therefore it is sometimes a useful strategy to initiate a second handshake during the connection in light of this new information.

Client Authentication

One common reason to renegotiate is to require client authentication. Many environments allow access to some resources by any client but require authentication to access others. Requiring SSL client authentication for all connections would exclude some clients and is therefore undesirable; however, it's a requirement for other connections.

One approach would be to use some variant of the separate ports approach and have a different port for connections that required client authentication. However, a more elegant approach is to allow clients to connect and request client authentication if a client requests access to a protected resource. This tactic is used by a number of Web servers.

The primary issue with renegotiation is arranging for it to happen at the right time. The SSL specification provides no real guidance as to when renegotiation is to occur, saying only that:

This message may be ignored by the client if it does not wish to renegotiate a session, or the client may, if it wishes, respond with a no_renegotiation alert. Since handshake messages are intended to have transmission precedence over application data, it is expected that the negotiation will begin before no more than a few records are received from the client.

In the client authentication case the situation is fairly simple. The server merely wants to ensure that the client is authenticated before it provides it any restricted services. Thus, the server should send a HelloRequest and then wait for the client to start the handshake. Any requests that the server receives between the time the HelloRequest is sent and the handshake completes should be queued and processed once the client has authenticated. Naturally, if authentication fails, the connection is closed or at least the requests are rejected.

Cipher Suite Upgrading

Another use of renegotiation is to upgrade to a stronger cipher suite. As with client authentication, the server might discover that the client is asking for especially sensitive data and wish to use stronger ciphers. The timing for cipher suite upgrading is more problematic. Imagine that some traffic to and from a server is more sensitive than other traffic. The server might choose to ordinarily negotiate DES or RC4 but upgrade to 3DES when this sensitive traffic is being passed. Renegotiation can be used for this purpose as well. It could also be used to negotiate a new connection with a new ephemeral DH key to ensure Perfect Forward Secrecy.

Timing can be much trickier in this case. If all you're concerned with is confidentiality for data the server transmits, then the server can simply transmit its HelloRequest and wait as it did for client authentication. However, if data transmitted by the client must be confidential, the situation becomes more problematic because there is no way to force the client to renegotiate immediately. About the only thing the server can do is terminate the connection if the client starts sending sensitive data before renegotiating. Because the client will transmit up to the size of its TCP window, even if the server sends an error as soon as it receives the first sensitive byte, quite a lot of sensitive data will likely be transmitted under the less-secure cipher suite.

Replenishment of Keying Material

One concern that implementors often have with SSL is whether they should renegotiate to replenish their keying material, typically to prevent large-scale attacks on long-lived connections. If really large amounts of data are being transferred, new keys must be occasionally generated to prevent CBC rollover. From an application perspective, timing isn't that critical because environments where this is a concern typically are moving megabytes of data. A kilobyte more or less sent before renegotiation isn't that big a deal.

Client Behavior

The discussion in the preceding sections suggests several cases in which servers will transmit HelloRequest messages and then stop waiting for a new connection. As a consequence, clients that receive HelloRequest messages should attempt to initiate a new handshake fairly immediately. Certainly, they should do so immediately if they have sent all their traffic and the server remains idle. Failing to do so risks deadlock.

7.18   Secondary Channels

Some protocols are designed to run over more than one TCP connection. FTP [Postel1985] provides a good example. The client initiates a connection to the server and logs in. This connection is called the *control connection*. Various commands are issued over this connection. Each time a file is transferred between the client and server, it's transmitted over a second connection called the *data connection*.

Typically, the data connection is created by the server. The client chooses an ephemeral port number and tells the server over the control connection. The server then opens a connection to that port and uses a secondary connection from the server to the client in order to transmit the data.

This case is confusing because the server is doing an active open: that is, it's acting the way traditional TCP clients do. Which side is the TLS client? FTP over SSL has never been standardized, but several drafts have been published and they take a stand on this issue (see [Ford-Hutchinson2000). The client *always* acts as the TLS client, regardless of who does the active open.

This choice makes the situation somewhat simpler because some implementations will do session resumption only in the same mode in which the session was created (i.e., if they were the TLS client for the first session, they must be the client for resumed sessions). More important, however, is to realize that the choice has to be made if you are to have interoperability.

7.19   Closure

Many protocols use the TCP connection close to indicate that no more data is on its way. From a security perspective, this is problematic because TCP FINs can be forged quite easily. To fix this problem, SSL provides its own closure mechanism: the close_notify alert. However, this is not the only secure approach. If the application-layer protocol has its own indication that the connection is about to close—and it's carried over SSL—then the close_notify is superfluous from a security perspective.

All protocols should do a full SSL closure handshake if for no other reason than that the specification requires it. Moreover, if you don't do it, you're technically forbidden to resume the connection—although many implementations violate this rule. That said, it's important to specify in your protocol design what the consequences of failure to complete the closure handshake are. In particular, some cases represent security risks and some do not.

Incomplete Close

Many protocols contain states in which one side knows that there will be no more data coming from the other side. Consider the case of data being transferred via FTP. The data channel is one-way only, so when the transmitting end is finished that means that there will be no more data transmitted at all.

In such cases, many implementations send a close_notify and then immediately close the connection. This generates a condition which RFC 2818 [Rescorla2000] calls an *incomplete close*. When the other side of the connection receives the close_notify, it responds with its own close_notify alert as required by section 7.2.1 of the TLS specification. However, because the connection has already been closed by the side that sent the first close_notify, the response is a TCP RST segment.

We've been using the term "closed" very loosely here. TCP supports a *half-close* in which one side is finished sending data but is still ready to receive. In the sockets API, this is implemented using the shutdown() call with the how value set to 1. Most other APIs provide similar functionality.

Most applications, however, simply use close(), which instructs the system not to accept any more data from the other side as well. This is the cause of the RST segment: the server received traffic after it had already closed the connection.

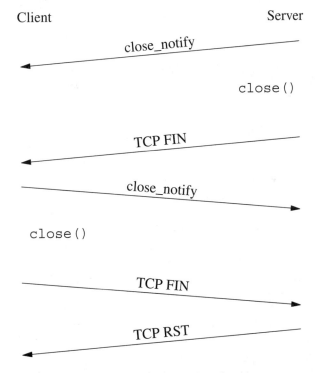

Figure 7.7 An incomplete close

Figure 7.7 shows a typical case. The server knows that the connection is finished and generates a close_notify. The server then calls close(), closing the connection completely (generating a FIN in the process). The client has no way of knowing that the server is not ready to receive more data (this might just be half-close) and sends its close_notify in response, followed by its own FIN. Because the socket is already closed on the server side, the server responds with an RST segment. Another way to get an RST is if the client has already written more data when it gets the close_notify. Note that RFC 2246 requires an implementation to stop transmitting data once it receives a close_notify, but the data might already be in the network buffers or on the wire.

An incomplete close does not necessarily present a security problem. In order to see this, consider the situation at both sides of the connection. The server knows that there will be no more protocol data (or at least that it isn't interested in any more) or it wouldn't have sent the close_notify in the first place. If there were somehow more data, this would represent a problem with the application protocol rather than the SSL connection. Whatever application data led the implementation to believe that there was no more data should have been protected just as securely as the close_notify would have been.

Now consider the view from the client's side of the connection The client knows for a fact that there will be no more data from the server because it's received an appropriate close_notify. It has generated an appropriate close_notify and had it rejected.

Premature Close

The second variety of closure failure to consider is the *premature close*. In premature close, one side closes the TCP connection (i.e., sends a FIN) without first sending a close_notify. Unlike an incomplete close, a premature close may very well represent a security threat. Recall that the close_notify exists to prevent a truncation attack. Without seeing the close_notify, the receiver cannot distinguish between a FIN segment generated by the sender and a FIN segment forged by an attacker, so a truncation attack may well be in progress.

It's worth distinguishing between two cases. In the first, the application protocol has its own end-of-data markers. If these markers are received before the FIN, then the receiver should assume that there has been an implementation error on the sender's side; this error presumably caused either the end-of-data markers to be sent too early or the close_notify to be omitted. As long as the end-of-data markers were sent over the SSL channel, they cannot have been forged.

By contrast, if the protocol does not contain end-of-data markers—or if it contains them but they were not received prior to the FIN—then it is very possible that a truncation attack is under way. It is not possible to distinguish this case from implementation errors on the sender's side. In this case, the application must treat this as an error. Under no circumstances should a session that ends in a premature close be resumed; the SSL specification clearly forbids it.

Note that failing to resume an improperly closed connection doesn't really add any security value. A premature close may indicate that the connection is under some attack, but it doesn't indicate that any of the keying material has been compromised.

Figure 7.8 summarizes the correct behavior for closure problems.

Case	Generate Error	Resume Session
Incomplete Close	No	Yes
Premature Close after End of Data	No	No
Premature Close w/o End of Data	Yes	No

Figure 7.8 Correct behavior for closure problems

7.20 Summary

This chapter has discussed the design of application protocols that use SSL. Although it's possible to achieve some security with a naive approach, getting maximal security requires paying attention to a number of important and tricky details.

Not all security services need to be provided via SSL. Although SSL is useful for securing a wide variety of protocols, there are some services it cannot perform. In particular, it can't provide security for static data. Sometimes it is useful to combine SSL with other security measures.

Both protocol selection mechanisms have value. Separate ports is easier to implement, but upward negotiation is somewhat more tasteful and has dramatically better security against passive attack.

Authenticate servers with certificates. We've discussed one special case in which servers can be authenticated using a password, but in general it's best to stick with server certificates.

Set client security expectations. In order to prevent active attacks, clients need to know what kind of security to expect from the server. This means references must include both the expected server identity and some indication that the server requires security.

Certificates are harder than passwords, but also stronger. Client authentication based on certificates presents significant deployment problems but is also far more secure than passwords, even when they are transmitted over SSL.

Define rehandshake semantics. Rehandshake can be a valuable tool, but the lack of clear specification for the timing of rehandshake can result in race conditions. Designers need to clearly specify the application protocol states in which rehandshake is allowed.

Closure is tricky. Some protocols have their own end-of-data markers, making the SSL close_notify unnecessary. Other protocols do not, making the close_notify vital to prevent a truncation attack. Designers need to carefully examine the closure behavior of their particular protocol.

8

Coding with SSL

8.1 Introduction

In previous chapters we've concentrated on SSL from a protocol perspective. For protocol designers and systems architects, this is the appropriate level of analysis. However, even the best protocol design is useless unless it can be implemented. Therefore, this chapter concentrates on SSL from the implementation perspective.

Chapter 7 examined a series of design problems commonly encountered when working with SSL. Most of these problems can be approached using one of several well-known design patterns. Similarly, implementors working with SSL need to perform many of the same implementation tasks regardless of which application protocol they're working with. This chapter is devoted to describing these tasks and to programming idioms that have proved successful in executing them.

8.2 SSL Implementations

Because SSL implementations are readily available for most common languages, most programmers will be using a toolkit rather than implementing SSL themselves. We assume that you have such a toolkit available. Although each SSL toolkit has its own *Application Programming Interface* (API), the interfaces designed for each language typically share a common style, making code written for one toolkit instructive even if you are using a different one.

For our purposes, we've chosen two freely available SSL toolkits, one in C and one in Java. For C, we've chosen OpenSSL, derived from Eric Young's SSLeay toolkit. For Java, we've chosen PureTLS, written by the author of this book. Both toolkits have APIs that are fairly typical for their respective languages. Moreover, both are readily available for download on the Internet. See Chapter 2 for details.

8.3   Sample Programs

The best way to learn programming techniques is to write programs. To that end, we'll write two programs—a client and server pair—in both C and Java for a total of four programs. Our intent is to demonstrate programming techniques rather than to provide a detailed guide to programming with PureTLS or OpenSSL, so in cases where the OpenSSL-based and PureTLS-based code is substantially identical we'll choose one version. However, where the idioms are dramatically different between C and Java, we'll show examples for both languages.

Platform Issues

The C programs were developed with OpenSSL 0.9.4 on FreeBSD. They also work with OpenSSL 0.9.5a. Only the most basic OpenSSL functions are used so they should continue to work with most past and future versions. They should compile and run without modification on FreeBSD and other UNIX and UNIX-like operating systems. Some modification will probably be required in order to compile them on Windows.

The Java programs were developed with PureTLS 0.9b1 on FreeBSD with JDK 1.1.8. They have been tested with JDK 1.2.2 on Windows NT. They should compile and run with future versions of PureTLS.

We've deliberately chosen to emphasize UNIX over Windows for a number of reasons. First, SSLeay's predecessor, OpenSSL was designed for UNIX and thus OpenSSL's interface more closely matches that of UNIX than that of Windows. Moreover, networking APIs even on non-UNIX systems are typically based on sockets, so writing sockets-based networking code is widely applicable. Windows's networking interface, Winsock, is based on sockets but is not identical to it.

The second reason is that Microsoft provides its own API for SSL: SChannel, described in [Microsoft2000]. SChannel's interface is rather different from those provided by other SSL implementations so showing example programs using it would be of limited use to non-Windows programmers. By contrast, code written using OpenSSL is of broad applicability. The UNIX code we show is sufficiently generic that it should be portable to Windows without too much trouble.

The final reason is simple taste. In the opinion of the author, the UNIX programming API is cleaner and allows a simpler exposition of the SSL issues with a minimum of operating specific issues.

Client Program

Our client is the simplest kind of interactive client. It initiates an SSL connection to the server on the other end and then simply forwards data between the user and the server. In other words, it reads data from the keyboard and sends that data to the server over the

SSL connection. Similarly, it reads data from the server over the SSL connection and writes that data to the screen.

Despite its simplicity, this sort of program can serve a useful debugging purpose. Many Internet protocols (SMTP, HTTP, IMAP, ...) consist of simple ASCII commands and responses. Thus, a simple client can be used to contact the server directly for debugging purposes. The UNIX `telnet` program—which opens a simple TCP connection—is often used for this sort of server debugging.

This client does have one idiosyncracy: data is sent to the server in *line-by-line* mode on many systems. The UNIX terminal driver (and some others) by default buffers keyboard data until the user presses the return key. This behavior can be changed but it doesn't serve any useful demonstration purpose to do so.

Server Program

The server program is a simple *echo server*. It waits for TCP connections from clients. When it accepts one it negotiates an SSL connection. Once the connection is negotiated, it reads data from the client and then retransmits it right back. Finally, when the client closes the connection the server closes its side of the connection.

Obviously, this isn't that useful a service—although standard UNIX systems do come with an echo server that does this job in an insecure fashion—but this program allows us to demonstrate the essential features of a network server: waiting for connections, servicing them, and cleaning up afterwards.

Programs in Action

Figure 8.1 shows the interaction of our simple client and server programs. The user types data on the keyboard and it's transmitted to the server. The server simply echos the data back to the client. Finally, the client program prints the data to the screen.

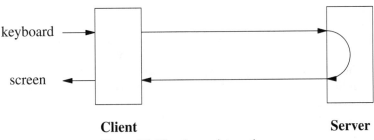

Client   **Server**

Figure 8.1 Client/server interaction

Figure 8.2 shows a demonstration run of our Java client (although the output of the C client would be nearly identical.)

```
[63] java SClient          Started the program
line 1                     Typed at keyboard
line 1                     Printed by client program
line 2                     Typed at keyboard
line 2                     Printed by client program
[64]                       Pressed Control-D to end program.
```

Figure 8.2 Sample run of SClient

Program Presentation

We've chosen to present only source code fragments in this chapter to illustrate the techniques we're discussing. Appendix A contains a complete source code listing for all the example programs as well as a road map to the various source files. You can tell which source file a given fragment comes from by examining the boundary lines at the top and bottom of the listing.

8.4   Context Initialization

The first task to perform when writing a program that uses SSL is to set up a context that will be used by the system. Most implementations do this by having a context object which the programmer needs to initialize. This context object is then used to create a new connection object for each new SSL connection. It is these connection objects which are used to do SSL handshakes, reads, and writes.

This approach has two advantages. First, the context object allows many structures to be initialized only once, saving time. In most applications, every SSL connection will use the same keying material, root list, etc. Rather than reloading this material for every connection, we simply load it into the context object at program startup. When we wish to create a new connection, we can simply point that connection to the context object.

The second advantage of having a single context object is that it allows multiple SSL connections to share data. The most obvious case where this is relevant is for SSL session resumption. Session data can be stored in the context object so that you can automatically resume a session merely by creating a new connection with the same context object.

Client Initialization

In general, a client will have to perform the following initialization tasks.

Load CAs. In nearly every SSL connection the server provides its certificate to identify itself. Obviously, in order to verify this certificate, the client needs to have a list of the CAs that it trusts to sign server certificates. Typically this list is stored in a file on disk somewhere and the client needs to load it.

Load client keying material. If the client has keys that it is using for client authentication, it will need to load them and their associated certificates as well. As we discussed in Chapter 5, these will usually be either in a file on disk or on some hardware device. In either case, the program will likely need to provide a password to access the keys.

Seed random number generator. Because every application environment is different, it is often difficult for toolkit programmers to generate good random seed data. For instance, screen or mouse data is often a good source of randomness, but some environments have neither a screen nor a mouse. Thus, many toolkits leave random number seeding up to the applications programmer. This usually means finding some source of randomness on your system and feeding it to the toolkit.

Set allowable cipher suites. Most toolkits have some set of cipher suites that they are prepared to negotiate by default. This may not suit your application and you should be prepared to change them. Many toolkits allow you to do this either at context setup time or on a per-connection basis.

The exact number of operations required to perform these actions depends on the particular toolkit you're using. For instance, SPYRUS's TLSGold loads all of its keying material from a single file in one operation whereas OpenSSL requires a number of different loading operations.

Server Initialization

In general, server initialization is a superset of client initialization. Although it's technically possible for a server that doesn't require client authentication not to have a list of CAs it trusts, it's good practice to check one's own certificates when initializing. This protects against data corruption and user error. Thus, loading a CA list is a good idea for servers as well. In addition, some server-specific initialization may be required.

Set DH group. If you're planning on using ephemeral DH mode, then the server needs to be loaded with the DH group to use. Since DH group generation is so slow, it's desirable to do this at startup time. Frequently, you'll want to store a long-term DH group on disk and then load it up at this time rather than generate a new group every time you start up.

Set ephemeral RSA keys. Similarly, if you plan to use ephemeral RSA (pretty much a requirement if you're using long RSA keys and supporting export cipher suites) you may want to load an ephemeral RSA key at this time. A lot of toolkits will generate one automatically as needed, but this approach avoids incurring that performance cost later.

Java Initialization

Demo.java

```
1       import COM.claymoresystems.sslg.*;
2       import COM.claymoresystems.ptls.*;

3       public class Demo {
4           public static final String host=  "localhost";
5           public static final int port=  4433;
6           public static final String root=  "root.pem";
7           public static final String random= "random.pem";

8           static SSLContext createSSLContext(String keyfile,String password){
9             SSLContext ctx=new SSLContext();

10            try {
11              ctx.loadRootCertificates(root);
12              ctx.loadEAYKeyFile(keyfile,password);
13              ctx.useRandomnessFile(random,password);
14            } catch (Exception e){
15              throw new InternalError(e.toString());
16            }

17            return ctx;
18          }
19        }
```

Demo.java

Figure 8.3 Demo source code

Demo.java, shown in Figure 8.3, contains all the generic initialization code we'll be using for PureTLS. It also contains a number of global definitions for things like the port number we're using. Our client and server programs are all subclasses of Demo.

Import other packages

1–2 The public interface of PureTLS lives in two Java packages. COM.claymoresyst ems.sslg contains interfaces and COM.claymoresystems.ptls contains the implementations.

Set constants

4–7 In a real program, variables like the locations of files, host names, and port numbers would be in a configuration file or input by the user. For our purposes we just hardwire them into the code.

Initialize context

9–18   PureTLS uses the `SSLContext` object to store its context. Once the context object is created, we need to load the root certificates and the key file we'll be using. Note that PureTLS requires a password to load its random file because the file is encrypted on disk. This prevents an attacker who can read the random file from reproducing the random stream.

C Initialization

`initialize_ctx()`, shown in Figure 8.4, serves the same purpose for OpenSSL as the `Demo` class does for PureTLS. This function is considerably longer than `Demo`, partly due to error checking each call: Java's exception mechanism does this for us with PureTLS. However, OpenSSL's setup is also somewhat more complicated, which complicates our example code.

Initialize global data

44-52   Before we can even create an SSL context we need to initialize the OpenSSL library itself using `SSL_library_init()`. The rest of this code allows us to display somewhat mnemonic error strings instead of error numbers by initializing the error list.

Initialize context

53-69   OpenSSL calls its SSL context variable an `SSL_CTX` (which presumably stands for SSL context). The initialization code is fairly straightforward, but a few fine points are worth comment. First, note the use of the `meth` parameter to `SSL_CTX_new()`. The purpose of this parameter is twofold. First, it allows us to set the SSL version that this context is prepared to negotiate.

More important, this technique allows us to link in only those sections of code that we need. Each `method` references the various functions and object files needed to implement it. In most systems, the linker links in only those library functions that are transitively referenced by `main()`. (That is to say, those functions that are referenced by `main()` or referenced by a function referenced by `main()`, and so on.) Thus, if you only specify `SSLv3_method()`, the SSLv2 and TLS functions are never even linked into the final object, reducing binary size. To write a client or server that would work with any SSL version you might use `SSLv23_method()`.

Also, notice the use of a password callback in lines 59–60. In PureTLS, passwords are provided directly to the library via API calls. In OpenSSL 0.9.4, OpenSSL, the library requests passwords from the user via a callback. In this case, we've replaced the default callback (which prompts the user via the terminal) with one that simply returns our hardwired password. In later versions of OpenSSL, it is possible for the programmer to pass in the password directly via an API call.

Common C Code

Our demo programs also use a number of other common subroutines and variables found in `common.c`. The function prototypes for these functions are found in `common.h`, which is included in all our other source files. `common.h` also includes a

common.c

```
38        SSL_CTX *initialize_ctx(keyfile,password)
39          char *keyfile;
40          char *password;
41          {
42            SSL_METHOD *meth;
43            SSL_CTX *ctx;

44            if(!bio_err){
45              /* Global system initialization*/
46              SSL_library_init();
47              SSL_load_error_strings();

48              /* An error write context */
49              bio_err=BIO_new_fp(stderr,BIO_NOCLOSE);
50            }

51            /* Set up a SIGPIPE handler */
52            signal(SIGPIPE,sigpipe_handle);

53            /* Create our context*/
54            meth=SSLv3_method();
55            ctx=SSL_CTX_new(meth);

56            /* Load our keys and certificates*/
57            if(!(SSL_CTX_use_certificate_file(ctx,keyfile,SSL_FILETYPE_PEM)))
58              berr_exit("Couldn't read certificate file");

59            pass=password;
60            SSL_CTX_set_default_passwd_cb(ctx,password_cb);
61            if(!(SSL_CTX_use_PrivateKey_file(ctx,keyfile,SSL_FILETYPE_PEM)))
62              berr_exit("Couldn't read key file");

63            /* Load the CAs we trust*/
64            if(!(SSL_CTX_load_verify_locations(ctx,CA_LIST,0)))
65              berr_exit("Couldn't read CA list");
66            SSL_CTX_set_verify_depth(ctx,1);

67            /* Load randomness */
68            if(!(RAND_load_file(RANDOM,1024*1024)))
69              berr_exit("Couldn't load randomness");

70            return ctx;
71          }
```

common.c

Figure 8.4 `initialize_ctx()`: initialization for OpenSSL

number of include files which we'll need in the other source files. Last, it includes a number of hardwired constants for things like the port number and the root file. We've reproduced `common.h` in Figure 8.5 for your viewing pleasure.

```
1       #ifndef _common_h
2       #define _common_h

3       #include <stdio.h>
4       #include <stdlib.h>
5       #include <errno.h>
6       #include <sys/types.h>
7       #include <sys/socket.h>
8       #include <netinet/in.h>
9       #include <netinet/tcp.h>
10      #include <netdb.h>
11      #include <fcntl.h>
12      #include <signal.h>

13      #include <openssl/ssl.h>

14      #define CA_LIST "root.pem"
15      #define HOST "localhost"
16      #define PORT 4433
17      #define BUFSIZZ 1024

18      extern BIO *bio_err;
19      int berr_exit (char *string);
20      int err_exit(char *string);

21      SSL_CTX *initialize_ctx(char *keyfile, char *password);
22      void destroy_ctx(SSL_CTX *ctx);

23      #endif
```

Figure 8.5 `common.h`

Server Initialization

Servers may require additional initialization steps that clients do not. As we discussed earlier, servers that need to do ephemeral keying will probably want to load either the DH group or the RSA key that they want to use. Also, in OpenSSL you need to explicitly activate session resumption for servers, which is done in lines 23–24. Figure 8.6 shows the additional server initialization steps required for OpenSSL.

```
19          /* Build our SSL context*/
20          ctx=initialize_ctx(KEYFILE,PASSWORD);
21          load_dh_params(ctx,DHFILE);
22          generate_eph_rsa_key(ctx);


23          SSL_CTX_set_session_id_context(ctx,(void*)&s_server_session_id_context,
24            sizeof s_server_session_id_context);
```

Figure 8.6 OpenSSL server initialization

8.5 Client Connect

Once the client has initialized the SSL context, it's ready to connect to the server. SSL toolkit APIs are typically closely modeled after normal networking APIs. Thus, C APIs closely resemble the Berkeley Sockets API with a series of SSL calls analogous to sockets calls. Java APIs typically subclass `java.net.Socket`—although Sun's JSSE [JavaSoft1999] takes a rather different approach which we won't show here.

Java Client Connect

PureTLS implements a class `SSLSocket` which subclasses `java.net.Socket`. As a consequence, it's trivial to make a simple SSL connection using code nearly identical to that you would use to make an ordinary socket connection. The primary additional wrinkle is that we need to check the distinguished name in the server's certificate against the hostname we want to connect to, as shown in Figure 8.7.

Extract Common Name

13–26   In order to check the server's certificate, we'll need to extract the Common Name from the DN. The `dnToCommonName()` method takes care of this. Recall that distinguished names are a sequence of *relative distinguished names* (RDNs). RDNs themselves are a list of *attribute value assertions* (AVAs). AVAs are just attribute-value pairs. In PureTLS, DNs are represented as `Vectors`. Their content RDNs are also `Vectors`, and the AVAs themselves are represented as arrays of `Strings` with the 0th element being the attribute and the first element being the value. Thus, this code takes the CN AVA out of the first (most local) RDN in the DN.

Connect to server

30   The connect itself is trivial. In the Java world, the connect is performed when you create a new `Socket`. `Socket` provides a constructor that automatically performs name resolution so we don't even need to look up the server's IP address.

```
                                                              ___ Client.java
13          private static String dnToCommonName(DistinguishedName dN)
14            throws IOException {
15            Vector dn=(Vector)dN.getName();
16            Vector rdn=(Vector)dn.lastElement();

17            if(rdn.size()!=1)
18              throw new IOException
19                ("DN forms with multiple AVAs per RDN are unacceptable");

20            String[] ava=(String [])rdn.firstElement();

21            if(ava.length!=2)
22              throw new IOException("Bogus AVA array");

23            if(!ava[0].equals("CN"))
24              throw new IOException("CN must be most local AVA");

25            return ava[1];
26          }

27          public static SSLSocket connect(SSLContext ctx,String host,int port)
28            throws IOException {
29            // Connect to the remote host
30            SSLSocket s=new SSLSocket(ctx,host,port);

31            // Check the certificate chain
32            Vector certChain=s.getCertificateChain();

33            // Length check
34            if(certChain.size()>2)
35              throw new IOException("Certificate chain too long");

36            // Hostname check (using Common Name)
37            Certificate cert=(Certificate)certChain.lastElement();
38            String commonName=dnToCommonName(cert.getSubjectName());
39            if(!commonName.equals(host))
40              throw new IOException("Host name does not match commonName");

41            return s;
42          }
                                                              ___ Client.java
```

Figure 8.7 PureTLS client connection

Check server certificate

31–42   Most of this function is taken up by checking the server's domain name against the server's certificate. Note that since we used the domain name to create the socket, PureTLS could theoretically perform this check for us. However, this would reduce programmer flexibility. The check shown here is about the most trivial possible. Note that we check the certificate chain length rather than relying on the Basic Constraints extension. Ideally, if Basic Constraints were universally available, PureTLS would check them for us. (It doesn't.)

C Client Connect

The OpenSSL API is considerably more complicated to use than the PureTLS API. In part this reflects the fact that Berkeley Sockets is substantially more complicated than Java networking. Additionally, we'll see that the OpenSSL API is somewhat more flexible than the PureTLS API.

Unlike PureTLS, OpenSSL requires us to create a TCP connection between client and server on our own and then use the TCP socket to create an SSL socket. We use the function `tcp_connect()` to do this job. This function (shown in Figure 8.8) should be familiar to anyone who's ever done any TCP programming: we use `gethostbyname()` to resolve the IP address of the server and then use `socket()` and `connect()`.

```
                                                                    client.c
3      int tcp_connect()
4      {
5          struct hostent *hp;
6          struct sockaddr_in addr;
7          int sock;

8          if(!(hp=gethostbyname(HOST)))
9            berr_exit("Couldn't resolve host");
10         memset(&addr,0,sizeof(addr));
11         addr.sin_addr=*(struct in_addr*)hp->h_addr_list[0];
12         addr.sin_family=AF_INET;
13         addr.sin_port=htons(PORT);

14         if((sock=socket(AF_INET,SOCK_STREAM,IPPROTO_TCP))<0)
15           err_exit("Couldn't create socket");
16         if(connect(sock,(struct sockaddr *)&addr,sizeof(addr))<0)
17           err_exit("Couldn't connect socket");
18         return sock;
19     }
                                                                    client.c
```

Figure 8.8 `tcp_connect()` function

Separating the TCP connection from the SSL connection has both advantages and disadvantages. The primary disadvantage is obvious: it's more difficult to program. However, functions like `tcp_connect()` are fairly common C idiom and any competent network programmer has likely written them many times. Moreover, if you're working with a preexisting network application it will already have such code and integrating this style of SSL API will be correspondingly easier.

However, separating the TCP connect and the SSL handshake means that the SSL API doesn't know the DNS name or port that the server is expected to have. This means that such a toolkit cannot (even in principle) automatically check the server's certificate against the DNS name. The application code must do the check. Also, as we'll see later, without the server's domain name, the client cannot know which session to attempt to resume, requiring the programmer to take care of client-side session resumption.

Requiring the programmer to do the TCP connect does have a number of flexibility advantages. Because an upward negotiation strategy requires that the application protocol have access to the socket in order to negotiate the transition to SSL, this sort of API is required if you want to do upward negotiation. Moreover, as we'll see in Chapter 9, some forms of proxying require that the application protocol have access to the socket before the SSL handshake.

C Client SSL Handshake

The `main()` function of `sclient.c`, shown in Figure 8.9 (see next page), is responsible for connecting to the server and performing the SSL handshake.

Create `SSL_CTX`

18–19   The first thing we need to do is construct the `SSL_CTX` object using `initialize_ctx()`. No further initialization is required on the client.

Connect to the server

20–21   We use our `tcp_connect()` function to connect to the server.

SSL handshake

22–28   Once we've created the TCP connection to the server, we need to turn on SSL. OpenSSL uses the `SSL` object to represent an SSL connection. The most important thing to notice about this stage is that we don't directly attach the `SSL` object to the socket. Rather, we create a `BIO` object using the socket and then attach the `SSL` object to the `BIO`. OpenSSL uses `BIO` objects to provide a layer of abstraction for I/O. As long as your object meets the `BIO` interface, it doesn't matter what the underlying I/O device is.

This abstraction layer provides even more flexibility than simply separating the TCP connect and the SSL handshake: It's perfectly possible with OpenSSL to do SSL handshakes on devices that aren't sockets at all—provided that you have an appropriate `BIO` object. For instance, one of the OpenSSL test programs connects an SSL client and server purely through memory buffers. A more practical use would be to support some protocol that can't be accessed via sockets. For instance, you could run SSL over a serial line.

```
10        int main(argc,argv)
11          int argc;
12          char **argv;
13          {
14            SSL_CTX *ctx;
15            SSL *ssl;
16            BIO *sbio;
17            int sock;

18            /* Build our SSL context*/
19            ctx=initialize_ctx(KEYFILE,PASSWORD);

20            /* Connect the TCP socket*/
21            sock=tcp_connect();

22            /* Connect the SSL socket */
23            ssl=SSL_new(ctx);
24            sbio=BIO_new_socket(sock,BIO_NOCLOSE);
25            SSL_set_bio(ssl,sbio,sbio);
26            if(SSL_connect(ssl)<=0)
27              berr_exit("SSL connect error");
28            check_cert_chain(ssl,HOST);

29            /* read and write */
30            read_write(ssl,sock);

31            destroy_ctx(ctx);
32          }
```

Figure 8.9 `sclient.c` `main()` function

Once we've established the SSL connection, we check the certificate chain in the now familiar fashion: we check the Common Name against the host name. The function `check_cert_chain()`, shown in Figure 8.10, is analogous to the certificate check we showed in Figure 8.7. Note, however, that we don't check the certificate chain length here. Instead, the length check is done automatically by OpenSSL as long as we set the maximum chain length using `SSL_CTX_set_verify_depth()`, as we did in `initialize_ctx()`.

```
                                                              _____ client.c
25        void check_cert_chain(ssl,host)
26          SSL *ssl;
27          char *host;
28          {
29            X509 *peer;
30            char peer_CN[256];

31            if(SSL_get_verify_result(ssl)!=X509_V_OK)
32              berr_exit("Certificate doesn't verify");

33            /*Check the cert chain. The chain length
34              is automatically checked by OpenSSL when we
35              set the verify depth in the ctx

36              All we need to do here is check that the CN
37              matches
38            */
39            /*Check the common name*/
40            peer=SSL_get_peer_certificate(ssl);
41            X509_NAME_get_text_by_NID(X509_get_subject_name(peer),
42              NID_commonName, peer_CN, 256);
43            if(strcasecmp(peer_CN,host))
44            err_exit("Common name doesn't match host name");
45          }
                                                              _____ client.c
```

Figure 8.10 check_cert_chain() function

8.6 Server Accept

The code for the server side of the SSL connection is conceptually similar to the client side. As before, the toolkit APIs mimic the programming idioms for the languages they're written in. Thus, the Java code uses a subclass of ServerSocket and the C code uses accept() and SSL_accept().

Java Server Accept

`java.net` uses a class called `ServerSocket` to accept connections as a server. `ServerSocket.accept()` returns a `Socket`. Sockets behave identically whether they were created using `ServerSocket.accept()` or `new Socket()`. PureTLS mimics this using a class called `SSLServerSocket`. The code to do an accept using PureTLS is shown in Figure 8.11.

```
                                                                      Server.java
23          SSLServerSocket listen=new SSLServerSocket(ctx,port);

24          while(true){
25            SSLSocket s=(SSLSocket)listen.accept();

26            // Process this connection in a new thread
27            ReadWrite rw=new ReadWrite(s,s.getInputStream(),
28              s.getOutputStream());
29            rw.start();
30          }
                                                                      Server.java
```

Figure 8.11 PureTLS server accept loop

This code is fairly simple. After we've created our `SSLServerSocket` we enter an infinite loop, calling `accept()` and then serve the resulting socket. The return value of `accept()` is a `Socket`. In fact, it's possible to SSL-enable a server even if it's completely SSL oblivious merely by passing it an `SSLServerSocket` rather than a `ServerSocket`. This is only possible because the PureTLS classes extend the `java.net` classes.

In practice, however, most applications want to be able to use `SSLSocket`-specific methods so they cast the return value of `accept()` to an `SSLSocket`, as we do in line 25. If we wanted, for instance, to discover the cipher suite we negotiated, this cast would be necessary. In line 25 we cast the return value of `accept()` to an `SSLSocket` because `accept()` returns a `Socket`. If we were willing to write all of our code simply in terms of `Socket`'s methods, then we would not make this cast, but would rather operate solely in terms of `Socket` methods.

C Server Accept

As with the C client accept, OpenSSL requires the programmer to perform the TCP accept. With the TCP socket in hand, we then create `BIO` and `SSL` objects, exactly as we did to connect. However, instead of calling `SSL_connect()` we instead call `SSL_accept()`, as shown in Figure 8.12.

```
                                                                    sserver.c
90          sock=tcp_listen();

91          while(1){
92           if((s=accept(sock,0,0))<0)
93             err_exit("Problem accepting");

94             sbio=BIO_new_socket(s,BIO_NOCLOSE);
95             ssl=SSL_new(ctx);
96             SSL_set_bio(ssl,sbio,sbio);

97             if((r=SSL_accept(ssl)<=0))
98               berr_exit("SSL accept error");

99             echo(ssl,s);
100         }
                                                                    sserver.c
```

Figure 8.12 OpenSSL server accept loop

One difference between the C code and the Java code that isn't instantly apparent is that `sserver` can handle only one client at a time. By contrast, `Server` (our Java server) can handle an arbitrary number of clients. The difference is hinted at in line 29 of Figure 8.11: The `ReadWrite` class that we use to echo data between client and server is subclassed from `Thread`. When we call `start()` it forks off a new thread to handle the new client, leaving the original thread to handle new clients.

   We could get a somewhat similar effect by calling `fork()` in `sserver`. However, we'd need to make a few more changes to get as clean a result as we get in Java. We'll cover this topic in more detail in Section 8.8.

8.7 Simple I/O Handling

Once we've established a SSL connection, we'd like to be able to send data over it. In principle, this can be done in a fashion analogous to sending data over TCP sockets. In practice, using SSL introduces some subtleties that need to be dealt with. We'll start with a simple task and build toward progressively more complex cases.

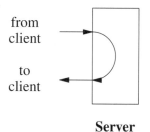

Server

Figure 8.13 Server I/O

The simplest example of SSL I/O in these programs is the server side. Figure 8.13 reprises the server-side of our diagram from Figure 8.1. As you can see, the server's job is very simple: read data from the client and echo it back. If there's no data available to write to the client, do nothing. Figure 8.14 shows this code.

The implementation of echo() should be familiar to anyone who's ever written a TCP server. It's mostly just the standard TCP read/write loop with calls to SSL_read() and SSL_write() replacing calls to read() and write(). This provides us with a nice illustration of how OpenSSL does things without having to concern ourselves with the new complexities introduced by SSL; we'll consider those in Section 8.9.

echo() is passed the SSL object to read from in the argument ssl. It's also passed the socket that ssl is attached to in the argument s. We don't use s for most of the function but we need it when we close down the socket at the very end.

Read data

10–20   The first thing we do in our loop is read some data from the client side of our SSL connection. This is easily done by choosing a buffer of appropriate size and calling SSL_read(). Note that buffer size isn't really that important here. The semantics of SSL_read(), like the semantics of read(), are that it returns the data that is available, even if it's less than the requested amount. On the other hand, if no data is available, then the call to read *blocks*—the call waits until some data is available and returns that.

The choice of BUFSIZZ, then, is basically a performance tradeoff. The tradeoff is quite different here than when we're simply reading from normal sockets. In that case, each call to read() requires a context switch into the kernel. Because context switches are expensive, programmers try to use large buffers to reduce them. However, when we're using SSL the number of calls to read()—and hence context switches—is largely determined by the number of records the data was written in rather than the number of calls to SSL_read().

For instance, if the client wrote a 1000-byte record and we call SSL_read() in chunks of 1 byte, then the first call to SSL_read() will result in the record being read

```
                                                                          echo.c
3        void echo(ssl,s)
4          SSL *ssl;
5          int s;
6          {
7            char buf[BUFSIZZ];
8            int r,len,offset;

9            while(1){
10             /* First read data */
11             r=SSL_read(ssl,buf,BUFSIZZ);
12             switch(SSL_get_error(ssl,r)){
13               case SSL_ERROR_NONE:
14                 len=r;
15                 break;
16               case SSL_ERROR_ZERO_RETURN:
17                 goto end;
18               default:
19                 berr_exit("SSL read problem");
20             }

21             /* Now keep writing until we've written everything*/
22             offset=0;

23             while(len){
24               r=SSL_write(ssl,buf+offset,len);
25               switch(SSL_get_error(ssl,r)){
26                 case SSL_ERROR_NONE:
27                   len-=r;
28                   offset+=r;
29                   break;
30                 default:
31                   berr_exit("SSL write problem");
32               }
33             }
34           }
35         end:
36           SSL_shutdown(ssl);
37           SSL_free(ssl);
38           close(s);
39         }
                                                                          echo.c
```

Figure 8.14 echo(): a simple server echo routine

in and the rest of the calls will just read it out of the SSL buffer. Thus, the choice of buffer size is less significant when we're using SSL than with normal sockets.

> Note that if the data were written in a series of small records, you might want to read all of them at once with a single call to read(). OpenSSL provides a flag SSL_CTRL_SET_READ_AHEAD that turns on this behavior.

Note the use of the switch on the return value of SSL_get_error() in line 12. The convention with normal sockets is that any negative number (typically −1) indicates failure and that one then checks errno to determine what actually happened. Obviously errno won't work here since that only shows system errors and we'd like to be able to act on SSL errors. Also, errno requires careful programming in order to be thread safe.

Instead of errno, OpenSSL provides the SSL_get_error() call. This call lets us examine the return value and figure out whether an error occurred and what it was. In this case, we're concerned with only one of three cases.

The return value was positive. In this case, we've read some data and we set the len value to that length in order to write it later.

The return value was zero. This does *not* mean that there was no data available. In that case, we would have blocked as discussed above. Rather, it means that the socket is closed and there will never be any data available to read. Thus, we exit the loop.

The return value was something negative. This signals some kind of error, but we need to use SSL_get_error() to find out exactly what. Since this program has no error handling, we simply default to berr_exit() which prints an error message and exits. A more sophisticated program would have more switch branches to determine exactly what kind of error had occurred and take appropriate action.

Note that in this case, since we handle all error conditions the same, we could simply have checked the return value for being positive, negative, or zero, and acted accordingly. Indeed, another perfectly good idiom would be to only enter the switch statement if the value were negative, handling the non-error cases directly inline. Also note that SSL_get_error() is an OpenSSL specific feature. Some other toolkits choose to use the return value directly to indicate the error value.

Write data

21–33   By the time we get to this section of the code we've definitely read some data from the client. That data is stored in buf (starting at position 0) and is of length len. The job of this code is to echo that data back to the client (i.e., to write it to ssl).

At first glance, the outer while() loop may seem puzzling. After all, there was no such loop when we were reading data from the network. The reason for this is simple: we want to write all the data to the network. The semantics of SSL_write() guarantee only that some data will be written, not necessarily all of it. The return value tells us how much. Thus, if not all the data is written in one call, we need to loop until we've written it all.

However, we want to write the data that we haven't written, not rewrite the data we've already written. In order to do this, we need to maintain a pointer to the end of the data that we've written (and hence to the beginning of the data we need to write). Thus, we keep the variable `offset`. At the beginning of this loop it is set to zero because we've written no data. However, once we write some data, we increment it by the length of the data written and decrement `len` accordingly. Finally, when `len` is zero (and `offset` points to the end of the buffer) we exit the loop.

Why is it so important to write all the data? Consider the case where the user types something and then waits for the server to respond. Now, the server goes to write the data but only succeeds in writing part of it. Without the loop at line 23, the server would jump back to line 9 and try to read data from the client. However, the client is waiting for the server, so there isn't any data to read. The server just blocks in the `SSL_read()`. We've now got a deadlock because the client is waiting for the server but the server is waiting for the client—even though there is something the server could be doing: writing the data.

The way out of this situation, of course, is for the server to finish writing all of its data before it waits for the client. Although ultimately in this situation the server will have to write all of its data first, there are other ways to arrange that than looping around the `SSL_write()`. We'll see another approach to this problem in Section 8.8.

> In practice, this call to `SSL_write()` should always write all the data before returning. By default, OpenSSL insists on this behavior. However, if the `SSL_MODE_ENABLE_PARTIAL_WRITE` flag is set, then it will return after writing one record even if there is more than one record's worth of data in the write buffer. Thus, if this flag was set and we were working with larger blocks than 1024 bytes, we might very well see partial writes.

As we did when reading, we use `SSL_get_error()` to process the return value. However, we're only concerned with two cases here:

The return value was positive. In this case, we wrote some data.

The return value was non-positive. In this case, some error occurred. Note that we shouldn't ever see a zero return value. If no data can be written then we'll block. If the socket is closed we should see an actual error.

Close the connection

36–39 When we reach the bottom of the loop then we know that we've read all the data that the client will send, so we are ready to close the socket. We call `SSL_shutdown()` to send the close_notify and then free the `SSL` structure and close the socket.

8.8 Multiplexed I/O Using Threads

The simple I/O discipline we saw in the previous section works fine for the server because its only source of input is the client. However, this approach is inadequate for the client. Consider Figure 8.15, which shows the inputs and outputs of the client. The client has to listen simultaneously to two sources of input, the keyboard and the server. Input from the keyboard and the server can appear *asynchronously*. That is to say that they can appear in any order. This means that a simple read/write discipline like we had for the server is fundamentally inadequate.

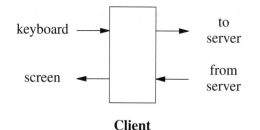

Figure 8.15 Client I/O

It's easy to see this, even with our simple server. Consider an I/O discipline analogous to the one we used in the server, represented by the pseudo-code in Figure 8.16.

```
1        while(1){
2            read(keyboard,buffer);
3            write(server,buffer);

4            read(server,buffer);
5            write(screen,buffer);
6        }
```

Figure 8.16 A broken client I/O discipline

Now, imagine that we have a slow server. The user types some input at the keyboard, which the client sends to the server. However, the server is slow and takes a while to respond. In the meantime, the user has typed in even more data—but the client can't read or write it because it's stuck at line 4, waiting to read from the server. Finally, the server writes the data and the client writes it to the screen. This frees the client to read the data from the client and send it to the server. Already, this behavior is kind of unpleasant. We could be writing data to the server but we can't because it's slow. On the other hand, this doesn't directly affect the user experience because our protocol is so simple—it's just unaesthetic. Now let's consider an example in which this behavior would cause serious problems: remote login.

Consider the case in which you're remotely logged into a machine and you request a directory listing. Your request is a single line (ls on UNIX boxes) but the response is a large number of lines. In general, these lines will be written in more than one write. Thus, it may very well take more than one read in order to read them from the server. However, if we use the I/O discipline in Figure 8.16, we'll run into a problem.

We read the command from the user and the first chunk of the server's response, but after that we get deadlocked. The client is waiting in line 2 for the user to type something but the user is waiting for the rest of the directory listing. We're deadlocked. Recognize that this is the dual of the deadlock we saw in Section 8.7 and the solution is the same: we need to read all the available data from the server.

However, the precise solution we employed before won't work. Recall that calling SSL_read() when there is no data available simply blocks waiting for the server. We can't have that because we'd just get stuck at the end of the server's data when what we actually need to do is read from the keyboard. Similar arguments can be used to show that no possible arrangement of sequenced reads and writes can work correctly. Instead, we need some way to ensure that we read data from either the keyboard or the server, depending on which one is ready.

The traditional solution to this problem depends on which language you're using. In languages like Java, the solution is to use threads. In languages like C, where threads support is nonexistent or non-standard, more complicated mechanisms have been developed. This section shows a threaded solution written in Java. The next section shows a solution in C using select().

Figure 8.17 shows the main() method for our Java client. Lines 12–14

SClient.java

```
11    public static void main(String []args)
12        throws IOException {
13        SSLContext ctx=createSSLContext(keyfile,password);
14        SSLSocket s=connect(ctx,host,port);

15        // This thread reads from the console and writes to the server
16        ReadWrite c2s=new ReadWrite(s,System.in,s.getOutputStream());
17        c2s.start();

18        // This thread reads from the server and writes to the console
19        ReadWriteWithCancel s2c=new ReadWriteWithCancel(s,
20            s.getInputStream(),System.out,c2s);
21        s2c.start();
22        s2c.setPriority(Thread.MAX_PRIORITY);
23        s2c.join();
24    }
```

SClient.java

Figure 8.17 Java client main()

just call the context and socket creation code we've seen before, so we ignore them. What's important is the rest of the function.

Start threads

15–23   The general structure of the client is simple. Instead of having a single read/write loop like the one in Figure 8.16, we have two such loops, each operating in a separate thread. Individually, the loops simply block when they don't have any data to read. However, this doesn't result in deadlock because the thread scheduler automatically runs whichever thread has data to read or write.

We accomplish this by instantiating two `ReadWrite` objects. (`ReadWrite-WithCancel` is a subclass of `ReadWrite` that we use to get the right behavior during connection closure. We'll examine this further in Section 8.10. For now think of `Read-WriteWithCancel` as `ReadWrite`.) `ReadWrite` subclasses `Thread` so when we call `start()` it automatically starts as a new thread.

> Line 22 shouldn't be necessary. It's a workaround for a problem in the JDK 1.1.8 thread scheduler. Without it, the `c2s` thread starves the `s2c` thread. This hack is not necessary in JDK 1.2.X. The `join()` in line 23 causes this thread to wait for the `s2c` thread to finish. This isn't strictly necessary in this case but would be if we wanted to know when the connection to the server was finished.

Figure 8.18 shows the relevant section of `ReadWrite`. We've omitted the closure code because we'll treat that in Section 8.10. The constructor simply creates the object and assigns the arguments to instance variables. Note that the arguments we provide include an `InputStream` and an `OutputStream`. These are standard Java I/O classes which PureTLS subclasses. Thus, this code is totally oblivious to PureTLS. It could be used exactly as-is with standard sockets!

```
                                                                  ReadWrite.java
8        public class ReadWrite extends Thread {
9            protected SSLSocket s;
10           protected InputStream in;
11           protected OutputStream out;

12           /** Create a ReadWrite object

13               @param s the socket we're using
14               @param in the stream to read from
15               @param out the stream to write to
16           */
17           public ReadWrite(SSLSocket s,InputStream in,OutputStream out){
18             this.s=s;
19             this.in=in;
20             this.out=out;
21           }
```

```
22          /** Copy data from in to out.*/
23          public void run() {
24              byte[] buf=new byte[1024];
25              int read;

26              try {
27                while(true){
28                  // Check for thread termination
29                  if(isInterrupted())
30                    break;

31                  // Read data in
32                  read=in.read(buf);

33                  // Exit if there is no more data available
34                  if(read==-1)
35                    break;

36                  // Write the data out
37                  out.write(buf,0,read);
38                }

39              } catch (IOException e){
40                // run() can't throw IOException
41                throw new InternalError(e.toString());
42              }

43              // Finalize
44              onEOD();
45          }
```

_____ ReadWrite.java

Figure 8.18 ReadWrite I/O handling

Read and write

22–45   Because ReadWrite is subclassed from Thread it has certain automatic behaviors. In particular, it inherits a method called start(). The start() method automatically creates a new thread and then calls run(). This is why the code that actually does the work of ReadWrite is in the run() method.

The run() method itself is simple. We simply read() off of the InputStream (in) and write to the OutputStream (out). Unlike OpenSSL, PureTLS guarantees that when you call write() all of the data will be delivered to the network before it returns. Thus, we don't need to even loop around write() the way we did in Figure 8.8. Obviously, this behavior would be disastrous if the whole program blocked on write(); because we're operating in our own thread, there's no problem at all.

PureTLS handles network problems differently from OpenSSL. Standard Java practice is to have network errors delivered via exceptions and PureTLS follows this practice. Thus, when we read data in lines 32–35 we don't need to check for read errors. All we need to do is distinguish a successful read from an end of data. This is easy since read() returns the length of the data read or a −1 for end of data. If we read some data, we fall through to the write code at line 37. Otherwise, we exit the loop and close the connection.

As we said, network errors are handled by throwing an IOException. In this program, we simply catch these errors, treat them as fatal, and throw an InternalError in response. In a real program, we'd make some attempt to determine fatal from non-fatal errors and report them to the user.

8.9   Multiplexed I/O with select()

Although the threaded approach works fine for Java, it is far less satisfactory for C. Threads support is not part of the C standard and so it's left up to the platform to provide whatever threading mechanisms it chooses. Windows provides fairly complete threading support and threads are the multiplexing method of choice on that platform.

Unfortunately, the situation on UNIX is far worse. UNIX threads support is not standardized and, worse yet, many C-based libraries on UNIX aren't thread safe. If you want portable code on UNIX, you have to avoid threads. This means that if you want to multiplex I/O you need to use select(). Although this use of select() is a pretty common UNIX idiom, the interaction of select() with SSL is far from clean and requires understanding some subtleties we've so far only hinted at.

Read

The basic problem we're facing is that SSL is a record-oriented protocol. Thus, even if we want to read only one byte from the SSL connection, we still need to read the entire record containing that byte into memory. Without the entire record in hand, the SSL implementation can't check the record MAC and so we can't safely deliver the data to the programmer. Unfortunately, this behavior interacts poorly with select(), as shown in Figure 8.19.

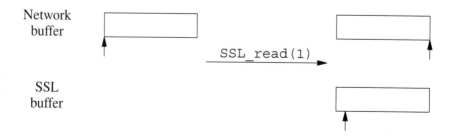

Figure 8.19 Read interaction with SSL

The left-hand side of Figure 8.19 shows the situation when the machine has received a record but it's still waiting in the network buffers. The arrow represents the read pointer which is set at the beginning of the buffer. The bottom row represents data decoded by the SSL implementation but not yet read by the program (the *SSL buffer*). This buffer is currently empty so we haven't shown a box. If the program calls `select()` at this point, it will return immediately indicating that a call to `read()` will succeed. Now, imagine that the programmer calls `SSL_read()` requesting one byte. This takes us to the situation at the right side of the figure.

As we said earlier, the SSL implementation has to read the entire record in order to deliver even a single byte to the program. In general, the application does not know the size of records and so its reads will not match the records. Thus, the box in the upper right-hand corner shows that the read pointer has moved to the end of the record. We've read all the data in the network buffer. When the implementation decrypts and verifies the record, it places the data in the SSL buffer. Then it delivers the one byte that the program asked for in `SSL_read()`. We show the SSL buffer in the lower right-hand corner. The read pointer points somewhere in the buffer, indicating that some of the data is available for reading but some has already been read.

Consider what happens if the programmer calls `select()` at this point. `select()` is concerned solely with the contents of the network buffer, and that's empty. Thus, as far as `select()` is concerned there's no data to read. Depending on the exact arguments it's passed, it will either return saying that there's nothing to read or wait for some more network data to become available. In either case we wouldn't read the data in the SSL buffer. Note that if another record arrived then `select()` would indicate that the socket was ready to read and we'd have an opportunity to read more data.

Thus, `select()` is an unreliable guide to whether there is SSL data ready to read. We need some way to determine the status of the SSL buffer. This can't be provided by the operating system because it has no access to the SSL buffers. It must be provided by the toolkit. OpenSSL provides exactly such a function. The function `SSL_pending()` tells us whether there is data in the SSL buffer for a given socket. Figure 8.20 shows `SSL_pending()` in action.

The logic of this code is fairly straightforward. `select()` has been called earlier, setting the variable `readfds` with the sockets that are ready to read. If the SSL socket is ready to read, we go ahead and try to fill our buffer. Once we've read some data, we write it to the console. Then we check with `SSL_pending()` to see if the record was longer than our buffer. If it was, we loop back and read some more data.

Note that we've added a new branch to our `switch` statement: a check for `SSL_ERROR_WANT_READ`. What's going on here is that we've set the socket for *nonblocking* operation. Recall that we said in Section 8.7 that if you called `read()` when the network buffers were empty, it would simply block (wait) until they weren't. Setting the socket to nonblocking causes it to return immediately saying that it *would have* blocked.

To understand why we've done this, consider what happens if an SSL record arrives in two pieces. When the first piece arrives, `select()` will signal that we're ready to read. However, we need to read the entire record in order to return any data so this is a

read_write.c

```
43              /* Now check if there's data to read */
44              if(FD_ISSET(sock,&readfds)){
45                do {
46                  r=SSL_read(ssl,s2c,BUFSIZZ);

47                  switch(SSL_get_error(ssl,r)){
48                    case SSL_ERROR_NONE:
49                      fwrite(s2c,1,r,stdout);
50                      break;
51                    case SSL_ERROR_ZERO_RETURN:
52                      /* End of data */
53                      if(!shutdown_wait)
54                       SSL_shutdown(ssl);
55                      goto end;
56                      break;
57                    case SSL_ERROR_WANT_READ:
58                      break;
59                    default:
60                      berr_exit("SSL read problem");
61                  }
62                } while (SSL_pending(ssl));
63              }
```

read_write.c

Figure 8.20 Reading data using `SSL_pending()`

false positive. Attempting to read all that data will block, leading to exactly the deadlock we were trying to avoid. Instead, we set the socket to nonblocking and catch the error, which OpenSSL translates to `SSL_ERROR_WANT_READ`.

Write

When we're writing to the network we have to face the same sort of inconsistency that we had when reading. Again, the problem is the all-or-nothing nature of SSL record transmission. For simplicity's sake, let's consider the case where the network buffers are mostly full and the program attempts to perform a modest-sized write, say 1K. This is illustrated in Figure 8.21.

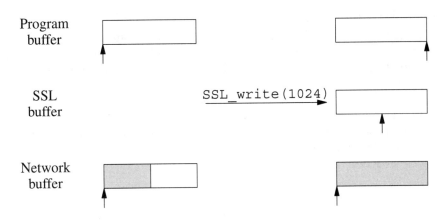

Figure 8.21 Write interaction with SSL

Again, the left-hand side of the figure represents our initial situation. The program has 1K to write in some buffer. The write pointer is set at the beginning of that buffer. The SSL buffers are empty. The network buffer is half-full (the shading indicates the full region). The write pointer is set at the beginning. We've deliberately obscured the distinction between the TCP buffers and the size of the TCP window because it's not relevant here. Suffice it to say that the program can safely write 512 bytes without blocking.

Now, the program calls `SSL_write()` with a 1024-byte block. The toolkit has no way of knowing how much data it can write safely, so it simply formats the buffer as a single record, thus moving the write pointer in the program buffer to the end of the buffer. We can ignore the slight data expansion from the SSL header and MAC and simply act as if the data to be written to the network was 1024 bytes.

Now, what happens when the toolkit calls `write()`? It successfully writes 512 bytes but gets a *would block* error when it attempts to write to the end of the record. As a consequence, the write pointer in the SSL buffer is moved halfway across—indicating that half of the data has been written to the network. The network buffer is shaded to indicate that it's completely full. The network write pointer hasn't moved.

We now need to concern ourselves with two questions: first, how does the toolkit indicate this situation to the user and, second, how does the user arrange that the SSL buffer gets flushed when space is available in the network buffer? The kernel will automatically flush the network buffer when possible so we don't need to worry about arranging for that. We can use `select()` to see when there is more space available in the network buffer and we should therefore flush the SSL buffer. There are at least two strategies for handling this situation. We'll describe the method that OpenSSL uses and then describe an alternate strategy.

OpenSSL Write Handling

Once OpenSSL has received a *would block* error from the network, it aborts and propagates that error all the way up to the application. Note that this does *not* mean that it throws away the data in the SSL buffer. This is impossible because part of the record might already have been sent.

In order to flush this buffer, the programmer must call `SSL_write()` again with the same buffer that it called the first time (it's permissible to extend the buffer but the start must be the same.) OpenSSL automatically remembers where the buffer write pointer was and only writes the data after the write pointer. Figure 8.22 shows this process in action.

```
                                                              _____ read_write.c
66            /* Check for input on the console*/
67            if(FD_ISSET(fileno(stdin),&readfds)){
68              c2sl=read(fileno(stdin),c2s,BUFSIZZ);
69              if(c2sl==0){
70                shutdown_wait=1;
71                if(!SSL_shutdown(ssl))
72                  return;
73              }
74              c2s_offset=0;
75            }

76            /* If we've got data to write then try to write it*/
77            if(c2sl && FD_ISSET(sock,&writefds)){
78              r=SSL_write(ssl,c2s+c2s_offset,c2sl);

79              switch(SSL_get_error(ssl,r)){
80                /* We wrote something*/
81                case SSL_ERROR_NONE:
82                  c2sl-=r;
83                  c2s_offset+=r;
84                  break;

85                /* We would have blocked */
86                case SSL_ERROR_WANT_WRITE:
87                  break;

88                /* Some other error */
89                default:
90                  berr_exit("SSL write problem");
91              }
92            }
                                                              _____ read_write.c
```

Figure 8.22 Client to server writes using OpenSSL

Read from console

66–75   The first thing we need to do is have some data to write. Thus, we check to see if the console is ready to read, and if so read whatever's there (up to BUFSIZZ bytes) into the buffer c2s, placing the length in the variable c2sl.

Write to network

76–92   If c2sl is nonzero and the network buffers are (at least partially) empty, then we have data to write to the network. As usual, we call SSL_write() with the buffer c2s. As before, if we manage to write some but not all of the data, we simply increment c2s_offset and decrement c2sl.

The new behavior here is that we check for the error SSL_ERROR_WANT_WRITE. This error indicates that we've got unflushed data in the SSL buffer. As we described above, we need to call SSL_write() again with the same buffer, so we simply leave c2sl and c2s_offset unchanged. Thus, the next time SSL_write() is called it will automatically be with the same data.

> OpenSSL actually provides a flag called SSL_MODE_ACCEPT_MOVING_WRITE_BUFFER which allows you to call SSL_write() with a different buffer after a would block error. However, this merely allows you to allocate a new buffer with the same contents. SSL_write() still seeks to the same write pointer before looking for new data.

An Alternative Nonblocking Strategy

SPYRUS's TLSGold toolkit (a commercial C-based toolkit) implements a somewhat different strategy for handling nonblocking I/O. As long as the toolkit is able to completely encode the program write buffer, it returns success—even if it can't completely flush the SSL buffer. The only case in which it returns indicating that it would block is if there is already data in the SSL buffers and it can't flush them entirely. This behavior more closely matches the semantics of UNIX sockets.

However, because the caller has no indication that the data actually went to the SSL buffer and not to the network directly, he has to take positive action. TLSGold provides a call SSL_IsMoreWriteData() which performs the same function for writes that we saw SSL_pending() perform for reads. Thus, when programming TLSGold, the programmer needs to check TSW_SSL_IsMoreWriteData() and attempt to flush the buffers when the network is ready to write. Flushing the write buffers is accomplished by calling TSW_SSL_Write() with a zero-length buffer.

A Complete `select()`-based Solution

Figure 8.23 shows the complete code of read_write(). We've seen most of these pieces before but it's useful to examine the function as a whole.

```
                                                                            _____ read_write.c
  8        void read_write(ssl,sock)
  9          SSL *ssl;
 10          {
 11            int width;
 12            int r,c2sl=0,c2s_offset=0;
 13            fd_set readfds,writefds;
 14            int shutdown_wait=0;
 15            char c2s[BUFSIZZ],s2c[BUFSIZZ];
 16            int ofcmode;

 17            /*First we make the socket nonblocking*/
 18            ofcmode=fcntl(sock,F_GETFL,0);
 19            ofcmode|=O_NDELAY;
 20            if(fcntl(sock,F_SETFL,ofcmode))
 21              err_exit("Couldn't make socket nonblocking");


 22            width=sock+1;

 23            while(1){
 24              FD_ZERO(&readfds);
 25              FD_ZERO(&writefds);

 26              FD_SET(sock,&readfds);

 27              /*If we've still got data to write then don't try to read*/
 28              if(c2sl)
 29                FD_SET(sock,&writefds);
 30              else
 31                FD_SET(fileno(stdin),&readfds);

 32              r=select(width,&readfds,&writefds,0,0);
 33              if(r==0)
 34                continue;

 35              /* Now check if there's data to read */
 36              if(FD_ISSET(sock,&readfds)){
 37                do {
 38                  r=SSL_read(ssl,s2c,BUFSIZZ);

 39                  switch(SSL_get_error(ssl,r)){
 40                    case SSL_ERROR_NONE:
 41                      fwrite(s2c,1,r,stdout);
 42                      break;
```

```
43              case SSL_ERROR_ZERO_RETURN:
44                /* End of data */
45                if(!shutdown_wait)
46                  SSL_shutdown(ssl);
47                goto end;
48                break;
49              case SSL_ERROR_WANT_READ:
50                break;
51              default:
52                berr_exit("SSL read problem");
53            }
54          } while (SSL_pending(ssl));
55        }

56        /* Check for input on the console*/
57        if(FD_ISSET(fileno(stdin),&readfds)){
58          c2sl=read(fileno(stdin),c2s,BUFSIZZ);
59          if(c2sl==0){
60            shutdown_wait=1;
61            if(SSL_shutdown(ssl))
62              return;
63          }
64          c2s_offset=0;
65        }

66        /* If we've got data to write then try to write it*/
67        if(c2sl && FD_ISSET(sock,&writefds)){
68          r=SSL_write(ssl,c2s+c2s_offset,c2sl);

69          switch(SSL_get_error(ssl,r)){
70            /* We wrote something*/
71            case SSL_ERROR_NONE:
72              c2sl-=r;
73              c2s_offset+=r;
74              break;

75            /* We would have blocked */
76            case SSL_ERROR_WANT_WRITE:
77              break;

78            /* Some other error */
79            default:
80              berr_exit("SSL write problem");
81          }
82        }
83
```

(continued)

```
84        Figure 8.23 (continued)

85            }
86        end:
87            SSL_free(ssl);
88            close(sock);
89            return;
90        }
```
                                                                    _____ read_write.c

Figure 8.23 read_write() function

Set nonblocking

17–21   The first thing we do is make the socket nonblocking. This is standard UNIX code.

Set up select() masks

24–34   We always want to be ready to read from the server, but we want to do flow control for data we write to the server. To that end, we always look for the server socket being ready to read, but we switch between looking for data on the keyboard and looking for being ready to write to the server. If c2sl is nonzero, then we have data to write to the server and so we tell select() to look for the server socket to be writeable. Otherwise, we wait for the keyboard to be readable.

Note that if we wanted to we could always wait for data to be available on the keyboard. However, this might mean that data came in on the keyboard while we still had data to write to the server. Then we would have to append this new data to the c2s buffer and would thus complicate the code. We definitely want to look for the server socket to be writeable only when we have data to write. Most of the time there is no data to write or read and so the server socket is writeable most of the time. Thus, if we listened for the server socket to be writeable we'd constantly be spinning through the select() loop, which is not the behavior we want. Rather, we want our program to sleep until it has something to do.

We've seen the rest of the function before, but one inefficiency is worth noting: once we've read data from the keyboard we have to reenter the select() before we even attempt to write it to the server. In most cases the server is ready to write, so it would be slightly faster to simply attempt the write immediately. However, this would complicate the code and be only a trivial optimization.

8.10 Closure

Now that we've seen the code for reading and writing data, we're ready to examine closure. We need to be concerned with two primary issues. First, we need to ensure that the program both sends and receives a close_notify—and that an error is thrown if a close_notify is not received. Second, we need to ensure that we handle an incomplete close correctly. First, let's examine the OpenSSL-based closure code in Figure 8.23.

OpenSSL Closure

We've already seen the closure behavior on the server, so now let's examine it on the client. There are two situations in which the client might need to shut down the connection. First, the client might receive an end of data via the keyboard. Second, the client might receive a close_notify from the server. (If the client receives a TCP FIN without a close_notify it just exits with an error at the end of SSL_read().) The only way that our server can terminate is if it receives a user end of data.

User end of data

59–63   If we receive an end of data from the keyboard, then we need to initiate the closure process. OpenSSL only has one function for doing this, SSL_shutdown(). It returns 1 if it was able to complete the closure process and 0 otherwise. The only condition in which it's likely to return 0 is if it hasn't received a close_notify yet. Thus, if we get a 0 return value, we have to wait for one. We set shutdown_wait to 1 and return to the select loop.

Wait for close

43–47   This section of code handles both the case where we receive an unsolicited close_notify from the server and the case where we receive one in delayed response to our close_notify. If the server socket is readable but we get a 0 return value we know that we've received a close_notify (because a bare TCP FIN would generate an error). If this is an unsolicited close_notify, then shutdown_wait will be zero and we need to use SSL_shutdown() to send our close_notify. On the other hand, if we have already sent our close_notify, then we simply jump out of the loop.

In the case of an unsolicited close_notify it's possible that the other side has completely closed the connection. In this case, our close_notify might trigger a TCP RST, which manifests itself on the sending end by raising a SIGPIPE signal. Because the default response to a SIGPIPE is to shut down the process, we have to arrange to ignore it. The call to signal() in Line 52 in common.c (Figure 8.4) takes care of this by setting up a dummy handler. Another approach would be to set the signal to be ignored. This approach allows us to catch the signal and potentially do something with it—like close the connection.

Clean up objects

84–88   Cleaning up consists of freeing the SSL object and closing the socket afterwards.

PureTLS closure

Unlike OpenSSL, PureTLS provides three methods for handling the SSL closure process. close() acts much like SSL_shutdown(), but sendClose() and recvClose() allow a finer control over what's going on. The sample code uses these rather than close().

Recall that we omitted the implementation of `ReadWrite.onEOD()` from our discussion in Section 8.8. We present it here in Figure 8.24.

ReadWrite

```
56        protected void onEOD(){
57          try {
58            s.sendClose();
59          } catch (IOException e){
60            ; // Ignore broken pipe
61          }
62        }
```

ReadWrite

Figure 8.24 `ReadWrite.onEOD()`

`onEOD()` is called at the end of `ReadWrite.run()`. Typically, this occurs when the thread has received an end of data from the keyboard. In that case, the thread sends a **close_notify** using `sendClose()` and exits. However, `ReadWrite.onEOD()` can also be called when an unsolicited **close_notify** is received from the server. This process is initiated by the class `ReadWriteWithCancel`, as shown in Figure 8.25.

ReadWriteWithCancel.java

```
11      public class ReadWriteWithCancel extends ReadWrite {
12          protected ReadWrite cancel;

13          public ReadWriteWithCancel(SSLSocket s,InputStream in,OutputStream out,
14            ReadWrite cancel){
15            super(s,in,out);
16            this.cancel=cancel;
17          }

18          protected void onEOD(){
19            if(cancel.isAlive()){
20              cancel.interrupt();
21              try {
22                cancel.join();
23              } catch (InterruptedException e){
24                throw new InternalError(e.toString());
25              }
26            }
27          }
```

ReadWriteWithCancel.java

Figure 8.25 `ReadWriteWithCancel` class

`ReadWriteWithCancel` differs from `ReadWrite` in that it overrides `onEOD()`. Recall from Section 8.8 that the thread listening to the server is an instance of `ReadWriteWithCancel`. When that thread sees an end of data from the server it knows that it's received a close_notify. (Bare TCP FINs cause an `IOException` to be thrown.) It responds to this by triggering the thread writing to the server to send its own close_notify. This ensures that we don't have two threads trying to write to the same socket at the same time, which could happen if `ReadWriteWithCancel` tried to call `sendClose()` itself.

The signalling is done by calling `cancel.interrupt()`. `ReadWrite` tests for the interrupt using the `interrupted()` call. If `interrupted()` returns `true` then the read/write loop exits and `onEOD()` is called. Meanwhile, the server-to-client thread waits for the client-to-server thread to exit and then exits itself.

Once again, if the other side sent an unsolicited close_notify we need to be concerned with getting an RST when we send our close_notify. This is why the call to `sendClose()` is wrapped in a `try/catch`. The RST triggers an `IOException` which is simply ignored.

8.11 Session Resumption

The last topic we'll treat in this chapter is session resumption. As we discussed in Section 4.10, when the client has the server's domain name, it's possible to do automatic session resumption. PureTLS does this. Figure 8.26 shows a PureTLS example class that does session resumption on the client side. The PureTLS server we've been using all along automatically loops and so needs no special support to demonstrate session resumption.

Java Session Resumption

```
                                                                      RClient.java
6        public class RClient extends Client {
7            public static void main(String []args)
8                throws IOException {
9                SSLContext ctx=createSSLContext(keyfile,password);

10               /* Connect and close*/
11               SSLSocket s=connect(ctx,host,port);
12               s.close();

13               /* Now reconnect: resumption happens automatically*/
14               s=connect(ctx,host,port);
15               s.close();
16           }
17       }
                                                                      RClient.java
```

Figure 8.26 Resuming sessions with PureTLS

Note that we haven't done anything special to enable session resumption. The `SClient` class that we were using simply didn't do it. This class does.

C Session Resumption

OpenSSL requires some additional support in order to do session resumption. We've seen the initialization code required on the server previously and we don't need to add any new code there. However, we do need to do some additional work on the client side. Figure 8.27 shows a client that does session resumption. The key code here is at line 27 and line 34. We use `SSL_get_session()` to get the session data from the first `SSL` object and then use `SSL_set_session()` to assign the data to the second `SSL` object. From there, we can simply call `SSL_connect()` again.

Of course, this code isn't suitable for a production application. You can only resume sessions with the same server that you created them with, and this code makes no attempt to discriminate between various servers—because the server name is hardwired. In a real application, you would want to have some sort of lookup table that maps hostname/port pairs to `SESSION` objects.

Finally, note that even without having the hostname and port passed into the SSL toolkit, it is still possible to automatically resume sessions. The toolkit can call `get-peername()` on the socket in order to get the remote host and port. However, because OpenSSL's `BIO` abstraction separates the SSL code from the socket, this isn't possible with OpenSSL. TLSGold fixes this problem by having a `getpeername()` function as part of its I/O abstraction. However, OpenSSL does not do this and so the application needs to handle resumption explicitly.

8.12 What's Missing?

As long as this chapter is, there are still some aspects of SSL programming that we've omitted. This section quickly summarizes them.

Better Certificate Checking

As we discussed in Chapter 7, a more sophisticated approach to checking server certificates against the server hostname is to use the X.509 subjectAltName extension. In order to make this check, you would need to extract this extension from the certificate and then check it against the hostname. This isn't extremely difficult but it is intricate and tightly bound to the certificate processing API of the SSL toolkit, which is why we've omitted it here. Additionally, it would be nice to be able to check host names against wildcarded names in certificates. We don't show how to do this either.

```
                                                            ____ rclient.c
6        int main(argc,argv)
7          int argc;
8          char **argv;
9          {
10            SSL_CTX *ctx;
11            SSL *ssl;
12            BIO *sbio;
13            SSL_SESSION *sess;
14            int sock;

15            /* Build our SSL context*/
16            ctx=initialize_ctx(KEYFILE,PASSWORD);

17            /* Connect the TCP socket*/
18            sock=tcp_connect();

19            /* Connect the SSL socket */
20            ssl=SSL_new(ctx);
21            sbio=BIO_new_socket(sock,BIO_NOCLOSE);
22            SSL_set_bio(ssl,sbio,sbio);
23            if(SSL_connect(ssl)<=0)
24              berr_exit("SSL connect error (first connect)");
25            check_cert_chain(ssl,HOST);

26            /* Now hang up and reconnect */
27            sess=SSL_get_session(ssl); /*Collect the session*/
28            SSL_shutdown(ssl);
29            close(sock);

30            sock=tcp_connect();
31            ssl=SSL_new(ctx);
32            sbio=BIO_new_socket(sock,BIO_NOCLOSE);
33            SSL_set_bio(ssl,sbio,sbio);
34            SSL_set_session(ssl,sess); /*And resume it*/
35            if(SSL_connect(ssl)<=0)
36              berr_exit("SSL connect error (second connect)");
37            check_cert_chain(ssl,HOST);

38            /*Now close everything down again*/
39            SSL_shutdown(ssl);
40            close(sock);
41            destroy_ctx(ctx);
42          }
                                                            ____ rclient.c
```

Figure 8.27 Resuming sessions with OpenSSL

/dev/random

An increasing number of UNIX systems support a device called /dev/random. In essence, /dev/random acts like a continuous source of random bytes. You simply open the device and read from it. /dev/random operates by examining a number of system variables, timers, and interrupts and mixing them into a pseudo-random number generator to produce high-quality randomness as output. On systems with /dev/random, it is a useful source of randomness, either in place of or in addition to the OpenSSL or PureTLS randomness file. Windows 2000 also has a similar facility. We haven't shown how to access these facilities for portability reasons, but they do deserve mention.

Multiprocess Operation

The most significant omission from these examples is a method for servers to support more than one client. As we mentioned, our PureTLS-based server starts a new thread to actually serve clients but the SSL accepts all happen in the main thread. This is undesirable in a high-traffic server. Our OpenSSL-based server is completely incapable of handling more than one client at a time. Handling this case cleanly comes up quite frequently in Web applications—where multiple simultaneous connections at low cost are very important—and so we'll take it up in the next chapter when we discuss HTTP over TLS.

Better Error Handling

Note that these applications handle errors simply by exiting with an error. A real application would, of course, be able to recognize errors and signal them to the user or some audit log rather than just exiting.

8.13   Summary

This chapter has discussed techniques for programming applications that use SSL. We've provided two sets of example programs, one written in C using OpenSSL and another written in Java using PureTLS. These examples illustrate a number of common idioms seen in applications that use SSL.

Programming language matters. As we saw, PureTLS and OpenSSL mimic the networking APIs for the languages they were written in. Moreover, the sort of I/O discipline that is most appropriate depends on the capabilities of your language.

Context objects allow one-time initialization. A number of initialization procedures such as keyfile loading and randomness generation are time consuming. In order to avoid performing them repeatedly for every SSL connection, we initialize a context object and use that to create our new connections.

Single-source I/O is easy. In simple server cases, we often need to simply read from the SSL connection, perform some service, and respond. In such cases programming the appropriate reads and writes is straightforward—nearly identical to programming with sockets.

Multiplexed I/O is hard. When we need to multiplex between several sources of input, we use either threads or `select()` to arrange that we service all I/O needs without starvation. This requires careful attention to correct record framing and closure behavior.

SSL record framing causes problems. SSL data must be read from and written to the network one record at a time. Because applications often want to read and write data in sizes other than a record, `select()` often gives incorrect answers about the amount of data available. In such cases, programmers must use toolkit-specific mechanisms to determine the state of the SSL read and write buffers.

Closure must be handled carefully. It's important to be able to handle both locally initiated and unsolicited closes. With a locally initiated close, we must not simply close the connection but rather wait until a close_notify is received. With an unsolicited close, the programmer must arrange to send a close_notify but be prepared to recover if it's answered with an RST.

Session resumption APIs vary widely. PureTLS automatically resumes sessions where appropriate. OpenSSL requires user intervention. Some other C-based toolkits do resumption automatically as well.

9

HTTP over SSL

9.1 Introduction

HTTP (*Hypertext Transfer Protocol*) provides a natural example of a protocol secured with SSL. It was the first protocol to use SSL and is still by far the most important secured protocol. The standard approach—found in nearly every Web browser and server—uses a separate ports strategy, whereas the IETF has standardized an upward negotiation technique for upgrading to TLS in HTTP.

This chapter starts with a discussion of the problem of Web security at a high level, including an introduction to the basic Web technologies. Then we discuss the traditional approach to HTTP with SSL (HTTPS, described in RFC 2818) and how it interacts with these Web technologies. This leads into a discussion of the newer HTTP Upgrade technique (described in RFC 2817), and how it compares to HTTPS. Finally, we discuss some programming issues commonly encountered when using HTTP with SSL.

9.2 Securing the Web

The prototypical Web security application is credit card submission to a Web server. The user browses some Web site and places a number of items in his virtual shopping cart. In general, this step is done without any security. It's assumed that this information isn't sensitive—although it might be if you were buying something embarrassing.

The requirement for security kicks in when the customer is ready to check out. In order to do so, the customer needs to provide his credit card number to the server. Because anyone who has the credit card number can pose as the user and initiate charges, it's obvious that we need to provide confidentiality for the credit card. Moreover, the user needs to be sure that he's submitting his credit card to the right server lest a fake server steal his credit card.

At checkout time, the server hands the user off to a secure page, where he can type in his credit card number and expiration date. After this information is submitted securely, the user needs to get a confirmation from the server that his order was received. This also needs to be securely delivered to prevent attackers from silently blocking orders.

For this application, our security requirements are very simple. We need to provide confidentiality for the data passing between client and server and the user needs to be sure that his client is connected to the right server. Other applications may have more advanced security needs, but any Web security protocol needs to at least satisfy these requirements.

Basic Technologies

Before we even discuss security, it's important to understand the basic technologies that make up the World Wide Web infrastructure. The three technologies that we need to consider are *HTTP*, *HTML*, and *URLs*.

HTTP

HTTP (*HyperText Transfer Protocol*) is the basic transport protocol of the Web. The Web is a client/server system and some mechanism needs to exist to move data between servers and clients. HTTP provides that mechanism. Most Web browsers speak other protocols, such as FTP, but the vast majority of Web traffic is moved by HTTP.

HTML

HTML (*HyperText Markup Language*) is the basic document format of the Web. HTML is basically an enhanced version of ASCII text. The two most important features it offers are the ability to structure the document to indicate paragraphs, line breaks, etc. and the ability to provide *links*. Links allow the user to click from one document to another.

URLs

URLs (*Uniform Resource Locators*) provide the references used in links. Every HTML link has an associated URL which tells the browser what to do when the user clicks on the link. In theory URLs can describe data fetched over any protocol but in practice they mostly refer to data to be fetched over HTTP.

Practical Considerations

There are several features of the real world Web environment that are not obvious from the simple client/server model that we've suggested so far. Three of these features turn out to have particular relevance when we consider the Web security problem: *connection behavior*, *proxies*, and *virtual hosts*.

Connection Behavior

Most Web pages contain a number of embedded ("inline") images on the page. These images must be fetched individually with their own HTTP request. As a performance improvement, most clients perform these fetches in parallel. Thus, fetching any page actually involves an extensive sequence of requests. To ensure reasonable performance, we need to ensure that per-request overhead is kept to a minimum.

Proxies

A very large number of Web transactions occur from large intranet environments. These intranets are often separated from the Internet by firewalls, and access to Internet resources is allowed only through proxies. A successful Web security solution must be able to pass through proxies.

Virtual Hosts

It's quite common for a single server (such as an ISP server) to host Web sites for a number of organizations. For instance, it's quite common for ISPs to offer combined Web hosting and credit card clearing for merchants too small to have their own merchant accounts. Naturally, each merchant would like to appear to have his own Web server even though multiple servers are in fact running on the same server as other merchants. A technique called *virtual hosts* makes this possible, but it can interact badly with security.

Security Considerations

Once we understand the sorts of transactions we'd like to perform and the Web protocols and environments in which they need to work, we can consider how to provide the appropriate security services. In particular, we need to figure out how we'll approach the important problems discussed in Chapter 7: *protocol selection*, *client authentication*, *reference integrity*, and *connection semantics*.

9.3 HTTP

This section provides a very brief overview of HTTP, described in [Fielding1999]. Our intent is not to provide a full description; that purpose is amply filled by a number of other sources, including [Stevens1994]. Rather, our intent is to describe enough of HTTP so that we can adequately talk about what it means to secure HTTP with SSL. Thus, we will focus on the details that are most relevant to security and SSL.

Conceptually, HTTP is a simple protocol. The basic unit of HTTP interaction is the request/response pair. The client opens a TCP connection to the server and writes the request. The server writes back the response. The server indicates the end of the response either with a length header or simply by closing the connection.

Requests

An HTTP request consists of three parts, the *request line*, *header*, and an optional *body*. The request line is simply a single line. The header is a series of colon-separated key-value pairs, and the body is arbitrary data. The header and the body are separated by a single blank line. Figure 9.1 shows a sample request.

```
GET / HTTP/1.0
Connection: Keep-Alive
User-Agent: Mozilla/4.7 [en] (X11; U; FreeBSD 3.4-STABLE i386)
Host: www.rtfm.com
Accept: image/gif, image/x-xbitmap, image/jpeg, image/pjpeg, image/png, */*
Accept-Encoding: gzip
Accept-Language: en
Accept-Charset: iso-8859-1,*,utf-8
(blank line)
```

Figure 9.1 An HTTP request

The request shown in Figure 9.1 consists simply of a request line and the header. The first line (starting with GET) is the request line. The rest of the request is header.

The format of an HTTP request line is

Method Request-URI HTTP-Version

The HTTP/1.1 RFC defines seven request methods: OPTIONS, GET, HEAD, POST, PUT, DELETE, TRACE. A number of other methods are defined by WEBDAV [Goland1999]. We don't need to be much concerned with the difference between various request methods. The two most common methods are GET and POST. The only relevant difference between them is that POSTs may have a message body whereas GETs do not.

The Request-URI should be thought of as the name of the resource that we're trying to access. In general, it looks like a UNIX path name, for instance /foo/bar/baz. It may also have a series of arguments on the end. Finally, the HTTP-Version will generally be either HTTP/1.0 or HTTP/1.1. HTTP/1.1 is the version that the IETF is standardizing on but we can mostly ignore the differences between the two versions.

A large number of header fields are possible but most of these don't have any interaction with SSL. The request in Figure 9.1 does have one header line that is relevant, however. The Connection header indicates that the client would like the server to keep the connection open after sending the response. Thus, keep-alive interacts with the SSL closure process. We'll discuss that interaction further in Section 9.15.

All the information that the client transmits to the server is in the client request. Thus, if we are to secure that data, we must ensure that the client's request is encrypted. Note that this necessarily includes securing the request line because the identity of the resource that the client is fetching may itself be sensitive. Obviously, providing this service requires that the client know it is talking to the correct server.

Responses

HTTP responses have a very similar format to requests. The only difference is that the request line is replaced with a status line which indicates how the server processed the request. The format of a status line is

HTTP-Version Status-Code Reason-Phrase

The HTTP-Version is the same as with the request. The Status-Code is a numeric code indicating the action the server took. In general this will be 200 for a successful request or some other number for failure (300 series codes are used to indicate some other non-error conditions in which the request isn't serviced.) We'll see a few more status codes when we discuss Upgrade in Section 9.21. The Reason-Phrase is simply a textual description of what happened. For a successful transaction this is usually OK. Figure 9.2 shows a successful HTTP response—the response to the request in Figure 9.1.

The response shown in Figure 9.2 illustrates a number of important points. First note the HTTP/1.1 200 OK status line, indicating that the request succeeded. Also, note the following three header fields:

```
Content-Length: 1650
Keep-Alive: timeout=15, max=100
Connection: Keep-Alive
```

The Keep-Alive and Connection: Keep-Alive header fields indicate that the server will not be closing the connection after sending the response. This means that the client will have to determine when the response ends from the contents of the response. The Content-Length header tells the clients how many bytes are in the body of the response. The Content-Type line tells us that the body of the message is of type text/html, indicating that the body is an HTML document.

Obviously, if securing HTTP transactions is to have any meaning at all, we must provide security for the response. This not only means ensuring that it is safe from viewing by attackers but also that no attacker can pose as the server in order to send data to the client or tamper with that data in transit.

9.4   HTML

HTML (*HyperText Markup Language*) is simply ASCII text decorated with a series of markers (called *tags*) that add structure to the document. For instance the <P> tag says to begin a new paragraph. A Web browser contains an *HTML parser* which takes the HTML as input and produces a formatted page as output. Note that because the markup

```
HTTP/1.1 200 OK
Date: Sat, 15 Jan 2000 05:15:54 GMT
Server: Apache/1.3.1 (UNIX)
Last-Modified: Tue, 22 Jun 1999 19:25:14 GMT
ETag: "2a99d-672-376fe31a"
Accept-Ranges: bytes
Content-Length: 1650
Keep-Alive: timeout=15, max=100
Connection: Keep-Alive
Content-Type: text/html

<!DOCTYPE HTML PUBLIC "-//W3C//DTD HTML 3.2 Final//EN">
<HTML>
 <HEAD>
  <TITLE>RTFM</TITLE>
 </HEAD>
<!-- Background white, links blue (unvisited), navy (visited), red (active) -->
 <BODY
  BGCOLOR="#FFFFFF"
  TEXT="#000000"
  LINK="#0000FF"
  VLINK="#000080"
  ALINK="#FF0000"
 >
<CENTER>
<A HREF="contact.html">
<IMG SRC="rtfm.gif" BORDER=0></A>
</CENTER>
```
Deleted text
```
RTFM in cooperation with Claymore Systems is releasing a free
Java SSLv3/TLS implementation: <A HREF="/puretls>PureTLS"</A>.
<P>
 
<CENTER>

<A HREF="contact.html">Contact Us</A>
</BODY>
</HTML>
```

Figure 9.2 An HTTP Response

mostly describes structure and not layout, there is more than one way to format a given page.

The only aspect of HTML that we need to be concerned with is the links that it contains. A link is merely a reference in the page to another piece of content. That content can in turn be fetched by the Web browser, usually using HTTP but sometimes via some other protocol.

Anchors

The most familiar type of link is what's referred to as an *anchor*. This is simply a section of the HTML (typically a region of text) that is tagged in such a way that it corresponds to a given reference. Clicking on the section of screen that corresponds to that section of HTML causes the browser to fetch the indicated content. When you're clicking the various highlighted and underlined links in your Web browser, you're using anchors. The HTML page in Figure 9.2 contains an anchor:

```
<A HREF="/puretls>PureTLS"</A>
```

What appears on the screen is the underlined text PureTLS. Clicking on the underlined section causes the browser to dereference the link by fetching the document pointed to by /puretls (on the Web server from which it fetched the original document: www.rtfm.com). The HREF="/puretls" is what specifies the target of the link. The target of the link (in this case the string /puretls) is called a *Uniform Resource Locator* (URL). We'll discuss URL syntax in Section 9.5. The link itself is defined by the region bracketed by <A HREF="/puretls"> (the *start tag*) and </A> (the *end tag*).

Inline Images

Another type of link is what's called an inline image. Unlike an anchor, which just sits there until the user clicks on it, the browser automatically fetches inline images and puts them into the Web page at the location in the HTML where the image tag appears. (Because the layout of the HTML page is determined in part by the browser, the whole idea of location is a rather fuzzy one.)

Whenever you see a picture in some Web page, that's an inline image of some sort. Even animated pictures are done with a variant of inline images. The HTML page in Figure 9.2 contains a reference to an inline image:

```
<IMG SRC="rtfm.gif" BORDER=0>
```

The IMG tag is basically like the A tag except that it uses the field SRC rather than HREF to carry the URL pointing to the content it's referencing. Thus, the picture contained in the file rtfm.gif (RTFM's logo) will be displayed in this page. This tag also contains a BORDER=0 attribute, indicating that the image should be presented without any border.

Note that the security properties of an inline image may not be the same as the security properties of the page that references it. Because images are often used as integral parts of the meaning of the page, the browser should clearly indicate if the security properties are different from that of the page in which they are embedded.

Forms

The final sort of link that we'll consider is what's generally referred to as a Web form. Although the implementation of a Web form is complicated, the idea is very simple and familiar. The Web page shows a number of user interface widgets such as text fields and pulldown menus. There's also a special button called the *submit button*. Sometimes it's even labeled "submit."

The user interacts with the widgets in some way, say by selecting which kind of credit card he has and filling in the credit card number and expiration of the card that he wants to pay with. When he's done he clicks the submit button. At this point some magic happens: the browser takes the current values of all the widgets and builds a string that carries their values. Then it makes a request to the server (to the URL associated with the form) and passes the values of the widgets with the request.

Forms (and indeed all links) can be labeled with a method type which represents the HTTP method type to use when dereferencing the link. The relevant two methods for forms are POST and GET. The important difference between them is simple: In a GET the values of the fields in the form are attached to the URI in the request line; in a POST it's sent in the message body.

Dynamic Content

Web pages can also contain a variety of types of dynamic content: code that is executed by the Web client. This code can either be directly in the HTML or can be referenced via a link similar to an inline image. This code can be in a variety of languages, including Java, JavaScript and VBScript. It is also possible to have a link that references a binary program which is then loaded into the memory space of the Web browser. This is called a *plug-in*.

9.5   URLs

URLs are the basic form of addressing in the World Wide Web. The idea behind a URL is to provide a single short string that identifies any network-accessible resource. URLs provide a unified interface for a wide variety of different access methods. A URL might reference a document accessible via HTTP, FTP, Gopher, or even instruct the browser to create a mail message. This saves the user from having to be familiar with the different conventions previously required to use any particular access method (for instance, anonymous FTP).

URLs can be extremely complicated, and they vary substantially between different access methods. (See [Berners-Lee1998] for a full description.) However, all the URLs that we'll be concerned with have a common form:

<scheme>://<host>[:<port>]/<path>[?<query>]

The scheme corresponds to the protocol being used to access the resource. Thus, for HTTP, it would be `http`, for FTP `ftp`, and so on. The host and port fields specify the server to connect to. The [ ] around the port field means that it's optional. Protocols usually have a default port defined, but access may be permitted on any port. The default port for HTTP is 80.

The path section of the URL provides the name (location) of the resource on the indicated server. Paths typically look like UNIX filenames (`/foo/bar/baz`). In theory, the fact that the path looks like a filename does not mean that the various parts correspond to directories, files, etc., but in practice this is often the case. In such cases, the server will serve the file that corresponds to the resource.

Finally, a URL might have a query at the end, set off by a ?. The query is intended to be resource specific and is "interpreted by the resource." Queries are most frequently used when the resource isn't a file but is rather a program that dynamically generates the resource in question. In such cases, the query part is used to provide the input to the program. For instance, an `ldap:` URL corresponds to an entry in an LDAP (*Lightweight Directory Access Protocol*) directory server. The query information can be used to identify the attributes that the client is interested in, the scope of the query, as well as other query parameters.

An Example

A simple URL might look something like Figure 9.3.

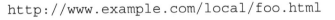

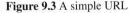

scheme   host   path

Figure 9.3 A simple URL

The resource described by this URL might be described as follows: Using HTTP, connect to the machine `www.example.com` on port 80. Request the resource `/local/foo.html`.

It's also possible to have a *relative* URL, such as `/local/foo.html`. In this case, the scheme and the host are assumed to be the same as those used to fetch the document containing the URL.

URIs versus URLs

The HTTP request line contains a URI. We've just seen what URLs are, but what's a URI? URI stands for *Uniform Resource Identifier*. URIs are a superset of URLs. A URI is simply a short string that refers to a given resource. A URL is a URI that contains explicit instructions about how to fetch the resource. It's possible to have URIs that uniquely identify a resource but don't provide instructions on how to fetch it. One such class of URIs is called a *Uniform Resource Name* (URN).

In general, any URI you're likely to see is a URL, because they describe how to use HTTP, FTP, etc., to fetch the resource. However, it's conceivable that the HTTP request line could contain a non-URL URI and therefore RFC 2616 uses the term URI. For the rest of this chapter we'll use the term URI when talking about the token that appears in the HTTP request and URL when talking about the token appearing in a link. See [W3C2000] for more information on this topic.

9.6   HTTP Connection Behavior

Consider a typical Web page. Such a page likely has between five and ten inline images. As we discussed in the previous section, each of these images requires a separate HTTP request/response pair. Because most older Web browsers and servers closed the connection to indicate the end of the response, it could potentially require as many as 11 separate TCP connections to fetch a single page.

Really old browsers such as Mosaic make all of these TCP connections sequentially, but the performance consequences of this procedure were terrible and Netscape soon introduced the technique of opening a number of simultaneous HTTP connections, one for each image up to a configurable upper limit.

In 1994 Spero [Spero1994] showed that the performance of using multiple connections (whether sequential or parallel) suffers badly from its interaction with TCP. First, each connection requires a three-way handshake to initiate (costing 1.5 round trips). Worse yet, TCP slow start (described in [Jacobsen1988]) can cause serious delays when the client's requests are longer than the server's maximum segment size.

In order to work around these problems, [Padmanabhan1995] and [Mogul1995] suggested keeping the TCP connection open after serving pages. This approach eventually emerged as the `Connection: Keep-Alive` header we saw in Section 9.1. As we saw, the end of data in that case is signalled with the `Content-Length` header. Although persistent connections reduce the number of connections made by browsers, many browsers still initiate a number of connections when they load a page with a large number of images to allow them to load all the images in parallel.

The use of a large number of parallel connections was one of the prime motivators for the session resumption feature of SSL. Because even simple pages cause a large number of connections within seconds of each other, SSL performance can be dramatically improved with session resumption.

9.7   Proxies

An HTTP proxy is a program that sits between a client and a server. It accepts the client request and then initiates its own request to the server. There are two primary reasons why proxies are useful: caching for multiple clients and as a pass-through for firewalls. The primary issue we face is to ensure that HTTP with SSL can operate even in proxied environments. This section provides some background on how proxies work.

The protocol traffic between a browser and a proxy is almost identical to the protocol traffic between a browser and a server. It is not, however, completely identical. The primary difference that we need to be concerned with is the difference in the request line. The problem is that the standard request line does not contain the identity of the server, which contains the resource but only the address of the resource on the server. Thus, when talking to a proxy, the client uses a fully qualified URL, containing the hostname as well as the path of the resource. For the request shown in Figure 9.1, the request line would be:

```
GET http://www.rtfm.com/ HTTP/1.0
```

When talking to the server, the proxy would remove the hostname and send the request as the client would have sent it to the server. There are a number of other subtleties in the proxy interaction, mainly having to do with the meaning of various header fields. Some header fields are intended for the proxy and the proxy should process (and remove) them when sending the request to the server. Others are intended for the server and the proxy should ignore them. We'll see an example of this distinction when we address Upgrade in Section 9.21.

Caching Proxies

The idea behind a caching proxy is simple. Many Web pages are both static and frequently fetched. If those pages are cached on the client machine, then server load and performance can be greatly improved. Most browsers now cache files on disk or in memory but this is useful only when a client repeatedly fetches the same data. Even so, this optimization is surprisingly useful: consider the case in which a single image such as a menu bar or a logo is used repeatedly throughout a site.

In an environment where many users are likely to fetch the same page, a more aggressive strategy can pay off. If caching is done at the proxy, then all users can benefit once a single user has fetched a page. Naturally, browsers must be configured to make connections to the cache rather than directly to the server. This configuration can be done manually but many browsers also provide auto-configuration features which allow IS administrators to configure proxies for all internal clients.

The primary problem that complicates caching proxy design and implementation is maintaining cache freshness. It is necessary to detect content that is dynamic and therefore cannot be cached as well as to periodically check whether a document has been updated on the server. HTTP contains complicated mechanisms for addressing this problem but they are largely irrelevant to SSL because the traffic from client to server is encrypted and therefore caching is impossible anyway.

Firewall Proxies

The purpose of a firewall is to restrict traffic between the inner (protected) network and the Internet as a whole. Although some firewalls allow arbitrary TCP connections between the inner network and the Internet, many do not. Such firewalls typically rely on application-layer proxies to enable the necessary (typically restricted) set of services.

The primary design goal for firewall proxies is of course security. To that end, the proxies are typically very simple and designed to be error free. Although a firewall HTTP proxy can also be a caching proxy, usually such proxies do not contain a cache. The primary issue for SSL/proxy interaction is to ensure that our HTTP over SSL traffic can pass through proxies safely without being damaged by the proxy.

9.8 Virtual Hosts

Consider the situation where a customer's Web site is being hosted by an *Internet Service Provider* (ISP). Even though an ISP may have many customers, it wants to have only a few server machines. This necessitates the ability to appear to have many Web servers on the same server machine.

Naturally, each customer wants to be able to have a separate Web address. Even if they are actually hosted on the server `www.provider.com`, they would like their clients to be able to access their home page at `http://www.customer.com/`. Because there is only one Web server, it will be receiving requests for multiple *virtual servers*. The problem now becomes how to distinguish which virtual server a given request is intended for. The Request-URI specifies only the path of the resource within the server, so other means are necessary.

Modern Web clients use the Host header to provide the hostname of the Web server that they believe they are connecting to. This permits the Web server to disambiguate multiple virtual servers on the same physical server. Obviously, a good design for HTTP over SSL should ensure that it doesn't break virtual hosts.

9.9 Protocol Selection

At the time that the first HTTP over SSL solutions were being designed, the upward negotiation strategy for SSL hadn't been invented. Also, an important design consideration for HTTP servers was that they were supposed to be *stateless*—each request/response pair was intended to be independent. Thus, a protocol model that required multiple round trips through the HTTP engine (as we'll see is required by Upgrade) was difficult to accept. The idea behind SSL, after all, was that you could simply replace your sockets calls with SSL calls and not change the rest of your code at all. If minimizing impact on the rest of the code is the overriding design goal (which it often is) a separate ports approach is the only workable strategy.

9.10   Client Authentication

Certificate-based client authentication is completely unnecessary for secure forms submission. In practice, most Web sites choose not to authenticate their users at all. The ones that do typically wish to use some external authenticator (such as a credit card number). As a consequence, certificate-based client authentication is not a high priority for Web applications.

Although client authentication in SSLv2 wasn't widely supported, most SSLv3 and TLS implementations do have support for client authentication. In certain restricted (intranet) environments, certificate-based authentication is very useful and practical. Thus, a Web security solution should also support certificates for clients.

It's possible to support certificates without any special protocol support from HTTP (as opposed to from SSL) because the server can simply request client authentication from the client in the SSL handshake. However, because the SSL handshake happens before the server knows which resource the client is attempting to access, this tends to be a rather all-or-nothing proposition. As we'll see in Section 9.18, it might be desirable for servers to be able to signal in the reference that they expect client authentication, thus allowing the client to offer it in the handshake.

9.11   Reference Integrity

The Web has a very clear reference model: resources are identified by URL. Thus, the obvious design choice for HTTP over SSL was simply to try to match the URL reference to the server's identity. This required that CAs issue certificates containing hostnames. This is the approach that the HTTPS designers chose.

A more sophisticated approach would be to have the references themselves contain an additional indicator of the expected server identity. This could be placed in the anchor (as was done in Secure HTTP [Rescorla1999a]; see Chapter 11) or it could be somewhere in the URL. The primary disadvantage of this approach is that it would make the common user activity of typing in URLs much harder. The primary advantage is that it would allow vastly more flexibility in terms of what sort of certificates servers could have. We'll see a case where that sort of flexibility would have been valuable when we discuss virtual servers in Section 9.17.

Connection Semantics

HTTP over SSL is essentially constrained to use HTTP's connection semantics. This was obviously problematic because SSL handshakes were far more expensive than TCP handshakes. Reducing this load was one of the primary motivators for the fast resumption mechanism. Unfortunately, resumption broke the stateless model of HTTP. In fact, as we'll see in Section 9.24, it placed quite a burden on the server because implementing resumption required interprocess communication of session state.

If we think of SSL as being designed without reference to HTTP and then applied to HTTP, this burden seems like an unfortunate outcome of the interaction of a general security protocol with HTTP. However, in reality SSL was largely designed for HTTP and modifications to reduce the state burden would have been possible, had the designers thought of them. We'll discuss a few such tricks when we discuss Secure HTTP in Chapter 11. Nevertheless, the stateless interaction model was already on its way out when SSL was designed, due to the TCP performance issues discussed in Section 9.6 and its unacceptable performance consequences on UNIX systems.

9.12 HTTPS

Now that we've covered the problem of Web security from a design perspective, we're prepared to understand HTTPS, the dominant approach used for HTTP with SSL. We're also prepared to evaluate how good a job it actually does at meeting the challenges we've discussed.

We begin by examining a simple request made with HTTPS to illustrate its basic features. Although the basic idea behind HTTPS is very simple, there are some technical points that need to be carefully defined: *connection closure* behavior and the use of URLs to provide *reference integrity*. With a clear definition of HTTPS in hand, we then consider its interaction with a number of confounding features faced in the real network: *proxies* and *virtual hosts*. We also discuss the problem of determining when to require certificate-based *client authentication* in a real Web environment.

Although HTTPS is basically secure, a number of attacks and limitations have been discovered. We describe these attacks and some techniques for avoiding them in Sections 9.19 and 9.20. Finally, we consider HTTP Upgrade, a newer alternative to HTTPS. HTTP Upgrade is intended to fix some known problems with HTTPS, but we'll see that it introduces a number of problems of its own.

9.13 HTTPS Overview

HTTP was the first application-layer protocol to be secured with SSL. The first public implementation of HTTP over SSL was in Netscape Navigator 2 in 1995. At the time, the separate ports strategy was the only one available and Netscape used it for HTTP as well as for NNTP and SMTP. The URLs for pages fetched via HTTP over SSL began with `https://` to disambiguate them from HTTP URLs, and this approach quickly became known as HTTPS.

> HTTPS stands for "HTTP Secure." This construction seems a little stilted but Netscape was prevented from using `shttp://` because Secure HTTP (see Chapter 11) already used that protocol name for its URL scheme.

Despite the wide deployment of SSL-enabled HTTP implementations, neither Netscape nor anyone else published a standard for HTTP over SSL until the IETF started considering the matter in 1998. Instead, it was widely assumed that there was only one obvious way to do things and the (somewhat nontrivial) details were passed around as lore. HTTPS was finally documented in RFC 2818 [Rescorla2000].

The HTTPS approach is very simple: The client makes a connection to the server, negotiates an SSL connection, and then transmits its HTTP data over the SSL application data channel. This description makes it sound very easy and in principle this is true. The only other piece of information that you need to have in order to create an interoperable (though not necessarily secure) HTTPS implementation is the port number. Because we're using a separate ports strategy, HTTPS connections need their own port. IANA assigned HTTPS port 443, so by default HTTPS connections happen on that port. Of course, it's still possible to specify a different port number in the URL.

Figure 9.4 shows an example HTTPS request in action between a Netscape 4.7 client and an Apache 1.3.9 server running mod_ssl 2.4.10. All the initial traffic (records 1–9) is the SSL handshake. This is a rather ordinary SSLv3 handshake except that the client is connecting using the SSLv2 backward-compatibility handshake. Even with modern Web browsers, this is still by far the most common case. Also, note that the client offered only SSLv3 not TLS. As of this writing, TLS support is still not available in Netscape.

```
New TCP connection: romeo(4577) <-> romeo(443)
1 948676151.6444 (0.0005) C>S SSLv2 compatible client hello
  Version 3.0
  cipher suites
      TLS_RSA_WITH_RC4_128_MD5
      value unknown: 0xffe0    Proprietary Netscape cipher suite
      TLS_RSA_WITH_3DES_EDE_CBC_SHA
      value unknown: 0xffe1    Proprietary Netscape cipher suite
      TLS_RSA_WITH_DES_CBC_SHA
      TLS_RSA_EXPORT1024_WITH_RC4_56_SHA
      TLS_RSA_EXPORT1024_WITH_DES_CBC_SHA
      TLS_RSA_EXPORT_WITH_RC4_40_MD5
      TLS_RSA_EXPORT_WITH_RC2_CBC_40_MD5
2 948676151.6495 (0.0051) S>C    Handshake
      ServerHello
        session_id[32]=
          15 07 d3 46 a9 40 bc bc 6f 54 f9 60
          40 d0 bf 2f 08 3e 1e 4e f4 1d 7c 52
          31 46 14 20 ad 95 5b 04
        cipherSuite           TLS_RSA_WITH_RC4_128_MD5
        compressionMethod            NULL
3 948676151.6495 (0.0000) S>C    Handshake
      Certificate
4 948676151.6495 (0.0000) S>C    Handshake
      ServerHelloDone
```

(continued)

Figure 9.4 *(continued)*

```
 5 948676151.6637 (0.0141) C>S    Handshake
          ClientKeyExchange
 6 948676151.6900 (0.0262) C>S    ChangeCipherSpec
 7 948676151.6900 (0.0000) C>S    Handshake
          Finished
 8 948676151.6921 (0.0020) S>C    ChangeCipherSpec
 9 948676151.6921 (0.0000) S>C    Handshake
          Finished
10 948676151.6933 (0.0012) C>S     application_data
     data: 284 bytes
     ------------------------------------
     GET /tmp.html HTTP/1.0
     Connection: Keep-Alive
     User-Agent: Mozilla/4.7 [en] (X11; U; FreeBSD 3.4-STABLE i386)
     Host: romeo
     Accept: image/gif, image/x-xbitmap, image/jpeg, image/pjpeg, ⌐
     image/png, */*
     Accept-Encoding: gzip
     Accept-Language: en
     Accept-Charset: iso-8859-1,*,utf-8


     ------------------------------------
11 948676151.7013 (0.0079) S>C     application_data
     data: 395 bytes
     ------------------------------------
     HTTP/1.1 200 OK
     Date: Mon, 24 Jan 2000 01:09:11 GMT
     Server: Apache/1.3.9 (Unix) mod_ssl/2.4.10 OpenSSL/0.9.4
     Last-Modified: Sun, 23 Jan 2000 23:08:11 GMT
     ETag: "58820-79-388b89db"
     Accept-Ranges: bytes
     Content-Length: 121
     Connection: close
     Content-Type: text/html

     <HTML>
      <HEAD>
       <TITLE>Test</TITLE>
      </HEAD>
      <BODY>
      <H1>
      Test Page
      </H1>
```

```
     This page is just a sample.
     <P>
     </BODY>
     </HTML>
     ------------------------------------
12 948676151.7063 (0.0050) S>C    Alert
        level          warning
        value          close_notify
Server FIN
13 948676151.8052 (0.0989) C>S    Alert
        level          warning
        value          close_notify
Client FIN
```

Figure 9.4 A Request with HTTPS

Record 10 contains the HTTP request. This request is essentially identical to the request we showed in Figure 9.1 except that it's for a different URL. Note that absolutely no client data is sent until the SSL connection has been negotiated. Shortly, we'll see how this can cause problems in transitioning HTTP systems to HTTPS.

Record 11 contains the HTTP response. Note that the HTTP response fits entirely in one record. Of course, if the Web page were longer, this might require spanning multiple records. This response is basically similar to the response we showed in Figure 9.2, except that the page itself is different.

The only significant difference is that instead of Connection: keep-alive, the server has sent a Connection: close header, indicating that it will close the connection after serving this page. We've configured the server not to use retained connections so that we can show the closure behavior.

As we'd expect, the server sends its close_notify followed by a TCP FIN. The client responds with its close_notify and a FIN. Technically, the server could withhold its FIN until after it had received the client's close_notify. The SSL spec is silent on this issue. However, in practice, early versions of Netscape would not respond to the close_notify until they had received the FIN, so sending it immediately is good practice.

9.14 URLs and Reference Integrity

The vast majority of HTTP connections are initiated by dereferencing some URL. Because HTTPS uses the separate ports strategy, the URL must indicate that the protocol to be used is HTTPS rather than HTTP. This is done simply by using the https protocol identifier rather than the http protocol identifier:

```
https://www.example.com/example.html
```

Downgrade Attacks

The use of the `https` protocol identifier protects against downgrade attacks. The client expects to initiate an SSL connection to the server—indeed, there is no way for the server (or an attacker) to indicate that it *won't* speak SSL. The attacker can only cause an error to be generated. Of course, as we discussed earlier, users can sometimes be tricked into retrying with an HTTP connection if the HTTPS connection fails.

However, the `https` identifier provides only one bit of information: The client should expect security. This doesn't provide any indication of what security properties to expect. With SSLv2, this presented a serious problem because SSLv2 had no protection against an attacker downgrading the connection to a weaker algorithm. However, SSLv3 and TLS do provide algorithm downgrade protection. Because SSLv3 and TLS also provide protection against downgrading to SSLv2, as long as the server speaks SSLv3 at all, the negotiation cannot be downgraded to a weaker algorithm.

As long as the server is correctly authenticated, then the handshake can be conducted securely. Thus, provided the client doesn't accept anonymous DH and adequately checks the server's identity as described in the next section, HTTPS (with SSLv3) is secure against downgrade attacks. However, if the server isn't authenticated correctly, the attacker can mount a man-in-the-middle attack.

End-point Authentication

The HTTPS spec provides a somewhat complicated algorithm for checking the server's identity. The intent is to accommodate a variety of special cases. In most cases the server's expected hostname will be available from the URL or some similar source. If the client has the server's expected hostname, it must check it against the server's certificate.

Alternatively, the client might have specific information about the server's certificate rather than the hostname, in which case it's required to check that. Finally, although it is explicitly allowed to perform no checks at all, this should really never be done because it leaves the connection open to an active attack.

Figure 9.5 shows a flowchart for the hostname checking procedure. If a subjectAlt-Name extension is present with type dNSName, that must be checked. Currently, no major CA issues certificates of this type but it is hoped that in the future they will do so, because this approach is far cleaner than using the Common Name—the Common Name approach requires an implicit agreement between the CA and users about the semantics of the Common Name, whereas the semantics of dNSName are clear.

If the dNSName is not present, however, the Common Name must be checked. Because a DN may have two RDNs which both specify Common Name values, the specification explicitly requires that the most local RDN be checked. No explicit rule is provided for the case in which a single RDN contains two Common Name values. The obvious choice is to accept the certificate if any of the names match.

RFC 2818 also allows wildcarded DNs. Part of the name is replaced by a "*". The "*" can match any string. Thus, if the Common Name is `*.example.com` this certificate would work for `foo.example.com`, `bar.example.com`, etc. Wildcarding only really works well if you have a number of virtual servers run by the same

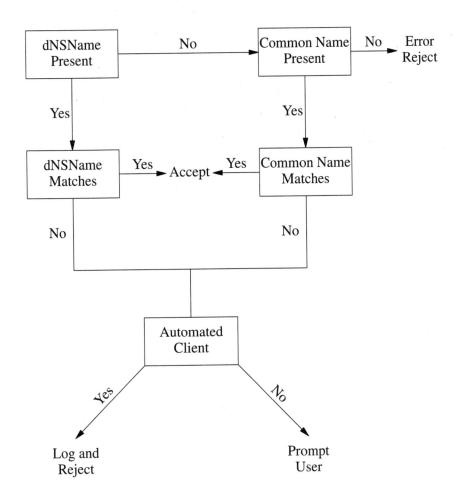

Figure 9.5 Certificate checking algorithm

organization. You can't use it to represent (say) www.domain.com and www.anotherdomain.com because any wildcard that matched both would also match other domains not owned by the certificate-holder.

Failure Behavior

The obvious response to a mismatch between the certificate and the server's expected identity is simply to terminate the connection. Unfortunately, this behavior has been found to be very irritating to users. Although such a mismatch may in principle reflect an active attack, in practice it more likely reflects a misconfiguration of the server.

Netscape Navigator has traditionally responded to mismatches (and to unverifiable certificates) by prompting the user with a dialog box identifying the error and offering to shut down the connection or continue. Older versions of Internet Explorer simply shut down the connection and refused to continue. However, newer versions of IE allow the user to continue.

The HTTPS specification provides a number of alternatives for handling a mismatch. A client such as a browser must at minimum notify the user of the mismatch. It may offer a choice to continue or simply terminate the connection. An automated client must log the error and should terminate the connection.

Although continuing in the face of a certificate mismatch is known to be insecure against active attack, it's important to remember that users will often attempt to refetch the page using HTTP if the HTTPS fetch fails. In cases in which the user will attempt an insecure fetch, then it is still better to accept the wrong certificate, because there is some chance that the problem is simply a configuration error. For example, the server administrator might have changed the DNS name of the server without getting a new certificate. Figure 9.6 shows the possible cases. As you can see, accepting the wrong certificate is never worse (and sometimes better) than having the user retry with HTTP.

| | Client Behavior | | |
Situation	Failure	Accept Certificate	Retry with HTTP
Configuration Error	Failure to communicate	Communication OK	Data transmitted in clear
Attack	Attack prevented	Successful attack	Data transmitted in clear

Figure 9.6 Results of various error handling strategies

Determining how to behave when certificate processing fails requires examining your security policy and the attitudes of your users. It's never appropriate to simply accept a certificate that the implementation knows to be wrong. However, in some circumstances it might be superior to allow the user to accept the certificate anyway. As Figure 9.6 shows, this may be superior to simply refusing to connect altogether. When certificate validation fails, both Netscape and Internet Explorer pop up a dialog to allow the user to continue with the connection.

User Override

As discussed above, Netscape and later versions of IE allow the user to continue even if the certificate does not match. From the user's perspective, they behave essentially identically. However, from a bits-on-the-wire perspective they behave rather differently.

Figure 9.7 shows a Netscape client connecting to a server with an unacceptable certificate. As you might expect, the client waits for the server to send the Certificate message and then holds the connection open while it prompts the user to accept the certificate or cancel the connection. In the trace shown in Figure 9.7, the user has chosen to accept the certificate, so the handshake continues.

Note that depending on what exactly is wrong with the certificate (bad hostname, unknown CA, expired, or maybe all three), the user may have to click through a number of dialogs to accept the certificate and continue. This can take a while and the server must therefore set its timeouts long enough that it doesn't time out during this process.

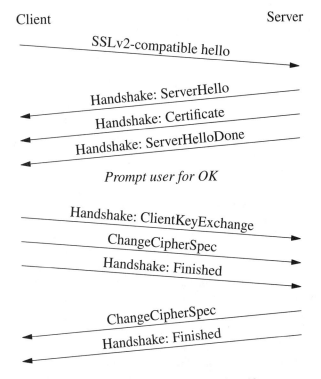

Figure 9.7 Netscape: user accepts bad certificate

Figure 9.8 shows Netscape's behavior when the user chooses to cancel the handshake. After the user presses the cancel button in the dialog, the client sends a bad_certificate alert to the server and terminates the connection.

IE's behavior is somewhat less obvious. When IE receives a bad certificate, it completes the handshake and then closes the connection, as shown in Figure 9.9. Once the connection is closed, IE prompts the user to accept or reject the certificate. If the certificate is rejected, the connection just stays closed. If the certificate is accepted, IE initiates a new connection to the server. Note that IE resumes the SSL session, thus avoiding the cost of a full new handshake.

Netscape's behavior is what you would expect from reading the spec. However, IE's behavior, though surprising, is not actually forbidden. The primary advantage of IE's behavior is that it does not consume server resources while the user is deciding whether or not to accept the certificate. Because server sockets are a somewhat limited resource,

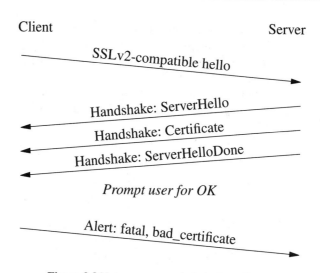

Figure 9.8 Netscape: user rejects bad certificate

this can be a valuable optimization for heavily loaded servers. However, since a server in heavy use should have a certificate from a well-known CA, this case isn't actually that important.

IE's approach has two disadvantages: First, the server doesn't get any feedback that the client didn't like its certificate. If the server administrator actually reads the log files, a bad_certificate alert would warn him that there was a problem. Second, if the server isn't using session caching or times out the client's session before the reconnect, a new full handshake will be required, which is expensive for both the client and the server.

Since responding to the accept/reject dialogs is irritating to the user, both Netscape and IE cache the user's acceptance of the certificate. Netscape also allows the user to specify that this certificate should be accepted permanently so that the user will never be bothered again. Deciding whether this is a bug or a feature is left up to the reader.

Reference Sources

It's important to note that reference integrity depends on the reference being safely delivered to the client. If the reference is delivered in such a way that it can itself be trusted, then the previously mentioned properties hold. For instance, the reference might itself be delivered over an HTTPS link. However, in cases where the reference is delivered over an unsecured link, then it's possible to mount active attacks by changing the page containing the reference. We'll see such an attack in Section 9.20. No possible reference integrity checking can prevent this form of attack.

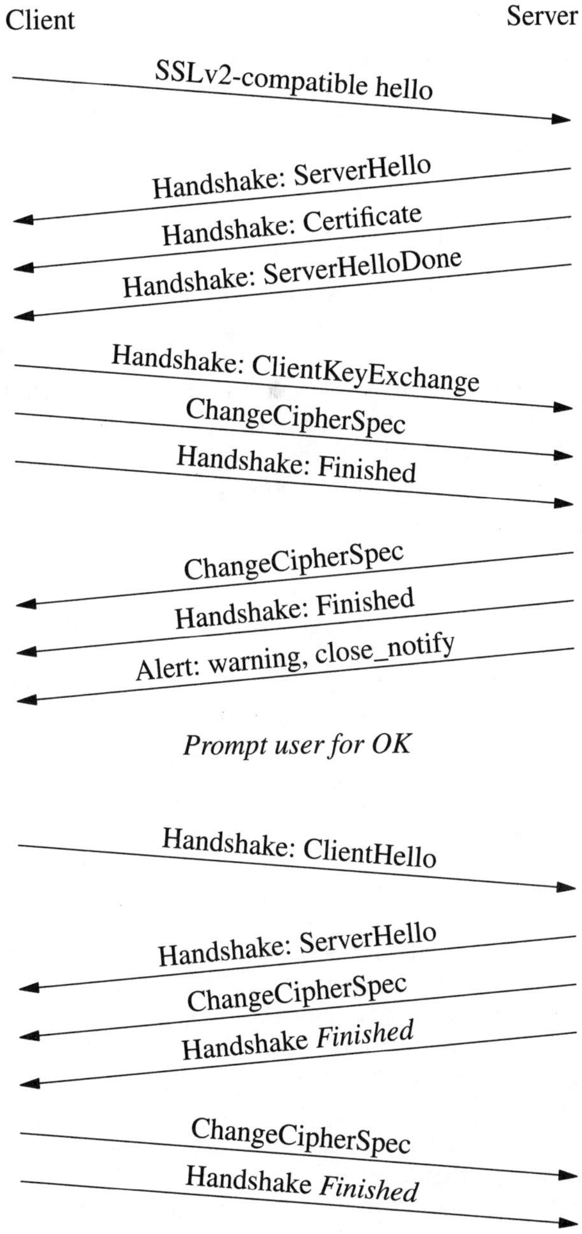

Client   Server

SSLv2-compatible hello

Handshake: ServerHello

Handshake: Certificate

Handshake: ServerHelloDone

Handshake: ClientKeyExchange

ChangeCipherSpec

Handshake: Finished

ChangeCipherSpec

Handshake: Finished

Alert: warning, close_notify

Prompt user for OK

Handshake: ClientHello

Handshake: ServerHello

ChangeCipherSpec

Handshake *Finished*

ChangeCipherSpec

Handshake *Finished*

Figure 9.9 IE: user accepts bad certificate

Client Identity

In some non-Web environments the "client" is actually another host. If the server knows that this is the case, then the server should perform the same sorts of checks that are described above.

9.15   Connection Closure

Finally, we must consider the issue of closure. The correct closure behavior is easily summarized: Whenever either side wishes to close the connection, it should send a close_notify and optionally wait for a close_notify. This is required both by the TLS and HTTPS RFCs. The issue that we need to be concerned with is how to behave when a TCP FIN is received without a close_notify. In some cases, this situation represents an obvious possible attack. In others, it may simply be a programming error. We'd like to be able to distinguish such cases in order to avoid recording a large number of spurious errors.

Session Resumption

Recall from our discussion in Chapter 7 that the rules about session resumption are clear. In no case should an SSL implementation resume a session when it has received a premature close. To do so would be to explicitly violate the SSL specification. However, it is permissible to send one's own close_notify and then shut down the connection without waiting for the other side's close_notify. In such a case, an SSL implementation may resume the session.

Error Handling

Primarily we're concerned with client behavior. First, HTTP semantics imply that errors are more serious for clients than servers. A server that receives an end of data during the request, whether via proper SSL closure or via a TCP FIN will behave in essentially the same way: abandon processing the request. Second, when servers encounter errors, they usually simply log them to audit logs. Thus, a server author can safely log anything out of the ordinary.

By contrast, clients often signal errors directly to users via dialog boxes and the like. It's therefore important to avoid both failure to report legitimate errors (because this hides important information from the user) and reporting non-errors (because this overwhelms the user and increases the chance that the user will ignore legitimate errors).

As a general rule we want to be able to distinguish between two classes of error:

Likely programming error. The HTTP traffic indicators about connection closure don't match the SSL behavior. We want to be forgiving when we receive a message that is broken but doesn't indicate a security problem.

Truncation attack. The client received a response that might be incomplete.

Likely Programming Error

Consider the case where the client expects the connection to close but then receives a premature close. For instance, the client receives a response from the server with the `Connection: close` header. The client reads the entire amount of data specified by the `Content-Length` header. Thus, the client expects the connection to close immediately. Now, the client receives a bare FIN without ever receiving a close_notify. It's possible that an attacker forged the FIN but it's more likely that the server has made an error and closed the connection incorrectly. We know that the client has received all the data that the server is supposed to send, so we don't need to worry that the page is damaged, and the client can display it without reporting an error.

A slightly more difficult class of cases involves those in which the client doesn't expect any traffic from the server but it also does not expect the server to close the connection. Imagine that the client receives a response with a `Content-Length` header and it has read all of that data. However, the client believes that it's using persistent connections and so does not know if the server will close the connection. (HTTP permits the server to close the connection without notifying the client.) Thus, if the client receives a premature close after reading the whole response, it's possible that an attacker is mounting a denial-of-service attack, but again it's more likely that the server is broken. In any case, the client knows that the response that it actually did receive is complete and can display it.

Finally, consider the case where a proper close_notify occurs before it is expected, for instance before the number of bytes specified by the `Content-Length` header has been read. This is an obvious programming error on the server because an attacker could neither forge a close_notify nor undetectably change the `Content-Length` header.

Truncation Attack

Recall that older versions of HTTP use connection closure to signal end of data. Thus, if a client expects to receive more data from the server but instead receives a premature close, it must signal an error. First, consider the case where no `Content-Length` header is present. Since the client has no indicator of when the response is finished other than the connection close, receipt of a close_notify is essential to know that the entire response was received.

Similarly, if the `Content-Length` header is present but a premature close is found before the full response has been read, this must be treated as an error. It's of course possible that the server has merely miscomputed the length, but there is no way to distinguish this case from an attack. Note that we handle this case differently from the case where the full length has been read, in which case we know that we've received the full response and any possible attack merely prevented us from receiving the next response.

In any case where there has been a possible truncation attack and a response might have been shortened, the client should warn the user, usually by printing an error message or popping up a dialog indicating that the connection closed unexpectedly and the data might be truncated. Particularly paranoid clients might refuse to display any of the response at all.

9.16   Proxies

HTTPS interacts uncleanly with proxies. The general problem is that HTTPS semantics imply that the client negotiated an SSL session with the target server. Once the client has done so, all the data that passes between the client and server are encrypted. The result is that caching proxies won't work. It's reasonable to regard this as a feature, because the data we're attempting to transmit between client and server are supposed to be confidential anyway. However, even in cases where no confidentiality is employed (i.e., cipher suites with only message integrity) no caching is possible.

CONNECT

A more serious problem is that the usual HTTP proxy semantics do not work with HTTPS. Recall that the proxy examines the client's request in order to determine which server to connect to. HTTPS requires that the client pass its request over the encrypted channel, so this approach is obviously no longer possible. This is a more serious issue than the inability to cache, because proxies are the only method available for traversing certain firewalls. Thus, without special support, HTTPS is incompatible with those firewalls.

The special support comes in the form of a new proxy method: CONNECT, documented in RFC 2817 [Khare2000]. The CONNECT method instructs the proxy to initiate a TCP connection to the specified remote server and then pass data between client and server without examining it or changing it. The client then transmits the SSL data to the proxy as if the proxy were the server. Figure 9.10 shows the beginning of such a connection up through the transmission of the ClientHello. Note that the client supplies the host and port of the specified server to the proxy in the Request-URI field of the request.

From the perspective of the HTTPS user or programmer, this approach appears to work well. However, from the perspective of the firewall administrator, the results are less positive. Firewall administrators are often concerned with controlling the sorts of traffic that traverse the firewall. For instance, they might wish to screen out particular types of Web content. Because traffic transmitted with CONNECT is supposed to be unexamined—and is in theory unreadable because it's encrypted—this type of screening is now impractical.

The protocols that can cross firewalls using CONNECT are not even limited to SSL over HTTP. Although in principle the firewall could attempt to determine that the traffic was SSL, in practice this is too difficult. Thus CONNECT method permits a client to punch a hole in the firewall and pass arbitrary traffic through that hole. An administrator can attempt to limit the hosts and port numbers to which a client connects, but this is a fairly weak sort of enforcement.

Man-in-the-Middle Proxies

As we've seen, in general proxies cannot view the traffic between client and server. However, it's possible to arrange matters so that the proxy can do so by having the proxy mount a man-in-the-middle attack on the connection. The proxy accepts the CONNECT request but instead of proxying the data it negotiates a pair of SSL

```
New TCP connection: romeo(2577) <-> romeo(80)
1 949442170.3636 (0.0002) C>S
data: 37 bytes
------------------------------------
CONNECT www.rtfm.com:443 HTTP/1.0


------------------------------------


2 949442170.3686 (0.0052) S>C
data: 102 bytes
------------------------------------
HTTP/1.0 200 Connection established
Proxy-agent: Apache/1.3.9 (Unix) mod_ssl/2.4.10 OpenSSL/0.9.4


------------------------------------


3 949442170.4403 (0.0769) C>S    Handshake
      ClientHello
        Version 3.1
        cipher suites
                    TLS_DHE_DSS_WITH_RC4_128_SHA
                    TLS_DHE_DSS_WITH_RC2_56_CBC_SHA
                    TLS_RSA_EXPORT1024_WITH_RC4_56_SHA
                    TLS_DHE_DSS_EXPORT1024_WITH_DES_CBC_SHA
                    TLS_RSA_EXPORT1024_WITH_DES_CBC_SHA
                    TLS_RSA_EXPORT1024_WITH_RC2_CBC_56_MD5
                    TLS_RSA_EXPORT1024_WITH_RC4_56_MD5
                    TLS_DHE_RSA_WITH_3DES_EDE_CBC_SHA
                    TLS_DHE_DSS_WITH_3DES_EDE_CBC_SHA
                    TLS_RSA_WITH_3DES_EDE_CBC_SHA
                    TLS_RSA_WITH_IDEA_CBC_SHA
                    TLS_RSA_WITH_RC4_128_SHA
                    TLS_RSA_WITH_RC4_128_MD5
                    TLS_DHE_RSA_WITH_DES_CBC_SHA
                    TLS_DHE_DSS_WITH_DES_CBC_SHA
                    TLS_RSA_WITH_DES_CBC_SHA
                    TLS_DHE_RSA_EXPORT_WITH_DES40_CBC_SHA
                    TLS_DHE_DSS_EXPORT_WITH_DES40_CBC_SHA
                    TLS_RSA_EXPORT_WITH_DES40_CBC_SHA
                    TLS_RSA_EXPORT_WITH_RC2_CBC_40_MD5
                    TLS_RSA_EXPORT_WITH_RC4_40_MD5
        compression methods
                    NULL
```

Figure 9.10 Using CONNECT with a proxy

connections, one to the client and one to the server. It then passes data between client and server but the data is available in cleartext form to the proxy. Figure 9.11 shows this process.

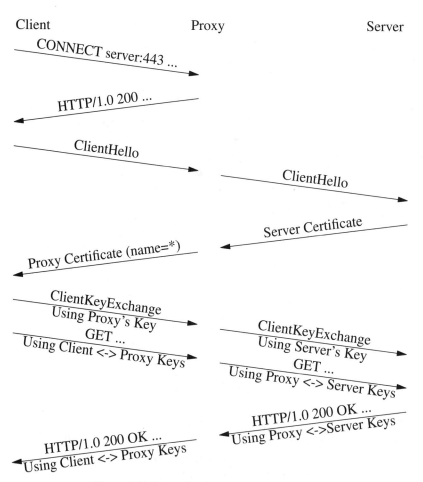

Figure 9.11 A man-in-the-middle proxy in action

But how is this possible, since SSL is supposed to be resistant to man-in-the-middle attacks? It requires the cooperation of the client. The proxy has a very special certificate that has "*" as its Common Name. Because the hostname match is wildcarded, the client will accept this certificate no matter which host it wants to connect to. Obviously, no legitimate CA will issue such a certificate because it would let the holder imperson-ate any server. To work around this, the administrator needs to run his own CA and install it into the browser. Because browsers that aren't under the control of the administrator won't have this CA in their list of trusted CAs, they can't be fooled by this dangerous certificate.

> Note that RFC 2818 forbids such certificates from being issued, since "*" can only match a single domain name component. However, as we'll see in Section 9.17, Netscape allows a "*" to match anything. In order to make this trick work with RFC 2818-compliant browsers, you would need to have a certificate containing a series of patterns: "*", "*.*", "*.*.*", ...

Note that this sort of proxy has serious drawbacks. If the proxy is compromised, the traffic of all clients is compromised. Because the proxy is outside (or part of) the firewall, it makes a good target for attack. Also, because the client does not connect directly to the server, SSL client authentication no longer works.

Cipher Suite Translation

Due to the old U.S. export regulations, a curious asymmetry exists between clients and servers. The two most popular browsers, Netscape and Internet Explorer, are both made by U.S. companies and thus were subject to strict U.S. export regulations. Because downloading the more secure "domestic" version of the browsers was difficult, many Americans have "export" browsers. As a consequence, there are a lot of browsers available with only weak cryptography.

By far the most popular Web server is Apache. Although Apache was written in the U.S., there are several easily available SSL/TLS patches for Apache written outside the U.S. Also, because Netscape's servers weren't free, getting the "domestic" Netscape server wasn't much harder than getting the "export" server. Thus, a fairly high percentage of the Netscape servers sold in the U.S. had strong cryptography. In general, most servers suppport strong cryptography.

C2 Net took advantage of this situation to offer a man-in-the-middle proxy called SafePassage. SafePassage runs on the same computer as the client. It allows "export" clients to connect to it with weak cryptography, but then itself uses strong cryptography to connect to the server. Because SafePassage was manufactured outside the U.S., foreigners could get a copy and upgrade their browsers. Thus, the weak cryptography is only used to encrypt data that never leaves the machine anyway.

The need for SafePassage dwindled with the introduction of Fortify, a patch to Netscape that upgraded "export" versions to support strong cipher suites, and finally vanished when the U.S. government liberalized its export regulations in January 2000. Nevertheless, SafePassage was the first example of a man-in-the-middle proxy and thus an innovative product. SPYRUS has used a similar approach to translate ordinary RSA-based cipher suites to cipher suites using the U.S. government's FORTEZZA card.

9.17 Virtual Hosts

HTTPS also interacts poorly with virtual hosts. Once again, the problem is that the SSL connection is established before any HTTP data is transmitted. Recall that ordinarily the server uses the `Host` header in the request to determine which virtual host is being accessed. Because the request is transmitted after the handshake occurs, the server must negotiate the SSL connection without the guidance of the `Host` header.

Consider the issue of which server certificate to present to the client. If the servers were in fact on separate machines, we would expect them to have different certificates and under normal circumstances we would expect each virtual server to have its own certificate. However, knowing which certificate to present requires knowing which virtual server the client is attempting to connect to. Similar considerations apply if the virtual servers have different security policies and want to negotiate different cipher suites.

However, there is another method of implementing virtual servers that is consistent with SSL. It is possible for a machine to be configured so that a single network interface has multiple IP addresses (called aliases). Each virtual server is assigned its own alias. Thus, when the server accepts the connection, it looks at the IP address that it accepted the connection on and uses that to determine which virtual server the client is attempting to access.

As we implied in Section 9.11, another approach would be to allow the anchor to specify the server's certificate, perhaps somewhere in the URL. Then a server could use the same certificate for all its virtual servers while still preserving reference integrity.

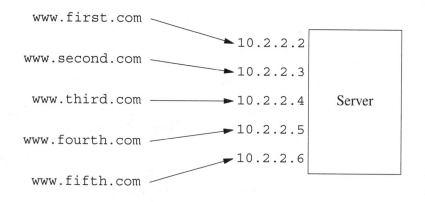

Figure 9.12 Virtual hosts using IP aliases

Figure 9.12 shows a sample virtual server configuration with five virtual servers. The DNS name `www.first.com` is assigned to 10.2.2.2, the name `www.second.com` is assigned to 10.2.2.3, etc. Note that this technique is distinctly different from using CNAME records. Although multiple Web addresses point to the same server, they don't point to the same DNS A record but rather to different A records with different IP addresses.

This situation can be considered a design flaw in SSL. It would be fairly straightforward for the client to signal the DNS name of the server it was trying to connect to in the ClientHello, thus allowing the server to behave appropriately. This change would not compromise confidentiality because it's fairly easy for an attacker to deduce from other public network data (the IP header and the rest of the handshake) which server the client expects to connect to. This is one of several proposed changes for the next version of TLS—if there ever is one.

Note that this change to SSL would not relieve the client of the obligation of checking the server's certificate against the expected identity. Failure to make that check *would* introduce a vulnerability. The only purpose of this change would be as a prehandshake hint to the server.

Multiple Names

Another slightly less tasteful approach to the virtual hosts problem is to allow a certificate to serve multiple hosts. RFC 2818 specifies how to do this using wildcarding. See Section 9.14 for more details.

Netscape supports wildcarding. In fact, Netscape's wildcarding approach is substantiallly more flexible (and complicated) than that described in RFC 2818. It supports

*—anything at all

?—any single character

—the end of a string

[abc]—one occurrence of a, b, or c

[A-Z]—any character in the range A to Z

[^ab]—any character other than a or b

~—negates the pattern that follows

(pattern1|pattern2)—either pattern1 or pattern2

In order to allow special characters to appear in patterns, Netscape also uses \ as an escape character. However, since none of the special characters can appear in domain names in any case, this isn't really necessary. Netscape's approach to wildcarding is described in [Netscape1995a].

In addition to wildcarding, Internet Explorer supports another approach. Each certificate is allowed to have multiple Common Names. Thus, the certificate could contain names for `foo.example.com` and `bar.example.com`. This approach has the advantage that a certificate can be issued for multiple unrelated domains. However, it has the disadvantage that if even a single new virtual host is added for a certificate, it must be totally reissued. By contrast, wildcarding allows the certificate to match any number of virtual hosts as long as they match the pattern.

9.18   Client Authentication

Finally, consider the decision of whether the server should request client authentication using certificates. Some servers require client authentication for all pages that are fetched via HTTPS but much more common is for only certain pages to require client authentication. This policy is difficult to support cleanly with HTTPS.

Yet again, the problem is that the SSL handshake must be completed before the HTTP request is transmitted to the server. Thus, the server cannot know what resource is being requested (and therefore whether to request client authentication) until after the time at which it would have liked to request client authentication.

One approach would be for the server to always request client authentication but to allow the client to connect without it. Then, if the request turns out to require client authentication and the client didn't provide it, to throw an error at that point. Although technically workable, this has unfortunate user interface consequences: Users are almost always prompted for which certificate to use when authenticating. Thus, always requesting client authentication inconveniences all users—even those who do not need to authenticate. This inconvenience is usually considered enough to disqualify this approach.

The commonly used approach is for the server to negotiate an ordinary SSL connection for all clients. Then, once the request has been received, the server determines whether client authentication is required. If it isn't required, the server simply services the request. If it is required, the server requests a rehandshake using HelloRequest. In this second handshake, the server requests client authentication. Figure 9.13 shows a connection where this has happened.

```
New TCP connection: romeo(4569) <-> romeo(443)
1 948675468.0084 (0.0005) C>S SSLv2 compatible client hello
  Version 3.0
  cipher suites
      TLS_RSA_WITH_RC4_128_MD5
      value unknown: 0xffe0 Proprietary Netscape cipher suite
      TLS_RSA_WITH_3DES_EDE_CBC_SHA
      value unknown: 0xffe1 Proprietary Netscape cipher suite
      TLS_RSA_WITH_DES_CBC_SHA
      TLS_RSA_EXPORT1024_WITH_RC4_56_SHA
      TLS_RSA_EXPORT1024_WITH_DES_CBC_SHA
      TLS_RSA_EXPORT_WITH_RC4_40_MD5
      TLS_RSA_EXPORT_WITH_RC2_CBC_40_MD5
2 948675468.0139 (0.0054) S>C   Handshake
  ServerHello
    session_id[32]=
        22 0f e0 2c 1e 63 a3 b2 cd 68 6a af
        6c f5 bc ff 0d 77 7d d4 dc bd e5 3f
        80 1e da 33 3c 79 f4 0d
    cipherSuite              TLS_RSA_WITH_RC4_128_MD5
    compressionMethod              NULL
```

3 948675468.0139 (0.0000) S>C   Handshake
        Certificate
4 948675468.0139 (0.0000) S>C   Handshake
        ServerHelloDone
5 948675468.0281 (0.0142) C>S   Handshake
        ClientKeyExchange
6 948675468.0796 (0.0515) C>S   ChangeCipherSpec
7 *948675468.0796 (0.0000) C>S   Handshake*
        Finished
8 948675468.0818 (0.0021) S>C   ChangeCipherSpec
9 *948675468.0818 (0.0000) S>C   Handshake*
        Finished
10 *948675468.0830 (0.0012) C>S   application_data*
        data: 291 bytes

        GET /secure/tmp.html HTTP/1.0
        Connection: Keep-Alive
        User-Agent: Mozilla/4.7 [en] (X11; U; FreeBSD 3.4-STABLE i386)
        Host: romeo
        Accept: image/gif, image/x-xbitmap, image/jpeg, image/pjpeg, image/png, */*
        Accept-Encoding: gzip
        Accept-Language: en
        Accept-Charset: iso-8859-1,*,utf-8

        ----
11 *948675468.0892 (0.0062) S>C   Handshake*
        HelloRequest
12 *948675468.0912 (0.0019) C>S   Handshake*
        ClientHello
          Version 3.0
          cipher suites
                    TLS_RSA_WITH_RC4_128_MD5
                    value unknown: 0xffe0 Proprietary Netscape cipher suite
                    TLS_RSA_WITH_3DES_EDE_CBC_SHA
                    value unknown: 0xffe1 Proprietary Netscape cipher suite
                    TLS_RSA_WITH_DES_CBC_SHA
                    TLS_RSA_EXPORT1024_WITH_RC4_56_SHA
                    TLS_RSA_EXPORT1024_WITH_DES_CBC_SHA
                    TLS_RSA_EXPORT_WITH_RC4_40_MD5
                    TLS_RSA_EXPORT_WITH_RC2_CBC_40_MD5
        compression methods
                    NULL

(continued)

Figure 9.13 *(continued)*

```
13 948675468.0928 (0.0016) S>C    Handshake
      ServerHello
        session_id[32]=
          20 60 4a f0 84 cb b4 7c 7e 9b af d0
          3c fe 70 4c 47 58 96 18 2e 02 89 39
          94 50 4b e2 77 b0 2c a8
        cipherSuite            TLS_RSA_WITH_RC4_128_MD5
        compressionMethod             NULL
14 948675468.0928 (0.0000) S>C    Handshake
      Certificate
15 948675468.1005 (0.0077) S>C    Handshake
      CertificateRequest
              certificate_types          rsa_sign
              certificate_types          dss_sign
        certificate_authority
          30 49 31 0b 30 09 06 03 55 04 06 13
          02 55 53 31 13 30 11 06 03 55 04 0a
          13 0a 52 54 46 4d 2c 20 49 6e 63 2e
          31 13 30 11 06 03 55 04 0b 13 0a 43
          6f 6e 73 75 6c 74 69 6e 67 31 10 30
          0e 06 03 55 04 03 13 07 54 65 73 74
          20 43 41
16 948675468.1005 (0.0000) S>C    Handshake
      ServerHelloDone
17 948675471.2692 (3.1687) C>S    Handshake
      Certificate
      ClientKeyExchange
        EncryptedPreMasterSecret[128]=
      CertificateVerify
        Signature[128]=
          77 db fe 35 67 0d fa 1d 7d ea 2e 70
          ae 8f b4 a8 6f 26 91 df 81 1b 8b c6
          e1 7a 94 67 ed 9c ad be be 1a 71 74
          6e 1b b1 ae c1 9e 26 81 d7 6c 30 ae
          67 54 b8 12 f5 cf 0a e2 71 81 ae 0e
          8a 14 ee 76 de 39 44 33 9b 6e fd e7
          19 51 73 43 67 28 5d bf d3 74 a2 b8
          4a f1 32 0a 02 c8 27 b7 bd eb 79 38
          ca 3f 91 c7 95 46 b0 c3 32 ff 07 0d
          7b 54 28 30 c3 f4 67 f1 f1 58 e9 7c
          61 4c a7 28 51 c5 ad 92
18 948675471.2997 (0.0304) C>S    ChangeCipherSpec
```

```
19 948675471.4797 (0.1800) C>S    Handshake
       Finished
20 948675471.4811 (0.0013) S>C    ChangeCipherSpec
21 948675471.4811 (0.0000) S>C    Handshake
       Finished
22 948675471.4848 (0.0037) S>C    application_data
   data: 423 bytes
   -----------------------------------
   HTTP/1.1 200 OK
   Date: Mon, 24 Jan 2000 00:57:48 GMT
   Server: Apache/1.3.9 (Unix) mod_ssl/2.4.10 OpenSSL/0.9.4
   Last-Modified: Sun, 23 Jan 2000 23:08:52 GMT
   ETag: "8e469-95-388b8a04"
   Accept-Ranges: bytes
   Content-Length: 149
   Connection: close
   Content-Type: text/html

   <HTML>
    <HEAD>
     <TITLE>Test</TITLE>
    </HEAD>
    <BODY>
    <H1>
    Client Auth Test Page
    </H1>
    This page must be fetched with client auth.
    <P>
    </BODY>
    </HTML>
   -----------------------------------
23 948675471.4895 (0.0047) S>C    Alert
        level        warning
        value        close_notify
Server FIN
24 948675471.5060 (0.0164) C>S    Alert
        level        warning
        value        close_notify
Client FIN
```

Figure 9.13 Rehandshake with client authentication

When the client first connects in Figure 9.13, the server does an ordinary SSL handshake, exactly as we saw before. Once the handshake is complete, the client sends the request in record 10. Again, this is identical to the request in Figure 9.4 except that we're requesting a different resource `/secure/tmp.html` instead of `/tmp.html`.

At this point, the server examines its access control information and determines that the resource being requested requires client authentication and that the current connection doesn't have client authentication. Thus, the server will need to request a rehandshake in order to force the client to authenticate with its certificate. This is accomplished by sending the HelloRequest in record 11.

The HelloRequest causes the client to initiate a new handshake. Although technically the client is not required to do so immediately, the client can't do anything else until the server sends its response. The server sending the HelloRequest is a good indicator that the server may be waiting for the new handshake before it responds, so in practice the client will initiate a new handshake immediately, sending the ClientHello in record 12.

From here on in, the handshake is just like the SSL client authentication handshake we saw in Chapter 4. Note, however, that this entire process is taking place over the encrypted channel established in the first handshake. Finally, when the handshake completes in records 18–22, the server sends its response back (using the freshly negotiated session) in record 22.

Performance Consequences

Note that the client does not offer to resume the session when it sends its second ClientHello. Although it could do so, session resumption is incompatible with client authentication and so the server would have to refuse to resume the session in any case. As a consequence, the client and the server need to perform an entirely new handshake. This highlights the major drawback of the renegotiation approach: It doubles the amount of work that the server must do in order to establish the connection—and HTTPS was already much slower than bare HTTP. (Assuming that the keys are RSA keys, most of the client's work is doing its signature, so the extra cost of the extra handshake over simply authenticating in the first handshake to the client is insignificant.)

Other Approaches

Clearly, this problem represents a mismatch between the behavior of SSL and common HTTP usage. It's tempting to call it an SSL design error, but it's important to recall that SSL is a general protocol and that it's inherent in SSL design that the cryptographic keys must be negotiated before the first piece of application data is transmitted. Remember that the request might contain sensitive information, so it must be protected.

Nevertheless, it would be possible to improve the situation. First, SSL could allow you to perform client authentication on a resumed session. This is quite technically feasible and is simply a matter of slightly changing the behavior of the SSL messages. A number of possible modifications are possible, but one would be to use ServerHelloDone even in case of session resumption. Then, the server would have the opportunity to send a CertificateRequest. This should not cause a performance problem because the entire set of server messages can be transmitted in one handshake record and hence one TCP segment.

We cannot use the approach that we used with virtual servers where we indicated which server the client wanted to connect to. To work for this problem, the client would have to transmit the Request-URI in the clear over the wire. But the Request-URI itself may be sensitive information and an attacker cannot necessarily deduce it from sniffing. Thus, this approach cannot be used securely.

Another approach would be to have an indication in the URL that client authentication is required. This would also require SSL to have a mechanism for the client to unilaterally offer client authentication. The client could then make that offer based on the URL. This approach has the problem that if a server changed its access control settings it would then need to arrange to change all the relevant references. However, it would always be possible to renegotiate if the client made a connection using an out of date URL. There is currently no standard for how to do this, but it would be fairly straightforward to design one.

9.19 Referrer

In 1997, Daniel Klein observed that the Referrer header enabled a passive sniffing attack on HTTPS connections. The Referrer header simply contains the URL of the page that the user was viewing when he clicked the link that referenced the current page. Referrer provided a convenient way for sites to see which other sites were pointing at them, which was useful for a variety of statistics gathering purposes.

The attack was a result of the interaction of HTTP GET and referrer. Recall that when HTML forms are being used with GET the arguments are placed on the end of the Request-URI. Thus, when the user clicked on any link on the page resulting from the forms submission, the arguments to the form appeared in the Referrer header. If the link was an HTTP link, then the arguments would be transmitted in the clear on the next request. However, even if the link was an HTTPS link but was to a site other than the site to which the user submitted the form, that site would get the arguments in the Referrer header.

A user might have been understandably upset if one of the form fields revealed was his credit card number. The general response to this attack is to use forms that submit with HTTP POST. POST puts the arguments in the message body instead, thus neatly thwarting the attack.

9.20 Substitution Attacks

Recall from Chapter 7 that reference integrity requires that the references be reliably obtained. A number of different attacks have been described based on this principle. The general idea is to mount a man-in-the middle attack on the Web page that contains the first reference to an HTTPS page. The attacker then replaces the HTTPS URL with a reference to his own site instead. Because the URL matches the attacker's certificate, this completely bypasses the client's reference integrity checks.

Of course, it's possible (though unlikely) that the user will examine the URL displayed by the browser to see if it's what's expected. To counter this, the attacker can obtain a Web site with a name that looks like the victim's Web site (e.g., www.foos0ft.com instead of www.foosoft.com. Only a very astute user will notice this sort of substitution.

User Overrides

As we discussed earlier, even in cases where the reference does not match the server's certificate, many browsers give the user the opportunity to continue the connection. It's easy to see how to take advantage of this behavior to mount an attack. The attacker simply arranges for a certificate that the user might believe was appropriate (for instance, the foos0ft substitution in the previous section) and then takes over the client's HTTPS connection. In many cases, the user will allow the connection to go through, in which case the attack has succeeded.

9.21   Upgrade

RFC 2817 [Khare2000] defines a method for using the HTTP/1.1 Upgrade header to do upward negotiation from HTTP to HTTP over TLS. This approach was intended to provide an alternative to the popular HTTPS approach, without requiring the allocation of a separate port. In practice, however, there has been essentially no deployment of the Upgrade approach in the Web context. Most of the interest in Upgrade appears to be for other protocols which use HTTP, in part because the IESG has resisted standardizing HTTP-based protocols which use separate ports for TLS.

Client Requested Upgrade

The simplest case to understand is one in which the client requests upgrade. The client simply includes the header Upgrade: TLS/1.0 in its request, as shown in Figure 9.14. Note that this request contains the Host header. Thus, the server knows which host the client intends to talk to and virtual hosting works properly without having multiple IP addresses. Note the use of the TLS/1.0 token. No SSL token was standardized so there is no official way to upgrade to SSL.

```
GET /foo.bar HTTP/1.1
Host: www.example.com
Upgrade: TLS/1.0
Connection: Upgrade
```
(blank line)

Figure 9.14 An Upgrade request

If the server is willing to upgrade, it sends a dummy response with the 101 response code, as shown in Figure 9.15. Immediately after sending the dummy response, it begins TLS negotiation. When the client receives the response, it is expected to send a ClientHello. Only after the TLS connection has been negotiated does the server send its response to the client's original request. Note that the server's Upgrade header contains both the TLS/1.0 and HTTP/1.1 tokens. The tokens are intended to be passed in "bottom-up" order. Thus, the server is saying that it will speak HTTP over TLS. However, the server could choose not to upgrade and simply respond to the client's message.

```
HTTP/1.1 101 Switching Protocols
Upgrade: TLS/1.0, HTTP/1.1
Connection: Upgrade
(blank line)
```

Figure 9.15 A response accepting an Upgrade request

One drawback of this approach that should be immediately obvious is that the client's original request is sent in the clear. This is problematic because the client's request might contain sensitive information. RFC 2817 provides a mechanism called *mandatory upgrade*. What this means is that the client sends a dummy request to the server so that the actual request won't be revealed. The request that's used is an OPTIONS request, which requests general information about the server. The specification isn't clear on this point, but presumably the server could refuse to upgrade even with a mandatory upgrade. In that case, the client would have an opportunity to close the connection without any sensitive information having been transmitted.

Server Requested Upgrade

The server also has an opportunity to request TLS upgrading. The server can advertise that it supports TLS in an informational fashion merely by including the appropriate Upgrade header in its normal responses. However, in certain circumstances, the server may wish to enforce the use of TLS. It can do so by responding to requests that require TLS with the 426 Upgrade Required error code, as shown in Figure 9.16.

```
HTTP/1.1 426 Upgrade Required
Upgrade: TLS/1.0, HTTP/1.1
Connection: Upgrade
(blank line)
```

Figure 9.16 A mandatory upgrade advertisement

The 426 response does not in and of itself initiate the TLS handshake. Rather, it's an error signaling that the client must use TLS to fetch this URL. When the client receives an Upgrade Required, it must use the methods described above to initiate an upgrade. Note that a mandatory upgrade advertisement is useful only in cases where only the data sent by the server is sensitive. The client has *already* transmitted *its* data over a clear channel, so if the request contained sensitive data, the damage has already been done.

HTTP Upgrade *does* allow HTTP over TLS to be negotiated over HTTP connections. In that sense, it can be considered a success. However, it has a number of problems that substantially reduce its attractiveness. First, its interaction with proxies is even worse than HTTPS's. Second, it doesn't provide for references to indicate that upgrade should be expected, thus creating security and performance problems.

Proxy Interactions

RFC 2616 [Fielding1999] defines the Upgrade header as a *hop-by-hop* header. This means that proxies are intended to act as if the header was intended for them. The intent is that clients should be able to negotiate better protocols with proxies (e.g., HTTP/1.1 from HTTP/1.0) even if the servers have not yet been upgraded.

However, because the client wishes to negotiate an end-to-end TLS connection with the server, the hop-by-hop nature of the Upgrade header presents a problem when upgrading to TLS. In order to work around this, the client needs to first use CONNECT to establish a tunnel to the server, just as it did with HTTPS. This is rather unfortunate because it means that clients can't upgrade to TLS at all without first creating a tunnel, which greatly reduces the value of proxies. A better approach would be to have a new end-to-end header to advertise client TLS support. Proxies would recognize this header (though not tamper with it) and if TLS were negotiated, then the proxy would go into a transparent mode.

No References

Another problem with HTTP Upgrade, is that there is no way for clients to be told in references that they should expect to be able to upgrade when they connect to the server. In fact, the specification specifically states that https behavior is totally unchanged: it still refers to HTTPS.

This omission has a number of unfortunate consequences. The first is the loss of even the minimal reference integrity protections provided by HTTPS. With Upgrade, the client cannot even detect that TLS should have been negotiated and wasn't. If the client wants to use TLS at all, even in an opportunistic mode, its only choice is to offer Upgrade on every connection. As we've said earlier, this means that the client must use CONNECT with any proxy, and thus proxies become completely ineffective.

Worse yet, unless the client is willing to accept worst-case performance behavior, the client's request is completely exposed. Recall that the client's request will contain the contents of any form submission and consider the case where the form submitted requests a credit card number. Moreover, the client software cannot tell when requests contain sensitive information because some sites put such information directly in URLs or in browser cookies.

Thus, for maximal security the client always needs to first try an OPTIONS request. However, in the common case where TLS is not supported, this simply means an extra request/response round trip for no benefit. Even in cases where the upgrade is successful, HTTPS is faster than Upgrade because it does not need the dummy request. Thankfully, this overhead need only be incurred the first time the browser connects to a site if the server doesn't support security—the client can cache the fact that the server will not Upgrade.

Finally, the lack of a distinguished reference makes HTTP Upgrade vulnerable to a downgrade attack where the attacker removes the upgrade tokens, thus forcing the client and the server to negotiate HTTP. This attack is not possible with HTTPS because the client is only prepared to do HTTPS when dereferencing an https:// URL.

All of these problems could be easily fixed with the introduction of a new URL method indicating that HTTP/TLS using Upgrade was expected. However, it would be unwise to attempt to co-opt https: for this purpose, since clients would then be unable to distinguish HTTP Upgrade-required servers from HTTPS servers.

9.22 Programming Issues

Chapter 8 discussed general programming issues with SSL, but each protocol is different and programming using HTTPS presents some specific problems. The rest of this chapter is devoted to covering two of these issues: implementing the HTTP CONNECT method discussed in Section 9.16 and supporting the large number of HTTPS connections that will be experienced by any active server.

9.23 Proxy CONNECT

The example programs we showed in Chapter 8 all connected directly to the server. As we discussed in Section 9.16, HTTPS clients often need to connect through a proxy rather than directly to the server. This requires that the programmer do some extra work. Figure 9.17 shows a new version of our client that connects through a proxy rather than directly to the server. Note that this client contains code only for connecting through a proxy. A real client would be able to switch-hit depending on configuration settings.

Programmer's note: Many firewalls allow the CONNECT method on port 443 only. We're using port 4433 for programming convenience because you can run servers on port 4433 without being root. However, you may find that you need to run your test servers on port 443 if you want to try proxying.

```
1        /* A proxy-capable SSL client.

2           This is just like sclient but it only supports proxies
3        */
4        #include <string.h>
5        #include "common.h"
6        #include "client.h"
7        #include "read_write.h"

8        #define PROXY "localhost"
9        #define PROXY_PORT 8080
10       #define REAL_HOST "localhost"
11       #define REAL_PORT 4433

12       int writestr(sock,str)
13         int sock;
14        char *str;
15         {
16          int len=strlen(str);
17          int r,wrote=0;

18          while(len){
19            r=write(sock,str,len);
20            if(r<=0)
21              err_exit("Write error");
22            len-=r;
23            str+=r;
24            wrote+=r;
25          }

26          return (wrote);
27        }

28       int readline(sock,buf,len)
29         int sock;
30        char *buf;
31        int len;
32         {
33          int n,r;
34          char *ptr=buf;

35          for(n=0;n<len;n++){
36            r=read(sock,ptr,1);
```

```
37                if(r<=0)
38                  err_exit("Read error");
39                if(*ptr=='\n'){
40                  *ptr=0;

41                  /* Strip off the CR if it's there */
42                  if(buf[n-1]=='\r'){
43                    buf[n-1]=0;
44                    n--;
45                  }

46                  return(n);
47                }

48                *ptr++;
49              }

50            err_exit("Buffer too short");
51          }

52      int proxy_connect(){
53          struct hostent *hp;
54          struct sockaddr_in addr;
55          int sock;
56          BIO *sbio;
57          char buf[1024];
58          char *protocol, *response_code;

59          /* Connect to the proxy, not the host */
60          if(!(hp=gethostbyname(PROXY)))
61            berr_exit("Couldn't resolve host");
62          memset(&addr,0,sizeof(addr));
63          addr.sin_addr=*(struct in_addr*)hp->h_addr_list[0];
64          addr.sin_family=AF_INET;
65          addr.sin_port=htons(PROXY_PORT);

66          if((sock=socket(AF_INET,SOCK_STREAM,IPPROTO_TCP))<0)
67            err_exit("Couldn't create socket");
68          if(connect(sock,(struct sockaddr *)&addr,sizeof(addr))<0)
69            err_exit("Couldn't connect socket");

70          /* Now that we're connected, do the proxy request */
71          sprintf(buf,"CONNECT %s:%d HTTP/1.0\r\n\r\n",REAL_HOST,REAL_PORT);
72          writestr(sock,buf);

73
```

(continued)

```
74      Figure 9.17 (continued)

75              /* And read the response*/
76              if(readline(sock,buf,sizeof(buf))==0)
77                err_exit("Empty response from proxy");

78              if((protocol=strtok(buf," "))<0)
79                err_exit("Couldn't parse server response: getting protocol");
80              if(strncmp(protocol,"HTTP",4))
81                err_exit("Unrecognized protocol");
82              if((response_code=strtok(0," "))<0)
83                err_exit("Couldn't parse server response: getting response code");
84              if(strcmp(response_code,"200"))
85                err_exit("Received error from proxy server");

86              /* Look for the blank line that signals end of header*/
87              while(readline(sock,buf,sizeof(buf))>0) {
88                ;
89              }

90              return(sock);
91           }

92      int main(argc,argv)
93        int argc;
94        char **argv;
95        {
96          SSL_CTX *ctx;
97          SSL *ssl;
98          BIO *sbio;
99          int sock;

100         /* Build our SSL context*/
101         ctx=initialize_ctx(KEYFILE,PASSWORD);

102         /* Connect the TCP socket*/
103         sock=proxy_connect();

104         /* Connect the SSL socket */
105         ssl=SSL_new(ctx);
106         sbio=BIO_new_socket(sock,BIO_NOCLOSE);
107         SSL_set_bio(ssl,sbio,sbio);
108         if(SSL_connect(ssl)<=0)
109           berr_exit("SSL connect error");
110         check_cert_chain(ssl,HOST);
```

```
111                    /* read and write */
112                    read_write(ssl,sock);

113                    destroy_ctx(ctx);
114               }
```

Figure 9.17 A proxy-capable client

A write function

12–27   Our proxy-capable client needs to be able to send the CONNECT request to the proxy server. We encapsulate the writing code in the `writestr()` function. This function simply takes an input string of arbitrary length and writes it to the specified socket.

A read function

28–51   We also need to be able to read the proxy server's response. The response should be a series of HTTP header lines separated by the carriage return (`0x0d`) and line feed (`0x0a`). The `readline()` function simply reads one line off the network into the buffer. This function is suitable only for demonstration purposes. It reads one byte from the network at a time, which is very inefficient. Moreover, it fails catastrophically if the buffer is too short to contain the line.

Connect to the proxy

52–69   The `proxy_connect()` function is intended to replace the `tcp_connect()` function that we used in Chapter 8. The beginning of the function simply replicates the connecting code that was in `tcp_connect()`. However, this time instead of connecting to the server, we connect to the proxy.

Write request

70–72   The first thing that the client needs to do is to construct the CONNECT request, containing the real host and port that we wish the proxy to connect to. The `"\r\n\r\n"` string at the end of the string signals the end of the HTTP header with a blank line. Then we simply use `writestr()` to transmit the request to the proxy.

Read response

73–88   Once the request has been transmitted to the proxy, we need to read back the response to make sure that the proxy successfully connected. We parse the first line of the response (the status line) to ensure that the protocol is HTTP and that the status code is 200. The rest of the header we simply read and throw away. Again, the end of the proxy's response is signaled by a blank line. Note that we must read all the header lines so that when the SSL engine looks for the ServerHello it doesn't read any of the proxy response.

main()

90–112   Our main() function is identical to the main() in sclient.c except that it calls proxy_connect() rather than connect() in line 101. Once the tunnel is established, the client can completely ignore the existence of the proxy.

Note that in order to use a proxy the client had to read and write directly to the TCP socket before doing the SSL handshake. This is possible with OpenSSL because the API requires that the programmer do the connect() first before starting the SSL session. However, if the connect() and the SSL handshake are integrated, as they are in PureTLS, this would not be possible.

> This problem is on the PureTLS known bug list, so with any luck the author will have fixed this problem by the time you read this.

9.24 Handling Multiple Clients

Any real server needs to be able to simultaneously handle multiple clients. This means being able to multiplex data reads and writes between those clients, serving clients that are ready to be served and ignoring those that aren't. Moreover, it needs to do so in a timely fashion, without serving only one client and starving the others. This is especially problematic in HTTPS where any given client may be requesting data on a number of separate connections.

It's possible to do this using the select() based I/O multiplexing technique we used in Chapter 8, but it's not very convenient. It turns out to be difficult to write programs this way, partly because it requires explicitly carrying a lot of state around.

To see this, consider the problem of reading the HTTP request. The server reads the data, but perhaps only part of the request is available. The server can't wait for the rest of it because it must serve other clients. Thus, it must store the data it has already read and finish reading the rest of the request when the client eventually sends it. This course requires creating an explicit context object for that client and somehow associating it with the client socket. This isn't especially difficult, but it is inconvenient.

The second problem is that the server needs to be very careful not to allocate too much time to a single operation. Imagine that a request requires performing some operation—such as a database query—that takes 5 seconds. Obviously, the requesting client must wait for the operation to complete, but equally obviously the server can't starve all the other clients because it's serving this particular client. Instead, it must break out of the operation and service other clients and then resume the operation. Again, this means carrying the operation state around explicitly rather than implicitly.

Moreover, the programmer must constantly be paying attention to how long various actions are expected to take, lest the server inadvertently fail to service other clients while performing a time-consuming operation. This can be a particular problem when using third-party libraries because they may not include facilities for breaking out of their API calls.

Multiprocess Servers

Unsurprisingly, most programmers choose a different approach toward serving multiple clients: Each client connection is assigned its own thread of control. On UNIX systems, this usually means a process and on Windows (or in Java) it means a thread. The scheduler is then responsible for distributing CPU time between the server processes/threads serving each client and can ensure that each client gets its fair share.

The traditional design for such a server is to have a single process/thread that listens for client connections. When it receives a new connection, it spawns off a new process/thread to handle that connection. Figure 9.18 shows pseudo-code for such a server.

The main server process simply loops forever. On each iteration of the loop, it calls `accept()`. If a new client connection has come in, `accept()` returns a socket corresponding to that new connection. Otherwise, the process is simply put to sleep until a new client comes in. Once a new connection is created, the server creates a new process to handle it. On UNIX, this is done using the `fork()` system call. On Windows, we'd be creating a new thread using `CreateThread()`. The parent process returns to the top of the loop and calls `accept()` again.

```
server_process() {
    server_socket=create_socket();

    for(;;){
      client=accept(server_socket);
      if(pid=fork()){
        /* Parent process */
        continue;
      }
      else {
        /* Child process */
        serve_request(client);
        exit(0);
      }
   }
}
```

Figure 9.18 A simple server

On UNIX, we'd actually need the parent process to `close()` the socket connected to the client in order to free up server resources. Any given process is allowed to have only a finite number of file descriptors open at any given time, and if we don't close the socket, the parent process will quickly run out. This has no effect on the socket in the child process.

The child process or thread simply serves the client. Because the scheduler automatically interrupts it to service other server control threads, the child can simply concentrate on serving its one client. In particular, it can safely use blocking I/O or perform time consuming operations without worrying about breaking out of those operations to serve other clients.

Multiprocess Servers Using SSL

When adding SSL to one of these multiprocess servers, we must be careful. It's tempting to simply replace all the socket calls with calls to SSL sockets. This will not work. In particular, the SSL handshake must be executed in the child process rather than in the parent process. Otherwise, the server will be able to execute only one SSL handshake at once. The handshake represents a substantial bottleneck, especially when the round-trip time between client and server is significant. This bottleneck is particularly troublesome with HTTP because the number of connections is so large.

In order to avoid this bottleneck, the server needs to perform the TCP accept() in the parent process but the SSL handshake in the child process. This is fairly straightforward to do with OpenSSL, because SSL_handshake() is its own call. Figure 9.19 shows a variant of the main loop in our OpenSSL server program that behaves in this way.

```
                                                                     mserver.c
24          while(1){
25            if((s=accept(sock,0,0))<0)
26              err_exit("Problem accepting");

27            if(pid=fork()){
28              close(s);
29            }
30            else {
31              sbio=BIO_new_socket(s,BIO_NOCLOSE);
32              ssl=SSL_new(ctx);
33              SSL_set_bio(ssl,sbio,sbio);

34              if((r=SSL_accept(ssl)<=0))
35                berr_exit("SSL accept error");

36              echo(ssl,s);
37            }
38          }
                                                                     mserver.c
```

Figure 9.19 A simple OpenSSL-based multiprocess server

The only really new code here is the call to fork() in line 27. This creates a new process (on UNIX). That process is able to run the SSL handshake independently. The code would be analogous on Windows but the call would be to CreateThread() instead of to fork().

Because PureTLS emulates Java's socket API, the `accept()` and SSL handshake all happen during the same API call. Thus, there is no way to arrange to execute the handshake in a child thread. This is an omission in PureTLS and a better approach would be to allow the programmer to tell `accept()` to just create the socket and then do the SSL handshake separately.

SSL Session Caching

Whenever we have a multiprocess or multithreaded server, we need to make accommodations in our session caching strategy. Session data is unique because it must be shared between all the different control threads and can also be updated by any process/thread. Other data, such as the SSL context data, may be shared by all processes/threads, but isn't constantly updated. Session cache data must be updated in at least two situations. First, whenever a new session is created, it must be added to the cache. Second, if a session is to be marked non-resumable (e.g., because an alert was received) it must be removed from the session cache. We need to ensure proper concurrency control so that simultaneous updates can't lead to cache corruption.

If we're using threads rather than processes, all of this is fairly simple. Because threads all share memory, we can simply use an in-memory representation for the session cache. However, it's still necessary to lock the cache data while reading and writing. The details of how to do this locking depend on the system and threading package being used. Java provides probably the simplest methods for doing this. Methods can be marked `synchronized`, in which case calls to those methods will be serialized. Figure 9.20 shows a fragment of PureTLS's internal session caching code, complete with synchronization.

```
                                                              SSLContext.java
438         protected synchronized void storeSession(String key,SSLSessionData sd){
439           SSLDebug.debug(SSLDebug.DEBUG_STATE,"Storing session under key"+key);
440           session_cache.put(key,(Object)sd);
441         }

442         protected synchronized SSLSessionData findSession(String key){
443           SSLDebug.debug(SSLDebug.DEBUG_STATE,"Trying to recover session using key"+key);
444           Object obj=session_cache.get(key);

445           if(obj==null)
446            return null;

447           return (SSLSessionData)obj;
448         }

449         protected synchronized void destroySession(String sessionLookupKey){
450           session_cache.remove(sessionLookupKey);
451         }
                                                              SSLContext.java
```

Figure 9.20 PureTLS synchronized session caching code

PureTLS stores the session data using a hash table (`session_cache`) which is an instance variable of the `SSLContext` class. This code fragment shows the minimal required three methods for accessing the cache: `storeSession()` creates an entry. `findSession()` looks up an entry and `destroySession()` deletes an entry from the cache.

Session Caching with Multiprocess Servers

If your server uses multiple processes rather than multiple threads, the situation becomes dramatically more difficult. Because processes do not share memory, it's not possible to simply have a pointer to some common structure that is accessed by all the processes. Instead, the server needs to rely on operating system services to carry the session data around.

There are a number of different techniques that can be used for this job. Most toolkits do not provide support for sharing session data between processes, so the problem usually needs to be solved on a server-by-server basis. One approach is to have a single *session server*. The session server stores all of its session data in memory. The SSL servers access the session server via *interprocess communication* mechanisms, typically some flavor of sockets. The major drawback to this approach is that it requires the creation of some entirely different server program to do this job, as well as the design of the SSL server to session server communications protocol. It can also be difficult to ensure access control so that only authorized server processes can obtain access.

Another approach is to use *shared memory*. Many operating systems provide some method of allowing processes to share memory. Once the shared memory segment is allocated, data can be accessed as if it were ordinary memory. Unfortunately, this technique isn't as useful as it sounds because there's no good way to allocate out of the shared memory pool, so the processes need to allocate a single large segment and then statically address inside of it. Worse yet, shared memory access is not easily portable.

The most commonly used approach is to simply store the data on a file on the disk. Then, each server process can open that file and read and write out of it. Standard file locking routines such as `flock()` can be used to provide synchronization and concurrency control. One might think that storing the data to disk would be dramatically slower than shared memory, but remember that most operating systems have disk caches and this data would likely be placed in such a cache.

A variant of this approach is to use one of the simple UNIX key-value databases (DBM and friends) rather than a flat file. This allows the programmer to simply create new session records and delete them without worrying about placing them in the file. If such a library is used, care must be taken to flush the library buffers after each write, because data stored in the buffers has not been written to disk.

OpenSSL does not provide any support for this sort of session caching at all, but it does provide hooks for programmers to use their own session caching code. ApacheSSL (based on OpenSSL) uses the session server approach. mod_ssl (also based on OpenSSL) can support either the disk-based database approach or a shared memory approach. The SPYRUS TLSGold toolkit uses the file-based approach without any database support. The code for all of these approaches is too complicated to show here, but Appendix A shows the mod_ssl session caching code.

Advanced Server Configurations

Early SSL servers operated as described earlier in this section. However, it was observed that the cost of the `fork()` on UNIX was very substantial. When Netscape introduced their server, they added a feature that *pre-forked* a number of child servers and arranged to distribute clients to those servers rather than creating a new process for each client. Most UNIX-based servers, including the popular free Apache server, now do this.

Later Netscape servers also operated multiple threads within the same server process. However, they continued to use multiple server processes as well. Thus, although these new configurations represented an improvement in HTTP server behavior, they still required that multiple processes be able to share session data.

9.25   Summary

SSL was designed for use with HTTP and so we'd expect them to work relatively well together. In general they do, as evidenced by the ubiquity of HTTPS clients and servers. However, when we examine the interaction in detail, we can see a number of situations in which clumsy workarounds have had to be used to compensate for deficiencies in SSL and HTTPS.

HTTPS is the dominant approach to securing HTTP. HTTPS is extremely simple to implement, which no doubt accounts for its rapid deployment. Despite a number of problems, it has yet to be replaced in any substantial way.

HTTPS uses hostnames for reference integrity. The HTTPS URLs contain the expected hostname for the server. The client is expected to check the hostname against the name in the server's certificate. No provision is made for certificates with names that don't match the host name.

Using HTTPS breaks proxies. When HTTPS is used, proxy caching is totally ineffective. Moreover, proxies require special support for the CONNECT method to be able to pass HTTPS at all.

Servers have trouble requesting different handshakes for different resources. Because the SSL handshake takes place before the server sees the request, the server has no way to condition its handshake on the resource to be requested. This can lead to expensive renegotiation.

HTTP Upgrade fixes some problems and introduces others. HTTP Upgrade helps reduce port consumption and works properly with virtual hosts. Unfortunately, its interaction with proxies is even worse than in HTTPS and it provides much weaker reference integrity.

Session caching is critical. Because so many Web page fetches require multiple HTTPS connections, SSL session caching is extremely important. Because Web servers often run as multiple processes, servers must share cache data between processes, creating implementation problems.

10

SMTP over TLS

10.1 Introduction

The second example protocol we'll consider is the *Simple Mail Transfer Protocol* (SMTP), described in RFC 821 [Postel1982]. SMTP is the basic protocol used to transport Internet electronic mail (e-mail). E-Mail is arguably the single most important Internet application and so securing it is an especially high priority. Thus, the standard for SMTP over TLS (RFC 2487 [Hoffman1999a]) was published essentially at the same time as the standard for TLS, RFC 2246.

As with the chapter on HTTP, we start by describing Internet mail and SMTP. We then consider the approach used by RFC 2487. As we'll see, it's very difficult to provide even basic security services for mail using TLS. This is not the fault of the author of RFC 2487. In fact, SMTP is an interesting case precisely because its security requirements are so poorly matched to the services that TLS is able to provide. Finally, we briefly discuss the programming issues involved in using SMTP with TLS.

10.2 Internet Mail Security

The process of sending e-mail should be familiar to most Internet users. The user has a program that permits him to enter the recipient and compose a message. When he's finished composing, he tells the program to send it. Usually, the sender has a local *mail server* to which he sends the mail. The mail server arranges for delivery to the recipient. The sender's security requirement is for confidentiality: He wants to ensure that the message goes to the intended recipient and that the contents are readable only by that recipient. He might also wish to know that the message arrived at the recipient undamaged.

Similarly, the recipient has a local mail server. The sender's mail server delivers the mail to the recipient's mail server. The recipient's mail program then obtains the mail from the mail server and displays it to the recipient. The recipient's security requirement is for message authentication and message integrity; he wants to know who sent the message and know that it has not been tampered with in transit.

343

Basic Technologies

In order to understand how electronic mail works—and thus any potential security solution—it's important to understand the basic technologies in the e-mail infrastructure. The major three technologies that we need to consider are *SMTP*, the *RFC 822* and *MIME* message formats, and *e-mail addresses*.

SMTP

SMTP is the basic transport protocol for e-mail. Its job is to transport messages between senders (either client programs or mail servers) and receiving mail servers. In the early days of the net there were other protocols that did this job but currently SMTP is the only major mail delivery protocol.

RFC 822 and MIME

SMTP just provides the transport for messages. The actual specification for messages appeared in RFC 822[Crocker1982]. However, RFC 822 only specified formats for ASCII text messages and eventually the *Multipurpose Internet Mail Extensions* (MIME) [Freed1996a, Freed1996b, Moore1996, Freed1996c, Freed1996d] were added to support other forms of content.

E-mail addresses

In order to send mail to someone, it's necessary not only to know the recipient's name but also their e-mail address. The address not only tells the sender which server to connect to but also tells the receiving server what to do when it gets the mail.

Practical Considerations

We also need to be concerned with some features of the mail environment that are not obvious from the description in the previous paragraphs. Four of these features turn out to have particular security relevance: *mail relaying*, *virtual hosting*, *MX records*, and *client mail access*.

Mail Relaying

It's fairly frequent for mail not to travel directly between two servers but rather to go through a series of *mail relays* on the way. The obvious security problem is maintaining security through these relays.

Virtual Hosts

As with Web servers, it's quite common for ISPs to maintain mail servers for people's personal domains or small corporate domains. This allows users to each have their own domain and e-mail addresses without even a direct connection to the Internet. The problem we face here is the same as that with HTTPS: making sure that the receiving server provides the appropriate certificate to the sender.

MX Records

Using mail relaying, it's possible to send mail to machines that are not currently connected to the Internet. The sender simply connects to the correct relay and trusts the relay to deliver the mail. *Mail Exchanger* (MX) records serve to identify which relay to connect to.

Client Mail Access

When most mail was read on UNIX machines, the mail server simply placed the mail on the disk and the user's client would read it off the disk. In modern networking environments, most mail clients are on PCs without access to the filesystem of the server. Those clients use a variety of network protocols to access the mail server and retrieve their mail.

Security Considerations

Once we understand the Internet mail environment, we can consider how to offer the appropriate security services. As before, we need to consider the important problems discussed in Chapter 7: *protocol selection*, *client authentication*, *reference integrity*, and *connection semantics*.

10.3   Internet Messaging Overview

Any Internet mail system consists of at least two types of entities: clients (known as *mail user agents* (MUAs)) and servers (*mail transport agents* (MTAs)). The mail client is the program the user interacts with. It displays his mail and permits him to compose and send new mail. However, most clients have nothing to do with either mail receipt or delivery. These jobs are accomplished by the MTAs.

As we said earlier, mail does not go directly from sender to recipient. Instead, it passes through a series of servers along the way. Figure 10.1 shows a simple mail system delivering a single piece of e-mail. The sending client on the left is sending a message to the receiving client on the right. The user composes a message and then his mail client transmits it using SMTP to his local mail server. The local mail server then transmits the message (again using SMTP) to the recipient's local mail server.

It's actually quite common for the mail client to transmit the message to the first hop server using something other than SMTP. On UNIX systems, the mail client often invokes the MTA (usually Sendmail) as a program. Sendmail then uses SMTP to deliver the message to the next hop server. When the MTA is Microsoft Exchange, clients often use *Mail Application Programming Interface* (MAPI) to talk to the MTA.

Figure 10.1 A simple mail system

The final link, from the recipient's local mail server to the recipient, is *not* accomplished via SMTP. A large number of protocols exist for reading mail, including *Post Office Protocol* (POP) [Myers1996] and *Internet Mail Access Protocol* (IMAP), defined in [Crispin1996]. On many UNIX systems, the mail server resides on the same machine that the recipient is using and the recipient can simply read the mail messages off of the disk. It is even possible to read one's mail using HTTP. In any case, this link does not use SMTP.

Consider what happens if the recipient's mail server is temporarily offline. The sender's local mail server will simply hold on to the mail, retrying every so often, until it can deliver it or the message times out. Similarly, the recipient need not be online at all for mail to be delivered to his local server. The local server will simply store the mail and wait for the recipient to pick it up. Thus, Internet mail systems handle disconnection gracefully in a way that HTTP does not. This is obviously necessary in order to accommodate users who do not have permanent Internet connections. This style of messaging is what's referred to as *store-and-forward*.

10.4 SMTP

As with HTTP, SMTP is conceptually simple but somewhat complicated in practice. The sending agent makes a connection to the receiving agent on TCP port 25. The sending and receiving agents then engage in a series of requests and responses to establish sending and receiving parameters, including the sender and the recipient. Finally, once all the parameters are established, the sending agent transmits the message to the server.

All communication is done in lockstep. The sending agent sends a command and the receiving agent sends a reply. Commands consist of a single line terminated by a CRLF. Responses consist of a three-digit number (the *reply code*) followed by some explanatory text. Responses can take up multiple lines. Each line except the last has a hyphen after the reply code to indicate that more lines are coming. Figure 10.2 shows a simple SMTP example.

```
New TCP connection: romeo(3094) <-> speedy(25)
1 949464306.6034 (0.0966) S>C
data: 101 bytes
--------------------------------------
220 speedy.rtfm.com ESMTP SendWhale 8.9.1/8.6.4 ready at 28.8K Tue, 1 ↵
Feb 2000 20:05:03 -0800 (PST)
--------------------------------------

2 949464306.6036 (0.0969) C>S
data: 21 bytes
--------------------------------------
EHLO romeo.rtfm.com
--------------------------------------
```

```
3 949464306.6089 (0.1022) S>C
data: 173 bytes
------------------------------------
250-speedy.rtfm.com Hello romeo.rtfm.com [216.98.239.227], pleased to ⏎
meet you
250-EXPN
250-VERB
250-8BITMIME
250-SIZE
250-DSN
250-ONEX
250-ETRN
250-XUSR
250 HELP
------------------------------------


4 949464306.6094 (0.1026) C>S
data: 41 bytes
------------------------------------
MAIL From:<ekr@romeo.rtfm.com> SIZE=224
------------------------------------


5 949464306.8004 (0.2937) S>C
data: 39 bytes
------------------------------------
250 <ekr@romeo.rtfm.com>... Sender ok
------------------------------------


6 949464306.8005 (0.2938) C>S
data: 24 bytes
------------------------------------
RCPT To:<ekr@rtfm.com>
------------------------------------


7 949464306.8302 (0.3234) S>C
data: 36 bytes
------------------------------------
250 <ekr@rtfm.com>... Recipient ok
------------------------------------


8 949464306.8303 (0.3236) C>S
data: 6 bytes
------------------------------------
DATA
------------------------------------
```

(continued)

Figure 10.2 *(continued)*

```
9 949464306.8570 (0.3502) S>C
data: 50 bytes
------------------------------------
354 Enter mail, end with "." on a line by itself
------------------------------------


10 949464306.8578 (0.3510) C>S
data: 445 bytes
------------------------------------
Received: from romeo.rtfm.com (localhost [127.0.0.1]) by romeo.rtfm.com ↵
(8.9.3/8.6.4) with ESMTP id UAA46227 for <ekr@rtfm.com>; Tue, 1 Feb ↵
2000 20:05:06 -0800 (PST)
Message-Id: <200002020405.UAA46227@romeo.rtfm.com>
To: ekr@rtfm.com
Subject: Test message
Mime-Version: 1.0 (generated by tm-edit 7.108)
Content-Type: text/plain; charset=US-ASCII
Date: Tue, 01 Feb 2000 20:05:06 -0800
From: Eric Rescorla <ekr@rtfm.com>

This is a test
------------------------------------


11 949464306.9991 (0.4924) C>S
data: 3 bytes
------------------------------------
.
------------------------------------


12 949464307.0654 (0.5587) S>C
data: 44 bytes
------------------------------------
250 UAA09843 Message accepted for delivery
------------------------------------


13 949464307.0864 (0.5797) C>S
data: 6 bytes
------------------------------------
QUIT
------------------------------------
```

```
14 949464307.1127 (0.6059) S>C
data: 40 bytes

------------------------------------
221 speedy.rtfm.com closing connection
------------------------------------


Client FIN
Server FIN
```

Figure 10.2 A simple SMTP example

When the sender first connects to the receiver, the receiver sends a banner with identifying information, usually including a hostname and a software version number. In this case, segment 1 shows that the server is Sendmail 8.9.1.

The first command that the sender sends should be either HELO or EHLO. Traditional SMTP as described in RFC 821 used the HELO command. RFC 1425 introduced a number of extensions to SMTP and the EHLO command indicates that a sender complies with that specification. Either command should contain the sender's hostname (as it believes it to be.) In this example, the sender's hostname is romeo.rtfm.com.

The receiver responds to the EHLO with its own hostname and a list of the extensions it supports. Thus, this server supports a number of extensions, including EXPN, VERB, and 8BITMIME.

The rest of the connection proceeds in a similar fashion. The sender identifies the user who sent the message using the MAIL command and the recipient of the message using the RCPT command. In both cases, the receiving server responds with the 250 status code to indicate that things are fine.

Once the sender and receiver have been accepted, the sending agent can send the actual message using the DATA command. The receiver responds with a 354 indicating that the sender should go ahead and send the message. The actual message appears in segment 10. SMTP uses a single line containing only a period (i.e., .CRLF) to indicate the end of data, and we see that in segment 11. In segment 12, the receiver indicates that it's accepted the message and it's ready to deliver it.

At this point, the sending agent could repeat the MAIL, RCPT, DATA sequence to send another message. In this trace, however, there is no other message to send, so the sending agent uses QUIT to close out the connection.

10.5 RFC 822 and MIME

RFC 822 style messages are very simple. They consist of a number of header lines followed by a message body. Each header line is simply the name of the header, followed by a colon and the value, like so:

```
From: ekr@rtfm.com
```

The message body contents are largely freeform. RFC 822 restricted the message body data to ASCII characters, but MIME opened it up to binary data. Figure 10.3 shows a simple example mail message sent from the author to himself. Note that the two long `Received` header lines have been broken up into multiple lines. If a header line begins with a whitespace character it is automatically *folded* onto the end of the previous line.

```
From ekr@Network-Alchemy.COM  Tue Feb  8 09:25:10 2000
Received: from Hydrogen.Network-Alchemy.COM (Hydrogen.Network-Alchemy.COM
  [199.46.17.130]) by speedy.rtfm.com (8.9.1/8.6.4) with ESMTP id JAA04954
  for <ekr@rtfm.com>; Tue, 8 Feb 2000 09:25:09 -0800 (PST)
Received: (from ekr@localhost)  by Hydrogen.Network-Alchemy.COM
  (8.8.7/8.8.8) id JAA05750 for ekr@rtfm.com; Tue, 8 Feb 2000 09:23:52
  -0800 (PST)  (envelope-from ekr)
Date: Tue, 8 Feb 2000 09:23:52 -0800 (PST)
From: Eric Rescorla <ekr@Network-Alchemy.COM>
Message-Id: <200002081723.JAA05750@Hydrogen.Network-Alchemy.COM>
To: ekr@rtfm.com
Subject: Test message

How about this?
```

Figure 10.3 An e-mail message

This format should look very familiar from our discussion of HTTP requests and responses. This isn't surprising because HTTP messages were explicitly modeled after e-mail messages. Look at the `Received` lines in this message. The SMTP servers along the mail path add new header lines of the message. In fact, only the last two header lines `To` and `Subject` were created by the client's MUA. As each server processes the data, it may add its own header lines to the front of the message.

Thus, when the client's MUA passed the message on to his local MTA at `hydrogen.network-alchemy.com`, the server automatically added the `Date` field to indicate when it sent the message, the `From` field to indicate who the sender was, and the `Message-Id` field to provide "tracking number" for this message. Note that the handling of the `From` field is inconsistent; some mail clients will generate it themselves and it will usually not be tampered with by the server.

The `From` line at the top of the message and the first `Received` header were added by the recipient's mail server at `speedy.rtfm.com`. This line is only added by certain UNIX mailers as part of the UNIX "mbox" storage format.

Received Lines

The `Received` lines provide a record of the path that the message took through the mail system. Each server adds its own `Received` line to the front of the message when it processes it.

Examining these headers, we can see that the original message was sent by the user `ekr` on the machine `hydrogen.network-alchemy.com`. The user directly invoked the mail server rather than connecting to it via SMTP. (Actually, the user used the `Mail` command, which invokes Sendmail.) `hydrogen.network-alchemy.com` connected directly to `speedy.rtfm.com` (the mail server for the `rtfm.com` domain) and delivered the message. `speedy` wrote the message on disk, ready for the user to read.

Sender Identity

As you can see, there are two indications in the message of who the sender was. The first is the `From` line at the top of the message. Note that this is not a header line; it has no colon. It's added by Sendmail before writing the data to disk. Other mailers may use a different format. This can be thought of as indicating the *transport identity*. It's the identity that the sending SMTP agent used in its `MAIL` command. The `From` line in the message should be thought of as the *message identity*. It's the identity that the sender of the message placed in the message. SMTP doesn't care about this identity at all.

In this case, the sending agent was invoked by the user as a program rather than over the network and so it is able to verify the user's identity and generate the appropriate `MAIL` command. By contrast, the user can write a new `From` header and have it simply carried by the sending agent. Thus, the `From` header is untrustworthy. As we'll see later, the contents of the `MAIL` command are untrustworthy as well.

10.6   E-Mail Addresses

The form of identification used by Internet mail is the e-mail address. It's used both to describe how to reach someone (a reference) and as an indication of sender identity. Thus, if we're to understand how to do either of these things securely, we need to be familiar with how addressing works.

Internet mail addressing can be fiendishly complex. In particular, addresses can contain all sorts of routing information telling the servers along the way which server to transfer the mail to next. Before the DNS and MX records, addresses were often specified with routing information contained in "bang paths," as in the following:

```
foo!bar!ekr
```

The above address means to send the mail to host `foo`. `foo` should send it to user `ekr` on host `bar`. Luckily, in the modern Internet such things have mostly vanished and addresses can be described fairly simply as follows:

```
local-part@domain
```

The domain can be thought of as simply the DNS domain name of the target machine. This isn't strictly correct as we'll see when we discuss mail relaying and MX records in Section 10.9, but it's a good approximation.

The local-part can be loosely thought of as the mailbox. Again, this isn't strictly correct, but it is a useful approximation. It certainly may not correspond to any actual user. For instance, it might correspond to a mailing list run off the server, or an alias to another user. For instance, machines are supposed to have a `postmaster` address but they usually do not have a `postmaster` user but rather alias the address to an administrator's account.

`postmaster@example.com`

local-part   domain

Figure 10.4 An e-mail address

Figure 10.4 shows an example e-mail address with pointers to the local-part and the domain. It refers to the mailbox `postmaster` at the domain `example.com`.

10.7 Mail Relaying

In the examples we've discussed so far, messages were sent directly from the sender's local mail server to the recipient's local mail server. However, in many cases there are other servers in between. This often occurs because of network segmentation, particularly from firewalls.

Recall from Chapter 7 that many firewalls only permit traffic to cross the firewall by way of proxy. This means that the firewall needs to have some sort of SMTP agent proxying the traffic. Unlike an HTTP proxy, an SMTP proxy is two-way. It receives messages from the outside world and sends them to the internal SMTP server as well as transferring messages from the inside world to outside servers. Thus, in an environment where both sender and receiver are behind firewalls, any message will pass through at least four SMTP servers: the sender's local server, the sender's firewall, the receiver's firewall, and the receiver's local server.

The security problem that we face whenever we have mail relaying is to ensure that malicious relays cannot read the mail or alter or forge mail. With HTTPS we solved this problem by simply cutting the relays out of the loop. The CONNECT method allowed us to make an end-to-end connection between client and server. Because SMTP is store-and-forward, this approach is infeasible. If we are to use SSL, we have to arrange that we connect only through trusted relays.

Organizational Servers

It's also quite common for companies to have multiple *organizational servers* so that different subunits of the same company may be hosted on different servers. For instance, accounting might be on one server and engineering might be on another. The engineering and accounting servers might even run different operating systems in order to accommodate their different needs, with the engineers on UNIX with Sendmail and the accountants on NT with Exchange.

Another reason to have organizational servers is for load sharing purposes. E-Mail often takes up quite a bit of disk space and a big organization may choose to have a number of machines with smaller disks rather than one machine with an enormous disk. This approach has the added benefit that it avoids having a single point of failure for the entire corporation.

However, it's often desirable to hide this complexity so that users can have a single mailbox that can be addressed from whichever organizational server they're actually hosted on. To implement this, all mail must go through some central server which dispatches it to the organizational servers. Figure 10.5 shows such a setup.

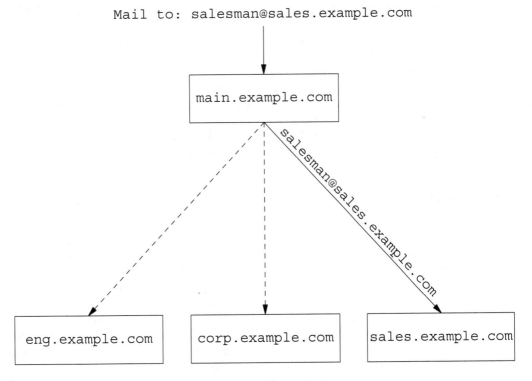

Figure 10.5 Organizational servers

In Figure 10.5, we have a single central server for the company ExampleCo (domain `example.com`). ExampleCo has three subdivisions, engineering, corporate management, and sales, each with its own SMTP server. When a message comes in addressed to `salesman`, it first goes to `main.example.com`, which figures out that it should relay it to `sales.example.com`.

One drawback of having all organizational servers have the same domain is the requirement to synchronize usernames between the servers. In order to avoid this, some organizations have organizational servers that serve separate domains. A typical e-mail address in such a system would be `foo@corp.example.com`. Such organizations might still choose to have a single mail server receive all mail from the outside purely for administrative or firewall reasons.

Smart Hosts

In a situation where organizations have their own mail servers, it's often desirable to have a single server that takes care of all transmissions to the outside world. The organizational servers are simply configured to relay all messages to that main server. This main server is often called a *smart host*.

The advantage of having a smart host is that all complicated mail configuration can be done at that single management point. The organizational mail servers are trivial to configure because routing is very simple: they always route to the smart host. In the modern Internet, mail routing is generally fairly simple, so this isn't as much of a problem as it used to be. However, smart hosts are still quite common because they allow a single administrative point for mail delivery.

Figure 10.6 shows the same server structure that we showed in Figure 10.5, but this time sending a message from a user of `eng.example.com` to the e-mail address `recipient@rtfm.com`. The machine `main.example.com` is the smart host, so `eng` sends the message to `main`, which arranges to send it to `rtfm.com`.

Open Relays

Before the rise of the Internet, it was extremely common for organizations not to have a full-time connection to other parts of the network. Rather, they might have an occasional connection to one or two other mail servers. These servers would accept mail for the network and relay their mail to the outside world. As a matter of tradition and courtesy, people would simply configure their mailers to accept mail traffic from any host to any host and do their best to deliver it. This configuration is called an *open relay*.

This sort of configuration has become much less common (though not yet nonexistent, especially outside the U.S.) but many mail agents are still configured as open relays. This has lately become an issue due to the rise of *spam*—unsolicited mass commercial e-mail—the e-mail equivalent of junk mail.

A common tactic to block spam is to simply refuse SMTP connections from the spammer's network. A number of organizations maintain lists of known spammers and you can configure your mailer to block mailers on those lists. In response, spammers send mail through innocent open relays. Administrators thus face the difficult choice of

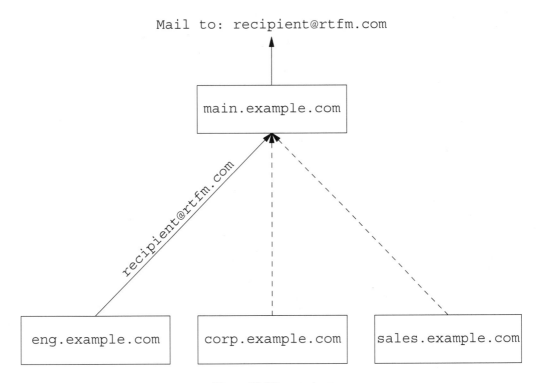

Figure 10.6 A smart host

blocking mail from legitimate machines or getting spam relayed through those machines. Those who choose to block can subscribe to lists of open relays in the same way as they subscribe to lists of known spammers.

The security problem here is to permit relaying for authorized machines—even if they are not part of your network—but to forbid relaying for unauthorized machines. SSL allows us to provide strong authentication for senders who want to use our server as a relay and only relay mail for senders who authenticate as an authorized machine.

10.8 Virtual Hosts

As indicated earlier, it's quite common for customers of ISPs to wish to have their own e-mail domain. Quite frequently, these customers are connected via dialup lines and therefore do not have a full-time connection to the Internet. In such cases, the ISP receives mail for them and the customers arrange to read the mail remotely. Because the SMTP RCPT command identifies the domain name of the mail recipient, supporting virtual hosts with SMTP is easy. However, as with HTTP, we need to be concerned that it works equally well when we add security to the mix.

10.9 MX Records

So far we've avoided the question of how one server knows which server to connect to in order to deliver mail to a certain recipient. Mail routing is conceptually simple but there are some subtleties we need to consider.

In general, mail servers consist of one of two types, dumb and smart. A dumb server is able to recognize mail destined for one of its mailboxes and deliver that. Any other kind of message is simply handed off to a smart host for delivery. Thus, dumb servers don't have a routing problem. They simply need to be configured to know what the smart host is.

One might think that smart host behavior would be fairly simple as well: look up the domain portion of the e-mail address and connect to the given server. However, consider the case of virtual hosts. For concreteness, let's assume that we have a single ISP server, `mail.exampleisp.com` and it's hosting the virtual domain `examplecustomer.com`. One approach would be to have a DNS A record pointing from `examplecustomer.com` to `mail.exampleisp.com`'s IP address. However, this would imply that other services such as Telnet were available to `examplecustomer.com` when in fact that machine isn't really on the net at all.

A better solution is to use a record specially designed for mail, the MX (*Mail Exchanger*) record. An MX record tells a sender that the target of the MX record is the mail relay for the requested domain. We can also have multiple MX records, as shown in Figure 10.7.

```
microsoft.com    preference = 10, mail exchanger = mail2.microsoft.com
microsoft.com    preference = 10, mail exchanger = mail3.microsoft.com
microsoft.com    preference = 10, mail exchanger = mail4.microsoft.com
microsoft.com    preference = 10, mail exchanger = mail5.microsoft.com
microsoft.com    preference = 10, mail exchanger = mail1.microsoft.com
```

Figure 10.7 MX records for `microsoft.com`

Figure 10.7 shows the MX records for the domain `microsoft.com` as fetched by `nslookup`. There are five records for machines `mail1` through `mail5`. Note that each record has a preference value. This can be used to indicate that the sender should try the mail servers in order. Thus, MX records can be used to preferentially direct traffic along certain links. This would not be possible if we'd used A records because they do not have preference values.

Unfortunately, this sort of mail relaying presents a security challenge. Because we can't trust the DNS we can't know that the MX records we're getting haven't been forged. Thus, just as with CNAMEs, we need to check the recipient's domain (e.g., `microsoft.com`) rather than the name of the mail exchanger (e.g., `mail1.microsoft.com`) against the server's certificate when we connect. As we'll see later, this presents an administrative problem.

10.10 Client Mail Access

Although many clients are on the same machine as their local mail server and can read data from disk, many must access their mail through network protocols such as POP or IMAP. Obviously, these connections must be conducted securely. Securing these protocols is out of scope for this chapter, but it's important to note that unless the client fetches mail securely, securing the inter-server links is useless. Naturally, client/server communication is often secured via SSL as described in [Newman1999]. As usual, each protocol has some subtleties that must be addressed when using SSL. The reader might find it instructive to examine these standards after reviewing the guidelines in Chapter 7.

10.11 Protocol Selection

As we saw in Figure 10.2, SMTP already has an extension mechanism. Thus, it's very natural to use this extension to implement an upward negotiation strategy. Moreover, this approach is much more palatable to systems administrators; since SMTP traffic nearly always needs to come in through firewalls in order to be delivered, it's attractive not to have to open up another port for secured SMTP traffic.

10.12 Client Authentication

In the mail environment, we're actually concerned with two kinds of client authentication: *authenticated relaying* and *originator authentication*. The purpose of authenticated relaying is to allow relaying but to restrict the service to certain sending servers. The purpose of originator authentication is to provide information to the recipient about who sent the message. As we indicated in Section 10.5, this is an important requirement for e-mail. The recipient would like to be able to authenticate the sender.

Unfortunately, the nature of SMTP makes originator authentication very difficult. Because the sending server is usually controlled not by the client but is rather a system process, it is not likely to have the user's keying material. Thus, the best service we are likely to be able to offer is authentication for the sending server. The sending server can, of course, assert the client's identity but the receiver must trust the sending server. As we'll see in Section 10.23, the situation becomes even worse when we consider the possibility of relays between client and server.

10.13 Reference Integrity

As we said earlier, Internet mail uses e-mail addresses as references. When we're concerned with reference integrity we're concerned with delivering mail to the right receiver. Unfortunately, the receiving mail server is likely to be some mail server not under direct control of the user. The user's machine may not even be on the net at the time of delivery. As with originator authentication, we're immediately forced to settle for something less desirable than we would like. At best, reference integrity can mean that we're delivering to the correct server and that we trust it to deliver the mail safely to the correct user.

10.14 Connection Semantics

Because the number of mail messages to a typical mail server is much fewer than the number of HTTP requests to a typical Web server, we don't have to worry about session resumption as much. We still have to be concerned with preventing truncation attacks, but SMTP's command-oriented nature works in our favor here. It's typically fairly clear when connections should be closed and when they should not.

10.15 STARTTLS

Now that we understand the problem of e-mail security from a design perspective, we're prepared to talk about STARTTLS. The standard approach to SMTP over SSL is described in RFC 2487 [Hoffman1999a]. We're also prepared to evaluate how well STARTTLS does at meeting the requirements discussed in the previous part of the chapter.

We begin by examining a simple transaction that uses STARTTLS. This allows us to see how the STARTTLS extension is used to upgrade from SMTP to SMTP over TLS. As usual, we'll discuss how to handle *connection closure*.

Once we have a clear picture of the behavior specified by RFC 2487, we can examine its interaction with some real world requirements. In particular, we'll examine the possibility of requiring messages to be transmitted with TLS as well as the interaction of STARTTLS with *virtual hosts*.

Finally, we'll consider what security protections STARTTLS actually provides. We'll examine the problem of providing *security indicators* that show what sort of protections were used for each link in the message path. We'll also consider the problems of providing *authenticated relaying*, *originator authentication*, and *reference integrity* with SMTP.

10.16 STARTTLS Overview

RFC 2487 was published roughly at the same time as the TLS specification, RFC 2246. Although SMTP over SSL had been in use for some time, RFC 2487 codified the rules for its use. A separate ports strategy (SMTPS) was briefly in use but did not see wide deployment and has been obsoleted by STARTTLS.

STARTTLS uses the SMTP extensions mechanism, documented in RFC 1869 [Klensin1995]. The server offers STARTTLS as one of its extensions, and the client can respond with the STARTTLS command. The client and the server then engage in a TLS handshake. Once the handshake is finished, they start over again with EHLO as if they had just connected.

```
New TCP connection: romeo(2515) <-> mike(25)
1 950072479.5489 (0.0225) S>C
data: 25 bytes
------------------------------------
220 mike.rtfm.com ESMTP
------------------------------------


2 950072479.5490 (0.0226) C>S
data: 21 bytes
------------------------------------
EHLO romeo.rtfm.com
------------------------------------


3 950072479.5495 (0.0231) S>C
data: 63 bytes
------------------------------------
250-mike.rtfm.com
250-PIPELINING
250-STARTTLS
250 8BITMIME
------------------------------------


4 950072479.5496 (0.0232) C>S
data: 10 bytes
------------------------------------
STARTTLS
------------------------------------


5 950072479.5536 (0.0272) S>C
data: 19 bytes
------------------------------------
220 ready for tls
------------------------------------


6 950072479.6269 (0.1004) C>S SSLv2 compatible client hello
  Version 3.1
  cipher suites
      TLS_DHE_DSS_WITH_RC4_128_SHA
      TLS_DHE_DSS_WITH_RC2_56_CBC_SHA
      TLS_RSA_EXPORT1024_WITH_RC4_56_SHA
      TLS_DHE_DSS_EXPORT1024_WITH_DES_CBC_SHA
      Cipher suite list trimmed
```

(continued)

Figure 10.8 *(continued)*

```
 7 950072479.7353 (0.1084) S>C    Handshake
        ServerHello
          session_id[32]=
              73 bf d5 04 ac 45 c1 7e a6 04 82 d0
              ae 5c ed db f8 8f b4 2b f5 9e d0 6c
              52 08 87 20 16 0e 4d 54
          cipherSuite             TLS_RSA_WITH_3DES_EDE_CBC_SHA
          compressionMethod            NULL
 8 950072479.7353 (0.0000) S>C    Handshake
        Certificate
 9 950072479.7353 (0.0000) S>C    Handshake
        ServerHelloDone
10 950072479.7380 (0.0027) C>S    Handshake
        ClientKeyExchange
11 950072479.7380 (0.0000) C>S    ChangeCipherSpec
12 950072479.7380 (0.0000) C>S    Handshake
        Finished
13 950072479.7702 (0.0321) S>C    ChangeCipherSpec
14 950072479.7702 (0.0000) S>C    Handshake
        Finished
```

Client restarts SMTP session with a new EHLO

```
15 950072479.7707 (0.0004) C>S    application_data
     data: 21 bytes
     -------------------------------------
     EHLO romeo.rtfm.com
     -------------------------------------
16 950072479.7714 (0.0007) S>C    application_data
     data: 49 bytes
     -------------------------------------
     250-mike.rtfm.com
     250-PIPELINING
     250 8BITMIME
     -------------------------------------
17 950072479.7716 (0.0002) C>S    application_data
     data: 32 bytes
     -------------------------------------
     MAIL FROM:<ekr@romeo.rtfm.com>
     -------------------------------------
18 950072479.7723 (0.0006) S>C    application_data
     data: 8 bytes
```

```
      ------------------------------------
      250 ok
      ------------------------------------
19 950072479.7724 (0.0001) C>S   application_data
      data: 29 bytes
      ------------------------------------
      RCPT TO:<ekr@mike.rtfm.com>
      ------------------------------------
20 950072479.7731 (0.0006) S>C   application_data
      data: 8 bytes
      ------------------------------------
      250 ok
      ------------------------------------
21 950072479.7732 (0.0001) C>S   application_data
      data: 6 bytes
      ------------------------------------
      DATA
      ------------------------------------
22 950072479.7749 (0.0016) S>C   application_data
      data: 14 bytes
      ------------------------------------
      354 go ahead
      ------------------------------------
```

   Client transmits actual message

```
23 950072479.7752 (0.0003) C>S   application_data
      data: 244 bytes
      ------------------------------------
      Received: (qmail 21198 invoked by uid 556); 9 Feb 2000 05:01:19 -0000
      Date: 9 Feb 2000 05:01:19 -0000
      Message-ID: <20000209050119.21197.qmail@romeo.rtfm.com>
      From: ekr@romeo.rtfm.com
      To: ekr@mike.rtfm.com
      Subject: test

      test message
      .
      ------------------------------------
24 950072479.8403 (0.0650) S>C   application_data
      data: 27 bytes
      ------------------------------------
      250 ok 950048042 qp 25454
      ------------------------------------
```

                                                        (continued)

Figure 10.8 *(continued)*

Client closes connection

```
25 950072479.8404 (0.0001) C>S    application_data
     data: 6 bytes   .
     ------------------------------------
     QUIT
     ------------------------------------
Client FIN
26 950072479.8412 (0.0007) S>C    application_data
     data: 19 bytes
     ------------------------------------
     221 mike.rtfm.com
     ------------------------------------
Server FIN
```

Figure 10.8 Upgrading with STARTTLS

The trace in Figure 10.8 shows the beginning of an SMTP connection that upgrades with STARTTLS. This trace was generated using the popular qmail mailer with a patch to support STARTTLS, but a similar trace would be generated by other mailers.

As before, in segment 1 the server sends the 220 response to identify itself. The client then sends the EHLO command. This time when the server responds it offers the STARTTLS extension, indicating that it is prepared to process the STARTTLS command (segment 3).

At this point in our original SMTP trace (Figure 10.2) the client issued the MAIL command to start sending the message. Here, however, it issues the STARTTLS command to initiate the TLS handshake in segment 4.

In segment 5 the server responds with 220 ready for tls, indicating that the client should proceed with the ClientHello. Note that the server could advertise START-TLS in response to the EHLO but refuse it when it was actually requested. In fact, this is exactly what qmail does when configured without a certificate.

Segment 6 contains the client's ClientHello. Note that the client actually offers an SSLv2 backward-compatible handshake. Unlike HTTP Upgrade, RFC 2487 isn't very clear on exactly what versions of SSL and TLS servers and clients are expected to support. The use of the term TLS implies that they support TLS but not SSLv2 or SSLv3. However, most of the currently available STARTTLS implementations are based on toolkits that support SSLv2 and SSLv3 as well, so they usually offer SSLv2.

The rest of the handshake (records 7–16) completes in the usual way. The one surprising feature is that the server never requests client authentication. This is a fairly common feature of STARTTLS implementations. Thus, the receiving server has no cryptographic way of identifying the sending server. In fact, the standard implies that it shouldn't. We'll see the reason for this in Section 10.18.

Once the handshake is finished, the client sends its EHLO encrypted over the newly negotiated TLS channel and the mail delivery proceeds as normal, except that it is encrypted using TLS.

10.17 Connection Closure

Note that the client simply closed the connection in Figure 10.8 without sending a close_notify. It just sent the QUIT command and then shut down its side of the connection. Similarly, the server sent its 221 response and then shut down its side of the connection. Recall that the purpose of the close_notify is to prevent truncation attacks. The question we need to ask is, does this represent a threat?

Obviously, this connection was not under attack, but is it possible that it could have been? The answer is no. The exchange of QUIT and 221 clearly indicates that both sides want to close the connection. These messages were sent over TLS so they could not have been tampered with by the attacker. Recall that in Chapter 7 we said that close_notify wasn't required if the application protocol has its own end-of-data markers. This is exactly such a case.

Other Situations

SMTP has the convenient property that both sides always know whose turn it is to talk and how long a command or response is. Thus, it's easy to determine whether an unexpected close has happened within a protocol message or between protocol messages.

Because mail servers automatically retry (after some timed interval) when they encounter errors, the appropriate response to most sorts of unexpected close is simply to log them and continue. However, a repeated pattern of premature closes may represent a denial-of-service attack and should be investigated.

In general, no agent should act on a partial message. Thus, if an agent receives only part of a command or an e-mail message, it should not process it. Similarly, senders should not assume that mail has been received by the receiver unless they actually see the 250 response indicating that the mail has been accepted for transmission.

Resumption

As required by the SSL specification, agents must not resume sessions that were closed without a close_notify. Thus, the session shown in Figure 10.8 cannot be resumed. This isn't as important an issue with SMTP as it is with HTTP because senders do not usually reconnect repeatedly within a short period of time. Nevertheless, a correct implementation would send a close_notify.

10.18 Requiring TLS

One might wish to configure one's mail server to require messages to be transmitted via TLS. Actually, it's technically possible to configure outgoing traffic and incoming traffic separately. You might choose to do this if you didn't care about who sent mail to you but you wanted to ensure that mail you transmitted was sent securely. Or, you might choose to accept mail only from authenticated sources but to transmit mail to anyone. Unfortunately, it's not really desirable to require TLS for either incoming or outgoing traffic.

Outgoing Traffic

Requiring TLS to transmit mail is easy. Simply refuse to connect to servers that don't offer the `STARTTLS` extension. However, because most servers don't support `START-TLS`, this means that the vast majority of the messages that you try to send will bounce. One might wish to allow users to require that a particular message be transmitted with TLS, but there's no standard way to do so because there is no standard way to mark messages for TLS transmission, so you can't require TLS on other MTAs in the relay chain.

Incoming Traffic

RFC 2487 provides support for requiring TLS for all incoming traffic. The receiving server simply responds to commands (other than `EHLO`, `NOOP`, `STARTTLS` and `QUIT`) with:

```
530 Must issue a STARTTLS command first
```

However, RFC 2487 also explicitly forbids publicly referenced mail servers from being configured this way, with one exception: servers may refuse to relay traffic unless it came over a proper TLS-authenticated channel (see Section 10.21). The intent of this rule is to prevent administrators from configuring their systems in such a way as to break interoperability; requiring TLS would cut off e-mail from most of the Internet. However, it also makes enforcement of security properties very difficult, because it prohibits receivers from requiring that mail senders be authenticated.

10.19 Virtual Hosts

We saw in Chapter 9 that an upward negotiation approach (Upgrade) made virtual hosts work properly with HTTP. We might expect that they would work similarly well with `STARTTLS`. Unfortunately, due to an oversight in the specification, they don't. In HTTP Upgrade, the client used the `Host` header to indicate the virtual host that it wished to connect to. Similarly, we'd expect the sender to identify the host somewhere in the first few segments.

However, nowhere in the TCP segments (1–5) that precede the TLS handshake does the sender identify the domain of the recipient (which identifies the virtual host). This only happens when the sender issues the RCPT command, which is too late since the TLS connection has already been negotiated.

The appropriate fix for this problem is for the sender to provide the recipient's domain as an argument to the STARTTLS command. It shouldn't provide the local-part because that's not necessary and we'd like to keep it secret. If this is done, virtual hosts will work properly. Note that this isn't a problem with the STARTTLS approach, it's merely a specification error, and it's been suggested that it be fixed before RFC 2487 advances to Draft Standard.

10.20 Security Indicators

It's clearly desirable for users to be able to determine the security properties that were used to transmit the message. Because messages are often written to disk and then read by the clients, the logical place to put this information is in the message headers. This also saves us the trouble of modifying our mail reading protocols to carry this information.

Figure 10.9 shows an example of this procedure. This is the same message we saw transmitted in Figure 10.8 as represented on disk after being delivered. Note the next-to-last Received header, which reads in part DES-CBC3-SHA encrypted SMTP. If the sender had used client authentication, this header line might also contain the certificate that the sender used to authenticate or some other equivalent indicator of the sender's identity.

```
From ekr@romeo.rtfm.com Tue Feb 08 22:14:02 2000
Return-Path: <ekr@romeo.rtfm.com>
Delivered-To: ekr@mike.rtfm.com
Received: (qmail 25454 invoked from network); 8 Feb 2000 22:14:02 -0000
Received: from romeo.rtfm.com (216.98.239.227)
   by mike.rtfm.com with DES-CBC3-SHA encrypted SMTP; 8 Feb 2000 22:14:02 -0000
Received: (qmail 21198 invoked by uid 556); 9 Feb 2000 05:01:19 -0000
Date: 9 Feb 2000 05:01:19 -0000
Message-ID: <20000209050119.21197.qmail@romeo.rtfm.com>
From: ekr@romeo.rtfm.com
To: ekr@mike.rtfm.com
Subject: test

test message
```

Figure 10.9 A message delivered with STARTTLS

Interpreting the Indicators

There are no standards for exactly how to place this sort of security information in headers. RFC 822 provides some guidance as to where in the header the information will come (after the `with` keyword) but other than that the implementation can arrange things more or less however it wants. Similarly, a client program could attempt to interpret them but will probably have to fall back on showing them to the user. Note that under normal circumstances, many clients don't even show the users `Received` headers unless they ask.

Last Hop

It's important to recognize that the headers are not cryptographically authenticated in any way. Thus, at the very best, the user has direct information about the last set of `Received` headers: those created by his local mail server on the *last hop*. The recipient must assume that his local mail server is trustworthy or he has no security. Thus, he can trust his mail server not to create false headers. However, any other headers may have been tampered with by any agent along the way.

Thus, in order to have any assurance about the security properties of the message all the way from sender to receiver, the connection must trust all hosts along the way. Moreover, those hosts must be cryptographically authenticated. Otherwise, an attacker might pose as a sender that you trust. Because the format of the `Received` fields isn't fixed, this evaluation can't really be made automatically and has to be made by the user.

10.21 Authenticated Relaying

There are two possible uses for certificate-based client authentication with STARTTLS: authenticated relaying and originator authentication. This section discusses authenticated relaying and the next discusses originator authentication.

The purpose of authenticated relaying is to allow a server to provide relaying services for servers it recognizes while denying those it does not. As we discussed in Section 10.7, open relays are often abused by spammers. Nevertheless, some sites need to relay mail. If the only machines that you relay from are behind the same firewall as your mail server, then you can often use IP-based authentication. However, often this isn't the case, either because there is no firewall or because your mail server needs to relay for machines at other places on the net.

In such cases, it's quite appropriate to use certificate-based client authentication to restrict relaying services. There are two interesting cases to consider. In the first, the sender has already connected with TLS. In the second, the sender has connected without TLS. In either case, the server will need to examine the `RCPT` command to see whether relaying has been requested.

If the sender has connected with TLS, then the server needs to check its certificate against the list of servers permitted to request relay. If no certificate has been presented, then the server will need to request a rehandshake. This is analogous to the case we saw in Chapter 9 where an HTTP server requested a rehandshake to cause the client to authenticate.

RFC 2487 isn't completely clear on what to do if the sender hasn't used TLS at all, but presumably the receiving server should send the 530 response, indicating that the sender must use TLS and then request client authentication during the TLS handshake.

10.22 Originator Authentication

The other possible use of client authentication is to provide originator authentication. The purpose of originator authentication is to provide the recipient assurance of the sender's identity. This is clearly valuable to recipients because they don't want to be fooled by forged e-mail. Unfortunately, originator authentication works very poorly with STARTTLS.

Because RFC 2487 forbids requiring TLS, it's clearly not possible to require client authentication via TLS. Thus, it's not really possible to enforce any sort of originator authentication. However, a server might choose to request client authentication whenever negotiating TLS. In that case, if the sending server uses STARTTLS and has a certificate, the receiving server will at least know who sent the data on the last hop. If the recipient is really lucky, every single hop will have used TLS and every sender will have client-authenticated to every receiver. In this case, the user has some hope of determining who the originator was.

In order to do this, however, the user will have to examine the Received headers to determine that every host that handled the message is trustworthy and should have been in the path of the message. This is particularly difficult because it is unlikely that each receiver server will add the entire certificate chain of each sender into the headers. Thus, the ultimate recipient cannot determine if the certificates used by the originator and each server in the path can be validated to a CA that he trusts.

At the end of the day, then, there is no good way to use SMTP with TLS to do originator authentication in most cases. This conclusion isn't restricted to the details of STARTTLS. It's a general problem with the interaction between TLS and the SMTP service model. Even if the various headers were standardized and it were thus technically possible to distinguish legitimate from illegitimate senders automatically, it would still require trusting every host along the way, which is a fundamentally unreasonable requirement. Thus, the receiver can have no assurance that the sender is who he says he is or even that the message was encrypted the entire way.

10.23 Reference Integrity Details

The situation with respect to reference integrity is little better. We said in Section 10.2 that the sender would like to be able to know that the message will be delivered to the recipient and that it will be protected in transit. Unfortunately, the mechanics of SMTP and STARTTLS make this nearly impossible.

Secure References

The first problem we face is that e-mail addresses don't contain any indication that you can send mail to them securely. It's obvious why this isn't the case: what would such an indication mean? The recipient doesn't know anything about the servers on the sender's side of the connection. The most he can possibly know about is the servers on his side of the connection.

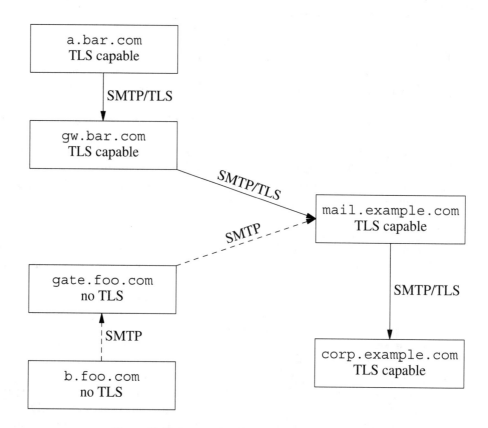

Figure 10.10 A network with secure and insecure servers

Consider the network setup shown in Figure 10.10 from the perspective of the user foo@corp.example.com. He knows that when servers look up the domain example.com they'll get an MX record pointing to mail.example.com. He also knows that mail.example.com and corp.example.com support TLS. Thus, he knows that the last hop will be delivered securely and that if the server connecting to mail is TLS-capable, then it might be able to connect securely, but that's the most he can be certain of.

In fact, two different senders get two different sets of security properties. A user on a.bar.com is able to have his mail sent over encrypted links all the way to corp.example.com. By contrast, mail sent from b.foo.com travels over insecure channels all the way to mail.example.com, where it's encrypted for the final hop to corp.example.com. There's no reasonable way for the recipient to predict what the behavior will be for any given sender.

Obviously, we could use a weak indicator that said essentially: "If you're TLS enabled, you should be able to send mail to me with TLS." However, this would necessarily involve a different form of e-mail address, because our current forms have no room for such an indication. This seems like a high cost for little benefit.

Enforcing Security

Imagine that the sender has some external information to the effect that the recipient would like to receive e-mail over a TLS connection. Furthermore, the sender knows that his local servers are TLS-capable. He can certainly configure his SMTP agent to do TLS only. However, this doesn't buy very much.

Again, consider the network in Figure 10.10. A user on a.bar.com would like to send mail to foo@corp.example.com. He knows that he's security capable and that the recipient is, so he configures his agent to do TLS, which it does, all the way to gw.bar.com. However, gw.bar.com doesn't know to negotiate TLS with mail.example.com, so an active attacker can downgrade the connection to regular SMTP. All this requires is tampering with the EHLO response to remove the offer of STARTTLS. The rest of the connection can be left unchanged.

Clearly, if we're to get anywhere we'll need some way to instruct every server along the way to do TLS. This could be done either by having a new mail header or (more likely) with some argument to the STARTTLS extension. Of course, such an extension would mean that if any server in the path between sender and receiver doesn't speak TLS then the mail will simply bounce, but sometimes sacrificing interoperability is the price we pay for security, so this might be worth it. However, as we'll soon see, it isn't.

Relaying versus Security

Unfortunately, the possibility of SMTP relaying more or less destroys any attempt to enforce TLS all along the message path. Again, consider the message we sent in Figure 10.10, but under a DNS spoofing attack where the attacker forges MX records for corp.example.com. Ordinarily, they would read something like

```
corp.example.com  preference = 10, mail exchanger=mail.example.com
```

The attacker substitutes this with

```
corp.example.com  preference = 10, mail exchanger=mail.attacker.com
```

Now, when the a.bar.com goes to deliver the message, we get the path shown in Figure 10.11 (assuming that the attacker bothers to deliver the message at all instead of just dropping it). Note that every hop in the delivery has still been transmitted with TLS.

Moreover, the contents of the MX record match the attacking server's certificate. We've simply added another relay in the chain. Clearly, then, requiring TLS alone is insufficient. We need servers to enforce the identity of the relays they're transmitting to. This shouldn't be surprising, because we said in Chapter 7 that just having a valid certificate isn't enough for reference integrity.

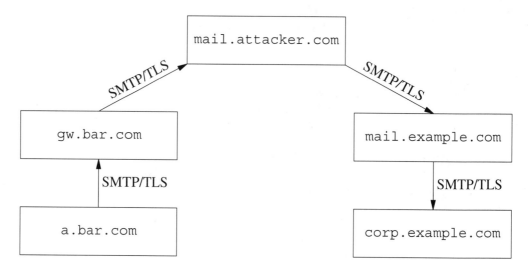

Figure 10.11 A fake mail exchanger

The problem we face is that there's nothing fundamentally wrong with the path shown in Figure 10.11. In this case, the extra relay is an attacker, but this sort of topology is relatively common. It's not even that uncommon for mail from organization A to organization B to be routed through a third organization, as we discussed in Section 10.7. Thus, we can't just check the hostnames on the certificates against the e-mail addresses in the RCPT command.

The only approach that's known to work at all is for every legitimate relay for a given host to have a certificate with that host's domain as its identity. Although this is secure, it's ultimately a configuration disaster, because every such relay must be manually configured. Worse yet, unless revocation is carefully done, the compromise of any such server compromises all traffic to the target domain permanently. If we had Secure DNS, then we could know that the MX records were correct and then we could check the name in the MX record against the server certificate. However, Secure DNS deployment has so far been minimal so this is not a real option.

At the end of the day, then, we're left with the conclusion that STARTTLS can't provide any real assurance to the sender of the security properties of the message he's sending. Even if he's willing to restrict himself to sending mail only over TLS, he can't be sure that the message will be securely delivered to the intended recipient. He certainly can't be sure that it was delivered undamaged. Once again, this problem doesn't have anything to do with the particular details of STARTTLS. It's simply inherent to using TLS to secure the hop-by-hop connections. Hop-by-hop security doesn't guarantee security between two endpoints.

10.24 Why Not CONNECT?

Clearly, the problems we're facing with SMTP are related to the existence of relays. HTTPS dealt with intermediaries like proxies by essentially bypassing them. The CONNECT method tells the proxy to get out of the way of the HTTPS connection. With an end-to-end channel between the client and server, HTTPS can guarantee the kind of security properties that STARTTLS can't.

This suggests the obvious question of whether it's possible to use some sort of CONNECT variant to tunnel through SMTP relays in the same way that we tunnel through Web proxies. Unfortunately, this is both technically and administratively problematic.

Technical Problems

One technical problem this approach faces is that this would completely break relaying for disconnected servers. As we said in Section 10.3, some organizations connect to the net only occasionally to get their mail. Such networks use a relay to store their mail for them. Clearly, it's not possible to tunnel to a server that's not connected to the net.

Conceivably, we could patch this problem by treating the final relay as if it were the recipient's local server. We'd issue it an appropriate certificate for the recipient's domain and allow it to negotiate the TLS connection with the sender. Because the alternative is for such networks not to receive encrypted mail at all, this might be acceptable.

Mail server software simply isn't designed to operate in this way. It expects to be able to queue messages and process them at leisure. This is important because it allows it to be robust against temporary network failures. Tunneling through the servers would entail major architectural changes to the software. Moreover, it would violate important invariants of the Internet mail environment; mail should be deliverable even if both networks are not online at the same time. That's what store-and-forward means.

Finally, consider the effect on the sending clients. In the current environment, mail is "fire and forget." A client can send mail to its local mail server and the user can disconnect from the network completely and still trust that his mail will be delivered. If the client is going to tunnel through to the end server, then it must remain online—and arrange to retry even if the recipient's server is temporarily down. Users frequently connect for only a few minutes at a time so this isn't really an acceptable result.

Administrative Problems

The more serious problems are administrative. Unlike Web servers, mail servers often are behind firewalls. HTTP CONNECT only allows clients to tunnel out from behind firewalls. The approach we're considering would allow senders to tunnel *in*. Allowing an encrypted connection to a mail machine behind the firewall understandably makes administrators quite nervous, especially because Sendmail, the dominant UNIX mail program, is notorious for having security problems.

10.25 What's STARTTLS Good For?

In Section 10.2, we named a number of desirable properties for an Internet mail security protocol. We wanted senders to be sure that their mail would be delivered securely to recipients. We wanted recipients to be able to authenticate the sender and know that messages hadn't been tampered with in transit. In Chapter 9, we saw that HTTPS met all of these goals, yet we've just seen that STARTTLS doesn't allow us to have any of these properties. Naturally, the question arises: What is STARTTLS good for?

Passive Attacks

The attacks that we've described for STARTTLS all rely on the attacker tampering with the network, typically either by playing man-in-the-middle or by contaminating the sender's DNS cache. In essence, they rely on the attacker pretending to be one of the communicating parties and thus subverting our security protections. This is a perfectly reasonable form of attack to worry about, but it's also comparatively difficult to mount. Moreover, the attacker needs to be online and transmitting data, which makes it easier to track him down. Thus, it's reasonable to consider what sorts of protection STARTTLS provides against passive attacks.

STARTTLS is useful if we're merely interested in opportunistic cryptography, that is if we ignore active attacks. Because senders no longer have to worry about connecting to the wrong gateway, all the attacks based on relay substitution disappear, as do the downgrade attacks. All we really have to worry about is whether or not servers support STARTTLS. If all the servers in the path of message support it, then the message can be delivered confidentially. Of course, we still need to trust the gateways not to read our mail. Depending on if they belong to a third party, this may or may not be a reasonable assumption.

We don't even need to have an "enforce TLS" flag. The servers will automatically upgrade where appropriate. However, it would be possible to introduce such a flag to indicate that servers should bounce mail if they can't deliver it securely.

Note that because we're not worrying about active attack, certificates add very little value in this situation. Recall that the major purpose of certificates is to prevent the active attacker from substituting his key for that of the legitimate receiver. Since we've ruled that attack out of scope, certificates aren't buying very much. We could dispense with them entirely and simply use anonymous DH. In some sense, this is making a virtue of necessity, because we saw in Section 10.8 that checking to see if a certificate represented the legitimate receiver was one of the hard problems with SMTP.

No Sender Authentication

Although we can have confidentiality, it's meaningless to talk about authentication or message integrity. The whole point of authentication is that it provides assurance of the message in the face of active attack. Since we've ruled that sort of attack out of scope, authentication and integrity are simply no longer relevant.

10.26 Programming Issues

Implementing SMTP over TLS doesn't really require any idioms that we haven't seen before. However, there are a few minor issues with SMTP that we didn't have to be concerned with when discussing HTTPS. The rest of this chapter describes two of these issues: implementing the STARTTLS extension and server startup. These issues aren't difficult enough to require sample code, but they are important enough to take note of.

10.27 Implementing STARTTLS

Conceptually, implementing STARTTLS is the same as implementing the CONNECT method for HTTPS. In both cases, the client needs to perform an application-layer handshake in the clear and then transition to SSL/TLS. The server code is analogous to the client code. However, STARTTLS is a little more complicated than CONNECT. HTTPS clients know that they are going to a proxy and CONNECT handling is simple enough that the client side can be written without actually invoking the HTTP engine. However, because STARTTLS is an upward-negotiation strategy, it typically gets wired directly into the SMTP engine.

State

The primary issue we need to be concerned with is SMTP-engine state. RFC 2487 is quite clear that any extensions advertised or negotiated before the TLS handshake no longer apply to the connection once the handshake has been completed. Thus, the implementation must be prepared to throw away all state and renegotiate extensions once the TLS handshake has completed. There are two reasons for this requirement: first, the attacker might have interfered with the extension advertisements. Second, the server might be willing to offer different services when TLS is being used.

Network Access

For efficiency reasons, it's quite common for SMTP implementations to want to buffer network reads and writes. Some implementations use stdio but some use their own network buffering code. In any case, the SSL implementation needs to be able to read and write to and from the network. Most SSL implementations provide some sort of abstract networking API which allows the application to provide its own I/O routines. OpenSSL does this using the BIO object, as shown in Figure 10.12.

```
                                                                    _____ sclient.c
26              ssl=SSL_new(ctx);

27              sbio=BIO_new_socket(sock,BIO_NOCLOSE);

28              SSL_set_bio(ssl,sbio,sbio);
                                                                    _____ sclient.c
```

Figure 10.12 OpenSSL BIO initialization

This abstraction allows the user to provide his own I/O routines as long as they can be represented as a BIO. sIn theory, PureTLS could do the same thing by having the user provide InputStream and OutputStream objects. However, as we discussed earlier, this functionality is not currently available in PureTLS. Note that if the buffering in the SMTP implementation is intended to read one line at a time, it will have to be deactivated before the TLS handshake because TLS data is not line-oriented.

If the SSL toolkit doesn't provide a replaceable networking API, it almost certainly reads and writes directly from sockets. In that case, the SMTP implementation will need to arrange to give a raw socket to the toolkit. This is relatively easy with STARTTLS because the length of commands and responses is always known, as is the start of the SSL handshake. Therefore, there is no need to be concerned that some of the SSL handshake will be trapped in the SMTP read/write buffers.

10.28 Server Startup

It's quite common to run mail servers in the same fashion as Web servers. We have a single server process that accepts connections from clients and then creates a new control thread to handle them. We already saw how to write this sort of program in Chapter 8. However, many mail servers on UNIX systems are configured differently. UNIX has a program called inetd. Inetd is a *superserver*. It listens for connections on a number of ports and has a configuration file that tells it which program to run to handle each kind of connection. Ordinarily, this approach works fine for a lightly loaded server, but it presents us with problems when we're using SSL.

Recall from Chapter 8 that SSL agents typically have a one-time initialization of an SSL context which contains keying material, randomness, etc. This context is then used for all subsequent connections. Clearly, if we're running our mail server out of inetd, we'll have to create our context object every time we receive a piece of e-mail. This presents two problems. First, we have to arrange to get access for the server to get access to its keying material. Second, we have to ensure that initialization is fast.

Keying Material

As we saw in Chapter 5, the standard way to protect keying material is to encrypt it under a passphrase. If we're running a single server process like an HTTPS server, we can simply prompt the user for the passphrase at system startup. This is somewhat inconvenient since it makes unattended startup difficult, but it's not unworkable. However, if our server runs out of inetd, this approach will no longer work.

The common approach to follow in these circumstances is simply to leave the private key on disk in the clear, but protected by file permissions or access control lists. A slightly more sophisticated solution is to have a single server process that is started at machine startup time. When it starts, it prompts the user for a password. The mail server program then contacts the server to obtain the keying material. Access to the server program is controlled via file permissions or ACLs.

The advantage of this approach is that the keying material is still encrypted on disk. Thus, if the machine is turned off, the passphrase will be needed to restart it. This provides some protection against server theft. Obviously, if the key is stored in hardware then the system will not be vulnerable to these attacks.

Fast Initialization

Recall that one of the major motivations for having a context object was so that time-consuming initialization could happen only once. Thus, if we have time-consuming initialization stages, they need to be somehow avoided. The common tasks that consume time at startup are generation of ephemeral keys and randomness seeding. This data can be precomputed and stored in files. As we saw in Chapter 9, our server can read this data from the files on startup.

10.29 Summary

Although the SSL designers intended that SSL could be used as a generic security layer, SSL was not specifically designed to work well with SMTP. However, the serious need for security for mail messages led to attempts to use SSL to secure SMTP, despite some serious mismatches between the SMTP model and the services SSL provides. In this chapter, we explored the standardized use of TLS with SMTP and examined some of the problems with this approach.

E-Mail is a store-and-forward system. The sending agent sends its message to the next server in the path using SMTP and that server then makes its best effort to deliver the message.

RFC 2487 specifies a method for using TLS to secure individual SMTP links. It introduces the STARTTLS extension which clients and servers can use to negotiate from a regular SMTP connection to SMTP over TLS.

Relays create problems. Because individual SMTP links are what is secured, each relay between client and server must be trusted. Moreover, because relay discovery is done via DNS, it's difficult to prevent attackers from posing as relays.

Senders can't determine security properties. Because e-mail addresses contain no information about the security of the transmission channel, a sender cannot know that his message will be sent confidentially.

Recipients can't get sender authentication. RFC 2487 forbids requiring TLS to receive mail. Even if TLS is used, the existence of relays makes it very difficult to determine the original sender.

STARTTLS provides protection against passive attack. If a sending and receiving server are both TLS capable, they will by default negotiate a TLS connection, thus protecting against sniffing.

11

Contrasting Approaches

"If you only have a hammer, you tend to see every problem as a nail."
—Abraham Maslow

11.1 Introduction

The previous chapters have focused on SSL. We've discussed its design goals, how it works, and how to use it. We've also examined two application-layer protocols that have been secured with SSL: HTTP and SMTP.

At this point, you should have a fairly good idea of how SSL works and what it can do. This, the final chapter, takes a broader view. As we saw in Chapters 9 and 10, certain security tasks can be very difficult to accomplish with SSL. In many cases, other security techniques can do the job much more cleanly and easily. Thus, it's important to be familiar with other techniques in order to be able to choose the best one. All too frequently, people use SSL to secure some application because it's the only approach they know about.

This chapter considers three other security protocols. First, we consider IPsec, which provides security for IP packets. IPsec operates at a lower layer than does SSL but provides many of the same security services. It also has some of the same limitations.

The second approach we consider is object security. Instead of encrypting the channel, object security sends protected objects over a clear channel. Because the individual protocol objects need to be secured, object security protocols are usually application specific. We'll examine Secure HTTP, which provides security for HTTP transactions and S/MIME, which provides security for Internet mail messages.

11.2 The End-to-End Argument

In this chapter we survey protocols at several layers of the protocol stack. As we'll see, the higher—closer to the application layer—we get in the protocol stack, the better security services we're able to provide. This is one instance of the end-to-end argument, best stated by Saltzer, Reed, and Clark [Saltzer1984] as:

> The function in question can completely and correctly be implemented only with the knowledge and help of the application standing at the end points of the communication system. Therefore, providing that questioned function as a feature of the communication system is not possible. (Sometimes an incomplete version of the function provided by the communication system may be useful as a performance enhancement.)

[Saltzer1984] is one of the great papers in computer science and is important reading for anyone who's interested in understanding networking. The argument can be summarized as follows: Any communications system involves intermediaries, such as network devices, computers, and programs which are unaware of the total context of the communication being involved. These intermediaries are therefore incapable of ensuring that the data is processed correctly. [Voydock1983] makes this point specifically in the context of security.

This argument has obvious intuitive appeal and it coincides with our experience with HTTP and SMTP. HTTPS and SMTP/TLS worked relatively well until we started introducing proxies and relays. In order to get HTTPS to work properly with proxies we had to tunnel through the proxy—in essence creating an end-to-end channel—and SMTP/TLS security is badly broken by relaying.

11.3 The End-to-End Argument and SMTP

It's easiest to understand the end-to-end argument with an example. Consider the case of SMTP over TLS. The application at the "end-points of the communications system" is the e-mail program used by the sender and recipient. However, SMTP/TLS provides security at a lower level: mail transport between mail relays. As a consequence, it is incapable of providing correct security services. This manifests itself in a variety of ways, but we'll consider only two: last-hop delivery and relaying.

Last-Hop Delivery

Recall that mail delivery to the end user is not accomplished via SMTP. Rather, it's done by some other protocol such as IMAP or POP or merely by reading the mail off the disk. This means that no possible SMTP/TLS measure can ensure integrity and confidentiality of the data between the local server and the mail reading client, because the communications channel between the server and mail reader might be compromised.

Even if we could somehow secure that protocol, say by running it over SSL, it would still be possible for the local server to be compromised, thus allowing the message to be compromised. No link-level security measures can protect us against this problem. By contrast, if the security is provided end-to-end by the mail programs, then this attack is no longer possible.

Relaying

The problem we face with relaying is similar. SMTP/TLS provides *link-level* security. The links between relays are secured but any given relay might be compromised. Worse yet, SMTP/TLS has no way of indicating that the next hop must be encrypted—or even what its identity is—so attackers can substitute themselves as a man-in-the-middle or downgrade the SMTP connection. Again, if the security were provided end-to-end, then we could prevent this attack.

An End-to-End Solution

The solution is to provide security end-to-end. Because there isn't an SMTP connection between the recipient and the local server, we can't establish an SMTP tunnel as we did with HTTP CONNECT. The correct approach is to create secure objects and transmit them via ordinary SMTP. As we'll see in Sections 11.17–11.21 this is exactly what S/MIME does.

11.4   Other Protocols

We'll be considering three protocols: IPsec, Secure HTTP, and S/MIME. Each protocol is capable of doing some but not all of the jobs that we've seen SSL do. IPsec is a general IP security solution. Thus, it can be used to provide generic security for any application that runs over IP in the same way that SSL can be used to provide security for any application that runs over a connection-oriented transport. Secure HTTP and S/MIME are both *object security* protocols designed for specific application layer protocols. Secure HTTP provides security for HTTP requests and responses by treating each request or response as an individual protected object. S/MIME provides security for individual e-mail messages.

Figure 11.1 shows the relationship of the various protocols in the protocol stack. Security protocols are shaded. At the bottom we have IP, over which we carry essentially all our data. IPsec is simply a set of extensions to IP which add security services. Thus, any application that can run over IP (and hence over TCP and UDP) can easily run over IPsec. Note that although UDP is shown layered only over IPsec, it can obviously run over IP as well.

Although SSL can in theory run over any connection-oriented transport, in practice it's nearly always used over TCP. Protocols that would ordinarily be layered over TCP

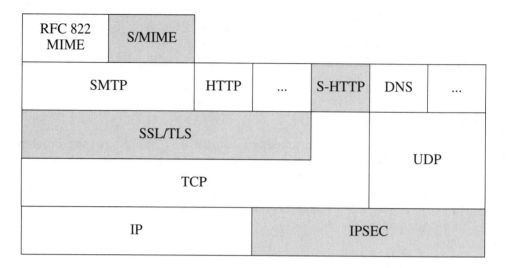

Figure 11.1 Where security fits in the protocol stack

can then be layered over SSL. Figure 11.1 shows three: SMTP, HTTP, and Secure-HTTP. Note that although we show them layered over SSL, of course HTTP and SMTP can be run directly over TCP.

At the top of Figure 11.1 we show RFC 822 and MIME messages, which are layered over SMTP. S/MIME messages are a specific kind of MIME message which provides cryptographic security. Thus, they can be carried over SMTP exactly as RFC 822/MIME messages are.

11.5 IPsec

IPsec is the umbrella term used for several different technologies standardized by the IETF IP Security working group and documented in RFC 2408: *Internet Security Association and Key Management Protocol* (ISAKMP) [Maughan1998]; RFC 2409: *Internet Key Exchange* (IKE) [Harkins1998]; RFC 2402: *Authentication Header* (AH) [Kent1998a]; and RFC 2406: *Encapsulating Security Payload* (ESP) [Kent1998b]. These technologies work together to provide security for IP traffic. RFC 2401 [Kent1998c] describes the architecture of IPsec.

Like SSL, IPsec has a key exchange and parameter management facility provided by ISAKMP and IKE and a data protection facility provided by AH and ESP. The glue between these facilities is provided by *security associations* (SAs). ISAKMP and IKE are used to establish SAs which are used by AH and ESP to protect the data. Unlike SSL, the key management and traffic protection functions are completely separate. It's possible to use AH and ESP without IKE, provided you have some other method of establishing SAs. Theoretically, it's possible to use IKE to exchange keys for non-IPsec protocols, but in practice this doesn't happen.

Our Approach

In order to compare IPsec and SSL, we first need to have a grasp of the fundamentals of how IPsec works. Thus, we first provide a high-level discussion of IPsec. We start by describing the three major components: *SAs, ISAKMP/IKE*, and *AH/ESP*. Then we'll examine how they work together to protect IP traffic. Finally, we'll compare secure communications with IPsec to SSL to see the advantages and disadvantages of each approach.

11.6 Security Associations

An IPsec SA loosely corresponds to an SSL session. It refers to a set of negotiated algorithms and keying material to be used to transmit data between two hosts. A security association differs from an SSL session in that it is unidirectional. In order for a pair of hosts to communicate securely, they must have two SAs, one for each direction. Each SA has a *security parameter index* (SPI): a 32-bit value identifying the SA. The SPI may not be globally unique but each SPI, source IP address, protocol (AH or ESP) triplet must be unique. SPIs are intentionally short because they are carried in each protected packet. A longer SPI would consume excessive network bandwidth.

11.7 ISAKMP and IKE

Before any data can be sent using either AH or ESP, an SA needs to be established. The IPsec architecture document (RFC 2401) provides for two methods of SA establishment: manual keying and ISAKMP/IKE. Manual keying means setting the keys and algorithms manually on both hosts. ISAKMP and IKE provide automatic key and session management in a similar way to the SSL handshake.

ISAKMP provides a generic framework for negotiating security associations and keys. It describes handshake phases and messages, as well as describing how to negotiate algorithms. However, it does not provide any specific key exchange methods. IKE provides key exchange methods based on Diffie-Hellman.

The IKE key exchange is based on STS [Diffie1992], Oakley [Orman1998], and SKEME [Krawczyk1995]. The two parties exchange Diffie-Hellman shares (public keys) and use the shared key to derive traffic encryption and message authentication keys. The DH shares can be authenticated using digital signature, public key encryption, or a shared secret. Note that because we're using DH we automatically get *perfect forward secrecy* (PFS). (See Chapter 5 for a discussion of PFS.) IKE defines a number of well-known DH groups; implementations can use private groups but most implementations use one of the public ones. By contrast, SSL leaves the choice of group up to the server.

Identity Protection

One of the unique features offered by IKE is identity protection for the parties in the exchange. In *Main Mode*, the DH shares are exchanged in the clear but the certificates and authenticating data for the shares are encrypted. Figure 11.2 shows this mode in operation.

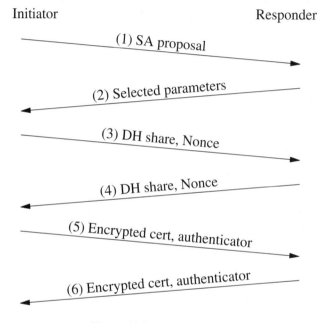

Figure 11.2 IKE Main Mode

IKE makes no distinction between client and server because this distinction does not exist at the IP layer. Instead, the sender of the first packet is called the *initiator* and the second the *responder*. We show the initiator on the left and the responder on the right. The handshake takes place in a series of *exchanges* where the initiator and responder each send a single message. Thus, Main Mode consists of three exchanges.

In the first exchange, we see the initiator sends a *proposal* for the algorithms that it's willing to support. The responder selects one from that set. In the second exchange, they each send a *nonce* (a random string analogous to the random values in SSL) and their respective DH shares. Finally, in the third exchange, they exchange signatures over the DH shares as well as over other parts of the exchange.

The end result of this handshake is roughly equivalent to an SSL handshake using DH and client authentication. The client and the server are mutually authenticated and they share an agreed upon set of keys and algorithms. There is no way in IKE to have one-way authentication in the way that SSL only authenticates the server.

The reason for having three exchanges in Main Mode is to protect the identity of the parties from sniffers. Identity protection is primarily useful where one host might have multiple identities and wants attackers to be unable to tell which one it's using for a specific handshake. By first doing an anonymous DH exchange and then conducting the rest of the exchange over an encrypted channel, IKE stops a passive attacker from determining the identities of the communicating parties. Although it's possible to provide this service in SSL by using an anonymous DH exchange followed by a normal exchange, this approach is far less clean than IKE Main Mode because it requires multiple key agreement phases. However, if this sort of protection is not desired, then all of these exchanges can be collapsed into a single exchange. This is called IKE *Aggressive Mode*.

Two-Phase Operation

Whereas SSL handshakes apply to a single connection, IKE is used to establish parameters for all traffic between two machines. It's very possible that different types of traffic will need different sorts of protection. For instance, Telnet sessions would probably need encryption, whereas DNS service needs only authentication.

In order to meet these different needs, IKE uses a *two-phase* approach. The first IKE handshake between two machines is used only to establish an ISAKMP SA. This SA is used only to transmit further IKE traffic. Thus, in order to actually transmit normal IP traffic, you need to do another IKE handshake to establish SAs for the particular type of traffic (protocol, port numbers, etc.) that you want to secure.

IKE provides a special *Quick Mode* for these new handshakes. Quick Mode is like SSL session resumption and can be used to generate new keying material from the original SA without doing a new key exchange. Alternatively, if PFS for the new SA is desired, a new DH key agreement can be performed. The authentication stages are still skipped. Because the exchanges take place over an authenticated channel, they are implicitly authenticated. Quick mode sets up a pair of SAs, one in either direction.

ISAKMP Transport

In SSL, the handshake happens in-band on the TCP connection that will be used to transport the data. Because ISAKMP is intended to establish communication parameters between two machines in general rather than over a single connection, this is obviously not possible. Instead, UDP port 500 has been designated for ISAKMP traffic.

Note that a result of using UDP is that there is no guarantee that packets will be delivered from sender to receiver. Thus, any ISAKMP implementation must maintain retransmit timers. If a given message is not responded to, the implementation must retransmit it. This adds some programming complexity not required by SSL.

One serious drawback to using UDP is the interaction of UDP with firewalls. Many firewalls block UDP entirely. Thus, if your IPsec host is behind a firewall, you'll need to configure your firewall to pass or proxy UDP traffic on port 500. This requires convincing your firewall administrator, which is often difficult, because holes in firewalls, especially for incoming UDP, are considered dangerous.

11.8   AH and ESP

Whereas SSL has a single unified record format, IPsec has two—AH and ESP—which do slightly different jobs. AH provides solely for message authentication and anti-replay. ESP provides for traffic encryption as well as optional message authentication and anti-replay.

AH

The idea behind AH is to provide a new IP header that authenticates the IP data and as much of the IP header as possible. It does this by MACing the data and most of the header. Because some of the header fields may change in transit, they are excluded from the MAC. Figure 11.3 thus shows a packet protected with AH, both before and after the addition of AH. MACed sections are shaded (note that even though the entire header is shaded, only parts of the header are MACed).

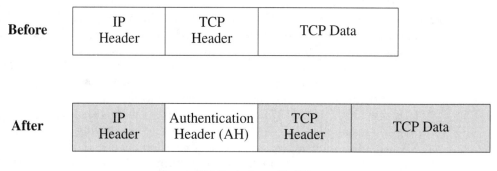

Figure 11.3 Protecting with AH

The AH header also contains a sequence number which is included in the MAC. This number can be used to provide replay detection. Note that normally functioning networks will sometimes see replays due to retransmission by intermediate routers. The purpose of replay detection is simply to ensure that the host's TCP and UDP layers see each packet only once. Replay prevention is primarily necessary for UDP, because TCP automatically handles and rejects replayed packets.

ESP

ESP provides encryption and optional authentication for the payload of an IP packet. Unlike AH, no protection is provided for the header at all. Only the payload of the message is protected. ESP can provide encryption, authentication, or both. Figure 11.4 shows a packet before and after ESP is applied. Protected sections of the packet are shaded.

IP Header	TCP Header	TCP Data

Before (label at left of first table)

IP Header	ESP Header	TCP Header	TCP Data

After (label at left of second table)

Figure 11.4 Protecting with ESP

Tunnel Mode

Note that because ESP provides no protection for the header, it's possible for an attacker to see (or change) the source or destination address. Both AH and ESP provide a mode called *tunnel mode* (the simpler mode we've just described is called *transport mode*) where the entire IP packet is protected. In essence, this is done by wrapping the packet to be protected in another packet which has AH or ESP applied. Figure 11.5 shows such a packet before and after ESP is applied.

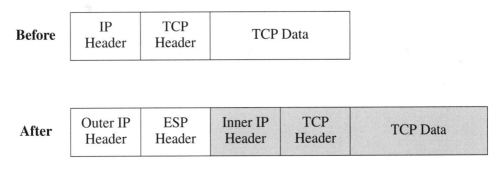

Before

IP Header	TCP Header	TCP Data

After

Outer IP Header	ESP Header	Inner IP Header	TCP Header	TCP Data

Figure 11.5 ESP in tunnel mode

In general, transport mode should be used for traffic between two hosts, because repeating the headers as in tunnel mode is unnecessary and wastes bandwidth. The sender and receiver address do not need to be cryptographically verified because they are implicit in the SA. Tunnel mode is primarily used in creating *virtual private networks* (VPNs). Two IPsec-capable routers can be configured to encrypt all traffic passing between them. This configuration acts as if the networks were directly connected via a private line, hence the term VPN. Tunnel mode should be used because the IP addresses may be that of any machine behind the router.

11.9 Putting It All Together: IPsec

Let's consider what happens when a host wishes to transmit a packet to another host with which it has never communicated. It can't do so until it has an SA set up to protect the data. Thus, it holds the packet while it performs the IKE exchanges necessary to set up the required SA. Once the SA is negotiated, it protects and transmits the packet.

When a packet is received, the host first needs to look at the SPI (in the AH or ESP header) to determine if it corresponds to a known SA. If it does, it reverses the applied protections and passes the data to the IP stack. Note that all of these behaviors can happen transparently to the application program. It just uses normal network calls and the data is automatically protected and unprotected.

Policy

So far, we've skipped over the question of how hosts decide what sorts of protections IKE should negotiate. In general, it's anticipated that there will be two mechanisms. First, system administrators will be able to set policies for a host. These policies would describe what sort of protections to negotiate based on the destination host, port, and protocol. Thus, applications can get some default security without any change to their code at all.

In some cases, applications will wish to have direct control of security services. To facilitate this, operating systems can offer extensions to the sockets API allowing the application to control the security to be negotiated for that socket. Of course, the application program must then be changed to use these extensions.

When we have multiple policies for different kinds of traffic, it is possible that although we have an SA for a given host, it has the wrong sort of protection. In that case, IKE will have to negotiate a new SA. Similarly, a host might receive a packet which has an SA that doesn't match the policy for the kind of packet it is. In such cases, the IP stack will have to reject the data, often generating some kind of ICMP error. Upon receiving such an error, the sender should negotiate an appropriate IPsec SA.

11.10 IPsec versus SSL

Note that despite a number of differences, IPsec and SSL are conceptually very similar. Each protocol has a handshake phase where it negotiates keys and parameters and then a data transfer phase where it protects traffic. IPsec behaves most like SSL when using ESP in transport mode. It provides authentication for the traffic data but not any of the IP headers. However, with IPsec, because the TCP messages are protected, TCP FINs can be used to close the connection securely. There is no need for special IPsec closure messages.

In many ways, IPsec can be thought of as SSL, only more so. SSL can be used to secure any traffic that goes over TCP, but IPsec can be used to secure any traffic that goes over IP, including UDP. SSL requires merely replacing socket calls with SSL socket calls but IPsec can be added without changing applications at all. Even if the application wishes to be IPsec aware, it can still use the basic socket calls without having to compensate for unusual I/O behavior due to SSL record framing. This is particularly convenient in situations where much of the network code is from a third party. Using SSL requires changing all of this code. IPsec requires changing essentially none of it.

Although IPsec does not require disrupting applications, it does require disrupting the operating system. The code for performing AH and ESP is necessarily part of the IP stack. In most systems, the stack is located in the operating system kernel. The ISAKMP/IKE code can be implemented in user space but must be able to create kernel table entries for SAs so that the AH/ESP code can access them. Thus, enabling IPsec can mean installing a whole new operating system.

Endpoint Authentication

Unlike SSL, ISAKMP requires that both sides authenticate. This is inconvenient because in many interactions the client identity isn't important. However, ISAKMP allows shared secret–based authentication whereas SSL does not. Note that these differences are simply design choices in the respective protocols. They're not inherent results of putting security at the transport or IP layers.

Intermediaries

We've seen that HTTPS can tunnel through proxies, but that SMTP over TLS must connect directly to relays and deliver the mail to them. The difference is due to the store-and-forward semantics of mail delivery. With IPsec, tunneling through intermediaries isn't even an option.

Recall that when we tunneled HTTPS through the proxy, we still had to make a TCP connection to the proxy. Thus, the proxy had to be able to read the TCP traffic—it was the application-layer traffic that it couldn't read. Because IPsec offers protection at the IP layer, this separation is no longer possible. The most that is possible is to offer IPsec to the intermediary. When application-level intermediaries are involved, IPsec can only offer link protection, whereas SSL can sometimes offer end-to-end protection.

Another approach to intermediaries would simply be for connections that are to be secured with IPsec to bypass the intermediaries entirely and connect directly to the target host. In general, however, this will not work. Firewall proxies are in place to control access, and punching holes—even for IPsec—negates this purpose. Moreover, in the case of SMTP, relays are a necessary part of the mail system and cannot be bypassed; the sending host doesn't know where to deliver the mail except to a relay.

Virtual Hosts

In Chapters 9 and 10, we saw that it was possible to use virtual hosts with SSL without IP aliasing, provided that we used an upward negotiation strategy that signaled the identity of the target host. With IPsec, however, because there is no application-layer protocol data transmitted before the IPsec SAs are established, there's no such thing as upward negotiation. Thus, IP aliasing is the only workable approach to virtual hosting.

NAT

IPsec completely breaks when a router is performing *Network Address Translation* (NAT). This technique allows a large number of machines to use a small number of IP addresses. Each machine is assigned its own private IP address and then the router automatically translates the private IP numbers to one of the assigned public IP numbers on transmission and from the public numbers to private numbers on receipt.

Naturally, because IPsec depends on establishing SAs to specific hosts, identified by IP address, NAT causes substantial problems if you want to run IPsec from a machine behind the NAT router. (Although if only a small number of hosts were to use IPsec, the router could be programmed to give them fixed addresses.) By contrast, SSL is completely unaffected by NAT. There is wide (and often acrimonious) debate about whether NAT is a good or a bad idea ([Rekhter1994, Lear1994, Rekhter1996]), so this is either a bug or a feature depending on your perspective. Nevertheless, NAT is widely deployed and so it's problematic that hosts behind NAT routers can't use IPsec.

Bottom Line

The dominant argument against IPsec is the need to change the TCP/IP stack. The dominant argument for it is not needing to change applications in order to secure them. In practice, because most applications don't really *need* security and changing operating systems is very inconvenient, it's better to simply use SSL on an application-by-application basis. However, IPv6 requires security support, so if it is ever widely deployed in end systems, that would be a good time to add security to IPv4 as well. Also, Windows 2000 comes with built-in IPsec support which makes IPsec a very attractive choice for Windows 2000–only applications.

The most common use of IPsec is to create VPNs, which it does very well. Upgrading a single router is fairly straightforward, and IPsec-capable routers are widely available. Installing such a router on your network makes it easy to produce a secure connection to remote networks. Thus, any traffic from one network to the other is automatically encrypted by the gateway routers. This is by far the most straightforward way to create a VPN.

If we assume that in the future IPsec will be widely available on end-user machines, then we can expect its widespread use for opportunistic security. As we saw in the case of SMTP over TLS, it can be useful to opportunistically negotiate security even without any protection against active downgrading. This provides protection against passive sniffing attacks with almost no configuration or management overhead. Thus, while it's difficult to replace HTTPS with HTTP/IPsec, replacing SMTP/TLS with SMTP/IPsec is quite attractive.

11.11 Secure HTTP

Secure HTTP (S-HTTP) [Rescorla1999a] provides a syntax for securing messages sent using HTTP. Unlike HTTPS, which largely ignores the content and boundaries of individual HTTP messages, S-HTTP treats each HTTP request or response as a single unit and protects it individually. This allows S-HTTP to protect different messages between client and server differently as well as to offer message-level digital signature and non-repudiation.

S-HTTP consists of two major components, a *message format* for encapsulating and protecting individual messages and a *negotiation syntax* which allows both client and server to express their opinions about how data should be protected and to provide keying material.

Full disclosure: I was one of the primary designers of Secure HTTP and for several years worked for a company that sold Secure HTTP toolkits. This gives me good perspective on the relative merits of Secure HTTP and SSL. However, it also introduces the suspicion of bias. Nevertheless, I've tried to present the pros and cons as objectively as I can.

Message Format

The S-HTTP message format is based on the *Cryptographic Message Syntax* (CMS), described in RFC 2630 [Housley1999b]. CMS is a variant of PKCS #7 [RSA1993c] designed for use with *Secure MIME* (S/MIME). In general, S-HTTP messages look like HTTP requests or responses, but the bodies are CMS messages. The protected body contains the actual HTTP request or response that the client or server sent. Thus, the headers and the message body are protected.

Cryptographic Options

One of the deliberate design goals of S-HTTP was that it have the same messaging model as HTTP. Thus, whereas SSL requires multiple round trips between client and server to perform the handshake, S-HTTP does not. Instead, Web pages containing S-HTTP links also contain negotiation information. This information is sufficient for the client to determine which protections to apply to a request generated by dereferencing a link—without first talking to the server. Similarly, S-HTTP clients put negotiation information in the headers of their requests. This information is sufficient to tell the server how to protect the response.

Our Approach

Our intent is to compare the HTTPS, discussed in Chapter 9, with S-HTTP. In order to do this, we need to understand how S-HTTP works well enough to appreciate the differences. Thus, we start with an overview of S-HTTP. First, we discuss CMS and then the format of S-HTTP messages. Then, we consider cryptographic options and the negotiation process. Finally, we discuss how negotiation and messaging work together to secure HTTP traffic and show an example.

With a firm understanding of S-HTTP established, we're ready to discuss the advantages and disadvantages with regard to HTTPS. In general, S-HTTP's message orientation provides greater flexibility than HTTPS. It is able to provide message-level signature and nonrepudiation, which HTTPS cannot. It also interacts more cleanly with proxies and virtual hosts. The primary disadvantage of S-HTTP is that it is substantially more complicated to implement, both on clients and servers.

11.12 CMS

CMS is a fairly typical protocol for cryptographically securing messages. It provides encryption and signature for arbitrary content. Every CMS message has a type that describes the form of cryptographic enhancement that has been applied. CMS messages may be recursively encapsulated in order to apply multiple types of enhancement. CMS defines six basic types, Data, SignedData, EnvelopedData, EncryptedData, and DigestedData. However, S-HTTP uses only SignedData and EnvelopedData, so we'll talk only about them.

SignedData

A SignedData message consists of some content and one or more signatures over that content. As usual, the content is digested and then the digest is signed with the sender's public key. The message can—and usually does—contain the appropriate certificates needed to certify the key(s) used to sign the message. The message can also contain CRLs needed to check the validity of the certificates.

It's also possible to have a SignedData message with no content. This is called a *detached signature* and represents a signature over some data which must be externally specified.

EnvelopedData

An EnvelopedData message contains encrypted data. The data is encrypted with a randomly generated symmetric *content encryption key* (CEK). The encrypted content is encapsulated in a wrapper that contains one or more RecipientInfo blocks. Each RecipientInfo block contains the CEK encrypted for a given recipient.

The CEK may be encrypted in any of three ways. If RSA is used, the CEK is simply encrypted under the recipient's public key. If DH is used, the CEK is encrypted under the sender and recipient's pairwise DH shared secret. Note that you don't encrypt the message directly under the pairwise DH shared secret because this would require reencrypting the entire message for each recipient. Encrypting the CEK under the pairwise secret allows the sender to just generate a new wrapped CEK for each recipient. Finally, it is possible to simply encrypt the CEK under a symmetric *key encryption key* (KEK) shared by sender and recipient. How such a key would be shared is outside the scope of

CMS. However, S-HTTP provides a way of establishing such keys, as we discuss in Section 11.14.

Signing and Encrypting

CMS does not provide any content type that provides both signature and encryption. To apply both enhancements, we must use recursively enhanced content. Thus, we take the data and sign it to produce a SignedData. Then we take the SignedData and use it as input to the encryption process to produce an EnvelopedData. Reading such a message simply reverses this procedure.

11.13 Message Format

Unlike HTTPS, S-HTTP messages use the same port as HTTP messages. They are designed so that a server can easily distinguish an S-HTTP request and remove the enhancements before processing the request. In order to do this, S-HTTP uses a special request method: Secure. Because the Request-URI might contain sensitive information, it is replaced with a "*". Figure 11.6 shows a typical S-HTTP request.

```
Secure * Secure-HTTP/1.4
Content-Type: message/http
Content-Privacy-Domain: CMS
```

Binary CMS message deleted

Figure 11.6 An S-HTTP message

The Content-Privacy-Domain: CMS line indicates that the (deleted) request body is a CMS message. This is necessary because S-HTTP also supports another (less popular) message security mechanism called *MIME Object Security Services* (MOSS). When the CMS message is unwrapped, its contents are the HTTP request that the client would have sent if S-HTTP were not being used. (This is what Content-Type: message/http means.)

S-HTTP responses follow a similar format to that of S-HTTP requests. Because the success or failure of the response is potentially sensitive, we wrap the entire HTTP response; the status line always reads

```
Secure-HTTP/1.4 200 OK
```

S-HTTP was originally designed using PKCS #7 and then adapted to CMS. Although CMS has suport for symmetric message authentication using MACs, PKCS #7 did not. Thus, S-HTTP also provides a MAC-Info header line which allows a MAC to be attached to the message.

11.14 Cryptographic Options

As we discussed in Chapter 9, HTTPS URLs can be distinguished from HTTP URLs by the `https` scheme. However, this is the only information provided to clients. The determination of which cipher suites to use is made during the SSL handshake. S-HTTP also has its own scheme: `shttp`. However, most of the information is given in cryptographic options. These options indicate what sorts of transformations the recipient expects the sender to use when sending a message.

The server's options are usually placed in the associated HTML anchor. RFC 2659 [Rescorla1999b] describes the procedure. The client's options are placed in the inner header—the HTTP header, not the S-HTTP header—of the request. When a client dereferences a URL, it first finds the corresponding options and uses them to determine what kind of message to send. When the server sends a response, it first examines the client's options in the HTTP header of the client's request.

S-HTTP doesn't have any real negotiation. Rather, the sender merges his own preferences with the receiver's preferences to come up with a jointly acceptable set of enhancements. He then applies those enhancements to the message and sends it. Except for the location of the cryptographic options, the client and server behave identically in this respect.

The cryptographic options contain two different kinds of information: *keying material* and *negotiation headers*. Keying material includes keys, certificates, etc., to be used when protecting a message. Negotiation headers contain preferences for what sorts of protection to use, including algorithms and key lengths.

Keying Material

The keying material options allow one side to send another side keying material to be used to respond to that message. Thus, a server could include its certificate in a link on a HTML page so that a client could use the certificate to encrypt its request for that link. S-HTTP also allows the sharing of a symmetric encryption key using the `Key-Assign` line. Because RSA encryption is expensive, it's better if any client and server pair only do it once. Thus, if a client encrypts to a server, it can provide the server with a symmetric key which the server can then use as a KEK to encrypt the CEK for its response.

Negotiation Headers

In SSL, all of the possible enhancement options come as a package: key exchange algorithm, authentication algorithm, encryption algorithm, and message authentication algorithm are all defined by the cipher suite. By contrast, S-HTTP has rather more options and they are specified more or less orthogonally.

S-HTTP allows negotiation of three different privacy enhancements: digital signature over the content (`sign`), encryption of the content (`encrypt`), and symmetric message authentication of the content (`auth`). These enhancements may be present in any combination, although the presence of `auth` and `sign` together seems redundant.

For each of these enhancements, the algorithm may be negotiated. Additionally, it is possible to negotiate key exchange algorithms (public key versus symmetric key) independently of content encryption algorithms. It is also possible to provide information about what sort of key the sender should sign with if digital signature is to be applied.

Finally, the negotiation headers can contain information about which enhancements an agent will use when sending. Thus, a server can tell a client what sort of message to expect in response to its request. The client should then compare the server's actual response to the behavior promised in the cryptographic options. Figure 11.7 shows an example of a single negotiation header sent by a server.

```
SHTTP-Symmetric-Content-Algorithms: orig-optional=DES-CBC, DES-EDE3-CBC;
     recv-require=DES-EDE3-CBC
```

Figure 11.7 A negotiation header

The header line in Figure 11.7 says that this link must be dereferenced with 3DES (`recv-require=DES-EDE3-CBC`) but that the server is willing to respond with either DES or 3DES (`orig-optional=DES-CBC, DES-EDE3-CBC`).

S-HTTP defines eight such negotiable items, so the cryptographic options can get rather long. To alleviate this problem, RFC 2660 provides defaults. If the value of an option matches the default, then that option may be omitted.

All in all, S-HTTP allows negotiation of the following parameters:

- Message format—CMS or MOSS
- Certificate type—X509, PKCS7 wrapped
- Key exchange algorithm—DH, RSA, Inband, Outband
- Signature algorithm—RSA, DSS
- Message digest algorithm—MD5, SHA-1, HMAC
- Symmetric content encryption algorithm—DES, 3DES, DESX, CDMF, IDEA
- Symmetric key encryption algorithm—DES, 3DES, DESX, CDMF, IDEA
- Privacy enhancements—signature, encryption, authentication, or some combination

Note that there are no specifications for use of DES, DESX, or CDMF with CMS. However, there's really only one obvious way to plug in new content encryption algorithms. By advertising support for these algorithms, S-HTTP implementations imply that they support this approach.

11.15 Putting It All Together: S-HTTP

The easiest way to see how S-HTTP works is to see an example. Figure 11.8 shows a page with a Secure-HTTP link on it. How the client got this page is irrelevant, but likely it was fetched via HTTP.

```
<CERTS FMT=PKCS-7>
Certificate deleted
</CERTS>

<A DN="CN=Test Server, O=RTFM, Inc., C=US"
    CRYPTOPTS="
      SHTTP-Privacy-Enhancements: recv-required=encrypt;
      SHTTP-Key-Exchange-Algorithms: recv-required=RSA;
      SHTTP-Symmetric-Content-Algorithms: recv-required=DES-EDE3-CBC"
    HREF="shttp://www.rtfm.com/test.html">
    Click here to dereference</A>
```

Figure 11.8 A page with an S-HTTP link

The CERTS element contains a base64-encoded PKCS #7 certificate chain. We've deleted it from this example. The anchor contains the relevant cryptographic options. The DN field contains the distinguished name of the server. Note that the server's certificate and distinguished name are provided separately. The CERTS element is just advisory. The DN attribute is what's used to find the server's key.

The CRYPTOPTS attribute contains the negotiation headers. In this case, the server requires the client to encrypt, using RSA for key exchange and 3DES for symmetric encryption. Finally, the HREF attribute contains the URL of the resource, as usual, but with an shttp scheme.

When the client dereferences the link, it encrypts the request, using RSA for key exchange and 3DES for encryption, as required. It also provides a symmetric key to the server using the Key-Assign header. The encrypted request is shown in Figure 11.9. This request (and all the messages shown throughout the rest of the chapter) are shown in *crypto-vision*. Rather than displaying the encrypted content as a blob of binary data, we show the inner content that you would see if you decrypted it. This content is presented in a *fixed-width italic* font to differentiate it from the rest of the message.

Note that the headers that would ordinarily have been in the HTTP request, such as Security-Scheme and User-Agent are in the inner encrypted request. Again, these headers are potentially sensitive, so they must be protected.

The last four header lines are the S-HTTP negotiation headers. The Key-Assign line provides an *inband* key. This key can be used to allow the server to respond with an encrypted message without performing another RSA operation. It also allows the client to receive encrypted messages without having a private key, just as it can with SSL. The client should generate a fresh key for each request. This key has the label 1.

The last three header lines tell the server that it must encrypt its response using 3DES. It must wrap the CEK using the inband key passed in this request, using 3DES. It must also provide a MAC over the entire message.

Finally, Figure 11.10 shows the server's response to this message, once again in crypto-vision. As instructed, the server has encrypted the message for the client with the key inband:1 as the CEK. This is hidden in the CMS wrapper. The server has also

```
Secure * Secure-HTTP/1.4
Content-Type: message/http
Content-Privacy-Domain: CMS

GET /secret HTTP/1.0
Security-Scheme: S-HTTP/1.4
User-Agent: Web-O-Vision 1.2beta
Accept: *.*
Key-Assign: Inband,1,reply,des-ecb,des-ede3-ecb;
      78787878787878787878787878787878787878787878787878
SHTTP-Privacy-Enhancements: recv-required=encrypt,auth
SHTTP-Symmetric-Content-Algorithms: recv-required=DES-EDE3-CBC
SHTTP-Key-Exchange-Algorithms: recv-required=inband
SHTTP-Symmetric-Header-Algorithms: recv-required=DES-EDE3-ECB
(blank line)
```

Figure 11.9 An S-HTTP request

used inband:1 to compute the HMAC value found in the MAC-Info line. Note that the real HTTP headers are encrypted and MACed. They potentially contain sensitive data and so must be protected. Thus, it's possible to have a S-HTTP response where the S-HTTP status line is OK but the interior HTTP status line indicates an error.

```
Secure-HTTP/1.4 200 OK
Content-Type: message/http
MAC-Info:31ff8122,rsa-sha-hmac,
      a51d612e5f3d0fbb3d8837ca351fcec879e5e3a6,inband:1
Content-Privacy-Domain: CMS

HTTP/1.0 200 OK
Security-Scheme: S-HTTP/1.4
Content-Type: text/html

Congratulations, you've won.
```

Figure 11.10 An S-HTTP response

Client Authentication

S-HTTP authenticates the client by authenticating the request message. There are two options for authenticating a message: digital signature over the message and MAC. Digital signature provides for nonrepudiation whereas a MAC merely provides a fast integrity and sender-authentication check. The digital signature binds the message's sender to the sender's certificate. The MAC allows the recipient to know that the message was sent by someone who has the MAC key.

Reference Integrity

Preserving S-HTTP reference integrity is very simple. Because the page containing the reference also contains the cryptographic information required to encrypt the request, the client can simply use that information. There is thus no requirement that the server's certificate actually matches the server's DNS name. All that is required is to check that the server's certificate verifies. The client knows the server's identity from its certificate.

Because each message is individually authenticated, we need to provide some way of binding the reference to the server's response. Otherwise, the attacker could replay an old response to the client. The way to do this is for the client to provide a key using `Key-Assign` and then require the server to encrypt or MAC its response using that key. Knowing the key depends on being able to decrypt the original request, which implies knowing the server's private key. Thus, the response is bound to the request.

Automatic Options Generation

The most notable feature of S-HTTP is that any given request, even for resources on the same site, might use a different set of cryptographic enhancements. Although this provides tremendous flexibility, it also presents a substantial burden on the administrator. Even with defaults, S-HTTP negotiation headers are difficult to write manually. Worse yet, writing the options into the HTML files means that if your policies ever change you have to edit all the pages with references to the affected resources.

A better approach is to have the server automatically create the options. To do this requires that the server have a primitive HTML parser capable of identifying links. When a link is found, the server then finds the access control policy associated with the resource and automatically emits the appropriate options along with that link. Unfortunately, early S-HTTP servers did not support this feature, making them very hard to administer.

Note the `Security-Scheme` header field in Figure 11.9. This is a new HTTP header added by S-HTTP. It allows a client to tell a server that it is S-HTTP capable. This allows the server to rewrite only pages destined for S-HTTP-capable browsers. Although S-HTTP's modifications to HTML are intended to be invisible when viewed in HTML compliant browsers, some browsers nevertheless displayed them as part of the page. This header prevented pages containing S-HTTP links from containing extra clutter in non-S-HTTP browsers.

Stateless Operation

We've shown how a client can use the `Key-Assign` header to provide the server with a symmetric encryption key for the server's response. Obviously, the server could do the same thing in its cryptographic options, but this would ordinarily require it to remember the key. Because we have to contend with multiple server processes, this means arranging to communicate this key between them. Recall that we faced a similar problem with SSL session caching.

With S-HTTP, however, this problem can be attacked without creating server state. The `Key-Assign` header allows the sender to assign the key an arbitrary name. We can leverage this name to avoid storing temporary keys. All of our server processes share a single *master* CEK. Then, when we create a new temporary key for use with `Key-Assign`, we arrange that we can generate that key from the label. The simplest way to do this is to simply encrypt the key with the master CEK and use that as the label.

$$Label = E(MasterCEK, Key)$$

Alternatively, we can randomly generate the label and use that to generate the key, like so:

$$Key = HMAC(MasterCEK, Label)$$

We could imagine using such a trick with SSL by using the encrypted master secret as the session ID. Unfortunately, this is impossible for two reasons. First, the session ID would need to be as long as the master secret, but it's only 32 bytes and the master secret is 48 bytes. Second, SSL requires us not to resume sessions that aren't closed properly. This requires us to be able to invalidate sessions, which would require inter-process communication. Note, however, that invalidating sessions doesn't really add that much security and that many implementations don't do it in any case. The major obstacle is that the session ID is too short.

11.16 S-HTTP versus HTTPS

In general, the closer to the application-layer protocol that you provide security, the more flexible and powerful security the services you are able to offer. However, this flexibility often comes at the cost of complexity and implementation effort. Thus, although S-HTTP is significantly more flexible than HTTPS, and interacts better with the Web environment, it's also significantly harder to implement and deploy.

Flexibility

The most noticeable difference between HTTPS and S-HTTP is that S-HTTP is far more flexible than HTTPS. In principle, every resource on an S-HTTP-enabled Web server can require a different set of cryptographic enhancements in order to be fetched. In practice, this much flexibility is rarely required, however it's quite common to want three to five policies. HTTPS has difficulty handling even this many policies and usually needs to resort to clumsy hacks like virtual hosts or multiple ports (one for each policy). As we saw in Chapter 9, requiring client authentication on only part of an HTTPS Web site requires an entire rehandshake for those pages. With S-HTTP it's a simple matter of changing the options for the appropriate links.

However, S-HTTP's flexibility comes at a high price. Having to make page-by-page decisions is daunting for administrators. This administrative burden can be minimized with good server design and user interface, but this requires substantially more programming than writing an HTTPS-enabled server.

Nonrepudiation

One S-HTTP feature that cannot be achieved with HTTPS is nonrepudiation. Since SSL knows nothing about the various HTTP message boundaries and uses MACs for message authentication, there is no way to provide proof that a given request or response was made. By contrast, because S-HTTP provides whole-message signature, this is a simple matter of signing the appropriate message. It's equally easy for the client and server to request this service by setting the appropriate option.

The signing feature of S-HTTP can also be used to allow servers to cache presigned documents. This allows the server to execute the signature once and simply hand out the same document repeatedly to multiple clients. This can be useful for static objects that need to be integrity protected but do not need to be secret.

Proxies

In the simplest case, S-HTTP proxies can behave exactly like HTTPS CONNECT proxies. However, because the message structure of S-HTTP is apparent to the proxy, a more sophisticated proxy can take advantage of this information. For instance, a proxy could notice where message boundaries are and shut down idle connections. A really sophisticated proxy can cache responses for static, unencrypted documents fetched with S-HTTP. Thus, it's possible for S-HTTP proxies to cache signed content such as programs or long-lived data files.

Virtual Hosts

S-HTTP's interaction with virtual hosts is simple. Because S-HTTP provides the DN of the server in the cryptographic options, there is no need to use different certificates for different virtual hosts. Even if this is desired, because the CMS message clearly indicates the DN of the recipient, the server can easily decrypt the message. Once the message is decrypted, the server has access to the Host header and can act accordingly.

User Experience

One drawback with the strategy of placing cryptographic options in anchors is that the URL now becomes insufficient to fetch a resource. The client also needs the cryptographic options from the anchor. Thus, it's possible for a user to type an https: URL into a browser directly, but a shttp: URL is much less useful. RFC 2660 describes a hack whereby the browser may ask the server for some generic cryptographic options, but because the server doesn't know what resource is being requested, S-HTTP is no more flexible than HTTPS in this case.

When S-HTTP and HTTPS were first introduced, the insufficiency of `shttp:` URLs seemed like a major drawback. Users are quite commonly in the habit of typing URLs directly into the browser and if the entire Web was to be secured then it was assumed that they would want to type in secure URLs. However, it turns out that most Web sites use security for only a very limited portion of the site, using `https:` links to transition from the insecure to secure portions. Thus, because the URL is nearly always found in an HTML page, there is a location to put the cryptographic options.

Ease of Implementation

The difficulty of implementing S-HTTP and SSL is roughly comparable. However, the difficulty of integrating them into preexisting software is not. We've already mentioned that S-HTTP requires extensive support from the server in order to rewrite HTML pages to insert cryptographic options. None of this effort is required with HTTPS. Note, however, that this means that Web designers need to explicitly edit the HTML to make resources accessible via HTTPS. With a rewriting strategy, such as should be employed with S-HTTP the administrator can change only the access control settings and the server will automatically convert pages to secure access as appropriate.

S-HTTP also requires substantially more support on the client side than does HTTPS. Primarily, the HTML parser needs to be modified in order to allow the cryptographic options to be extracted. None of this work is necessary with HTTPS. Also, because S-HTTP allows more operational modes, the user interface should reflect exactly what sorts of processing a given message had, whereas with HTTPS it's more realistic to simply indicate *secure* or *insecure*.

Whether this is a bug or a feature depends on your perspective. The reason it's insufficient to say *secure* or *insecure* with S-HTTP is that S-HTTP has a far more flexible security model. Thus, if you think that the additional features that S-HTTP adds are worth having, then you need some way to represent them to the user. On the other hand, if you think the features are unnecessary, then they just make extra user interface effort.

In sum, implementing S-HTTP requires substantially more programming effort than does HTTPS. Moreover, this programming effort cannot be isolated into a toolkit but requires tight integration with the browser and server. This difference isn't surprising, because S-HTTP is far more tightly integrated with HTML and HTTP than HTTPS.

Bottom Line

In terms of technical merits, S-HTTP's greater flexibility and tight integration with the Web is both a cost and a benefit. It allows S-HTTP to offer features that HTTPS cannot, such as nonrepudiation and pre-signed data. It also means that S-HTTP's interaction with virtual hosts and proxies is far cleaner. However, it also means that implementing S-HTTP is far harder than implementing HTTPS.

Moreover, the subtleties involved in implementing HTTPS involve making it totally secure. The subtleties involved in implementing S-HTTP involve making it usable. Thus, a naive HTTPS implementation might fail to deal with closure or reference integrity properly. A naive S-HTTP implementation might require the administrator to manually edit HTML documents in a particularly unpleasant way. Because users tend to value convenience over security, a naive S-HTTP implementation is much less valuable than a naive HTTPS implementation.

In 1995 and 1996, there was substantial doubt as to whether HTTPS or S-HTTP would become the dominant Web security protocol. There is no longer any doubt; HTTPS is the undisputed winner. Whatever their respective technical merits, every major browser and server implements HTTPS whereas none implement S-HTTP. Thus, there isn't really a choice of whether to use S-HTTP or HTTPS.

11.17 S/MIME

S/MIME provides message-oriented security services for e-mail messages. Before the Web, e-mail was—and arguably still is—the most important networking service. Thus, many attempts have been made to standardize it. In the IETF alone, there have been no less than four e-mail security standards: PEM, MOSS, OpenPGP, and S/MIME. All of these protocols take essentially the same approach. They treat an e-mail message as a single object and provide security services for that object. The differences between them are largely details of message format and trust model.

S/MIME version 2 [Dusse1998] was originally developed by RSA Labs and used RSA's PKCS #7 [RSA1993c] cryptographic messaging format. PKCS #7 supported only RSA for key exchange and thus S/MIME v2 only had support for RSA. When the IETF S/MIME working group was created to standardize S/MIME v3 [Ramsdell1999], one of the primary goals was to add support for other algorithms. Thus, PKCS #7 was revised to create CMS [Housley1999b], which also supported other key exchange and signature algorithms.

Our Approach

Our intent is to compare securing e-mail transport via SMTP/TLS with S/MIME. As with S-HTTP, we'll first present enough detail to explain how S/MIME works. We've already covered CMS in Section 11.12, but there are some subtleties in S/MIME's use of CMS, particularly when data is signed but not encrypted. Finally, we'll cover S/MIME algorithm selection; because e-mail is store-and-forward, ensuring that the sender knows which algorithm to use takes some special thought.

With our knowledge of S/MIME in hand, we then discuss its advantages and disadvantages over SMTP over TLS. As we discussed in Chapter 10, SMTP over TLS really doesn't do that good a job of securing e-mail. S/MIME, however, does an excellent job. The only real advantage that SMTP over TLS has is that it doesn't require as much client-side support.

11.18 Basic S/MIME Formatting

MIME allows e-mail messages to carry arbitrary content through the use of a `Content-Type` line. S/MIME uses the `application/pkcs7-mime` content type to indicate that the content type is a CMS-encapsulated MIME message. That is to say, when the CMS body is unwrapped, it itself contains a MIME body. Figure 11.11 shows such an example, once again in crypto-vision.

```
From: ekr@rtfm.com
Subject:Test message
Content-Type: application/pkcs7-mime; smime-type=enveloped-data


Content-Type: text/plain


This is an encrypted message.
```

Figure 11.11 An encrypted S/MIME message

Note that the `Subject` line of the message appears in the unencrypted portion. Thus, the `Subject` is not cryptographically protected in any way. In fact, none of the normal mail headers are. If they are to be protected, they must appear in the header section of the inner content.

11.19 Signing Only

Figure 11.11 showed an encrypted message. The simplest way to prepare a signed message would be to do exactly the same thing as before, except using the CMS SignedData type. Of course, the `smime-type` parameter would now be `signed-data`. This approach is simple but has a substantial drawback. The message can't be read by a non-S/MIME-capable client. An encrypted message by definition requires an encryption-capable client to read it. This is not the case with a carefully structured signed message.

If a message is signed but not encrypted, then it's desirable for it to be readable by recipients without S/MIME-capable clients. This would encourage senders to sign messages whether or not the recipient was S/MIME capable. One could also send signed messages to multiple recipients—a useful feature when some of them can verify the message but it must be readable by all.

However, simply presenting the message as a CMS SignedData using `application/pkcs7-mime` defeats this purpose. Most MIME readers simply save content with unrecognized types to disk. Moreover, even if the reader attempts to view the data, since CMS is a binary format, it's very inconvenient to distinguish the CMS wrapper from the data. Often, standard tools will not display binary data at all.

Multipart/Signed

The solution to this problem is to make use of CMS detached signatures. We also need to use a different wrapping method, `multipart/signed`. As well as arbitrary data content types, MIME allows multiple content types to exist in a single message, using the `multipart` types. A `multipart/signed` message contains two parts. The first part is the actual object as it would have appeared if it weren't S/MIME wrapped. The second is a CMS detached signature over the message. Figure 11.12 shows an example of this.

```
Content-Type: multipart/signed; protocol="application/pkcs7-signature";
    micalg=sha1; boundary=boundaryYYY

--boundaryYYY
Content-Type: text/plain

This is a clear-signed message.
--boundaryYYY
Content-Type: application/pkcs7-signature
Content-Transfer-Encoding: base64

Signature deleted
--boundaryYYY--
```

Figure 11.12 A multipart/signed message

The `--boundaryYYY` lines indicate the breaks between various body parts. Note that any MIME-compliant agent can notice that the first body part is of type `text/plain` and display it to the user. It can either ignore the second body part or offer to save it to disk. In either case the user will be able to read the signed message without the signature getting in the way. Even if the user does not have a MIME-compliant mailer, he will have a much better chance of viewing the content if the signed data is separated from the binary clutter of the CMS wrapper.

S/MIME and S-HTTP

S/MIME encapsulation provides essentially the same set of features as S-HTTP's message format. The reason that S-HTTP provides its own message format is that it was designed before S/MIME. It would be perfectly possible to use S/MIME encapsulation with S-HTTP negotiation, and this would be the best choice if S-HTTP were being designed today.

11.20 Algorithm Choice

Because of the store-and-forward nature of e-mail, it's not possible for the sender and recipient to negotiate algorithms or keys. In principle, it's possible that the sender and recipient have never communicated before. The sender needs only to have the recipient's public key, which he could have gotten from a directory.

However, when the first message has been sent, the sender has an opportunity to communicate to the recipient what sorts of enhancements he would like the recipient to use when he replies. This is particularly important in order to ensure interoperation between export and domestic clients. Thus, S/MIME signed messages can include a *capabilities* attribute which indicate the signer's preferences.

Capabilities

The SMIMECapabilities attribute is used to indicate which cryptographic algorithms the sender supports. It's simply a list of the algorithms that the sender wishes to advertise. It can include at minimum the following types of algorithm:

- signature algorithms
- symmetric encryption algorithms
- key encipherment algorithms (how the CEK is encrypted)

The capabilities attribute is a fairly general mechanism for advertising a user's preferences. Algorithms are intended to be listed in order of preference so a user can describe not only what he supports but the order in which he wants it used. It's even possible to represent that you would prefer people to sign the messages they sent you, using the preferSignedData capability. Implementations are supposed to ignore capability identifiers they don't recognize, so the set can be extended in the future.

Algorithm Choice

The only algorithm choice that we really have to be concerned with is the encryption algorithm. The key establishment algorithm is defined by the recipient's key, so there is no choice to be made there, except in the unlikely case where the recipient has multiple keys—in which case the sender can choose either one. Theoretically, there might be an issue of which digest algorithm to use, but in practice support for SHA-1 is nearly universal. However, there is substantial variation in encryption algorithm support. In particular, there are a large number of exportable clients that support only RC2-40. For obvious reasons, it's important to encrypt your message with an algorithm the recipient supports. RFC 2633 details three cases.

Known capabilities. In the case where a sender knows the recipient's capabilities, the situation is simple. It should choose one of the recipient's supported algorithms. As a matter of courtesy, the RFC 2633 says that it should use the recipient's most preferred cipher. However, a sender might choose to use a cipher that the recipient liked less but the sender liked more. If a directory exists, then it is quite likely that the sender would be able to get the recipient's capabilities when it fetches the certificate.

Unknown capabilities, known use of encryption. In the case where the sender has received an encrypted message from the recipient but doesn't know any capabilities, then it's fairly safe to use the same encryption algorithm as the recipient used in that message.

Unknown capabilities. S/MIME v3 required support for 3DES, so if the sender knows that the recipient supports S/MIME v3, then it's safest to send using 3DES. However, S/MIME v2 required support for RC2-40 and many export clients supported only that, so absolutely maximal interoperability (at a tremendous security cost) can be achieved by using RC2-40. In general, RC2-40 is so weak that it's generally best to use 3DES.

Capability Discovery

The result of these rules is that over the course of several e-mail exchanges, the parties develop an understanding of their respective capabilities and a sort of algorithm negotiation takes place. Consider the case where we have two parties, Alice and Bob. They both have RSA keys and support 3DES, but neither knows the other's capabilities. The first three messages they send are shown in Figure 11.13.

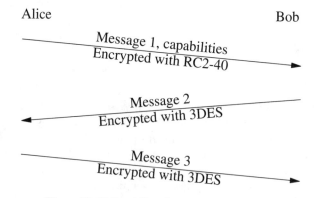

Figure 11.13 Capability discovery with S/MIME

Alice wants to be absolutely sure that Bob can read the first message she sends, so she sends it using RC2-40. (She could also send it in the clear.) She supports 3DES, so she also includes a capabilities attribute indicating that she does. Thus, when Bob replies, he encrypts with 3DES. Now, he doesn't even have to include capabilities for Alice to know that he supports 3DES—he just used it—so Alice's final message also uses 3DES.

11.21 Putting It All Together: S/MIME

Now that we've seen the various components of S/MIME, let's examine how they work together to provide a coherent set of security services. Imagine that Alice wants to send a message to Bob. She already has his certificate and his capabilities, presumably by obtaining them from some directory.

Endpoint Identification

Alice has fetched Bob's certificate from the directory and verified it, but how does she know that it really is Bob's certificate? Recall that with SSL we often faced the problem of comparing a certificate to a DNS name. Here, we have a similar problem but we want to compare to an e-mail address. The solution is also similar: certificates can contain e-mail addresses either as a portion of the distinguished name or in the emailAddress value of the subjectAltName extension. Thus, Bob's certificate is the one that contains Bob's e-mail address in one of these locations.

Message Sending

With Bob's certificate in hand, generating a message that can only be read by Bob is simple. Alice encrypts the message under a randomly generated CEK and encrypts the CEK under Bob's public key, as usual. Optionally, she signs the message before encryption. She then transmits it—over any channel at all—to Bob. At this point it's perfectly safe to use normal unencrypted SMTP.

Sender Authentication

Once Bob receives the message, he wants to be able to do two things: read the message and authenticate the message and its sender. Reading the message is trivial. As usual, he simply decrypts the CEK using his private key and the message using the CEK. Naturally, all this is done automatically by his MUA.

Verifying the message signature is equally straightforward. First, Bob verifies the cryptographic identity of the message. However, as we saw in Chapter 10, e-mail messages also contain non-cryptographic indicators of the message sender in the From header. Because this header is under the control of the sender, the receiver's MUA must verify that it matches the certificate that was used to sign the message. If it doesn't, the MUA must somehow inform the user to prevent him from being fooled.

Multiple Signers

In certain circumstances, it's desirable to have a message signed by multiple senders. Consider the case where a message is really being sent by two people. In an ordinary letter, they would both sign it. Similarly, with a digitally signed message, we'd like both to sign it. This is trivial with S/MIME, even if the signers are on totally separate networks and computers, because CMS supports multiple signatures on a single message.

Multiple Recipients

Even more common than multiple signers is multiple recipients. It's very common to want to send a message to a number of recipients, while encrypting to all of them. This is very efficient in S/MIME. One simply encrypts the message with a single CEK and then encrypts the CEK individually for each recipient in a separate RecipientInfo structure. Thus, the message needs to be encrypted only once, saving both CPU time and bandwidth. For large mailing lists, S/MIME even includes a feature allowing the whole mailing list to share a single symmetric *mailing list key* under which the CEK is encrypted.

Receipts

One nice feature offered by S/MIME is the ability to provide a receipt, as described in RFC 2634 [Hoffman1999b]. Receipts allow a sender to be sure that the recipient received a message and that it was undamaged. A sender can use an attribute to indicate that he would like a receipt from the recipient. When the recipient receives the message, he generates a signed response containing the receipt. Note that the sender cannot force the recipient to generate a receipt. It requires the cooperation of the recipient. Although the recipient's software should generate the receipt automatically, this feature can be bypassed. Thus, although a receipt proves that the recipient received the mail, the lack of a receipt is not evidence that he did not.

11.22 Implementation Barriers

Being able to use S/MIME requires having three things: an S/MIME-capable client, a certificate, and access to the certificates of others. S/MIME-capable clients are becoming ubiquitous; S/MIME is no more difficult to implement than SSL, and many of the browsers that support SSL now support S/MIME, including Netscape Communicator and Microsoft's Outlook Express. As of this writing, OpenSSL even has some S/MIME support. However, the requirements for certificates and certificate access are more problematic.

Certificates

Certificates are fairly widely available from commercial CAs. However, S/MIME differs fundamentally from any system we've discussed so far in that it requires end users—not just servers—to have certificates. This is a significant entry barrier because the number of users far exceeds the number of servers. Thus, to date, deployment of certificates has been slow.

One problem with certificate deployment is that the certificates need to vouch for the e-mail addresses of users. This presents a social problem because it's not clear who can vouch for the claim that a user has a particular e-mail address. Clearly the user can't be trusted. Theoretically the owner of the domain in which the e-mail address lives should vouch for the user's identity, but this requires the system administrator to be involved, which is highly inconvenient.

A weak but fairly common approach is for the CA to force the the user to prove that he can receive mail at a given e-mail address. Typically, the CA e-mails the user a random string which must be returned in order to get a certificate. This protocol is obviously subject to various kinds of attack, including simple sniffing, but because it has to be done only once for a given user, it's not completely worthless. Nevertheless, better certificate issuance procedures, probably rooted in Secure DNS, are needed.

Certificate Discovery

The second deployment problem is obtaining the certificates of others. It's obviously impossible to send encrypted mail to someone unless you have his certificate. In a perfect world, certificates would be available from a directory service, but despite some deployment, directories are far from ubiquitous.

In the absence of global directories, the best strategy is to sign every message one sends. Thus, anyone who receives a message from you will have your certificate and be able to encrypt to you. When you receive a signed message, you remember the e-mail address to certificate mapping. Thus, you can send encrypted e-mail to anyone from whom you've ever received e-mail. Over time, most people you communicate with will have your certificate and can send you encrypted e-mail. Until directories are ubiquitous, local caching is probably the best we can do.

11.23 S/MIME versus SMTP/TLS

In Chapter 10, we saw that SMTP/TLS wasn't very good at securing e-mail. By contrast, S/MIME does an excellent job. This is largely due to approaching the problem at the right layer of abstraction, the sender and recipient MUAs.

End-to-End Security

S/MIME provides end-to-end security. Messages are encrypted and signed by the sender and decrypted and verified by the recipient. They transit the network in a protected form. By contrast, with SMTP/TLS, we were often unable to protect the "last hop" link between the mail client and its local server because these links didn't use SMTP at all but rather some other protocol such as MAPI or POP. With S/MIME this is no problem because the encrypted messages are simply MIME data and can use any transport.

Nonrepudiation

SSL and TLS are completely unable to provide nonrepudiation because they use MACs for message integrity. Because S/MIME uses digital signature and signs the whole message, signed S/MIME messages can be forwarded from one recipient to another while leaving the signature intact and verifiable.

Relays

Even if both the sender's and recipient's local mail servers support SMTP/TLS, if the mail has to pass through a non-TLS relay along the way, then the message won't be secured. By contrast, S/MIME doesn't require any of the mail servers to be security capable. It merely requires support for S/MIME in the end user programs.

S/MIME does require one sort of support from relays; they must not damage the content. Because the signature is over a specific representation of bytes, if the relays damage the byte stream, then the signature will no longer verify. SMTP-compliant relays do not cause this problem, but mail often passes through other kinds of relays. To some extent, S/MIME is hardened against known transformations, but it is still possible for a relay to damage the message beyond repair. However, such relays would surely not be SMTP/TLS compliant, so the situation for S/MIME is no worse than for SMTP/TLS in this case.

Virtual Hosts

S/MIME doesn't require any special support from the mail servers at all, so virtual hosts work perfectly. And because the sender and recipient certificates are bound to their addresses, not to any particular server, users can easily move from ISP to ISP without changing any of their credentials.

Bottom Line

In general, S/MIME is a far superior solution to SMTP/TLS. The only significant barriers to using S/MIME are deployment barriers. However, S/MIME-capable mail clients are becoming increasingly popular and certificates are now available if not ubiquitous. The only significant advantage that SMTP/TLS offers over S/MIME is the ability to opportunistically secure e-mail in transit. However, this need would ultimately be better met using IPsec.

11.24 Choosing the Appropriate Solution

Now that we've seen a number of alternative approaches, we have enough information to draw some more general conclusions about when SSL is appropriate and when we'd be better served by attacking the problem at some higher or lower layer.

In general, SSL works well when the communications model is simple. Communications model simplicity has a number of aspects, but in general what we mean is that the interaction should be as much like a direct TCP connection between the two end parties as possible. The more complicated the environment is, the more difficult providing adequate security with SSL becomes.

Direct Connection

Providing adequate security with SSL more or less requires having a direct connection between client and server. Many of the problems we encountered with SMTP occurred because we didn't have a direct connection. With HTTPS we were able to get adequate results only because we were able to simulate a direct connection by convincing the proxy to provide us with a tunnel.

Whenever we don't have a direct connection, an object security solution suits us better. S-HTTP interacts somewhat better than SSL with proxies and S/MIME is of course completely oblivious to mail relaying. In general, as long as you can avoid your objects being damaged by intermediaries, an object security protocol is a better choice.

TCP Only

Consider a protocol such as DNS that communicates via UDP. Because SSL requires a TCP channel, it's impossible to secure it with SSL. However, because IPsec lives at a lower layer in the protocol stack, it's capable of providing security for UDP data. Similarly, an object security protocol such as DNSSEC (described in RFC 2535 [Eastlake1999]) that secures the actual DNS data works fine with UDP. In this case, DNSSEC is a better solution because it doesn't require setting up an IPsec channel just to do name resolution.

Only Two Communicating Parties

Because SSL connections are inherently one-to-one, SSL works best if there are only two communicating parties. Object security tends to support many-to-many communications much more cleanly. Even when we can simulate a many-to-many interaction with SSL, it is usually far clumsier than the corresponding object security solution.

Consider the case of sending a message to a large number of recipients. With SSL, we need to reencrypt the message every time we send to a new person. With an object solution, we can simply rewrap the CEK for each new recipient. This saves both CPU time and bandwidth. If the message is simply signed, then we don't even need to reencrypt the CEK. We can simply transmit the same message to multiple recipients. This capability is especially important when we're repeatedly transmitting the same signed content, such as a signed software distribution. We can sign the content offline and then have the pre-signed file on some insecure server. Thus, even if the server is compromised, the attacker cannot create a fake distribution.

Simple Security Services

SSL works best when the security services to be provided are simple. Because it doesn't know anything about the objects being transmitted it can't offer services like nonrepudiation, timestamping, or return receipt. These services require an object security protocol, which is inherently an application-layer service.

11.25 Summary

SSL is a useful and flexible security tool, but it is not the only tool in our toolbox. It's important to understand our other alternatives in order to know when to choose the right one. This chapter has surveyed three other security protocols—IPsec for securing arbitrary network data, Secure HTTP for securing HTTP transactions, and S/MIME for securing e-mail messages—in order to provide this perspective.

The end-to-end argument requires that correct security for applications be provided by the application. Because HTTP and e-mail are application-layer protocols, security for them must be provided at the application layer. HTTPS mostly meets this test. SMTP/TLS does not, which accounts for many of its shortcomings.

Higher-level security protocols are more flexible. In accordance with the end-to-end argument, higher-level protocols are more capable of providing exactly the security that an application needs. In particular, object security protocols can provide advanced features such as nonrepudiation. In general, if it's not too much trouble, it's better to use a higher-level security mechanism.

Lower-level security protocols are more general. The lower in the protocol stack that we put security, the more traffic it can account for. Thus, whereas S-HTTP and S/MIME can secure only one service, SSL can secure anything running on TCP and IPsec can secure any TCP/IP traffic.

IPsec provides security for any network data. Unlike SSL, IPsec provides security for any traffic between two hosts. This means that once IPsec is installed, all applications gain some security. However, because IPsec is lower in the protocol stack than is SSL, it is even more sensitive to interference by intermediaries in the communications channel.

Secure-HTTP provides security for HTTP transactions. S-HTTP treats each HTTP request or response as an individual message. This allows more flexible negotiation of security properties as well as object security for the messages.

S/MIME provides security for e-mail messages. Each individual message is protected. This allows end-to-end message protection and fits well with the e-mail store-and-forward model. It also allows true sender and recipient authentication.

SSL works well with real-time TCP services. If the communicating parties are directly connected using TCP, then SSL works well. If they are using something other than TCP, then IPsec should probably be used. If they are not directly connected, then an application-level security protocol is more appropriate. SSL is a compromise between application security, which offers better protection, and IP security, which offers more generality.

Appendix A

Example Code

A.1   Chapter 8

This section contains complete versions of the example programs from Chapter 8. Machine readable versions of these programs can also be downloaded from the author's Web site at http://www.rtfm.com/sslbook/examples.

A.1.1 C Examples

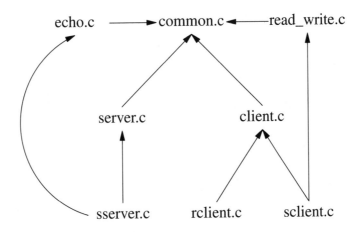

The above picture shows the dependency graph for the various C source files in the examples.

common.c provides a set of common utility functions including a common initializer for client and server and error exit routines.

server.c provides server utility functions, mainly for initialization but also the tcp_listen() encapsulation for creating and binding sockets.

client.c provides our tcp_connect() wrapper for connect() and the check_cert_chain() verification routine.

echo.c contains the main server echo loop.

sserver.c contains the server main program which arranges to listen on a socket and then loops between accept() and echo().

read_write.c contains multiplexed select()-based I/O handling for the client.

sclient.c is our main client program. It connects to the server and then uses read_write() to move data back and forth.

rclient.c is a stub client that demonstrates how to do session resumption with OpenSSL.

--- common.h

```
1      #ifndef _common_h
2      #define _common_h

3      #include <stdio.h>
4      #include <stdlib.h>
5      #include <errno.h>
6      #include <sys/types.h>
7      #include <sys/socket.h>
8      #include <netinet/in.h>
9      #include <netinet/tcp.h>
10     #include <netdb.h>
11     #include <fcntl.h>
12     #include <signal.h>

13     #include <openssl/ssl.h>

14     #define CA_LIST "root.pem"
15     #define HOST "localhost"
16     #define RANDOM   "random.pem"
17     #define PORT 4433
18     #define BUFSIZZ 1024

19     extern BIO *bio_err;
20     int berr_exit (char *string);
21     int err_exit(char *string);

22     SSL_CTX *initialize_ctx(char *keyfile, char *password);
23     void destroy_ctx(SSL_CTX *ctx);

24     #endif
```

```
1       #include "common.h"

2       BIO *bio_err=0;
3       static char *pass;
4       static int password_cb(char *buf,int num,int rwflag,void *userdata);
5       static void sigpipe_handle(int x);

6       /* A simple error and exit routine*/
7       int err_exit(string)
8         char *string;
9         {
10          fprintf(stderr,"%s\n",string);
11          exit(0);
12        }

13      /* Print SSL errors and exit*/
14      int berr_exit(string)
15        char *string;
16        {
17          BIO_printf(bio_err,"%s\n",string);
18          ERR_print_errors(bio_err);
19          exit(0);
20        }

21      /*The password code is not thread safe*/
22      static int password_cb(char *buf,int num,int rwflag,void *userdata)
23        {
24          if(num<strlen(pass)+1)
25            return(0);

26          strcpy(buf,pass);
27          return(strlen(pass));
28        }

29      static void sigpipe_handle(int x){
30        }

31      SSL_CTX *initialize_ctx(keyfile,password)
32        char *keyfile;
33        char *password;
34        {
35          SSL_METHOD *meth;
36          SSL_CTX *ctx;
```

```
37              if(!bio_err){
38                 /* Global system initialization*/
39                 SSL_library_init();
40                 SSL_load_error_strings();

41                 /* An error write context */
42                 bio_err=BIO_new_fp(stderr,BIO_NOCLOSE);
43              }

44              /* Set up a SIGPIPE handler */
45              signal(SIGPIPE,sigpipe_handle);

46              /* Create our context*/
47              meth=SSLv3_method();
48              ctx=SSL_CTX_new(meth);

49              /* Load our keys and certificates*/
50              if(!(SSL_CTX_use_certificate_file(ctx,keyfile,SSL_FILETYPE_PEM)))
51                berr_exit("Couldn't read certificate file");

52              pass=password;
53              SSL_CTX_set_default_passwd_cb(ctx,password_cb);
54              if(!(SSL_CTX_use_PrivateKey_file(ctx,keyfile,SSL_FILETYPE_PEM)))
55                berr_exit("Couldn't read key file");

56              /* Load the CAs we trust*/
57              if(!(SSL_CTX_load_verify_locations(ctx,CA_LIST,0)))
58                berr_exit("Couldn't read CA list");
59              SSL_CTX_set_verify_depth(ctx,1);

60              /* Load randomness */
61              if(!(RAND_load_file(RANDOM,1024*1024)))
62                berr_exit("Couldn't load randomness");

63              return ctx;
64            }

65        void destroy_ctx(ctx)
66          SSL_CTX *ctx;
67          {
68            SSL_CTX_free(ctx);
69          }
```

```
                                                                    echo.h
1        #ifndef _echo_h
2        #define _echo_h

3        void echo(SSL *ssl,int sock);

4        #endif
```
                                                                    echo.h
```
                                                                    echo.c
1        #include "common.h"

2        void echo(ssl,s)
3          SSL *ssl;
4          int s;
5          {
6            char buf[BUFSIZZ];
7            int r,len,offset;

8            while(1){
9              /* First read data */
10             r=SSL_read(ssl,buf,BUFSIZZ);
11             switch(SSL_get_error(ssl,r)){
12               case SSL_ERROR_NONE:
13                 len=r;
14                 break;
15               case SSL_ERROR_ZERO_RETURN:
16                 goto end;
17               default:
18                 berr_exit("SSL read problem");
19             }

20             /* Now keep writing until we've written everything*/
21             offset=0;

22             while(len){
23               r=SSL_write(ssl,buf+offset,len);
24               switch(SSL_get_error(ssl,r)){
25                 case SSL_ERROR_NONE:
26                   len-=r;
27                   offset+=r;
28                   break;
29                 default:
30                   berr_exit("SSL write problem");
31               }
```

```
32                  }
33                }
34            end:
35              SSL_shutdown(ssl);
36              SSL_free(ssl);
37              close(s);
38            }
```

_____ echo.c

_____ read_write.h

```
1        #ifndef _read_write_h
2        #define _read_write_h

3        void read_write(SSL *ssl,int sock);

4        #endif
```

_____ read_write.h

_____ read_write.c

```
1        #include "common.h"

2        /* Read from the keyboard and write to the server
3           Read from the server and write to the keyboard

4           we use select() to multiplex
5        */
6        void read_write(ssl,sock)
7          SSL *ssl;
8          {
9             int width;
10            int r,c2sl=0,c2s_offset=0;
11            fd_set readfds,writefds;
12            int shutdown_wait=0;
13            char c2s[BUFSIZZ],s2c[BUFSIZZ];
14            int ofcmode;

15            /*First we make the socket nonblocking*/
16            ofcmode=fcntl(sock,F_GETFL,0);
17            ofcmode|=O_NDELAY;
18            if(fcntl(sock,F_SETFL,ofcmode))
19              err_exit("Couldn't make socket nonblocking");


20            width=sock+1;
```

```
21              while(1){
22                FD_ZERO(&readfds);
23                FD_ZERO(&writefds);

24                FD_SET(sock,&readfds);

25                /*If we've still got data to write then don't try to read*/
26                if(c2sl)
27                  FD_SET(sock,&writefds);
28                else
29                  FD_SET(fileno(stdin),&readfds);

30                r=select(width,&readfds,&writefds,0,0);
31                if(r==0)
32                  continue;

33                /* Now check if there's data to read */
34                if(FD_ISSET(sock,&readfds)){
35                  do {
36                    r=SSL_read(ssl,s2c,BUFSIZZ);

37                    switch(SSL_get_error(ssl,r)){
38                      case SSL_ERROR_NONE:
39                        fwrite(s2c,1,r,stdout);
40                        break;
41                      case SSL_ERROR_ZERO_RETURN:
42                        /* End of data */
43                        if(!shutdown_wait)
44                          SSL_shutdown(ssl);
45                        goto end;
46                        break;
47                      case SSL_ERROR_WANT_READ:
48                        break;
49                      default:
50                        berr_exit("SSL read problem");
51                    }
52                  } while (SSL_pending(ssl));
53                }

54                /* Check for input on the console*/
55                if(FD_ISSET(fileno(stdin),&readfds)){
56                  c2sl=read(fileno(stdin),c2s,BUFSIZZ);
57                  if(c2sl==0){
58                    shutdown_wait=1;
59                    if(SSL_shutdown(ssl))
```

```
60              return;
61           }
62         c2s_offset=0;
63       }

64       /* If we've got data to write then try to write it*/
65       if(c2sl && FD_ISSET(sock,&writefds)){
66         r=SSL_write(ssl,c2s+c2s_offset,c2sl);

67         switch(SSL_get_error(ssl,r)){
68           /* We wrote something*/
69           case SSL_ERROR_NONE:
70             c2sl-=r;
71             c2s_offset+=r;
72             break;

73             /* We would have blocked */
74           case SSL_ERROR_WANT_WRITE:
75             break;

76             /* Some other error */
77           default:
78             berr_exit("SSL write problem");
79         }
80       }


81       }
82     end:
83       SSL_free(ssl);
84       close(sock);
85       return;
86     }
```

_____ read_write.c

_____ server.h

```
1      #ifndef _server_h
2      #define _server_h

3      #define KEYFILE "server.pem"
4      #define PASSWORD "password"
5      #define DHFILE "dh1024.pem"

6      int tcp_listen(void);
7      void load_dh_params(SSL_CTX *ctx,char *file);
```

```
8          void generate_eph_rsa_key(SSL_CTX *ctx);

9          #endif
```

```
1          #include "common.h"
2          #include "server.h"

3          int tcp_listen()
4            {
5              int sock;
6              struct sockaddr_in sin;
7              int val=1;

8              if((sock=socket(AF_INET,SOCK_STREAM,0))<0)
9                err_exit("Couldn't make socket");

10             memset(&sin,0,sizeof(sin));
11             sin.sin_addr.s_addr=INADDR_ANY;
12             sin.sin_family=AF_INET;
13             sin.sin_port=htons(PORT);
14             setsockopt(sock,SOL_SOCKET,SO_REUSEADDR,&val,sizeof(val));

15             if(bind(sock,(struct sockaddr *)&sin,sizeof(sin))<0)
16               berr_exit("Couldn't bind");
17             listen(sock,5);

18             return(sock);
19           }

20         void load_dh_params(ctx,file)
21           SSL_CTX *ctx;
22           char *file;
23           {
24             DH *ret=0;
25             BIO *bio;

26             if ((bio=BIO_new_file(file,"r")) == NULL)
27               berr_exit("Couldn't open DH file");

28             ret=PEM_read_bio_DHparams(bio,NULL,NULL,NULL);
29             BIO_free(bio);
30             if(SSL_CTX_set_tmp_dh(ctx,ret)<0)
31               berr_exit("Couldn't set DH parameters");
```

```
32            }

33        void generate_eph_rsa_key(ctx)
34          SSL_CTX *ctx;
35          {
36            RSA *rsa;

37              rsa=RSA_generate_key(512,RSA_F4,NULL,NULL);

38              if (!SSL_CTX_set_tmp_rsa(ctx,rsa))
39                berr_exit("Couldn't set RSA key");

40              RSA_free(rsa);
41          }
```

_____ server.c
_____ client.h

```
1        #ifndef _client_h
2        #define _client_h

3        #define KEYFILE "client.pem"
4        #define PASSWORD "password"

5        int tcp_connect(void);
6        void check_cert_chain(SSL *ssl,char *host);

7        #endif
```

_____ client.h
_____ client.c

```
1        #include "common.h"

2        int tcp_connect()
3        {
4            struct hostent *hp;
5            struct sockaddr_in addr;
6            int sock;

7            if(!(hp=gethostbyname(HOST)))
8              berr_exit("Couldn't resolve host");
9            memset(&addr,0,sizeof(addr));
10           addr.sin_addr=*(struct in_addr*)hp->h_addr_list[0];
11           addr.sin_family=AF_INET;
```

```
12            addr.sin_port=htons(PORT);

13            if((sock=socket(AF_INET,SOCK_STREAM,IPPROTO_TCP))<0)
14              err_exit("Couldn't create socket");
15            if(connect(sock,(struct sockaddr *)&addr,sizeof(addr))<0)
16              err_exit("Couldn't connect socket");

17            return sock;
18          }

19       /* Check that the common name matches the host name*/
20       void check_cert_chain(ssl,host)
21         SSL *ssl;
22         char *host;
23         {
24           X509 *peer;
25           char peer_CN[256];

26           if(SSL_get_verify_result(ssl)!=X509_V_OK)
27             berr_exit("Certificate doesn't verify");

28           /*Check the cert chain. The chain length
29             is automatically checked by OpenSSL when we
30             set the verify depth in the ctx

31             All we need to do here is check that the CN
32             matches
33           */
34           /*Check the common name*/
35           peer=SSL_get_peer_certificate(ssl);
36           X509_NAME_get_text_by_NID(X509_get_subject_name(peer),
37             NID_commonName, peer_CN, 256);
38           if(strcasecmp(peer_CN,host))
39           err_exit("Common name doesn't match host name");
40          }
```

_____ client.c

_____ sserver.c

```
1        /* A simple SSL echo server */
2        #include "common.h"
3        #include "server.h"
4        #include "echo.h"

5        static int s_server_session_id_context = 1;
```

```
6        int main(argc,argv)
7          int argc;
8          char **argv;
9          {
10           int sock,s;
11           BIO *sbio;
12           SSL_CTX *ctx;
13           SSL *ssl;
14           int r;

15           /* Build our SSL context*/
16           ctx=initialize_ctx(KEYFILE,PASSWORD);
17           load_dh_params(ctx,DHFILE);
18           generate_eph_rsa_key(ctx);

19           SSL_CTX_set_session_id_context(ctx,(void*)&s_server_session_id_context,
20             sizeof s_server_session_id_context);

21           sock=tcp_listen();

22           while(1){
23             if((s=accept(sock,0,0))<0)
24               err_exit("Problem accepting");

25             sbio=BIO_new_socket(s,BIO_NOCLOSE);
26             ssl=SSL_new(ctx);
27             SSL_set_bio(ssl,sbio,sbio);

28             if((r=SSL_accept(ssl)<=0))
29               berr_exit("SSL accept error");

30             echo(ssl,s);
31           }
32           destroy_ctx(ctx);
33           exit(0);
34         }
```
_____ sserver.c

_____ sclient.c
```
1        /* A simple SSL client.

2           It connects and then forwards data from/to the terminal
3           to/from the server
4        */
5        #include "common.h"
6        #include "client.h"
7        #include "read_write.h"
```

```
8          int main(argc,argv)
9           int argc;
10          char **argv;
11          {
12            SSL_CTX *ctx;
13            SSL *ssl;
14            BIO *sbio;
15            int sock;

16            /* Build our SSL context*/
17            ctx=initialize_ctx(KEYFILE,PASSWORD);

18            /* Connect the TCP socket*/
19            sock=tcp_connect();

20            /* Connect the SSL socket */
21            ssl=SSL_new(ctx);
22            sbio=BIO_new_socket(sock,BIO_NOCLOSE);
23            SSL_set_bio(ssl,sbio,sbio);
24            if(SSL_connect(ssl)<=0)
25              berr_exit("SSL connect error");
26            check_cert_chain(ssl,HOST);

27            /* read and write */
28            read_write(ssl,sock);

29            destroy_ctx(ctx);
30          }
```
——————————————————————————————————————— sclient.c

——————————————————————————————————————— rclient.c
```
1          /* SSL client demonstrating session resumption */
2          #include "common.h"
3          #include "client.h"
4          #include "read_write.h"

5          int main(argc,argv)
6           int argc;
7           char **argv;
8           {
9            SSL_CTX *ctx;
10           SSL *ssl;
11           BIO *sbio;
12           SSL_SESSION *sess;
13           int sock;

14            /* Build our SSL context*/
```

```
15            ctx=initialize_ctx(KEYFILE,PASSWORD);

16            /* Connect the TCP socket*/
17            sock=tcp_connect();

18            /* Connect the SSL socket */
19            ssl=SSL_new(ctx);
20            sbio=BIO_new_socket(sock,BIO_NOCLOSE);
21            SSL_set_bio(ssl,sbio,sbio);
22            if(SSL_connect(ssl)<=0)
23              berr_exit("SSL connect error (first connect)");
24            check_cert_chain(ssl,HOST);

25            /* Now hang up and reconnect */
26            sess=SSL_get_session(ssl); /*Collect the session*/
27            SSL_shutdown(ssl);
28            close(sock);

29            sock=tcp_connect();
30            ssl=SSL_new(ctx);
31            sbio=BIO_new_socket(sock,BIO_NOCLOSE);
32            SSL_set_bio(ssl,sbio,sbio);
33            SSL_set_session(ssl,sess); /*And resume it*/
34            if(SSL_connect(ssl)<=0)
35              berr_exit("SSL connect error (second connect)");
36            check_cert_chain(ssl,HOST);

37            /*Now close everything down again*/
38            SSL_shutdown(ssl);
39            close(sock);
40            destroy_ctx(ctx);
41          }
```

A.1.2 Java Examples

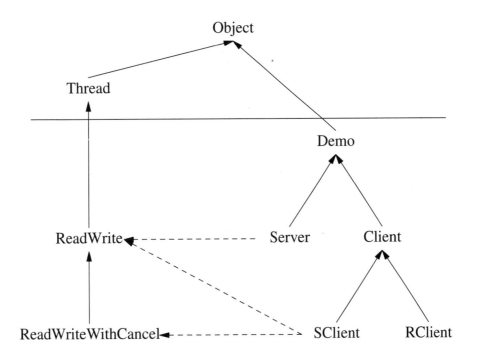

The above picture shows the class hierarchy for the Java classes in the examples. Classes above the line are standard Java classes. Classes below the line are classes in the examples. Dashed lines indicate non-inheritance dependencies. So, Server extends Demo but simply uses ReadWrite.

Demo provides a set of common constant definitions and our common initialization routine.

ReadWrite provides a thread instance that copies data from an InputStream and to an OutputStream. When it receives an end of data on the InputStream it sends a close_notify down the OutputStream.

ReadWriteWithCancel is a specialization of ReadWrite that notifies another thread when it receives an end of data.

Server is our server program. It creates an SSLServerSocket and then loops between accept() and ReadWrite.

Client provides common client functionality. In particular, it contains our generic connect function and the server certificate check.

SClient is our main client program. It connects to the server and uses ReadWrite and a ReadWriteWithCancel to copy data to and from the server.

RClient is a stub client that demonstrates session resumption using PureTLS.

```
1          import COM.claymoresystems.sslg.*;
2          import COM.claymoresystems.ptls.*;
3          import java.io.*;

4          /** This class simply copies anything from the in InputStream
5              to the out OutputStream
6          */
7          public class ReadWrite extends Thread {
8              protected SSLSocket s;
9              protected InputStream in;
10             protected OutputStream out;

11             /** Create a ReadWrite object

12                 @param s the socket we're using
13                 @param in the stream to read from
14                 @param out the stream to write to
15             */
16             public ReadWrite(SSLSocket s,InputStream in,OutputStream out){
17               this.s=s;
18               this.in=in;
19               this.out=out;
20             }

21             /** Copy data from in to out.*/
22             public void run() {
23               byte[] buf=new byte[1024];
24               int read;

25               try {
26                 while(true){
27                   // Check for thread termination
28                   if(isInterrupted())
29                     break;

30                   // Read data in
31                   read=in.read(buf);

32                   // Exit if there is no more data available
33                   if(read==-1)
34                     break;
```

```
35                    // Write the data out
36                    out.write(buf,0,read);
37                  }

38              } catch (IOException e){
39                // run() can't throw IOException
40                throw new InternalError(e.toString());
41              }

42              // Finalize
43              onEOD();
44            }

45            protected void onEOD(){
46              try {
47                s.sendClose();
48              } catch (IOException e){
49                ; // Ignore broken pipe
50              }
51            }
52          }
```

_____ ReadWrite.java

_____ ReadWriteWithCancel.java

```
1        import COM.claymoresystems.sslg.*;
2        import COM.claymoresystems.ptls.*;
3        import java.io.*;


4        /** This class is a simple extension of ReadWrite.

5            When it receives an end of data on its in socket it
6            sends an interrupt to the 'cancel' thread.
7        */
8        public class ReadWriteWithCancel extends ReadWrite {
9            protected ReadWrite cancel;

10           public ReadWriteWithCancel(SSLSocket s,InputStream in,OutputStream out,
11             ReadWrite cancel){
12             super(s,in,out);
13             this.cancel=cancel;
14           }

15           protected void onEOD(){
16             if(cancel.isAlive()){
17               cancel.interrupt();
```

```
18              try {
19                cancel.join();
20              } catch (InterruptedException e){
21                throw new InternalError(e.toString());
22              }
23            }
24          }
25        }
```
—— ReadWriteWithCancel.java

—— Demo.java

```
1        import COM.claymoresystems.sslg.*;
2        import COM.claymoresystems.ptls.*;

3        public class Demo {
4            public static final String host=  "localhost";
5            public static final int port=  4433;
6            public static final String root=  "root.pem";
7            public static final String random= "random.pem";

8            static SSLContext createSSLContext(String keyfile,String password){
9              SSLContext ctx=new SSLContext();

10             try {
11               ctx.loadRootCertificates(root);
12               ctx.loadEAYKeyFile(keyfile,password);
13               ctx.useRandomnessFile(random,password);
14             } catch (Exception e){
15               throw new InternalError(e.toString());
16             }

17             return ctx;
18           }
19         }
```
—— Demo.java

```
1      /** This class is a simple SSL echo server */
2      import COM.claymoresystems.sslg.*;
3      import COM.claymoresystems.ptls.*;
4      import java.io.*;

5      public class Server extends Demo {
6          protected static final String keyfile="server.pem";
7          protected static final String password="password";
8          protected static final String dh="dh1024.pem";
9          protected static boolean requireclientauth=true;

10         protected SSLSocket sock;
11         protected InputStream in;
12         protected OutputStream out;

13         public static void main(String []args)
14           throws IOException {
15           SSLContext ctx=createSSLContext(keyfile,password);

16           // Load our DH group
17           ctx.loadDHParams(dh);

18           SSLServerSocket listen=new SSLServerSocket(ctx,port);

19           while(true){
20             SSLSocket s=(SSLSocket)listen.accept();

21             // Process this connection in a new thread
22             ReadWrite rw=new ReadWrite(s,s.getInputStream(),
23               s.getOutputStream());
24             rw.start();
25           }
26         }
27      }
```

```
1      /* A simple SSL client.

2         It connects and then forwards data from/to the terminal
3         to/from the server
4      */
5      import COM.claymoresystems.sslg.*;
6      import COM.claymoresystems.ptls.*;
7      import java.io.*;
```

```
8        public class SClient extends Client {
9            public static void main(String []args)
10             throws IOException,InterruptedException {
11             SSLContext ctx=createSSLContext(keyfile,password);
12             SSLSocket s=connect(ctx,host,port);

13             // This thread reads from the console and writes to the server
14             ReadWrite c2s=new ReadWrite(s,System.in,s.getOutputStream());
15             c2s.start();

16             // This thread reads from the server and writes to the console
17             ReadWriteWithCancel s2c=new ReadWriteWithCancel(s,
18               s.getInputStream(),System.out,c2s);
19             s2c.start();
20             s2c.setPriority(Thread.MAX_PRIORITY);
21             s2c.join();
22         }
23     }
```

_____ SClient.java

_____ RClient.java

```
1        /* SSL client demonstrating session resumption */
2        import COM.claymoresystems.sslg.*;
3        import COM.claymoresystems.ptls.*;
4        import java.io.*;

5        public class RClient extends Client {
6            public static void main(String []args)
7              throws IOException {
8              SSLContext ctx=createSSLContext(keyfile,password);

9              /* Connect and close*/
10             SSLSocket s=connect(ctx,host,port);
11             s.close();

12             /* Now reconnect: resumption happens automatically*/
13             s=connect(ctx,host,port);
14             s.close();
15         }
16     }
```

_____ RClient.java

A.2   Chapter 9

This section contains complete versions of the example programs from Chapter 9: `pclient.c` and `mserver.c`. It also contains the section of mod_ssl responsible for doing cross-process session caching.

A.2.1 HTTPS Examples

The programs presented in Chapter 9 demonstrated various SSL idioms that are commonly used with HTTPS. They build on the same common framework as the programs from Chapter 8. Again, machine readable versions of these programs can also be downloaded from the author's Web site at `http://www.rtfm.com/sslbook/examples`.

`pclient` is a proxy-capable client. It uses the HTTP CONNECT method to connect to a proxy and then tunnel through to the server.

`mserver` is an SSL server capable of handling multiple clients simultaneously in different server process. Essentially, this is the same job that `Server` does in Java.

```
                                                                    pclient.c
1        /* A proxy-capable SSL client.

2           This is just like sclient but it only supports proxies
3        */
4        #include <string.h>
5        #include "common.h"
6        #include "client.h"
7        #include "read_write.h"

8        #define PROXY "localhost"
9        #define PROXY_PORT 8080
10       #define REAL_HOST "localhost"
11       #define REAL_PORT 4433

12       int writestr(sock,str)
13         int sock;
14         char *str;
15         {
16           int len=strlen(str);
17           int r,wrote=0;

18           while(len){
19             r=write(sock,str,len);
20             if(r<=0)
21               err_exit("Write error");
```

```
22              len-=r;
23              str+=r;
24              wrote+=r;
25            }

26          return (wrote);
27        }

28      int readline(sock,buf,len)
29        int sock;
30        char *buf;
31        int len;
32        {
33          int n,r;
34          char *ptr=buf;

35          for(n=0;n<len;n++){
36            r=read(sock,ptr,1);

37            if(r<=0)
38              err_exit("Read error");

39            if(*ptr=='\n'){
40              *ptr=0;

41              /* Strip off the CR if it's there */
42              if(buf[n-1]=='\r'){
43                buf[n-1]=0;
44                n--;
45              }

46              return(n);
47            }

48            *ptr++;
49          }

50          err_exit("Buffer too short");
51        }

52      int proxy_connect(){
53          struct hostent *hp;
54          struct sockaddr_in addr;
55          int sock;
56          BIO *sbio;
```

```
57          char buf[1024];
58          char *protocol, *response_code;

59          /* Connect to the proxy, not the host */
60          if(!(hp=gethostbyname(PROXY)))
61            berr_exit("Couldn't resolve host");
62          memset(&addr,0,sizeof(addr));
63          addr.sin_addr=*(struct in_addr*)hp->h_addr_list[0];
64          addr.sin_family=AF_INET;
65          addr.sin_port=htons(PROXY_PORT);

66          if((sock=socket(AF_INET,SOCK_STREAM,IPPROTO_TCP))<0)
67            err_exit("Couldn't create socket");
68          if(connect(sock,(struct sockaddr *)&addr,sizeof(addr))<0)
69            err_exit("Couldn't connect socket");

70          /* Now that we're connected, do the proxy request */
71          sprintf(buf,"CONNECT %s:%d HTTP/1.0\r\n\r\n",REAL_HOST,REAL_PORT);
72          writestr(sock,buf);

73          /* And read the response*/
74          if(readline(sock,buf,sizeof(buf))==0)
75            err_exit("Empty response from proxy");

76          if((protocol=strtok(buf," "))<0)
77            err_exit("Couldn't parse server response: getting protocol");
78          if(strncmp(protocol,"HTTP",4))
79            err_exit("Unrecognized protocol");
80          if((response_code=strtok(0," "))<0)
81            err_exit("Couldn't parse server response: getting response code");
82          if(strcmp(response_code,"200"))
83            err_exit("Received error from proxy server");

84          /* Look for the blank line that signals end of header*/
85          while(readline(sock,buf,sizeof(buf))>0) {
86              ;
87          }

88          return(sock);
89        }

90      int main(argc,argv)
91        int argc;
92        char **argv;
93        {
```

```
94              SSL_CTX *ctx;
95              SSL *ssl;
96              BIO *sbio;
97              int sock;

98              /* Build our SSL context*/
99              ctx=initialize_ctx(KEYFILE,PASSWORD);

100             /* Connect the TCP socket*/
101             sock=proxy_connect();

102             /* Connect the SSL socket */
103             ssl=SSL_new(ctx);
104             sbio=BIO_new_socket(sock,BIO_NOCLOSE);
105             SSL_set_bio(ssl,sbio,sbio);
106             if(SSL_connect(ssl)<=0)
107               berr_exit("SSL connect error");
108             check_cert_chain(ssl,HOST);

109             /* read and write */
110             read_write(ssl,sock);

111             destroy_ctx(ctx);
112           }
```

_____ pclient.c

_____ mserver.c

```
1       /* A multiprocess SSL server */
2       #include "common.h"
3       #include "server.h"
4       #include "echo.h"

5       int main(argc,argv)
6         int argc;
7        char **argv;
8         {
9          int sock,s;
10         BIO *sbio;
11         SSL_CTX *ctx;
12         SSL *ssl;
13         int r;
14         pid_t pid;

15             /* Build our SSL context*/
16             ctx=initialize_ctx(KEYFILE,PASSWORD);
```

```
17              load_dh_params(ctx,DHFILE);
18              generate_eph_rsa_key(ctx);

19              sock=tcp_listen();

20              while(1){
21                if((s=accept(sock,0,0))<0)
22                  err_exit("Problem accepting");

23                if(pid=fork()){
24                  close(s);
25                }
26                else {
27                  sbio=BIO_new_socket(s,BIO_NOCLOSE);
28                  ssl=SSL_new(ctx);
29                  SSL_set_bio(ssl,sbio,sbio);

30                  if((r=SSL_accept(ssl)<=0))
31                    berr_exit("SSL accept error");

32                  echo(ssl,s);
33                }
34              }
35              destroy_ctx(ctx);
36              exit(0);
37            }
```
_____ mserver.c

A.2.2 mod_ssl Session Caching

mod_ssl is a module for the popular Apache Web server. It uses OpenSSL to add SSL/TLS support to Apache. Apache is primarily used on UNIX systems and thus uses multiple processes to handle multiple clients at the same time. As we discussed in Chapter 9, we thus need special support in order to share sessions between these processes. The rest of this section examines this code.

OpenSSL provides its own session caching code that works within a single program. In order to accommodate application programs with more sophisticated needs, it provides a number of hooks which allow programs to provide their own session handling code. We first examine the hooks that mod_ssl installs.

Next, we consider the actual session caching code in mod_ssl. Actually, mod_ssl provides two kinds of session caching support. The first (more portable) version uses dbm to save the session ids to disk. The second (faster) version uses shared memory segments. mod_ssl's hooks call generic functions which switch-hit between the different implementations.

Hooks

```
                                                              ssl_engine_kernel.c
167      /*
168       *  This callback function is executed by OpenSSL whenever a new SSL_SESSION is
169       *  added to the internal OpenSSL session cache. We use this hook to spread the
170       *  SSL_SESSION also to the inter-process disk-cache to make share it with our
171       *  other Apache pre-forked server processes.
172       */
173      int ssl_callback_NewSessionCacheEntry(SSL *ssl, SSL_SESSION *pNew)
174      {
175          conn_rec *conn;
176          server_rec *s;
177          SSLSrvConfigRec *sc;
178          long t;
179          BOOL rc;

180          /*
181           * Get Apache context back through OpenSSL context
182           */
183          conn = (conn_rec *)SSL_get_app_data(ssl);
184          s    = conn->server;
185          sc   = mySrvConfig(s);

186          /*
187           * Set the timeout also for the internal OpenSSL cache, because this way
188           * our inter-process cache is consulted only when it's really necessary.
189           */
```

```
190            t = sc->nSessionCacheTimeout;
191            SSL_set_timeout(pNew, t);

192            /*
193             * Store the SSL_SESSION in the inter-process cache with the
194             * same expire time, so it expires automatically there, too.
195             */
196            t = (SSL_get_time(pNew) + sc->nSessionCacheTimeout);
197            rc = ssl_scache_store(s, pNew, t);

198            /*
199             * Log this cache operation
200             */
201            ssl_log(s, SSL_LOG_TRACE, "Inter-Process Session Cache: "
202                    "request=SET status=%s id=%s timeout=%ds (session caching)",
203                    rc == TRUE ? "OK" : "BAD",
204                    ssl_scache_id2sz(pNew->session_id, pNew->session_id_length),
205                    t-time(NULL));

206            /*
207             * return 0 which means to OpenSSL that the pNew is still
208             * valid and was not freed by us with SSL_SESSION_free().
209             */
210            return 0;
211        }


212     /*
213      * This callback function is executed by OpenSSL whenever a
214      * SSL_SESSION is looked up in the internal OpenSSL cache and it
215      * was not found. We use this to lookup the SSL_SESSION in the
216      * inter-process disk-cache where it was perhaps stored by one
217      * of our other Apache pre-forked server processes.
218      */
219     SSL_SESSION *ssl_callback_GetSessionCacheEntry(
220         SSL *ssl, unsigned char *id, int idlen, int *pCopy)
221     {
222         conn_rec *conn;
223         server_rec *s;
224         SSL_SESSION *pSession;

225         /*
226          * Get Apache context back through OpenSSL context
227          */
228         conn = (conn_rec *)SSL_get_app_data(ssl);
229         s    = conn->server;
```

```
230              /*
231               * Try to retrieve the SSL_SESSION from the inter-process cache
232               */
233              pSession = ssl_scache_retrieve(s, id, idlen);

234              /*
235               * Log this cache operation
236               */
237              if (pSession != NULL)
238                  ssl_log(s, SSL_LOG_TRACE, "Inter-Process Session Cache: "
239                          "request=GET status=FOUND id=%s (session reuse)",
240                          ssl_scache_id2sz(id, idlen));
241              else
242                  ssl_log(s, SSL_LOG_TRACE, "Inter-Process Session Cache: "
243                          "request=GET status=MISSED id=%s (session renewal)",
244                          ssl_scache_id2sz(id, idlen));

245              /*
246               * Return NULL or the retrieved SSL_SESSION. But indicate (by
247               * setting pCopy to 0) that the reference count on the
248               * SSL_SESSION should not be incremented by the SSL library,
249               * because we will no longer hold a reference to it ourself.
250               */
251              *pCopy = 0;
252              return pSession;
253          }

254      /*
255       *  This callback function is executed by OpenSSL whenever a
256       *  SSL_SESSION is removed from the the internal OpenSSL cache.
257       *  We use this to remove the SSL_SESSION in the inter-process
258       *  disk-cache, too.
259       */
260      void ssl_callback_DelSessionCacheEntry(
261          SSL_CTX *ctx, SSL_SESSION *pSession)
262      {
263          server_rec *s;

264          /*
265           * Get Apache context back through OpenSSL context
266           */
267          s = (server_rec *)SSL_CTX_get_app_data(ctx);
268          if (s == NULL) /* on server shutdown Apache is already gone */
269              return;
```

```
270              /*
271               * Remove the SSL_SESSION from the inter-process cache
272               */
273              ssl_scache_remove(s, pSession);

274              /*
275               * Log this cache operation
276               */
277              ssl_log(s, SSL_LOG_TRACE, "Inter-Process Session Cache: "
278                      "request=REM status=OK id=%s (session dead)",
279                      ssl_scache_id2sz(pSession->session_id,
280                      pSession->session_id_length));

281              return;
282          }
```

——— ssl_engine_kernel.c

OpenSSL provides for three session caching hooks: *session creation*, *session fetching*, and *session_deletion*. The mod_ssl hook functions are basically wrappers around the cache functions that we'll discuss in the next section. All they really do is call the cache functions and log the results.

Session creation

173–211 The session creation code is the only complicated hook. mod_ssl's interprocess cache is intended to be used only if the OpenSSL internal cache fails. Thus, if a session was created by the same process that it's being resumed in, we don't have to go to the interprocess cache to resume it. However, because entries have to be created in both caches, ssl_callback_NewSessionCacheEntry() is always called when a new session is created. It does three jobs: sets the timeout in the internal cache, creates an interprocess cache entry using ssl_scache_store(), and logs the results.

Session fetching

219–253 ssl_callback_GetSessionCacheEntry() is called whenever a client requests session resumption but OpenSSL can't find the session in the internal cache. It calls ssl_scache_retrieve() to get the cache entry and then logs the result.

Session deletion

260–282 ssl_callback_DelSessionCacheEntry() is called whenever a session becomes invalid, such as when we catch an alert or have a premature close. It simply calls ssl_scache_remove() to delete the session and then logs the result.

Generic Session Caching Code

```
                                                                    ssl_engine_scache.c
108    BOOL ssl_scache_store(server_rec *s, SSL_SESSION *pSession, int timeout)
109    {
110        SSLModConfigRec *mc = myModConfig();
111        ssl_scinfo_t SCI;
112        UCHAR buf[MAX_SESSION_DER];
113        UCHAR *b;
114        BOOL rc = FALSE;

115        /* add the key */
116        SCI.ucaKey = pSession->session_id;
117        SCI.nKey   = pSession->session_id_length;

118        /* transform the session into a data stream */
119        SCI.ucaData    = b = buf;
120        SCI.nData      = i2d_SSL_SESSION(pSession, &b);
121        SCI.tExpiresAt = timeout;

122        /* and store it... */
123        if (mc->nSessionCacheMode == SSL_SCMODE_DBM)
124            rc = ssl_scache_dbm_store(s, &SCI);
125        else if (mc->nSessionCacheMode == SSL_SCMODE_SHM)
126            rc = ssl_scache_shm_store(s, &SCI);

127    #ifdef SSL_VENDOR
128        ap_hook_use("ap::mod_ssl::vendor::scache_store",
129                    AP_HOOK_SIG3(void,ptr,ptr), AP_HOOK_ALL, s, &SCI);
130    #endif

131        /* allow the regular expiring to occur */
132        ssl_scache_expire(s, time(NULL));

133        return rc;
134    }

135    SSL_SESSION *ssl_scache_retrieve(server_rec *s, UCHAR *id, int idlen)
136    {
137        SSLModConfigRec *mc = myModConfig();
138        SSL_SESSION *pSession = NULL;
139        ssl_scinfo_t SCI;
140        time_t tNow;

141        /* determine current time */
```

```
142            tNow = time(NULL);

143            /* allow the regular expiring to occur */
144            ssl_scache_expire(s, tNow);

145            /* create cache query */
146            SCI.ucaKey    = id;
147            SCI.nKey      = idlen;
148            SCI.ucaData   = NULL;
149            SCI.nData     = 0;
150            SCI.tExpiresAt = 0;

151            /* perform cache query */
152            if (mc->nSessionCacheMode == SSL_SCMODE_DBM)
153                ssl_scache_dbm_retrieve(s, &SCI);
154            else if (mc->nSessionCacheMode == SSL_SCMODE_SHM)
155                ssl_scache_shm_retrieve(s, &SCI);

156    #ifdef SSL_VENDOR
157            ap_hook_use("ap::mod_ssl::vendor::scache_retrieve",
158                        AP_HOOK_SIG3(void,ptr,ptr), AP_HOOK_ALL, s, &SCI);
159    #endif

160            /* return immediately if not found */
161            if (SCI.ucaData == NULL)
162                return NULL;

163            /* check for expire time */
164            if (SCI.tExpiresAt <= tNow) {
165                if (mc->nSessionCacheMode == SSL_SCMODE_DBM)
166                    ssl_scache_dbm_remove(s, &SCI);
167                else if (mc->nSessionCacheMode == SSL_SCMODE_SHM)
168                    ssl_scache_shm_remove(s, &SCI);
169    #ifdef SSL_VENDOR
170                ap_hook_use("ap::mod_ssl::vendor::scache_remove",
171                            AP_HOOK_SIG3(void,ptr,ptr), AP_HOOK_ALL, s, &SCI);
172    #endif
173                return NULL;
174            }

175            /* extract result and return it */
176            pSession = d2i_SSL_SESSION(NULL, &SCI.ucaData, SCI.nData);
177            return pSession;
178        }
```

```
179         void ssl_scache_remove(server_rec *s, SSL_SESSION *pSession)
180         {
181             SSLModConfigRec *mc = myModConfig();
182             ssl_scinfo_t SCI;

183             /* create cache query */
184             SCI.ucaKey      = pSession->session_id;
185             SCI.nKey        = pSession->session_id_length;
186             SCI.ucaData     = NULL;
187             SCI.nData       = 0;
188             SCI.tExpiresAt = 0;

189             /* perform remove */
190             if (mc->nSessionCacheMode == SSL_SCMODE_DBM)
191                 ssl_scache_dbm_remove(s, &SCI);
192             else if (mc->nSessionCacheMode == SSL_SCMODE_SHM)
193                 ssl_scache_shm_remove(s, &SCI);

194     #ifdef SSL_VENDOR
195             ap_hook_use("ap::mod_ssl::vendor::scache_remove",
196                         AP_HOOK_SIG3(void,ptr,ptr), AP_HOOK_ALL, s, &SCI);
197     #endif

198             return;
199         }

200         void ssl_scache_expire(server_rec *s, time_t now)
201         {
202             SSLModConfigRec *mc = myModConfig();
203             SSLSrvConfigRec *sc = mySrvConfig(s);
204             static time_t last = 0;

205             /*
206              * make sure the expiration for still not-accessed session
207              * cache entries is done only from time to time
208              */
209             if (now < last+sc->nSessionCacheTimeout)
210                 return;
211             last = now;

212             /*
213              * Now perform the expiration
214              */
215             if (mc->nSessionCacheMode == SSL_SCMODE_DBM)
216                 ssl_scache_dbm_expire(s, now);
```

```
217              else if (mc->nSessionCacheMode == SSL_SCMODE_SHM)
218                  ssl_scache_shm_expire(s, now);

219              return;
220          }
```
                                                                    _ ssl_engine_scache.c

The mod_ssl session caching code is divided between the generic code and the underlying implementations of interprocess sharing. In particular, the generic code arranges for expiration to happen at the appropriate times and makes sure that expired sessions can't be resumed. Other than that, the heavy lifting is all done by the underlying interprocess sharing code.

Session storage

108–134 ssl_scache_store() arranges to serialize the session object. It then calls the appropriate session caching method to actually share the session. Finally, it calls the cache expiration function.

Session retrieval

135–178 ssl_scache_retrieve() first calls the appropriate session caching method to load the session object. If the object is found, it then checks to see if it's expired. If the session is expired, it automatically removes it from the cache. Otherwise, it deserializes the object and returns it.

Session deletion

179–199 ssl_scache_remove() merely calls the underlying cache methods to remove the cache entry.

Cache expiry

200–245 ssl_scache_expire() is never called directly by the mod_ssl session caching hooks. However, it's necessary that we occasionally go through the session cache and delete old entries, otherwise the session cache would grow without bound. Instead, it's automatically called whenever a new session object is created. mod_ssl allows the administrator to set expiries to happen after a certain interval, so most calls to ssl_scache_expire() are within that interval and return at line 210. Otherwise, ssl_scache_expire() calls the appropriate expiration method.

DBM Session Caching

```
368        BOOL ssl_scache_dbm_store(server_rec *s, ssl_scinfo_t *SCI)
369        {
370            SSLModConfigRec *mc = myModConfig();
371            DBM *dbm;
372            datum dbmkey;
373            datum dbmval;

374            /* be careful: do not try to store too much bytes in a DBM file! */
375        #ifdef SSL_USE_SDBM
376            if ((SCI->nKey + SCI->nData) >= PAIRMAX)
377                return FALSE;
378        #else
379            if ((SCI->nKey + SCI->nData) >= 950 /* at least less than approx. 1KB */)
380                return FALSE;
381        #endif

382            /* create DBM key */
383            dbmkey.dptr  = (char *)(SCI->ucaKey);
384            dbmkey.dsize = SCI->nKey;

385            /* create DBM value */
386            dbmval.dsize = sizeof(time_t) + SCI->nData;
387            dbmval.dptr  = (char *)malloc(dbmval.dsize);
388            if (dbmval.dptr == NULL)
389                return FALSE;
390            memcpy((char *)dbmval.dptr, &SCI->tExpiresAt, sizeof(time_t));
391            memcpy((char *)dbmval.dptr+sizeof(time_t), SCI->ucaData, SCI->nData);

392            /* and store it to the DBM file */
393            ssl_mutex_on(s);
394            if ((dbm = ssl_dbm_open(mc->szSessionCacheDataFile,
395                                    O_RDWR, SSL_DBM_FILE_MODE)) == NULL) {
396                ssl_log(s, SSL_LOG_ERROR|SSL_ADD_ERRNO,
397                        "Cannot open SSLSessionCache DBM file '%s' for writing (store)",
398                        mc->szSessionCacheDataFile);
399                ssl_mutex_off(s);
400                free(dbmval.dptr);
401                return FALSE;
402            }
403            if (ssl_dbm_store(dbm, dbmkey, dbmval, DBM_INSERT) < 0) {
404                ssl_log(s, SSL_LOG_ERROR|SSL_ADD_ERRNO,
405                        "Cannot store SSL session to DBM file '%s'",
```

```
406                         mc->szSessionCacheDataFile);
407             ssl_dbm_close(dbm);
408             ssl_mutex_off(s);
409             free(dbmval.dptr);
410             return FALSE;
411         }
412         ssl_dbm_close(dbm);
413         ssl_mutex_off(s);

414         /* free temporary buffers */
415         free(dbmval.dptr);

416         return TRUE;
417     }

418     void ssl_scache_dbm_retrieve(server_rec *s, ssl_scinfo_t *SCI)
419     {
420         SSLModConfigRec *mc = myModConfig();
421         DBM *dbm;
422         datum dbmkey;
423         datum dbmval;

424         /* initialize result */
425         SCI->ucaData    = NULL;
426         SCI->nData      = 0;
427         SCI->tExpiresAt = 0;

428         /* create DBM key and values */
429         dbmkey.dptr  = (char *)(SCI->ucaKey);
430         dbmkey.dsize = SCI->nKey;

431         /* and fetch it from the DBM file */
432         ssl_mutex_on(s);
433         if ((dbm = ssl_dbm_open(mc->szSessionCacheDataFile,
434                             O_RDONLY, SSL_DBM_FILE_MODE)) == NULL) {
435             ssl_log(s, SSL_LOG_ERROR|SSL_ADD_ERRNO,
436                     "Cannot open SSLSessionCache DBM file '%s' for reading (fetch)",
437                     mc->szSessionCacheDataFile);
438             ssl_mutex_off(s);
439             return;
440         }
441         dbmval = ssl_dbm_fetch(dbm, dbmkey);
442         ssl_dbm_close(dbm);
443         ssl_mutex_off(s);
```

```
444            /* immediately return if not found */
445            if (dbmval.dptr == NULL || dbmval.dsize <= sizeof(time_t))
446                return;

447            /* copy over the information to the SCI */
448            SCI->nData   = dbmval.dsize-sizeof(time_t);
449            SCI->ucaData = (UCHAR *)malloc(SCI->nData);
450            if (SCI->ucaData == NULL) {
451                SCI->nData = 0;
452                return;
453            }
454            memcpy(SCI->ucaData, (char *)dbmval.dptr+sizeof(time_t), SCI->nData);
455            memcpy(&SCI->tExpiresAt, dbmval.dptr, sizeof(time_t));

456            return;
457        }

458        void ssl_scache_dbm_remove(server_rec *s, ssl_scinfo_t *SCI)
459        {
460            SSLModConfigRec *mc = myModConfig();
461            DBM *dbm;
462            datum dbmkey;

463            /* create DBM key and values */
464            dbmkey.dptr  = (char *)(SCI->ucaKey);
465            dbmkey.dsize = SCI->nKey;

466            /* and delete it from the DBM file */
467            ssl_mutex_on(s);
468            if ((dbm = ssl_dbm_open(mc->szSessionCacheDataFile,
469                                    O_RDWR, SSL_DBM_FILE_MODE)) == NULL) {
470                ssl_log(s, SSL_LOG_ERROR|SSL_ADD_ERRNO,
471                        "Cannot open SSLSessionCache DBM file '%s' for writing (delete)",
472                        mc->szSessionCacheDataFile);
473                ssl_mutex_off(s);
474                return;
475            }
476            ssl_dbm_delete(dbm, dbmkey);
477            ssl_dbm_close(dbm);
478            ssl_mutex_off(s);

479            return;
480        }

481        void ssl_scache_dbm_expire(server_rec *s, time_t tNow)
```

```
482        {
483            SSLModConfigRec *mc = myModConfig();
484            DBM *dbm;
485            datum dbmkey;
486            datum dbmval;
487            pool *p;
488            time_t tExpiresAt;
489            int nElements = 0;
490            int nDeleted = 0;
491            int bDelete;
492            datum *keylist;
493            int keyidx;
494            int i;

495            /*
496             * Here we have to be very carefully: Not all DBM libraries are
497             * smart enough to allow one to iterate over the elements and at the
498             * same time delete expired ones. Some of them get totally crazy
499             * while others have no problems. So we have to do it the slower but
500             * more safe way: we first iterate over all elements and remember
501             * those which have to be expired. Then in a second pass we delete
502             * all those expired elements. Additionally we reopen the DBM file
503             * to be really safe in state.
504             */

505        #define KEYMAX 1024

506            ssl_mutex_on(s);
507            for (;;) {
508                /* allocate the key array in a memory sub pool */
509                if ((p = ap_make_sub_pool(NULL)) == NULL)
510                    break;
511                if ((keylist = ap_palloc(p, sizeof(dbmkey)*KEYMAX)) == NULL) {
512                    ap_destroy_pool(p);
513                    break;
514                }

515                /* pass 1: scan DBM database */
516                keyidx = 0;
517                if ((dbm = ssl_dbm_open(mc->szSessionCacheDataFile,
518                                        O_RDWR, SSL_DBM_FILE_MODE)) == NULL) {
519                    ssl_log(s, SSL_LOG_ERROR|SSL_ADD_ERRNO,
520                            "Cannot open SSLSessionCache DBM file '%s' for scanning",
521                            mc->szSessionCacheDataFile);
522                    ap_destroy_pool(p);
```

```
523                     break;
524                 }
525             dbmkey = ssl_dbm_firstkey(dbm);
526             while (dbmkey.dptr != NULL) {
527                 nElements++;
528                 bDelete = FALSE;
529                 dbmval = ssl_dbm_fetch(dbm, dbmkey);
530                 if (dbmval.dsize <= sizeof(time_t) || dbmval.dptr == NULL)
531                     bDelete = TRUE;
532                 else {
533                     memcpy(&tExpiresAt, dbmval.dptr, sizeof(time_t));
534                     if (tExpiresAt <= tNow)
535                         bDelete = TRUE;
536                 }
537                 if (bDelete) {
538                     if ((keylist[keyidx].dptr = ap_palloc(p, dbmkey.dsize)) != NULL) {
539                         memcpy(keylist[keyidx].dptr, dbmkey.dptr, dbmkey.dsize);
540                         keylist[keyidx].dsize = dbmkey.dsize;
541                         keyidx++;
542                         if (keyidx == KEYMAX)
543                             break;
544                     }
545                 }
546                 dbmkey = ssl_dbm_nextkey(dbm);
547             }
548             ssl_dbm_close(dbm);

549             /* pass 2: delete expired elements */
550             if ((dbm = ssl_dbm_open(mc->szSessionCacheDataFile,
551                                     O_RDWR, SSL_DBM_FILE_MODE)) == NULL) {
552                 ssl_log(s, SSL_LOG_ERROR|SSL_ADD_ERRNO,
553                         "Cannot re-open SSLSessionCache DBM file '%s' for expiring",
554                         mc->szSessionCacheDataFile);
555                 ap_destroy_pool(p);
556                 break;
557             }
558             for (i = 0; i < keyidx; i++) {
559                 ssl_dbm_delete(dbm, keylist[i]);
560                 nDeleted++;
561             }
562             ssl_dbm_close(dbm);

563             /* destroy temporary pool */
564             ap_destroy_pool(p);
```

```
565              if (keyidx < KEYMAX)
566                  break;
567          }
568          ssl_mutex_off(s);

569          ssl_log(s, SSL_LOG_TRACE, "Inter-Process Session Cache (DBM) Expiry: "
570                  "old: %d, new: %d, removed: %d", nElements, nElements-nDeleted, nDeleted);
571          return;
572      }
```
                                                                        ssl_engine_scache.c

DBM is a standard UNIX package that offers a simple key-value database. It allows the creation of arbitrary pairs of lookup keys and data values in a one-to-one association. Essentially, it's a large, self-resizing hash table. However, the data is stored in disk files so it can be shared between processes.

DBM maintains an index of all the keys for fast lookups. Unfortunately, DBM was not designed for concurrent access. Therefore, there's no way for it to detect that the database has been updated and reload the index. The only time the index is reloaded is when the database is opened. Similarly, portions of the database may be cached and get written out only when it is closed. Thus, for multiple processes to use the database, they must open and close it each time they want to access some data. Most of the complication in the mod_ssl DBM code is concerned with arranging this.

Session creation

368–417 The first job is to create the DBM keys and values. The key is simply the session ID. The value contains the time and the serialized session object. Because the value must be a single byte string, they must be packed together, which is done in lines 385-391. Once the key and value are ready to store, the database must be locked so that no other process can write to it. mod_ssl has an interprocess mutex that it uses for this purpose (line 393). Once the database is locked, mod_ssl can open the database and then store our key-value pair. When this is all finished, mod_ssl closes the database and releases the lock.

Session retrieval

418–457 Session retrieval is just session storage in reverse. Note that mod_ssl makes no distinction between mutexes for reading and writing. It's generally safe for two processes to read the same DBM file at the same time. In an active system with a lot more session resumption than session creation, it would pay to have a read lock and a write lock. Thus, multiple readers would be able to read the database concurrently rather than blocking each other. Once the session is fetched, the expiry time and the session object must be unpacked and returned to the caller (lines 448–453).

Session removal

458–480 `ssl_scache_dbm_remove()` follows a now familiar pattern. The database is locked and then the deletion is performed. Then the database is unlocked.

Cache expiry

481–572 Session deletion is tricky. In theory, we'd like to do a linear scan of the database and delete the expired elements as we go. Unfortunately, many old DBM implementations would corrupt the database if you tried to scan and delete at the same time. Thus, expiration is done in two passes. In the first pass (lines 515–548) the database is scanned and a list of all the sessions to be expired is created. In the second pass (lines 549–567) each entry on the list is deleted. This is inefficient, and you'd like not to do it very often.

Shared Memory Session Caching

DBM session caching is very slow. Every cache store or fetch requires us to lock the database, open two files (the index and data files), read data from the disk, close the files, and unlock the database. This adds a very substantial amount of overhead to the process. Thus, mod_ssl has a faster approach based on shared memory. The general idea is to create a key-value database that stores its data in memory rather than on disk. Then this memory can be located in a shared memory segment so that multiple processes can access it.

_____ ssl_session_cache.c

```
752        BOOL ssl_scache_shm_store(server_rec *s, ssl_scinfo_t *SCI)
753        {
754            SSLModConfigRec *mc = myModConfig();
755            void *vp;

756            ssl_mutex_on(s);
757            if (table_insert_kd(mc->tSessionCacheDataTable,
758                            SCI->ucaKey, SCI->nKey,
759                            NULL, sizeof(time_t)+SCI->nData,
760                            NULL, &vp, 1) != TABLE_ERROR_NONE) {
761                ssl_mutex_off(s);
762                return FALSE;
763            }
764            memcpy(vp, &SCI->tExpiresAt, sizeof(time_t));
765            memcpy((char *)vp+sizeof(time_t), SCI->ucaData, SCI->nData);
766            ssl_mutex_off(s);
767            return TRUE;
768        }

769        void ssl_scache_shm_retrieve(server_rec *s, ssl_scinfo_t *SCI)
770        {
771            SSLModConfigRec *mc = myModConfig();
```

```
772              void *vp;
773              int n;

774              /* initialize result */
775              SCI->ucaData    = NULL;
776              SCI->nData      = 0;
777              SCI->tExpiresAt = 0;

778              /* lookup key in table */
779              ssl_mutex_on(s);
780              if (table_retrieve(mc->tSessionCacheDataTable,
781                                 SCI->ucaKey, SCI->nKey,
782                                 &vp, &n) != TABLE_ERROR_NONE) {
783                  ssl_mutex_off(s);
784                  return;
785              }

786              /* copy over the information to the SCI */
787              SCI->nData   = n-sizeof(time_t);
788              SCI->ucaData = (UCHAR *)malloc(SCI->nData);
789              if (SCI->ucaData == NULL) {
790                  SCI->nData = 0;
791                  ssl_mutex_off(s);
792                  return;
793              }
794              memcpy(&SCI->tExpiresAt, vp, sizeof(time_t));
795              memcpy(SCI->ucaData, (char *)vp+sizeof(time_t), SCI->nData);
796              ssl_mutex_off(s);

797              return;
798          }

799      void ssl_scache_shm_remove(server_rec *s, ssl_scinfo_t *SCI)
800      {
801          SSLModConfigRec *mc = myModConfig();

802          /* remove value under key in table */
803          ssl_mutex_on(s);
804          table_delete(mc->tSessionCacheDataTable,
805                       SCI->ucaKey, SCI->nKey, NULL, NULL);
806          ssl_mutex_off(s);
807          return;
808      }

809      void ssl_scache_shm_expire(server_rec *s, time_t tNow)
```

```
810          {
811              SSLModConfigRec *mc = myModConfig();
812              table_linear_t iterator;
813              time_t tExpiresAt;
814              void *vpKey;
815              void *vpKeyThis;
816              void *vpData;
817              int nKey;
818              int nKeyThis;
819              int nData;
820              int nElements = 0;
821              int nDeleted = 0;
822              int bDelete;
823              int rc;

824              ssl_mutex_on(s);
825              if (table_first_r(mc->tSessionCacheDataTable, &iterator,
826                              &vpKey, &nKey, &vpData, &nData) == TABLE_ERROR_NONE) {
827                  do {
828                      bDelete = FALSE;
829                      nElements++;
830                      if (nData < sizeof(time_t) || vpData == NULL)
831                          bDelete = TRUE;
832                      else {
833                          memcpy(&tExpiresAt, vpData, sizeof(time_t));
834                          if (tExpiresAt <= tNow)
835                              bDelete = TRUE;
836                      }
837                      vpKeyThis = vpKey;
838                      nKeyThis  = nKey;
839                      rc = table_next_r(mc->tSessionCacheDataTable, &iterator,
840                                      &vpKey, &nKey, &vpData, &nData);
841                      if (bDelete) {
842                          table_delete(mc->tSessionCacheDataTable,
843                                      vpKeyThis, nKeyThis, NULL, NULL);
844                          nDeleted++;
845                      }
846                  } while (rc == TABLE_ERROR_NONE);
847              }
848              ssl_mutex_off(s);
849              ssl_log(s, SSL_LOG_TRACE, "Inter-Process Session Cache (SHM) Expiry: "
850                      "old: %d, new: %d, removed: %d", nElements, nElements-nDeleted, nDeleted);
851              return;
852          }
```

The shared memory session caching code is extremely similar to the DBM-based code. The primary difference from a programming perspective is that it uses a hash table (`table_insert_kd()` and friends) instead of DBM. However, because DBM's API is essentially a hash table, the primary difference is which functions to call.

Session storage

752–769 As with the DBM code, we first lock the cache with `ssl_mutex_on()` and then store the data. The primary difference here is that we don't have to actually open the database, as we did with DBM. Clearly, this is a significant performance improvement.

Session retrival

769–898 The same comments apply here.

Session removal

799–808 Same here.

Cache expiry

809–852 Cache expiry is substantially simpler than with DBM. Because the hash table implementation correctly handles deletions in the middle of a scan, the expiry can be accomplished in one pass. Otherwise, the code is fairly similar to the DBM code.

Appendix B

SSLv2

B.1   Introduction

The focus of this book has been on SSLv3 and TLS. However, most SSLv3 implementations are also SSLv2 implementations and some significant Web sites still support only SSLv2. This appendix thus provides an introduction to SSLv2, described in [Hickman1995]. We start by providing an overview of how SSLv2 works. However, we won't be discussing SSLv2 at anywhere near the level of detail we used for SSLv3. Rather, we'll stay at more or less the same level of abstraction we used for discussing IPSEC, S-HTTP, and S/MIME.

By the time that SSLv3 was designed, Netscape employed security professionals including the noted cryptographer Taher Elgamal. SSLv3 itself was designed with the assistance of a security consultant (Paul Kocher). However, at the time that SSLv2 was designed, Netscape (then Mosaic Communications) didn't employ any security experts. In the absence of real expertise, Kipp Hickman, an employee without notable security credentials or experience, was tasked to do the design. Unsurprisingly then, SSLv2 contained a number of security flaws which ultimately led to the design of SSLv3.

Our next order of business will be to explore the ways in which SSLv2 was flawed. First, SSLv2 is missing several features. Second, it has a number of security flaws. Though none of these is crippling for simple credit card submission, they are nevertheless quite serious. We'll discuss these problems. We've seen how they were fixed in SSLv3, but it's instructive to look at how Microsoft fixed them in *Private Communications Technology* (PCT). Finally, we'll briefly discuss what happened to SSLv1.

B.2   SSLv2 Overview

SSLv2 uses the same model as SSLv3. There is a handshake phase to establish keys and negotiate algorithms. After the handshake is completed, the keys and algorithms are used to encrypt the application data traffic. In fact, many of the messages in the SSLv2 handshake have similar names and field values to the SSLv3 handshake. (No doubt by the intent of the SSLv3 designers.) Figure B.1 shows a sample SSLv2 handshake.

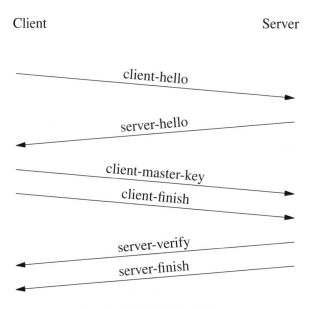

Client Server

client-hello

server-hello

client-master-key

client-finish

server-verify

server-finish

Figure B.1 SSLv2 handshake

CLIENT-HELLO

In the CLIENT-HELLO message, the client sends a list of the ciphers it supports, a random CHALLENGE, and possibly a session ID. The CHALLENGE plays much the same role as the random value in SSLv3: it provides freshness for the session keys and allows the client to detect replay attacks. As with SSLv3, the session ID is used for session resumption.

SERVER-HELLO

In the SERVER-HELLO message, the server provides its certificate as well as the subset of the client's ciphers that it supports. Unlike SSLv3, the client ultimately chooses which cipher to use. However, the server can delete any ciphers that it doesn't support. The server also provides a CONNECTION-ID which serves much the same purpose as the server random value in SSLv3.

CLIENT-MASTER-KEY

The CLIENT-MASTER-KEY provides the master key encrypted under the server's public key. In order to handle exportable ciphers, the master key is split into an encrypted section and a clear section. Thus, to do 40-bit RC4, you would encrypt 40 bits and have 88 bits in the clear. Digest functions are then used to convert the master key to encryption and MAC keys. This message also provides the IV if necessary for the cipher. The IV is transmitted in the clear.

CLIENT-FINISH

The CLIENT-FINISH message is the first encrypted message. It contains the CONNEC-TION-ID and proves that the client knows the encryption keys.

SERVER-VERIFY

The SERVER-VERIFY message contains the encrypted challenge. This proves that the server knows the encryption keys.

SERVER-FINISH

The SERVER-FINISH message contains the session ID. The client will use that if it wishes to resume the session.

Session Resumption

SSLv2 also has a session resumption mode. If the server recognizes the client's session ID, it sets a flag in its SERVER-HELLO. When resuming a session, the client simply omits the CLIENT-MASTER-KEY message and the client and server reuse the master key.

Client Authentication

SSLv2's client authentication is fairly simple. The server has an additional message called REQUEST-CERTIFICATE which it uses to request client authentication. The message contains a challenge that is used to generate the data signed by the client. The client responds with a CLIENT-CERTIFICATE message, which contains the client's certificate and a signature over the challenge, the client's encryption key, and the server's encryption key.

Data Transmission

SSLv2 data transmission is analogous to SSLv3 data transmission, although the details are different. The data are broken up into a series of records. Each record is invidually MACed and encrypted. The MAC is an ad hoc function rather than HMAC, but it doesn't have any known serious weaknesses.

B.3   Missing Features

SSLv2 was missing a number of features that seemed desirable. None of these features are absolutely necessary, but their absence was inconvenient and they were added when SSLv3 was designed.

Certificate Chaining

SSLv2 permitted the client and server to send only one certificate each. Thus, this certificate had to be directly signed by the root. As we discussed in Chapter 5, it's quite convenient to have one root CA that signs a number of CAs who themselves certify users. This is not possible in SSLv2. SSLv3 allows clients and servers to have arbitrary-length certificate chains.

Same RSA Key for Export and Domestic Clients

At the time that SSLv2 was designed, U.S. export regulations forbade the use of RSA keys longer than 512 for key exchange in exportable software. However, 1024- and 512-bit keys were already standard for moderate- to high-security applications. Thus, if you wanted your server to handle strong (128-bit) ciphers, you clearly wanted to have a 1024-bit RSA key. However, because that key would also be used for key exchange, you couldn't serve export clients with the same key. Rather, your server would need two keys.

However, when Netscape first delivered SSLv2 in Navigator, they omitted the test for long keys from the export client. The *exportable* Navigator supported 1024-bit RSA. Nevertheless, they somehow got export approval. It's not clear (at least to the author) whether NSA didn't know about this problem when they reviewed Navigator, or if they just ignored it. In any case, this set a precedent and several other vendors got similar approval.

However, when SSLv3 was designed, there were indications that the NSA would be less forgiving. Thus, SSLv3 complied with the regulations by using the long RSA key to sign a 512-bit ephemeral RSA key. With this trick, it was possible both to have only one key and to comply with regulations.

B.4   Security Problems

Export Message Authentication

SSLv2 uses the same keys for message authentication as for encryption. Thus, if we're using RC4 in export mode, the encryption and MAC keys are based on only 40 bits of secret data and have 40 bits of entropy as well. Thus, in export mode, it's no more difficult to mount an integrity attack than to mount a confidentiality attack. The attacker simply exhaustively searches all 40 bits of secret master key. Exhaustively searching a 40-bit keyspace is within the means of fairly modest attackers.

By contrast, SSLv3 uses a large master key and does the entropy reduction in the key derivation stage. You can exhaustively search the encryption keys, but this doesn't allow you to work backwards to the master secret. Thus, the MAC keys are strong, even if encryption is weak—or nonexistent. In SSLv3, even if weak ciphers are used, mounting an integrity attack is intractable.

Weak MACs

Although no really good attacks are known on SSLv2's MAC, it certainly isn't as strong as HMAC. In particular, it relies solely on MD5. There's no way to use SHA-1. There's been some recent concern about the strength of MD5 [Dobbertin1996] and so this is rather undesirable, though not fatal. In this instance, at least, the designers can be forgiven somewhat. The attacks on MD5 and the development of HMAC happened after SSLv2 was published. However, not having the ability to negotiate to SHA is unnecessarily inflexible in any case.

Downgrade

SSLv2 doesn't have any protection for the handshake. Thus, it's possible for an attacker to force the parties to negotiate to a weak cipher even if they both support a stronger cipher. SSLv3 solves this problem with the Finished messages, which contain a message digest over the entire handshake.

Truncation Attacks

SSLv2 simply uses the TCP connection close to indicate end of data. This means that it's susceptible to truncation attacks. The attacker can simply forge TCP FINs and the recipient can't tell that it's not a legitimate end of data. SSLv3 fixes this problem by having an explicit closure alert.

Client Authentication Transfer

The PCT specification [Benaloh1995] describes a subtle but serious attack on SSLv2 client authentication. Consider the problem of securing a Web site where part of the content can be accessed by a normal SSL connection but part requires client authentication. Because SSLv2 message authentication is so weak when using export ciphers, the server will want to require a strong cipher for the protected sections of the Web site. Otherwise, the attacker can just crack the connection and pose as the client.

Imagine that we have a situation in which the client has already connected to the server using an export cipher. The attacker has cracked the connection by exhaustively searching the 40-bit keyspace and so knows the master key and the read/write keys. Eventually, the client is likely to reconnect to the server to make another request. The attack then proceeds as shown in Figure B.2.

The attacker intercepts the TCP connection between client and server and reads the client's CLIENT-HELLO. The attacker then opens up its own connection to the server, offering a 128-bit cipher but using the client's challenge. It sends its own SERVER-HELLO to the client agreeing to resume the connection. The attacker then sends his own CLIENT-MASTER-KEY message to the server using the same master key as in the original connection, but this time with the entire key encrypted under the server's RSA key. At this point, the client-attacker and server-attacker master keys are both the same as the master key in the original connection because the client has resumed that connection.

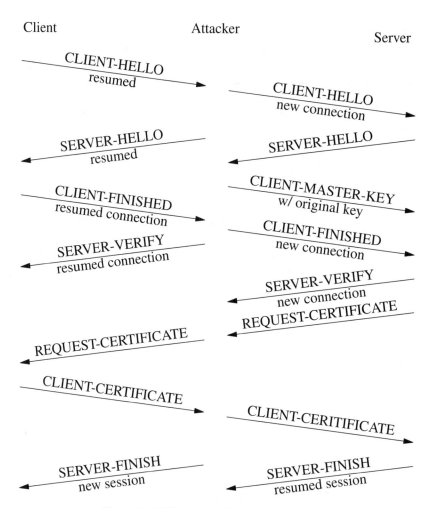

Figure B.2 SSLv2 authentication transfer attack

The server asks for client authentication using a REQUEST-CERTIFICATE message which the attacker forwards to the client. The client responds with a CLIENT-CERTIFICATE message. Recall that the data that is signed consists of the client write key, the server write key, and the challenge. All of these are the same in the client-attacker connection and the attacker-server connection. Thus, the attacker can simply forward the CLIENT-CERTIFICATE message to the server and the attacker has what appears to the server to be a client-authenticated connection with strong encryption—except that actually it's a connection to the attacker. This attack is impossible in SSLv3 and TLS because of the separation of authentication keys from encryption keys.

B.5   PCT

Microsoft's response to the security errors in SSLv2 was to design their own protocol, a variant of SSLv2 called *Private Communications Technology* (PCT). PCT fixed the most severe security flaws in SSLv2. In particular, it fixed the downgrade and client authentication vulnerabilities. It also simplified the handshake somewhat, thus reducing the number of round trips that were required in order to establish a connection. Finally, it incorporated more flexible cipher suite selection.

Verify Prelude

SSLv3 used the Finished messages to prevent a downgrade attack by an active attacker. PCT uses a verify-prelude field in the CLIENT-MASTER-KEY message to provide the same protection. The verify-prelude contains a MAC of the client and server hello messages. Thus, the server can detect if the connection has been downgraded. Because the verify-prelude is sent with the key exchange, the server can immediately reject the connection if any tampering has occurred—unlike with SSLv3, where the entire connection has to be completed before the attack can be detected.

Strengthened Message Integrity

PCT made message authentication orthogonal to security. As with SSLv3, a long master key was transmitted and this key was used to generate the MAC and encryption keys independently. Even if a 40-bit encryption key was being used, the MAC key was full strength. Thus, even if the encryption keys were broken, message integrity would be intact.

Improved Client Authentication

The authentication transfer attack on SSLv2 depended on the CLIENT-CERTIFICATE message being the same no matter what cipher suite was used. PCT fixed this attack by having the client's certificate sign the verify-prelude field. Because this field depends on the cipher suite, the transfer attack no longer works. Moreover, the transfer attack depends on being able to recover the master secret for a connection using a 40-bit cipher suite. This is no longer possible in PCT because the master key is always long even if export encryption is used.

Orthogonal Cipher Suite Negotiation

Whereas SSLv2, SSLv3, and TLS all have a single cipher suite value which defines all the cryptographic parameters in use, PCT specifies the cipher, hash, certificate, and key exchange algorithms separately. Moreover, the cipher specifications are themselves orthogonal so that an encryption algorithm can be specified independently of the key length. The advantage of this approach is that it's not necessary to register a cipher suite for every desired combination of algorithms.

The argument used by the SSLv3 designers against this approach was that specifying algorithms orthogonally allowed inappropriate or insecure combinations to be constructed. I don't find this argument that compelling. Even when cipher suites are monolithic, it's possible to create inappropriate combinations (4096-bit RSA keys with DES, for instance). By contrast, we've seen in previous chapters that the failure to specify cipher suites orthogonally in SSLv3 led to some useful combinations not being registered (e.g., DH/DSS with RC4).

Backward Compatibility

As with SSLv3, it was desirable that PCT be backward-compatible with SSLv2. Thus, the PCT CLIENT-HELLO had to be representable as an SSLv2 CLIENT-HELLO. However, because Microsoft didn't have control of the version number space, they couldn't just use version 3 as Netscape did. Instead, PCT was forced to use a hack: the designers specified a new cipher suite that indicated that the client supported PCT. Thus, an SSLv2 server that saw this cipher suite wouldn't recognize it and would continue with SSLv2, but a PCT server would be able to do the PCT handshake.

The second backward-compatibility problem was support for PCT's orthogonal algorithm selection. The approach used by the designers was to represent the algorithms all as SSLv2 cipher suites and then to use bit masks to distinguish the various classes. Figure B.3 shows a dump of part of a PCT-compatible CLIENT-HELLO.

This CLIENT-HELLO is actually compatible with SSLv2, PCT, and SSLv3/TLS. Thus SSLv3/TLS cipher suites (represented as SSLv2 cipher suites) also appear in this message. Line 1 indicates that the client speaks PCT. Lines 2–3 indicate that it supports both X.509 certificate chains as well as bare X.509 certificates. Lines 4–5 indicate that both MD5 and SHA are supported. Line 6 indicates support for RSA key exchange.

Pay special attention to lines 10–11 and lines 21–22. The PCT specifications for the encryption and MAC algorithms are four bytes long and so must be represented as two SSLv2 cipher suites, with the first half appearing in one and the second in the next. Thus lines 10–11 specify 128-bit RC4 with a 128-bit MAC. This hack is required because the orthogonal PCT cipher suites can't fit into the 3-byte space provided by SSLv2.

Bottom Line

At the time that PCT was introduced, Netscape was by far the dominant Web browser and so SSLv3 became far more important than PCT. Thus, no major vendor other than Microsoft implemented PCT. Although Microsoft Internet Explorer eventually became the dominant Web browser, the defeat of Netscape happened far too late to save PCT. Although it's arguable that PCT embodies more elegant design choices than SSLv3/TLS, it doesn't contain any features sufficiently important to justify using it in face of the far wider deployment of SSLv3.

1	8f 80 01	PCT_SSL_COMPAT | PCT_VERSION_1
2	80 00 03	PCT_SSL_CERT_TYPE | PCT1_CERT_X509_CHAIN
3	80 00 01	PCT_SSL_CERT_TYPE | PCT1_CERT_X509
4	81 00 01	PCT_SSL_HASH_TYPE | PCT1_HASH_MD5
5	81 00 03	PCT_SSL_HASH_TYPE | PCT1_HASH_SHA
6	82 00 01	PCT_SSL_EXCH_TYPE | PCT1_EXCH_RSA_PKCS1
7	00 00 04	TLS_RSA_WITH_RC4_128_MD5
8	00 00 05	TLS_RSA_WITH_RC4_128_SHA
9	00 00 0a	TLS_RSA_WITH_3DES_EDE_CBC_SHA
10	83 00 04	PCT_SSL_CIPHER_TYPE_1ST_HALF | PCT1_CIPHER_RC4
11	84 80 40	PCT_SSL_CIPHER_TYPE_2ND_HALF | PCT1_ENC_BITS_128 | PCT1_MAC_BITS_128
12	01 00 80	SSL2_RC4_128_WITH_MD5
13	07 00 c0	SSL2_DES_192_EDE3_CBC_WITH_MD5
14	03 00 80	SSL2_RC2_128_CBC_WITH_MD5
15	00 00 09	TLS_RSA_WITH_DES_CBC_SHA
16	06 00 40	SSL2_DES_64_CBC_WITH_MD5
17	00 00 64	TLS_RSA_EXPORT1024_WITH_RC4_56_SHA
18	00 00 62	TLS_RSA_EXPORT1024_WITH_DES_CBC_SHA
19	00 00 03	TLS_RSA_EXPORT_WITH_RC4_40_MD5
20	00 00 06	TLS_RSA_EXPORT_WITH_RC2_CBC_40_MD5
21	83 00 04	PCT_SSL_CIPHER_TYPE_1ST_HALF | PCT1_CIPHER_RC4
22	84 28 40	PCT_SSL_CIPHER_TYPE_2ND_HALF | PCT1_ENC_BITS_40 | PCT1_MAC_BITS_128
23	02 00 80	SSL2_RC4_128_EXPORT40_WITH_MD5
24	04 00 80	SSL2_RC2_128_CBC_EXPORT40_WITH_MD5
25	00 00 13	TLS_DHE_DSS_WITH_3DES_EDE_CBC_SHA
26	00 00 12	TLS_DHE_DSS_WITH_DES_CBC_SHA
27	00 00 63	TLS_DHE_DSS_EXPORT1024_WITH_DES_CBC_SHA

Figure B.3 PCT CLIENT-HELLO

B.6   What about SSLv1?

At this point, you're probably thinking "I've heard about SSLv3 and SSLv2, but what about SSLv1?" Netscape never actually delivered a specification or a public implementation of SSL version 1. We've just seen that SSLv2 contains a number of modest security flaws that could have been avoided by careful engineering. The drafts of SSLv1 that circulated for review had all these security flaws but also contained a very serious security flaw: weak integrity protection.

The very first SSLv1 draft didn't have any message integrity protection at all. Almost unbelievably, it also used RC4, with the effect that an attacker could make predictable changes in the plaintext. Moreover, it didn't have any sequence numbers, so it was totally vulnerable to replay attack.

Later versions added a sequence number and a checksum, but used a *cyclic redundancy check* (CRC) as the checksum. Unfortunately, CRC isn't non-invertible or collision free the way that MD5 is, so it didn't prevent message integrity attacks when RC4 was used. Finally, right before releasing SSLv2, the designers figured out about integrity attacks and changed the MAC to MD5, which solved the problem. Credit for these changes largely goes to Martin Abadi, who pointed out the problems to Netscape.

Bibliography

All RFCs are freely downloadable via the Web as described in Section 2.2.

[Abbott1988] Abbott, S., and Keung, S., *CryptoSwift (ver.2) Performance on Netscape Enterprise Server* (April, 1988).

```
http://isglabs.rainbow.com/isglabs/NS351-CSv2-NT-perf/⏎
NS351-CSv2.html
```

Describes performance behavior of a commercial (though somewhat outdated) server with and without hardware acceleration.

[Anderson1999] Anderson, R., Biham, A., and Knudsen, L., *Serpent: A Proposal for the Advanced Encryption Standard* (1999).

```
http://csrc.nist.gov/encryption/aes/round2/AESAlgs/Serpent/⏎
Serpent.pdf
```

[ANSI1985] ANSI, "American National Standard for Financial Institution Key Management (wholesale)," ANSI X9.17 (1985).

Describes 3DES.

[ANSI1986] ANSI, "American National Standard for Financial Institution Message Authentication (Wholesale)," ANSI X9.9 (Revised) (1986).

One of many descriptions of DES-CBC MAC.

[ANSI1995] ANSI, "Public key cryptography for the financial services industry — Certificate management," ANSI X9.57 (1995).

[ANSI1998] ANSI, "Agreement of Symmetric Keys Using Diffie-Hellman and MQV Algorithms," ANSI X9.42 draft (1998).

[Atkins1996] Atkins, D., Stallings, W., and Zimmermann, P., "PGP Message Exchange Formats," RFC 1991 (August 1996).

[Balenson1993] Balenson, D., "Privacy Enhancement for Internet Electronic Mail: Part III: Algorithms, Modes, and Identifiers," RFC 1423 (February 1993).

[Banes1999] Banes, J., and Harrington, R., "56-bit Export Cipher Suites for TLS," draft-ietf-tls-56-bit-ciphersuites-00.txt (April 1999).

[Banes2000] Banes, J., *Personal communication.* (2000).

[Bellare1995] Bellare, M., and Rogaway, P., "Optimal asymmetric encryption padding," *Advances in Cryptology — Eurocrypt 94 Proceedings,* Springer-Verlag, Berlin (1995).

[Bellovin1995] Bellovin, S.M., "Using the Domain Name System for System Break-ins" in *5th USENIX UNIX Security Symposium,* p. 199–208, USENIX, Salt Lake City, UT (June 5–7, 1995).

[Benaloh1995] Benaloh, J., Lampson, B., Simon, D., Spies, T., and Yee, B., "Private Communication Technology Protocol," draft-microsoft-PCT-01.txt (September 1995).
The second PCT draft

[Berners–Lee1994] Berners–Lee, T., Masinter, L., and McCahill, M., "Uniform Resource Locators," RFC 1738 (December 1994).

[Berners-Lee1998] Berners-Lee, T., Fielding, R., and Masinter, L., "Uniform Resource Identifiers (URI)," RFC 2396 (August 1998).

[Biham1991a] Biham, E., Shamir, A., and Differential Cryptanalyis of DES-like Cryptosystems, *Advances in Cryptology—CRYPTO '90 Proceedings,* p. 2–21, Springer-Verlag, Berlin (1991).

[Biham1991b] Biham, E., Shamir, A., and Differential Cryptanalyis of DES-like Cryptosystems, *Journal of Cryptology,* 4, 1, p. 3–72 (1991).

[Biham1993a] Biham, E., and Shamir, A., "Differential Analysis of the Full 16-Round DES," *Advances in Cryptology—CRYPTO '92 Proceedings,* p. 487–496, Springer-Verlag, Berlin (1993).

[Biham1993b] Biham, E., and Shamir, A., *Differential Analysis of the Data Encryption Standard,* Springer-Verlag, New York, N.Y. (1993).

[Blaze1996] Blaze, M., Diffie, W., Rivest, R., Schneier, B., Shimomura, T., Thompson, E., and Weiner, M., *Minimal Key Lengths for Symmetric Ciphers to Provide Adequate Commercial Security* (January 1996).

[Blaze1999] Blaze, M., Feigenbaum, J., Ionnidis, J., and Keromytis, A., "The Keynote Trust Management System, Version 2," RFC 2704 (September 1999).

[Bleichenbacher1998] Bleichenbacher, D., "Chosen Ciphertext Attacks against Protocols Based on RSA Encryption Standard PKCS #1," *Advances in Cryptology — CRYPTO 98,* p. 1–12 (1998).

[Bleichenbacher1999] Bleichenbacher, D., *Personal communication.* (1999).

[Boe1999] Boe, M., "TLS-based Telnet Security," draft-ietf-tn3270-telnet-tls-03.txt (October, 1999).
Telnet over TLS has never been standardized, but this document describes the best current practice.

[Burwick1999] Burwick, C., Coppersmith, D., D'Avignon, E., Genarro, R., Halevi, S., Jutla, C., Matyas, S.M. Jr., O'Connor, L., Peyravian, M., Safford, D., and Zunic, N., *MARS, a Candidate Cipher for AES,* IBM Corporation (September 1999).
`http://csrc.nist.gov/encryption/aes/round2/AESAlgs/MARS/⏎`
`mars.pdf`

[Cocks1973] Cocks, C., "A Note on Non-Secret Encryption," CESG Report, CESG (1973).
`http://www.cesg.gov.uk/about/nsecret/notense.htm`
Describes CESG's invention of what we call RSA.

[Crispin1996] Crispin, M., "Internet Message Access Protocol—Version 4rev1," RFC 2060 (December 1996).

[Crocker1982] Crocker, D., "Standard for the Format of ARPA Internet Text Messages," RFC 822 (August 1982).
The basic standard for internet email messages.

[Daemen1999] Daemen, J., and Rijmen, V., *AES Proposal: Rijndael* (March 1999).
`http://csrc.nist.gov/encryption/aes/round2/AESAlgs/Rijndael/⏎`
`Rijndael.pdf`

[Dai2000] Dai, W., *Crypto++ 3.1 Benchmarks* (2000).
`http://www.eskimo.com/~weidai/benchmarks.html`
Wei Dai's benchmarks for his Crypto++ package.

[Dierks1999] Dierks, T., and Allen, C., "The TLS Protocol Version 1.0," RFC 2246 (January 1999).

[Diffie1976] Diffie, W., and Hellman, M.E., "New directions in cryptography," *IEEE Transactions on Information Theory,* 22, 6, p. 655–654 (1976).

[Diffie1992] Diffie, W., van Oorschot, P.C., and Wiener, M.J., "Authentication and Authenticated Key Exchanges," *Designs, Codes, and Cryptography,* 2, p. 102–125 (1992).
Describes the Station to Station protocol (STS), a form of authenticated DH upon which IKE is based.

[Dobbertin1996] Dobbertin, H., "The Status of MD5 After a Recent Attack," *CryptoBytes,* 2, 2, RSA Laboratories (Summer 1996).

[Dusse1998] Dusse, S., Hossman, P., Ramsdell, B., Lundblade, L., and Repka, L., "S/MIME Version 2 Message Specification," RFC 2311 (March 1998).

[Eastlake1994] Eastlake, D. 3rd., Crocker, S., and Schiller, J., "Randomness Recommendations for Security," RFC 1750 (December 1994).

[Eastlake1999] Eastlake, D., 3rd., "Domain Name System Security Extensions," RFC 2535 (March 1999).

[Ellis1970] Ellis, J.H., *The Possibility of Non-Secret Encryption,* CESG (1970).
`http://www.cesg.gov.uk/about/nsecret/possnse.htm`

[Ellis1987] Ellis, J.H., *The Story of Non-Secret Encryption,* CESG (1987).
`http://www.cesg.gov.uk/about/nsecret/ellis.htm`

[Ellison1999] Ellison, C., Frantz, B., Lampson, B., Rivest, R., Thomas, B., and Ylonen, T., "SPKI Certificate Theory," RFC 2693 (September 1999).

[Fielding1999] Fielding, R., Gettys, J., Mogul, J., Frystyk, H., Masinter, L., Leach, P., and Berners-Lee, T., "Hypertext Transfer Protocol," RFC 2616 (June 1999).

[Ford-Hutchinson2000] Ford-Hutchinson, Paul, Carpenter, M., Hudson, T., Murray, E., and Wiegand, V., "Securing FTP with TLS," draft-murray-auth-ftp-ssl-05.txt (January 2000).
FTP over TLS has never been standardized. This document describes the de facto standard.

[Freed1996a] Freed, N., and Borenstein, N., "Multipurpose Internet Mail Extensions (MIME) Part One: Format of Internet Message Bodies," RFC 2045 (November 1996).

[Freed1996b] Freed, N., and Borenstein, N., "Multipurpose Internet Mail Extensions (MIME) Part Two: Media Types," RFC 2046 (November 1996).

[Freed1996c] Freed, N., Klensin, J., and Postel, J., "Multipurpose Internet Mail Extensions (MIME) Part Four: Registration Procedures," RFC 2048 (November, 1996).

[Freed1996d] Freed, N., and Borenstein, N., "Multipurpose Internet Mail Extensions (MIME) Part Five: Conformance Criteria and Examples," RFC 2049 (November 1996).

[Freier1996] Freier, A.O., Karlton, P., and Kocher, P.C., *The SSL Protocol Version 3.0* (November 1996).
http://home.netscape.com/eng/ssl3/draft302.txt
The last published draft of SSLv3. Note that SSLv3 was never published as an IETF RFC of any kind. This document combined with Netscape's implementation represent the de facto standard.

[Gilmore1998] Gilmore, J. (Ed.), *Cracking DES: Secrets of Encryption Research, Wiretap Politics & Chip Design,* O'Reilly & Associates (May 1998).
Describes how to build a dedicated hardware DES search engine.

[Goland1999] Goland, Y., Whitehead, E., Faizi, A., Carter, S., and Jensen, D., "HTTP Extensions for Distributed Authoring—WEBDAV," RFC 2518 (February 1999).

[Goldberg1996] Goldberg, I., and Wagner, D., "Randomness and the Netscape Browser," *Dr. Dobb's Journal* (January 1996).
The paper that described the weakness in Netscape PRNG seeding.

[Harkins1998] Harkins, D., Carrel, D., and The Internet Key Exchange (IKE), RFC 2409 (November 1998).

[Hennessey1996] Hennessey, J., Goldberg, D., and Patterson, D.A., *Computer Architecture: A Quantitative Approach, 2ed.,* Morgan Kaufmann (January 1996).
The standard book on processor design by some of the inventors of RISC.

[Hickman1995] Hickman, K., *The SSL Protocol* (February 1995).
http://www.netscape.com/eng/security/SSL_2.html
The specification for SSLv2.

[Hoffman1999a] Hoffman, P., "SMTP Service Extension for Secure SMTP over TLS," RFC 2487 (January 1999).
The standard for SMTP over TLS.

[Hoffman1999b] Hoffman, P., "Enhanced Security Services for S/MIME," RFC 2634 (June 1999).

[Housley1999a] Housley, R., Ford, W., Polk, W., and Solo, D., "Internet X.509 Public Key Infrastructure Certificate and CRL Profile," RFC 2459 (January 1999).

[Housley1999b] Housley, R., "Cryptographic Message Syntax," RFC 2630 (June 1999).
CMS is a variant of PKCS #7 that has been extended to support Diffie-Hellman. and DSA.

[IANA] IANA, *Well Known Ports.*
`http://www.iana.org/numbers.htm`
A list of all the assigned well known ports.

[ITU1988a] ITU, "The Directory—Authentication Framework," ITU Recommendation X.509 (1988).

[ITU1988b] ITU, "The Directory—Models," ITU Recommendation X.500 (1988).

[ITU1988c] ITU, "Specification of Abstract Syntax Notation One (ASN.1)," ITU Recommendation X.208 (1988).

[ITU1988d] ITU, "Specification of Basic Encoding Rules for Abstract Syntax Notation One (ASN.1)," ITU Recommendation X.209 (1988).

[Jablon1996] Jablon, D., "Strong Password-only Authenticate Key Exchange," *ACM Computer Communications Review,* 26, 5 (October 1996).

[Jacobsen1988] Jacobsen, V., "Congestion Avoidance and Control," *Computer Communication Review,* 18, 4, p. 314–329 (August 1988).

[JavaSoft1999] JavaSoft, *Java Secure Socket Extension (JSSE 1.0)* (1999).
`http://java.sun.com/products/jsse/`
Sun's free "non-commercial" quality implementation of SSL/TLS.

[Johnson1993] Johnson, D.B., Matyas, S.M., Le, A.V., and Wilkins, J.D., "Design of the Commercial Data Masking Facility Data Privacy Algorithm" in *1st ACM Conference on Computer and Communications Security,* p. 93–96, ACM Press (1993).

[Joncheray1995] Joncheray, L., "A Simple Active Attack Against TCP" in *5th USENIX UNIX Security Symposium,* p. 7–19, USENIX, Salt Lake City, UT (June 5-7, 1995).

[Kaliski1993] Kaliski, B., "Privacy Enhancement for Internet Electronic Mail: Part IV: Key Certification and Related Services," RFC 1424 (February 1993).

[Kaliski1998a] Kaliski, B., and Staddon, J., "PKCS #1: RSA Cryptography Specifications Version 2.0," RFC 2437 (October 1998).

[Kaliski1998b] Kaliski, B.S., Jr., "Compatible cofactor multiplication for Diffie-Hellman primitives," *Electronics Letters,* 34, 25, p. 2396–2397 (December 1998).

[Kaufman1995] Kaufman, C., Perlman, R., and Speciner, M., *Network Security: Private Communications in a Public World,* Prentice-Hall, Englewood Cliffs, NJ (1995).
An excellent introduction to cryptography and network security. Focuses on the application of cryptography to communications security.

[Kelsey1999] Kelsey, J., Schneier, B., and Ferguson, N., "Notes on the Design and Analysis of the Yarrow Cryptographic Pseudorandom Number Generator" in *Sixth Annual Workshop on Selected Areas in Cryptography,* Springer-Verlag, Berlin (August 1999).

[Kent1993] Kent, S., "Privacy Enhancement for Internet Electronic Mail: Part II: Certificate-Based Key Management," RFC 1422 (February 1993).

[Kent1998a] Kent, S., and Atkinson, R., "IP Authentication Header," RFC 2402 (November, 1998).

[Kent1998b] Kent, S., Atkinson, R., and RFC 2406, *IP Encapsulating Security Payload (ESP)* (November 1998).

[Kent1998c] Kent, S., and Atkinson, R., "Security Architecture for the Internet Protocol," RFC 2401 (November 1998).

[Keung] Keung, S., *Cryptoswift performance under SSL with file transfer* (19XX).
`http://isglabs.rainbow.com/isglabs/SSLperformance/`↵
`SSL+file%20performance.html`

[Khare2000] Khare, R., and Lawrence, S., "Upgrading to TLS Within HTTP/1.1," RFC 2817 (May 2000).

[Klein1990] Klein, D.V., *"Foiling the Cracker": A Survey of and Improvements to Password Security* (1990).
A good description of how easy it is to crack passwords when users choose them.

[Klensin1995] Klensin, J., Freed, N., Rose, M., Stefferud, E., and Crocker, D., "SMTP Service Extensions," RFC 1869 (November 1995).

[Kocher1996a] Kocher, P., *A Quick Introduction to Revocation Trees* (1996).
`http://www.valicert.com/pdf/Certificate_revocation_trees.pdf`

[Kocher1996b] Kocher, P., *Timing Attacks on Implementation of Diffie-Hellman, RSA, DSS, and Other Systems* (1996).

[Kocher1999] Kocher, P., and Jun, B., *The Intel Random Number Generator* (April 1999).
This paper describes an analysis of the Intel hardware PRNG in the Pentium III.

[Krawczyk1995] Krawczyk, H., *SKEME: A Versatile Secure Key Exchange Mechanism for Internet* (August 1995).

[Krawczyk1996] Krawczyk, H., *Personal communication.* (1996).
HMAC is believed to be immune to Dobbertin's attacks on MD5.

[Krawczyk1997] Krawczyk, H., Bellare, M., and Canetti, R., "HMAC: Keyed-Hashing for Message Authentication," RFC 2104 (February 1997).

[Lear1994] Lear, E., Fair, E., and Kessler, T., "Network 10 Considered Harmful (Some Practices Shouldn't be Codified)," RFC 1627 (June 1994).
The RFC that launched an extremely acrimonious debate over NAT.

[Lim1997] Lim, C.H., and Lee, P.J., "A key recovery attack on discrete log-based schemes using a prime order subgroup" in *Advances in Cryptology—Crypto 97,* p. 249–263, Springer-Verlag, Berlin (1997).

[Linn1993] Linn, J., "Privacy Enhancement for Internet Electronic Mail: Part I: Message Encryption and Authentication Procedures," RFC 1421 (February 1993).

[Maughan1998] Maughan, D., Schertler, M., Schneider, M., and Turner, J., "Internet Security Association and Key Management Protocol (ISAKMP)," RFC 2408 (November 1998).

[Medvinsky1999] Medvinsky, A., and Hur, M., "Addition of Kerberos Cipher Suites to Transport Layer Security (TLS)," RFC 2712 (October 1999).

[Menezes1996] Menezes, A.J., van Oorschot, P.C., and Vanstone, S.A., *Handbook of Applied Cryptography,* CRC Press, Boca Raton, FL (1996).
> Not a useful introduction but an extremely useful technical reference to cryptography.

[Microsoft2000] Microsoft, *Security Support Provider Interface* (2000).
> `http://msdn.microsoft.com/library/default.asp?URL=/library/psdk/↵`
> `secspi/portalsspi_1545.htm`
> Documents Microsoft's built-in security services including SChannel.

[Miller1987] Miller, S., Neumann, B., Schiller, J., and Saltzer, J., "Kerberos Authentication and Authorization System," *Project Athena Technical Plan,* MIT Project Athena (December 1987).

[Mockapetris1987a] Mockapetris, P.V., "Domain Names—Concepts and Facilities," RFC 1034 (November 1987).

[Mockapetris1987b] Mockapetris, P.V., "Domain Names—Implementation and Specification," RFC 1035 (November 1987).

[Moeller1998] Moeller, B., "Export-PKC attacks on SSL 3.0/TLS 1.0," *Message to IETF-TLS mailing list* (October 1998).
> `http://www.imc.org/ietf-tls/mail-archive/msg01671.html`

[Mogul1995] Mogul, Jeffrey C., "The Case for Persistent-Connection HTTP," Research Report 95/4 (May 1995).
> `http://www.research.digital.com/abstracts/95.4.html`
> An early paper showing the benefits of HTTP retained connections.

[Moore1996] Moore, K., "MIME (Multipurpose Internet Mail Extensions) Part Three: Message Header Extensions for Non-ASCII," RFC 2047 (November 1996).

[Myers1996] Myers, J., and Rose, M., "Post Office Protocol—Version 3," RFC 1939 (May 1996).

[Myers1999] Myers, M., Ankney, R., Malpani, A., Galperin, S., and Adams, C., " X.509 Internet Public Key Infrastructure Online Certificate Status Protocol—OCSP," RFC 2560 (June 1999).

[Nagle1984] Nagle, J., "Congestion Control in IP/TCP Internetworks," RFC 0896 (Jan 1984).

[Needham1978] Needham, R.M., and Schroeder, M.D., "Using Encryption for Authentication in Large Networks of Computers," *Communications of the ACM,* 21, p. 993–999 (December 1978).

[Netcraft2000] Netcraft, *Netcraft Secure Web Server Survey* (January 2000).
> Netcraft kindly provided me with a copy of this survey.

[Netscape1995a] Netscape Communications Corp, *SSL 2.0 Certificate Usage* (1995).
> `http://www.netscape.com/eng/security/ssl_2.0_certificate.html`
> Describes Netscape's wildcarding technique.

[Netscape1999a] Netscape Communications Corp., *Netscape Certificate Extensions, Communicator 4.0 Version* (1999).
> `http://www.netscape.com/eng/security/comm4-cert-exts.html`

[Neumann1951] von Neumann, J., "Various Techniques Used in Connection with Random Digits," *Applied Mathematics Series,* 12, p. 36–38, U.S. National Bureau of Standards (1951).

[Newman1999] Newman, C., "Using TLS with IMAP, POP3 and ACAP," RFC 2595 (June 1999).
Provides upward negotiation mechanisms for IMAP, POP and ACAP.

[NIST1993a] National Institute of Standards and Technology (NIST), "Data Encryption Standard," FIPS PUB 46-2, U.S. Department of Commerce (December 1993).
This is the reissued DES document. It's essentially identitical to the document published in 1977.

[NIST1994a] National Institute of Standards and Technology (NIST), and Secure Hash Standard, FIPS PUB 180-1, U.S. Department of Commerce (May 1994).
The revised SHA draft that describes SHA-1.

[NIST1994b] National Institute of Standards and Technology, "Security Requirements for Cryptographic Modules," FIPS PUB 140-1, U.S. Department of Commerce (January 1994).
Describes four levels of secure modules, ranging from Level 1 (requiring approved algorithms but running on general purpose computers) to Level 4 (full tamperproofing.)

[Orman1998] Orman, H., "The OAKLEY Key Determination Protocol," RFC 2412 (November 1998).

[Padmanabhan1995] Padmanabhan, V.N., "Improving World Wide Web Latency," UCB/CSD 95-875, Computer Science Division, University of California, Berkeley (May 1995).

[Postel1982] Postel, J., "Simple Mail Transfer Protocol," RFC 821 (August 1982).
The base standard for Internet mail transport.

[Postel1985] Postel, J., and Reynolds, J.K., "File Transfer Protocol," RFC 959 (October 1985).

[Postel1991a] Postel, J., "Internet Protocol," RFC 791 (September 1991).
The IETF standard for IP.

[Postel1991b] Postel, J., "Internet Control Message Protocol," RFC 792 (September 1991).

[Postel1991c] Postel, J., "Transmission Control Protocol," RFC 793 (September 1991).
The IETF standard for TCP.

[Ramsdell1999] Ramsdell, B., "S/MIME Version 3 Message Specification," RFC 2633 (June 1999).

[Rekhter1994] Rekhter, Y., Moskowitz, B., Karrenberg, D., de Groot, G.J., and RFC 1597, *Address Allocation for Private Internets* (March 1994).
The original RFC describing NAT and Network 10.

[Rekhter1996] Rekhter, Y., Moskowitz, B., Karrenberg, D., de Groot, G.J., and Lear, E., RFC 1918 (February 1996).
This document represents a truce of sorts in the NAT debate.

[Relyea1996] Relyea, B., *Appendix A—SSL Protocol Version 3.0 Specification Errata for Fortezza Implementations* (November, 1996).
http://www.armadillo.huntsville.al.us/Fortezza_docs/ssl_fortezza.pdf
Describes how to make SSLv3 work with FORTEZZA.

[Rescorla1999a] Rescorla, E., and Schiffman, A., "The Secure HyperText Transfer Protocol," RFC 2660 (August 1999).

[Rescorla1999b] Rescorla, E., and Schiffman, A., "Security Extensions for HTML," RFC 2659 (August 1999).

[Rescorla2000] Rescorla, E., "HTTP over TLS," RFC 2818 (May 2000).

[Rivest1979] Rivest, R.L., Shamir, A., and Adelman, L.M., "On Digital Signatures and Public Key Cryptosystems," Technical Report, MIT/LCS/TR-212, MIT Laboratory for Computer Science (January 1979).

[Rivest1983] Rivest, R., Shamir, A., and Adelman, L.M., "Cryptographic communications system and method," US Patent 4405829 (September 1983).
The RSA Patent.

[Rivest1992] Rivest, R., "The MD5 Message-Digest Algorithm," RFC 1321 (April 1992).

[Rivest1995] Rivest, R., Robshaw, M.J.B., Sidney, R., and Yin, Y.L., *The RC6^{TM} Block Cipher* (August 1995).
http://csrc.nist.gov/encryption/aes/round2/AESAlgs/RC6/cipher.pdf

[Rivest1998] Rivest, R., "A Description of the RC2(r) Encryption Algorithm," RFC 2268 (January 1998).

[RSA1993a] Kaliski, B.S., Jr., "A Layman's Guide to a Subset of ASN.1, BER, and DER," Technical Note, RSA Laboratories (November 1993).
Provides a readable introduction to ASN.1, BER, and DER.

[RSA1993b] RSA Laboratories, "RSA Encryption Standard," PKCS #1 (November 1993).

[RSA1993c] RSA Laboratories, "Cryptographic Message Syntax Version 1.5," PKCS #7 (November 1993).

[RSA1993d] RSA Laboratories, "Password Based Encryption Standard," PKCS #5 (November 1993).

[RSA1999a] RSA Laboratories, "Personal Information Exchange Syntax," PKCS #12 (June 1999).

[RSA1999b] RSA Laboratories, "Password Based Encryption Standard," PKCS #5v2.0 (March 1999).

[Saltzer1984] Saltzer, J.H., Reed, D.P., and Clark, D.D., "End-to-End Arguments in System Design," *ACM Transactions in Computer Systems,* 2, 4, p. 277–288 (November 1984).
The classic description of the end-to-end argument, a basic networking design principle.

[Schneier1996a] Schneier, B., *Applied Cryptography, 2ed.,* John Wiley & Sons, New York, N.Y. (1996).
The standard text on cryptography.

[Schneier1996b] Schneier, B., and Wagner, D., "Analysis of the SSL 3.0 Protocol," *The Second USENIX Workshop on Electronic Commerce Proceedings,* p. 29–40, USENIX Press (November 1996).

[Schneier1998] Schneier, B., Kelsey, J., Whiting, D., Wagner, D., Hall, C., and Ferguson, N., *Twofish: A 128-Bit Block Cipher* (June 1998).
`http://csrc.nist.gov/encryption/aes/round2/AESAlgs/Twofish/⏎` Twofish.pdf

[Schnorr1991] Schnorr, K., "Method for Identifying Subscribers and for Generating and Verifying Electronic Signatures in a Data Exchange System," US Patent 4995082 (Feb 1991).

[Shamir1999] Shamir, A., "Factoring Large Numbers with the TWINKLE Device," *Eurocrypt '99 Rump Session* (1999).

[Spero1994] Spero, S., *Analysis of HTTP Performance Problems* (1994).
`http://sunsite.unc.edu/mdma-release/http-prob.html`

[Stevens1994] Stevens, W.R., *TCP/IP Illustrated, Volume 1: The Protocols,* Addison-Wesley, Reading, MA (1994).
The classic book on TCP/IP.

[Voydock1983] Voydock, V., and Kent, S.T., "Security mechanisms in high-level network protocols," *ACM Computing Surveys,* 15, p. 135–171 (1983).
An early survey of various mechanisms for providing cryptographic security in networks. Voydock and Kent discuss many of the same issues that we've seen in this chapter in the context of early network protocols. Kent has been a key figure in the design of a number of important public and classified security protocols, including IPsec and PEM.

[W3C2000] W3C, *Naming and Addressing: URIs, URLs, ...* (2000).
`http://www.w3.org/Addressing/`
A good guide to the relationship between URIs and URLs.

[WAP1999a] Wireless Application Protocol Forum, *WAP WTLS* (Nov 1999).

[Williamson1974] Williamson, M., *Non-Secret Encryption Using a Finite Field,* CESG (1974).
`http://www.cesg.gov.uk/about/nsecret/secenc.htm`
Describes CESG's invention of a system which is essentially Diffie-Hellman.

[Williamson1976] Williamson, M., *Thoughts on Cheaper Non Secret Encryption,* CESG (1976).
`http://www.cesg.gov.uk/about/nsecret/cheapnse.htm`

[Wu1998] Wu, T., "The Secure Remote Password Protocol," *Proceedings of the 1998 Internet Society Network and Distributed Systems Security Symposium,* p. 97–111 (March 1998).

Index

As is the case with many technical books, a large number of the terms we use are acronyms. In this index, the primary entry for each term is indexed under the acronym with the expansion in parentheses. The index entry for the expanded term refers the reader to the acronym. For convenient reference, a list of important acronyms with the page where they are first explained follows the index.

ACRONYMS

3DES	Triple DES, p. 6
ACL	Access Control List, p. 236
AES	Advanced Encryption Standard, p. 31
AH	Authentication Header, p. 380
ANSI	American National Standards Institute, p. 44
API	Application Programming Interface, p. 46
ASN.1	Abstract Syntax Notation 1, p. 14
AVA	Attribute-Value Assertion, p. 258
BER	Basic Encoding Rules, p. 14
BXA	Bureau of Export Administration, p. 24
CA	Certificate Authority, p. 9
CBC	Cipher Block Chaining, p. 28
CDMF	Commercial Data Masking Facility, p. 25
CESG	Communications-Electronics Security Group, p. 9
CFB	Cipher Block Feedback, p. 28
CMS	Cryptographic Messaging Syntax, p. 390
CN	Common Name, p. 13
CRC	Cyclic Redundancy Check, p. 464
CRL	Certificate Revocation List, p. 13
DER	Distinguished Encoding Rules, p. 14
DES	Data Encryption Standard, p. 6
DH	Diffie-Hellman, p. 34
DHCP	Dynamic Host Configuration Protocol, p. 108
DN	Distinguished Name, p. 12
DNS	Domain Name System, p. 156
DNSSEC	DNS Security, p. 409
DSA	Digital Signature Algorithm, p. 37
DSS	Digital Signature Standard, p. 37
EC	Elliptic Curve, p. 103
ECB	Electronic Code Book, p. 28
EDE	Encrypt-Decrypt-Encrypt, p. 30
EEE	Encrypt-Encrypt-Encrypt, p. 30
ESP	Encapsulating Security Payload, p. 380
FIPS	Federal Information Processing Standard, p. 37
FTP	File Transfer Protocol, p. 244
HTML	Hypertext Markup Language, p. 295
HTTP	Hypertext Transfer Protocol, p. 293
HTTPS	traditional HTTP over SSL, p. 304
I/O	Input/Output, p. 177
IANA	Internet Assigned Numbers Authority, p. 225
IE	Internet Explorer, p. 54
IESG	Internet Engineering Steering Group, p. 50
IETF	Internet Engineering Task Force, p. 43
IIS	Internet Information Server, p. 54
IKE	Internet Key Exchange, p. 380
IMAP	Internet Mail Access Protocol, p. 346
IP	Internet Protocol, p. 46
IPsec	Internet Protocol Security, p. 380
ISAKMP	Internet Security Association and Key Management Protocol, p. 380
ISO	International Standards Organization, p. 15
ISP	Internet Service Provider, p. 302
ITU	International Telecommunications Union, p. 44
IV	Initialization Vector, p. 28
JCA	Java Cryptographic Architecture, p. 200
JDK	Java Development Kit, p. 200
JSSE	Java Secure Sockets Extension, p. 258
KDC	Key Distribution Center, p. 8
KDF	Key Derivation Function, p. 20
KEA	Key Exchange Algorithm, p. 105

Register Your Book

at www.aw.com/cseng/register

You may be eligible to receive:

- Advance notice of forthcoming editions of the book
- Related book recommendations
- Chapter excerpts and supplements of forthcoming titles
- Information about special contests and promotions throughout the year
- Notices and reminders about author appearances, tradeshows, and online chats with special guests

Contact us

If you are interested in writing a book or reviewing manuscripts prior to publication, please write to us at:

Editorial Department
Addison-Wesley Professional
75 Arlington Street, Suite 300
Boston, MA 02116 USA
Email: AWPro@aw.com

Addison-Wesley

Visit us on the Web: http://www.aw.com/cseng

SSL/TLS cipher suites

Cipher Suite	Auth	Key Exchange	Encryption	Digest	Number
TLS_RSA_WITH_NULL_MD5	RSA	RSA	NULL	MD5	0x0001
TLS_RSA_WITH_NULL_SHA	RSA	RSA	NULL	SHA	0x0002
TLS_RSA_EXPORT_WITH_RC4_40_MD5	RSA	RSA_EXPORT	RC4_40	MD5	0x0003
TLS_RSA_WITH_RC4_128_MD5	RSA	RSA	RC4_128	MD5	0x0004
TLS_RSA_WITH_RC4_128_SHA	RSA	RSA	RC4_128	SHA	0x0005
TLS_RSA_EXPORT_WITH_RC2_CBC_40_MD5	RSA	RSA_EXPORT	RC2_40_CBC	MD5	0x0006
TLS_RSA_WITH_IDEA_CBC_SHA	RSA	RSA	IDEA_CBC	SHA	0x0007
TLS_RSA_EXPORT_WITH_DES40_CBC_SHA	RSA	RSA_EXPORT	DES40_CBC	SHA	0x0008
TLS_RSA_WITH_DES_CBC_SHA	RSA	RSA	DES_CBC	SHA	0x0009
TLS_RSA_WITH_3DES_EDE_CBC_SHA	RSA	RSA	3DES_EDE_CBC	SHA	0x000A
TLS_DH_DSS_EXPORT_WITH_DES40_CBC_SHA	RSA	DH_DSS_EXPORT	DES_40_CBC	SHA	0x000B
TLS_DH_DSS_WITH_DES_CBC_SHA	DSS	DH	DES_CBC	SHA	0x000C
TLS_DH_DSS_WITH_3DES_EDE_CBC_SHA	DSS	DH	3DES_EDE_CBC	SHA	0x000D
TLS_DH_RSA_EXPORT_WITH_DES40_CBC_SHA	RSA	DH_EXPORT	DES_40_CBC	SHA	0x000E
TLS_DH_RSA_WITH_DES_CBC_SHA	RSA	DH	DES_CBC	SHA	0x000F
TLS_DH_RSA_WITH_3DES_EDE_CBC_SHA	RSA	DH	3DES_EDE_CBC	SHA	0x0010
TLS_DHE_DSS_EXPORT_WITH_DES40_CBC_SHA	DSS	DHE_EXPORT	DES_40_CBC	SHA	0x0011
TLS_DHE_DSS_WITH_DES_CBC_SHA	DSS	DHE	DES_CBC	SHA	0x0012
TLS_DHE_DSS_WITH_3DES_EDE_CBC_SHA	DSS	DHE	3DES_EDE_CBC	SHA	0x0013
TLS_DHE_RSA_EXPORT_WITH_DES40_CBC_SHA	RSA	DHE_EXPORT	DES_40_CBC	SHA	0x0014
TLS_DHE_RSA_WITH_DES_CBC_SHA	RSA	DHE	DES_CBC	SHA	0x0015
TLS_DHE_RSA_WITH_3DES_EDE_CBC_SHA	RSA	DHE	3DES_EDE_CBC	SHA	0x0016
TLS_DH_anon_EXPORT_WITH_RC4_40_MD5	-	DH_EXPORT	RC4_40	MD5	0x0017
TLS_DH_anon_WITH_RC4_128_MD5	-	DH	RC4_128	MD5	0x0018
TLS_DH_anon_EXPORT_WITH_DES40_CBC_SHA	-	DH	DES_40_CBC	SHA	0x0019
TLS_DH_anon_WITH_DES_CBC_SHA	-	DH	DES_CBC	SHA	0x001A
TLS_DH_anon_WITH_3DES_EDE_CBC_SHA	-	DH	3DES_EDE_CBC	SHA	0x001B
TLS_RSA_EXPORT1024_WITH_DES_CBC_SHA †	RSA	RSA	DES_CBC	SHA	0x0062
TLS_DHE_DSS_EXPORT1024_WITH_DES_CBC_SHA †	RSA	RSA	DES_CBC	SHA	0x0063
TLS_RSA_EXPORT1024_WITH_RC4_56_SHA †	RSA	RSA	RC4_56	SHA	0x0064
TLS_DHE_DSS_EXPORT1024_WITH_RC4_56_SHA †	RSA	RSA	RC4_56	SHA	0x0065
TLS_DHE_DSS_WITH_RC4_128_SHA †	RSA	RSA	RC4_56	SHA	0x0066

Cipher suites marked with a † are 56-bit export ciphers defined in [Banes1999] not in RFC 2246.